THE
Christian
BED & BREAKFAST
DIRECTORY

1998–99 EDITION

DAN HARMON, EDITOR

BARBOUR
PUBLISHING, INC.
Uhrichsville, Ohio

THE
Christian
BED & BREAKFAST
DIRECTORY

1998–99 EDITION

© MCMXCVIII by Barbour Publishing, Inc.

ISBN 1-57748-022-8

Published by Barbour Publishing, Inc.
P.O. Box 719
Uhrichsville, Ohio 44683
http://www.barbourbooks.com

 Member of the
Evangelical Christian
Publishers Association

Printed in the United States of America.

TABLE OF CONTENTS

How To Use This Book

Have you ever dreamed of spending a few days in a rustic cabin in Alaska? Would you like to stay in an urban town house while taking care of some business in the city? Would your family like to spend a weekend on a midwestern farm feeding pigs and gathering eggs? Maybe a romantic Victorian mansion in San Francisco or an antebellum plantation in Mississippi is what you've been looking for. No matter what your needs may be, whether you are traveling for business or pleasure, you will find a variety of choices in the 1998-1999 edition of *The Christian Bed & Breakfast Directory*.

In the pages of this guide you will find over 1,400 bed and breakfasts, small inns, and homestays. All of the information has been updated from last year's edition, and many entries are listed for the first time. Although not every establishment is owned or operated by Christians, each host has expressed a desire to welcome Christian travelers.

The directory is designed for easy reference. At a glance, you can determine the number of rooms available at each establishment and how many rooms have private (PB) and shared (SB) baths. You will find the name of the host or hosts, the price range for two people sharing one room, the kind of breakfast that is served, and what credit cards are accepted. There is a "Notes" section to let you know important information that may not be included in the description. These notes correspond to the list at the bottom of each page. The descriptions have been written by the hosts. The publisher has not visited these bed and breakfasts and is not responsible for inaccuracies.

General maps are provided to help you with your travel plans. Included are the towns where our bed and breakfasts are located, some reference cities, major highways, and major recreational lakes. Please use your road map for additional assistance and details when planning your trip.

It is recommended that you make reservations in advance. Many bed and breakfasts have small staffs or are run single-handedly and cannot easily accommodate surprises. Also ask about taxes, as city and state taxes vary. Remember to ask for directions, and if your special dietary needs can be met, and confirm check-in and check-out times.

Whether you're planning a honeymoon, family vacation, or business trip, *The Christian Bed & Breakfast Directory* will make any outing out of the ordinary.

DAN HARMON, EDITOR

ALABAMA

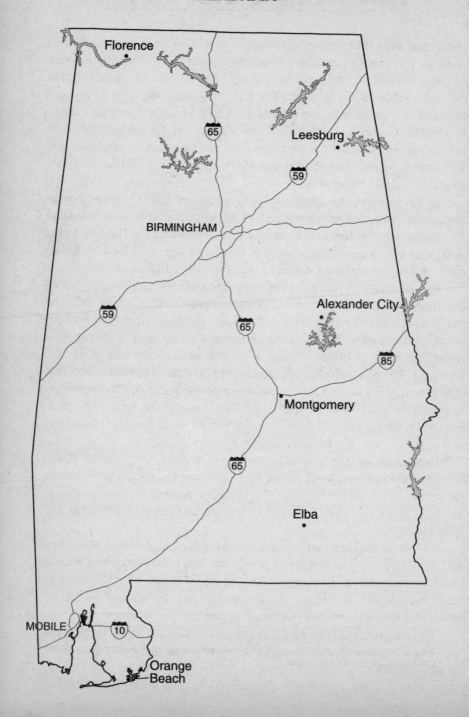

Alabama

ALSO SEE RESERVATION SERVICES UNDER MISSISSIPPI AND TENNESSEE.

ALEXANDER CITY

Mistletoe Bough Bed and Breakfast

497 Hillabee Street, 35010
(205) 329-3717; FAX (205) 234-0094
Web site: http://www.bbonline.com/al/mistletoe

Mistletoe Bough Bed and Breakfast

Mistletoe Bough is an elegant Queen Anne house built in 1890 for the family of Reuben Herzfeld. The bed and breakfast offers guests a retreat into years gone by with all the comforts and conveniences of modern days. Listed on the National Register of Historic Places, this lovely Victorian home offers elegance and charm you sense the moment you enter.

Hosts: Carlice E. and Jean H. Payne
Rooms: 5 (PB) $70-95
Full Breakfast
Credit Cards: none
Notes: 2, 5, 7 (over 10), 9, 10, 12

ELBA

Aunt B's Bed and Breakfast

717 W. Davis Street, 36323
(334) 897-6918 (voice and FAX)

This historic country Victorian built in 1910 has survived two floods, in 1920 and 1990. Restored in 1993. Three guest rooms: the Angel Room (king-size bed decorated with Battenburg lace), the Cowboy Room (two full-size beds decorated with handmade quilts), and the

---

NOTES: Credit cards accepted: A Master Card; B Visa; C American Express; D Discover; E Diners Club; F Other; 2 Personal checks accepted; 3 Lunch available; 4 Dinner available; 5 Open all year; 6 Pets welcome; 7 Children welcome; 8 Tennis nearby; 9 Swimming nearby; 10 Golf nearby; 11 Skiing nearby; 12 May be booked through travel agent.

Mayberry Room (twin or king beds decorated with ruffles). All have private baths. The shaded backyard has a hammock near the goldfish pond. Country breakfast. Shop "Aunt B's Closet" for gifts, baskets, and collectibles.

Hosts: Barbara and Bobby Hudson
Rooms: 3 (PB) $40-50
Full Breakfast
Credit Cards: A, B
Notes: 2, 5, 7, 8, 9, 10, 12

FLORENCE

Natchez Trace Bed and Breakfast Reservation Service

PO Box 193, **Hampshire, TN** 38461
(615) 285-2777; (800) 377-2770

This reservation service is unusual in that all the homes listed are close to the Natchez Trace, the delightful National Parkway running from Nashville, Tennessee, to Natchez, Mississippi. Kay Jones can help you plan your trip along the Trace, with homestays in interesting and historic homes along the way. Locations of homes include Ashland City, Columbia, FairView, Franklin, Hohenwald, and Nashville, **Tennessee**; Florence and Cherokee, **Alabama**; and Church Hill, Corinth, French Camp, Kosciusko, Lorman, Natchez, New Albany, Tupelo, and Vicksburg, **Mississippi**. Rates $60-125.

Wood Avenue Inn

658 N. Wood Avenue, 35630
(205) 766-8441

This grand Victorian mansion offers 1889 splendor in the heart of Florence's historic

Wood Avenue Inn

district. Guests can walk to restaurants, art galleries, and shopping, or stroll the beautiful campus of the University of North Alabama. Relax in the lovely gardens observing a variety of birds while they sing you a song! Romantic, quiet, and comfortable.

Hosts: Gene and Alvern Greeley
Rooms: 5 (4PB, 1SB) $63-98
Full Breakfast
Credit Cards: A, B
Notes: 2, 5, 8, 9, 10, 12

LEESBURG

The Secret Bed and Breakfast Lodge

Route 1, Box 82, 35983-9732
(205) 523-3825; FAX (205) 523-6455
Web site: http://www.bbonline.com/~bbonline/al/
    thesecret

At The Secret Bed and Breakfast Lodge, guests have a scenic view of seven cities and two states, overlooking Weiss Lake from Shinbone Ridge. Rooftop pool and vaulted ceiling in lodge area. Fireplace. King/queen-sized beds, TVs, private baths, VCRs. AAA star rating. A spe-

NOTES: Credit cards accepted: A Master Card; B Visa; C American Express; D Discover; E Diners Club; F Other; 2 Personal checks accepted; 3 Lunch available; 4 Dinner available; 5 Open all year; 6 Pets

cial place—a secret—with a view as spectacular in the day as it is enchanting at night. Come. Discover. Enjoy!

Hosts: Carl and Diann Cruickshank
Rooms: 4 (PB) $85-105
Full Country Breakfast
Credit Cards: A, B
Notes: 2, 5, 8, 9, 10

Red Bluff Cottage

MONTGOMERY

Red Bluff Cottage

551 Clay Street, PO Box 1026, 36101
(334) 264-0056; fax (334) 263-3054
E-mail: RedBlufBnB@aol.com
Web site: http://www.bbonline.com/al/redbluff

Anne and Mark Waldo invite you to share the comforts and pleasures of Red Bluff Cottage, high above the Alabama River in Montgomery's historic Cottage Hill District. Red Bluff is a raised cottage, built in 1987 as a B&B inn. The guest rooms are all on the ground floor, with easy access from the parking area, gazebo, and fenced play yard. The kitchen, dining room, living room, sitting room with TV, and music room with piano and harpsichord are on the second floor; guests are urged to enjoy these public rooms. A deep upstairs porch offers a panoramic view of the river

plain and downtown Montgomery, including a unique view of the state capitol. Each of the four guest rooms has a private bath and is furnished with family antiques. Anne is a cook and gardener and Mark, a retired Episcopal priest, is the handyman and assistant.

Hosts: Mark and Anne Waldo
Rooms: 4 (PB) $55-65
Full Breakfast
Credit Cards: A, B, D, E
Notes: 2, 7

ORANGE BEACH

The Original Romar House

23500 Perdido Beach Boulevard (Hwy 182), 36561
(334) 974-1625; 1-800-487-6627;
FAX (334) 974-1163
E-mail: original@gulftel.com
Web site: http://www.bbonline.com/al/romarhouse

Quaint and romantic 1920s seaside inn with each room decorated in art-deco furniture and named after a local festival like the Mardi Gras Room, the Shrimp Festival Room or the Red Snapper Festival Room. Enjoy private beach bicycles, hot tub spa and full southern breakfast. Read a book in a swing on the deck, curl up in the hammock, or walk on the beach, picking up seashells. We have golf, tennis, fishing, and entertainment nearby at this award-winning inn.

Hosts: Darrell Finley and Jerry Gilbreath
Rooms: 7 (PB) $ 89-120
Full Breakfast
Credit Cards: A, B, C
Notes: 2, 5, 8, 9, 10

welcome; 7 Children welcome; 8 Tennis nearby; 9 Swimming nearby; 10 Golf nearby; 11 Skiing nearby; 12 May be booked through travel agent.

ALASKA

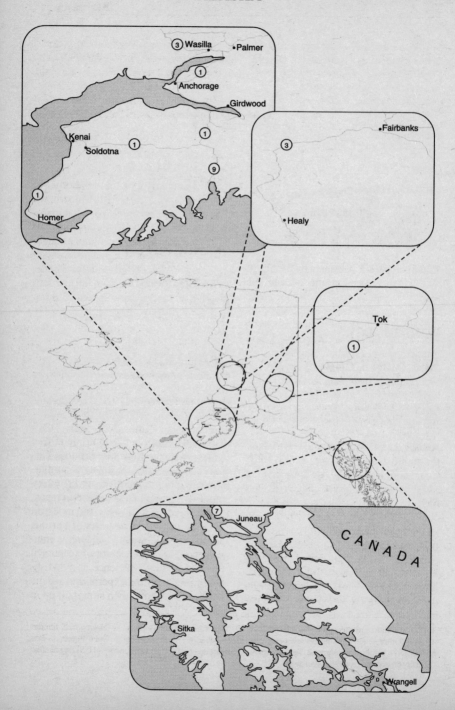

Alaska

ANCHORAGE

Elderberry B&B

8340 Elderberry, 99502
(907) 243-6968 (voice and FAX)

Elderberry B&B is located by the airport and has three guest rooms with private baths. We cater to each one of our guests on an individual basis. Situated on the greenbelt in Anchorage where moose often can be spotted. We serve full, homemade breakfasts. Linda and Norm, the hosts, love to talk about Alaska and are very active in their church.

Hosts: Norm and Linda Seitz
Rooms: 3 (PB) $50-75
Full Breakfast
Credit Cards: A, B
Notes: 2, 5, 7, 11, 12

Homestays at Homesteads

807 G, Suite 250, 99501
(907) 272-8644; FAX (907) 274-8644

A statewide reservation service, Homestays at Homesteads features delightful folks who enjoy opening their homes to you. From wilderness to downtown, we know Alaska: where to go, what to do, how and when to do it. Let us make all your travel and bed and breakfast arrangements. Almost four hundred rooms with private and shared baths are available, priced from $65 to 130. Both full and continental breakfasts are served. Sharon Kelly, coordinator.

Hospitality Plus

7722 Anne Circle, 99504-4601
(907) 333-8504; FAX (907) 337-1718
E-mail: jbudai@alaska.net
Web site: http://www.alaska.net/%7Ejbudai/

Envision a comfortable home, delightful and thematically decorated rooms, caring and knowledgeable hosts, a sumptuous breakfast elegantly served every morning, a mountain range within reach, a profusion of wildflowers, and moose in the yard. Add to that years of various and intriguing Alaskan adventures, a Hungarian refugee's escape story, exceptional tour and guiding experience, an avid fisherman, story-telling experts, and artistic achievements, and then sum it all up in

---

NOTES: Credit cards accepted: A Master Card; B Visa; C American Express; D Discover; E Diners Club; F Other; 2 Personal checks accepted; 3 Lunch available; 4 Dinner available; 5 Open all year; 6 Pets welcome; 7 Children welcome; 8 Tennis nearby; 9 Swimming nearby; 10 Golf nearby; 11 Skiing nearby; 12 May be booked through travel agent.

one word: *hospitality*. It doesn't get better than this!

Hosts: Charles and Joan Budai
Rooms: 3 (1PB; 2SB) $60-85
Full Breakfast
Credit Cards: D
Notes: 2, 5, 7, 8, 9, 11, 12

White Goose Inn

3060 Admiralty Bay Circle, 99515
(907) 349-1022; FAX (907) 564-5132
E-mail: wgoosein@alaska.net
Web site: http://www.alaska.net/~wgoosein

Located in a quiet neighborhood convenient to the airport, shopping, dining, downtown, and the mountains, where you truly can relax. The White Goose Inn is within walking distance of tennis courts and biking/jogging trails, and only minutes from golf courses, hiking, and ski trails. Room features a queen-size brass bed with cable TV, telephone, bathrobes and adjoining private bath. Extended/hearty continental breakfast. Smoke-free environment. Fully licensed. Hosts have lived in Alaska more than twenty years and want to share their beautiful state with you.

Hosts: Jim and Judy Buono
Rooms: 1 (PB) $65-85 (seasonal)
Continental Breakfast
Credit Cards: A, B
Notes: 2, 5, 8, 9, 10, 11, 12

FAIRBANKS

7 Gables Inn

PO Box 80488, 99708
(907) 479-0751; FAX (907) 479-2229
E-mail: gables7@alaska.net
Web site: http://www.alaska.net/~gables7

Historically, Alaska's 7 Gables Inn was a fraternity house located within walking dis-

tance of the University of Alaska/Fairbanks campus, near the river and airport. The ten-thousand-square-foot Tudor-style inn features a floral solarium, an antique stained glass-decorated foyer with an indoor waterfall, cathedral ceilings, and rooms with dormers. Amenities include full gourmet breakfasts, private Jacuzzi baths, cable TV/VCRs, phones, a conference room, a library, Alaskana videos, laundry, bikes, canoes, and skis.

Hosts: Paul and Leicha Welton
Rooms: 9 (PB) $50-130
Full Breakfast
Credit Cards: A, B, C, D, E
Notes: 2, 5, 7, 11, 12

Cook's Cove Bed and Breakfast

424 Glacier Avenue, 99701
(907) 452-3442
E-mail: bcook@mosquitonet.com
Web site: http://www.fireweed.com/COOK

The Cook family crest bears the inscription "He showeth a safe road"—an appropriate direction for the weary traveler seeking a safe night's lodging. Located in the "Golden Heart of Alaska," Cook's Cove is decorated in the style of a Victorian country cottage. The atmosphere is peaceful and cozy, and the hospitality of your hosts is warm and friendly. Dick loves to share Alaska stories, and Betty serves up a hearty breakfast, with fresh-baked scones a specialty.

Hosts: Dick and Betty Cook
Rooms: 2 1/2 (SB) $50-65
Full Breakfast
Credit Cards: none
Notes: 2, 5, 7, 9 (indoor), 10, 11 (winter)

NOTES: Credit cards accepted: A Master Card; B Visa; C American Express; D Discover; E Diners Club; F Other; 2 Personal checks accepted; 3 Lunch available; 4 Dinner available; 5 Open all year; 6 Pets

Eleanor's Northern Lights Bed and Breakfast

360 State Street, 99701
(907) 452-2598

We are Christian folks, part of the Wels Lutheran Church.

Host: Laverne Wood
Rooms: 6 (4PB; 2SB) $50-65
Full or Continental Breakfast
Credit Cards: A, B, C, D
Notes: 2, 3 (self-serve, $3), 5, 7, 8, 9, 10, 11, 12

Lennie's Lair Bed and Breakfast

2034 Eagan Avenue, 99701
(907) 456-5931

In the heart of the city, with a partial forest setting. Close to Alaskaland, public bus routes, and restaurant.

Hosts: Leneve (Lennie) Johnson
Rooms: 2 (PB) $85
Continental Breakfast
Credit Cards: A, B
Notes: 2, 5

GIRDWOOD

"A Cross Country Meadows" Bed and Breakfast

PO Box 123, Timberline and Alta Drive, 99587
(907) 783-3333; FAX (907) 783-3335
E-mail: crosscountrymeadowsbb@juno.com

The "A Cross Country Meadows" Bed and Breakfast was designed and built specifically as a B&B and furnished for the convenience of our guests. We cater to those who seek quiet, peaceful accom-

"A Cross Country Meadows" B&B

modations with a luxurious and private atmosphere. Our home is a place for guests to rest from their travels or regroup for another nearby adventure. Our B&B is a great place for staging day trips, for a romantic retreat, or for just mixing business with pleasure. Sylvia and Brent's warm hospitality and their love of crafts graciously accent this cozy, charming B&B. Their home is decorated beautifully. All the top-floor guest rooms have a panoramic view of surrounding meadows, Alyeska ski slopes and awesome, snow-capped glaciers. Each deluxe bedroom has cathedral ceilings and shares a private loft and sitting area.

Hosts: Brent and Sylvia Stonebraker
Rooms: 2 (PB with king-sized beds) $95-100
"Country Style" Continental Breakfast
Credit Cards: A, B, C
Notes: 5, 11, 12

HEALY

Rustic Ridge Bed and Breakfast

PO Box 46, 99743
(907) 683-2921

Here at Rustic Ridge, you'll have twelve hundred square feet of newly constructed,

welcome; 7 Children welcome; 8 Tennis nearby; 9 Swimming nearby; 10 Golf nearby; 11 Skiing nearby; 12 May be booked through travel agent.

secluded, affordable accommodations. Our place is ideal for two couples traveling together. Some amenities include queen-size beds, private entrance, laundry facilities, large Jacuzzi tub, fully equipped kitchen, queen-size hide-a-bed, and private patio with an incredible view. We are fifteen miles from the entrance to Denali National Park. Pond nearby. Our family and friendly dog team would enjoy meeting you!

Hosts: Tim and Karla MacIver
Rooms: 2 + hideaway bed in living room (SB) $80-140
Continental Breakfast
Credit Cards: none
Notes: 2, 5, 6, 7

HOMER

Brass Ring
Bed and Breakfast

PO Box 2090, 99603
(907) 235-5450; FAX (907) 235-4930
E-mail: vanbrass@ptialaska.net
Web site: http://www.ptialaska.net/~vanbrass

Located in the heart of Homer, our Alaskan log home has three rooms with private baths and two sharing one bath. A honeymoon suite is available. Our full cooked breakfasts include fresh ground coffee and fresh fruit. Sourdough pancakes are our specialty. At the end of the day, relax in our outdoor hot tub.

Hosts: Vicki and Dave VanLiere
Rooms: 5 (3PB; 2SB) $70-100
Full Breakfast
Credit Cards: A, B, D
Notes: 2, 12

Three Moose Meadow Wilderness Bed and Breakfast

PO Box 15291, 99603
(907) 235-0755

With the help of the Lord, we've taken the bed and breakfast concept to a new level. Understanding that travelers to Alaska want to experience Alaska, we offer you a newly constructed log cabin in a wilderness setting. Your cozy cottage is nestled in the woods and overlooks a meadow with snow-capped mountains beyond. You'll enjoy a covered porch complete with a swing. Our bed and breakfast also features a large deck, TV with VCR, kitchen, bath, and open-view woodstove for guests. Very private. Call for a brochure.

Hosts: Jordan and Jennie Hess
Rooms: 2 (PB) $85
Full Breakfast
Credit Cards: none
Notes: 2, 5, 6 (outdoor), 7

JUNEAU

Alaska Wolf House

PO Box 21321, 99802
(907) 586-2422; (888) 586-9053;
FAX (907) 586-9053
E-mail: akwlfhs@ptialaska.net
Web site: http://www.wetpage.com/akwlfhse

Alaska Wolf House is a four thousand-square-foot western red cedar log home located one mile from downtown Juneau. Built on the side of Mt. Juneau, it features a southern exposure enabling the viewing

---

NOTES: Credit cards accepted: A Master Card; B Visa; C American Express; D Discover; E Diners Club; F Other; 2 Personal checks accepted; 3 Lunch available; 4 Dinner available; 5 Open all year; 6 Pets

of sunrises and sunsets over busy Gastineau Channel and the moon rising over the statuesque mountains of Douglas Island. Hosts Philip and Clovis Dennis serve an excellent breakfast in the Glassroom overlooking the channel and mountains. Within a short walk is the Glacier hiking-jogging-biking trail and public transportation. Smoke-free rooms are available with private or shared bathrooms. Suites have kitchens. Plan to enjoy all the amenities of home while experiencing "Our Great Land of Foreverness."

Hosts: Philip and Clovis Dennis
Rooms: 6 (4PB; 2SB) $75-135
Full Breakfast
Credit Cards: A, B
Notes: 2, 5, 7, 8, 9, 10, 11, 12

The Lost Chord

2200 Fritz Cove Road, 99801
(907) 789-7296; (907) 780-6275

The Lost Chord was a music business we started in our home when Alaska was still a territory. It was a unique enterprise, with a quality of its own. In 1983, we moved to a new home on the waterfront and the music business, along with many other items, were lost. But the uniqueness and character of the Lost Chord have emerged again as a beautiful bed and breakfast situated on an exquisite private beach. There are rivers for you to cross, mountains to hike, and a bed and breakfast we promise you'll like.

Hosts: Jess and Ellen Jones
Rooms: 4 (1PB; 3SB) $60-125
Full Breakfast
Credit Cards: A, B
Notes: 2, 5, 6, 7, 8, 9, 10, 11, 12

Pearson's Pond Luxury Inn and Garden Spa

4541 Sawa Circle, 99801-8723
(907) 789-3772; FAX (907) 789-6722
E-mail: pearsons.pond@juneau.com
Web site: http://www.juneau.com/pearsons.pond

This award-winning bed and breakfast resort is a perfect getaway for nature and privacy lovers. Enjoy a hot tub and massage at your breathtaking waterfront retreat overlooking Mendenhall Glacier. Photograph wildlife between naps on the dock, or row the peaceful pond surrounded by gardens and sparkling fountains. Bike or walk the adjacent river trail. Garden- or water-view minisuites have private entry, kitchens and every imaginable amenity. Guests enjoy health club access. Frommer's "Best B&B of Alaska." AAA/ABBA Excellence.

Hosts: Steve and Diane Pearson
Rooms: 3 (PB) $99-199
Continental Breakfast
Credit Cards: A, B, C, D, E, F
Notes: 2, 5, 7, 8, 9, 10, 11, 12

KENAI

Eldridge Haven Bed and Breakfast

2679 Bowpicker Lane, 99611
(907) 283-7152; FAX (907) 283-7152

Eldridge Haven Bed and Breakfast is hospitality at its best! Peaceful, clean, friendly. Excellent food: giant Alaskan pancake, steaming gingered bananas, stuffed scones, etc. It's in a wooded area surrounded by prime habitat for moose, caribou, bald

welcome; 7 Children welcome; 8 Tennis nearby; 9 Swimming nearby; 10 Golf nearby; 11 Skiing nearby; 12 May be booked through travel agent.

eagles, and waterfowl. You can walk to the beach. Cross-country skiing is convenient. The lodging is close to all Peninsula points, including Seward and Homer. So eliminate packing and unpacking; stay with the best and visit the rest. Children are treasured; guests are pampered. Eldridge Haven Bed and Breakfast is open year-round. We've been serving satisfied guests since 1987.

Hosts: Marta and Barry Eldridge
Rooms: 2 (1PB; 1SB) $65-80
Full Breakfast
Credit Cards: A, B
Notes: 2, 5, 7, 8, 9, 10, 11 (cross-country), 12

PALMER

Hatcher Pass Bed and Breakfast

HC 05, Box 6797-D, 99645
(907) 745-6788; FAX (907) 745-6787
E-mail: Hejl@juno.com

Located at the base of beautiful Hatcher Pass, our private log cabins offer the warmth and charm of Alaskan decor and hospitality. Each cabin has a private shower and kitchenette. We are open year-round to accommodate your winter sporting needs as well as your summer activities and visits to the Matanuski-Susitna Valley. We look forward to seeing you at Hatcher Pass Bed and Breakfast. We pledge to work to make you glad you stayed with us.

Hosts: Dan and Liz Hejl
Rooms: 3 (PB) $75
Continental Breakfast
Credit Cards: A, B
Notes: 2, 5, 6, 7, 11, 12

Beyond the Boardwalk Inn of Pelican

PELICAN

Beyond the Boardwalk Inn of Pelican

Summer: PO Box 12, Pelican, 99832
   (907) 735-2463
Winter: PO Box 60, Indianola, WA 98342
   (360) 297-3550

Our home resides in a small boardwalk fishing town in a deep fjord, ninety miles west of Juneau. My wife and I, being teachers, enjoy opening our home in June, July, and August, when you can appreciate the solitude and beauty of waterfalls, hiking, fishing, wonderful food, and Christian fellowship. Our home, decorated uniquely Alaskan, features a log cabin with hot tub and three guest rooms. A truly Christian, rural Alaskan adventure.

Hosts: Ted and AnneBeth Whited
Rooms: 3 (1PB; 2SB) $90
Full Breakfast
Credit Cards: A, B, C, D, E
Notes: 2, 4

SITKA

Alaska Ocean View B&B

1101 Edgecumbe Drive, 99835
(907) 747-8310 (voice and FAX)

An outstanding lodging rated one of "Alaska's best!" Drift off to sleep in an exceptionally comfortable king/queen bed under a fluffy down comforter after a relaxing, massaging soak in the patio Jacuzzi. Awake to the wonderful aroma of a generous gourmet breakfast cooking, fresh-ground coffee brewing, and bread baking. The in-room TV/VCR, stereo, phone, robe, library, and view, and the friendly hosts all help make your stay one to remember.

Yukon Don's Bed and Breakfast

Hosts: Carole and Bill Denkinger
Rooms: 3 (PB) $89-139
Full Breakfast
Credit Cards: A, B, C
Notes: 2, 5, 7, 8, 9, 12

SOLDOTNA

Denise Lake Lodge

PO Box 1050, 99669
(907) 262-1789; (800) 478-1789;
FAX (907) 262-7184
E-mail: Jehanson@ptialaska.net
Web site: http://www.bbonline.com/ak/deniselake

Denise Lodge is located in a quiet, friendly atmosphere nestled in a setting of white birches overlooking Denise Lake. Our lodge offers a variety of options. These include a log lodge with a large covered deck and gas barbecue on the lake side. There are loons and ducks on the lake and an occasional moose feeding in the front yard. We have a spacious dining area with two large windows facing the lake. All rooms and cabins have private baths. No smoking indoors.

Hosts: Jim and Elaine Hanson
Rooms: 12 (PB)
Full Breakfast
Credit Cards: A, B, C, D
Notes: 2, 7, 10, 12

WASILLA

Yukon Don's Bed and Breakfast

1830 E. Parks Hwy., Suite 386, 99654
(907) 376-7472; (800) 478-7472;
FAX (907) 376-6515

When you're traveling in Alaska, or to and from Denali National Park, you don't want to miss staying at Yukon Don's Bed and Breakfast, "Alaska's most acclaimed B&B Inn." Each spacious, comfortable guest room is decorated with authentic Alaskana; stay in the Iditarod, Fishing, Denali or Hunting rooms, or select the Matanuska or Yukon executive suites. Our guests relax in the Alaska room, complete with an Alaskan historic library, video library, pool table, cable TV, and gift bar. The all-glass-view room on the second floor offers the grandest view in the Matanuska Valley, complete with fireplace, chairs and observation deck. We offer phones in each room, Yukon Don's own expanded continental breakfast bar, sauna, exercise room, and, according to Commissioner Glenn Olds (world traveler) "the grandest view he has ever seen from a home." Judge William Hungate of St.

welcome; 7 Children welcome; 8 Tennis nearby; 9 Swimming nearby; 10 Golf nearby; 11 Skiing nearby; 12 May be booked through travel agent.

Louis, Missouri, said, "It's like seeing Alaska without leaving the house." Wasilla is home of the international Iditarod sled dog race.

Hosts: "Yukon" Don and Kristan Tanner
Rooms: 8 (3PB; 5SB) $79-125
Continental Breakfast
Credit Cards: A, B, C, D
Notes: 2, 5, 7, 8, 10, 11, 12

WRANGELL

Grand View Bed and Breakfast

PO Box 927, 99929
(907) 874-3225; FAX (907) 874-3225
Web site: www.wrangell.com/business/grand/
   view.htm

Nestled in the woods, quiet and secluded. A private suite has its own entrance, one bedroom, private bath, kitchen/dining area, living room, color cablevision, telephone, microwave. Smoke-free environ-

Grand View Bed and Breakfast

ment, view with lots of maritime activity to watch and beautiful sunsets. We will work with you to customize a package for the activities that best suit your needs, such as biking, charter fishing, kayaking, jet boat tours, guided walking tours, car rental, golf, tennis, or swimming. We'll leave the light on for you.

Hosts: Judy and John Baker
Rooms: 1 (PB) $65
Full or Continental Breakfast
Credit Cards: none
Notes: 2, 3, 5, 8, 9, 10, 12

NOTES: Credit cards accepted: A Master Card; B Visa; C American Express; D Discover; E Diners Club; F Other; 2 Personal checks accepted; 3 Lunch available; 4 Dinner available; 5 Open all year; 6 Pets

Arizona

Advance Reservations Inn Arizona and Old Pueblo Homestays, RSO

PO Box 13603, **Tucson**, 85732
(520) 790-0030; (800) 333-9776;
FAX (520) 790-2399
E-mail: JAWS1926@aol.com
Web site: http://azres.com

A **statewide** B&B reservation service featuring accommodations in individual homes, inns, and guest ranches in **Arizona**, ranging from the very modest to luxurious, including continental to gourmet breakfast. Some provide facilities for group meetings, weddings, reunions, etc. Brochure $3 with SASE. MC, Visa and Discover accepted. William A. Janssen, coordinator.

Arizona Trails B&B Reservation Service

PO Box 18998, **Fountain Hills**, 85269-8998
(602) 837-4284; (888) 799-4284;
FAX (602) 816-4224

The convenient and easy way to make your bed and breakfast reservations free of charge. **Statewide** accommodations. Specializing in traditional bed and breakfasts and inns, romantic getaways and unique, luxurious B&B experiences as well as corporate travel and small group accommodations. All properties are personally inspected and approved to ensure a quality visit. "Stay out West with the folks who know it best." Major credit cards and personal checks accepted. Roxanne and Hank Boryczki, owners.

Mi Casa Su Casa Bed and Breakfast Reservation Service

PO Box 950, **Tempe**, 85280-0950
(602) 990-0682; (800) 456-0682 (reservations);
FAX (602) 990-3390
E-mail: ruthy2425@aol.com

Since 1981, we proudly have listed inspected, clean, comfortable B&B homestays, inns, cottages and ranches in Arizona and the Southwest. We list about two hundred modest-to-luxurious, historic-to-contemporary B&Bs. In **Arizona**, listings include Ajo, Benson, Bisbee, Cave Creek, Cottonwood, Flagstaff, Globe, Mesa, Page, Patagonia, Paradise (near Portal), Payson, Phoenix, Prescott, Rimrock, Scottsdale, Sedona, Sierra Vista, Sonoita, Tempe, Tucson, Tombstone, Willcox, Williams and other cities. (See also our entries in Nevada, New Mexico and Utah.) We also represent two luxury

welcome; 7 Children welcome; 8 Tennis nearby; 9 Swimming nearby; 10 Golf nearby; 11 Skiing nearby; 12 May be booked through travel agent.

ARIZONA

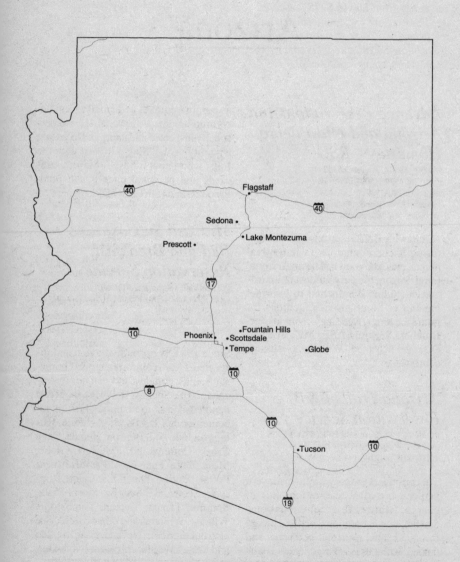

villas, one in Puerto Vallarto, **Mexico**, and the second in the Costa Brava area of **Spain**. Most rooms have private baths and range from $50 to $275, based on double-occupancy. Continental to gourmet breakfasts. A book with individual descriptions and pictures is available for $9.50. Ruth Young, coordinator.

Birch Tree Inn Bed and Breakfast

FLAGSTAFF

Birch Tree Inn Bed and Breakfast

824 W. Birch Avenue, 86001-4420
(520) 774-1042; 1-888-774-1042;
FAX (520) 774-8462
E-mail: birch@flagstaff.az.us
Web site: www.flagstaff.az.us/birch

Offering a quiet respite, this comfortable home has warm and friendly innkeepers. Each guest room has its own personality, and the swing on the wraparound porch awaits you. Fresh-baked muffins or breads are a part of the hearty, down-home breakfasts served each morning. Four seasons of beauty in the mountain town of Flagstaff encourage guests to fully explore its wonder.

Hosts: Sandy and Ed Znetko, and Donna and
   Rodger Pettinger
Rooms: 5 (3PB, 2SB) $69-109
Full Breakfast
Credit Cards: A, B, C, D
Notes: 2, 5, 7, 8, 10, 11, 12

Comfi Cottages

1612 N. Aztec Street, 86001
(520) 774-0731; (888) 774-0731;
FAX (520) 779-1008
E-mail: Comfie@infomagic.com
Web site: http://www.virtualflagstaff.com/comfi

Near the Grand Canyon, great for families. Five individual cottages with antiques and English country motif. Three cottages are two-bedroom, one bath; one is a one-bedroom honeymoon cottage and two are three-bedroom, two baths. All have gas fireplaces. Fully equipped with linens, towels, blankets. Kitchens have dishes, pots, pans, coffeepot, etc. Ready-to-prepare breakfast foods in fridge. Color cable television and telephone. Bicycles on premises, washer/dryer, picnic tables, and barbecue grills at each cottage. *Arizona Republic's*

Comfi Cottages

NOTES: Credit cards accepted: A Master Card; B Visa; C American Express; D Discover; E Diners Club; F Other; 2 Personal checks accepted; 3 Lunch available; 4 Dinner available; 5 Open all year; 6 Pets welcome; 7 Children welcome; 8 Tennis nearby; 9 Swimming nearby; 10 Golf nearby; 11 Skiing nearby; 12 May be booked through travel agent.

choice as "Best Weekend Getaway" for November 1995.

Hosts: Pat and Ed Wiebe
Rooms: 8 (PB) $75-195 (for entire cottage)
Guest-Prepared Full Breakfast
Credit Cards: A, B, D
Notes: 2, 5, 7, 8, 9, 10, 11, 12

The Inn at 410

410 N. Leroux Street, 86001
(520) 774-0088; (800) 774-2008;
FAX (520) 774-6354

Explore the Grand Canyon, Indian Country, Sedona, and the San Francisco Peaks while relaxing at "the Place with the Personal Touch." The Inn at 410 offers four seasons of hospitality in a charming 1907 Craftsman home. Scrumptious gourmet breakfasts and afternoon cookies and tea. Uniquely decorated guest rooms, all with private baths, some with fireplaces and oversize Jacuzzi tubs; one room wheelchair accessible. Walk two blocks to shops, galleries, and restaurants in historic downtown Flagstaff.

Hosts: Howard and Sally Krueger
Rooms: 9 (PB) $125-175
Full Breakfast
Credit Cards: A, B
Notes: 2, 5, 7, 10, 11, 12

Jeanette's Bed and Breakfast

3380 E. Lockett Road, 86004-4043
(520) 527-1912; (800) 752-1912

Relax and enjoy while you step back in time. Architecture of the post-Victorian era recalls Arizona's first statehood days. Experience Jeanette's four rooms filled with signs of the time. Private baths re-

Jeanette's Bed and Breakfast

flect the style of the era and a "breakfast so divine" is served with the flair and detail of a fine Sunday dinner. Flagstaff is the place to be for sights, sounds, and the smell of cool, clean, pine-scented mountain air. So come, stay a day or stay a week at "Jeanette's."

Hosts: Jeanette and Ray West
Rooms: 4 (PB) $65 winter - $85 summer
Full Breakfast
Credit Cards: A, B
Notes: 2, 5, 7 (over 7), 8, 9, 10, 11, 12

GLOBE

Cedar Hill B&B

175 East Cedar, 85501
(520) 425-7530

Cedar Hill B&B was built in 1903 by the Trojanavich family. They were owners of a lumber company, which accounts for the wainscoting walls in the kitchen and rear porch. The property has many fruit trees, flower beds and a grape arbor for the enjoyment of our guests. Guests may enjoy both a front porch with swings and our back patio with shade trees. The backyard is fenced for the protection of children and pets you may wish to bring! Cable TV and VCR are available in the

NOTES: Credit cards accepted: A Master Card; B Visa; C American Express; D Discover; E Diners Club; F Other; 2 Personal checks accepted; 3 Lunch available; 4 Dinner available; 5 Open all year; 6 Pets

living room. Within driving distance of both Tuscon and Phoenix. Discounts for seniors and for stays longer than overnight.

Hostess: Helen Gross
Rooms: 2 (SB) $40-50
Full Breakfast
Credit Cards: none
Notes: 2, 5, 6, 7, 9

Cedar Hill Bed and Breakfast

LAKE MONTEZUMA

Whispering Waters Bed and Breakfast

PO Box 5633, 86342
(520) 567-4540

Discover an unforgettable getaway. Whispering Waters sits on nearly one acre "on the banks of Beaver Creek." Nature is bountiful—see the many species of birds, including the Golden Eagle and numerous waterfowl. Enjoy afternoon tea on the ninety-foot covered deck or next to a cozy fire. Walk or bicycle around the picturesque community and visit the many area attractions. No smoking indoors.

Hostess: Mona Marszaiek
Rooms: 3 (1PB; 2SB) $85-110
Full Country Breakfast
Credit Cards: A, B, C
Notes: 2, 5, 7, 8, 9, 10, 11, 12

PHOENIX

The Villa on Alvarado

2031 N. Alvarado Road, 85004
(602) 253-9352

Located in a quiet, historic neighborhood, the Villa features a spacious guest house with two bedrooms, two baths, and a kitchenette. The deck overlooks the manicured gardens and a sparkling pool. If royalty is your preference, our English tower will be perfect for you. It has a private entrance, sitting room, curved stairway that leads to a magnificent, canopied king-sized bed, private bath, and balcony.

Hosts: Kay and Chris King
Rooms: 3 (PB) $80-125
Continental Breakfast
Credit Cards: none
Notes: 5, 8, 9, 10

PRESCOTT

Hassayampa Inn

122 E. Gurley St., 86301
(520) 778-9434; (800) 322-1927;
FAX (520) 445-8590
E-mail: inn@primenet.com

Times have changed, but the Inn, now listed on the National Register of Historic places, still retains the charm of yesteryear with the amenities of today. The classic overnight rooms, lace curtains, oak period furniture, and modern bathrooms, along with exceptional service provided by a caring staff, will enhance your visit. Discriminating travelers will find the Inn the ideal destination, just steps from the center of town, Courthouse square, antique shops, museums, and stately Victorian

welcome; 7 Children welcome; 8 Tennis nearby; 9 Swimming nearby; 10 Golf nearby; 11 Skiing nearby; 12 May be booked through travel agent.

homes. For the finest in cuisine visit the acclaimed Peacock Room; for a light snack and beverage relax in the quaint Bar and Grill; or just sit back and enjoy the beauty of the magnificent lobby at the Hassayampa Inn.

Hosts: Bill and Georgia Teich, J.L. Jernegan
Rooms: 68 (PB) $99-175
Full Breakfast
Credit Cards: A, B, C, D, E
Notes: 2, 3, 4, 5, 7, 8, 9, 10, 12

Mount Vernon Inn

204 N. Mt. Vernon Avenue, 86301
(520) 778-0886; FAX (520) 778-7305
E-mail: mtvrnon@primenet.com
Web site: http://prescottlink.com/mtvrnon/
    index.htm

Built in 1900 and listed on the National Register of Historic Places, the Mount Vernon Inn is one of Prescott's "Victorian Treasures." The four spacious guest rooms with private baths and three beautiful country cottages offer charming alternatives to conventional lodging and are designed for your comfort and relaxation. Breakfast is served in the guest rooms. The inn is situ-

Mount Vernon Inn

ated just a few blocks from the town square. Come and enjoy the hospitality of our inn!

Hosts: Michele and Jerry Neumann
Rooms: 7 (PB) $90-120
Full Breakfast
Credit Cards: A, B, D
Notes: 2, 5, 8, 9, 10, 12

SCOTTSDALE

Valley O' the Sun Bed and Breakfast

PO Box 2214, 85252
(602) 941-1281; (800) 689-1281;
FAX (800) 689-1281

"Cead Mile Failte" is the slogan in Gaelic on the doormat of the Valley O' the Sun Bed and Breakfast. They mean "100,000 welcomes." This bed and breakfast is more than just a place to stay. Kathleen wants to make your visit to the great Southwest a memorable one. Ideally located in the college area of Tempe, but still close enough to Scottsdale to enjoy the glamour of its shops, restaurants, and theaters. Two guest rooms can comfortably accommodate four people. One bedroom has a full-size bed and the other has twin beds. Each room has its own TV. Within minutes of golf, horseback riding, picnic area, swimming, bicycling, shopping, and tennis. Within walking distance of Arizona State University.

Hostess: Kathleen Curtis
Rooms: 2 (SB) $40
Continental Breakfast
Credit Cards: none
Notes: 2 (restricted), 5, 7 (over 10), 8, 9, 10, 11, 12

NOTES: Credit cards accepted: A Master Card; B Visa; C American Express; D Discover; E Diners Club; F Other; 2 Personal checks accepted; 3 Lunch available; 4 Dinner available; 5 Open all year; 6 Pets

The Graham Bed and Breakfast Inn

SEDONA

The Graham Bed and Breakfast Inn

150 Canyon Circle Drive, 86351
(520) 284-1425; (800) 228-1425;
FAX (520) 284-0767
E-mail: graham@sedona.net
Web site: http://www.sedonasfinest.com

The Graham Bed and Breakfast Inn is an award-winning Inn with a swimming pool, hot tub, and exceptional theme rooms. Room features include fireplaces, Jacuzzi tubs, private balconies with red rock views, and television/VCRs. Four new luxury, adobe-style casitas are now available; each one has a waterfall shower, bath fireplace, and one-of-a-kind furnishings. Guests check in to the aroma of fresh-baked bread; each casita has its own bread maker.

Hosts: Carol and Roger Redenbaugh
Rooms: 10 (PB) $109-369
Full Breakfast
Credit Cards: A, B, D
Notes: 2, 5, 7, 8, 9, 10, 12 (no fee)

Territorial House Bed and Breakfast

65 Piki Drive, 86336
(520) 204-2737; (800) 801-2737;
FAX (520) 204-2230

Our large stone and cedar house has been tastefully decorated to depict Arizona's territorial era. Each room recalls different stages of Sedona's early history. Some rooms have private balcony, Jacuzzi tub, or fireplace. An enormous stone fireplace graces the living room and a covered veranda welcomes guests at the end of a day of sightseeing. Relax in our outdoor hot tub. A full hearty breakfast is served at the harvest table each morning. All of this is served with Western hospitality.

Hosts: John and Linda Steele
Rooms: 4 (PB) $109-159
Full Breakfast
Credit Cards: A, B, C, D
Notes: 2, 5, 7, 8, 9, 10, 11, 12

TUCSON

Casa Alegre Bed and Breakfast

316 E. Speedway Boulevard, 85705
(520) 628-1800; (800) 628-5654;
FAX (520) 792-1880

Casa Alegre is a charming 1915 Craftsman-style bungalow featuring mahogany,

Casa Alegre

welcome; 7 Children welcome; 8 Tennis nearby; 9 Swimming nearby; 10 Golf nearby; 11 Skiing nearby; 12 May be booked through travel agent.

leaded glass, built-in cabinetry, and hardwood floors. The serene gardens, pool, and hot tub make an oasis of comfort in central Tucson, just minutes from the University of Arizona. A scrumptious full breakfast is served. Private baths. AAA- and Mobil-rated.

Hostess: Phyllis Florek
Rooms: 5 (PB) $60-105
Full Breakfast
Credit Cards: A, B, C, D
Notes: 2, 5, 8, 9, 10, 11, 12

El Presidio
Bed and Breakfast Inn

297 N. Main Avenue, 85701
(520) 623-6151; (800) 349-6151;
FAX (520) 623-3860

Experience southwestern charm in a desert oasis with the romance of a country inn. Garden courtyards with the Old Mexico ambience of lush, floral displays, fountains, and cobblestone surround a richly appointed guest house and suites. Enjoy antique decor, robes, complimentary beverages, fruit, snacks, TVs, and telephones. The 1880s Victorian adobe mansion has been featured in numerous magazines and in the book *The Desert Southwest*. The inn is located in a historic district. You can walk to fine restaurants, museums, shops, and the arts district. El Presidio is located close to downtown. Mobil and AAA three-star rated.

Hostess: Patti Toci
Rooms: 3 suites (PB) $85-110
Full Breakfast
Credit Cards: none
Notes: 2, 5, 8, 9, 10, 12

Elizabeth's
Bed and Breakfast

1931 W. Calle Campana de Plata, 85745
(520) 884-8874

This modest, attractively decorated home is within walking distance of a bus stop, regional park, and golf courses. The comfortable home is in a quiet neighborhood three miles west of the University of Arizona. The hostess is a world traveler who enjoys meeting new people. She takes pride in her home and will make you very welcome. The guest bedroom has a queen-size bed, large closet, dresser space, TV, radio, and telephone.

Hostess: Elizabeth Woolery
Rooms: 1 (PB) $45-55
Full Breakfast
Credit Cards: none
Notes: 2, 3, 5, 8, 9, 10, 12

Hacienda
Bed and Breakfast

5704 E. Grant Road, 85712
(520) 290-2224; (888) 236-4421
FAX (520) 721-9066
E-mail: Hacienda97@aol.com
Web site: http://members.aol.com/Hacienda97/
    INDEX.html

Four quiet, air-conditioned rooms with private baths. Two have TV/VCRs and private entrances; one offers handicap access and has a refrigerator, coffeemaker and full hide-a-bed. Two bedrooms share a sitting room with TV/VCR and table and chairs. A full is breakfast served. Guests may use the private courtyard, barbecue, pool/spa, exercise room, computer, FAX,

NOTES: Credit cards accepted: A Master Card; B Visa; C American Express; D Discover; E Diners Club; F Other; 2 Personal checks accepted; 3 Lunch available; 4 Dinner available; 5 Open all year; 6 Pets

copier, fireproof file for valuables. Lots of hiking, biking, and bird-watching in the area. Smoke-free. No pets. Supervised children welcome. AAA-rated; member of Tucson Convention Bureau and Chamber of Commerce, and of AABBI.

Hosts: Barbara and Fred Shamseldin
Rooms: 4 (PB) $85-105
Full Breakfast
Credit Cards: A, B, C, D
Notes: 2 (traveler's checks), 5, 10, 11 (short season), 12

Jeremiah Inn

10921 E. Snyder Road, 85749
(520) 749-3072

For centuries travelers have paused at quiet inns to refresh themselves before continuing life's journey. The Jeremiah Inn is one such place (Jeremiah 9:2a). Santa Fe style with spacious contemporary comforts are offered in this 1995-constructed inn, a 3.3-acre desert retreat in the shadows of the Catalina Mountains. Birding, stargazing, hiking, swimming, queen beds, afternoon cookies, and smoke-free premises are offered.

Hosts: Bob and Beth Miner
Rooms: 3 (PB) $55-100
Full Breakfast
Credit Cards: A, B
Notes: 2, 5, 7, 8, 9, 10, 11, 12

June's Bed and Breakfast

3212 W. Holladay Street, 85746
(520) 578-0857

Mountainside home with pool. Majestic, towering mountains. Hiking in the desert.

Sparkling city lights. Beautiful rear yard and patio. Suitable for receptions.

Hostess: June Henderson
Rooms: 3 (1PB; 2SB) $45-55
Continental Breakfast
Credit Cards: none
Notes: 8, 9, 10, 11, 12

La Posada del Valle

1640 N. Campbell Avenue, 85719
(520) 795-3840; FAX (520) 795-3840
Web site: http://www.arizonaguide.com/visitpremier

La Posada del Valle, surrounded by orange trees and lush gardens, is an elegant inn built in 1929. Five guest rooms with private baths and private entrances are furnished with antiques from the 1920s and '30s. Breakfast is served in the dining room with its glorious Catalina Mountain views. Guests gather for afternoon tea. The University of Arizona, University Medical Center, shops, restaurants, etc., are all within walking distance. *Wir sprechen Deutsch.* La Posada del Valle is AAA three-diamond-rated.

Rooms: 5 (PB) $90-135
Full Breakfast
Credit Cards: A, B
Notes: 2, 5, 7, 8, 9, 10, 11, 12

Redbud House Bed and Breakfast

7002 E. Redbud Street, 85715
(520) 721-0218

Cozy home in northeast Tuscon. Helpful hosts. All proceeds go to hosts' churches. Convenient to bus line, restaurants, Sabino Canyon; only fifteen miles from airport. An Olympic-size pool is available within

welcome; 7 Children welcome; 8 Tennis nearby; 9 Swimming nearby; 10 Golf nearby; 11 Skiing nearby; 12 May be booked through travel agent.

walking distance. Off-street parking. Cannot accommodate children or pets.

Hosts: Ken and Wanda Mayer
Rooms: 1 (PB) $55
Full Breakfast
Credit Cards: none
Notes: 2, 9, 10

Rincon Valley Retreat Bed and Breakfast

7080 S. Camino Loma Alta, 85747
(520) 647-3335
E-mail: valleyretreat@theriver.com

Charming country ranchlike atmosphere. Enjoy quiet solitude overlooking the beautiful Saguaro National Park. Arizona artists Sharon Maia and Larry Wilson invite you to relax in the warm accommodations of their home. Walls graced with paintings and photography of the Southwest add to the enchantment of this southern Arizona retreat. Fireplaces, TV/VCR in common areas. Incredible views. Hearty, healthy breakfasts. Miles of hiking trails just steps from the front door. Bicycles available; horseback riding close by.

Hosts: Sharon and Larry Wilson
Rooms: 2 (PB) $75-85
Full Breakfast
Credit Cards: A, B
Notes: 2, 3 and 4 (picnic baskets, on request), 5, 7

Shadow Mountain Ranch Bed and Breakfast Inn

8855 N. Scenic Drive, 85743
(520) 744-7551; (888) 9-SHADOW
E-mail: shadmtn@aol.com
Web site: members.aol.com/shadmtn/ranch.html

Enjoy a paradise in the desert, nestled high in the Tucson Mountains. A place you must see to believe. Magical, romantic, secluded. Pool, spa. A great location, minutes from our many historic and popular attractions. Shadow Mountain Ranch is a nature and outdoor lover's dream location. Hiking, jogging, birding, and biking. Horseback riding can be arranged. Innkeeper Lyn Nelson warmly welcomes guests to her beautiful and environmentally sensitive home, along with her two lovable indoor cats Benson and Patches. She enjoys sharing her "paradise of peace" and knowledge of area sights.

Hostess: Lyn Nelson
Rooms: 5 (3SB; 2PB)
Continental Breakfast
Credit Cards: none
Notes: 2, 6 (in guest house), 7, 10

Arkansas

CALICO ROCK

Happy Lonesome Log Cabins

HC 61, Box 72, 72519
(870) 297-8764
E-mail: cjeck@juno.com

Happy Lonesome offers secluded comfort and charm. Enjoy our natural and relaxing location surrounded by the Ozark National Forest. The cabins are provided with milk, juice, coffee, cereal, and homemade bread, and are decorated with the past in mind while providing modern comforts. Each cabin has a comfortable sleeping loft, kitchenette including microwave, downstairs living area, bath, hide-a-bed, woodstove, and air-conditioning. Outside is a covered porch with swing or double rocker; an outdoor grill is nearby. Enjoy a breathtaking view of the White River from the two-hundred-foot bluff locations. Relax on the wide porch and delight in the panoramic view of the river valley, forest, and wildlife.

Hosts: Christian and Carolyn Eck
Rooms: 4 (2PB; 2SB) $52.50
Continental Breakfast
Credit Cards: A, B, D
Notes: 2, 7, 8, 9, 10

Beaver Lake Bed and Breakfast

EUREKA SPRINGS

Beaver Lake B&B

1234 CR 20, 72632
(501) 253-9210; (888) 253-9210
Web site: http://www.bbonline.com/ar/beaverlake

Our comfortable country home has an awe-inspiring view of Beaver Lake and the surrounding Ozark Mountains from every room! Experience peace and beauty away from the crowds and the stress of your daily life. Swim, fish, hike, or just relax on the wraparound porch and let gracious hosts pamper you—the perfect place to renew your spirit. Accommodations are for nonsmoking adults only. Request our brochure or look for us on the Internet. Closed Christmas to New Year's Day.

Hosts: David and Elaine Reppel
Rooms: 4 (PB) $65-85
Full Gourmet Breakfast
Credit Cards: A, B, D
Notes: 2, 5, 9, 10, 12

---

welcome; 7 Children welcome; 8 Tennis nearby; 9 Swimming nearby; 10 Golf nearby; 11 Skiing nearby; 12 May be booked through travel agent.

ARKANSAS

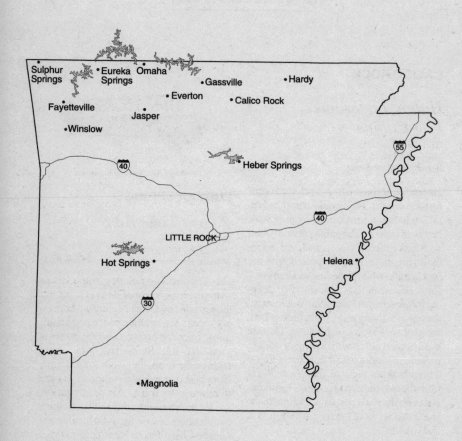

Bonnybrooke Farm Atop Misty Mountain

Route 2, Box 335A, 72631
(501) 253-6903

If your heart's in the country—or longs to be—we invite you to share the sweet quiet and serenity that awaits you in your place to come home to. Five cottages, distinctly different in their pleasure to tempt you. Fireplace and Jacuzzi for two, full glass fronts and mountaintop views, shower under the stars, wicker porch swing in front of the fireplace . . . you're gonna love it! In order to preserve privacy, the location is given to registered guests only.

Hosts: Bonny and Josh Pierson
Rooms: 5 cottages (PB) starting at $95
Continental Breakfast
Credit Cards: none
Notes: 2, 5, 9, 12

The Brownstone Inn

75 Hillside Avenue, 72632
(501) 253-7505; (800) 973-7505
Web site: http://www.eureka-usa.com/lodging/brownstone.html

A present part of Eureka's past in this historical limestone building, located on the trolley route to historic downtown and an easy, short drive to the Great Passion Play. Victorian accommodations, private outside entrances, private baths, and gourmet breakfasts with coffee, tea, or juice at your doorstep before breakfast. Featured in *Best Places to Stay in the South.*

Hosts: Marvin and Donna Shepard
Rooms: 4 (PB) $90-105
Full Breakfast
Closed January and February
Credit Cards: A, B
Notes: 2, 5, 10, 12

Crescent Cottage Inn

Crescent Cottage Inn

211 Spring Street, 72632
(501) 253-6022; 1-800-223-3246;
FAX (501) 253-6234
E-mail: raphael@ipa.net
Web site: http://www.eureka-usa.com/crescott/index.html

Famous 1881 Victorian on National Register of Historic Places. The oldest, most historic and photographed bed and breakfast. Special features include a great arch, antiques, hand-painted ceiling decorations, and crystal chandeliers such as those that were in the home of the first governor of Arkansas after the Civil War. Towers and sunbursts grace this Queen Anne home. All rooms have private Jacuzzis, baths, queen beds, TV/VCRs, and FM-AM radios. Best view of the mountains and forests. It's only a short walk or the trolley to downtown.

Hosts: Ralph and Phyllis Becker
Rooms: 4 (PB) $93-130
Full Breakfast
Credit Cards: A, B, D
Notes: 2, 5, 7, 8, 9, 10, 12

NOTES: Credit cards accepted: A Master Card; B Visa; C American Express; D Discover; E Diners Club; F Other; 2 Personal checks accepted; 3 Lunch available; 4 Dinner available; 5 Open all year; 6 Pets welcome; 7 Children welcome; 8 Tennis nearby; 9 Swimming nearby; 10 Golf nearby; 11 Skiing nearby; 12 May be booked through travel agent.

Enchanted Cottages

18 Nut Street, Historic District, 72632
(501) 253-6790; (800) 862-2788

Romantic storybook cottages hidden in the historic district of Eureka Springs. Jacuzzi for two or private outdoor hot tub, cozy fireplaces, queen- or king-size beds, cable TV, kitchen and patios with grills. These cottages have been featured on Eureka Springs' Homes Tour. Special honeymoon and anniversary packages.

Hosts: Barbara Kellogg and David Pettit
Rooms: 3 (PB) $75-129
Continental Breakfast
Credit Cards: A, B
Notes: 5, 9, 10, 12

Gardeners Cottage

c/o 11 Singleton, 72632
(501) 253-9111; (800) 833-3394

Tucked away in a private, wooded historic district, the delightful Gardeners Cottage features charming country decor with romantic touches, cathedral ceilings, skylight, full kitchen, and a Jacuzzi for two. The spacious porch with its swing and hammock is perfect for leisurely lounging. Great for honeymooners or for a long, peaceful stay.

Hostess: Barbara Gavron
Rooms: 1 cottage (PB) $95-115
No Breakfast
Closed January-March
Credit Cards: A, B, C, D
Notes: 2, 9, 10, 12

Heart of the Hills Inn

5 Summit, 72632
(501) 523-7468; (800) 523-7468

This 1883 Victorian inn has two guest suites, each with private bath and en-

trance. Antiques, china, refrigerator, cable TV, coffeemaker, and double Jacuzzi are found in the honeymoon suite. A separate country cottage features a sitting loft, kitchenette, stereo. Evening wine or sparkling juice and cheese are available for our guests. A continental breakfast is each morning served in your room or on a private deck. Enjoy the lovely garden that overlooks a wooded area. Smoking outside only.

Hosts: Jim and Kathy Vanzandt
Rooms: 3 (PB) $95-125
Continental Breakfast
Credit Cards: A, B, C, D, F
Notes: 2, 5, 9, 10, 11

The Heartstone Inn and Cottages

35 Kings Highway, 72632
(501) 253-8916; (800) 494-4921;
FAX (501) 253-6821

An award-winning inn with all private baths, private entrances, and cable TV. King and queen beds. Antiques galore. Renowned gourmet breakfasts. In-house massage therapy studio. Golf privileges. Large decks and gazebo under the trees; great for bird-watching. Recommended by: *The New York Times, Country Home Magazine, America's Wonderful Little Hotels and Inns, Recommended Inns of the South*, and many more.

Hosts: Iris and Bill Simantel
Rooms: 10 + a 1-bedroom cottage and a 2-bedroom cottage (PB) $65-120
Full Gourmet Breakfast
Closed Christmas through January
Credit Cards: A, B, C, D
Notes: 2, 9, 10, 12

NOTES: Credit cards accepted: A Master Card; B Visa; C American Express; D Discover; E Diners Club; F Other; 2 Personal checks accepted; 3 Lunch available; 4 Dinner available; 5 Open all year; 6 Pets

Inn at Rose Hall

56 Hillside, 72632
(501) 253-5405 (voice and FAX); (800) 828-4255
E-mail: rosehall@ipa.net
Web site: www.pimps.com/eureka/lodging/
    everose.html#rose

An elegant Victorian mansion offering elegance and grandeur that will make your stay the difference between ordinary and legendary. Premier accommodations are designed to offer ambience as well as comfort. Experience the luxuriousness of Victorian furnishings, grand fireplaces, Jacuzzis for two, resplendent stained glass, fresh flowers, chocolates, and designer linens. A gourmet three-course breakfast is served each morning, and complimentary beverages await each evening. *No smoking or pets.* Rose Hall is unsurpassed for its wedding, honeymoon, and anniversary accommodations. Catering to small wedding and reception groups (up to twenty), we offer the perfect romantic experience. A special place for that special time.

Hostess: Sandy Latimer
Rooms: 5 (PB) $125-150
Full Breakfast
Credit Cards: A, B, C, D, E
Notes: 2, 5, 9, 10, 12

Piedmont House Bed and Breakfast

165 Spring Street, 72632
(501) 253-9258; (800) 253-9258
Web site: http://www.pimps.com/eureka/lodging/
    piedlake.html#piedmont

Built as travelers' lodging in 1880, Piedmont House is located in the heart of the Victorian historic district. Each room has private baths, air-conditioning, ceiling fans, and private entrance from the wraparound porches. Best mountain views and just a short walk to historic downtown shopping and great restaurants. A home away from home with the warmest hospitality you could ever find. Delicious full breakfasts served each morning.

Hosts: Sheri and Ron Morrill
Rooms: 8 (PB) $79-129
Full Breakfast
Credit Cards: A, B, C, D
Notes: 2, 5, 7 (over 12), 10

Ridgeway House B&B

28 Ridgeway, 72632
(501) 253-6618; (800) 477-6618;
FAX (501) 253-2499 (call first)

Prepare to be pampered! Sumptuous breakfasts, luxurious rooms, antiques, desserts, quiet street within walking distance of eight churches, five-minute walk to historic downtown, trolley one block away. Porches, decks, private Jacuzzi suites for anniversaries/honeymoons. All our guests are VIPs! Open all year.

Hosts: Becky and "Sony" Taylor
Rooms: 5 (3PB; 2SB) $79-139
Full Breakfast
Credit Cards: A, B, D
Notes: 2, 5, 7, 12

Ridgeway House B&B

---

welcome; 7 Children welcome; 8 Tennis nearby; 9 Swimming nearby; 10 Golf nearby; 11 Skiing nearby; 12 May be booked through travel agent.

Singleton House Bed and Breakfast

Singleton House Bed and Breakfast

11 Singleton, 72632
(501) 253-9111; (800) 833-3394

This old-fashioned Victorian house with a touch of magic is whimsically decorated and has an eclectic collection of treasures and antiques. Breakfast is served each morning on the balcony overlooking a wildflower garden and fishpond. You can walk one block to the historic district, shops, and cafés. Passion Play and Holy Land tour reservations can be arranged. A guest cottage with a Jacuzzi is available at a separate location. A hands-on apprenticeship program also is available for our guests! The Singleton House Bed and Breakfast has been featured in more than fifteen bed and breakfast guidebooks. We currently are celebrating our fourteenth year of operation!

Hostess: Barbara Gavron
Rooms: 5 (PB) $60-95; cottage $95-115
Full Breakfast
Closed January and February
Credit Cards: A, B, C, D
Notes: 2, 5, 7, 9, 10, 12

EVERTON

Clear Creek Cabin

4075 Crawford Road, 72633
(870) 429-6592

Charming 1850s log cabin lovingly restored and furnished with modern conveniences. Nestled on the banks of sparkling Clear Creek. Its peaceful setting on 345 scenic acres is perfect for fishing, swimming, hiking, cave exploring, and quiet relaxation. A living room with fireplace, bedroom, bath, fully equipped kitchen, and large porch with swing welcome you. Day excursions include Branson, Eureka Springs, Silver Dollar City, Buffalo National River, and White River (famous for trout).

Hostess: Marilyn Eaton
Rooms: 3-room log cabin (PB) $80
No Meals
Credit Cards: none
Notes: 2, 5, 9

Clear Creek Cabin

FAYETTEVILLE

Hill Avenue Bed and Breakfast

131 Hill Avenue, 72701
(501) 444-0865

This century-old home is located in a residential neighborhood near the University of Arkansas, downtown square, the

---

NOTES: Credit cards accepted: A Master Card; B Visa; C American Express; D Discover; E Diners Club; F Other; 2 Personal checks accepted; 3 Lunch available; 4 Dinner available; 5 Open all year; 6 Pets

Walton Art Center, and the Bud Walton Arena. Accommodations are smoke-free and feature king beds and private baths.

Hosts: Cecelia and Dave Thompson
Rooms: 3 (PB) $60
Continental Breakfast
Credit Cards: none
Notes: 5

GASSVILLE

Lithia Springs Bed and Breakfast Lodge

593 Highway 126 N., 72635
(879) 435-6100

A lovingly restored, early Ozark health lodge, six miles southwest of Mountain Home in north central Arkansas. Fishing, boating, and canoeing in famous lakes and rivers. Scenic hills, valleys, and caverns. Silver Dollar City, Branson, and Eureka Springs are within driving distance. Enjoy walking in the meadow and woods and browse through the adjoining Country Treasures Gift Shop.

Hosts: Paul and Reita Johnson
Rooms: 4 (P&SB) $50-70
Full Breakfast
Credit Cards: A, B
Notes: 2, 5, 8, 9, 10, 12

Lithia Springs Bed and Breakfast Lodge

HARDY

Hideaway Inn B&B

Route 1, Box 199, 72542
(870) 966-4770; (888) 966-4770
Web site: http://www.bbonline.com/ar/hideaway

Hideaway Inn is a modern bed and breakfast on 376 acres. It offers three guest rooms with queen beds and central air. Gourmet breakfast and evening snack served. TV/VCR in common area. Beautiful setting, picnic sites, and outdoor pool. Children welcome. Log cabin with two bedrooms, two baths, living/dining/kitchenette combo. Located ten miles from Hardy and Spring River.

Hostess: Julia Baldridge
Rooms: 5 (3PB; 2SB) $55-95
Full Breakfast
Credit Cards: A, B, C, D
Notes: 2, 5, 7, 9, 10, 12

Olde Stonehouse Bed and Breakfast

511 Main Street, 72542
(501) 856-2983

This native stone house is located in the historic district one block the from Spring River and Old Hardy Town's quaint antique and craft shops. Guests enjoy the antiques, queen beds, private baths, central heat/air, ceiling fans, unusual stone fireplace with "Arkansas Diamonds," and player piano. A full breakfast is served family-style each morning. There is a separate 1904 cottage with opulant Victorian-inspired suites. Nearby, you will find the Country Music-Comedy Theater with outdoor musicals, Antique Car and

welcome; 7 Children welcome; 8 Tennis nearby; 9 Swimming nearby; 10 Golf nearby; 11 Skiing nearby; 12 May be booked through travel agent.

Veterans Museums, golfing, canoeing, trail rides, Mammoth Springs and Grand Gulf state parks.

Hosts: Peggy & David Johnson
Rooms: 7 + 2 suites (PB) $55-95
Full Breakfast
Credit Cards: A, B, C, D
Notes: 2, 3, 4, 5, 8, 9, 10, 12

HEBER SPRINGS

The Anderson House Inn

201 E. Main Street, 72543
(501) 362-5266; (800) 264-5279;
FAX (501) 362-2326
E-mail: innkeepr@cswnet.com
Web site: http://www.bbonline.com/ar/anderson

The Anderson House is a country Inn in the bed and breakfast tradition. Enjoy a wonderful lodging alternative in a beautiful Ozark foothills setting. Convenient to Greens Ferry Lake and Little Red River fishing and water sports. Trophy trout fishing is available. We feature handmade quilts, antiques, and a southern flavor. Our great room has a large-screen TV for guests to enjoy.

Hosts: Jim and Susan Hildebrand
Rooms: 16 (PB) $68-94
Full Breakfast
Credit Cards: A, B, C, D
Notes: 2, 5, 8, 9, 10, 11, 12

HELENA

Foxglove

229 Beech, 72342
(870) 338-9391; (800) 863-1926

On a ridge overlooking historic Helena and the Mississippi River, stunning antiques abound in this nationally registered inn. Parqueted floors, quartersawn oak woodwork, stained glass, and six original fireplaces are complemented by private marble baths, whirlpool tubs, phones, cable, FAX, air-conditioning, and other modern conveniences. Points of interest include Delta Cultural Center, Confederate cemetery, antique shops, and casino, all within five minutes. A complimentary evening beverage and snack are included in the price.

Host: John Butkiewicz
Rooms: 8 (6PB; 2SB in suites) $69-109
Full Breakfast
Credit Cards: A, B, C
Notes: 2, 5, 12

HOT SPRINGS

Vintage Comfort Bed and Breakfast

303 Quapaw, 71901
(501) 623-3258; (800) 608-4682

Situated on a tree-lined street, a short walk from Hot Springs' historic Bath House Row, art galleries, restaurants, and shopping. Guests enjoy a comfortably restored Queen Anne house built in 1907. Four spacious rooms are available upstairs, each with private bath, ceiling fan, and period furnishings. A delicious full breakfast is served each morning in the inn's dining room. Vintage Comfort B&B is known for its comfort and gracious southern hospitality.

Hostess: Helen Bartlett
Rooms: 4 (PB) $65-90
Full Breakfast
Credit Cards: A, B, C
Notes: 2, 5, 7 (over 6 years), 8, 9, 10, 12

NOTES: Credit cards accepted: A Master Card; B Visa; C American Express; D Discover; E Diners Club; F Other; 2 Personal checks accepted; 3 Lunch available; 4 Dinner available; 5 Open all year; 6 Pets

JASPER

Cliff House Inn

HCR 31 Box 85, 72641
(870) 446-2292

Our inn overlooks the deepest valley in Arkansas. The view from the rooms and dining room is spectacular. The Ozark Mountains are known for the beauty of wildflowers and fall foliage. All rooms are nonsmoking. Excellent food, beautiful gifts and crafts. See the Glory of God from the highest peak.

Hosts: Neal and Karen Heath
Rooms: 5 (PB) $45-55
Continental Breakfast
Credit Cards: A, B, D
Notes: 2, 3, 4, 7

MAGNOLIA

Magnolia Place

510 E. Main, 71753
(870) 234-6122; (800) 237-6122;
FAX (870) 234-1254
E-mail: magnoliaplace@msn.com
Web site: http://www.bbonline.com/ar/magnolia

Your secure comfort and enjoyment is our main priority in five beautiful guest rooms, each decorated with spectacular antiques and each having a private bath, telephone, and TV. Imagine a refreshing breeze as you relax on the large wraparound porch and enjoy the rockers and swing, just like the old days. Stroll along the flagstone path through the flower garden. Savor a full gourmet breakfast served in the elegant formal dining room, featuring an 1820 dining table once used by President Harding.

Magnolia Place

Experience the charm and hospitality of the Old South in exquisite surroundings.

Hosts: Carolyne Hawley and Ray Sullivent
Rooms: 5 (PB) $89-99
Full Breakfast
Credit Cards: A, B, C, D, E
Notes: 5, 9, 10, 12

OMAHA

Aunt Shirley's Sleeping Loft

7250 Shirley Lane, 72662
(870) 426-5408

Quiet, relaxed atmosphere. Rustic country setting with the convenience of home. Air-conditioning, private bath, clean. Beautiful view with walkways, patio. Gas grill, campfires available. Swings under the trees. *Big* country breakfast, lots of southern hospitality. Children welcome. Ten miles north of Harrison, twenty-four miles south of Branson, Missouri. Near Eureka Springs, Buffalo River, Tablerock Lake, Bull Shoals Lake. Member of Harrison Chamber of Commerce.

Hosts: Buddy and Shirley LeBleu
Rooms: 2 + cabin (PB) $50-60
Full Breakfast
Credit Cards: A, B
Notes: 2, 5, 6, 7, 9, 10

welcome; 7 Children welcome; 8 Tennis nearby; 9 Swimming nearby; 10 Golf nearby; 11 Skiing nearby; 12 May be booked through travel agent.

SULPHUR SPRINGS

Harbor House
400 E. Patterson, PO Box 66, 72768
(501) 298-3354

Turn-of-the-century holistic healing center and bathhouse converted to a quaint bed and breakfast, furnished with antiques. Situated on 137 acres in the beautiful northwest corner of Arkansas. Convenient to Eureka Springs, Branson and many area lakes. Our own private lake comes with a beautiful two-bedroom log cabin, totally private. Experience the warmth and hospitality of days gone by—peaceful, relaxing, and restoring.

Hosts: Dwayne and Vivian Barber
Rooms: 5 (1PB, 4SB) + cabin; $35-125
Full Breakfast
Credit Cards: none
Notes: 2, 4, 5, 7, 8, 9, 10

WINSLOW

Sky-Vue Lodge
22822 N. Highway 71, 72959
(501) 634-2003; (800) 782-2003

Located on Scenic 71 near Fayetteville, Sky-Vue Lodge offers a twenty-five-mile view of the Ozarks. Enjoy the spectacular view from the porch of your charming cabin, which has heating and AC for year-round comfort. Hike our eighty-three acres, or enjoy activities at two nearby state parks. Family oriented, alcohol free. Ideal for retreats, conferences, reunions, and weddings. Full breakfast included; other meals available.

Hosts: Glenn and Janice Jorgenson
Rooms: 7 cabins (PB) $45-55
Full Breakfast
Credit Cards: A, B, C, D
Notes: 2, 4, 5, 6, 7, 8, 9

NOTES: Credit cards accepted: A Master Card; B Visa; C American Express; D Discover; E Diners Club; F Other; 2 Personal checks accepted; 3 Lunch available; 4 Dinner available; 5 Open all year; 6 Pets

California

AHWAHNEE

Silver Spur
Bed and Breakfast

44625 Silver Spur Trail, 93601
(209) 683-2896

Silver Spur Bed and Breakfast is nestled in the Sierra Nevadas of California, just off historic Highway 49—key to the California Gold Country, near the south and west gates of famed Yosemite National Park, and minutes from many outdoor sports. We feature beautiful, clean rooms with private baths and entrances, tastefully decorated in American Southwest style. Outdoor rest and dining areas boast outstanding views of the Sierra Nevadas. A continental breakfast is served daily. Come enjoy the grandeur of Yosemite and be treated to old-fashioned hospitality and great value!

Hosts: Patty and Bryan Hays
Rooms: 2 (PB) $45-60
Expanded Continental Breakfast
Credit Cards: A, B, D
Notes: 2, 5, 6 (sometimes), 7, 9, 10, 11, 12

ALAMEDA

Garratt Mansion

900 Union, 94501
(510) 521-4779; FAX (510) 521-6796
E-mail: garrattm@pacbell.net

This 1893 Victorian halts time on the tranquil island of Alameda. Only twenty miles to Berkeley or downtown San Francisco. We'll help maximize your vacation plans or leave you alone to regroup. Our rooms are large and comfortable, and our breakfasts are nutritious and filling.

Hosts: Royce and Betty Gladden
Rooms: 7 (5PB; 2SB) $80-130
Full Breakfast
Credit Cards: A, B, C, D, E
Notes: 2, 5, 8, 9, 10, 12

Garratt Mansion

---

welcome; 7 Children welcome; 8 Tennis nearby; 9 Swimming nearby; 10 Golf nearby; 11 Skiing nearby; 12 May be booked through travel agent.

CALIFORNIA (NORTHERN)

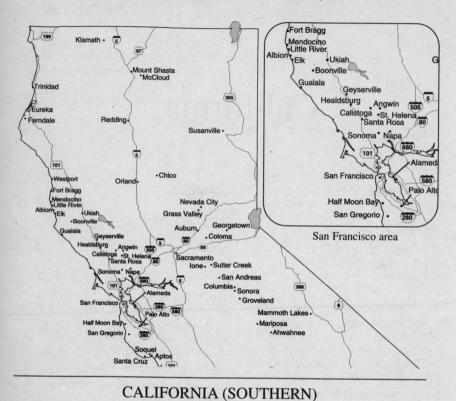

San Francisco area

CALIFORNIA (SOUTHERN)

Los Angeles area

AVALON

Gull House
Bed and Breakfast Home

344 Whittley Avenue, PO Box 1381, 90704-1381
(310) 510-2547; FAX (310) 510-9569

Two deluxe suites are on the lower level of our contemporary home, each with separate entrance, large living room with gas log fireplace, morning room with refrigerator and table, bedroom, and bath. Two large guest rooms overlook a patio, pool, and spa, with baths. Breakfast is served on the patio. Within walking distance of island activities—beaches, golf, tennis, boating, fishing, biking, horseback riding, and picnic facilities. Full payment ten days prior to arrival. This is our fifteenth year. AAA-rated, two diamonds. Open March-December.

Hosts: Bob and Hattie Michalis
Rooms: 5 (4PB; 1SB) $110-145
Continental Plus Breakfast
Credit Cards: none
Notes: 2 (traveler's checks, money orders), 8, 9 (on premises), 10, 11 (water), 12

BIG BEAR LAKE

Truffles Bed and Breakfast

43591 Bow Canyon Drive, PO Box 130649, 92315
(909) 585-2772 (voice and FAX; call before FAXing)

Gracious hospitality in peaceful surroundings describe this elegant, country manor inn nestled on three-fourths acre at a seven thousand-foot-high mountain resort. Skiing, golf, hiking, and lake close by. Five guest rooms are individually appointed with private baths and feathertop beds. Full breakfasts, afternoon appetizers, and

evening desserts topped off with truffles on bedtime pillows make for a memorable stay. This spacious lodging includes comfortable traditional and antique furnishings with attention to detail. No smoking.

Hosts: Marilyn Kane and Carol Bracey
Rooms: 5 (PB) $115-140
Full Breakfast
Credit Cards: A, B, C, D
Notes: 2, 5, 7 (over 12), 10, 11

BOONVILLE

Anderson Creek Inn

12050 Anderson Valley Way, PO Box 217, 95415
(707) 895-3091

Delightfully blending elegance with rustic, this lovely inn is spacious and quiet, surrounded by spectacular valley views and rolling pastures full of friendly farm animals. There are five gracious guest rooms with king beds and private baths. Prices include wine, hors d'oeuvres, and a full gourmet breakfast. Some rooms have fireplaces; all have wonderful views and plenty of privacy.

Hosts: Rod and Nancy Graham
Rooms: 5 (PB) $110-165
Full Breakfast
Credit Cards: A, B
Notes: 2, 5, 6 (with prior approval), 7, 8, 9 (pool), 10

CALISTOGA

Calistoga Wayside Inn

1523 Foothill Boulevard, 94515
(707) 942-0645; (800) 845-3632;
FAX (707) 942-4169

A warm, inviting Mediterranean-style home, built in the 1920s and situated in a

---

NOTES: Credit cards accepted: A Master Card; B Visa; C American Express; D Discover; E Diners Club; F Other; 2 Personal checks accepted; 3 Lunch available; 4 Dinner available; 5 Open all year; 6 Pets welcome; 7 Children welcome; 8 Tennis nearby; 9 Swimming nearby;   10 Golf nearby; 11 Skiing nearby; 12 May be booked through travel agent.

Calistoga Wayside Inn

secluded garden setting. Guest rooms have king- or queen-size beds and private baths. Enjoy the garden and patio, or curl up by the fireplace. Guests savor a Calistoga country breakfast, afternoon refreshments, and herb tea in the evening. Restaurants, shops, wineries, and spas are nearby. Gift certificates.

Hosts: Jan Balcer and Kathryn Lamm
Rooms: 3 (PB) $100-150
Full Breakfast
Credit Cards: A, B, C, D
Notes: 2, 5, 8, 9, 10

Foothill House

3037 Foothill Boulevard, 94515
(707) 942-6933; (800) 942-6933;
FAX (707) 942-5692

"The romantic inn of the Napa Valley," according to the *Chicago Tribune* travel editor. In a country setting, located in the western foothills just north of Calistoga, the Foothill House offers spacious suites individually decorated with antiques. All suites have private baths and entrances, fireplaces, small refrigerators, and AC. Some of the suites have Jacuzzis. A luxurious cottage is also available. A gourmet breakfast is served each morning and appetizers and refreshments each evening. Foothill House recently received the

American Bed & Breakfast Association's highest award for 1997 (four crowns—whiche places it in the top 5 percent in United States).

Hosts: Doris and Gus Beckert
Rooms: 4 (PB) $135-275
Full Breakfast
Credit Cards: A, B, C, D
Notes: 2, 5, 8, 9, 10, 12

Hillcrest Bed and Breakfast

3225 Lake County Highway, 94515
(707) 942-6334

Secluded hilltop country home with breathtaking views of the lush Napa Valley. Swimming, hiking, and fishing on forty acres. The property has been in the family since 1860. The home is filled with antique furnishings. Rooms have balconies and HBO. Large pool and outdoor Jacuzzi.

Hostess: Debbie O'Gorman
Rooms: 6 (4PB; 2SB) $45-90
Continental Breakfast
Credit Cards: none
Notes: 2, 5, 6, 8, 9, 10, 11 (water), 12

CAMBRIA

The Pickford House Bed and Breakfast

2555 MacLeod, 93428
(805) 927-8619

Eight large rooms are done in antiques. All have private baths with claw-foot tubs and showers. The front three rooms have

---

NOTES: Credit cards accepted: A Master Card; B Visa; C American Express; D Discover; E Diners Club; F Other; 2 Personal checks accepted; 3 Lunch available; 4 Dinner available; 5 Open all year; 6 Pets

fireplaces and a view of the mountains and valley. All rooms have a TV and king- or queen-size bed. Wine and fruitbreads are served at 5 PM. The Pickford House is located near beaches and wineries, only seven miles from the Hearst Castle. Third person only $20. A full breakfast is served from 8 to 9 AM in our antique dining room with its cozy fireplace and 1860 antique bar. Gift certificates are offered. An abundance of parking space is available for guests. Check in after 3 PM, check out at 11 AM.

Hostess: Anna Larsen
Rooms: 8 (PB) $89-130
Full Breakfast
Credit Cards: A, B
Notes: 2, 5, 7

CAPISTRANO BEACH

Capistrano Seaside Inn

34862 Pacific Coast Highway, 92624
(714) 496-1399; (800) 25-BEACH;
FAX (714) 240-8977
E-mail: beach@pacific-ocean.com
Web site: www.seaside-inn.com

Enjoy Capistrano State Beach, the "Riviera of California," located directly across the street from the Seaside Inn. Our rooms offer views of the ocean and have private patios. Most rooms have a wood-burning fireplace, in-room coffee, and refrigerator. We have an outdoor Jacuzzi for your comfort and a friendly and efficient staff.

Rooms: 29 (PB) $49-129
Continental Breakfast
Credit Cards: A, B, C
Notes: 5, 7, 9, 10, 12

CARMEL

Stonehouse Inn

PO Box 2517, 8th below Monte Verde, 93921
(408) 624-4569; (800) 748-4418

A touch of old Carmel. Experience this luxurious country house in a quiet neighborhood setting. The Stonehouse Inn offers restful bedrooms that are light and airy; some have a view of the ocean through the trees. Each room is decorated in soft colors featuring antiques, cozy comforters, fresh flowers and special touches for guests' comfort. A generous breakfast is served in the sunny dining room. Come join us at the Stonehouse Inn for a special, warm and memorable experience.

Hosts: Kevin and Terri Navaille
Rooms: 6 (2PB; 4SB) $110-189
Full Breakfast
Credit Cards: A, B
Notes: 5, 7 (over 12), 8, 9, 10

Stonehouse Inn

Sunset House

PO Box 1925, 93921
(408) 624-4884 (voice and FAX)

Sunset House, a romantic inn located on a quiet residential street, captures the essence of Carmel. Experience the sound

welcome; 7 Children welcome; 8 Tennis nearby; 9 Swimming nearby; 10 Golf nearby; 11 Skiing nearby; 12 May be booked through travel agent.

of the surf—you are close to the beach and yet only two blocks away from the quaint shops, restaurants, and galleries that make Carmel famous. A special breakfast tray is brought to the room, allowing guests to relax and enjoy the glow of the fire and the beauty of the view. Each guest room is uniquely decorated with considerable thought and care to ensure an enjoyable stay.

Hosts: Camille and Dennis Fike
Rooms: 5 (PB) $130-190
Expanded Continental Breakfast
Credit Cards: A, B, C, D
Notes: 2, 5, 6, 7, 8, 9, 10, 12

CARMEL VALLEY

The Valley Lodge
Carmel Valley Road at Ford Road, PO Box 93, 93924
(408) 659-2261; (800) 641-4646;
FAX (408) 659-4558

A warm Carmel Valley welcome awaits the two of you, a few of you, or a small conference. Relax in a garden patio room or a cozy one- or two-bedroom cottage with fireplace and kitchen. Enjoy a sumptuous continental breakfast, our heated pool, sauna, hot spa, and fitness center. Tennis and golf are nearby. Walk to fine restaurants and quaint shops in Carmel Valley village, or just listen to your beard grow.

Hosts: Peter Coakley
Rooms: 31 (PB) $99-169
Expanded Continental Breakfast
Credit Cards: A, B, C
Notes: 2, 5, 6 ($10 fee), 7, 8, 9 (on site), 10, 12

CHICO

L'abri Bed and Breakfast
14350 Highway 99, 95973
(916) 893-0824; (800) 489-3319
Web site: http://now2000.com/labri

Our ranch-style home is located on two and a half acres. We have established an assortment of outside places for you to find the relaxation that is so much a part of "getting away." You may enjoy sitting on the patio or back lawn, watching the various birds that visit us throughout the year. A seasonal creek provides a restful rhythm as it flows through the property. Perhaps reclining on bales of hay and taking in the sunset over an expanse of western sky sounds more to your liking. Feed and pet our barnyard friends. Miles of hiking trails are nearby. All guest quarters have outside entrances. Breakfast is served in your room, if desired.

Hosts: Sharon and Jeff Bisaga
Rooms: 3 (PB) $65-90
Full Breakfast, weekends; Continental, weekdays
Credit Cards: A, B, D
Notes: 2, 5, 8, 9, 10

COLOMA

The Coloma Country Inn
PO Box 502, 345 High Street, 95613
(916) 622-6919

Built in 1852, this country Victorian farmhouse is surrounded by five acres of private gardens amid a three-hundred-acre state park. The main house has five guest rooms and the carriage house has two suites. All rooms feature country decor,

---

NOTES: Credit cards accepted: A Master Card; B Visa; C American Express; D Discover; E Diners Club; F Other; 2 Personal checks accepted; 3 Lunch available; 4 Dinner available; 5 Open all year; 6 Pets

including quilts, stenciling, American antiques, and fresh flowers. You can hot-air balloon with your host from the backyard meadow or white-water raft from the South Fork American River, one block from the Inn.

Hosts: Alan and Cindi Ehrgott
Rooms: 7 (5PB; 2SB) $90-130
Full Breakfast
Credit Cards: none
Notes: 2, 5, 7, 9, 12

COLUMBIA

Columbia Fallon Hotel

PO Box 1870, 95310
(209) 532-1479; (800) 532-1479;
FAX (209) 532-7027
E-mail: info@cityhotel.com
Web site: http://www.cityhotel.com

Join us as we step back in time to an era filled with grand promises and false hopes—an era that saw struggle and hardship turn into wealth and riches, an era when fortunes were made and lost quickly.

Columbia Fallon Hotel

Since 1857, the Fallon Hotel has played an important role in the rise and fall of Columbia. It has been restored authentically by the State of California to its Victorian grandeur. Many of the antiques and furnishings are original to the Hotel, from the petite and intimate hall rooms to the grand bridal suite. Breakfast is served in the downstairs parlor; fresh coffee, tea, orange juice, cereals, freshly baked breads, muffins, and rolls will start your morning on the right track. Fallon Theatre, home of one of the finest theatrical companies in the West, is adjacent to the hotel. The delightful, highly acclaimed City Hotel Restaurant is just a few steps away.

Host: Tom Bender
Rooms: 14 (1PB; 13SB) $55-95
Expanded Continental Breakfast
Credit Cards: A, B, C, D
Notes: 2, 4, 5, 7, 8, 9, 10, 11, 12

CORONADO

Glorietta Bay Inn

1630 Glorietta Blvd., 92118
(619) 435-3101; (800) 283-9383;
FAX (619) 435-6182
E-mail: rooms@gloriettabayinn.com
Web site: www.gloriettabayinn.com

The Inn is located on Coronado Island, a resort community offering a small-town lifestyle, yet conveniently across the street from the world-famous Hotel del Coronado and across the bay from San Diego. Now a Coronado historic landmark, it was once the home of sugar baron John Spreckels. The mansion was built in 1908 and includes seven bedrooms, three suites, and a penthouse. All accommodations include a private bath and AC. Adjacent

welcome; 7 Children welcome; 8 Tennis nearby; 9 Swimming nearby; 10 Golf nearby; 11 Skiing nearby; 12 May be booked through travel agent.

are five contemporary wings. The bed and breakfast rooms are located inside the mansion.

Rooms: 11 (PB) $155-300
Continental Breakfast
Credit Cards: A, B, C
Notes: 2, 5, 8, 9, 10, 12

Traveller's Repose Bed and Breakfast

DESERT HOT SPRINGS

Traveller's Repose Bed and Breakfast

66920 First Street, PO Box 655, 92240
(760) 329-9584

Bay windows, gingerbread trim, stained glass, and a white picket fence decorate this two-story Victorian home. Guest rooms are individually decorated: a rose room with antiques and lace accessories, a blue and white room with a heart motif, and a green room with handcrafted pine furniture. Tea is served midafternoon in the guest parlor. Located twelve miles north of Palm Springs.

Hostess: Marian Relkoff
Rooms: 3 (PB) $65-85
Continental Breakfast
Credit Cards: none
Notes: 2, 8, 9, 10, 12

ELK

Elk Cove Inn

PO Box 367, 95432
(707) 877-3321; (800) 275-2967;
FAX (707) 877-1808
E-mail: elkcove@mcn.org
Web site: http://www.elkcoveinn.com

A uniquely romantic bed and breakfast with dramatic ocean views, located in the town of Elk just an easy five-minute walk from the sandy beach. All rooms are provided with complimentary port wine and chocolates, fluffy robes, coffeemakers, featherbeds and down comforters. Our suites have separate living and bedroom areas, fireplaces, large baths with spa tubs and balconies.

Host: Elaine Bryant
Rooms: 15 (PB) $108-298
Full Breakfast
Credit Cards: A, B, C
Notes: 2, 4, 5, 10, 12

ESCONDIDO

The Parsonage Bed and Breakfast

239 S. Maple Street, 92025
(760) 741-9160; FAX (760) 741-2630
E-mail: Parsonage5@Juno.com

Built in 1910 as the parsonage of the First Congregational Church, this home has been restored to its original glory. Relax in a claw-foot tub, sleep on queen-size beds (down comforters and featherbeds are available on request), and enjoy dessert every evening on the front porch. The Parsonage is within thirty minutes of all San

---

NOTES: Credit cards accepted: A Master Card; B Visa; C American Express; D Discover; E Diners Club; F Other; 2 Personal checks accepted; 3 Lunch available; 4 Dinner available; 5 Open all year; 6 Pets

The Parsonage Bed and Breakfast

Diego attractions and within walking distance of the Columbia Center for the Arts, fine restaurants, and antique stores.

Hosts: Robert and Ann McQuead
Rooms: 3 (1PB; 2SB) $75-95
Full Breakfast
Credit Cards: none
Notes: 2, 5, 7 (over 12), 8, 9, 10

EUREKA

Abigail's "Elegant Victorian Mansion" B&B Lodging Accommodations

1406 "C" Street, 95501-1765
(707) 444-3144; FAX (707) 442-5594
Web sites: http://www.bnbcity.com/inns/20016
http://www.innaccess.com/evm

An award-winning 1888 national historic landmark of opulence, grace, and grandeur, featuring spectacular gingerbread exteriors, opulent Victorian interiors, antique furnishings, and an acclaimed French gourmet breakfast. Exclusively for the nonsmoking traveler, this is a "living history house-museum" for the discriminating connoisseur of authentic Victorian decor who also has a passion for quality, service, and the extraordinary. Breathtakingly authentic, with all the nostalgic trimmings of a century ago, this meticulously restored Victorian masterpiece offers both history and hospitality, combined with romance and pampering. Enjoy the regal splendor of this spectacular state historic site, and indulge in four-star luxury. With complimentary horseless carriage rides, bicycles, sauna, and laundry service, the Inn is recommended by AAA, Mobil, Fodor's, and more. Arthur Frommer calls it "The very best that California has to offer—not to be missed."

Hosts: Doug and Lily Vieyra
Rooms: 4 (2PB; 2SB) $95-185
Full French Gourmet Breakfast
Credit Cards: A, B
Notes: 5, 8, 9, 10, 11, 12

The Cornelius Daly Inn

1125 "H" Street, 95501
(707) 445-3638; (800) 321-9656;
FAX (707) 444-3636
E-mail: dalyinn@humboldt1.com
Web site: http://www.humboldt1.com/~dalyinn

This exquisite Colonial Revival mansion, built in 1905, has four fireplaces, lovely Victorian gardens, and a third-floor "Christmas Ballroom," and is completely furnished with turn-of-the-century antiques. We are known for our wonderful breakfasts and making our guests feel at home in a quiet, romantic atmosphere. Eureka's Old Town, with its wonderful shops and restaurants, is within walking distance. The majestic redwoods and the Pacific Ocean are only minutes away.

welcome; 7 Children welcome; 8 Tennis nearby; 9 Swimming nearby; 10 Golf nearby; 11 Skiing nearby; 12 May be booked through travel agent.

The Cornelius Daly Inn

Wine and cheese each evening. AAA-approved, three-diamond rating.

Hosts: Sue and Gene Clinesmith
Rooms: 5 (3PB; 2SB) $80-140
Full Breakfast
Credit Cards: A, B, C, D, E
Notes: 2, 5, 7, 8, 10, 12

FERNDALE

The Gingerbread Mansion Inn

400 Berding Street, 95536
(707) 786-4000; (800) 952-4136;
FAX (707) 786-4381
E-mail: kenn@humboldt1.com
Web site: http://www.gingerbread-mansion.com

Nestled between giant redwoods and the rugged Pacific Coast is one of California's best-kept secrets: the Victorian village of Ferndale. A state historic landmark listed on the National Historic Register, Ferndale is a community frozen in time, with Victorian homes and shops relatively unchanged since their construction in the mid-to-late 1800s. One of Ferndale's most well-known homes is the Gingerbread Mansion Inn. Decorated with antiques, the

eleven romantic guest rooms offer private baths, some with old-fashioned clawfoot tubs, and fireplaces. Also included is a full breakfast, high tea, four parlors, and formal English gardens. Rated four diamonds by AAA.

Host: Ken Torbert
Rooms: 10 (PB) $140-350
Full Breakfast
Credit Cards: A, B, C
Notes: 2, 5, 10, 12

FORT BRAGG

Avalon House

561 Stewart Street, 95437
(707) 964-5555 (voice and FAX);
(800) 964-5556

A 1905 Craftsman home in a quiet residential neighborhood, three blocks from the ocean and two blocks from the Skunk train. Rooms with private baths, fireplaces, whirlpool tubs, down comforters, and ocean views. Enjoy all the romance of the Mendocino coast, even if you never leave your room. No smoking allowed.

Hostess: Anne Sorrells
Rooms: 6 (PB) $70-135
Full Breakfast
Credit Cards: A, B, C, D
Notes: 2, 5, 7, 8, 9, 10, 12

Grey Whale Inn

615 N. Main Street, 95437
(707) 964-0640; (800) 382-7244;
FAX (707) 964-4408
E-mail: gwhale@mcn.org

Handsome four-story Mendocino Coast landmark since 1915. Cozy to expansive, all rooms have private baths, TVs, phones,

---

ocean, garden, hill or town views. Some rooms have fireplaces; one has a Jacuzzi tub. Recreation area with pool table/library, fireside lounge, and TV/VCR room. Sixteen-person conference room. Full buffet breakfast features blue-ribbon coffee cakes. Friendly, helpful staff. Relaxed seaside charm, situated six blocks from the beach. Celebrate your special occasion on the fabled Mendocino Coast!

Hosts: Colette and John Bailey
Rooms: 14 (PB) $90-180
Full Breakfast
Credit Cards: A, B, C, D, F
Notes: 2, 5, 7, 8, 9, 10, 12

GEORGETOWN

Historic American River Inn

PO Box 43, 95634
(916) 333-4499; (800) 245-6566;
FAX (916) 333-9253

Innkeepers Will and Maria Collin carry on the century-old tradition of graciousness in a setting far removed from the fast pace of modern living. You are invited to cool off in a beautiful mountain pool or relax in the spa. Some may choose a day of bicycling amid the colorful, breathtaking daffodils, irises, and brilliant, yellow-gold scotch broom. The bicycles are provided. The historic Queen Anne inn specializes in ladies and couples retreats/seminars and corporate meetings with fifteen to forty people.

Hosts: Will and Maria Collin
Rooms: 18 (12PB; 6SB) $85-115
Full Gourmet Breakfast
Credit Cards: A, B, C, D, E, F
Notes: 2, 3, 5, 7, 8, 9, 10, 11, 12

GEYSERVILLE

Campbell Ranch Inn

1475 Canyon Road, 95441
(707) 857-3476; (800) 959-3878;
FAX (707) 857-3239

A thirty-five-acre country setting in the heart of the Sonoma County wine country between the Alexander Valley and Dry Creek Valley wine regions. Spectacular view, beautiful gardens, tennis court, swimming pool, hot tub, and bicycles. The inn has four spacious rooms and a private cottage, private baths, king beds, and balconies. Quiet and peaceful. Full breakfast is served on the terrace, and an evening dessert of homemade pie or cake is offered. Visit wineries and Lake Sonoma for water sports, fishing, and hiking. The wine country destination resort. Color brochure available.

Hosts: Jerry and Mary Jane Campbell
Rooms: 5 (PB) $100-165
Full Breakfast
Credit Cards: A, B, C
Notes: 2, 5, 10, 12

GRASS VALLEY

Elam Biggs Bed and Breakfast

220 Colfax Avenue, 95945
(916) 477-0906

This 1892 beautiful Queen Anne Victorian is set admist a large yard surrounded by grand shade trees and a rose-covered picket fence. It's just a short stroll from historic downtown Grass Valley. In the

Elam Biggs B&B

morning, enjoy brewed coffee and a hearty breakfast served in the lovely dining room or outside on the private porch.

Hosts: Peter and Barbara Franchino
Rooms: 5 (PB); $75-110
Full Breakfast
Credit Cards: A, B
Notes: 2, 5, 7, 8, 9, 10, 11, 12

Murphy's Inn

318 Neal Street, 95945
(916) 273-6873; 1-800-895-2488;
FAX (916) 273-5157

Murphy's Inn offers the discriminating traveler a return to the splendor of the Victorian era. Your first glimpse of the Inn is the giant sequoia tree standing amidst well-kept grounds, and the ivy baskets surrounding the veranda. Eight bedrooms with lace curtains, antiques, and private baths make your stay comfortable. A full breakfast is included. Chocolate chip cookies and soft drinks always available.

Hosts: Ted and Nancy Days, Linda Jones
Rooms: 8 (PB) $95-150
Full Breakfast
Credit Cards: A, B, C
Notes: 5, 7, 8, 9, 10, 11, 12

GUALALA

North Coast Country Inn

34591 S. Highway 1, 95445
(707) 884-4537; (800) 959-4537

Picturesque redwood buildings on a forested hillside overlooking the Pacific Ocean. The large guest rooms feature fireplaces, private baths, queen beds, decks, and minikitchens and are furnished with authentic antiques. Two penthouse guest rooms, added in 1997, are surrounded by the hillside forest of pine, redwood and fir; the rooms are wood-paneled with high ceilings and picture windows, fireplaces, private bathrooms, whirlpool tubs, king beds and private decks. Breakfast and evening sherry are served in the common room by the fireplace. A TV and VCR are available. Enjoy a beautiful hilltop gazebo garden and romantic hot tub under the pines.

Hosts: Loren and Nancy Flanagan
Rooms: 6 (PB) $135-175
Full Breakfast
Credit Cards: A, B, C
Notes: 2, 5, 8, 10, 12

HEALDSBURG

The Honor Mansion

14891 Grove Street, 95448
(707) 433-4277; (800) 554-4667;
FAX (707) 431-7173
Web site: http://www.honormansion.com

A beautifully restored 1883 "Italianate" Victorian in the heart of the Sonoma County wine country. Enjoy the comfort

NOTES: Credit cards accepted: A Master Card; B Visa; C American Express; D Discover; E Diners Club; F Other; 2 Personal checks accepted; 3 Lunch available; 4 Dinner available; 5 Open all year; 6 Pets

of immaculate guest rooms, a dip in the pool, or a peaceful rest beside the Koi pond waterfall. Wonderful food; warm hospitality. Your best vacation ever!

Hosts: Cathi & Steve Fowler
Rooms: 6 (PB) $120-220
Full Breakfast
Credit Cards: A, B, D
Notes: 2, 5, 8, 9, 10, 12

IDYLLWILD

The Pine Cove Inn
PO Box 2181, 23481 Highway 243, 92549
(909) 659-5033; (888) 659-5033;
FAX (909) 659-5034

Enjoy clean air with great views of Mt. San Jacinto and Mt. Tahquitz. Our units are spacious and tastefully appointed in a variety of styles. Relax, read a book, or hike on seventy-five miles of marked trails in the San Jacinto wilderness area. New apartment unit above the lodge has a full kitchen, television, and fireplace. Get acquainted with paradise.

Hosts: Bob and Michelle Bollmann
Rooms: 10 (PB) $70-100
Full Breakfast
Credit Cards: A, B, C
Notes: 2, 5, 7, 10, 12

Wilkum Inn Bed and Breakfast
PO Box 1115, 92549-1115
(909) 659-4087; (800) 659-4086

Come home to warm hospitality and personal service in a friendly mountain ambiance. The two-story, shingle-sided Inn is

nestled among pines, oaks, and cedars. Warm, knotty pine interiors and a cozy river rock fireplace are enhanced by the innkeepers' antiques and collectibles. Expanded continental breakfast of fruits and breads such as crepes, Belgian waffles, or abelskivers fortify guests for a day of hiking or visiting unique shops and art galleries.

Hostesses: Annamae Chambers and Barbara Jones
Rooms: 4 (PB) $65-95
Expanded Continental Breakfast
Credit Cards: none
Notes: 2, 5, 12

The Heirloom

IONE

The Heirloom
214 Shakeley Lane, 95640
(209) 274-4468; (888) 628-7896

Travel down a country lane to a spacious, romantic English garden and a petite colonial mansion built circa 1863. The house features balconies, fireplaces, and heirloom antiques, along with gourmet breakfasts and gracious hospitality. The Heirloom is located in the historic gold country, close to all major northern California cities. The

welcome; 7 Children welcome; 8 Tennis nearby; 9 Swimming nearby; 10 Golf nearby; 11 Skiing nearby; 12 May be booked through travel agent.

area abounds with antiques, wineries, and historic sites. Within walking distance of a golf course.

Hostesses: Melisande Hubbs and Patricia Cross
Rooms: 6 (4 PB; 2 SB); $60-92
Full Breakfast
Credit Cards: A, B, C
Closed Thanksgiving and Christmas
Notes: 2, 5, 8, 9, 10

JULIAN

Butterfield Bed and Breakfast

2284 Sunset Drive, PO Box 1115, 92036
(619) 765-2179; (800) 379-4262
FAX (619) 765-1229

Butterfield Bed and Breakfast captures the gold mining and apple growing heritage of the historic mountain hamlet of Julian. The inn's five guest rooms, each with private bath, offer guests day's-end luxury in the French Bedroom Suite, Country Rose, Feathernest Room, Apple "Sweet," or Rosebud Cottage. Each morning guests are treated to a gourmet breakfast. Butterfield offers holiday specials, carriage rides, and candlelight dinner, or just a quiet place to relax. From the lilac and apple blossoms of spring, the wildflowers of summer, and the glorious hues of fall to the white frosting of winter, Butterfield Bed and Breakfast delivers a mother lode of hospitality all year long.

Hosts: Ray and Mary Trimmins
Rooms: 5 (PB) $105-135
Full Breakfast
Credit Cards: A, B, C, D
Notes: 2, 4, 5, 7, 8, 10, 12

Eden Creek Orchard Bed and Breakfast

1052 Julian Orchards Drive, 92036
(760) 765-2102; FAX (760) 943-7959
E-mail: eden_bb@ramonamall.com
Web site: http://www.ramonamall.com/eden_bb.html

Two romantic cottage suites on our ten-acre apple orchard in historic Julian, a gold mining town in the mountains one hour east of downtown San Diego. The Eden Creek Suite is an eight-hundred-square foot, two-bedroom charmer with fireplace, kitchenette, patios, fountain and swing. The Orchard Suite, five hundred square feet, is above "the barn" and is luxury and privacy made to order. The romantic ambience includes canopy bed, fireplace, antique tub, and kitchenette. Both suites have TV, VCR, and stereo with CD. The outdoor Jacuzzi overlooks the orchard and has a spectacular view of Volcan Mountain. The only winery in Julian is right next door. Complimentary carriage rides with a two-night booking. The ground floor of the barn is spacious and cozy and is ideal for weddings, reunions, or relaxing. Suites are nonsmoking.

Hosts: Gary and Lee Simons
Rooms: 3 (PB) $95-135 (AAA, senior, military discounts)
Full or Continental Breakfast
Credit Cards: A, B, C, D, E, F
Notes: 2

Julian Gold Rush Hotel

PO Box 1856, 2032 Main Street, 92036
(760) 765-0201; (800) 734-5854 (CA only);
FAX (760) 765-0327

Built in 1897 by a freed slave and his wife, the Hotel fit beautifully into the emerging

---

NOTES: Credit cards accepted: A Master Card; B Visa; C American Express; D Discover; E Diners Club; F Other; 2 Personal checks accepted; 3 Lunch available; 4 Dinner available; 5 Open all year; 6 Pets

Victorian society of the 1890s. The Hotel often was called the "Queen of the Black Country" and was a frequent stopping place of Lady Bronston, Adm. Nimitz, the Scripps, and the Whitneys. The hotel register boasts the presence of many a senator and congressman. Popular also with the townfolk, the hotel served as a Julian social center after the monthly town hall dances, when Margaret Robinson hosted and prepared much-anticipated midnight feasts.

Hosts: Steve and Gig Ballinger
Rooms: 14 (PB) $72-160
Full Breakfast
Credit Cards: A, B, C
Notes: 2, 5, 7, 8, 9, 10, 12

Leucadia Inn-by-the-Sea

P.O. Box 1115, 92036
(760) 942-1668; (800) 942-1668

Leucadia Inn-by-the-Sea is a boutique bed and breakfast hotel tucked in the seaside village of Leucadia. Its seven theme rooms, queen beds, and private baths are just a block from the ocean. Walk sandy beaches, wade in ocean waters or surf majestic waves. Sea World, San Diego

Leucadia Inn-by-the-Sea

Zoo and Wild Animal Park, Del Mar Race Track, and Carlsbad Flower Fields are nearby. Visit the quaint towns of Carlsbad and Encinitas.

Hosts: Ray and Mary Trimmins
Rooms: 7 (PB) $69-129
Continental Breakfast
Credit Cards: A, B, C, D

KERNVILLE

Kern River Inn Bed and Breakfast

PO Box 1725, 119 Kern River Drive, 93238-1725
(760) 376-6750; (800) 986-4382;
FAX (760) 376-6643
E-mail: kribb@kernvalley.com
Web site: http://www.travelassist.com/reg/
ca111.html

A charming, classic country riverfront bed and breakfast located on the wild and scenic Kern River in the quaint little town of Kernville within the Sequoia National Forest in the southern Sierra Mountains. We specialize in romantic getaways. All guest rooms have private baths and feature river views; some have fireplaces and whirlpool tubs. A full breakfast is served. You can walk to restaurants, shops, parks, and the museum. It's only a short drive to giant redwood trees. This is an all-year vacation area with white-water rafting, hiking, fishing, biking, skiing, and Lake Isabella water activities.

Hosts: Jack and Carita Prestwich
Rooms: 6 (PB) $79-99
Full Breakfast
Credit Cards: A, B, C
Notes: 2, 5, 7, 9, 10, 11, 12

welcome; 7 Children welcome; 8 Tennis nearby; 9 Swimming nearby; 10 Golf nearby; 11 Skiing nearby; 12 May be booked through travel agent.

LAGUNA BEACH

Eiler's Inn

741 South Coast Highway, 92651
(714) 494-3004; FAX (714) 497-2215

Twelve rooms with private baths and a courtyard with gurgling fountain and colorful blooming plants are within walking distance of town and most restaurants; half block from the beach.

Host: Nico, Diana, Cynthia and Tracey Wirtz
Rooms: 12 (PB) $85-195
Full Breakfast
Credit Cards: A, B, C, D
Notes: 2, 5, 8, 9, 10, 12

LAKE ARROWHEAD

Romantique Lakeview Lodge

28051 Highway 189, PO Box 128, 92352
(909) 337-6633; (800) 358-5253;
FAX (909) 337-5966

The Romantique Lakeview Lodge is centrally located right across from the Lake Arrowhead Village and the lake. Our nine beautifully appointed rooms all are decorated differently, giving you a chance to come back again and again. All have their own private baths and color TV/VCRs. Some have gas log Victorian fireplaces. Continental breakfast with our huge cinnamon rolls is served daily. We are a smoke-free inn.

Hostesses: Megan McElrath and Linda Womack
Rooms: 9 (PB) $65-225
Continental Breakfast
Credit Cards: A, B, C, D
Notes: 5, 7, 8, 9, 10, 11, 12

LITTLE RIVER

The Victorian Farmhouse Inn

7001 N. Highway, 95456
(707) 937-0697; (800) 264-4723

Built in 1877 as a private residence, the Inn has been completely renovated and furnished in period antiques to enhance its beauty and Victorian charm. All rooms have private baths, and most have fireplaces. Breakfast is served in your room. The Inn has a country setting with redwoods and fir trees, and the ocean is just across the street. Located two miles south of Mendocino.

Hostess: Carole Molnar
Rooms: 12 (PB) $90-175
Full Breakfast
Credit Cards: A, B, C, D, E
Notes: 5, 6, 7, 8, 10, 12

LONG BEACH

Lord Mayor's B&B Inn

435 Cedar Avenue, 90802
(562) 436-0324 (voice and FAX)
E-mail: innkeepers@lordmayors.com
Web site: http://www.lordmayors.com

An award-winning historical landmark, the 1904 home of the first mayor of Long Beach invites you to enjoy the ambiance of years gone by. Rooms have ten-foot ceilings and are decorated with period antiques. Each unique bedroom has its private bath and access to a large sundeck. Full breakfast is served in the dining room or on the deck overlooking the garden. Located near beaches, close to major attractions, within walking distance of convention and civic center and special events

---

NOTES: Credit cards accepted: A Master Card; B Visa; C American Express; D Discover; E Diners Club; F Other; 2 Personal checks accepted; 3 Lunch available; 4 Dinner available; 5 Open all year; 6 Pets

held downtown. The right touch for the business and vacation traveler.

Hosts: Laura and Reuben Brasser
Rooms: 11 (PB) $80-125
Full Breakfast
Credit Cards: A, B, C
Notes: 2, 5, 7, 9, 10, 12

MAMMOTH LAKES

Snow Goose Inn Bed and Breakfast

PO Box 387, 57 Forest Trail, 93546
E-mail: snowgoose@qnet.com
Web site: http://mammothweb.com/lodging/
    snowgoose/snowgoose.html

Mammoth's first bed and breakfast. Enjoy yesterday's charm with today's convenience. Many antiques and quilts. Full breakfast, evening appetizers, private bath, telephone, and TV. Outside hot tub. Close to restaurants and shops.

Hosts: Bob and Carol Roster
Rooms: 19 (PB) $63-98
Full Breakfast
Credit Cards: A, B, D
Notes: 2, 5, 7, 8, 9, 10, 11, 12

MARIPOSA (GOLD COUNTRY AND YOSEMITE NATIONAL PARK)

Finch Haven

4605 Triangle Road, 95338
(209) 966-4738 (voice and FAX)

A quiet country home on nine acres with panoramic mountain views. Birds, deer, and other abundant wildlife. Two rooms with private bath and private deck. Queen and twin beds. Nutritious breakfast. In the heart of the California Gold Rush country near historic attractions. Convenient access to the spectacular Yosemite Valley and Yosemite National Park. A restful place to practice Mark 6:31 and to enjoy Christian hospitality.

Hosts: Bruce and Carol Fincham
Rooms: 2 (PB) $75
Full Breakfast
Credit Cards: none
Notes: 2, 5, 7, 8, 9, 11, 12

Shiloh Bed and Breakfast (Guest House)

Shiloh Bed and Breakfast

3265 Triangle Park Road, 95338
(209) 742-7200
Web site: http://www.sierranet.net/web/shiloh

An old, peaceful farmhouse with a private guest house nestled among Ponderosa pines in the foothills of Yosemite National Park. Two quaint knotty pine bedrooms in the main house share a private bath. The pleasantly decorated guest house sleeps five or six and has a full kitchen, living room, and deck. Playground for children, plus swimming pool and horseshoe pits. Historic gold rush country and Yosemite to explore. Christian hospitality.

Hosts: Ron and Joan Smith
Rooms: 3 (1PB; 2SB) $55-85
Expanded Continental Breakfast
Credit Cards: A, B, C, D
Notes: 2, 5, 7, 9, 10

welcome; 7 Children welcome; 8 Tennis nearby; 9 Swimming nearby; 10 Golf nearby; 11 Skiing nearby; 12 May be booked through travel agent.

Winsor Farms Bed and Breakfast

5636 E. Whitlock Road, 95338
(209) 966-5592

A country home seven miles north of Mariposa, just off Highway 140 to Yosemite National Park. This peaceful hilltop retreat among majestic pines and rugged oaks offers two rooms decorated for your comfort and convenience. An extended continental breakfast is served. The town of Mariposa is the gateway to the Mother Lode gold country, with famous courthouse, museums, and history center. Yosemite National Park is a scenic wonder of the world with waterfalls, granite cliffs, Sequoia Big Trees, birds, and animal life.

Hosts: Donald and Janice Haag
Rooms: 2 (SB) $40-50
Extended Continental Breakfast
Credit Cards: none
Notes: 2, 5, 7 (restricted)

MENDOCINO

Antioch Ranch

39451 Comptche Road, 95460
(707) 937-5570; FAX (707) 937-1757

Antioch Ranch, providing a Christian atmosphere of peace, is a place for refreshment and renewal. Located just five and a half miles inland from the picturesque town of Mendocino, the Ranch features four guest cottages on twenty acres of rolling hills, redwoods, and apple orchards. Each cottage has its own style and ambiance. Rustic, yet comfortable, each features woodstoves, complete kitchen with

a microwave, two bedrooms, bath, and open living/dining room.

Hosts: Jerry and Pat Westfall
Rooms: 4 two-bedroom cottages (PB) $65-85
Breakfast on Request
Credit Cards: none
Notes: 2, 5, 7, 8, 9 (beach), 10

Fensalden Inn

PO Box 99, **Albion**, 95410
(707) 937-4042; (800) 957-3850;
FAX (707) 937-2416
E-mail: Scottb@mcn.org
Web site: http://www.fensalden.com

Overlooking the Pacific Ocean from twenty tree-lined pastoral acres, Fensalden Inn offers a quiet respite for the perfect getaway. A former stagecoach way station, the inn offers a restful yet interesting stay. Eight guest quarters; some are suites with fireplaces and kitchens; all have private baths with showers or tubs; most have beautiful ocean views. Whale-watch, join the deer on a stroll through our meadow, or just relax and enjoy!

Hosts: Scott and Frances Brazil
Rooms: 8 (PB) $100-145
Full Breakfast
Credit Cards: A, B, D
Notes: 2, 5, 8, 10, 12

The Seafoam Lodge

PO Box 68, 95460
6751 N. Highway, **Little River**, 95456
(707) 937-1827; (800) 606-1827
FAX (707) 937-0744
Web site: http://touristguide.com/b&b/ca/seafoam

Panoramic ocean views and breathtaking sunsets await our guests from every room. A forested hillside provides the backdrop for the lodge, which is perched on six acres of coastal gardens and pines above the inn of Buckhorn Cove. The comfortable guest rooms have king- or queen-size beds, telephones, refrigerators, coffeemakers, color televisions, and VCRs. Some guest rooms have kitchens or fireplaces. Hot tubs in the open air, or enclosed in our gazebo.

Hosts: Dennis and Kathy Smith and Hazel Perry
Rooms: 24 (PB) $95-150
Continental Breakfast
Credit Cards: A, B, C, D
Notes: 2, 5, 6, 7, 8, 10, 12

Whitegate Inn Bed and Breakfast

PO Box 150, 499 Howard Street, 95460
(707) 937-4892; (800) 531-7282
FAX (707) 937-1131
E-mail: staff@whitegateinn.com
Web site: http://www.whitegateinn.com

Circa 1883. Old-world charm, atmosphere, and elegance in the heart of the village of Mendocino. Surrounded by gorgeous gardens and views of the rugged Pacific Coast, the Inn is a splendid example of classic, meticulously restored Victorian architecture. Step inside and enjoy a sense of informal luxury. The decor is elegant, set off by fresh flowers and striking French and Victorian antiques. In the morning, step into the handsomely furnished, sunlit dining room and enjoy a delicious, splendidly presented breakfast. Come and join us and experience sophistication, grace, and charming hospitality, presented in traditional European style.

Hosts: George and Carol Bechtloff
Rooms: 6 (PB) $129-249
Full Breakfast
Credit Cards: A, B, C, D, E, F
Notes: 2, 5, 8, 9, 10, 12

The Jabberwock

MONTEREY

The Jabberwock

598 Laine Street, 93940
(408) 372-4777; (888) 428-7253;
FAX (408) 655-2946
Web site: http://www.innaccess.com/jwi/

Alice's wonderland in a 1911 Craftsman-style home located just four blocks above Cannery Row and the Monterey Bay Aquarium. The Jabberwock has a half acre of beautiful gardens with a waterfall. Off-street parking is available for guests. Rooms have down pillows and comforters; most rooms have fine views of the bay. Guests may expect a full breakfast, hors d'oeuvres at 5 PM and homemade cookies and milk at bedtime.

Hosts: Joan and John Kiliany
Rooms: 7 (5PB; 2SB) $105-190
Full Breakfast
Credit Cards: A, B
Notes: 2, 5, 8, 9, 10, 12

welcome; 7 Children welcome; 8 Tennis nearby; 9 Swimming nearby; 10 Golf nearby; 11 Skiing nearby; 12 May be booked through travel agent.

MT. SHASTA

Mt. Shasta Ranch Bed and Breakfast

1008 W. A. Barr Road, 96067
(916) 926-3870; FAX (916) 926-6882

The inn is situated in a rural setting with a majestic view of Mt. Shasta and features a main lodge, carriage house, and cottage. Group accommodations are available. Our breakfast room is ideally suited for seminars and retreats, with large seating capacity. The game room includes piano, ping-pong, pool table, and board games. Guests also enjoy an outdoor Jacuzzi. Nearby recreational facilities include Alpine and Nordic skiing, fishing, hiking, mountain bike rentals, surrey rides, and museums. Call for pastor's discount.

Hosts: Bill and Mary Larsen
Rooms: 9 + 1 cabin (5PB; 5SB) $55-95
Full Breakfast
Credit Cards: A, B, C, D
Notes: 2, 5, 7, 8, 9, 10, 11, 12

NAPA

Belle Epoque

1386 Calistoga Avenue, 94559
(707) 257-2161; (800) 238-8070;
FAX (707) 226-6314

Elaborate Queen Anne architecture and extensive use of stained glass are complemented by elegant period furnishings. This century-old Victorian boasts six tastefully decorated guest rooms, each with private bath and two with fireplaces. A generous gourmet breakfast is offered each morning either by fireside in the formal dining room or in the more relaxed atmosphere of the inn's plant-filled sunroom. Complimentary evening wine and appetizers on the premises. Wine tasting room/cellar. Walk to Old Town, Wine Train, and the Opera House. On-grounds parking. Air-conditioned throughout.

Hostess: Georgia Jump
Rooms: 6 (PB) $125-185
Full Gourmet Breakfast
Credit Cards: A, B, C, D
Notes: 2, 5, 8, 9, 10, 12

Blue Violet Mansion

443 Brown Street, 94559
(707) 253-2583; (800) 959-2583;
FAX (707) 257-8205

1996 Gold Award: Best B&B in North America/OHG. Cross the threshold of this graceful Queen Anne Victorian mansion and return to the elegance of the 1880s. Situated on a quiet street with an acre of private gardens in historic Old Town Napa, the Mansion is within walking distance of downtown shops and restaurants. This lovingly restored inn is an intimate and romantic home with large, cheerful faux- and mural-painted rooms with fireplaces, balconies, private baths or spas, and more. Guests are encouraged to feel at home in the grand front rooms and enjoy the new courtyard garden with fountains, a stained-glass skylight, and a swimming pool. Enjoy an evening of romantic elegance with a private candlelight champagne dinner, picnic lunches, bicycles, and much more. Hot-air ballooning and golf packages are available. Located near the Wine Train. The Mansion is described by Bill Gleason in his book *50 Most Romantic Places in*

NOTES: Credit cards accepted: A Master Card; B Visa; C American Express; D Discover; E Diners Club; F Other; 2 Personal checks accepted; 3 Lunch available; 4 Dinner available; 5 Open all year; 6 Pets

Northern California as the cabernet of Napa Valley's inns.

Hosts: Bob and Kathy Morris
Rooms: 14 (PB) $145-285
Full Breakfast
Credit Cards: A, B, C, D, E, F
Notes: 2, 3, 4, 5, 7, 8, 9, 10, 12

The Napa Inn

1137 Warren Street, 94559
(707) 257-1444; (800) 435-1144;
FAX (707) 257-0251

This beautiful Queen Anne Victorian built in 1899 and furnished with antiques is reminiscent of a bygone era when life was simpler and the pace more relaxed. Your cares and worries will melt away as you bask in the warmth and ambience of this lovely Inn. Relax in one of our six beautifully appointed guest rooms, each with its own private bathroom.

Hosts: Ann and Denny Mahoney
Rooms: 6 (PB) $130-190
Full Breakfast
Credit Cards: A, B, C, D, E
Notes: 2, 5, 8, 10, 12

The Old World Inn

1301 Jefferson Street, 94559
(707) 257-0112; FAX (707) 257-0118
Web site: http://www.napavalley.com/napavalley/
    lodging/inns/oldworld

The Old World Inn was built in 1906 by contractor E.W. Doughty for his private town residence. The home is an eclectic combination of architectural styles detailed with wood shingles; wide, shady porches; clinker brick; and leaded and beveled glass. The Inn is furnished throughout with painted antique furniture. The eight guest

The Old World Inn

rooms have been decorated individually with coordinated linens and fabrics. All have private bathrooms, most of them complete with Victorian claw-foot tubs and showers; one has a private spa tub. Bright, fresh Scandinavian colors. A complimentary carafe of Napa Valley wine awaits in your room. Satisfy your urge for a mid-afternoon snack and join us for tea and an assortment of homemade cookies. The Inn is air-conditioned. A large, custom Jacuzzi is available outside.

Host: Sam Van Hoeve
Rooms: 8 (PB) $110-160
Full Breakfast
Credit Cards: A, B, C, D
Notes: 2, 5, 8, 9, 10, 12

NAPA VALLEY

Bartels Ranch and B&B Country Inn

1200 Conn Valley Road, **St. Helena**, 94574
(707) 963-4001; FAX (707) 963-5100

"Heaven in the Hills." Situated in the heart of the world-famous Napa Valley wine country is this secluded, romantic, elegant country estate overlooking a "hundred-acre valley with a ten thousand-acre view."

welcome; 7 Children welcome; 8 Tennis nearby; 9 Swimming nearby; 10 Golf nearby; 11 Skiing nearby; 12 May be booked through travel agent.

Honeymoon "Heart of the Valley" suite has sunken Jacuzzi, sauna, shower, stone fireplace, and private deck with vineyard view. Romantic, award-winning accommodations, expansive entertainment room, poolside lounging, personalized itineraries, afternoon refreshments, pool table, fireplace, library, and terraces overlooking the vineyard. Bicycle to nearby wineries, lake, golf, tennis, fishing, boating, mineral spas, and bird-watching. Come dream awhile!

Hostess: Jami Bartels
Rooms: 4 (PB) $165-365 (winter discounts)
Full Breakfast
Credit Cards: A, B, C, D, E, F
Notes: 2, 3, 4 (catered), 5, 7, 8, 9, 10, 12

NEVADA CITY

The Parsonage Bed and Breakfast Inn

427 Broad Street, 95959
(916) 265-9478; (916) 265-8147
Web sites: http://www.virtualcities.com/ons/ca/g/
cag9504.htm
http://www.go-native.com/Inns/0033.html

History comes alive in this 125-year-old home in Nevada City's historic district. Cozy guest rooms, parlor, and dining and family rooms all are lovingly furnished with the innkeeper's pioneer family antiques. Breakfast is served on the veranda or in the formal dining room. Enjoy lunch or dinner at one of the twenty-six restaurants in the four-block area.

Hostesses: Deborah Dane and Pam Ashton
Rooms: 6 (PB) $70-135
Full Breakfast
Credit Cards: A, B
Notes: 2, 4, 5, 7, 11, 12

ORLAND

Inn at Shallow Creek Farm

4712 Road DD, 95963
(530) 865-4093; (800) 865-4093

The Inn offers bed and breakfast at a working farm and orange orchard. Our two-story farmhouse has spacious rooms furnished with antiques, creating a blend of nostalgia and comfortable country living. Our breakfasts feature home-baked breads and an assortment of fruit and juice from our own trees. Delicious homemade jams and jellies complement our farm breakfasts. Nearby Black Butte Lake and Sacramento National Wildlife Refuge offer outdoor recreation activities. French, German, and Spanish are spoken.

Hosts: Mary and Kurt Glaeseman
Rooms: 4 (2PB; 2SB) $55-75
Full Breakfast
Credit Cards: A, B
Notes: 2, 5, 9, 10, 12

PACIFIC GROVE

Gatehouse Inn

225 Central Avenue, 93950
(408) 649-8436; (800) 753-1881;
FAX (408) 648-8044
E-mail: lew@redshift.com
Web site: http://www.sueandlewinns.com

The Gatehouse Inn, built in 1884 as a summer retreat for Sen. Langford, features nine guest rooms, each with a different theme. Take a journey through the past in rooms such as the Steinbeck, Langford, or Victorian, all with Victorian elegance. For a different feel, try the Cannery Row Room, Turkish Room, or Italian Room. Whichever room you choose, enjoy our sump-

---

NOTES: Credit cards accepted: A Master Card; B Visa; C American Express; D Discover; E Diners Club; F Other; 2 Personal checks accepted; 3 Lunch available; 4 Dinner available; 5 Open all year; 6 Pets

Gatehouse Inn

tuous food, breathtaking views and romantic elegance.

Hostess: Lois DeFord
Rooms: 9 (PB) $110-150
Full Breakfast
Credit Cards: A, B, C, D
Notes: 2, 5, 7 (8 and older), 8, 9, 10, 12

Grand View Inn

557 Ocean View Boulevard, 93950
(408) 372-4341

Built in 1910, the Inn is at the edge of Monterey Bay. It was completely restored in 1994 by the Flatley family, owners of the Seven Gables Inn next door. Warm personal service, spectacular natural surroundings, comfortably appointed rooms, irresistible breakfasts, and sociable gatherings at afternoon tea. Quiet elegance. Along with unsurpassed views of Monterey Bay from each room, guests enjoy the comfort of marble-tiled private baths, patterned hardwood floors, beautiful antique furnishings, and lovely grounds.

Hosts: Susan Flatley and Ed Flatley
Rooms: 10 (PB) $125-185
Full Breakfast
Credit Cards: A, B
Notes: 2, 5, 7 (over 12), 8, 9, 10, 12

The Old St. Angela Inn Bed and Breakfast

321 Central Avenue, 93950
(408) 372-3246; (800) 748-6306;
FAX (408) 372-8560
E-mail: lew@redshift.com
Web site: http://www.sueandlewinns.com

Cape Cod-style bed and breakfast. Front sitting room with ocean view. Has large cut-stone fireplace. A full breakfast is served each morning. Late afternoon snacks with complimentary wine are served in the front sitting room. Located between Monterey and Pebble Beach near the Monterey Bay Aquarium. The Inn is within walking distance of many fine restaurants and an easy drive to world-class golf.

Hosts: Lewis Shaefer and Susan Kuslis
Rooms: 8 (PB) $100-150
Full Breakfast
Credit Cards: A, B, D
Notes: 2, 5, 6, 7, 8, 9, 10, 12

The Old St. Angela Inn Bed and Breakfast

Seven Gables Inn

555 Ocean View Boulevard, 93950
(408) 372-4341

Crashing waves, rocky shorelines, sea otters, whales, and beautiful sunsets are seen

welcome; 7 Children welcome; 8 Tennis nearby; 9 Swimming nearby; 10 Golf nearby; 11 Skiing nearby; 12 May be booked through travel agent.

from each guest room at century-old Seven Gables Inn. Such a romantic setting on the edge of Monterey Bay is enhanced by a dazzling display of fine European antiques, a sumptuous breakfast, afternoon tea, the comfort of all-private baths, and excellent service. Nearby attractions include the Monterey Bay Aquarium, Pebble Beach, Carmel, and Big Sur. Seven Gables Inn is Mobil Travel Guide four-star-rated.

Hosts: Susan Flatley and Ed Flatley
Rooms: 14 (PB) $135-250
Full Breakfast
Credit Cards: A, B
Notes: 2, 5, 7 (over 12), 8, 9, 10, 12

art galleries, and many restaurants. Or stay "home" to enjoy the desert sun in and around the pool and spa. The guest rooms feature queen or king beds, climate controls, ceiling fans, and color televions. They are uniquely decorated in southwestern style. Lemonade and iced tea are always available. Snacks served in the late afternoons. AAA three-diamond-rated; ABBA-rated A+.

Hosts: Karen and Terry Bennett
Rooms: 4 (PB) $70-170
Continental Breakfast
Credit Cards: A, B
Notes: 2, 5, 8, 9, 10, 12

PALM SPRINGS

Casa Cody Bed and Breakfast Country Inn

175 S. Cahuilla Road, 92262
(760) 320-9346; (800) 231-2639;
FAX (760) 325-8610

A romantic, historic hideaway is nestled against the spectacular San Jacinto Mountains in the heart of Palm Springs Village. Completely redecorated in Santa Fe decor, it has twenty-three ground-level units consisting of hotel rooms, studio suites, and one- and two-bedroom suites with private patios, fireplaces, and fully equipped kitchens. Cable television and private phones; two pools; secluded, tree-shaded whirlpool spa.

Hosts: Therese Hayes, Frank Tysen, and
        Elissa Goforth
Rooms: 23 (PB) $49-199
Continental Breakfast
Credit Cards: A, B, C
Notes: 2, 5, 6 and 7 (limited), 8, 9, 10, 11

Tres Palmas Bed and Breakfast

PALM DESERT

Tres Palmas Bed and Breakfast

73135 Tumbleweed Lane, 92260
(760) 773-9858; (800) 770-9858;
FAX (760) 776-9159

Tres Palmas is located just one block south of El Paseo, the "Rodeo Drive of the Desert," where you will find boutiques,

---

NOTES: Credit cards accepted: A Master Card; B Visa; C American Express; D Discover; E Diners Club; F Other; 2 Personal checks accepted; 3 Lunch available; 4 Dinner available; 5 Open all year; 6 Pets

REDDING

Palisades Paradise B&B

1200 Palisades Avenue, 96003
(530) 223-5305
Web site: http://www.awwwsome.com/paradise

Enjoy a breathtaking view of the Sacramento River, city, and mountains from this beautiful, contemporary home with its garden spa, fireplace, wide-screen TV/VCR, and homelike atmosphere. You are always made to feel "special" here. Travelers and business people alike seek out the comfort and relaxed atmosphere in this quiet, peaceful neighborhood. Palisades Paradise is a serene setting for a quiet hideaway, yet is conveniently located one mile from shopping and I-5, with water-skiing and river rafting nearby. Moderately priced. Major credit cards are accepted. Advanced reservations desired; five-day cancellation policy.

Hostess: Gail Goetz
Rooms: 2 (SB) $70-85
Expanded Continental Breakfast
Credit Cards: A, B, C
Notes: 2, 5, 6, 7 (when booking both rooms), 8, 9, 10, 11, 12

REDLANDS

Cress Grove Manor

10956 Walnut Street, 92374
(909) 389-9958; FAX (909) 424-0235

A Mediterranean villa. Fountains and statuary abound throughout five acres of orange grove. Amenities include a heated spa and pool. Queen beds in the guest rooms. Sports TV room with sixty-two-inch screen; satellite available. Elegant, romantic, secluded. Spacious great room with marble floors, staircase, twenty-two-foot fireplace and windows.

Hosts: Don and Cress Bracci
Rooms: 4 (3PB; 1SB) $138-155
Continental Breakfast
Credit Cards: none
Notes: 2 (in advance), 5, 9, 11

REDONDO BEACH

Breeze Inn

122 S. Juanita Avenue, 90277
(213) 316-5123

Located in a quiet, modest neighborhood. Large suite with private entrance, private bath with spa, antiques, Oriental carpet, California king bed, breakfast area with microwave and toaster oven, and stocked refrigerator for continental breakfast. Good ventilation with skylight and ceiling fan. Outside patio. One room available with twin beds and private bath. Brochure available with map. Near Los Angeles, Disneyland, Universal City, and approximately five blocks to pier and beach.

Host: Betty Binding
Rooms: 2 (PB) $45-65 (2-night minimum)
Continental Breakfast (extra charge for Full)
Credit Cards: none
Notes: 2, 5, 7 (over 5), 8, 9, 10

RIDGECREST

BevLen Haus

809 N. Sanders Street, 93555
(760) 375-1988; (800) 375-1988;
FAX (760) 375-6871

"Once a guest, always a friend." Gracious, quiet, safe, and comfortable; your "secret

welcome; 7 Children welcome; 8 Tennis nearby; 9 Swimming nearby; 10 Golf nearby; 11 Skiing nearby; 12 May be booked through travel agent.

high desert hideaway." Nearly two thousand square feet, furnished with antiques, handmade quilts, and comforters in winter! Paved parking. Cooling air in summer. Old-fashioned kitchen has antique cast-iron cookstove, hand-hammered copper sink. In full-service community. Close to Sierra Nevada, Death Valley, Naval Air Warfare Center, China Lake, ghost towns, movie sites, and ancient Indian cultural sites. Wildflowers in spring. No smoking.

Hosts: Bev and Len de Geus
Rooms: 3 (PB) $45-65
Full Breakfast
Credit Cards: A, B, C, D
Notes: 2, 5, 8, 9, 10, 12

ST. HELENA

Erika's Hillside

285 Fawn Park, 94574
(707) 963-2887

A Swiss chalet, European charm, and hospitality in a peaceful, wooded country setting on a three-acre hillside estate on the eastern side of the Napa Valley. Beautifully landscaped flower gardens, terraced rock walls among established oak trees. Magnificent views of the valley's vineyards and wineries. A setting in harmony with its natural topography, only five minutes from downtown St. Helena. Some of the local attractions include wineries, spas, the Napa Valley Wine Train, balloon rides, and glider flights.

Hostess: Erika Cunningham
Rooms: 3 (PB) $95-275
Semicontinental Breakfast
Credit Cards: A, B, C
Notes: 2, 5, 7, 8, 9, 10, 12

Hilltop House
Bed and Breakfast

9550 St. Helena Road, PO Box 726, 94574
(707) 944-0880; FAX (707) 571-0263

Poised at the very top of the ridge that separates the famous wine regions of Napa and Sonoma, Hilltop House is a country retreat with all the comforts of home and a view that you must see to believe. Annette and Bill Gevarter built their contemporary home with this mountain panorama in mind. The vast deck lets you enjoy it at your leisure with a glass of wine in the afternoon, breakfast in the morning, or a long soak in the hot tub. From this vantage point, sunrises and sunsets are amazing. You'll cherish the natural setting, caring hospitality, and prize location.

Hostess: Annette Gevarter
Rooms: 4 (PB) $105-175
Full Breakfast
Credit Cards: A, B, C
Notes: 2, 5, 8, 9, 10, 12

La Fleur
Bed and Breakfast

1475 Inglewood Avenue, 94574
(707) 963-0233
Web site: http://www.lafleurinn.com

A charming 1882 Queen Anne Victorian nestled in the heart of Napa Valley's collection of fine wineries. Spacious, beautifully appointed rooms featuring old-world charm, private baths, spectacular views, and fireplaces will provide a most comfortable visit. Our breakfast of gourmet delights is elegantly served in the solarium while hot-air balloons drift above the adjacent vineyards. Your stay at La Fleur will include a private tour of neighboring

Villa Helena Winery and an introduction to award-winning winemaker Don McGrath. Join us for our many special events and classes, including winemaking and wine appreciation.

Hosts: Kay Murphy and Staff
Rooms: 7 (PB) $150
Expanded Continental Breakfast
Credit Cards: none
Notes: 2, 5, 8, 9, 10, 12

Carole's Bed and Breakfast

SAN ANDREAS

The Robin's Nest

PO Box 1408, 95249
(209) 754-1076; FAX (209) 754-3975
Web site: http://touristguide.com/b&b/ca/robinsnest

A traditional yet informal Victorian bed and breakfast country inn in the heart of the gold country. Eight hundred square feet of interior common space—ideal for group gathering. One and a third acres of gardens and fruit orchards with several seating areas. Central heat and air, hot spa and five-course gourmet breakfast.

Hosts: Karen and William Konietzny
Rooms: 9 (7PB; 2SB) $55-105
Full Breakfast
Credit Cards: A, B, C, D
Notes: 4 (with reservations, minimum 4 people), 5, 7, 8, 9, 10, 11, 12

SAN DIEGO

Carole's Bed and Breakfast

3227 Grim Avenue, 92104
(619) 280-5258; (800) 975-5521
Web site: http://www.wholesalewebpages.com/usa/caroles.htm

Built in 1904 by Mayor Frary, this historic site has the handsome style and craftsman-

ship of its time. It has been restored by the present owners, who live on site, giving it constant loving care. The decor is of its period, with antiques and comfort as the focus. Amenities include a spa, black-bottom pool, and rose garden. Carole's Bed and Breakfast is within walking distance of Balboa Park, an assortment of small shops and restaurants.

Hosts: Carole Dugdale and Michael O'Brian
Rooms: 10 (4PB; 6SB) $65-150
Continental Plus Breakfast
Credit Cards: A, B, C, D, F
Notes: 5, 7, 8, 9, 10, 12

Ellsbree House Bed and Breakfast

5054 Narragansett, 92107
(619) 226-4133; FAX (619) 223-4133
E-mail: ktelsbree@juno.com
Web site: http://www.oceanbeach-online.com/elsbree/b&b

This lovely New England-style home with "English garden" landscaping provides a secluded feeling, yet is near and convenient to all San Diego has to offer. It provides meticulous bed and breakfast rooms, as well as a three-bedroom, three-bath luxury condo that is completely furnished and rents by the week.

Hosts: Katie and Phil Elsbree
Rooms: 6 (PB)
Continental Breakfast
Credit Cards: A, B
Notes: 2, 5, 8, 9, 10, 12

SAN FRANCISCO

Dolores Park Inn

3641 Seventeenth Street, 94114
(415) 621-0482; (415) 553-6060

This charming, two-story Italianate Victorian mansion was built in 1874. It sits in a subtropical garden behind a wrought iron fence in the sunny part of San Francisco. The guest rooms are appointed with antiques, queen-size beds, and color TVs. A full breakfast is served in the formal dining room, and an evening beverage is served either on the patio or by the fireplace. Within walking distance to international restaurants, antique streetcars, and easy transportation to the heart of San Francisco.

Host: Bernie H. Vielwerth
Rooms: 4 (1PB; 3SB) $95-165
Full Breakfast
Credit Cards: A, B
Notes: 5, 8, 12

The Monte Cristo

600 Presidio Avenue, 94115
(415) 931-1875; FAX (415) 931-6005

The Monte Cristo has been part of San Francisco since 1875, located two blocks from the elegantly restored Victorian shops, restaurants, and antique stores on Sacramento Street. There is convenient transportation to downtown San Francisco and to the financial district. Each room is elegantly furnished with authentic period pieces.

Host: George Yuan
Rooms: 14 (11PB; 3SB) $63-108
Full Buffet Breakfast
Credit Cards: A, B, C, D, E
Notes: 5, 7

The Monte Cristo

The Red Victorian

1665 Haight Street, 94117
(415) 864-1978; FAX (415) 863-3293
E-mail: redvic@linex.com
Web site: http://www.redvic.com

A century-old Victorian hotel, now a B&B "home in San Francisco" to creative, loving people from everywhere. The Rose Garden Room, Peace Room, Sunshine Room, Rainbow Room, Redwood Forest Room and thirteen others celebrate nearby Golden Gate Park and the "Summer of Love." Meditation room, Peace

---

NOTES: Credit cards accepted: A Master Card; B Visa; C American Express; D Discover; E Diners Club; F Other; 2 Personal checks accepted; 3 Lunch available; 4 Dinner available; 5 Open all year; 6 Pets

Apple Farm Inn

Arts gift shop. On colorful Haight Street in the geographic heart of San Francisco.

Hostess: Sami Sunchild
Rooms: 18 (4PB; 14SB) $95-200
Continental Buffet Breakfast
Credit Cards: A, B, C
Notes: 4, 5, 8, 12

SAN GREGORIO

Rancho San Gregorio

Route 1, Box 54, 5086 La Honda Road (Highway 84), 94074
(415) 747-0810; FAX (415) 747-0184
E-mail: rsgleebud@aol.com

Five miles inland from the Pacific Ocean is an idyllic rural valley where Rancho San Gregorio welcomes travelers to share relaxed hospitality. Picnic, hike, or bike in wooded parks or on ocean beaches. Our country breakfast features local specialties. Located forty-five minutes from San Francisco, Santa Cruz, and the Bay area. Smoking outdoors only.

Hosts: Bud and Lee Raynor
Rooms: 4 (PB) $75-145 (extra person $15)
Full Breakfast
Credit Cards: A, B, C, D
Notes: 2, 5, 7, 9, 10, 12 (10%)

SAN LUIS OBISPO

Apple Farm Inn

2015 Monterey Street; 93401
(805) 544-2040; (800) 255-2040;
FAX (805) 546-9495
Web site: http://www.applefarm.com

The comforts of a four-diamond hotel and atmosphere of a country inn blend to create the charming Apple Farm Inn. On a creekside setting surrounded by lavish gardens, the Inn is an elegant and peaceful retreat. Rich decor, distinctive beds and a fireplace that conveys warmth and hospitality give each room its own identity. Enjoy a pleasant meal in our restaurant, browse in the Gift Shop, or step back in time in our authentic Millhouse.

Hosts: Katy and Bob Davis
Rooms: 69 (PB) $109-239
Breakfast (extra fee)
Credit Cards: A, B, C, D
Notes: 2, 3, 4, 5, 7, 8, 9, 10, 12

SANTA BARBARA

Long's Seaview B&B

317 Piedmont Road, 93105
(805) 687-2947

Overlooking the ocean and Channel Islands. Quiet neighborhood with lovely

welcome; 7 Children welcome; 8 Tennis nearby; 9 Swimming nearby; 10 Golf nearby; 11 Skiing nearby; 12 May be booked through travel agent.

homes. Breakfast usually served on huge patio. Large bedroom with king-size bed. Private entrance, private bath. Convenient to all attractions and Solvang. Local information and maps. Great patio views.

Hostess: LaVerne Long
Rooms: 1 (PB) $80
Full Breakfast
Credit Cards: none
Notes: 2, 5, 8, 9, 10, 12

The Mary May Inn

111 W. Valerio Street, 93101
(805) 569-3398
Web site: http://www.silcom.com/~ricky/
mary.htm

Perhaps Santa Barbara's best-kept secret! Situated in a residential neighborhood sixteen blocks from the beach, two historical properties dating to the 1800s have been restored to their original elegance. The interiors are reminiscent of a time when life was slower. Each of the Mary May rooms shares a distinctive ambience. The Inn is a showcase for extraordinary furnishings. Some rooms have canopied beds, wood-burning fireplaces, or Jacuzzi tubs. Queen beds and private baths.

Hosts: Kathleen M. Pohring and Mark S. Cronin
Rooms: 12 (PB) $85-180
Full and Continental Breakfast
Credit Cards: A, B, C
Notes: 2, 5, 6 (owner's discretion), 7, 8, 9, 10, 12

Montecito B&B

167 Olive Mill Road, 93108
(805) 969-7992; FAX (805) 969-7992

Enjoy a spacious room with private bath, private entrance, TV, phone, desk, and eating area. Patio Jacuzzi is available for your use. Includes homemade continental breakfast and coffee. Room has garden atmosphere and looks out on a vista of trees and mountains. Located close to Westmont College and just above coastal village shopping and restaurants. Approximately one-half mile to the beach.

Hosts: Rick and Linda Ryan
Rooms: 1 (PB) $60-70
Continental Breakfast
Credit Cards: none
Notes: 2, 5, 7, 8, 9, 10, 12

The Old Yacht Club Inn

431 Corona Del Mar Drive, 93103
(805) 962-1277; (800) 676-1676 (U.S.);
(800) 549-1676 (California only);
FAX (805) 962-3989

The Inn at the beach! These 1912 California Craftsman and 1925 homes house nine individually decorated guest rooms furnished with antiques. Bicycles, beach chairs, and towels are included, and an evening social hour is provided. Gourmet dinner is available on Saturdays.

Hostesses: Nancy Donaldson and Sandy Hunt
Rooms: 10 (PB) $95-185
Full Breakfast
Credit Cards: A, B, C, D
Notes: 2, 4 (Saturdays), 5, 7, 8, 9, 10, 12

The Parsonage

1600 Olive Street, 93101
(805) 962-9336; (800) 775-0352;
FAX (805) 962-2285
E-mail: Parsonage1@aol.com

A quiet and peaceful setting awaits your arrival. Architecturally designed in Queen Anne Victorian motif, this famous landmark was built for the parson of Trinity Episcopal Church. The Parsonage hosts some of the finest antiques and furnishings in the area. Each room is elegantly decorated and distinctive to the period. The Parsonage is nestled between downtown Santa Barbara and the upper east foothills. Let "the ultimate bed and breakfast" take care of your every whim.

Hostess: Linda Minke
Rooms: 6 (PB) $130-280
Full Breakfast
Credit Cards: A, B, C
Notes: 5, 8, 9, 10, 12

The Upham Hotel and Garden Cottages

1404 De la Vina Street, 93101
(805) 962-0058; (800) 727-0876;
FAX (805) 963-2825

Established in 1871, the beautifully restored Upham Hotel offers a unique setting that combines the quaint ambience of a bed and breakfast with the professionalism of a full-service hotel. Seven buildings surround an acre of lovely gardens and house fifty guest rooms and suites, some with fireplaces and private patios or porches. Located in the heart of downtown within walking distance of museums, theaters, shopping, and restaurants.

Hostess: Jan Martin Winn
Rooms: 50 (PB) $130-360
Continental Breakfast
Credit Cards: A, B, C, D, E
Notes: 3 (Monday-Friday), 4 (Monday-Saturday), 5, 7, 8, 9, 10, 12

SANTA CRUZ

Chateau Victorian

118 First Street, 95060
(408) 458-9458

Chateau Victorian was turned into an elegant bed and breakfast with a warm, friendly atmosphere in 1983. Built around 1885, the Inn is only one block from the beach. All seven rooms have a queen-size bed; a private, tiled bathroom—one of which has a clawfoot tub with overhead shower; and a fireplace, with fire logs provided. Each room has its own heating system, controlled by the guest. The guest rooms are decorated and furnished in individual color schemes. The whole inn is carpeted. Wine and cheeses are available for guests in the late afternoon. Chateau Victorian is within walking distance of downtown, the Municipal Wharf, the Boardwalk Amusement Park, and both fine and casual dining.

Hostess: Alice June
Rooms: 7 (PB) $110-140
Expanded Continental Breakfast
Credit Cards: A, B, C
Notes: 2, 5, 8, 9, 10, 12 (no commissions)

Pleasure Point Inn

2-3665 E. Cliff Drive, 95062
(408) 475-4657; (800) 872-3029;
FAX (408) 464-3045
Web site: http://www.mcn.org/b&b/b&b.html

On the water overlooking the beautiful Monterey Bay. Fantastic views from three of our rooms. Fireplaces and whirlpool tubs. Boat charters are underway daily for fishing or cruising. Your host is an accomplished captain of the *Margaret Mary* and your hostess is more than willing to arrange dinner reservations at a fine, local restaurant, or point you to historic landmarks in the area. Within walking distance of the beaches and shopping villages.

Hosts: Margaret and Sal Margo
Rooms: 4 (PB) $125-155
Continental Breakfast
Credit Cards: A, B
Notes: 5, 8, 9, 10, 12

welcome; 7 Children welcome; 8 Tennis nearby; 9 Swimming nearby; 10 Golf nearby; 11 Skiing nearby; 12 May be booked through travel agent.

Valley View

PO Box 67438, 95067
(415) 321-5195; FAX (415) 325-5121

Unhosted retreat with two bedrooms and two baths. Luxurious getaway with walls of floor-to-ceiling glass and a large deck with spa. Overlooks a twenty-thousand-acre valley of redwoods. Full, self-serve breakfast in fridge. You have the entire house to yourselves! One or two couples, same price. Twelve minutes to Santa Cruz beaches. No indoor smoking.

Hostess: Tricia Young
Rooms: 2-bedroom house (PB) $195
Full Breakfast
Credit Cards: A, B, C, D, E, F

SANTA ROSA (WINE COUNTRY)

Pygmalion House Bed and Breakfast

331 Orange Street, 95401
(707) 526-3407 (voice and FAX)

Pygmalion House is a lovely Victorian (1880s) furnished with many of Gypsy Rose Lee's antiques and memorabilia. All the spacious guest rooms are sound-proofed, quiet and nicely decorated; all have private baths with tubs and showers, and queen- or king-size beds. The double parlor has a beautiful fireplace and a sitting room with octagonal windows. Our prices are most reasonable—you get the "mostest for the leastest." Guests return again and again.

Hostess: Carolyn E. Berry
Rooms: 6 (PB) $65-105
Full Country Breakfast
Credit Cards: A, B
Notes: 2, 5, 8, 9, 10

SEAL BEACH

The Seal Beach Inn and Gardens

212 5th Street, 92740
(562) 493-2416; (800) HIDEAWAY;
FAX (562) 799-0483

Elegant, historic Southern California inn, one block from the ocean beach in a charming, prestigious, seaside town next to Long Beach. Lush gardens, lovely estate appearance. The rooms and suites are exquisite. Pool, library, and kitchens are available. Free full breakfast/social hour. Modern amenities. Short walk to restaurants, shops, and beach pier. Three freeways close by. Easy drive to Disneyland and other major Los Angeles attractions and business centers. Meeting rooms available (twenty-four maximum). Convenient to LAX, Long Beach, and Orange County airports.

Hosts: Marjorie Bettenhausen-Schmaehl and Harty Schmaehl
Rooms: 23 (PB) $125-195
Full Gourmet Breakfast
Credit Cards: A, B, C, D, E, F
Notes: 3, 4, 5, 8, 9, 10, 12

SEQUOIA NATIONAL PARK

Mesa Verde Plantation Bed and Breakfast

33038 Sierra Highway 198, **Lemon Cove**, 93244
(209) 597-2555; (800) 240-1466;
FAX (209) 597-2551
E-mail: mvpbb@psnw.com
Web site: www.psnw.com/~mvpbb

Nestled among the peaceful foothills of the Sierra Nevada Mountains among acres of orange groves. The rooms are named af-

NOTES: Credit cards accepted: A Master Card; B Visa; C American Express; D Discover; E Diners Club; F Other; 2 Personal checks accepted; 3 Lunch available; 4 Dinner available; 5 Open all year; 6 Pets

ter characters from *Gone With the Wind* and decorated accordingly. Located only sixteen miles from Sequoia National Park. Heated swimming pool open all year, along with hot tub located in the orchard. Fireplaces, whirlpool tub, verandas, gazebos, and wedding facilities.

Hosts: Scott and Marie Munger
Rooms: 8 (6PB; 2SB) $70-125
Full Breakfast
Credit Cards: A, B, C, D, E
Notes: 2, 5, 9, 10, 11, 12

The Alisal Guest Ranch and Resort

SOLVANG

The Alisal Guest Ranch and Resort

1054 Alisal Road, 93463
(805) 688-6411; (800) 425-4725;
FAX (805) 688-2510
E-mail: sales@alisal.com
Web site: www.alisal.com

The Alisal Guest Ranch and Resort is a working cattle ranch and full-service resort that has been privately owned and operated since 1946. A ten-thousand-acre ranch with seventy-three guest cottages offers a high level of accommodation. The facilities include two eighteen-hole championship golf courses, seven tennis courts, a ninety-six-acre fishing/boating lake, horseback riding over miles of scenic trails, heated swimming pool, variety of children's activities, rodeos, barbecues, winemaker dinners, and meeting facilities for two hundred delegates. Located outside Solvang, approximately two hours from Los Angeles and forty minutes from Santa Barbara.

Host: David S. Lautensack
Rooms: 73 (PB) $325-400
Full or Continental Breakfast
Credit Cards: A, B, C, E
Notes: 2; 3; 4 (included); 5; 7; 8, 9, 10 (on premises); 12

SONOMA

The Hidden Oak Bed and Breakfast Inn

214 E. Napa Street, 95476
(707) 996-9863; (800) 969-4667
E-mail: hidenoak@pacbell.net
Web site: www.virtualcities.com/ca/hiddenoak.htm

A romantic hideaway just one block from "The Plaza," where you can relax and enjoy wine country life. The wisteria-adorned, Craftsman-style home was built in 1913 and is located within the historic residential area of downtown Sonoma. The Inn features three spacious guest rooms upstairs, all with queen-size beds and private baths, and a suite downstairs with a king-size bed, private bath, private parlour and private patio. A full three-course breakfast and afternoon refreshments are served in the dining room. Complimentary bicycles are available for local

welcome; 7 Children welcome; 8 Tennis nearby; 9 Swimming nearby; 10 Golf nearby; 11 Skiing nearby; 12 May be booked through travel agent.

The Hidden Oak Bed and Breakfast

touring. Two-night minimum on weekends, April through October, and some holidays. Children and wedding parties by arrangement. Sorry, no pets.

Hosts: Erin and Kurt Heeley
Rooms: 4 (PB) $110-210
Full or Continental Breakfast
Credit Cards: C, D
Notes: 2, 5, 10, 12

Sonoma Hotel

110 W. Spain Street, 95476
(707) 996-2996; (800) 468-6016;
FAX (707) 996-7014

Sonoma Hotel is a wonderful place, an hour's drive from San Francisco but a hundred years away. On Sonoma's tree-lined plaza, this vintage hotel offers accommodations and dining to the discriminating guest. To spend an evening here is to step back into a romantic period in history. Each antique-furnished room evokes a distinct feel of early California; the emphasis on comfort is decidedly European. Short walks to wineries, historic landmarks, art galleries, and unique shops.

Hosts: Dorene and John Musilli
Rooms: 17 (5PB; 12SB) $75-125
Continental Breakfast
Credit Cards: A, B, C
Notes: 2, 3, 4, 5, 7, 10, 12

Sparrow's Nest Inn

424 Denmark Street, 95476
(707) 996-3750; FAX (707) 938-5569
E-mail: sprrwsnest@aol.com
Web site: http://www.innsandouts.com/property/
    sparrows_nest_inn.html

Historic Sonoma is only one mile from this delightful cottage. It's just right for rest or romance. Pretty English country decor, fresh flowers, chocolates, cozy bed, scrumptious breakfast, privacy, garden and courtyard for sunning and reading. The "Nest" is complete with bedroom, bath, small kitchen fully equipped, living room (including sofa bed), phone, cable TV/VCR, and air-conditioning. Within three miles are five wineries, historic sites, wonderful restaurants and little shops.

Hosts: Thomas and Kathleen Anderson
Rooms: 1 single cottage (PB) $85-115
Full or Continental Breakfast
Credit Cards: A, B, C, D
Notes: 2, 5, 6 (special arrangements), 7, 8, 9, 10

SONORA

Barretta Gardens Bed and Breakfast Inn

700 S. Barretta Street, 95370
(209) 532-6039; (800) 206-3333;
FAX (209) 532-8257
E-mail: Barretta@mlode.com
Web site: http://www.sonnet.com/dancers/bandb/
    barretta

This elegant turn-of-the-century Victorian bed and breakfast sits on a hillside acre of gardens and lawns overlooking historic downtown Sonora and gold country sunsets. Fully air-conditioned with three parlors, a formal dining room, an enclosed solarium, a living room with fireplace and

NOTES: Credit cards accepted: A Master Card; B Visa; C American Express; D Discover; E Diners Club; F Other; 2 Personal checks accepted; 3 Lunch available; 4 Dinner available; 5 Open all year; 6 Pets

wraparound porches. Barretta Gardens Inn is special not only for its unique history and style, but also for its countless private places for guests to relax and watch hummingbirds feed or snowflakes fall.

Hostess: Nancy Brandt
Rooms: 5 (PB) $95-105
Full Breakfast
Credit Cards: A, B
Notes: 2, 5, 7, 9, 10, 11, 12

Lavender Hill Bed and Breakfast Inn

683 S. Barretta, 95370
(209) 532-9024; (800) 446-1333 Ext. 290

Come home . . . to a 1900s Victorian home overlooking the historic gold rush town of Sonora. At sunset you can watch the world from a wraparound porch, enjoy a country walk through year-round flower gardens, and relax on a covered patio (ideal for a small wedding). In the morning, you wake to a home-cooked breakfast and have the opportunity to listen and share experiences with others, perhaps planning your day to include hiking in Yosemite, fishing, biking, river rafting, or even a scenic steam train ride. Afternoons and evenings could include a stroll to downtown antique shops and boutiques, fine dining, and a performance at one of the professional repertory theaters. We will be glad to plan a dinner-theater package for your stay. Gift certificates are available. One visit will have you longing to return "home."

Hosts: Jean and Charlie Marinelli
Rooms: 4 (PB) $75-95
Full Breakfast
Credit Cards: A, B, C
Notes: 2, 5, 7, 8, 9, 10, 11, 12

SOQUEL

Blue Spruce Inn

2815 Main Street, 95073
(408) 464-1137; (800) 559-1137;
FAX (408) 475-0608
E-mail: pobrien@BlueSpruce.com
Web site: http://BlueSpruce.com

Spa tubs, fireplaces, quiet gardens, and original local art foster relaxation for our guests. The Blue Spruce is four miles south of Santa Cruz and one mile inland from Capitola Beach—an ideal location that blends the flavor of yesteryear with the comfort of today. Hike or bike through the redwoods or country fields. Walk to fine dining, then relax in the outdoor hot tub. Visit us soon!

Hosts: Pat and Tom O'Brien
Rooms: 6 (PB) $90-150
Full Breakfast
Credit Cards: A, B, C, D
Notes: 2, 5, 8, 9, 10, 12

SUMMERLAND

Inn on Summer Hill

PO Box 376, 2520 Lillie Avenue, 93067
(805) 969-9998; (800) 845-5566;
FAX (805) 565-9946

One of America's top-rated bed and breakfasts awaits you with visually captivating English country decor and world-class amenities. Set in the seaside village of Summerland, just five minutes south of Santa Barbara, this California Craftsman-style, award-winning Inn, built in 1989, offers sixteen minisuites with ocean views, fireplaces, Jacuzzis, canopy beds, video

welcome; 7 Children welcome; 8 Tennis nearby; 9 Swimming nearby; 10 Golf nearby; 11 Skiing nearby; 12 May be booked through travel agent.

players, and original art and accessories. A sumptuous, full gourmet breakfast is served each morning. Hors d'oeuvres and desserts add to the uncompromising comfort and charm of the inn. The guest rooms provide a directory of local activities along with concierge service and special packages for the discerning traveler who is in the mood for something out of the ordinary. Both the Automobile Club and *Country Inns Magazine* have rated the Inn on Summer Hill as one of the "Best in the Country."

Hostess: Denise LeBlanc
Rooms: 16 (PB) $170-325
Full Breakfast
Credit Cards: A, B, C, D
Notes: 3 (picnic only), 5, 8, 9, 10, 12

SUSANVILLE

The Roseberry House

609 North Street, 96130
(916) 257-5675

The Roseberry House lives up to its name, with roses in profusion in the carpets, wallpapers, and vases. It features an unusual collection of antiques, with each guest room distinctly different. Enjoy a tastefully prepared full breakfast in the formal dining room. This is our home and we want you to be comfortable here. Located just two blocks from Main Street in historic uptown Susanville and near a variety of Northern California recreational activities.

Hosts: Bill and Maxine Ashmore
Rooms: 4 (PB) $55-85
Full Breakfast
Credit Cards: A, B, C
Notes: 2, 5, 8, 9, 10, 11

SUTTER CREEK

The Foxes in Sutter Creek

77 Main Street, PO Box 159, 95685
(209) 267-5882; (800) 957-3344
FAX (209) 267-0712
E-mail: foxes@cdepot.net
Web site: http://www.foxesinn.com

Foxes Bed and Breakfast Inn, formerly known as "The Brinn House," originated in 1857 during the gold rush. Since then it has undergone substantial changes and now features seven beautiful guest accommodations. Sutter Creek is known as "the nicest town in the Mother Lode." Within walking distance, you'll find many interesting antique shops, restaurants, specialty shops and art galleries. The local countryside abounds with interesting sights and exciting activities. Explore the many shops in quaint villages nearby.

Hosts: Pete and Min Fox
Rooms: 7 (PB) $105-160
Full Breakfast
Credit Cards: A, B, D
Notes: 2, 5, 8, 10, 12

The Hanford House

PO Box 1450; Highway 49, 61 Hanford Street, 29685
(209) 267-0747; (800) 871-5839;
FAX (209) 267-1825
E-mail: bobkat@hanfordhouse.com
Web site: http://www.hanfordhouse.com

A two-and-a-half-story, ivy-covered, red brick country manor inn that is a tranquil counterpoint to the demands of everyday life. Ten rooms, all with private full baths, fully air-conditioned, Jacuzzi tub, fireplaces, twenty-four-hour guest pantry. Full gourmet breakfast. Conference facilities on site. A serene and cozy haven filled

The Hanford House

with light, laughter, great food, personal attention, and thoughtful friends.

Hosts: Bob and Karen Tierno
Rooms: 10 (PB) $89-149
Full Breakfast
Credit Cards: A, B, D
Notes: 2, 5, 7 (well-behaved), 8, 9, 10, 11 (90 minutes), 12

Sutter Creek Inn

75 Main Street, PO Box 385, 95685
(209) 267-5606; FAX (209) 267-9287
E-mail: info@suttercreekinn.com
Web site: http://www.suttercreekinn.com

Built in 1859, the Inn is surrounded by tree-shaded lawns and gardens. It is within walking distance of shopping and dining in the historic gold rush town of Sutter Creek. The Inn features seventeen rooms, all with private baths. Many rooms offer fireplaces or private patios. Enjoy the peace and quiet of our hammocks and chaise lounges during the summer, or the patter of rain on our tin roofs in the winter. A full country breakfast is served family-style in our dining room each morning. Wineries, golf, hiking, biking, gold pan-

ning, and historical sites are nearby. Massages are available by appointment.

Host: Jane Way
Rooms: 17 (PB) $65-175
Full Breakfast
Credit Cards: A, B, C, D
Notes: 2, 5, 8, 9, 10, 11, 12

TEMECULA

Loma Vista B&B

33350 La Serena Way, 92591
(909) 676-7047; FAX (909) 676-0077 (call first)

Loma Vista is a contemporary California mission-style house surrounded by vineyards and citrus groves. It offers six guest rooms, each with a private bath and some with private balconies. We serve a champagne breakfast each day, wine and cheese each evening. The house is air-conditioned and is in a fantastic setting with gardens for guests to enjoy.

Hosts: Betty and Dick Ryan
Rooms: 6 (PB) $95-135
Full Breakfast
Credit Cards: A, B, D
Notes: 2, 5, 8, 9, 10, 12

welcome; 7 Children welcome; 8 Tennis nearby; 9 Swimming nearby; 10 Golf nearby; 11 Skiing nearby; 12 May be booked through travel agent.

UKIAH

Vichy Hot Springs

2605 Vichy Springs Road, 95482
(707) 462-9515; FAX (707) 462-9516

Vichy Springs is a delightful two-hour drive north of San Francisco. Historic cottages and rooms await you with delightful vistas from all locations. Vichy Hot Springs features naturally sparkling, 90-degree mineral baths, a communal 104-degree pool, and an Olympic-size pool. Guests can explore seven hundred private acres with trails and roads for hiking, jogging, picnicking, and mountain bicycling. Vichy's idyllic setting provides a quiet, healing environment for travelers. This is California State Landmark #980.

Hosts: Gilbert and Marjorie Ashoff
Rooms: 20 (PB) $135-185
Full Breakfast
Credit Cards: A, B, C, D, E, F
Notes: 2, 3, 4, 5, 7, 8, 9, 10, 12

VENTURA

Bella Maggiore Inn

67 S. California Street, 93001
(805) 652-0277; (800) 525-8479
FAX (805) 648-5670

Bella Maggiore is an intimate, European-style bed and breakfast, one hour north of Los Angeles. It features a garden courtyard with a fountain and a lobby with a fireplace and piano. Comfortable rooms with suites; some have fireplaces and spa tubs. A full breakfast is served in our courtyard restaurant, Nona's. Special rates are offered for business travelers and groups. We are only three blocks from the beach and within walking distance of several fine restaurants.

Hosts: Tom and Cyndi Wood
Rooms: 28 (PB) $75-150
Full Breakfast
Credit Cards: A, B, C, D, E, F
Notes: 3, 4, 5, 7, 9, 10, 12

La Mer Bed and Breakfast

411 Poli Street, 93001
(805) 643-3600; FAX (805) 653-7329
Web site: http://www.vcol.net/lamer

Built in 1890, this is a romantic European getaway in a Victorian Cape Cod home, a historic landmark nestled on a green hillside overlooking the spectacular California coastline. The distinctive guest rooms, all with private entrances and baths, are each a European adventure, furnished in European antiques to capture the feeling of a specific country. Bavarian buffet-style breakfast and complimentary refreshments; midweek packages; antique horse carriage rides. La Mer is AAA- and Mobil-approved.

Hosts: Gisela and Michael Baida
Rooms: 5 (PB) $80-155
Full Breakfast
Credit Cards: A, B, C
Notes: 2, 5, 8, 9, 10, 12

WESTPORT

Howard Creek Ranch

40501 N. Highway One, PO Box 121, 95488
(707) 964-6725, FAX (707) 964-1603
Web site: http://www.howardcreekranch.com

Howard Creek Ranch is a historic, four-thousand-acre, oceanfront farm dating to

NOTES: Credit cards accepted: A Master Card; B Visa; C American Express; D Discover; E Diners Club; F Other; 2 Personal checks accepted; 3 Lunch available; 4 Dinner available; 5 Open all year; 6 Pets

Howard Creek Ranch

1867, bordered by miles of **beach and** mountains in a wilderness area. **Flower** gardens, antiques, fireplaces, **redwoods,** a seventy-five-foot swinging **footbridge** over Howard Creek, cabins, hot tub, sauna, heated pool, and nearby horseback riding are combined with comfort, hospitality, and good food.

Hosts: Charles and Sally Grigg
Rooms: 11 (8PB; 3SB) $55-145
Full Breakfast
Credit Cards: A, B, C
Notes: 2, 5, 6 (by prior arrangement), 9 (on site)

YOSEMITE NATIONAL PARK (GROVELAND)

Yosemite River Resort (Formerly Lee's Middle Fork Resort)

11399 Cherry Lake Road, **Groveland** 95321
(209) 962-7408; (800) 626-7408;
FAX (209) 962-7400
E-mail: LMR@sonnet.com
Web site: http://www.sonnet/usr/yosemite

Conveniently located eleven miles from Big Oak Flat entrance to Yosemite National Park, Yosemite River Resort is the perfect place to stay for beautiful scenic landscapes while you vacation or simply pass through the charming Yosemite area. Relax and enjoy the restful atmosphere as you discover why Yosemite is so acclaimed for its beauty. While there, you have the opportunity to gaze upon some of the most amazing rock formations and the most stunning waterfalls, or enjoy an afternoon of activities which include hiking, well-stocked river fishing, swimming, or white-water rafting. For winter guests there is downhill and cross-country skiing. Come visit Yosemite River Resort and discover for yourself the real meaning of paradise.

Hosts: Roland and Robin Hilarides
Rooms: 20 (PB) $59-150
Continental Breakfast
Credit Cards: A, B, C, D, E
Notes: 3, 4, 5, 7, 8, 9, 10, 11, 12

welcome; 7 Children welcome; 8 Tennis nearby; 9 Swimming nearby; 10 Golf nearby; 11 Skiing nearby; 12 May be booked through travel agent.

COLORADO

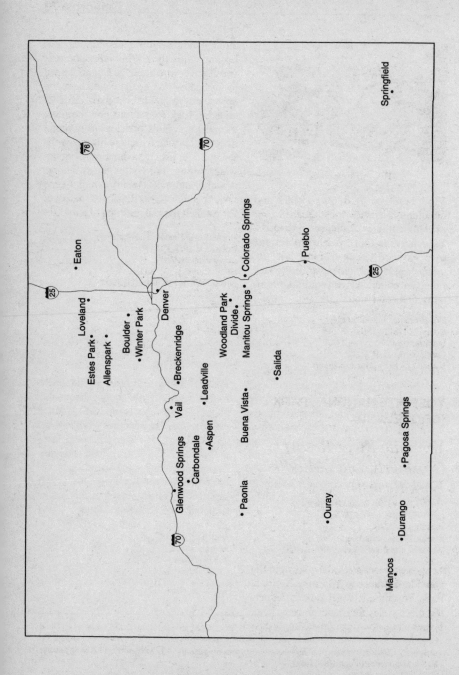

Colorado

ALLENSPARK

Allenspark Lodge and Crystal Springs Cabins

PO Box 247, 184 Main Street, 80510
(303) 747-2552
Web site: http://www.virtualcities.com/ons/co/e/
    coe2602.htm

Allenspark Lodge provides classic, high mountain quarters nestled in a lovely, flower-starred village. Comfortable guest rooms, warm hospitality, and magnificent surroundings combine to make our historic, cozy, beautifully remodeled Lodge the ideal place for that special vacation weekend, reception, reunion, or retreat. Come, let the magic begin! A hot tub and game room are available for our guests. The Lodge is located near Rocky Mountain National Park. Three small cabins are also available.

Hosts: Mike and Becky Osmun
Rooms: 12 (5PB; 9SB) $45-90
Continental Breakfast
Credit Cards: A, B
Notes: 2, 5, 11

Christmas Inn

ASPEN

Christmas Inn

232 W. Main Street, 81611
(970) 925-3822; (800) 625-5581
FAX: (970) 925-3328

This comfortable inn features attractive rooms with private baths, direct-dial phones, cable TVs, sundeck, off-street parking. Amenities include whirlpool and sauna (winter), daily housekeeping, complimentary breakfast, and afternoon refreshments. Walk to the quaint shops and restaurants of Aspen or use the free shuttle service to the Music Tent (summer), to four ski mountains, and around town.

Host: David Schlesinger
Rooms: 24 (PB) $56-110
Full Breakfast
Credit Cards: A, B, C
Notes: 5, 7, 8, 9, 10, 11, 12

NOTES: Credit cards accepted: A Master Card; B Visa; C American Express; D Discover; E Diners Club; F Other; 2 Personal checks accepted; 3 Lunch available; 4 Dinner available; 5 Open all year; 6 Pets welcome; 7 Children welcome; 8 Tennis nearby; 9 Swimming nearby; 10 Golf nearby; 11 Skiing nearby; 12 May be booked through travel agent.

Little Red Ski Haus

118 E. Cooper Avenue, 81611
(970) 925-3333

We are a quaint, historic lodge that has had only one owner for thirty-six years. The 110-year-old Victorian house has additional rooms for a total of twenty-one bedrooms. Christian hosts look forward to welcoming you to their lodge. Located in the center of Aspen and surrounded by impressive, 14,000-foot peaks of the Rocky Mountains. Nonsmoking lodge. Christian retreats welcome.

Hosts: Marjorie Babcock (owner) and Derek Brown (manager)
Rooms: 21 (4PB; 17SB) $52-118
Full Breakfast (winter); Continental (summer)
Credit Cards: A, B
Notes: 7, 9, 10, 11

BOULDER

Briar Rose Bed and Breakfast

2151 Arapahoe Avenue, 80302
(303) 442-3007; FAX (303) 786-8440
E-mail: brbbx@aol.com

English country cottage close to the University of Colorado and downtown Boulder. Nine unique rooms offer featherbed comforters, telephones, period antiques, fresh flowers, and good books. Friendly, attentive service includes afternoon and evening tea with our own shortbread cookies. Hearty, home-baked breakfast served in the dining room or on the sunporch. Schedule a ten- to fifteen-person retreat for the winter months.

Brair Rose Bed and Breakfast

Hosts: Margaret and Bob Weisenbach
Rooms: 9 (PB) $89-140
Continental Breakfast
Credit Cards: A, B, C
Notes: 2, 5, 8, 10, 11, 12

BRECKENRIDGE

Allaire Timbers Inn

9511 Highway 9, PO Box 4653, 80424
(970) 453-7530; (800) 624-4904;
FAX (970) 453-8699

Award-winning log bed and breakfast, combining contemporary and rustic log furnishings in an intimate setting. Guest rooms have private baths and decks with mountain views. Suites have private fireplaces and hot tubs. The great room has a fireplace, sunroom, loft, and outdoor hot tub. Enjoy the spectacular views of the Colorado Rockies. A hearty breakfast and afternoon refreshments are served each day. Wheelchair-accessible. Breckenridge offers an abundance of year-round activities. Featured on the Travel Channel's "Romantic Inns in America."

Hosts: Jack and Kathy Gumph
Rooms: 10 (PB) $125-275
Full Breakfast
Credit Cards: A, B, C, D
Notes: 2, 5, 10, 11, 12

NOTES: Credit cards accepted: A Master Card; B Visa; C American Express; D Discover; E Diners Club; F Other; 2 Personal checks accepted; 3 Lunch available; 4 Dinner available; 5 Open all year; 6 Pets

BUENA VISTA

The Adobe Inn

303 N. Highway 24, 81211
(719) 395-6340

The Adobe Inn offers a unique experience for the discriminating traveler. Three rooms and two suites provide a delightful range of styles and amenities. Each room has a private bath and cable TV, and you can relax in the two-person Jacuzzi down the hall. Each morning at the Adobe Inn begins with a bountiful breakfast of fresh fruit or juice, a tasty entrée, and your choice of teas, freshly brewed coffee, or Mexican hot chocolate.

Hosts: Paul, Marjorie, and Michael Knox
Rooms: 5 (PB) $59-89
Full Breakfast
Credit Cards: A, B
Notes: 2, 3, 4, 5, 7, 8, 9, 10, 11, 12

CARBONDALE

Mt. Sopris Inn

PO Box 126, 81623
(970) 963-2209; (800) 437-8675;
FAX (970) 963-8975
Email: mt.soprisinn@juno.com
Web sites: http://colorado-bnb.com/mtsopris
    http://www.virtualcities.com/mtsopris

At Mt. Sopris Inn, country elegance surrounds the visitor who appreciates our extraordinary property. Central to Aspen, Redstone, and Glenwood Springs, the Inn offers fifteen private rooms and baths, professionally decorated. All rooms have king- or queen-size bed, TV, and telephone; some have fireplaces, Jacuzzis, and steam baths. Guests may use the swimming pool, whirlpool, pool table, library,

great rooms, and seven-foot grand piano. The Inn is open to all.

Hostess: Barbara Fasching
Rooms: 14 (PB) $ 85-175
Full Breakfast
Credit Cards: A, B
Notes: 5, 9, 10, 11, 12

The Hearthstone Inn

COLORADO SPRINGS

The Hearthstone Inn

506 N. Cascade Avenue, 80903
(719) 473-4413; (800) 521-1885;
(719) 473-1322

Bright Victorian colors, friendly people, delightful breakfasts and period antiques. Rooms with wood-burning fireplaces or secluded porches are especially popular. Walk to quaint shops, coffeehouses, bookstores, and restaurants or enjoy the nearby four-mile park trail and neighborhood stately mansions. Located next door to Young Life Ministries; a short drive from *Focus on the Family*. We look forward to welcoming you!

Hostess: Dot Williams
Rooms: 25 (23PB; 2SB) $85-160
Full Breakfast
Credit Cards: A, B, C
Notes: 2, 5, 7, 8, 9, 10, 12

welcome; 7 Children welcome; 8 Tennis nearby; 9 Swimming nearby; 10 Golf nearby; 11 Skiing nearby; 12 May be booked through travel agent.

Holden House—1902 Bed and Breakfast Inn

1102 W. Pikes Peak Avenue, 80904
(719) 471-3980; FAX (719) 471-4740
E-mail: HoldenHouse@worldnet.att.net
Web site: http://www.bbonline.com/co/holden

Discover a Pikes Peak treasure! These 1902 storybook Victorians are filled with antiques and family heirlooms. Each guest suite boasts feather pillows, period furnishings, queen bed, in-room fireplace and oversize bubble bath "tub for two." Centrally located in a residential area near historic Old Colorado City. You can enjoy shopping, restaurants, and attractions nearby. Experience "The Romance of the Past With the Comforts of Today." Inn cats "Mingtoy" and "Muffin" are in residence. AAA/Mobil-rated.

Hosts: Sallie and Welling Clark
Rooms: 5 (PB) $110-120
Full Gourmet Breakfast
Credit Cards: A, B, C, D, E
Notes: 2, 5, 8, 9, 10, 12

The Painted Lady Bed and Breakfast Inn

1318 W. Colorado Avenue, 80904
(719) 473-3165; (800) 370-3165
FAX (719) 635-1396
E-mail: PaintedLadyInn@worldnet.att.net
Web site: http://www.bbonline.com/co/
    paintedlady

1894 Traditional Victorian inns close to Pikes Peak attractions and the business district. Suites can accommodate families (children over 4). An outdoor hot tub, wraparound porches, and a tub-for-two are just some of our extras! You'll meet our friendly resident cat and enjoy hearty breakfasts. A nonsmoking inn. AC. Homey atmosphere.

Hosts: Valerie and Zan Maslowski
Rooms: 4 (PB); $85-125
Full Breakfast
Credit Cards: A, B, C, D
Notes: 2, 5, 7 (over 4), 8, 9, 10, 12

Room at the Inn

618 N. Nevada Avenue, 80903
(719) 442-1896; (888) 442-1896;
FAX (719) 442-6802
Web site: http://www.indra.com/fallline/rai

Experience a peek at the past in this elegant Victorian. Enjoy the charm of a classic, three-story, turreted, antique-filled Queen Anne featuring original wall murals, oak staircase and pocket doors. Experience the romance of fireplaces, plush robes and whirlpool tubs for two. Gracious hospitality includes full breakfasts, afternoon tea, and turn-down service. AC, a hot tub and off-street parking are available for guests. A romantic retreat in the heart of the city. Mobil three-star-rated.

Hosts: Chick and Jan McCormick
Rooms: 7 (PB) $85-135
Full Breakfast
Credit Cards: A, B, C, D, E
Notes: 2, 5, 8, 9, 10, 12

DENVER

Capitol Hill Mansion

1207 Pennsylvania Street, 80203
(303) 839-5221; (800) 839-9329;
FAX (303) 839-9046

Award-winning 1891 Victorian mansion with eight individually decorated guest rooms featuring antiques mixed with mod-

Capitol Hill Mansion

ern amenities such as cable television, refrigerators, complimentary beverages, hair dryers, telephones, desks, private baths, off-street parking, and breakfast. Whirlpool tubs, fireplaces, and balconies are available. A short walk to downtown, government offices, museums, galleries, shops, and restaurants; a short drive to major sports venues and the Rocky Mountains. Perfect for business or romance.

Hostess: Kathy Robbins
Rooms: 8 (PB) $90-165
Full Breakfast
Credit Cards: A, B, C, D
Notes: 2 (with ID), 5, 7, 8, 9, 10, 11, 12

Castle Marne— A Luxury Urban Inn

1572 Race Street, 80206
(303) 331-0621; (800) 92 MARNE;
FAX (303) 331-0623
E-mail: themarne@ix.netcom.com
Web site: http://www.bedandbreakfastinns.org/
    castle

Chosen by *Country Inns Magazine* as one of the "Top 12 Inns in North America." Come fall under the spell of one of Denver's grandest historic mansions. Your stay at the Castle Marne combines Old World elegance with modern-day convenience and comfort. Each guest room is a unique experience in pampered luxury. All rooms have private baths. Two suites have Jacuzzi tubs for two. Three rooms have private balconies and hot tubs. Afternoon tea and a full gourmet breakfast are served in the cherry-paneled dining room. Castle Marne is a certified Denver Landmark and is on the National Register of Historic Structures.

Hosts: The Peiker Family
Rooms: 9 (PB) $85-210
Full Breakfast
Credit Cards: A, B, C, D, E, F
Notes: 2, 3, 4, 5, 7 (over 10), 8, 9, 10, 11, 12

Queen Anne Bed and Breakfast Inn

2147 Tremont Place, 80205
(800) 432-INNS (4667); FAX (303) 296-2151
E-mail: queenanne@worldnet.att.net
Web site: http://www.bedandbreakfastinns.org/
    queenanne

Facing quiet Benedict Fountain Park in downtown Denver are two side-by-side National Register Victorian homes with fourteen guest rooms, including four gallery suites. Flowers, chamber music, phones, period antiques, and private baths are in all rooms. Six rooms have special tubs; one has a fireplace. AC, free parking. Located within walking distance of the capitol, 16th Street Pedestrian Mall, the Convention Center, Larimer Square, restaurants, shops, and museums. Among its many awards: Best 12 B&Bs Nationally, Ten Most Romantic, Best of Denver, and Best 105 in Great American Cities. Now in its eleventh year, it is inspected

welcome; 7 Children welcome; 8 Tennis nearby; 9 Swimming nearby; 10 Golf nearby; 11 Skiing nearby; 12 May be booked through travel agent.

and approved by major auto clubs and *Distinctive Inns of Colorado*.

Hosts: The King Family
Rooms: 14 (PB) $75-175
Full Breakfast
Credit Cards: A, B, C, D, E, F
Notes: 2, 5, 7, 8, 9, 10, 11, 12

DIVIDE

Silver Wood B&B

463 County Road 512, 80814
(719) 687-6784; (800) 753-5592;
FAX (719) 687-1007
E-mail: silver1007@aol.com

Silver Wood is a newly constructed, contemporary home located in rural Colorado near Divide. Your drive to Silver Wood winds through strands of aspen, open meadows, pine trees, and fantastic views of mountains. Only twenty-two miles from Cripple Creek, thirty miles from Colorado Springs, and seven miles from Mueller State Park. Silver Wood offers a multitude of sight-seeing opportunities in the Pikes Peak area, with country quiet. Non-smoking residence.

Hosts: Larry and Bess Oliver
Rooms: 2 (PB) $65
Full Breakfast
Credit Cards: A, B, D
Notes: 2, 5, 7, 12

DURANGO

Logwood Bed and Breakfast and Lodge

35060 U.S. Highway 550 N., 81301
(970) 259-4396; (800) 369-4082;
FAX (970) 259-7812

Built in 1988, this forty-eight-hundred-square-foot red, cedar log home sits on

Logwood Bed and Breakfast Lodge

fifteen acres amid the beautiful San Juan Mountains beside the Animas River. Guest rooms are decorated with a southwestern flair. Homemade country quilts adorn the country-made, queen-size beds. Private baths in all guest rooms. A large, river rock fireplace warms the elegant living and dining areas in winter. Award-winning desserts are served in the evening. The entire Lodge may be rented, with full kitchen. Pamper yourselves. Come home to Logwood.

Hosts: Greg and Debby Verheyden
Rooms: 8 (PB) $65-125
Full Breakfast
Credit Cards: A, B
Notes: 2, 5, 7 (over 8), 9, 10, 11, 12

Scrubby Oaks Bed and Breakfast Inn

PO Box 1047, 81302
(970) 247-2176

Located on ten acres overlooking the Animas River Valley, this sprawling ranch-style inn has a quiet country feel with the convenience of being three miles from downtown Durango. Scrubby Oaks is beautifully furnished with family antiques, artworks, and fine books. Lovely gardens and patios frame the outside, where guests can relax after a day of sight-seeing around the Four Corners area. Snacks are offered

---

NOTES: Credit cards accepted: A Master Card; B Visa; C American Express; D Discover; E Diners Club; F Other; 2 Personal checks accepted; 3 Lunch available; 4 Dinner available; 5 Open all year; 6 Pets

in the afternoons, and a full country breakfast is served each morning.

Hostess: Mary Ann Craig
Rooms: 7 (3PB; 4SB) $70-80
Full Breakfast
Credit Cards: none
Open end of April to end of October
Notes: 2, 7, 8, 9, 10, 12

EATON

The Victorian Veranda Bed and Breakfast

515 Cheyenne Avenue, 80615
(970) 454-3890

We want to share with you our beautiful two-story Queen Anne home with a wraparound porch. It also has a view of the Rocky Mountains, forty-five minutes away. Our guests enjoy the spacious and comfortable rooms, balcony, fireplaces, bicycles-built-for-two, and baby grand player piano. One room has a private whirlpool bath. We are just fifty minutes from North Denver. A memorable and elegant stay for a moderate price.

Hosts: Nadine and Dick White
Rooms: 3 (1PB; 2SB) $45-60
Full Breakfast
Credit Cards: none
Notes: 2, 5, 7, 9, 10, 12

ESTES PARK

The Quilt House Bed and Breakfast

PO Box 339, 80517
(970) 586-0427

A beautiful view can be enjoyed from every window of this sturdy mountain home.

It is just a fifteen-minute walk from downtown Estes Park and only four miles from the entrance of Rocky Mountain National Park. There are three bedrooms upstairs, plus a lounge where guests can read, look at the mountains, and have a cup of coffee or tea. A guest house beside the main house has a kitchenette. The hosts gladly help with information concerning hiking trails, car drives, wildlife viewing, shopping, etc. No smoking.

Hosts: Hans and Miriam Graetzer
Rooms: 4 (PB) $52-62
Full Breakfast
Credit Cards: none
Notes: 2, 5, 8, 9, 10, 11

Romantic River Song Inn

Romantic River Song Inn

PO Box 1910, 80517
(970) 586-4066; FAX (970) 577-1961
E-mail: riversng@frii.com
Web site: http://www.starsend.com/getaway/
rivers~1/rspge1.htm

This stunning Craftsman-style inn is secluded at the end of a country road on twenty-seven wooded acres. All nine guest rooms have private baths and fireplaces. They are creatively designed and feature waterfall showers in the rooms. Fireside dinners and backpack picnic lunches are available for your Rocky Mountain National Park excursions.

welcome; 7 Children welcome; 8 Tennis nearby; 9 Swimming nearby; 10 Golf nearby; 11 Skiing nearby; 12 May be booked through travel agent.

Snowshoe weddings can be conducted by the innkeeper-minister.

Hosts: Gary and Sue Mansfield
Rooms: 9 (PB) $135-250
Continental Breakfast
Credit Cards: A, B
Notes: 4, 5, 10, 11, 12

GLENWOOD SPRINGS

Back in Time Bed and Breakfast

927 Cooper, 81601
(970) 945-6183

A spacious Victorian home built in 1903 and filled with antiques, family quilts, and clocks. A full breakfast is served in the dining room: a hot dish accompanied by fresh hot muffins, fruit, and a specialty of June's mouth-watering cinnamon rolls.

Hosts: June and Ron Robinson
Rooms: 3 (PB) $80-85
Full Breakfast
Credit Cards: A, B, C
Notes: 2, 5, 8, 9, 10, 11, 12

LEADVILLE

The Ice Palace Inn Bed and Breakfast

813 Spruce Street, 80461
(719) 486-8272; (800) 754-2840
Web site: http://colorado-bnb.com/icepalace

This gracious Victorian inn was built at the turn of the century, using the lumber from the famous Leadville Ice Palace. Romantic guest rooms, elegantly decorated with antiques, featherbeds and quilts, each with an exquisite private bath, are named after the original rooms of the Ice Palace. Begin your day with a delicious gourmet breakfast served at individual tables in this historic inn. Afternoon teas and goodies are available every day. Turn-down service in the evening.

Hosts: Giles and Kami Kolakowski
Rooms: 6 (PB) $79-139
Full Gourmet Breakfast
Credit Cards: A, B, C, D
Notes: 2, 5, 7, 8, 9, 10, 11, 12

Wood Haven Manor

Wood Haven Manor

809 Spruce, 80461
(719) 486-0109; (800) 748-2570;
FAX (719) 486-0210
E-mail: woodhavn@rmi.net
Web site: http://colorado-bnb.com/woodhavn

Enjoy the taste and style of Victorian Leadville by stepping back one hundred years in this beautiful home located in the prestigious "Banker's Row." Each room is distinctively decorated in Victorian style with private bath. One suite has a whirlpool tub. Spacious dining room; comfortable living room with fireplace. Historic city with a backdrop of Colorado's high-

---

NOTES: Credit cards accepted: A Master Card; B Visa; C American Express; D Discover; E Diners Club; F Other; 2 Personal checks accepted; 3 Lunch available; 4 Dinner available; 5 Open all year; 6 Pets

est mountains. Enjoy snowmobiling, biking, hiking, and more.

Hosts: Bobby and Jolene Wood
Rooms: 8 (PB) $59-129
Full Breakfast
Credit Cards: A, B, C, D
Notes: 2, 5, 7, 8, 9, 10, 11, 12

LOVELAND

Derby Hill Inn

2502 Courtney Drive, 80537
(970) 667-3193; (800) 498-8086;
FAX: (970) 667-3193
E-mail: derbyhilll@aol.com
Web site: http://www.questinns.com/derbyhill

Located in a quiet residential neighborhood close to retail and antique shops, art galleries, four-star golf course, and Rocky Mountain National Park. Art, sculpture, and antiques enhance the decor and homelike atmosphere. Well-decorated, comfortable rooms with private baths feature queen beds, phones, and TVs. Computer and fax available. A gourmet breakfast is served. Our friendly hospitality will make the casual and business traveler feel welcome. Members of PAII and BBIC.

Hosts: Dale and Bev McCue
Rooms: 2 (PB)
Full Breakfast
Credit Cards: A, B, C, E
Notes: 2, 5, 8, 9, 10, 12

The Lovelander B&B Inn

217 W. 4th Street, 80537
(970) 669-0798; (800) 459-6694;
FAX (970) 669-0797
E-mail: love@ezlink.com
Web sites: http://www.innbook.com/love.html
    http://www.bedandbreakfastinns.org/loveland/
    index.html

An elegant, eleven-room Victorian inn providing contemporary comfort. Each room has its own private bath and includes a memorable gourmet breakfast. Fresh-baked cookies and lemonade or hot cider greet you upon arrival. Come prepared to relax and enjoy the genuine hospitality of all of our innkeepers.

Hosts: Lauren and Gary Smith
Rooms: 11 (PB) $90-135
Full Breakfast
Credit Cards: A, B, C, D
Notes: 2, 3, 4, 5, 10, 12

MANCOS

Riversbend Bed and Breakfast

42505 Highway 160, 81328
(970) 533-7353
Web site: http://subee.com/rb/home.html

Located on the San Juan Skyway just seven miles from Mesa Verde National Park and twenty-seven miles from the Durango/Silverton Narrow Gauge Railroad. Riversbend is in a central location for exploring southwestern Colorado. Two-story log inn nestled under tall cottonwood trees on the bank of the Mancos River. Loft-style guest rooms and the entire inn are furnished comfortably with antiques and quilts reflecting days gone by. When guests return to Riverbend after a day exploring the area, they find porch swings, wooden rockers, and a relaxing hot tub waiting. Riversbend offers two common areas to guests at all times. You may read, relax in conversation with other guests, or . . . it's totally up to you!

Hostess: Gaye Curran
Rooms: 5 (1PB; 4SB) $62-85
Full Breakfast
Credit Cards: A, B, D
Notes: 2, 10, 11, 12

MANITOU SPRINGS

Frontier's Rest
Bed and Breakfast

341 Ruxton Avenue, 80829
(719) 685-0588; (800) 455-0588;
FAX (719) 685-1519
Web site: http://www.bbonline.com/co/frontier

"Old West" hospitality, creative breakfasts and unique rooms with period antiques all come together at this bed and breakfast at the foot of Pike's Peak, one of America's most famous landmarks. Located just four miles from downtown Colorado Springs and three blocks from downtown Manitou Springs, this historic property is within footsteps of major attractions, shopping, and fine dining. Yet it is wonderfully quiet at night. With lots of extras and a caring owner, you'll take home great memories from Frontier's Rest Bed and Breakfast.

Hostess: Jeanne Vrobel
Rooms: 4 (PB) $75-110
Full Breakfast
Credit Cards: A, B, C, D
Notes: 2, 5, 7, 8, 9, 10, 11, 12

Frontier's Rest

OURAY

The Damn Yankee
Country Inn

PO Box 410, 100 Sixth Avenue, 81427
(970) 325-4219

Relax your body. Ten uniquely appointed rooms await, each with a private bath and entrance, some with fireplaces. Cabins along the river are available. Drift off to the soothing music of a mountain stream from your luxurious queen-size bed. Snuggle under a plush down comforter. Most rooms have fireplaces. Sit back and watch your favorite film on cable TV. Drink in the fresh mountain air. Relax in our hot tub. Or gather around the parlor with friends and sing along to music from a baby grand piano. Feast your senses. Enjoy afternoon snacks in our towering observatory. And savor a hearty, gourmet breakfast as you watch the sun glint over the mountaintops.

Hosts: Matt and Julie Croce
Rooms: 10 (PB) $68-165
Full Hearty Gourmet Breakfast
Credit Cards: A, B, C, D
Notes: 2, 3, 4 (winter), 5, 8, 9, 10, 11, 12

Ouray 1898 House

322 Main Street, PO Box 641, 81427
(970) 325-4871
E-mail: bates@netzone.com
Web site: http://colorado-bnb.com/mainst

This one hundred-year-old house has been carefully renovated and combines the old with the comfortable amenities of today. Each room features antique furnishings, cable TV, and a private bath. From the deck off each guest room is a spectacular view of the San Juan Mountains—or en-

---

NOTES: Credit cards accepted: A Master Card; B Visa; C American Express; D Discover; E Diners Club; F Other; 2 Personal checks accepted; 3 Lunch available; 4 Dinner available; 5 Open all year; 6 Pets

joy this view from the unique Victorian gazebo and soothing spa. A full breakfast is served with a "variety for every appetite." Ouray is known as the "Jeep Capital of the World" and also is known for its natural hot springs and marvelous hiking trails.

Hosts: Lee and Kathy Bates
Rooms: 4 (PB) $58-100
Full Breakfast
Credit Cards: A, B, C
Notes: 2, 8, 9, 10

PAGOSA SPRINGS

Be Our Guest— A B&B/Guesthouse

19 Swiss Village Drive, 81147-9736
(970) 264-6814; (800) 484-2275/6595
FAX (970) 264-6953

We aim to please! We've added walls, doors, and two full baths to meet the needs of guests. Though rustic, our lodge-style home offers great convenience and relaxed comfort. Choose "one room or the whole house" (up to thirty). We have great group rates. So please, "Be Our Guest!"

Hosts: Tom and Pam Schoemig
Rooms: 5 (3PB; 2SB) $47.50-65
Full Breakfast
Credit Cards: none
Notes: 2, 5, 6 (by prior arrangement), 9, 10, 11

Davidson's Country Inn

PO Box 87, 81147
(970) 264-5863; FAX (970) 264-5492

Davidson's Country Inn is a three-story log house located at the foot of the Rocky Mountains on thirty-two acres. The inn provides a library, playroom, game room, and outdoor activities. A two-bedroom cabin is also available. The inn is tastefully decorated with family heirlooms and antiques, with a warm country touch to make you feel at home. Located two miles east of Highway 160.

Host: Gilbert Davidson
Rooms: 8 (3PB; 5SB) $59-95
Full Breakfast
Credit Cards: A, B, C, F
Notes: 2, 5, 6 (by arrangement), 7, 8, 9, 10, 11, 12

PAONIA

Pitkin Mesa Bed and Breakfast

3954 "P" Road, 81428
(970) 527-7576

Pitkin Mesa Bed and Breakfast is in the mild climate of Paonia's fruit-growing area. Guests enjoy restful views of the North Fork of Gunnison Valley and nearby mountains. They can hike or bike to shops and restaurants. This is a newer home in a semirural area with an indoor, heated swimming pool and spa. From the porch swing on our spacious deck you can take in the view of Mt. Lamborn (Romans 5:12). We are close to Black Canyon, scenic byways, and Grand Mesa's lakes. Tobacco- and alcohol-free. Children under 14 by special arrangement only. Open June-October.

Hosts: Dale and Barbara Soucek
Rooms: 3 (1PB; 2SB) $55-65
Full Breakfast
Credit Cards: A, B
Notes: 2, 8, 9

welcome; 7 Children welcome; 8 Tennis nearby; 9 Swimming nearby; 10 Golf nearby; 11 Skiing nearby; 12 May be booked through travel agent.

PUEBLO

Abriendo Inn

300 W. Abriendo Avenue, 81004
(719) 544-2703; FAX (719) 542-6544

Experience the elegance of an estate home as you delight in the pleasure of personal attention and hospitality. Get away to yesterday with the conveniences you expect of today. Breakfast is always hearty, home-baked, and served in the oak-wainscoted dining room or on one of the picturesque porches. The inn is located within walking distance of restaurants, shops, and galleries—all in the heart of Pueblo. All rooms have air-conditioning, king/queen beds, TVs, and telephones; some have whirlpool tubs.

Hostess: Kerrelyn M. Trent
Rooms: 10 (PB) $59-115
Full Breakfast
Credit Cards: A, B, C, E
Notes: 2, 5, 8, 9, 10, 12

SALIDA

Gazebo Country Inn

507 E. 3rd., 81201
(719) 539-7806; (800) 565-7806

A 1901, restored Victorian home with magnificent deck and porch views. Gourmet breakfasts and private baths. Located in the heart of the Rockies. White-water rafting on the Arkansas River and skiing at the Monarch Mountain Lodge are a few of the amenities. We are committed to your comfort and relaxation.

Hosts: BJ and Don Johannsen
Rooms: 3 (PB) $50-75
Full Breakfast
Credit Cards: A, B, C
Notes: 2, 5, 7 (over 8), 9, 10, 11, 12

The Tudor Rose

The Tudor Rose

PO Box 89, 81201
(719) 539-2002; (800) 379-0889;
FAX (719) 530-0345
E-mail: tudorose@rmi.net
Web site: http://www.bbonline.com/co/tudorose

Stately country manor, high on a pinon hill, surrounded by thirty-seven acres. Six distinctive rooms, including the Henry Tudor Suite with its raised Jacuzzi, highlight the inn. A formal Queen Anne living room, formal dining room, relaxing "wolf's" den, deck with sunken spa, and full hot breakfast are all complimentary. Facilities include a barn, fenced paddocks, access to thousands of federal acres, and outdoor dog accommodations.

Hosts: John and Terré Terrell
Rooms: 6 (4PB; 2SB) $50-105
Full Breakfast
Credit Cards: A, B, D
Notes: 2, 3, 5, 6, 7, 8, 9, 10, 11, 12

SPRINGFIELD

Plum Bear Ranch

PO Box 241, 81073
(719) 523-4344; FAX (719) 523-4324
E-mail: plumbear@ria.net

Plum Bear Ranch provides guests with an atmosphere of comfort and freedom—the

NOTES: Credit cards accepted: A Master Card; B Visa; C American Express; D Discover; E Diners Club; F Other; 2 Personal checks accepted; 3 Lunch available; 4 Dinner available; 5 Open all year; 6 Pets

opportunity for city dwellers to share in the bounty of the range. It's an ideal place to relax, with panoramic views and peaceful country settings. Gorgeous sunrises, spectacular sunsets.

Hosts: Todd and Lisa Ecton
Rooms: 7 (3PB; 4SB) $40-50
Full Breakfast
Credit Cards: A, B
Notes: 2, 5, 6, 7, 10

VAIL

Bed and Breakfast Reservations/Summit

2488 Garmisch Drive, 81657
(970) 476-6705; (800) 437-7330
E-mail: bbresser@vail.net

A bed and breakfast reservation agency offering the finest properties in Colorado. We specialize in the resort areas, including Summit County, Vail, Aspen, and Crested Butte, in both summer and winter. Private homestays or inns are available for travelers who desire something extraordinary.

Hosts: Narda Reigel and Beverly Miller
Credit Cards: A, B, C, D, E
Notes: 2

WINTER PARK

Candlelight Mountain Inn

PO Box 600, 80482
(970) 887-2877; (800) KIM-4-TIM (546-4846)

Nestled on a mountainside among pine and aspen trees, the Candlelight Mountain Inn is located in Colorado's beautiful Fraser Valley. Married couples, retired folks, and families will enjoy the comfortable beds, full breakfasts, candlelit lane, game and toy room, hot tub under the stars, glider swings around the campfire, the beautiful view, and other surprises. Our inn is situated in the heart of a vacation paradise; it's just fifteen minutes to the ski slopes, thirty minutes to Rocky Mountain National Park, and only three minutes to the Pole Creek Golf Course and the YMCA of the Rockies . . . a fantastic family vacation spot.

Hosts: Kim and Tim Onnen
Rooms: 4 (PB) $65-95
Full Breakfast
Credit Cards: none
Notes: 2, 5, 7, 8, 9, 10, 11

Pikes Peak Paradise

WOODLAND PARK

Pikes Peak Paradise

236 Pinecrest Road, 80863
(719) 687-6656; (800) 728-8282;
FAX (719) 687-9008
E-mail: ppp@cyber-bbs.com
Web site: http://www.cyber-bbs.com/ppp

All room rates include incredible Pikes Peak views, complimentary beverages and snacks, gourmet breakfasts daily, private

welcome; 7 Children welcome; 8 Tennis nearby; 9 Swimming nearby; 10 Golf nearby; 11 Skiing nearby; 12 May be booked through travel agent.

attached baths, and full use of the outdoor hot tub. National parks, shops, Olympic training center, skiing, white-water rafting, wildlife and many other attractions nearby. Open all year.

Hosts: Priscilla Arthur
Rooms: 6 (PB) $95-195
Full Breakfast
Credit Cards: A, B, C, D
Notes: 2, 4, 5, 6

Woodland Inn Bed and Breakfast

159 Trull Road, 80863
(719) 687-8209; (800) 226-9565;
FAX (719) 687-3112

Guests enjoy the relaxing, homelike atmosphere and fantastic views of Pikes Peak from this cozy country inn in the heart of the Rocky Mountains. Peacefully secluded on twelve private acres of woodlands, the Woodland Inn is convenient to a variety of attractions, some of which include limited-stakes gambling in Cripple Creek, Pikes Peak, the Cog Railway and highway, hiking, biking, golf, trail riding, and cross-country skiing. Hot-air ballooning with the host is also available! We welcome small wedding retreats and seminars; the Inn can accommodate fifteen to twenty overnight guests and up to fifty people at gatherings.

Hosts: Frank and Nancy O'Neil
Rooms: 7 (PB) $60-90
Full Breakfast
Credit Cards: A, B, C, D
Notes: 2, 5, 7, 8, 10, 11, 12

NOTES: Credit cards accepted: A Master Card; B Visa; C American Express; D Discover; E Diners Club; F Other; 2 Personal checks accepted; 3 Lunch available; 4 Dinner available; 5 Open all year; 6 Pets

Connecticut

Bed and Breakfast, Ltd.

759 Quinnipiac Ave., **New Haven**, 06513
(203) 469-3260
Web site: http://members.aol.com/bandbltd/
    master.htm

Bed and Breakfast, Ltd., offers more than
125 listings of private homes and small
inns throughout **Connecticut** (with additional locations in **Massachusetts** and
Rhode Island)—from elegantly simple
to simply elegant. Affordable and varied. A quick phone call assures up-to-
the-minute descriptions and availability.

Director: Jack M. Argenio
Rooms: 125+ (75PB, 50SB) $65-149
Full and Continental Breakfast
Credit Cards: (at some) A, B, C
Notes: (at some) 2, 4, 5, 6, 7, 8, 9, 10, 11

CLINTON

Captain Dibbell House

21 Commerce Street, 06413
(860) 669-1646; FAX (860) 669-2300

Our 1886 Victorian, just two blocks from
the shore, features a wisteria-covered, century-old footbridge and gazebo on our half
acre of lawn and gardens. Spacious living
rooms and bedrooms are comfortably furnished with antiques and family heirlooms,
fresh flowers, fruit baskets, and home-baked
treats. There are bicycles, nearby beaches,
and marinas to enjoy.

Hosts: Helen and Ellis Adams
Rooms: 4 (PB) $75-105
Full Breakfast
Credit Cards: A, B
Notes: 2, 8, 9, 10, 12

ESSEX

Griswold Inn

36 Main Street, 06426
(860) 767-1776; FAX (860) 767-0481

Warm up to the potbelly stove or gaze into
one of many fireplaces as you sense the
spirit of the "Gris." It is a kaleidoscope of
nostalgic images—a lovely country place
with a myriad Currier-and-Ives steamboat
prints, a Taproom described by Lucius
Beebe as probably the most handsome
barroom in America, and a library of fire-
arms dating from the 15th century. Historic collections of marine art and dining
rooms await you. The cuisine is unmatched for its genuineness and purity.

Hosts: Douglas and Joan Paul
Rooms: 30 (PB); $90-185
Continental Breakfast
Credit Cards: A, B, C
Notes: 2, 3, 4, 5, 6, 7, 8, 9, 10

welcome; 7 Children welcome; 8 Tennis nearby; 9 Swimming nearby; 10 Golf nearby; 11 Skiing nearby;
12 May be booked through travel agent.

CONNECTICUT

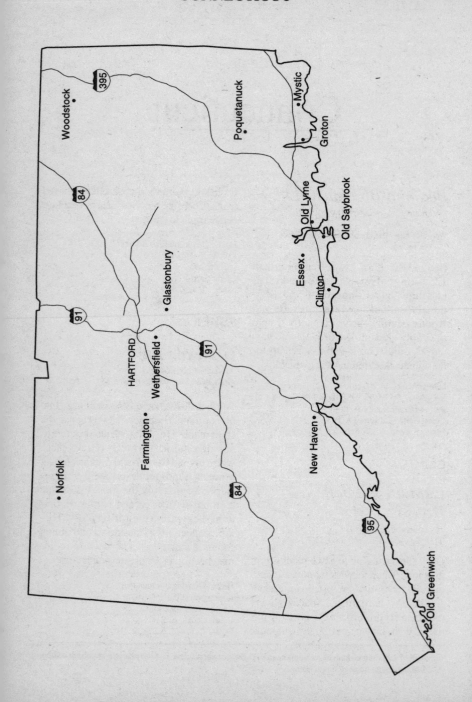

The Farmington Inn

FARMINGTON

The Farmington Inn

827 Farmington Avenue, 06032
(860) 677-2821; (800) 648-9804;
FAX: (860) 677-8332
E-mail: Classic.HTL@aol.com

Beautiful rooms, charming decor, exquisite amenities, convenient location. Outstanding restaurants and personal attention. Intimate bridal suites, hospitality rooms, and an exceptional breakfast. Fresh flowers in a picture-perfect lobby with antiques and original paintings.

Rooms have cable, VCR, movies, PPV available. Covered parking, concierge service. Myriad recreational activities.

Rooms: 72 (PB) $99-129
Continental Breakfast
Credit Cards: A, B, C, D, E
Notes: 5, 6, 7, 8, 9, 10, 11, 12

GLASTONBURY

Butternut Farm

1654 Main Street, 06033
(860) 633-7197; FAX (860) 659-1758

This 18th-century architectural jewel is furnished in period antiques. Prize-winning dairy goats, pigeons, and chickens roam in an estate setting with trees and herb gardens. Enjoy fresh eggs for breakfast. The farm is located ten minutes from Hartford by expressway; one and one half hours to any place in Connecticut. Private baths. No pets, no smoking.

Host: Don Reid
Rooms: 3 + suite and apartment (PB) $70-90
Full Breakfast
Credit Cards: C
Notes: 2, 5, 7, 8, 9, 10, 11

Butternut Farm

NOTES: Credit cards accepted: A Master Card; B Visa; C American Express; D Discover; E Diners Club; F Other; 2 Personal checks accepted; 3 Lunch available; 4 Dinner available; 5 Open all year; 6 Pets welcome; 7 Children welcome; 8 Tennis nearby; 9 Swimming nearby; 10 Golf nearby; 11 Skiing nearby; 12 May be booked through travel agent.

GROTON

Bluff Point Bed and Breakfast

26 Fort Hill Road, 06340
(860) 445-1314

A restored colonial bed and breakfast (circa 1850) located on U.S. Route 1 and adjacent to Bluff Point State Park Coastal Preserve. Conveniently located four miles from Mystic Seaport Museum. Large common area with shared TV is available for our guests. Our home is equipped with a central fire sprinkler system. No smoking or pets. We give warm and friendly service.

Hosts: Walter and Edna Parfitt
Rooms: 3 (PB) $85-95
Continental Breakfast
Credit Cards: A, B, C
Notes: 2, 5, 8, 9, 10

MYSTIC

The Adams House of Mystic

382 Cow Hill Road, 06355
(860) 572-9551

Historic 1749 colonial home close to Mystic Seaport and Mystic Aquarium. Seven rooms with queen beds, private baths and AC. Hearty breakfast included. Smoke-free. The large yard has gardens and a patio.

Hosts: Mary Lou and Gregory Peck
Rooms: 7 (PB) $95-175
Full Breakfast
Credit Cards: A, B, C, D
Notes: 2, 5, 7, 9, 10

The Adams House of Mystic

Harbour Inne and Cottage

15 Edgemont Street, 06355
(860) 572-9253

The Harbour Inne and Cottage is located on the Mystic River, two blocks from historic downtown Mystic. Six rooms and a cottage. The three-room cottage has a fireplace and two double beds in the bedroom. A sleeper sofa and color TV are in the living room, with glider doors opening onto a deck with a hot tub spa. Shower/lavatory facilities, kitchen and dining area. The guest house has five rooms, each with double bed, color TV, shower or bath, and air-conditioning. Guests have an equipped

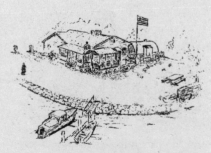

Harbour Inne and Cottage

NOTES: Credit cards accepted: A Master Card; B Visa; C American Express; D Discover; E Diners Club; F Other; 2 Personal checks accepted; 3 Lunch available; 4 Dinner available; 5 Open all year; 6 Pets

galley and dining area, as well as a social area with fireplace and antique piano.

Host: Charles Lecouras, Jr.
Rooms: 6 and cottage (PB) $75-250
Self-Catered Breakfast
Credit Cards: none
Notes: 5, 6, 7, 8, 9, 10

Red Brook Inn

PO Box 237, 06372
(860) 572-0349

Nestled on seven acres of old New England wooded countryside, lodging is provided in two historic buildings. The Haley Tavern, circa 1770, is a colonial built by sea captain Nathaniel Crary. Each room is appointed with period furnishings, including canopy beds. There are many working fireplaces throughout the Inn and guest rooms. A hearty breakfast is served family-style in the ancient keeping room. Enjoy a quiet atmosphere near Mystic Seaport Museum, antique shops, Foxwoods Casino, and Aquarium. Colonial dinner weekends available, November-December. No smoking.

Hostess: Ruth Keyes
Rooms: 10 (PB) $129-229
Full Breakfast
Credit Cards: A, B, C, D
Notes: 2, 5, 7, 8, 9, 10

NORFOLK

Greenwoods Gate Bed and Breakfast Inn

105 Greenwoods Road E., 06058
(860) 542-5439

Warm hospitality greets you in this beautifully restored 1797 colonial home. The Inn is small and elegant with four exquisitely appointed guest suites, each with private bath (one with Jacuzzi). Fine antiques, fireplaces, and sumptuous breakfasts indulge you. Afternoon tea and refreshments are served before going out to dinner. *Yankee Magazine* calls this "New England's most romantic Bed and Breakfast." *Country Inns Bed and Breakfast Magazine* says: "A Connecticut Jewel." Come join us at the home of Yale's summer music festival.

Host: George E. Schumaker
Rooms: 4 suites (PB) $175-235
Gourmet Breakfast
Credit Cards: none
Notes: 5, 7, 8, 9, 11, 12

OLD GREENWICH

Harbor House Inn

165 Shore Road, 06870
(203) 637-0145; FAX (203) 698-0943
Web site: http://www.HHInn.com

Harbor House Inn is located in Old Greenwich, surrounded by charm that speaks of times long ago. It is a short stroll from the beach and the lovely park that adjoins it—and yet only minutes from restaurants, stores, the train station, and I-95, and a mere forty-five minutes from New York City. If you just want to trade in the hectic hotel atmosphere for a relaxing time on your next business trip, the Harbor House Inn welcomes you.

Hostesses: Dolly Stuttig and Dawn Browne
Rooms: 23 (17PB; 6SB) $99-149
Continental Breakfast
Credit Cards: A, B, C
Notes: 2, 5, 7, 8, 9, 10, 12

welcome; 7 Children welcome; 8 Tennis nearby; 9 Swimming nearby; 10 Golf nearby; 11 Skiing nearby; 12 May be booked through travel agent.

Old Lyme Inn

OLD LYME

Old Lyme Inn

85 Lyme Street, 06371
(860) 434-2600; (800) 434-5352;
FAX (860) 434-5352
E-mail: olinn@aol.com

A fine 19th-century home restored to full
grandeur. A tree-shaded lawn leads to
the banistered front porch where guests
can relax. Built as a farmhouse, the Inn is
now a lodging with five guest rooms and
eight suites, furnished in Empire and Victorian style with antiques, and equipped
with air-conditioning, telephones, and TVs.

Hostess: Diana Atwood-Johnson
Rooms: 13 (PB) $99-158
Continental Breakfast
Credit Cards: A, B, C, D, E
Notes: 2, 3, 4, 5, 6, 7, 8, 9, 10, 12

OLD SAYBROOK

Deacon Timothy Pratt Bed and Breakfast

325 Main Street, 06475
(860) 395-1229
E-mail: shelley.nobile@snet.net
Web site: www.virtualcities.com/ct/pratthouse.htm

Step back in time and enjoy the splendor of
yesteryear at the Deacon Timothy Pratt

House. Guest rooms are romantically furnished in period style with working fireplaces. A full country breakfast is served
in the elegant dining room. Located in Old
Saybrook, where the Connecticut River
meets Long Island Sound, the Pratt House
is conveniently located in the historic and
shopping district. Walk to shops, restaurants, theaters, town green, and Saybrook
Point. Located near beaches, antique
shops, museums, Mystic Seaport and
Aquarium, Foxwoods Casino, Good-
speed Opera House, Ivoryton Playhouse,
Essex Steam Train and Riverboat, and
Gillette Castle State Park.

Hostess: Shelley C. Nobile
Rooms: 3 (PB) $105-140
Full Breakfast
Credit Cards: A, B, C
Notes: 2, 3, 5, 7, 8, 9, 10, 11, 12

PRESTON

Captain Grant's, 1754

109 Route 2A; 06365
(860) 887-7589; (800) 982-1772;
FAX (860) 892-9151
Web site: http://www.bbonline.com/ct/
captaingrants

Enjoy the austere gentility of a bygone era.
Captain Grant's, 1754, is located in a Na-

NOTES: Credit cards accepted: A Master Card; B Visa; C American Express; D Discover; E Diners
Club; F Other; 2 Personal checks accepted; 3 Lunch available; 4 Dinner available; 5 Open all year; 6 Pets

tional Historic District near the famous whaling village of Mystic, the Naval Submarine Museum, and the world's largest casinos. Each authentically restored guest room includes a private bath and color cable television. A library, keeping room and deck are for our guests' exclusive use. The morning greets you with a full candlelit breakfast and the evening with complimentary wine.

Hosts: Ted and Carol
Rooms: 4 (PB); $80-150
Full Breakfast
Credit Cards: A, B, C, D, F
Notes: 5, 7 (6 and over), 8, 9, 10, 12

WETHERSFIELD

Chester Bulkley House Bed and Breakfast

184 Main Street, 06109
(860) 563-4236; FAX (860) 257-8266
Web site: http://www.choice-guide.com/ct/bulkley

Nestled in the historic village of Old Wethersfield, this classic Greek Revival house has been restored lovingly by innkeepers Frank and Sophie Bottaro to provide a warm and gracious New England welcome to the vacationer, traveler, or businessperson. Built in 1830, the house boasts five delightfully airy guest rooms, each with a unique character and decorated with period antiques and vintage design details.

Hosts: Frank and Sophie Bottaro
Rooms: 5 (3PB; 2SB) $70-85
Full Breakfast
Credit Cards: A, B, C, D
Notes: 2, 5, 7, 8, 9, 10, 12

WOODSTOCK

Taylor's Corner Bed and Breakfast

880 Route 171, 06281-2930
(860) 974-0490; FAX (860) 974-0498
E-mail: taylors@neca.com
Web site: http://www.neguide.com/taylors

Taylor's Corner Bed and Breakfast, a romantic, 18th-century colonial home with eight working fireplaces, is on the National Register of Historic Places. Common areas and air-conditioned guest rooms with private baths are furnished with antiques. Originally a farmhouse, Taylor's Corner maintains its pastoral setting, surrounded by gardens and towering trees. Breakfast is served on fine Danish porcelain. The home is located just off Scenic Route 169 in Connecticut's "Quiet Corner." We're only five minutes from terrific antiquing in Putman or twenty minutes to Old Sturbridge Village.

Hosts: Peggy and Doug Tracy
Rooms: 4 (3PB; 1SB) $80-90
Full Breakfast, weekend; Continental, weekday
Credit cards: none
Notes: 2, 5, 7 (over 12), 9, 10, 11 (cross-country), 12

Taylor's Corner Bed and Breakfast

---

welcome; 7 Children welcome; 8 Tennis nearby; 9 Swimming nearby; 10 Golf nearby; 11 Skiing nearby; 12 May be booked through travel agent.

DELAWARE

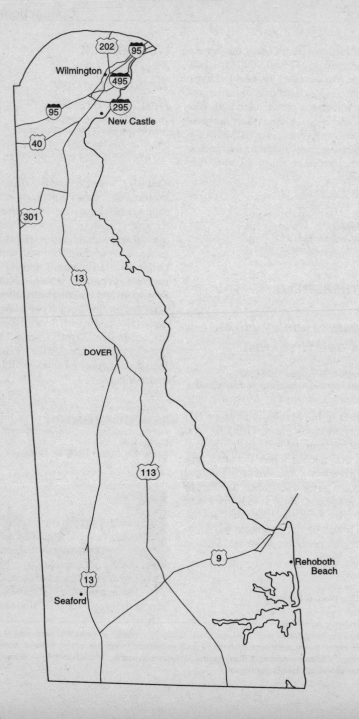

Delaware

NEW CASTLE

Armitage Inn

2 The Strand, 19720
(302) 328-6618; FAX (302) 324-1163
E-mail: armitageinn@earthlink.net

Built in 1732, the Armitage Inn is beautifully situated on the bank of the Delaware River in historic New Castle. Elegantly furnished, air-conditioned guest rooms, all with private baths and most with whirlpool tubs, overlook the picturesque vistas of the grand Delaware River, the acres of parkland surrounding the Inn, and a peaceful walled garden. A gourmet buffet breakfast is served in the grand dining room or in the garden. The Inn is conveniently located in the heart of this historic town. New Castle was established in 1651 and functions today as a living museum, with buildings dating back to its founding years. New Castle is situated in the heart of the Brandywine Valley, a region noted for its numerous museums and attractions.

Hosts: Stephen and Rina Marks
Rooms: 5 (PB) $105-150
Breakfast Buffet
Credit Cards: A, B, C, D
Notes: 5, 8, 10, 12

William Penn Guest House

206 Delaware Street, 19720
(302) 328-7736

Visit historic New Castle and stay in a charmingly restored home, circa 1682, close to museums and major highways. Rates are $60 for shared baths and $85 for private baths.

Hosts: Irma and Richard Burwell
Rooms: 4 (2PB; 2SB) $60-85
Continental Breakfast
Credit Cards: none
Notes: 2, 8

REHOBOTH BEACH

The Royal Rose Inn Bed and Breakfast

41 Baltimore Avenue, 19971
(302) 226-2535

A charming and relaxing 1920s beach cottage, this bed and breakfast is tastefully furnished with antiques and a romantic rose theme. A scrumptious breakfast of fresh fruit cups, homemade breads, muffins, and egg entrées is served on a screened porch. Air-conditioned guest

---

NOTES: Credit cards accepted: A Master Card; B Visa; C American Express; D Discover; E Diners Club; F Other; 2 Personal checks accepted; 3 Lunch available; 4 Dinner available; 5 Open all year; 6 Pets welcome; 7 Children welcome; 8 Tennis nearby; 9 Swimming nearby; 10 Golf nearby; 11 Skiing nearby; 12 May be booked through travel agent.

rooms, guest refrigerator, and off-street parking are real pluses for guests. The Royal Rose Inn is centrally located one and one-half blocks from the ocean and boardwalk. Midweek specials, weekend packages, and gift certificates. Open April through November, other times by chance.

Hosts: Kenny and Cindy Vincent
Rooms: 7 (3PB; 4SB) $55-125
Full Breakfast
Credit Cards: none
Notes: 2, 7 (over 6), 8, 9, 10

Tembo
Bed and Breakfast

100 Laurel Street, 19971
(302) 227-3360

Tembo, named after Gerry's elephant collection, is a white frame beach cottage set among old shade trees in a quiet residential area just one block from the beach. Furnished with comfortable antique furniture, hand-braided rugs, paintings, and carvings by Delaware artists. A cozy ambience pervades the home's casual, hospitable atmosphere.

Hosts: Don and Gerry Cooper
Rooms: 6 (1PB; 5SB) $75-125
Continental Breakfast
Credit Cards: none
Notes: 2, 7 (over 12), 8, 9, 10

SEAFORD

Nanticoke House

121 S. Conwell Street, 19973
(302) 628-1331

Nanticoke House is a one-hundred-year-old home located on the Nanticoke River in the central Delmarva Peninsula. It is convenient to ocean beaches, the Delaware and Chesapeake bays, Cape May-Lewis Ferry, and the barrier islands of Assateague and Chincoteague. There are many historical points of interest, antique shops, and outlet stores. Guests enjoy the river view, flower gardens, and relaxing, congenial atmosphere. Plenty of good food, fun, and fellowship. Nonsmoking residence. A God-given home we enjoy sharing (Hebrews 13:2).

Hosts: Bob and Dianne Seiler
Rooms: 3 (1PB; 2SB) $55-65
Full Breakfast
Credit Cards: none
Notes: 2, 5, 7, 9, 10

WILMINGTON

The Boulevard
Bed and Breakfast

1909 Baynard Boulevard, 19802
(302) 656-9700; FAX (302) 656-9701

This beautifully restored city mansion was built in 1913. An impressive foyer and magnificent staircase lead to a landing that features a window seat and large leaded-glass windows flanked by fifteen-foot columns. A full breakfast is served on the screened porch or in the formal dining room. Bedrooms are furnished with antiques and family heirlooms. Located near the business district and area attractions.

Hosts: Judy and Charles Powell
Rooms: 6 (4PB; 2SB) $65-80
Full Breakfast
Credit Cards: A, B, C
Notes: 2, 5, 7, 8, 10

NOTES: Credit cards accepted: A Master Card; B Visa; C American Express; D Discover; E Diners Club; F Other; 2 Personal checks accepted; 3 Lunch available; 4 Dinner available; 5 Open all year; 6 Pets

District of Columbia

ALSO SEE LISTINGS UNDER MARYLAND AND VIRGINIA.

Adams Inn

1744 Lanier Place NW, 20009
(202) 745-3600; (800) 578-6807;
FAX (202) 319-7958

This turn-of-the-century town house is in the Adams-Morgan neighborhood with more than forty ethnic restaurants. It has clean, comfortable, home-style furnishings. Adams Inn, located north of the White House and near the National Zoo, is convenient to transportation (Woodley Park Zoo Metro), convention sites, government buildings, and tourist attractions.

Hosts: Gene and Nancy Thompson
Rooms: 25 (14PB; 11SB) $45-90
Expanded Continental Breakfast
Credit Cards: A, B, C, D, E
Notes: 2, 5, 7, 12

Dupont at the Circle

1606 19th Street NW, 20009
(202) 332-5251, FAX (202) 408-8308
E-mail: skvirskya@tatc.com

This restored Victorian town house combines the charm of yesteryear with today's conveniences. Its rooms all have private baths, some with Jacuzzis and televisions. The location is perfect—one-half block to the Metro; shops, wonderful restaurants, the White House, and museums are within walking distance. All the guest rooms are air-conditioned.

Hosts: Alan and Anexora Skvirsky
Rooms: 8 (7PB; 1SB); $95-130
Continental Breakfast
Credit Cards: A, B, C
Notes: 2, 5, 8, 9, 12

Dupont at the Circle

Kalorama Guest House at Kalorama Park

1854 Mintwood Place NW, 20009
(202) 667-6369; FAX (202) 319-1262

Enjoy Washington, DC, the right way! Try bed and breakfast in a charming Victorian

---

welcome; 7 Children welcome; 8 Tennis nearby; 9 Swimming nearby; 10 Golf nearby; 11 Skiing nearby; 12 May be booked through travel agent.

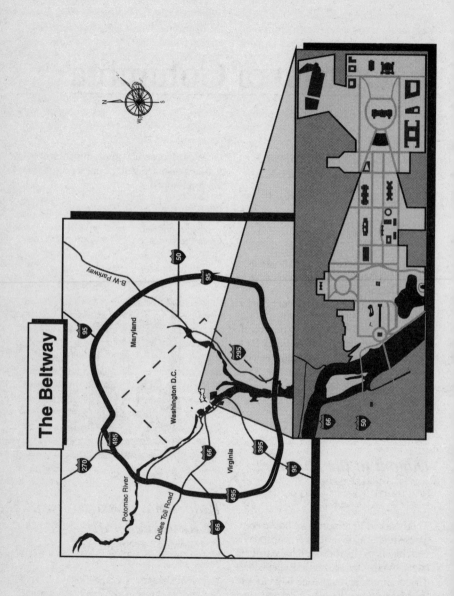

town house. Lodge downtown, within an easy walk of the restaurants, clubs, and nightlife of Adams Morgan and Dupont Circle. Walk to the Metro (subway). Allow us to provide you with a complimentary continental breakfast when you awake, and an evening aperitif when you return to your "home away from home." Most tourist attractions are only ten minutes away.

Hosts: Tami, Carlotta, Michael, and Steve
Rooms: 31 (12PB; 19SB) $55-125
Continental Breakfast
Credit Cards: A, B, C, D
Notes: 5, 7, 8, 12

Kalorama Guest House

Kalorama Guest House at Woodley Park

2700 Cathedral Avenue NW, 20008
(202) 328-0860; FAX (202) 328-8730

This charming Victorian inn offers a cozy home away from home. Located on a quiet street in a lovely downtown residential neighborhood, the House is a stroll from the Metro (subway), neighborhood restaurants, and shops. Guest rooms are tastefully decorated in period. Enjoy your breakfast in a sun-filled room and relax with an aperitif at day's end. Our hospitality and personal service are nationally known. Most of the popular tourist attractions in the nation's capital are only ten minutes away.

Hosts: Mike, Maryanne and Patty
Rooms: 19 (12PB; 7SB) $55-125
Continental Breakfast
Credit Cards: A, B, C, D
Notes: 5, 12

Swiss Inn

1204 Massachusetts Avenue NW, 20005
(202) 371-1816; (800) 955-7947;
FAX (202) 371-1816

The Swiss Inn is a charming turn-of-the-century Victorian town house located in Washington, DC. Amenities include bay windows, high ceilings, and fully equipped kitchenettes. The small, family-owned-and-operated inn is within walking distance of the White House, FBI, National Geographic, Chinatown, Convention Center, Smithsonian Museums, Ford's Theater, Women in the Arts Museum, subway, and many other attractions. We are also just two blocks from the main business district. Grocery stores are within walking distance, as are many churches, including St. Matthew's Cathedral.

Host: Ralph and Kelley
Rooms: 7 (PB) $58-108
No Breakfast
Credit Cards: A, B, C, D
Notes: 2, 5, 6, 7, 12

NOTES: Credit cards accepted: A Master Card; B Visa; C American Express; D Discover; E Diners Club; F Other; 2 Personal checks accepted; 3 Lunch available; 4 Dinner available; 5 Open all year; 6 Pets welcome; 7 Children welcome; 8 Tennis nearby; 9 Swimming nearby; 10 Golf nearby; 11 Skiing nearby; 12 May be booked through travel agent.

FLORIDA

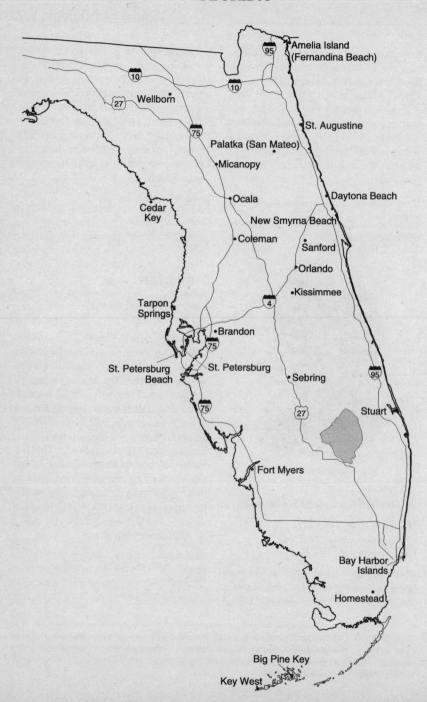

Florida

Bailey House

AMELIA ISLAND/ FERNANDINA BEACH

Bailey House

28 S. 7th Street, **Amelia Island**, 32034
(904) 261-5390; (800) 251-5390;
FAX (904) 321-0103
Web site: http://www.1895baileyhouse.com

Visit an elegant Queen Anne home furnished in Victorian period decor. The beautiful home, with its magnificent stained-glass windows, turrets, and wraparound porch, was built in 1895 and is on the National Register of Historic Places.

The recently renovated home offers the comforts of air-conditioning and private baths. The location in Fernandina's historic district is within walking distance of excellent restaurants, antique shopping, and many historic churches. No smoking or pets, please.

Hosts: Jenny and Tom Bishop
Rooms: 9 (PB) $85-135
Full Breakfast
Credit cards: A, B, C
Notes: 2, 5, 8, 9, 10, 12

AMELIA ISLAND

Elizabeth Pointe Lodge

98 S. Fletcher Avenue, 32034
(904) 261-1137; (800) 772-3359;
FAX (904) 277-6500
E-mail: Eliz.pt@worldnet.att.net
Web site: http://www.Elizabethpointelodge.com

The main house of the lodge is constructed in an 1890s Nantucket shingle style with a strong maritime theme, broad porches, rockers, sunshine, and lemonade. Located prominently on the Atlantic Ocean, the Lodge is only steps from often-deserted beaches. Suites are available for families. A newspaper is delivered to your room in the morning, and breakfast is served over-looking the ocean.

Hosts: David and Susan Caples
Rooms: 25 (PB) $120-225
Full Breakfast
Credit Cards: A, B, C, D
Notes: 2, 3, 5, 7, 8, 9, 10, 12

BAY HARBOR ISLANDS

The Bay Harbor Inn

9660 E. Bay Harbor Drive, 33154
(305) 868-4141; FAX (305) 867-9094

The Bay Harbor Inn is located in the heart of the beautiful Bay Harbor Islands situated by the Intracoastal Waterway next to a galaxy of art galleries and fine restaurants. The Inn is across from the world-famous Bal Harbor shops, one-fourth mile from the Atlantic Ocean and sandy beaches. Ten minutes north of downtown Miami along Collins Avenue, twenty minutes from Miami International Airport and Port Everglades. Seven rooms are handicap-accessible.

Hosts: Lior Dagan
Rooms: 38 (PB)

BIG PINE KEY

Deer Run

PO Box 431, 33043
(305) 872-2015
E-mail: deerrunbb@aol.com

Deer Run is a Florida Cracker-style home nestled in lush native trees on the ocean-front on Big Pine Key. It is furnished with antiques, wicker, and rattan. The upstairs rooms have high ceilings, Bahama fans, and French doors. Air-conditioned for guests' comfort. Breakfast is served on the big veranda overlooking the ocean. You can dive Looe Key, fish the flats, or charter a boat to fish the Gulf Stream. Bahia Honda State Park, which is only minutes away, is regarded as one of the most beautiful beaches in Florida.

Hostess: Sue Abbott
Rooms: 3 (PB) $85-125
Full Breakfast
Notes: 5

BRANDON

Behind the Fence Bed and Breakfast Inn

1400 Viola Drive, 33511
(813) 685-8201; (800) 44-TAMPA

Retreat into the simplicity and tranquillity of life in a bygone era with all the conveniences of today's world. Come to Florida and choose your accommodations, from a cottage by our pool to a private room in our antique-filled New England saltbox house. Nearby parks and river canoeing offer lots of opportunities for family activities. Homemade Amish sweet rolls are featured, and "relaxing" is the word most guests use to refer to their stay "behind the fence." Country furniture is for sale. Tours available upon request. AAA- and 3-star approved.

Hosts: Larry and Carolyn Yoss
Rooms: 5 (3PB; 2SB) $69-79
Expanded Continental Breakfast
Credit Cards: none
Notes: 2, 5, 6 (some), 7, 8, 9, 10

NOTES: Credit cards accepted: A Master Card; B Visa; C American Express; D Discover; E Diners Club; F Other; 2 Personal checks accepted; 3 Lunch available; 4 Dinner available; 5 Open all year; 6 Pets

Island Hotel

CEDAR KEY

Island Hotel

2nd and B Street, PO Box 460, 32625
(352) 543-5111; FAX (352) 543-6949
E-mail: ishotel@gnv.fdt.net
Web site: http://gnv.fdt.net/~ishotel/

Built in 1859, this country inn is on the
National Register of Historic Places. Constructed from seashell tabby with oak sup-
ports, with its sloping wood floors. Sit on
a rocker on the long balcony, or relax in
our cozy lounge bar painted with murals
of Cedar Key from the 1940s. Dine in
our gourmet restaurant serving a distinctively Cedar Key menu.

Hosts: Dawn and Tony Coosins
Rooms: 13 (11PB; 2SB) $85-110
Full Breakfast
Credit Cards: A, B, D
Notes: 4, 5, 7, 9, 12

COLEMAN

The Son's Shady Brook Bed and Breakfast

PO Box 551, 33521
(352) PIT-STOP (748-7867)

A refreshing change for all who seek solitude and tranquillity in a therapeutic, sce-

nic setting. An escape from the humdrum
of everyday life. Exclude the ordinary and
enjoy the beautiful wooded area with a rap-
idly flowing creek. Atmosphere condu-
cive to reading, writing, table games, or
just relaxing. Comfortable beds with other
interesting and enjoyable amenities. Delicious breakfasts. Central Florida attractions are about fifty miles away. Brochures
and gift certificates available.

Hostess: Jean Lake Martin
Rooms: 4 (PB) $50-60
Full Breakfast
Credit Cards: A, B, C
Notes: 2, 5, 8, 9, 10

The Son's Shady Brook Bed and Breakfast

DAYTONA BEACH

Live Oak Inn B&B and Restaurant

444-448 South Beach Street, 32114
(904) 252-4667; (800) 881-4667;
FAX (904) 239-0068

Live Oak Inn stands where Mathias Day
founded Daytona. Two carefully restored
houses—both listed in the National Register of Historic Places (1871 and 1881)—
are among Florida's top ten historic inns
and are the cornerstone of the Daytona

welcome; 7 Children welcome; 8 Tennis nearby; 9 Swimming nearby; 10 Golf nearby; 11 Skiing nearby;
12 May be booked through travel agent.

historic district. Each of the inn's rooms celebrates one of the people or events that helped shape Florida's history. All have private baths, king- or queen-size beds, and either Jacuzzis or Victorian soaking tubs with showers. The Inn has a restaurant and lounge, and is nonsmoking. It offers the best of Daytona! Located across the street from the downtown Halifax Harbor Marina and the restful atmosphere of the Intracoastal Waterway. The excitement of the "World's Most Famous Beach" is only one mile away. The Inn is one of those pleasant-memory, return-again places where hospitality is treated as an art.

Hosts: Jessie and Del Glock
Rooms: 14 (PB) $75-150
Continental Breakfast
Credit Cards: Call
Notes: 2, 3, 4, 5, 8, 9, 10, 12

FORT MYERS

Island Rover *Sailing Ship*
Mailing: 11470 S. Cleveland Avenue, 33907
(941) 936-2311; FAX (941) 936-7391
Web site: http://www.IslandRover.com

The *Island Rover* is a seventy-two-foot sailing ship, Coast Guard-approved for forty-nine passengers. Four staterooms accommodate passengers overnight. Located under the Sky Bridge at Ft. Myers Beach on the beach side. We are a tall ship, designed like a 19th-century pirate vessel. Relax and sail with us!

Rooms: 4 (1PB; 3SB) $99-149
Continental Breakfast
Credit Cards: A, B, C, D, E
Notes: 2, 5, 7, 8, 9, 10

Windsong Garden and Art Gallery
5570-4 Woodrose Court, 33907
(941) 936-6378

This town house-type home is designed to be your home away from home. Spacious accommodations include a bright and cheery suite with a large, private bath and dressing area. Located fifteen minutes from the beaches, Sanibel and Captiva Islands, fine shopping, good restaurants, and the University of Florida. Resident cat.

Hostess: Embe Burdick
Rooms: 1 (PB) $75
Continental Breakfast
Credit Cards: none
Notes: 2, 5, 8, 9, 10

HOMESTEAD

Room at the Inn
15830 SW 240 Street, 33031
(305) 246-0492; FAX (305) 246-0590

Rated superior small lodging by the International Hotel/Motel Guide, Room at the Inn is nestled in the heart of South Florida's prime agricultural community. This charming, custom-designed country ranch, built in 1972, truly exceeds its description as a "quiet place on a country estate." Attracting both vacationing and business visitors from around the globe, the bed and breakfast is an ideal retreat and a gateway for those venturing into the Florida Keys or Everglades National Parks. Guest rooms are nonsmoking and air-conditioned.

Host: Sally Robinson
Rooms: 4 + cottage (3PB; 2SB) $75-150
Full Breakfast
Credit cards: none
Notes: 2, 5, 8, 9, 10

NOTES: Credit cards accepted: A Master Card; B Visa; C American Express; D Discover; E Diners Club; F Other; 2 Personal checks accepted; 3 Lunch available; 4 Dinner available; 5 Open all year; 6 Pets

KEY WEST

Center Court Historic Inn and Cottages

916 Center Street, 33040
(305) 296-9292; (800) 797-8787;
FAX (305) 294-4104
E-mail: centerct@aol.com
Web site: http://www.centercourtkw.com

Center Court Historic Inn and Cottages offers affordable, elegant, Historic Preservation Award-winning accommodations nestled in quiet, tropical gardens just one-half block off Duval! We have fourteen rooms and cottages with queen and king beds, TVs, phones, air-conditioning, fans, private baths, and hair dryers. Enjoy breakfast each morning overlooking the heated pool, Jacuzzi, exercise pavilion and fishpond with its waterfall. Be pampered in our secret paradise! Center Court Historic Inn and Cottages is three-diamond AAA-rated.

Hostess: Naomi Van Steelandt
Rooms: 14 (PB) $88-168
Expanded Continental Breakfast
Credit Cards: A, B, C, D
Notes: 2, 5, 6, 7, 8, 9, 10, 12

Walden Guest House

717 Caroline Street (office: 223 Elizabeth Street), 33040
(305) 296-7161

Walden Guest House is in the historic seaport district in Old Towne, downtown Key West. We are totally accessible to all old town attractions, lower Duval Street, Sloppy Joe's Bar, restaurants, museums, boating, beaches, fishing, and night life. Let us be your vacation hosts for a getaway. Stay in old Key West.

Host: Richard Jabour
Rooms: 6 (2PB; 4SB) $54-105
No Breakfast
Credit Cards: A, B, D
Notes: 5, 7, 8, 9, 10, 12

Whispers B&B

409 William Street, 33040
(305) 294-5969; (800) 856-SHHH;
FAX (305) 294-3899

Whispers sits in the heart of Olde Town Key West, within view of the Gulf Harbor and surrounded by a thirty-block historic district of distinctive 19th-century homes. Ceiling fans whirl above rooms filled with antique furnishings. Guests enjoy the cool porches and lush garden. Take advantage of our complimentary membership in a local resort with private beach, pool, and health spa. Enjoy our tropical fish, birds, and gourmet breakfast creations. Come to paradise. Come home to Whispers.

Host: John Marburg
Rooms: 7 (PB) $69-150
Full Gourmet Breakfast
Credit cards: A, B, C, D
Notes: 2, 5, 8, 9, 10, 12

Whispers Bed and Breakfast

welcome; 7 Children welcome; 8 Tennis nearby; 9 Swimming nearby; 10 Golf nearby; 11 Skiing nearby; 12 May be booked through travel agent.

KISSIMMEE (ORLANDO)

The Unicorn Inn English Bed and Breakfast

8 S. Orlando Avenue, 34741
(407) 846-1200; (800) 865-7212;
FAX (407) 846-1773
E-mail: unicorn@gate.net
Web site: http://touristguide.com/b&b/florida/
    unicorn

The Unicorn—the only bed and breakfast in Kissimmee—is located in historic downtown off the Broadway. A safe, peaceful, relaxing district three hundred yards from Lake Tohopekalegia (fishing boats and other boats can be rented), the Unicorn is close to golf courses, horseback riding, and other attractions like Disney World (a fifteen-minute drive), Sea World, and Wet and Wild. Orlando airport is a twenty-five-minute drive. Amtrak and Greyhound stations are nearby. Guest rooms have TVs and air-conditioning. Kitchen facilities provide complimentary tea and coffee. Restored to its full grandeur, the Inn has antique pottery, prints, and furniture. Many churches are located nearby. British-owned and run by Fran and Don Williamson of Yorkshire, England. Our only rule is: "Make Yourself at Home." Airport pickups are available. The inn is

The Unicorn Inn

AAA three-diamond-rated; Mobil two-star-rated. A member of the Inn Route of Florida.

Hosts: Don and Fran Williamson
Rooms: 8 (including a 2-room suite) (PB) $75-85
Full Gourmet Breakfast
Credit Cards: A, B
Notes: 2 (deposit only), 5, 8, 9, 10, 12

Herlong Mansion

MICANOPY

Herlong Mansion

PO Box 667, 32667
(352) 466-3322; (800) 437-5664;
FAX (352) 466-3322

"Easily Florida's most elegant bed and breakfast"—*Florida Trend*, 11/89. Located in historic Micanopy, twelve miles south of Gainesville, Herlong Mansion is a three-story, brick, Greek Revival historic house with four suites, six rooms, and two cottages.

Host: H.C. (Sonny) Howard Jr.
Rooms: 12 (PB) $55-160
Full Breakfast
Credit Cards: A, B
Notes: 2, 5, 7, 12

NOTES: Credit cards accepted: A Master Card; B Visa; C American Express; D Discover; E Diners Club; F Other; 2 Personal checks accepted; 3 Lunch available; 4 Dinner available; 5 Open all year; 6 Pets

Shady Oak
Bed and Breakfast

PO Box 327, 32667
(352) 466-3476

The Shady Oak Bed and Breakfast stands majestically in the center of historic downtown Micanopy. A marvelous canopy of old live oaks, quiet, shaded streets, and many antique stores offer visitors a memorable connection to Florida's past. This three-story, 19th-century-style mansion features five beautiful, spacious suites, private baths, porches, Jacuzzi, Florida room, and widow's walk. Three lovely, historic churches are within walking distance. Local activities include antiquing, bicycling, canoeing, bird-watching, and much more. "Playfully elegant accommodations, where stained glass, antiques, and innkeeping go together as kindly as warm hugs with old friends."

Hosts: Frank James
Rooms: 6 (PB) $75-125
Full Breakfast
Credit Cards: A, B, D
Notes: 2, 3, 4, 5, 7, 12

NEW SMYRNA BEACH

Indian River Inn
and Conference Center

1210 S. Riverside Drive, 32168
(904) 428-2491; (800) 541-4529;
FAX (904) 426-2532

Built in 1916, this Inn is the oldest extant hotel in Volusia County. It has been lovingly restored and remodeled to meet all current standards of security, comfort, and convenience without sacrificing its charm and character. A gracious atmosphere of warmth and friendliness, unsurpassed in today's often frantic lifestyle, can be found here. We are located on the Atlantic Intracoastal Waterway, minutes from I-95 and I-4 between Daytona Beach and the Kennedy Space Center. Church groups and buses welcomed.

Hosts: Ed and Donna Ruby
Rooms: 27 + 15 suites (PB) $50-115
Continental Breakfast
Credit Cards: A, B, D
Notes: 2, 3 and 4 (available Thanksgiving-Easter), 5,
7, 8, 9 (on premises), 10, 12

Night Swan Intracoastal
Bed and Breakfast

512 S. Riverside Drive, 32168
(904) 423-4940; (800) 465-4261
FAX (904) 427-2814
E-mail: NightSwanB@aol.com

Come watch the pelicans, dolphins, sailboats, and yachts along the Atlantic Intracoastal Waterway from our beautiful front room, our wraparound porch, our 140-foot dock, or your room. Our spacious, three-story home has kept its character and charm of 1906 in the historic district of New Smyrna Beach, with its central fireplace and its intricate natural wood in every room. We are located between Daytona Beach and Kennedy Space Center on the Indian River, just two miles from the beach. AAA-approved.

Hosts: Martha and Chuck Nighswonger
Rooms: 8 (PB) $80-200
Full Breakfast
Credit Cards: A, B, C, D
Notes: 2, 5, 7, 8, 9, 10, 12

welcome; 7 Children welcome; 8 Tennis nearby; 9 Swimming nearby; 10 Golf nearby; 11 Skiing nearby; 12 May be booked through travel agent.

OCALA

Seven Sisters Inn

820 SE Fort King Street, 34471
(352) 867-1170; (800) 250-3496;
FAX (352) 867-5266

Seven Sisters Inn, chosen "Inn of the Month" by *Country Inns Bed and Breakfast Magazine*, is located in the heart of Ocala's historic district. Built in 1888, this Queen Anne-style Victorian house has been lovingly restored to its original stately elegance, with beautiful period furnishings. Each guest room has private bath, carefully chosen, elegant decor, sitting rooms, fireplaces, and much more. The owners, both airline pilots, have traveled all over the world, collecting suberb recipes. It's no wonder their gourmet dishes are received with such enthusiasm! Triple-Crown ABBA-, AAA three-diamond-, and three-star Mobil-rated.

Hosts: Ken and Bonnie Oden
Rooms: 8 (PB) $105-165
Full Breakfast
Credit Cards: A, B, C, D
Notes: 2, 5, 9, 10, 12

Seven Sisters Inn

ORLANDO

Meadow Marsh Bed and Breakfast

940 Tildenville School Road, **Winter Garden**, 34787
(407) 656-2064; (888) 656-2064

Peace and tranquillity surround you as God's beauty unfolds in twelve acres of ol' Florida. Giant oaks, stately palms, and abundant wildlife make your stay at Meadow Marsh one for relaxing and renewing your spirit. The spacious lawn invites a romantic picnic or hand-in-hand walk through the meadow to the adjacent rails-to-trails path. Old-fashioned swings, croquet, and badminton add to the feeling of yesteryear. You'll enjoy the 1877 Victorian farmhouse where cozy fireplaces, hardwood floors, and lace curtains add to the warmth and beauty of this country estate. Suites offer two-person whirlpools, while the smaller bedrooms have antique tubs. Pamper yourselves for a moment in an atmosphere of a sweeter time that existed not so very long ago.

Hosts: Cavelle and John Pawlack
Rooms: 4 + separate cottage (PB) $95-199
Full Three-Course Breakfast
Credit Cards: A, B, D
Notes: 2, 3, 5, 8, 10, 12

PerriHouse Bed and Breakfast Inn

10417 Centurion Court, 32836
(407) 876-4830; (800) 780-4830;
FAX (407) 876-0241

PerriHouse is a quiet, country estate inn secluded on three acres of land adjacent

---

NOTES: Credit cards accepted: A Master Card; B Visa; C American Express; D Discover; E Diners Club; F Other; 2 Personal checks accepted; 3 Lunch available; 4 Dinner available; 5 Open all year; 6 Pets

to the Walt Disney World Resort. Surrounded by trees, grassy fields, and orange groves, the PerriHouse estate is a natural bird sanctuary; bird feeders and baths make viewing birds in their natural activities a delight. Five minutes to Disney Village, Pleasure Island and EPCOT Center. Upscale continental breakfast, pool, hot tub. Eight guest "nests" with private baths, entrances. Four birdhouse cottages are planned by late 1998, featuring king-size canopy beds and whirlpool tubs for two. Three-, five- and seven-day vacation packages will be offered.

Hosts: Nick and Angi Perretti
Rooms: 8 (PB) $89-119
Continental Breakfast
Credit Cards: A, B, C, D, E
Notes: 2 (2 weeks ahead), 5, 7, 8, 9, 10, 12

ST. AUGUSTINE

Castle Garden Bed and Breakfast

15 Shenandoah Street, 32084
(904) 829-3839; FAX (904) 829-9049

Stay at a castle and be treated like royalty! Relax and enjoy the peace and quiet of "royal treatment" at our newly restored, one-hundred-year-old castle of the Moorish Revival design. The only sounds you'll hear are the occasional roar of a cannon shot from the old fort two hundred yards to the south, or the creak of solid wood floors. Awaken to the aroma of freshly baked goodies as we prepare a full, mouth-watering, country breakfast just like "Mom used to make." The unusual coquina stone exterior remains virtually untouched. The interior of the former Castle Warden Carriage House boasts two beautiful bridal suites complete with soothing in-room Jacuzzi and sunken bedrooms! Amenities: complimentary wine, chocolates, bikes, and private parking. Packages and gift baskets are available. We believe every guest is a gift from God.

Hosts: Kimmy VanKooten Kloeckner and Bruce Kloeckner
Rooms: 7 (PB) $75-150
Full Breakfast
Credit Cards: A, B, C, D
Notes: 2, 5, 7, 8, 10, 12

The Cedar House Inn

79 Cedar Street, 32084
(904) 829-0079; (800) 233-2746;
FAX (904) 829-0079
Web site: http://www.CedarHouseInn.com

Capture romantic moments at our 1893 Victorian home in the heart of the ancient city. Escape into your antique-filled bedroom with private whirlpool bath or clawfooted tub; enjoy the comfortable parlor with its fireplace, player piano and antique Victrola; or sit on the shady veranda. Elegant full breakfast, evening snack, parking on premises, Jacuzzi spa, and bicycles. Walk to historical sites or bicycle to the beach. AAA-approved, three-diamond rated. Smoke-free home.

Hosts: Russ and Nina Thomas
Rooms: 5 + 1 suite (PB) $59-150
Full Breakfast
Credit Cards: A, B, C, D
Notes: 2, 3 (picnic), 4, 5, 7 (over 10), 8, 9, 10, 12

The Kenwood Inn

38 Marine Street, 32084
(904) 824-2116; FAX (904) 824-1689
Web site: http://www.travelbase.com/destinations/
st-augustine/kenwood

Since 1886, the Kenwood Inn has stood as "a classic old Florida inn." After you

welcome; 7 Children welcome; 8 Tennis nearby; 9 Swimming nearby; 10 Golf nearby; 11 Skiing nearby; 12 May be booked through travel agent.

The Kenwood Inn

experience the charm and romance of our nation's oldest city, continue your stroll through the past at the Kenwood Inn. Located in a quiet section of the historic waterfront district in walking distance of all attractions, the Inn offers a swimming pool, walled-in courtyard and continental buffet breakfast featuring homemade breads, cakes, and muffins.

Hosts: Mark and Kerrianne Constant
Rooms: 14 (PB) $85-150
Continental Breakfast
Credit Cards: A, B, D
Notes: 2, 5, 7 (over 8), 8, 9, 10, 12

The Old Powder House Inn

38 Cordova Street, 32084
(904) 824-4149; (800) 447-4149;
FAX (904) 825-0143
E-mail: ahowes@aug.com

Escape to a romantic getaway in this charming, turn-of-the-century Victorian inn. Lace curtains and hardwood floors adorn antique-filled rooms. Towering pecan and oak trees shade verandas with rockers, from where you can watch the passing horse-drawn buggies. Or you may relax by the fountain in our courtyard. Amenities include a full gourmet breakfast, hors d' oeuvres, Jacuzzi, cable TV,

parking on site, bicycles, special packages and weddings, and owner hospitality.

Hosts: Al and Eunice Howes
Rooms: 8 (PB) $79-150
Full Gourmet Breakfast
Credit Cards: A, B, D
Notes: 2, 5, 7, 8, 9, 10, 12

St. Francis Inn

279 St. George Street, 32084
(904) 824-6068; (800) 824-6062;
FAX (904) 810-5525
E-mail: innceasd@aug.com

Built in 1791, the inn is a beautiful Spanish Colonial building. The courtyard garden provides a peaceful setting for traditional hospitality. Accommodations range from double rooms and suites to a five-room cottage—all with private bath, cable TV, and central air/heat; many have fireplaces. The Inn is centrally located in the historic district within easy walking distance of restaurants, shops, and sites.

Host: Joe Finnegan
Rooms: 14 (PB) $65-175
Continental Plus Breakfast
Credit cards: A, B, C, D
Notes: 2, 5, 8, 9, 10, 12

Victorian House Bed and Breakfast

11 Cadiz Street, 32084
(904) 824-5214

The Victorian House, built in 1897, is in the heart of historic St. Augustine, within walking distance of fine restaurants, the waterfront, shops, museums, and the plaza. Rooms have private baths and/or showers. Limited off-street parking. Breakfast, served in the dining room, may include home-cooked sweetbreads, granola, casserole, fruit, juice, and coffee.

Hostess: Daisy Morden Davis
Rooms: 8 (PB) $80-115
Hearty Continental Breakfast
Credit Cards: A, B, C
Notes: 2, 5, 7, 12

ST. PETE BEACH

Island's End Resort

1 Pass-a-Grille Way, 33706
(813) 360-5023; FAX (813) 367-7890

The compelling appeal of all that paradise can offer abounds at Island's End. Deep blue sky, turquoise waters, exotic sunrise, and sweets all work in concert to relax and entertain you. Island's End features six unique, well-appointed guest homes, including a fantastic three-bedroom house with atrium and private pool. Try your hand at fishing day or night from one of the best docks on Florida's west coast. Small private beach only a half block from our beautiful five-mile beach.

Hosts: Jone and Millard Gamble
Rooms: 5 cottages + 1 house (PB) $65-175
Continental served Tues., Thurs., and Saturday
Credit cards: A, B
Notes: 2, 5, 8, 9

ST. PETERSBURG

Mansion House

105 Fifth Avenue NE, 33701
(813) 821-9391 (voice and FAX);
(800) 274-7520 (reservations)
E-mail: mansion1@ix.netcom.com
Web site: http://www.mansionbandb.com

Mansion House, built in 1904 and beautifully restored, has five rooms with private

baths in the main house. A sixth room, the Carriage House, has a cathedral ceiling, four-poster bed, phone, and TV. Common areas include a library/TV room with VCR, sun porch, living room, and patio. Guests have access to kitchen and 24-hour snacks. Antiques from around the world are dispersed throughout the house. Convenient to cultural and sports attractions, water, restaurants, and shopping. Private boat cruises are available on the bay or gulf, with your host as captain. Portuguese is spoken. ABBA 1997 Excellence Award, three crowns. Superior Small Lodging, St. Petersburg/Clearwater Visitors and Convention Bureau. InnPoints travel incentives are awarded to guests. Mansion House offers travel agent commissions and online reservations through ASTRA Net, B&B Direct Worldcom/Places to Stay, and our Web site.

Hosts: Rose Marie and Robert Ray
Rooms: 6 (PB) $95-150
Full Breakfast
Credit Cards: A, B, C
Notes: 2, 5, 7, 8, 9, 10, 12

SAN MATEO

Ferncourt
Bed and Breakfast

150 Central Avenue, PO Box 758, 32187
(904) 329-9755

Built in 1889, this centurian "painted lady" with its seventeen-plus rooms has been restored lovingly by your host and hostess. They delight in sharing this small piece of Florida history with others. You will be served a complimentary gourmet breakfast in our dining room, breakfast room,

welcome; 7 Children welcome; 8 Tennis nearby; 9 Swimming nearby; 10 Golf nearby; 11 Skiing nearby; 12 May be booked through travel agent.

Ferncourt Bed and Breakfast

or, if you choose, on our spacious wrap-around veranda. Located in north central Florida, historic San Mateo was a thriving little town just before the turn of the century. Now only a sleepy hamlet, it offers a quiet place to get away. You are only minutes away from many of Florida's attractions. St. Augustine is only twenty-five minutes away.

Hosts: Jack and Dee Morgan
Rooms: 5 (PB) $55-75
Full Breakfast
Credit Cards: A, B, C, D
Notes: 2, 5, 10, 12

SANFORD

The Higgins House Bed and Breakfast

420 Oak Avenue, 32771
(407) 324-9238; (800) 584-0014;
FAX (407) 324-5060

Enjoy the romance of a bygone era at this 102-year-old Queen Anne Victorian bed and breakfast. Three guest rooms and a cottage all have private baths. Enjoy the Victorian gardens and hot tub. The Higgins

House Bed and Breakfast is located in historic Sanford near beautiful Lake Monroe and the St. Johns River. Antique shops are nearby.

Hosts: Walter and Roberta Padgett
Rooms: 3 + cottage (PB) $95-125
Continental Plus Breakfast
Credit Cards: A, B, C, D
Notes: 2, 5, 8, 10, 12

SEBRING

Kenilworth Lodge

836 SE Lakeview Drive, 33870
(941) 385-0111; (800) 423-5939;
FAX (914) 385-4686
E-mail: mark@ct.net
Web site: http://www.kenlodge.com

The Kenilworth Lodge is a historic inn that was built for "the well-to-do" in 1916 by George Sebring. The Kenilworth maintains its historic status (it soon is expected to be listed on the National Historic Register) while adding the modern conveniences of air-conditioning, satellite TVs, direct-dial phones, and refrigerators in the guest rooms. The Kenilworth Lodge specializes in golf packages, reunions, retreats, dance groups, murder-mystery getaways, and other leisure activities. Its central location makes the Kenilworth an ideal home base for your family's vacation. The Kenilworth Lodge is the perfect bed and breakfast property for the historic-minded traveler who enjoys the independence of an inn.

Hosts: Mark and Madge Stewart
Rooms: 130 (PB) $45-99
Expanded Continental Breakfast
Credit Cards: A, B, C, D
Notes: 2, 3, 4, 5, 7, 8, 9, 10, 11 (water), 12

NOTES: Credit cards accepted: A Master Card; B Visa; C American Express; D Discover; E Diners Club; F Other; 2 Personal checks accepted; 3 Lunch available; 4 Dinner available; 5 Open all year; 6 Pets

STUART

The Homeplace Bed and Breakfast

501 Akron Avenue, 34994
(561) 220-9148; (800) 251-5473;
FAX (561) 221-3265

The Homeplace, Stuart's premier bed and breakfast inn, was built in 1913 and lovingly restored in 1989. The inn is best known for its romantic ambience, quality, and unequaled graciousness. Four guest rooms are air-conditioned and appointed comfortably with antiques. The "wickered" sunporch and turn-of-the-century parlor create a Victorian setting in which to recall pleasurable reminiscences. The lush patio garden, pool, and heated spa beckon you. Stroll or bike to Stuart's newly restored historic area for shopping and fine dining. Located on two-and-a-half acres bordering Frazier Creek.

Hosts: Suzanne and Michael Pescitelli
Rooms: 4 (PB) $85-95 (subject to change)
Full Breakfast
Credit Cards: A, B
Notes: 2, 5, 8, 9 (on site), 10, 12

TARPON SPRINGS

East Lake Bed and Breakfast

421 Old East Lake Road, 34689
(813) 937-5487
E-mail: LittleFlower@Prodigy.com

Private home on two-and-a-half acres, situated on a quiet road along Lake Tarpon, close to the Gulf of Mexico. The hosts are retired businesspeople who en-

joy new friends and are well informed about the area. The room and adjoining bath are at the front of the house, away from the family quarters. The room has central air, color TV, and telephone. Breakfast includes fresh fruit, juice, entrée, and homemade breads and jams. Close to many Florida attractions.

Hosts: Dick and Marie Fiorito
Rooms: 1 (PB) $35 single, $40 double
Full Home-Cooked Breakfast
Credit Cards: none
Notes: 2, 5, 8, 9, 10

WELLBORN

1909 McLeran House Bed and Breakfast

12408 County Road 137, 32094
(904) 963-4603

The 1909 McLeran House offers guests a glimpse into the north Florida (Suwannee River Valley) of a century ago. Restoration of the home has been extensive and meticulous, including central air/heat. There are a huge wraparound front porch and six fireplaces, each with a curly-pine mantle. Furnishings are a tasteful and appropriate blend of old and new. A cedar gazebo crowns the garden area, which includes swing, fountain, arbor, walkways, goldfish pond, the original open well, and lush landscaping. Many local attractions nearby, including the Stephen Foster Folk Culture Center.

Hosts: Robert and Mary Ryals
Rooms: 2 (PB) $65-80
Deluxe Continental Breakfast
Credit Cards: none
Notes: 2, 5, 9, 10

welcome; 7 Children welcome; 8 Tennis nearby; 9 Swimming nearby; 10 Golf nearby; 11 Skiing nearby; 12 May be booked through travel agent.

GEORGIA

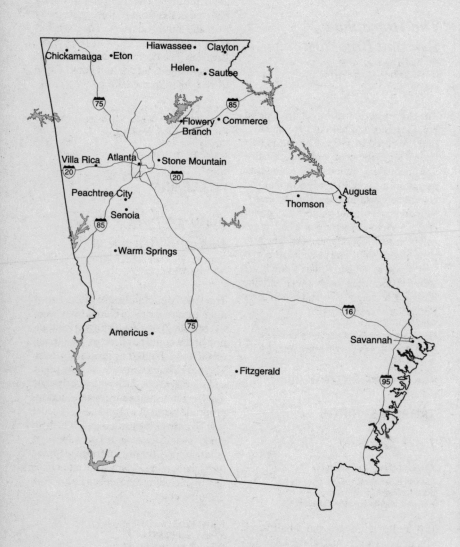

Georgia

RSVP GRITS, INC.

541 Londonberry Rd. NE, **Altlanta**, 30327
(404) 843-3933; (800) 823-7787
FAX (404) 252-8886
E-mail: innfo@aol.com
Web site: http://www.bbonline.com/ga/rsvpgrits

RSVP GRITS, INC. (Great Reservations in the South) represents a select group of B&Bs and inns in the **Atlanta** area, within two hundred miles of Atlanta, in **North Georgia**, and as far east as **Augusta**. We provide personal service and help you plan getaway weekends, romantic retreats, or small seminars. All properties are properly licensed and inspected. Free service. More than forty inns are represented, with private baths. $85-250. MC, Visa, personal checks are accepted. Marty Barnes, coordinator. Free brochure.

AMERICUS

1906 Pathway Inn

501 S. Lee Street, 31709
(912) 928-2078 (voice and FAX);
(800) 889-1466
E-mail: pathway@sowega.net
Web site: http://www.bestinns.net/usa/ga/
    pathway.html

Parlors, porches, whirlpools, down comforters, fireplaces, friends, muffins, and

1906 Pathway Inn

more await you at a 1906 Greek Revival-style inn with stained glass and a sumptuous, candlelit breakfast. Situated between Plains (home of President Carter) and Civil War Andersonville. The Inn is just thirty minutes west of I-75, two-and-a-half hours south of Atlanta. Home of Habitat for Humanity. We spoil business travelers the same as tourists and honeymooners. You will enjoy the candlelit, four-course, silver-service breakfast. On Sunday, attend church and hear President Carter teach Sunday school.

Hosts: David and Sheila Judah
Rooms: 5 (PB) $77-107
Full Breakfast
Credit Cards: A, B
Notes: 2, 5, 6, 7, 8, 10, 12

NOTES: Credit cards accepted: A Master Card; B Visa; C American Express; D Discover; E Diners Club; F Other; 2 Personal checks accepted; 3 Lunch available; 4 Dinner available; 5 Open all year; 6 Pets welcome; 7 Children welcome; 8 Tennis nearby; 9 Swimming nearby; 10 Golf nearby; 11 Skiing nearby; 12 May be booked through travel agent.

ATLANTA

Beverly Hills Inn

65 Sheridan Drive, 30305
(404) 233-8520; (800) 331-8520;
FAX (404) 233-8659
Web site: http://www.beverlyhillsinn.com

The Beverly Hills Inn is a charming, European-style hotel with eighteen suites uniquely decorated with period furnishings. We offer fresh flowers, a continental breakfast, and the little things that count to a traveler. We're a morning star, not a constellation; a solitary path, not a highway. Only some will understand, but then, we don't have room for everybody.

Hosts: Bonnie and Lyle Klienhans
Rooms: 18 (PB) $90-160
Continental Breakfast
Credit Cards: A, B, C, D, E
Notes: 2, 5, 6, 7, 12

Shellmont Bed and Breakfast Lodge

Shellmont Bed and Breakfast Lodge

821 Piedmont Avenue NE, 30308
(404) 872-9290; FAX (404) 872-5379

The Shellmont Bed and Breakfast Lodge is an impeccably restored 1891 National Register mansion located in midtown Atlanta's theater, restaurant and cultural district. It is a virtual treasure chest of stained, leaded and beveled glass, intricately carved woodwork, and hand-painted stenciling. Accommodations are furnished with antiques, Oriental rugs and period wall treatments. Shellmont's wicker-laden verandas overlook beautifully manicured lawns and gardens—including a lovely Victorian fishpond. We believe you will find your experience here to be unforgettable.

Hosts: Ed and Debbie McCord
Rooms: 5 (PB) $105-150
Full Breakfast
Credit Cards: A, B, C, F
Notes: 2, 5, 7 (limited), 8, 10, 12

The Woodruff Bed and Breakfast Inn

223 Ponce de Leon Avenue, 30136
(404) 875-9449; (800) 473-9449;
FAX (404) 875-2882

Prepare yourself for southern charm, hospitality, and a full southern breakfast. The Woodruff Bed and Breakfast Inn is conveniently located in midtown Atlanta. It is a 1906 Victorian home built by a prominent Atlanta family and fully restored by the current owners. Each room has been meticulously decorated with antiques. The Woodruff has a very colorful past, which lends to the charm and history of the building and the city. Close to everything. Ya'll come!

Hosts: Douglas and Joan Jones
Rooms 14 (10PB; 4SB) $89-149
Full Breakfast
Credit Cards: A, B, C, D
Notes: 2, 5, 7, 9, 12

NOTES: Credit cards accepted: A Master Card; B Visa; C American Express; D Discover; E Diners Club; F Other; 2 Personal checks accepted; 3 Lunch available; 4 Dinner available; 5 Open all year; 6 Pets

AUGUSTA

Perrin Guest House Inn

208 LaFayette Drive, 30909
(706) 731-0920; (800) 668-8930;
FAX (706) 731-9009

The Perrin Place is an old cotton plantation home established in 1863. The plantation has long since become the Augusta National Golf Course, home of the Masters, while the three acres of the home place remains a little spot of magnolia heaven surrounded by shopping, golfing, and fine dining. Our guest house has beautifully redecorated bedrooms that feature fireplaces, Jacuzzis, antiques, and comforters. Enjoy the privacy of your own fireplace in spacious accommodations, or share the pleasure of a front porch rocker, the comfort of a cozy parlor, or the cool of a scuppernong arbor with other guests. Weddings, receptions, and other social functions become treasured events when held at the Perrin. Available by reservation only.

Hosts: Ed and Audrey Peel
Rooms: 10 (PB), $75-125
Continental Breakfast
Credit Cards: A, B, C
Notes: 5, 8, 10, 12

CHICKAMAUGA

New Dawn Farm Bed and Breakfast

363 South Cedar Lane, 30707
(706) 539-2235; (888) 775-6689;
E-mail: 103210,3666@compuserve.com

Serene, rural setting within one hour of major recreation lakes, ski slope, historic Chickamauga Military Park, and state parks. Located only thirty minutes from Chattanooga, Tennessee. New Dawn Farm is a modest, newly renovated, four-bedroom home with living room, dining room, and kitchen. Participate in seasonal farm chores or request an old-fashioned wiener roast and hayride (no extra charge). Comfortable, affordable, and offering the most beautiful scenery anywhere. Reservations are requested.

Hostesses: Jennie Everett Chandler and Dedra
    Everett
Rooms: 4 (1PB; 3SB) $30-60
Continental Plus Breakfast
Credit Cards: none
Notes: 2, 5, 6, 7, 10, 11

CLAYTON

English Manor Inns

U.S. 76 East, 30525
(706) 782-5789; (800) 782-5780;
FAX (706) 782-5780 (call ahead)

Each of our seven inns, secluded in a 7.2-acre garden park, includes an impressive, well-appointed living room-dining room area and fully-equipped kitchen, cable television, deck, and covered porch with rockers. Enjoy the perfect romantic getaway or honeymoon in a suite with an oversize Jacuzzi tub. We host church groups, choir retreats, and family reunions. Enjoy wholesome recreation in a relaxing atmosphere. Shopping, restaurants and fast food are nearby.

Hosts: Susan and English Thornwell
Rooms: 42 (PB) $99-169
Full Breakfast
Credit Cards: none
Notes: 2, 5, 7, 8, 9, 10, 11, 12

welcome; 7 Children welcome; 8 Tennis nearby; 9 Swimming nearby; 10 Golf nearby; 11 Skiing nearby;
12 May be booked through travel agent.

The Pittman House Bed and Breakfast

COMMERCE

The Pittman House Bed and Breakfast

81 Homer Road, 30529
(706) 335-3823

The Pittman House Bed and Breakfast is located in the beautiful, rolling hill country of northeastern Georgia in the bustling town of historic Commerce. We invite you to come rock with us on the wraparound porch of our restored 1890s four-square Colonial house, which is furnished throughout with antiques that take you back to a quieter time and enhance the hominess of The Pittman House. Conveniently located within minutes of the University of Georgia, boating, historic Hurricane Shoals, shopping, vineyards, restaurants, and more. Only an hour from Atlanta and its attractions. Three-diamond AAA rating. A seventy-two-hour cancellation notice is required.

Hosts: Tom and Dot Tomberlin
Rooms: 4 (2PB; 2SB) $50-65
Full Breakfast
Credit Cards: A, B
Notes: 2, 5, 7, 8, 9, 10, 11, 12

ETON

Ivy Inn

PO Box 406, 245 Fifth Avenue E., 30724
(706) 517-0526; (800) 201-5477;
FAX (706) 517-0526

Historic 1908 country home was one of the first homes built in Eton. Rocking chair porches offer a break from a busy day shopping for antiques, clothes, or carpet; Eton is part of the carpet capital of the world. Hiking in Cohutta Wilderness or bicycling on the Inn's bikes refreshes the weary soul. In-room telephone and TV. Day trips to Atlanta, Chattanooga, and Ocoee River. Horses/stabling next door to the Inn. Restricted smoking.

Hosts: Gene and Juanita Twiggs
Rooms: 3 (PB) $87
Full Southern Breakfast
Credit Cards: A, B, C
Notes: 2, 5, 9, 10, 11 (water), 12

Ivy Inn

FITZGERALD

Dorminy Massee House

516 W. Central Avenue, 31750
(912) 423-3123; FAX (912) 423-2226

This family-owned, 1915 colonial-style home was designed by architect T.F.

Dorminy Massee House

Lockwood. It includes eight charmingly furnished, air-conditioned bedrooms, each with private bath, television, telephone, and computer modem. Our guests can read, relax, and converse in the elegant dining, living, and parlor areas. Spacious, beautifully landscaped grounds contain fishpool, gazebo, smokehouse, carriage house, and private parking. Walk three blocks to the Blue-Gray Museum and learn about Fitzgerald's unique history—the only town "colonized" by Union and Confederate veterans.

Hosts: Sherry and Mark Massee
Rooms: 8 (PB) $75-85
Continental Breakfast
Credit Cards: A, B
Notes: 2, 5, 7, 8, 10

FLOWERY BRANCH

Whitworth Inn

6593 McEver Road, 30542
(770) 967-2386; FAX (770) 967-2649
E-mail: visit@whitworthinn.com
Web site: http://www.whitworthinn.com

The Whitworth Inn is a contemporary country Inn on five wooded acres offering a relaxing atmosphere. Ten uniquely decorated guest rooms have their own baths.

Two guest living rooms are available. A full country breakfast is served in a large, sunlit dining room. Meeting/party space is available. The Inn is located thirty minutes northeast of Atlanta at Lake Lanier. Nearby attractions and activities include boating, golf, beaches, and water parks. Close to Road Atlanta and Chateau Elen Winery/Golf Course. Easily accessible from major interstates. Three-diamond AAA rating.

Hosts: Ken and Christine Jonick
Rooms: 10 (PB) $55-69
Full Breakfast
Credit Cards: A, B, C
Notes: 2, 5, 7, 8, 9, 10, 12

HELEN

Chattahoochee Ridge Lodge and Cabins

PO Box 175, 30545
(706) 878-3144; (800) 476-8331

Alone on a woodsy mountain above a waterfall, the Lodge has five new rooms and suites (kitchens and fireplaces) with private entrances, TV, air-conditioning, free phones, and Jacuzzi; plus double insulation and back-up solar for stewards of the earth. In the lodge and cabins you'll like the quiet seclusion, large windows, and deep-rock water. We'll help you plan great vacation days. Decor includes wide-board knotty pine, brass beds, full carpeting, and paddle fans.

Hosts: Bob and Mary Swift
Rooms: 5 + cabins (PB) $50-85
Credit Cards: A, B, C, D
Notes: 2, 5, 7, 8, 9, 10

---

welcome; 7 Children welcome; 8 Tennis nearby; 9 Swimming nearby; 10 Golf nearby; 11 Skiing nearby; 12 May be booked through travel agent.

Henson Cove Place Bed and Breakfast

HIAWASSEE

Henson Cove Place Bed and Breakfast

3840 Car Miles Road, 30546-9585
(706) 896-6195; (800) 714-5542;
FAX (706) 896-5252
E-mail: nle@yhc.edu
Web site: http://www.yhc.edu/users/nle

Henson Cove Place Bed and Breakfast is a unique lodging in northeast Georgia near Hiawassee in the mountains. Guests can relax on the front porch swing or rockers and view Kelly Ridge or watch the cows nearby. A full breakfast is prepared on a 1929 Tappan gas range. A cabin in the woods is also available. Come and stay with us—we treat you like family.

Hosts: Bill and Nancy Leffingwell
Rooms: 2 (PB) $60
Full Breakfast
Credit Cards: A, B
Notes: 2, 5, 8, 9, 10, 11

PEACHTREE CITY

Everhill Manor

114 Kirton Turn, 30269
(770) 631-4369

Located forty minutes from the heart of Atlanta. Colonial-style home offers an-

tique furnishings in two large guest rooms with private baths. Full breakfast in the dining room or on the screened porch overlooking the garden. Our unique community is noted for its sixty-five miles of recreational paths for walking, biking, or driving a golf cart to shopping areas, fishponds, playgrounds, and quiet spots beside the lake. Scenic and historical sites nearby. Guided tours available.

Hosts: Janet and David Hendry
Rooms: 2 (PB) $55
Full Breakfast
Credit Cards: none
Notes: 5, 7, 8, 9, 10

SAUTEE

The Stovall House Country Inn and Restaurant

1526 Highway 225 N., 30571
(706) 878-3355

Our 1837 Victorian farmhouse, restored in 1983, is listed on the National Register of Historic Places. Located on twenty-six acres in the historic Sautee Valley, the Inn has views of the mountains in all directions. The recipient of several awards for its attentive restorations, the Inn is furnished with family antiques and decorated with hand-stenciling. The restaurant, open to the public, features regional cuisine prepared with a fresh difference and served in an intimate yet informal setting. It's a country experience!

Host: Hamilton (Ham) Schwartz
Rooms: 5 (PB) $64-80
Continental Breakfast
Credit Cards: A, B
Notes: 2, 4, 5, 7, 8, 9, 10

NOTES: Credit cards accepted: A Master Card; B Visa; C American Express; D Discover; E Diners Club; F Other; 2 Personal checks accepted; 3 Lunch available; 4 Dinner available; 5 Open all year; 6 Pets

SAVANNAH

Bed and Breakfast Inn

117 W. Gordon Street at Chatham Square, 31401
(912) 238-0518; FAX (912) 238-0518
E-mail: b&binn@biztrac.com

Experience the charm of Savannah as a guest in our restored 1853 Federal row house on historic Gordon Row. Located in the heart of Savannah's historic district overlooking beautiful Chatham Square, the Bed and Breakfast Inn is situated amidst noble old mansions, museums, restaurants, churches and antique shops. Enjoy our southern hospitality—from the warm greeting upon entering the Inn, to a visit in our lovely gardens, to a good night's rest and a hearty home-style breakfast.

Host: Bob McAlister
Rooms: 14 (11PB; 3SB) $45-95
Full Breakfast
Credit Cards: A, B, C, D
Notes: 2, 5, 6, 7, 8, 9, 10, 12

Eliza Thompson House

5 West Jones Street, 31401
(912) 236-3620; (800) 348-9378;
FAX (912) 238-1920
E-mail: Elizath@aol.com
Web site: http://www.bbonline.com

Built in 1847, our elegant inn is in the heart of Savannah's historic district. Our twenty-three lovely guest rooms offer four-poster beds, antiques, and private baths. Enjoy breakfast and evening wine and cheese in our beautiful courtyard, as well as dessert after dinner in our parlor.

Host: Carol L. Day
Rooms: 23 (PB) $89-189
Full Breakfast
Credit Cards: A, B
Notes: 2, 5, 9, 12

Joan's on Jones Bed and Breakfast

17 W. Jones Street, 31401
(912) 234-3863; (800) 407-3863
FAX (912) 234-1455

In the heart of the historic district, two charming bed and breakfast suites grace the garden level of this three-story Victorian, private home. Each suite has a private entry, off-street parking, bedroom, sitting room, kitchen, bath, private phone, and cable TV. Note the original heart pine floors, period furnishings, and Savannah gray brick walls. Innkeepers Joan and Gary Levy, restaurateurs, live upstairs and invite you for a tour of their home if you're staying two nights or more.

Hosts: Joan and Gary Levy
Rooms: 2 suites (PB) $115-130
Continental Breakfast
Credit Cards: none
Notes: 2, 5, 6 (limited), 7, 8, 9, 10, 12

Lion's Head Inn

120 E. Gaston Street, 31401
(912) 232-4580 (voice and FAX); (800) 355-5466

The stately 19th-century mansion is in a quiet neighborhood just north of picturesque Forsyth Park. This lovely, 9,200-square-foot home is exquisitely appointed with four-poster beds, private baths, period furnishings, fireplaces, televisions, and phones. Each morning, enjoy a deluxe continental breakfast. Each evening, have wine and cheese on the veranda overlooking the marbled courtyard.

Hostess: Christy Dell'Orco
Rooms: 7 (PB) $90-190
Continental Deluxe Breakfast
Credit Cards: A, B, C, D
Notes: 2, 5, 7, 8, 9, 10, 12

---

welcome; 7 Children welcome; 8 Tennis nearby; 9 Swimming nearby; 10 Golf nearby; 11 Skiing nearby; 12 May be booked through travel agent.

SENOIA

Culpepper House B&B

35 Broad Street, 30276
(770) 599-8182

Step back 120 years to casual Victorian elegance. Enjoy a four-poster canopy bed next to a fireplace, with sounds of the night coming through the window. Wake to a gourmet breakfast, then take a tandem bike ride through the historic town of Senoia, visit area shops and tour the picturesque countryside, or just sit on the porch and rock. We are only thirty minutes from Atlanta.

Hostesses: Maggie and Barb
Rooms: 3 (PB) $85
Full Gourmet Breakfast
Credit Cards: A, B, C, D
Notes: 2, 5, 8, 9, 10, 12

The Village Inn Bed and Breakfast

STONE MOUNTAIN

The Village Inn B&B

992 Ridge Avenue, 30083
(770) 469-3459; (800) 214-8385;
FAX (770) 469-1051

We welcome you to our circa-1850 bed and breakfast in the quaint village of Stone Mountain, just outside Stone Mountain State Park (fifteen miles east of Atlanta). Five charming bedrooms and one suite have private baths. Guests enjoy whirlpool tubs, fireplaces, period antiques, ceiling fans, and central air-conditioning. One block from shopping, restaurants, and churches. Full country breakfast served family-style. Complimentary snacks and turn-down. Come experience true southern hospitality!

Hosts: Rob and Deandra Bailey
Rooms: 6 (PB) $85-125
Full Breakfast
Credit Cards: A, B, C, D
Notes: 2, 7, 8, 9, 10, 12

THOMSON

1810 West Inn

254 N. Seymour Drive, 30824
(800) 515-1810
Web site: http://www.bbonline.com/ga/1810west

The property includes a historic, restored farmhouse, circa 1810, and accompanying renovated country houses on twelve landscaped acres. All rooms have private baths, central air and heat, antique furnishings, and fireplaces. Enjoy the country kitchen, screened veranda, strolling peacocks, and nature trails. A continental breakfast is served. The Inn is ideal for business retreats. It has been featured in *Country Inns Magazine* and was named a "Great Inn of Georgia." It is convenient to I-20 and Augusta; two hours from Atlanta.

Hostess: Virginia White
Rooms: 10 (PB) $60-79
Extended Continental Breakfast
Credit Cards: A, B, C, D, F
Notes: 2, 5, 8, 9, 10, 12

NOTES: Credit cards accepted: A Master Card; B Visa; C American Express; D Discover; E Diners Club; F Other; 2 Personal checks accepted; 3 Lunch available; 4 Dinner available; 5 Open all year; 6 Pets

VILLA RICA

Twin Oaks Bed and Breakfast Cottages

9565 E. Liberty Road, 30180
(770) 459-4374; FAX (770) 459-5156

A uniquely intimate bed and breakfast located on a twenty-three-acre farm only thirty minutes from Atlanta. There are two exquisite guest cottages ideal for honeymoons or celebrating anniversaries. Cottages have CD/tape players; we furnish blues and jazz CDs. There are also two private suites on the property. All accommodations have hot tubs or Jacuzzis, fireplaces, private bathrooms, queen-size beds, TVs, VCRs, refrigerators, microwaves, and coffeemakers. Guests may enjoy a swimming pool, walking trails, horseback riding, and lots of exotic animals for feeding and viewing. (Our pet pig, "Elmer Leroy," enjoys scraps from supper!) Located near Six Flags Over Georgia and the projected *Gone With the Wind* theme park.

Hosts: Earl and Carol Turner
Rooms: 2 suites; 2 cottages (PB) $100-145
Full Breakfast
Credit Cards: C
Notes: 2, 5, 9, 10, 12

WARM SPRINGS

Hotel Warm Springs Bed and Breakfast Inn

PO Box 351, 31830
(706) 655-2114; (800) 366-7616;
FAX (706) 655-2771

"Presidents, passion and the past." Relive history and the Roosevelt Era in our 1907 hotel, ice cream parlor, and gift shops. Authentically restored and beautifully decorated with Roosevelt furniture and family antiques. Featuring our cozy honeymoon suite with king bed, suspended canopy, Victorian antiques, red heart tub, gold fixtures, breakfast in bed, flowers, champagne, and chocolates. Our large living room and dining room with Queen Anne furniture, Oriental rugs, and crystal teardrop chandelier is ideal for group meetings. Nestled in quaint Warm Springs Village—a shopper's paradise, home of FDR's Little White House, fourteen miles from Callaway Gardens and one hour from Atlanta. Award-winning cheese grits and homemade peach ice cream.

Host: Gerrie Thompson
Rooms: 14 (PB) $70-167
Full Breakfast
Credit Cards: A, B, C, D
Notes: 2, 5, 7, 8, 9, 10, 12

welcome; 7 Children welcome; 8 Tennis nearby; 9 Swimming nearby; 10 Golf nearby; 11 Skiing nearby; 12 May be booked through travel agent.

HAWAII

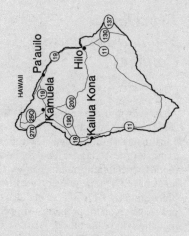

Hawaii

Pacific-Hawaii Bed and Breakfast Reservation Service

99-1661 Aiea Heights Drive, 96701
(800) 999-6026 (voice and FAX); (888) 262-6026

Reservation Service since 1982. Unique accommodations on all Hawaiian islands. We'll match your requirements for vacation homes, cottages, or bed and breakfasts. We seek to provide the traveler with a sense of connecting with a new friend, and strive for you to establish a bond with the local people here in Hawaii. We also can meet your language requirements; some of our hosts speak German, Spanish, Japanese, French. Three-day minimum stay. From $60 for two guests for B&B studio units. Doris Reichert, coordinator.

HAWAII—HILO

Hale Kai Bjornen

111 Honolii Pali, 96720
(808) 935-6330; FAX (808) 935-8439

Beautiful four-star bed and breakfast on the ocean bluff facing Hilo Bay and Honolii surfing beach. All rooms face the ocean and have private baths. There are fresh flowers in all rooms and bathrooms. A full gourmet breakfast is served, with such items as macadamia nut waffles, sausage, huge fruit platters, local juices, and kona coffee. Swimming pool and hot tub. Two miles from downtown. Very quiet area. Hosts help with directions, restaurants. Friendly Christians. We also have a two-bedroom, two-and-a-half-bath condo available on the ocean in Hilo for weekly or monthly rental.

Hosts: Evonne and Paul Bjornen
Rooms: 5 (PB) $85-105
Full Gourmet Breakfast
Credit Cards: none
Notes: 2, 5, 7, 8, 9, 10, 11, 12

HAWAII—KAMUELA

Kamuela Inn

PO Box 1994, 96743
(808) 885-4243; (800) 555-8968;
FAX (808) 885-8857

The Kamuela Inn offers comfortable, cozy rooms and suites with private baths, with or without kitchenettes, all with cable, color television. A complimentary continental breakfast is served in our coffee lanai each

---

NOTES: Credit cards accepted: A Master Card; B Visa; C American Express; D Discover; E Diners Club; F Other; 2 Personal checks accepted; 3 Lunch available; 4 Dinner available; 5 Open all year; 6 Pets welcome; 7 Children welcome; 8 Tennis nearby; 9 Swimming nearby; 10 Golf nearby; 11 Skiing nearby; 12 May be booked through travel agent.

morning. The inn is situated in a quiet, peaceful setting just off Highway 19. It is conveniently located near shops, retail outlets, banks, theaters, parks, tennis courts, museums, restaurants, and the post office. The big island's famous white sand beaches, golf courses, horseback rides, and valley and mountain tours are only minutes away.

Hostess: Carolyn Cascavilla
Rooms: 31 (PB) $54
Continental Breakfast
Credit Cards: A, B, C, D, E
Notes: 2, 5, 7, 8, 9, 10, 11, 12

HAWAII—PA'AUILO

Sud's Acres Bed and Breakfast

43-1973 Paauilo Mauka Road, 96776
(808) 776-1611 (voice and FAX);
(800) 735-3262

Our cozy two-bedroom cottage, with its complete kitchen and microwave oven, comfortably sleeps a family of five. It is situated on a macadamia nut farm at an elevation of eighteen hundred feet on the slopes of Mauna Kea. In our main house we have additional guest accommodations and provide wheelchair access. Sud's Acres Bed and Breakfast is are located forty miles north of Hilo airport, twenty miles from Waimea, and thirty miles from some of Hawaii's best beaches.

Hosts: "Suds" and Anita Suderman
Rooms: 3 (PB) $65
Continental Breakfast
Credit Cards: A, B, D, E
Notes: 5, 7, 9, 10, 12

KAILUA—KONA

Kiwi Gardens Bed and Breakfast

74-4920 Kiwi Street, 96740
(808) 326-1559; FAX (808) 329-6618
E-mail: kiwi@ilhawaii.net
Web site: http://www.keycommunications.com/ hawaii

We are located on the Big Island of Hawaii, nine miles southeast of Kona airport. We are on an acre with more than a hundred plants and fruit trees. Fresh fruit served from our grounds. First-floor (no steps) Master Suite has private bath (large shower and tub), king-size bed, French doors to sunset view of lanai, TV, refrigerator. Queen Room has queen bed and French doors to lanai; shares bath (shower) with Wicker Room—two beds, TV. Garden Tiki Room is in our back gardens. Private phone line for guests. No smoking.

Hosts: Shirlee and Ron
Rooms: 4 (2PB; 2SB) $65-85
Continental Breakfast
Credit Cards: none
Notes: 5, 7, 8, 9, 10, 11, 12

KAUAI—PRINCEVILLE

Hale 'Aha— "House of Gathering"

3875 Kamehameha Drive, PO Box 3370, 96722
(808) 826-6733; (800) 826-6733;
FAX (808) 826-9052
E-mail: kauai@pixi.com
Web site: http://oceandream.com/kauai/hale_aha

Vacation, honeymoon, or retreat in this peaceful resort setting on the golf course,

---

NOTES: Credit cards accepted: A Master Card; B Visa; C American Express; D Discover; E Diners Club; F Other; 2 Personal checks accepted; 3 Lunch available; 4 Dinner available; 5 Open all year; 6 Pets

overlooking the ocean and majestic mountains of the Garden Isle. On one side enjoy Hanalei, where *South Pacific* was filmed, with one beach after another leading you to the famous, lush, Napoli Coast hiking trails. Hale 'Aha has been written about in many books and magazines, but only a brochure can tell it all. Enjoy bananas, papayas, and pineapple from your hosts' garden.

Hosts: Herb and Ruth Bockelman
Rooms: 2 + 2 suites (PB) $85-220
"More Than" Continental Breakfast
Credit Cards: A, B
Notes: 2, 5, 8, 9, 10, 12

MAUI—KULA

Elaine's Up Country Guest Rooms

2112 Noalae Road, 96790
(808) 878-6623

Located in a quiet country setting with splendid ocean and mountain views. All rooms have private baths, full kitchens, and sitting room privileges. Guests are welcome to cook breakfast or whatever meals they like. Next to our main house is a delightful cottage made to order for a family; it has one bedroom with queen-size bed and twin beds in the loft. Large kitchen. We ask that our guests do not smoke or drink.

Hosts: Elaine and Murray Gildersleeve
Rooms: 3 + cottage (PB) $55-110
No Breakfast
Credit Cards: none
Notes: 2, 5, 7, 9, 10, 12

MAUI—LAHAINA

The Guesthouse

1620 Ainakea Road, 96761
(808) 661-8085; (800) 621-8942;
FAX (808) 661-1896
E-mail: 76725, 3473@compuserve.com
Web site: http://ourworld.compserve.com/
    homepages/guesthouse

Conveniently located between the historic whaling town of Lahaina and the beach resort of Kaanapali, the Guesthouse offers a choice of five guest rooms, each with a different touch of Aloha. All have air conditioning, televisions, and refrigerators; a private Jacuzzi has been added to our honeymoon suites. You may enjoy the conveniences of home with our modern kitchen and laundry facilities. Relax at poolside or take a short stroll to the beach. We know your visit will be special, so expect outstanding accommodations at moderate prices.

Hosts: Tanna Swanson, Tammy and Raphael Djoa
Rooms: 5 (4PB; 1SB) $59-89
Full Breakfast
Credit Cards: A, B, C, D
Notes: 2, 5, 7 (over 12), 8, 9, 10, 12

Old Lahaina House

PO Box 10355, 96761
(808) 667-4663; (800) 847-0761
FAX (808) 667-5615
Web site: http://www.mauiweb.com/maui/olhouse

We are on the outskirts of Lahaina, one minute from the beach. Two rooms with king-size beds; two rooms with two twin beds each. All rooms are air-conditioned and have television, phone, and private bath. We also offer one budget room for

welcome; 7 Children welcome; 8 Tennis nearby; 9 Swimming nearby; 10 Golf nearby; 11 Skiing nearby; 12 May be booked through travel agent.

one person at $50, with shared bath. Pool and tropical courtyard.

Hosts: John and Sherry Barbier
Rooms: 5 (4PB; 1SB) $69-95
Continental Breakfast
Credit Cards: A, B, C
Notes: 2, 5, 7, 8, 9, 10, 12

OAHU—AIEA

Pacific-Hawaii Bed and Breakfast

99-1661 Aiea Heights Drive, 96701
(800) 999-6026 (voice and FAX); (888) 262-6026

Enjoy picturesque Kailua and Lanikai, bordering a beautiful mountain range. Some consider it the finest beach in the USA. The bed and breakfast is located in a small residential community, yet within a half hour's drive of the night life of Waikiki. It offers a studio unit and one-bedroom apartment with a separate entrance in a private residence. Quarters are completely furnished and comfortable. Make this your home away from home. Come alone to this quaint hideaway, or bring your family.

Hostess: Doris Reichert
Rooms: 2 (PB) $60-100
Continental Breakfast
Credit Cards: A, B
Notes: 5, 7, 8, 9, 10, 12

NOTES: Credit cards accepted: A Master Card; B Visa; C American Express; D Discover; E Diners Club; F Other; 2 Personal checks accepted; 3 Lunch available; 4 Dinner available; 5 Open all year; 6 Pets

Idaho

COEUR D'ALENE

Gregory's McFarland House Bed and Breakfast

601 Foster Avenue, 83814
(208) 667-1232

Gregory's McFarland House

Surrender to the elegance of this award-winning historical home, circa 1905. The full breakfast is gourmet to the last crumb. Guests will be delighted by an ideal blending of beauty, comfort, and clean surroundings. Jerry Hulse, travel editor for *The Los Angeles Times*, wrote, "Entering Gregory's McFarland House is like stepping back one hundred years to an unhurried time when four posters were in fashion and lace curtains fluttered at the windows." Guest rooms offer private baths and are air-conditioned. This is a nonsmoking house. If you're planning a wedding, our resident minister and professional photographer are available to make your special day beautiful.

Hosts: Winifred, Carol, and Stephen Gregory
Rooms: 5 (PB) $85-125
Full Gourmet Breakfast
Credit Cards: A, B
Notes: 2, 5, 8, 9, 10, 11, 12

Katie's Wild Rose Inn

E. 5150 Couer d'Alene Lake Drive, 83814
(208) 765-9474; (800) 371-4345

Looking through the pine trees to Lake Coeur d'Alene, Katie's Wild Rose Inn is a haven for the weary traveler. Less than a mile from the public dock and beach, the inn has four cozy rooms, one with its own Jacuzzi. Guests can relax in the family room beside the fireplace or enjoy a game of pool. A full breakfast is served on the deck or in the dining room where you can admire the view.

Hosts: Lee and Joisse Knowles
Rooms: 4 (2PB; 2SB) $55-117
Full Breakfast
Credit Cards: A, B
Notes: 2, 5, 8, 9, 10, 11

---

welcome; 7 Children welcome; 8 Tennis nearby; 9 Swimming nearby; 10 Golf nearby; 11 Skiing nearby; 12 May be booked through travel agent.

IDAHO

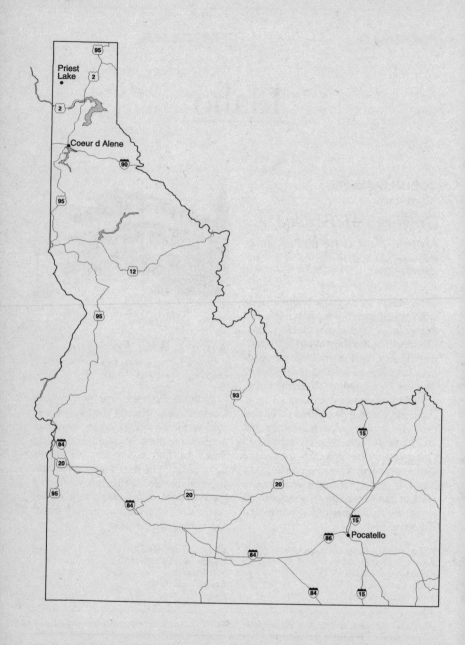

POCATELLO

Back o' Beyond
Bed and Breakfast Inn

404 S. Garfield Avenue; 83204
(208) 232-3825; FAX (208) 232-2771

An 1893 Victorian home, restored with lovely antiques. "Your home along the Oregon Trail" features three comfortable rooms with private baths and a pioneer patio to hear the author discuss his book about the Trail. The old-fashioned front porch beckons guests to linger with cookies, tea or lemonade. A full country breakfast is served in the old dining. The Inn is near downtown Old Pocatello, skiing, and the Fort Hall Replica.

Hosts: Jay and Sherrie Mennenga
Rooms: 3 (PB) $65
Full Breakfast
Credit Cards: A, B, C, D
Notes: 2, 3, 4, 5, 8, 10, 11, 12

PRIEST LAKE

Whispering Waters
Bed and Breakfast

HCR 5, Box 125 B, 83856
(208) 443-3229
Web site: http://www.nidlink.com/
  ~rocktrav.wwbb.html

Located on the secluded shores of Priest Lake's Outlet Bay. Just minutes away from golf course, hiking, cross-country skiing and snowmobiling trails, gift shops, resorts, and restaurants. Three guest rooms; each has private bath, sitting area with parlor stove, view, outside access, and covered patio. Early morning juice or coffee delivered to the rooms.

Hosts: Lana and Ray Feldman
Rooms: 3 (PB) $85
Full Breakfast
Credit Cards: A, B, D
Notes: 2, 5, 9, 10, 11 (cross country), 12

NOTES: Credit cards accepted: A Master Card; B Visa; C American Express; D Discover; E Diners Club; F Other; 2 Personal checks accepted; 3 Lunch available; 4 Dinner available; 5 Open all year; 6 Pets welcome; 7 Children welcome; 8 Tennis nearby; 9 Swimming nearby; 10 Golf nearby; 11 Skiing nearby; 12 May be booked through travel agent.

ILLINOIS

Illinois

ALGONQUIN

Victorian Rose Garden Bed and Breakfast

314 Washington Street, 60102
(847) 854-9667; (888) 854-9667;
FAX (847) 854-3236
Web site: http://www.7comm.com/rosegarden

Built in 1886, the Victorian Rose Garden invites guests to relax on its wraparound porch, to read by the fireplace, to play the baby grand piano, and to enjoy the old-fashioned barber corner. Bedrooms are individually decorated with antiques and collectibles. A delicious breakfast is served formally in the dining room each morning. Nearby are golf courses, antiques, a bike trail, restaurants, and a dinner boat. Chicago is only one hour away. The Victorian Rose Garden is a nonsmoking, nonalcoholic, animal-free residence. Special guest packages are available. Let us pamper you!

Hosts: Don and Sherry Brewer
Rooms: 5 (3PB; 2SB) $65-135
Full Breakfast
Credit Cards: A, B, C
Notes: 2, 5, 7 (over 12), 10, 12

ARCOLA

Curly's Corner Bed and Breakfast

425 E. County Road 200 N., 61910
(217) 268-3352

Our ranch-style, centrally air-conditioned farmhouse is in the heart of prairie farmland in a quiet Amish community. Hosts Warren and Maxine Arthur are dedicated to cordial hospitality and gladly will share information about the area and provide a suggested tour of Amish businesses. Curly's Corner Bed and Breakfast has four lovely and comfortable guest bedrooms with queen-size beds, televisions, etc. In the morning, you may enjoy a wonderful breakfast of homemade biscuits, fresh country sausage, bacon, eggs, etc. Curly's Corner is one-half mile north of beautiful Rockome Gardens; it also is close to three universities and various historical sites.

Hosts: Warren and Maxine Arthur
Rooms: 3 (2PB; 1SB) $50-60
Full Breakfast
Credit Cards: none
Notes: 2, 5, 7 (over 10), 8, 9, 10

NOTES: Credit cards accepted: A Master Card; B Visa; C American Express; D Discover; E Diners Club; F Other; 2 Personal checks accepted; 3 Lunch available; 4 Dinner available; 5 Open all year; 6 Pets welcome; 7 Children welcome; 8 Tennis nearby; 9 Swimming nearby; 10 Golf nearby; 11 Skiing nearby; 12 May be booked through travel agent.

ARTHUR

Heart and Home

137 E. Illinois Street, 61911
(217) 543-2910

Heart of Illinois Amish country. Built in 1911, it is a Victorian filled with the warmth of oak floors and stained-glass windows. Large front porch and second-story sunporch for your relaxation. Three nice guest rooms, one with a pull-out Murphy bed ideal for an additional guest. All rooms are upstairs (not handicap-accessible). Smoke- and alcohol-free. Two blocks from downtown. Central air. Open Thursdays, Fridays, and Saturdays, April through October.

Hosts: Don and Amanda Miller
Rooms: 3 (1PB; 2SB) $50-60
Full Breakfast
Credit Cards: none
Notes: 2, 8

BELLEVILLE

Swans Court Bed and Breakfast

421 Court Street, 62220
(618) 233-0779

Swans Court Bed and Breakfast is located in a federal historic district. Built in 1883, the house was restored in 1995. Furnished in period antiques, it reflects the gracious lifestyle of an earlier time without sacrificing modern amenities. Swans Court is within walking distance of shops, restaurants, and historical houses. Besides the many nearby attractions of southwestern

Swans Court Bed and Breakfast

Illinois, it is an easy twenty-minute drive to the recreational attractions of downtown St. Louis.

Hostess: Monty Dixon
Rooms: 4 (2PB; 2SB) $65-80
Full Breakfast
Credit Cards: A, B
Notes: 2, 5, 10, 12

BLOOMINGTON

Vrooman Mansion— A Bed and Breakfast Hospitality Establishment

701 E. Taylor, 61701
(309) 828-8816; (800) 524-6782;
FAX (309) 828-3148

A historic retreat in Italianate grandeur. Come stay at a fabulous mansion with original woodwork and stained-glass windows. This historic mansion was built in 1869 and added onto in 1900. Many dignitaries and other famous individuals have stayed and dined at the home.

Hosts: John and Nanako McEntire
Rooms: 5 (1PB; 4SB) $75-90
Gourmet Continental Breakfast
Credit Cards: A, B

NOTES: Credit cards accepted: A Master Card; B Visa; C American Express; D Discover; E Diners Club; F Other; 2 Personal checks accepted; 3 Lunch available; 4 Dinner available; 5 Open all year; 6 Pets

CHAMPAIGN

Grandma Joan's Homestay

2204 Brett Drive, 61821
(217) 356-5828
E-mail: jge@uiue.edu

This comfortable, contemporary home features multilevel decks, outdoor spa, screened-in porch, two fireplaces, and a collection of modern and folk art. Grandma pampers you with cookies and milk at bedtime and a healthy breakfast in the morning. Ten minutes from the University of Illinois and several parks and recreational options. Let this be your home away from home.

Hostess: Joan Erikson
Rooms: 3 (1PB; 2SB) $50-80
Full Breakfast
Credit Cards: none
Notes: 2, 5, 8, 9, 10

CHICAGO

Amber Creek's Chicago Connection

1260 N. Dearborn, Chicago;
Mail: 122 S. Bench Street, Galena, 61036
(815) 777-8400; FAX (815) 777-8446

A charming apartment on Chicago's Gold Coast in a quiet, secure building. Services on the main floor include Chicago's most popular coffeehouse. Tastefully decorated, spacious living room with nice views, including the lake. Full kitchen and bath. Romantic bedroom with king-size bed, down quilts, and extra pillows. Linens and towels provided. Walk to lake, restaurants, night life, Water Tower, and

Michigan Avenue shopping. Half block to airport limousine and public transportation. Parking garage next door. Ideal for one couple. Queen-size futon provides sleeping for additional guests.

Hosts: Kate Freeman
Rooms: 1 (PB) $89-129
Continental Breakfast
Credit Cards: A, B, C, D, E
Notes: 2, 3, 5, 7, 9, 12

Bed and Breakfast/ Chicago, Incorporated

PO Box 14088, 60614
(312) 951-0085; FAX (312) 649-9243
E-mail: BnBChicago@aol.com

A reservation service providing comfortable, reasonably priced lodging in private homes; furnished, "self-catering" apartments; and guest houses. Most are in the center of Chicago or close to it.

Host: Mary Shaw
Rooms: 150 (99 percent PB)
Continental Breakfast
Credit Cards: A, B, C, D
Notes: 2, 5, 7

ELDRED

Bluffdale Vacation Farm

Route 1, Box 145, 62027
(217) 983-2854

Our new hideaway cottage in the woods is secluded and luxurious. Soak in the whirlpool while you watch the sun set or gaze at the stars, then pop on a robe and enter your room where the fireplace is blazing. From this location at the base of the bluffs, you'll have two hundred acres of woodlands to explore by foot or horse. Whatever your recreational and culinary

welcome; 7 Children welcome; 8 Tennis nearby; 9 Swimming nearby; 10 Golf nearby; 11 Skiing nearby; 12 May be booked through travel agent.

desires, you'll find them at Bluffdale in the warmth and hospitality of your hosts.

Hosts: Bill and Lindy Hobson
Rooms: 2 (PB) $85
Full Breakfast
Credit Cards: none
Notes: 2, 3, 4, 5, 7, 9, 10, 12

GALENA

Avery Guest House

606 S. Prospect Street, 61036
(815) 777-3883
E-mail: avery@galenalink.com
Web site: http://www.worksweb.com/avery

This Pre-Civil War home located near Galena's main shopping and historic buildings is a homey refuge after a day of exploring. Enjoy the view from our porch swing, feel free to watch TV, or join a table game. Sleep soundly on comfortable queen beds. Our delicious full breakfast is served in our sunny dining room with a bay window overlooking the valley. Mississippi riverboats nearby.

Hosts: Gerry and Armon Lamparelli
Rooms: 3 (1PB; 2SB) $65-85
Full Breakfast
Credit Cards: A, B, D
Notes: 2, 5, 8, 9, 10, 11

Avery Guest House

Belle Aire Mansion Guest House

11410 Route 20 West, 61036
(815) 777-0893

Belle Aire Mansion Guest House is a pre-Civil War Federal home surrounded by eleven well-groomed acres that include extensive lawns, flowers, and a block-long, tree-lined driveway. Whirlpool and fireplace suites available. We do our best to make our guests feel they are special friends.

Hosts: Jan and Lorraine Svec
Rooms: 5 (PB) $70-160
Full Breakfast
Credit Cards: A, B, D
Notes: 2, 7, 8, 10, 12

Bielenda's Mars Avenue Guest Home

Bielenda's Mars Avenue Guest Home

515 Mars Avenue, 61036
(815) 777-2808; FAX (815) 777-1157
E-mail: bmarsbb@galenalink.com
Web site: http://homepage.interaccess.com/
~marsbbl

Bielenda's Mars Avenue Guest Home was built in 1855. It is a Federal-style home in

---

NOTES: Credit cards accepted: A Master Card; B Visa; C American Express; D Discover; E Diners Club; F Other; 2 Personal checks accepted; 3 Lunch available; 4 Dinner available; 5 Open all year; 6 Pets

the historic district of Galena. Three guest suites all have private baths. Country decor and antiques are displayed throughout. The unique, customized stenciling adds a special touch. A fireplace warms the living room, and a large porch offers a swing. Breakfast is full and plenty. Coffee is served to guest rooms an hour before breakfast. Cookies and desserts are available in the afternoon and evening.

Hosts: Michael and Joanne Bielenda
Rooms: 3 (PB) $85-95
Full Breakfast
Credit Cards: A, B, D
Notes: 2, 5

Brierwreath Manor B&B

216 N. Bench Street, 61036
(815) 777-0608

Brierwreath Manor, circa 1884, is just one block from Galena's Main Street and has a dramatic, inviting wraparound porch that beckons after a hard day. The house is furnished in an eclectic blend of antique and early American. You'll not only relax but feel right at home. Two suites offer gas log fireplaces. Central air-conditioning, ceiling fans, and cable TV add to your enjoyment.

Hosts: Mike and Lyn Cook
Rooms: 3 (PB) $85-105
Full Breakfast
Credit Cards: none
Notes: 2, 5, 8, 9, 10, 11

Cottage at Amber Creek

122 S. Bench Street, 61036
(815) 777-8400; FAX (815) 777-8446

Three hundred acres of woods and meadows will be yours to explore on this horse ranch secluded in hills twenty minutes from Galena. The Cottage at Amber Creek is a comfortable, one-bedroom cottage with a fireplace, whirlpool and full kitchen, set behind the main house with trees all around. A deck with grill for dining al fresco, sunbathing, or just relaxing faces a private garden with a fountain. The meadow beyond provides wonderful views of the stars and Milky Way at night. In the evening, roast marshmallows around the campfire while the owls, frogs, and coyotes serenade you.

Hostess: Kate Freeman
Rooms: 1 (PB) $89-149
Continental Breakfast
Credit Cards: A, B, C, D, E
Notes: 2, 5, 6, 8, 9, 10, 11, 12

Eagle's Nest

122 S. Bench Street, 61036
(815) 777-8400; FAX (815) 777-8446

The Eagle's Nest is a charming 1842 Federal brick cottage tucked into a wooded hillside in the historic district, within walking distance of shops and restaurants. It has been faithfully restored and furnished with period antiques. It includes a living room with fireplace, master bedroom with queen-size bed, and second bedroom with double bed. Guests have a fully equipped kitchen, bath with shower and double whirlpool, TV, stereo, deck, and grill. Linens and towels are provided. Perfect for history and antique buffs. Ideal for one couple; will accommodate two couples or a small family.

Hostess: Kate Freeman
Rooms: 1 (PB) $89-149
Credit Cards: A, B, C, D, E
Notes: 2, 5, 6, 7, 8, 9, 10, 11

welcome; 7 Children welcome; 8 Tennis nearby; 9 Swimming nearby; 10 Golf nearby; 11 Skiing nearby; 12 May be booked through travel agent.

Forget-Me-Not Bed and Breakfast

Forget-Me-Not Bed and Breakfast

1467 N. Elizabeth Scales Mound Road,
Elizabeth 61028
(815) 858-3744 (voice and FAX, call first)
E-mail: forget-me-not@juno.com

New country ridge home with old-world ambience on twenty-three acres overlooking a forest valley and panoramic countryside, away from the city stress. Only minutes from historic Galena, Apple Canyon Lake and Eagle Ridge Territory—scenic routes. Each guest room features a private bath, private entrance and private patio, queen-size bed, AC and heat control. Our home is spacious and romantically decorated to suit all occasions . . . anniversaries, birthdays, honeymoons, etc. Full, hearty breakfast, large great room, TV, games, huge fireplace, hillside picnic area, nature trails and spectacular views overlooking miles of countryside from a screened deck. Hostess speaks English and German. Handicap room. Older children welcome. No pets. Smoking on decks. Gift certificates available.

Hosts: Christa and Richard Grunert
Rooms: 3 (PB) $65-95
Full Breakfast
Credit Cards: A, B
Notes: 2, 5, 7 (12 and older), 8, 9, 10, 11

Hellman Guest House

318 Hill Street, 61036
(815) 777-3638; FAX (815) 777-3658
E-mail: hellman@galenalink
Web site: http://www.galena.com/hellman

An 1859 Queen Anne Victorian with wraparound porch overlooking downtown and countryside, the Hellman has stained- and beveled-glass windows, original woodwork, pocket doors, and period decor. For guests' comfort and convenience, there are queen-size beds, private baths, central air-conditioning, parlor fireplaces, complimentary early morning coffee or tea, a full breakfast, and afternoon beverages.

Hostess: Merilyn Tommaro
Rooms: 4 (PB) $99-149
Full Breakfast
Credit Cards: A, B, D
Notes: 2, 5, 7 (over 10), 8, 9, 10, 11

Hellman Guest House

Park Avenue Guest House

208 Park Avenue, 61036
(815) 777-1075; (800) 359-0743;
FAX (815) 777-1097
E-mail: parkave@galenalink.com
Web site: http://www.galena.com/parkave

1893 Queen Anne Painted Lady. Wraparound, screened porch, gardens, and ga-

---

NOTES: Credit cards accepted: A Master Card; B Visa; C American Express; D Discover; E Diners Club; F Other; 2 Personal checks accepted; 3 Lunch available; 4 Dinner available; 5 Open all year; 6 Pets

zebo for summer. Fireplace and opulent Victorian Christmas in winter. One suite sleeps three, and there are three antique-filled guest rooms, all with queen-size beds and fireplaces. Located in quiet residential area, it is only a short walk to Grant Park or across footbridge to Main Street shopping and restaurants.

Hosts: John and Sharon Fallbacher
Rooms: 4 (PB) $70-105
Hearty Continental Breakfast
Credit Cards: A, B, D
Notes: 2, 5, 7, 8, 9, 10, 11

Pine Hollow Inn

4700 N. Council Hill Road, 61036
(815) 777-1071

Pine Hollow is located on a secluded 120-acre Christmas tree farm a mile from Main Street, Galena. Roam around the grounds and enjoy the wildlife, or put your feet up, lean back and enjoy the country from our front porch. We provide all the comforts of home in a beautiful country setting. Each of our rooms is decorated in a country style with four-poster, queen-size bed, fireplace, and private bath. Whirlpool bath suites are available.

Hosts: Larry and Sally Priske
Rooms: 5 (PB) $75-120
Continental Breakfast
Credit Cards: A, B, D
Notes: 2, 5, 7 (over 12), 8, 9, 10, 11, 12

Wisconsin House Stage Coach Inn

2105 E. Main, **Hazel Green, WI**, 53811
(608) 854-2233

Built as a stage coach inn in 1846, the Inn now offers six rooms and two suites for

your comfort. Join us for an evening's rest. Dine and be refreshed in the parlor where Gen. Grant spent many evenings with his friend Jefferson Crawford. Most conveniently located for all the attractions of the tri-state area. Galena, Illinois, is ten minutes away; Dubuque, Iowa, fifteen miles away; and Platteville twenty miles away.

Hosts: Ken and Pat Disch
Rooms: 8 (6PB; 2SB) $55-110
Full Breakfast
Credit Cards: A, B, D
Notes: 2, 4, 5, 7, 12

HIGHLAND

Tibbetts House Bed and Breakfast

801 Ninth Street, 62249
(618) 654-4619; FAX (618) 654-8355

Highland, known as "Neu-Schweizerland," is just thirty minutes east of St. Louis. The inn was built around the turn of the century and is close to the town square, stores, shops, and restaurants. In the square is a gazebo where festivals and music concerts are held in the summer. At Christmas, the square and gazebo are decorated for the season. Home of Pet Milk Company; tours are given of the Latzer Homestead with Pet Milk memorabilia. Other landmarks include Lindendale Park and Fairgrounds, and Wicks Organ Company. Each room is uniquely decorated. Smoking only on the deck. No alcoholic beverages permitted.

Hostess: Ruth Ann Ernst
Rooms: 5 (3PB; 2SB) $59-69
Full Breakfast
Credit Cards: A, B, C, D
Notes: 1, 2, 7

welcome; 7 Children welcome; 8 Tennis nearby; 9 Swimming nearby; 10 Golf nearby; 11 Skiing nearby; 12 May be booked through travel agent.

JERSEYVILLE

The Homeridge B&B

1470 North State Street, 62052
(618) 498-3442

Beautiful, warm, brick 1867 Italianate Victorian private home on eighteen acres in a comfortable country atmosphere. Drive through stately iron gates and a pine-lined driveway to the fourteen-room historic estate of Sen. Theodore Chapman. Expansive, pillared front porch; hand-carved, curved stairway to spacious guest rooms. Twenty- by forty-foot swimming pool. Central AC. Located between Springfield, Illinois, and St. Louis, Missouri.

Hosts: Sue and Howard Landon
Rooms: 4 (PB) $75-85
Full Breakfast
Credit Cards: A, B, C
Notes: 2, 5, 7 (over 14), 8, 9 (on grounds), 10

MACOMB

The Pineapple Inn, Inc.

204 W. Jefferson, 61455
(309) 837-1914

The Pineapple Inn, Inc., is located in Old Town Macomb, within walking distance of the central business district and the historic courthouse, forty-five miles from Nauvoo. The Inn is a Queen Anne Victorian built in the late 1800s. It has central AC/heating. The pineapple is a symbol of warmth and hospitality; we care that our guests experience true hospitality.

Hosts: Dr. K. Dale and Wanda P. Adkins
Rooms: 5 (PB) $59.50-125
Full Breakfast
Credit Cards: none
Notes: 2, 5, 7, 8, 9, 10, 12

MOUNT CARMEL

The Poor Farm Bed and Breakfast

Poor Farm Road, 62863-9803
(618) 262-HOME (4663);
(800) 646-FARM (3276); FAX (618) 262-8199
E-mail: poorfarm@midwest.net

From 1857 to 1949, the Wabash Country Poor Farm served as a home for the homeless. Today the Poor Farm B&B is a home for the traveler who enjoys a warm, friendly atmosphere and a gracious glimpse of yesteryear. Located next to a twenty-five-acre park with a well-stocked lake; within walking distance of perhaps the finest eighteen-hole municipal golf course in Illinois. A fifteen-minute drive lands you in the spectacular 640-acre Beall Woods Conservation Area and Nature Preserve!

Hosts: Liz and John Stelzer
Rooms: 5 (2 suites and 3 doubles) (PB) $49-89
Full Country Breakfast
Credit Cards: A, B, C, D
Notes: 2, 3 and 4 (for groups of 10-30), 5, 7, 8, 9, 10, 12

OAKLAND

Inn on the Square

3 Montgomery Street, 61943
(217) 346-2289

Located twenty minutes from Eastern Illinois University, the Inn specializes in fine food and friendly atmosphere. Best of all is the return of bed and breakfast tourism. Blending the old with the new, we offer warm hospitality and simple country pleasures, as well as historical sites, recreational activities, shopping, and plain old

---

NOTES: Credit cards accepted: A Master Card; B Visa; C American Express; D Discover; E Diners Club; F Other; 2 Personal checks accepted; 3 Lunch available; 4 Dinner available; 5 Open all year; 6 Pets

sittin' and rockin'. Three upstairs bedrooms are comfortably furnished for country living, each with a private bath.

Hosts: Gary and Linda Miller
Rooms: 3 (PB) $45-50
Full Breakfast
Credit Cards: A, B
Notes: 2, 3 (Monday-Saturday), 4 (Friday-Sunday), 5, 7, 9, 10, 12

ONARGA

Dairy on the Prairie

1437 N. State Route 49, 60955-9505
(815) 683-2774

Situated among miles of corn and soybean fields on God's prairie is this recently remodeled homestead that has been "in the family" since 1892. Two tall silos and Holstein cows await you at the modern dairy/grain family farm. Enjoy the piano, organ, or keyboard along with hearty food, "down on the farm" hospitality, and a Christian atmosphere.

Hosts: Kenneth and Martha Redeker
Rooms: 3 (SB) $40-60
Full Breakfast (Continental on request)
Credit Cards: none
Notes: 2, 5, 7, 8, 9, 10

OTTAWA

Prairie Rivers B&B

121 E. Prospect Avenue, 61350
(815) 434-3226

Historic 1890 Queen Anne cottage nestled on a bluff at the confluence of the Illinois and Fox rivers. Postcard views. Central AC, three fireplaces, common areas. Luxurious bed and breakfast appointments. The atmosphere here is casual and friendly. A satisfying breakfast is served using fresh ingredients. Four state parks, five golf courses, and three marinas are located within fifteen minutes. Public boat launch. Restaurants, shops, and the historic I&M Canal are within an easy walk.

Hosts: Carol and Ed Mayer
Rooms: 4 (2PB; 2SB) $65-100
Expanded Continental Breakfast
Credit Cards: A, B
Notes: 2, 5, 8, 10, 11 (cross-country)

PEORIA (MOSSVILLE)

Old Church House Inn

1416 East Mossville Road, **Mossville** 61552
(309) 579-2300

Take sanctuary from the cares of life in our 1869 "country church." It includes a

Dairy on the Prairie

welcome; 7 Children welcome; 8 Tennis nearby; 9 Swimming nearby; 10 Golf nearby; 11 Skiing nearby; 12 May be booked through travel agent.

Historic Building Survey, eighteen-foot ceilings, library loft, Victorian antiques, classical music, afternoon tea, crackling fire, pillow chocolates, featherbeds, and flower garden. Nearby are the Rock Island Bike Trail, tearooms, antiques, riverboat cruises, fine dining, scenic drives, and sweet memories. On Peoria's north side in the scenic Illinois River Valley.

Hosts: Dean and Holly Ramseyer and Family
Rooms: 2 (SB) or 1 (PB) $75-105
Gourmet Continental Plus Breakfast
Credit Cards: A, B, D
Notes: 2, 5, 7 (by arrangement), 8, 9, 10, 11, 12

PETERSBURG

A Bit of Country Bed and Breakfast

122 W. Sheridan, 62675
(217) 632-3771

The nostalgia of country Victorian comes alive as you enter this 1868 home lovingly restored by your hosts. Our house has the warmth of country and the romance of Victorian living. A lovely collection of period furniture and beautifully decorated rooms combine to achieve authenticity as well as a feeling of being home. We are located in the historic district, two miles from Lincoln's New Salem. Twenty miles from Springfield and other Lincoln historic sites. Before a day of sight-seeing, guests enjoy a full, delicious breakfast featuring Mary Lou's famous muffins. Experience our personal service in one of the oldest homes in Petersburg. "Our guests enter strangers and depart friends."

Hosts: Jay and Mary Lou Jackson
Rooms: 2 (PB) $65
Full Breakfast
Notes: 2, 5, 7, 8, 9, 10

QUINCY

The Kaufmann House Bed and Breakfast

1641 Hampshire Street, 62301
(217) 223-2502

Nestled among majestic trees and lush gardens, our eclectic Queen Anne is in the heart of the historic district. We have lovingly restored it and filled it with abundant antiques. Your comfort and pleasure are of utmost importance. You'll delight in your breakfast of fresh pastries and fruit and our special blend of piping-hot coffee. Relax and prepare to be pampered.

Hosts: Emery and Bettie Kaufmann
Rooms: 3 (PB) $70
Continental Breakfast
Notes: 2, 5, 7, 8, 9, 10

ROCKFORD

The Barn of Rockford

6786 Guilford Road, 61107
(815) 395-8535
E-mail: barnrkfd@juno.com

Come experience country living within the city limits of Illinois's second-largest city. We are just minutes from a wide variety of shopping, fine dining, and one of the Midwest's best selections of antiques. Relax and explore our 110-year-old restored and converted barn. Enjoy a walk through the perennial gardens or a swim in the indoor pool. Then start your day with a sure-to-delight breakfast!

Hosts: Ken and Karen Sharp
Rooms: 4 (1PB; 3SB) $65-95
Full Breakfast
Credit Cards: A, B
Notes: 2, 5, 8, 9, 10, 11

NOTES: Credit cards accepted: A Master Card; B Visa; C American Express; D Discover; E Diners Club; F Other; 2 Personal checks accepted; 3 Lunch available; 4 Dinner available; 5 Open all year; 6 Pets

WEST SALEM

Thelma's Bed and Breakfast

201 S. Broadway, 62476
(618) 456-8401

This prairie-style brick house has twelve rooms, four bedrooms for guests, large front porch, back deck, and hot tub. Full breakfast with special attention to dietary needs. The only Moravian church in Illinois is located nearby.

Hostess: Thelma Lodwig
Rooms: 4 (SB) $40
Full Breakfast
Credit Cards: none
Notes: 2, 5, 7, 8

WHEATON

The Wheaton Inn

301 W. Roosevelt Road, 60187
(630) 690-2600; (800) 447-4667;
FAX (630) 690-2623

The Wheaton Inn is an urban inn built in 1987 of an architectural design that replicates Colonial Williamsburg. The inn is located approximately twenty-five miles

The Wheaton Inn

west of Chicago. Several of the sixteen rooms feature a Jacuzzi tub or gas fireplace. All offer a private bath with European towel warmers and amenities. There are several common rooms, including a living room with fireplace, a breakfast atrium room with French doors leading onto the patio, and lower-level conference rooms. A full breakfast and afternoon refreshments are offered daily. Explore the historic town of Wheaton or nearby Geneva for shopping and unique restaurants. Nearby attractions include Morton Arboretum, Cantigny War Museum, McCormick Mansion, Wheaton Water Park, and the Billy Graham Center on the Wheaton College Campus.

Host: Dennis Stevens
Rooms: 16 (PB) $99-215
Full Breakfast
Credit Cards: A, B, C, D, E
Notes: 2, 5, 7, 8, 9, 10, 11, 12

welcome; 7 Children welcome; 8 Tennis nearby; 9 Swimming nearby; 10 Golf nearby; 11 Skiing nearby; 12 May be booked through travel agent.

INDIANA

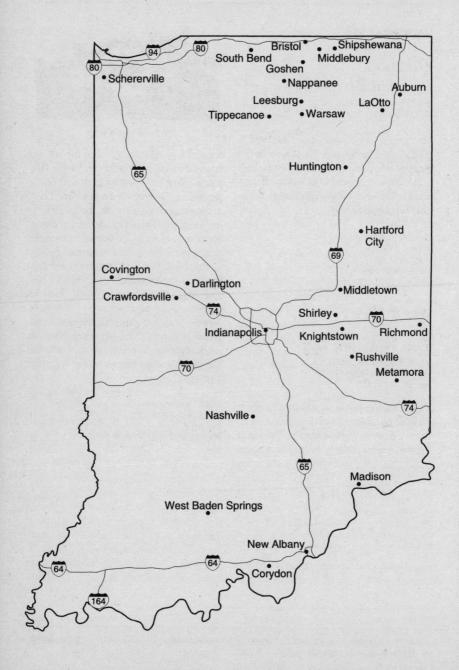

Indiana

AUBURN

Hill Top Country Inn

1733 County Road 28, 46706
(219) 281-2298

The Hill Top Country Inn offers a quiet
and beautiful setting with country porches,
wicker furniture, walking areas, small fishpond with fountain, and distinctive bed
chambers and sitting room. Our rooms are
decorated with a variety of quilts, stenciling, and country antiques. You'll find a formal dining room and farm kitchen with an
old-fashioned cook stove. Places to visit
in the area include antique shops, a car
museum, lakes, and parks.

Hosts: Chuck and Becky Derrow
Rooms: 4 (2PB; 2SB) $60-75
Full Breakfast
Credit Cards: none
Notes: 2, 5, 7, 12

BRISTOL

Rust Hollar B&B

55238 CR 31, 46507-9569
(219) 825-1111; FAX (219) 825-4614
E-mail: rusthollar@rusthollar.com
Web site: http://www.rusthollar.com

Rust Hollar Bed and Breakfast is a rustic
log home on a peaceful country road in a

Rust Hollar Bed and Breakfast

wooded "hollar." You may enjoy bird-
watching or a country walk. A full, hot
breakfast with homemade breads and
muffins is served each morning. The B&B
is located in Amish country. Shipshewana,
Middlebury (Das Essenhaus), Goshen,

NOTES: Credit cards accepted: A Master Card; B Visa; C American Express; D Discover; E Diners
Club; F Other; 2 Personal checks accepted; 3 Lunch available; 4 Dinner available; 5 Open all year; 6 Pets
welcome; 7 Children welcome; 8 Tennis nearby; 9 Swimming nearby; 10 Golf nearby; 11 Skiing nearby;
12 May be booked through travel agent.

Elkhart, South Bend, and Nappanee are within a half-hour drive.

Hosts: Tim and Janine Rust
Rooms: 4 (SB) $65-85
Full Breakfast
Credit Cards: A, B, D
Notes: 2, 5, 7, 10

CORYDON

The Kintner House Inn

101 S. Capital Avenue, 47112
(812) 738-2020; FAX (812) 738-7430

Historic bed and breakfast built in 1873, restored in 1986. Fifteen elegant rooms, all with private baths and TVs, five with fireplaces, and eight with VCRs. Antique furnishings in all the rooms. Nonsmoking building. Open year-round. First floor is handicap-accessible. Listed on the National Register of Historic Places and featured on two 1991 Hallmark™ Christmas cards. A hideaway for romantics, located in historic downtown Corydon, Indiana's first state capital.

Hostess: Mary Jane B. Reed
Rooms: 15 (PB) $49-89
Full Breakfast

COVINGTON

Green Gables
Bed and Breakfast

504 Fancy Street, 47932
(765) 793-7164

Covington's first bed and breakfast offers three guest rooms, each with private bath, including the spacious loft with two queen-size beds. Each room has a television; new air-conditioning throughout the house.

Home-cooked breakfasts are served by the private, in-ground pool or by one of two fireplaces in this hilltop home near I-74 in western Indiana. Only five miles from Indiana's finest steakhouse. ArtFest in May and AppleFest in October, both on the courthouse lawn.

Hosts: Marsha and Bill Wilkinson
Rooms: 3 (PB) $65
Full Breakfast
Credit Cards: A, B, C
Notes: 2, 5, 8, 9, 10

CRAWFORDSVILLE

Sugar Creek Queen Anne
Bed and Breakfast

PO Box 726, 901 W. Market, 47933
(317) 362-4095

Sugar Creek's decor is Victorian with a French Provincial touch. The turn-of-the-century home has two guest rooms with private baths and a honeymoon suite with a private sitting room and private bath. Guests enjoy our Victorian tearoom and snacks. Behind the house is a beautiful rose garden and a fourth guest room with private bath, a Jacuzzi, and a fitness center. The house has been newly remodeled with originality and creativity. A limo-narrated tour of Crawfordsville is available. Sugar Creek Bed and Breakfast is a member of the Indiana Bed and Breakfast Association. No smoking or alcohol inside the building.

Hosts: Mary Alice and Hal Barbee
Rooms: 4 (PB) $65
Full Breakfast
Credit Cards: none
Notes: 2, 5, 7

NOTES: Credit cards accepted: A Master Card; B Visa; C American Express; D Discover; E Diners Club; F Other; 2 Personal checks accepted; 3 Lunch available; 4 Dinner available; 5 Open all year; 6 Pets

DARLINGTON

Our Country Home

RR1, Box 103, 47940
(mail: PO Box 51762, Indianapolis, 46251)
(765) 794-3139

Escape to the country.... Enjoy Hoosier
hospitality at its best! A full country breakfast can be followed by a quiet walk along
the creek, a bike ride, or horseback riding.
There's even a bicycle built for two for
our guests to enjoy. Swimming, relaxing
in the hot tub, a carriage ride, or a sleigh
ride add further enjoyment to your day.
A telescope for star-watching is provided.
Our guests always arrive as visitors and
leave as friends.

Hosts: The Smith Family (Jim, Debbie, and Chris)
Rooms: 3+ (SB) $75-130
Full Breakfast
Credit Cards: A, B, C, D
Notes: 2, 3, 4, 5, 7, 9, 10, 12

GOSHEN

Coterie Bed and Breakfast

66083 State Road 15 S., 46526
(219) 533-8961

You will find us just two miles south of
Goshen College and one hour's drive
south of Notre Dame. We are also near
the Shipshewana World-Famous Flea
Market and Amish Acres. We have two
large bedrooms with private baths. One
bedroom overlooks our backyard, which
is home to Canadian geese and ducks.
We have air-conditioned rooms in summer and a fireplace for winter evenings.

We serve a full breakfast in our formal dining room.

Hosts: Dean and Kathy Sheeley
Rooms: 3 (2PB; 1 SB) $50
Full Breakfast
Credit Cards: none
Notes: 2, 5, 7, 8, 9, 10, 11

Indian Creek Bed and Breakfast

Indian Creek Bed and Breakfast

20300 County Road 18, 46528-9513
(219) 875-6606; FAX (219) 875-3968
E-mail: 71224.1462@compuserve.com
Web site: http://www.bestinns.net/usa/in/
     indiancreek.html

Come and enjoy our newly built country
Victorian home in the middle of Amish
country. It is decorated with family antiques. Walk back to the woods or sit on
the deck to watch for deer. Also enjoy
the great room, game room, and family
room. Full breakfast. Children welcome.
Handicap-accessible.

Hosts: Shirley and Herman Hochstetler
Rooms: 5 (PB) $79
Full Breakfast
Credit Cards: A, B, C, D
Notes: 2, 5, 7, 8, 9, 10, 12

welcome; 7 Children welcome; 8 Tennis nearby; 9 Swimming nearby; 10 Golf nearby; 11 Skiing nearby;
12 May be booked through travel agent.

De'Coy's Bed and Breakfast

HARTFORD CITY

De'Coy's Bed and Breakfast

1546 W. 100 N., 47348
(765) 348-2164 (voice and FAX)

Situated just west of Hartford City, De'Coy's Bed and Breakfast is conveniently located near Taylor University, Ball State University, and Indiana Wesleyan College. This charming country home offers its guests extraordinarily attractive accommodations with many extra special Hoosier touches. Visitors can relax in the quiet rural atmosphere of this old, restored home, enriched with many amenities not customary to the typical motel or hotel setting. Each room demonstrates its own character with antique furnishings and comfortable arrangements.

Hosts: Christopher and Tiann Coy
Rooms: 5 (1PB, 4SB) $48-60
Full Breakfast
Credit Cards: none
Notes: 2, 5, 7, 10, 12

HUNTINGTON

Purviance House Bed and Breakfast

326 S. Jefferson Street (SR 5 and U.S. 224), 46750
(219) 356-4218

Built in 1859, this beautiful home is on the National Register of Historic Places. It features a winding staircase, ornate ceilings, unique fireplaces, and parquet floors. It has been lovingly restored and decorated with antiques and period furnishings. Amenities include televisions in the guest rooms, snacks, beverages, kitchen privileges, and a library. Purviance House Bed and Breakfast is located near recreational areas with swimming, boating, hiking, bicycling. Historic tours are available. We are half hour from Fort Wayne, two hours from Indianapolis.

Hosts: Robert and Jean Gernand
Rooms: 5 (2PB; 3SB) $50-65
Full Breakfast
Credit Cards: A, B, D
Notes: 2, 5, 7, 8, 9, 10, 12

INDIANAPOLIS

Carriage House Bed and Breakfast

6440 N. Michigan Road, 46268
(317) 255-2276

Relax and enjoy all the amenities of home in your own spacious, private suite. Our Inn is decorated with your comfort in mind. We are located within twenty minutes of most Indianapolis events. Our deluxe upstairs suite includes a kitchenette and double whirlpool bath. Our facilities are smoke-free. If you're looking for a luxurious getaway at a modest price, try us. Our guests agree. Monthly and group rates available.

Hosts: David and Sue Wilson
Rooms: 2 (PB) $65-200
Full Breakfast
Credit Cards: none
Notes: 2, 5, 7, 10

NOTES: Credit cards accepted: A Master Card; B Visa; C American Express; D Discover; E Diners Club; F Other; 2 Personal checks accepted; 3 Lunch available; 4 Dinner available; 5 Open all year; 6 Pets

The Old Northside Bed and Breakfast

The Old Northside Bed and Breakfast

1340 N. Alabama Street, 46202
(317) 635-9123; (800) 635-9123 reservations only;
FAX (317) 635-9243
E-mail: oldnorth@indy.net
Web site: http://www.hofmeister.com/b&b.htm

The Old Northside Bed and Breakfast is an 1885 luxurious Victorian mansion in historic downtown, convenient to I-65, I-70, and city attractions. It represents the city's finest example of Romanesque Revival architecture with an elegant European turn-of-the-century decor. The home features themed rooms with Jacuzzi tubs in private baths—two with fireplaces. Guests may use the exercise room, conference room, and corporate services. A personal coffee service is delivered to your room before your full gourmet breakfast each morning. Complimentary snack and exceptional service.

Hostess: Susan Berry
Rooms: 6 (PB) $85-155
Full Gourmet Breakfast With Beverage Service
Credit Cards: A, B, C, D
Notes: 2, 5, 8, 9, 10, 12

KNIGHTSTOWN

Old Hoosier House Bed and Breakfast

7601 S. Greensboro Pike, 46148
(765) 345-2969; (800) 775-5315

Central Indiana's first and favorite country bed and breakfast, located in historic Knightstown, midway between Indianapolis and Richmond. The Old Hoosier House is ideally situated for sight-seeing and shopping in Indiana's "Antique Alley." Our guests may enjoy golf on the adjoining eighteen-hole Royal Highlands golf course; a golf package is available. The bed and breakfast is handicap-accessible. It is a member of the Indiana Bed and Breakfast Association and the American Historic Inn, Inc.

Hosts: Tom Lewis and Jean Lewis
Rooms: 4 (PB) $60-70
Full Breakfast
Credit Cards: none
Notes: 2, 5, 7, 8, 9, 10, 12

LAOTTO

Tea Rose Bed and Breakfast

7711 E. 500 S., 46763
(219) 693-2884

Enjoy a home-style breakfast on the spacious deck while watching the birds. Our air-conditioned country log home features a large great room, comfortable bedroom, and front porch. It's a short drive to the state park, zoo, Auburn Cord Dusenberg Museum, and Shipshewanna. Take a country drive to a quiet and more serene

welcome; 7 Children welcome; 8 Tennis nearby; 9 Swimming nearby; 10 Golf nearby; 11 Skiing nearby; 12 May be booked through travel agent.

lifestyle. Stop and smell the roses or sit on the porch awhile.

Hosts: Adrian and Anne Ledger
Rooms: 1 (PB) $55
Full Breakfast
Credit Cards: none
Notes: 2, 5, 7, 10

LEESBURG

Prairie House Bed and Breakfast

495 E. 900 N., 46538
(219) 658-9211; FAX (219) 453-4787

Come enjoy a peaceful farm atmosphere. Four tastefully decorated rooms with air, television, VCR. Close to Grace College, Wagon Wheel Playhouse, Shipshewana Flea Market, Amish Acres, antique browsing, the Old Bag Factory at Goshen, swimming, boating, and golfing. Excellent dining in the area. Tours of the farm available. Let us pamper you!

Hosts: Everett and Marie Tom
Rooms: 4 (2PB; 2SB) $55-65
Full Breakfast
Credit Cards: A, B
Notes: 2, 5, 7, 8, 9, 10

MADISON

Schussler House Bed and Breakfast

514 Jefferson Street, 47250
(812) 273-2068; (800) 392-1931

Experience the quiet elegance of a circa 1849 Federal/Greek Revival home taste-

Schussler House Bed and Breakfast

fully combined with today's modern amenities. Located in Madison's historic district, where antique shops, historic sites, restaurants, and churches are within a pleasant walking distance. This gracious home offers spacious rooms decorated with antiques and reproductions and carefully selected fabrics and wall coverings. A sumptuous breakfast in the sun-filled dining room begins your day.

Hosts: Judy and Bill Gilbert
Rooms: 3 (PB) $99
Full Breakfast
Credit Cards: A, B, D
Notes: 2, 5, 8, 9, 10, 11, 12

METAMORA

The Thorpe House Country Inn

19049 Clayborne Street, PO Box 36, 47030
(765) 647-5425

Visit the Thorpe House in historic Metamora, where the steam engine still brings passenger cars and the gristmill still grinds cornmeal. Spend a relaxing evening in the 1840 canal town home. The guest rooms are tastefully furnished with antiques and

---

NOTES: Credit cards accepted: A Master Card; B Visa; C American Express; D Discover; E Diners Club; F Other; 2 Personal checks accepted; 3 Lunch available; 4 Dinner available; 5 Open all year; 6 Pets

country accessories. Enjoy a hearty breakfast before visiting more than one hundred shops in this quaint village. Our family-style dining room is also open to the public.

Hosts: Mike and Jean Owens
Rooms: 4 + 2-room suite (PB) $70-125
Full Breakfast
Credit Cards: A, B, C, D
Notes: 2, 3, 6, 7, 10, 12

Bee Hive Bed and Breakfast

MIDDLEBURY

Bee Hive
Bed and Breakfast

Box 1191, 46540
(219) 825-5023

Come visit Amish country and enjoy our Hoosier hospitality. The Bee Hive is a two-story, open floor plan with exposed, hand-sawn, red oak beams and a loft. Enjoy our collection of antique farm machinery and other collectibles. Snuggle under handmade quilts and wake to the smell of freshly baked muffins. A guest cottage is available. Be one of many of our return guests, and become a friend.

Hosts: Herb and Treva Swarm
Rooms: 4 (1PB; 3SB) $52-70
Full Breakfast
Credit Cards: A, B
Notes: 2, 5, 7, 8, 9, 10, 11

Bontreger Guest Rooms

10766 CR 16, 46540
(219) 825-2647

Located between Middlebury and Ships-hewana on a county road in an Amish neighborhood. Cozy rooms and common room located away from family space. Continental breakfast in sunroom. Private bath. Smoke-free.

Hosts: Tom and Ruby Bontreger
Rooms: 2 (PB) $50
Continental Plus Breakfast
Credit Cards: none

The Country Victorian

435 South Main Street, 46540
(219) 825-2568; (888) BNB-STAY;
FAX (219) 825-3411
E-mail: mark@michianatoday.com

Come celebrate one hundred years of lovely Victorian living. Our large home is a fully updated Victorian with lots of charm and original style, located in the heart of Amish country. Relax on the front porch and watch buggies drive by. In colder months, sit by the fireplace to chat or curl up with a good book. Get pampered and experience the loving family atmosphere where children are a pleasure! Honey-moon suite with Jacuzzi. Bicycle rental. Special packages available. Very accessible to Indiana's toll road (I-80/90) and close to Shipshewana. Other attractions include Amish-style restaurants and crafters, community festivals, University of Notre Dame, and Goshen College.

Hosts: Mark and Becky Potterbaum
Rooms: 5 (PB) $69-109
Full Breakfast
Credit Cards: A, B, C, D
Notes: 2, 5, 7, 8, 10, 11, 12

welcome; 7 Children welcome; 8 Tennis nearby; 9 Swimming nearby; 10 Golf nearby; 11 Skiing nearby; 12 May be booked through travel agent.

A Laber of Love

11030 County Road 10, 46540
(219) 825-7877

This Cape Cod home is located in northern Indiana Amish farm country on three acres, two of which are wooded. A screened-in gazebo in the woods is ideal for quiet time or just relaxing. Guest quarters offer queen-size beds and private baths. A common game/sitting room is available for guests. Air-conditioned for year-round comfort. (Guest rooms are located upstairs.) A Laber of Love is situated close to a large flea market, open from May to October on Tuesdays and Wednesdays. Visitors will find lots of shopping in Middlebury and Shipshewana. Home-baked cinnamon rolls highlight breakfast each morning. This is a smoke-free bed and breakfast.

Hostess: Lori Laber
Rooms: 2 (PB) $55
Continental Breakfast
Credit Cards: none
Notes: 2, 5, 10, 12

The Patchwork Quilt Inn

11748 CR 2, 46540
(219) 825-2417; FAX (219) 825-5172

Relax and enjoy the simple grace and charm of our one-hundred-year-old farmhouse. Sample our country cooking with homemade breads and desserts. Complete your visit with one of our four-hour guided Amish back road tours. Our knowledgeable guides will drive you along little-known byways deep in the heart of Amish country near our inn. Come visit our Amish handmade quilt and wall-hanging shop. Inquire about our hands-on quilt

and craft projects. Fifteen smoke-free, charming rooms.

Hosts: Ray and Rosetta Miller
Rooms: 15 (PB) $70-100
Full Breakfast
Credit Cards: A, B
Notes: 2, 3 (Tuesday-Saturday), 4, 5 (B&B only), 10, 11 (cross-country), 12

Yoder's Zimmer Mit Frühstück Haus

PO Box 1396, 46540
(219) 825-2378; (219) 825-7378

We enjoy sharing our Amish-Mennonite heritage in our spacious Crystal Valley home. The rooms feature handmade quilts and antiques. Antiques and collectibles can be seen throughout the home. Three of our rooms can accommodate families. There are several common rooms available for relaxing, reading, TV, games, or socializing. Facilities are also available for pastor-elder retreats. AC, playground, swimming pool.

Hosts: Wilbur and Evelyn Yoder
Rooms: 5 (SB) $52.50
Full Breakfast
Credit Cards: A, B
Notes: 2, 5, 7, 8, 9, 10, 11, 12

Zimmer Haus Bed and Breakfast

130 Orpha Drive, 46540
(219) 825-7288

Relax and enjoy watching our llamas grazing and playing in the pasture after you have explored the many unique shops and sights of the Middlebury/Shipshewana area. Retreat to air-conditioned facilities, which

---

NOTES: Credit cards accepted: A Master Card; B Visa; C American Express; D Discover; E Diners Club; F Other; 2 Personal checks accepted; 3 Lunch available; 4 Dinner available; 5 Open all year; 6 Pets

include a common area with cable TV. Top the evening off with complimentary beverages and snacks. A full breakfast begins the new day's adventure. Member of Four Seasons B&B Association and Indiana B&B Association.

Hosts: Bob & Carolyn Emmert
Rooms: 2 (PB) $50-55
Full Breakfast
Credit Cards: none
Notes: 2, 7 (limited), 8, 10

MIDDLETOWN

Cornerstone Guest House

705 High Street, 47356
(765) 354-6004; (800) 792-6004;
FAX (765) 354-6057

Set in the small, quiet town of Middletown, the Cornerstone Guest House is an elegant place to stay. The ninety-year-old prairie-style home has original oak woodwork and flooring and is decorated tastefully with styles from the period. Coffee is brought to your room an hour before breakfast, and a full breakfast is served in the formal dining room. Cornerstone Guest House is ten minutes from Interstate 69 and forty minutes northeast of Indianapolis.

Hosts: Dave and Debbie Lively
Rooms: 4 (3PB, 1SB) $60-75
Full Breakfast
Credit Cards: A, B
Notes: 2, 5, 10

Country Rose Bed and Breakfast

5098 N. Mechanicsburg Road, 47356
(317) 779-4501; (800) 395-6449

A small town bed and breakfast looking out on berry patches and a flower garden.

Awake early or late to a delicious full breakfast. Fifty minutes to Indianapolis, twenty minutes to Anderson and Ball State universities.

Hosts: Rose and Jack Lewis
Rooms: 2 (1 suite, 1SB) $55-75
Full Breakfast
Credit Cards: none
Notes: 2, 5, 7, 8, 9, 10, 12

NAPPANEE

Victorian Guest House

302 E. Market Street, 46550
(219) 773-4383

Antiques, stained-glass windows, and pocket doors highlight this 1887 Historical Register mansion. Nestled amongst the Amish countryside where antique shops abound. A warm welcome awaits as you return to gracious living with all the ambience of the 1800s. Everything has been designed to make your bed and breakfast stay a memorable one. Close to Notre Dame and Shipshewana. Two hours from Chicago. Complimentary evening tea and sweets. "Prepare for a memory."

Hosts: Bruce and Vickie Hunsberger
Rooms: 6 (PB) $49-89
Full Breakfast
Credit Cards: A, B, D
Notes: 2, 5, 8, 9, 10

NASHVILLE

Day Star Inn

Box 361, 87 E. Main Street, 47448
(812) 988-0430

A friendly, homey atmosphere awaits as you retreat to the heart of Nashville's unique shopping downtown area. Short drive to Brown County State Park, golf courses, and other recreational areas. Five clean rooms can accommodate up to twenty-two guests (including children, if well-supervised). Air-conditioning, cable television, private bath and parking for guests. No smoking, alcoholic beverages or pets permitted, please.

Host: Edwin K. Taggart
Rooms: 5 (PB) $80-95
Continental Breakfast
Credit Cards: A, B, D
Notes: 2, 5, 7, 8, 9, 10, 11, 12

NEW ALBANY

Honeymoon Mansion Bed and Breakfast Inn and Wedding Chapel

1014 E. Main Street, 47150
(812) 945-0312; (800) 759-7270

Honeymoon Mansion has six lovely suites with private baths, marble Jacuzzis, and eight-foot-high marble columns. Our guests will enjoy queen-size, hand-carved cherry beds with lace-covered canopies. Stained-glass windows, grand staircase. Our wedding chapel seats seventy and has an ordained minister on staff; guests can marry or renew their vows. The mansion, built in 1850, is on the National Register of Historic Homes. A ten-percent discount is offered Sunday through Thursday. Senior citizens' discount.

Hosts: Franklin and Beverly Dennis
Rooms: 6 (PB) $70-140
Full Country Breakfast
Credit Cards: A, B, F
Notes: 2, 5, 8, 9, 10, 11, 12

RICHMOND

Norwich Lodge and Conference Center

920 Earlham Drive, 47374
(765) 983-1575; FAX (765) 983-1576
E-mail: mondiki@earlham.edu

Surrounded by four hundred acres of woods and streams, Norwich Lodge is open year-round and provides the ideal getaway for anyone who wants to escape life's daily routine. Outside the Lodge, a choice of paths can lead you on a fascinating escapade through one of nature's most scenic and beautiful playgrounds. You can hike along winding creeks, pause to watch the abundant wildlife, or spot a variety of birds that inhabit the surrounding countryside.

Hostess: Kim Mondics
Rooms: 14 (PB)
Continental Breakfast
Credit Cards: A, B
Notes: 2, 5, 7, 8, 9, 10

Philip W. Smith Bed and Breakfast

2039 E. Main Street, 47374
(765) 966- 8972; (800) 966-8972

Elegant Queen Anne Victorian family home located in East Main-Glen Miller Park Historic District, right on the Indiana-Ohio border off I-70. Built in 1890 by Philip W. Smith, the two-and-a-half-story brick home has Romanesque details and features stained-glass windows and ornate-carved wood. Four distinctive guest rooms: two with full-size beds, two with queen-size beds. Unwind in the evening

---

NOTES: Credit cards accepted: A Master Card; B Visa; C American Express; D Discover; E Diners Club; F Other; 2 Personal checks accepted; 3 Lunch available; 4 Dinner available; 5 Open all year; 6 Pets

Philip W. Smith Bed and Breakfast

with homemade snacks, coffee, and tea. Awaken to a breakfast highlighting fresh, regional ingredients. Stroll through historic districts, listen to outdoor concerts in the park, hike Whitewater River Gorge, relax in the garden, and shop at Richmond and "Antique Alley." AAA-approved.

Hosts: Chip and Chartley Bondurant
Rooms: 4 (PB) $65-75
Full Breakfast
Credit Cards: A, B
Notes: 2, 5, 7, 8, 10, 11, 12

RUSHVILLE

Greystone Inn Bed and Breakfast

525 N. Main Street, 46173
(765) 932-5922; (888) 270-0022;
FAX (765) 932-2192

The Greystone Inn Bed and Breakfast is an inn dedicated to providing a charming, unique place of hospitality where visitors can find the time to be refreshed, spiritually and physically. It is an inn of conservative eloquence, and those who share

that particular lifestyle will find it a haven to nourish their souls. "It is dedicated to Jesus Christ." The Inn was Jasper Case's mansion, built in 1918. Ranny and Denise Grady invite you to step back in time as you enter the door of this stately, twenty-five-room stone mansion. You will be greeted and enchanted by the eight beautiful Rookwood Pottery tiled fireplaces, the recreation/fitness room (in the basement), and the six elegant guest rooms, each named after a flower and decorated with antiques that have been chosen specifically reflect its unique name.

Hosts: Ranny and Denise Grady
Rooms: 25
Full Breakfast
Credit Cards: A, B
Notes: 2, 5, 8, 9, 10

SCHERERVILLE

Sunset Pines Bed and Breakfast

862 Sunset Drive, 46375
(219) 322-3322; (800) 458-0919, 19

Sunset Pines Bed and Breakfast is hidden away on the edge of a fifty-acre forest. Guests enjoy a country setting while still in the heart of town. We serve a generous continental or full-service breakfast. Our nonsmoking rooms offer every comfort, at prices ranging from $55 to 95 per night. Queen beds, whirlpool tubs. Our outdoor pool is open during the summer season. We are recommended by the Lake County Indiana Visitors Center.

Hosts: Clayton and Nikki Foster
Rooms: 2 (PB) $55-95
Full or Continental Breakfast
Credit Cards: A, B, C, D, E
Notes: 5, 7, 8, 9, 10

welcome; 7 Children welcome; 8 Tennis nearby; 9 Swimming nearby; 10 Golf nearby; 11 Skiing nearby; 12 May be booked through travel agent.

SHIPSHEWANA

Morton Street Bed and Breakfast, Inc.

PO Box 775, 140 Morton Street, 46565
(219) 768-4391; (800) 447-6475;
FAX (219) 768-7468

These three old homes are located on
Morton Street, in the heart of Amish country in Shipshewana. You will experience
the comfort of country, antique, or Victorian stylings. You find yourself within walking distance of the town's country quilt and
craft shops and the famous Shipshewana
flea market. Special winter and weekend
rates available.

Hosts: Esther Mishler, Joel and Kim Mishler
Rooms: 10 (PB) $80-100
Full Breakfast
Credit Cards: A, B, D
Notes: 2, 4, 5, 7, 10, 11, 12

SHIRLEY

Sweet's Home Sweet Home

402 Center Street, 47384
(317) 737-6357; (800) 418-2076

This is a large, comfortable home specializing in small-town hospitality. It features
a large yard with a rose garden and is
within walking distance of Shirley's historic district. Sweet's Home Sweet Home
is centrally located within an easy drive of
several attractions. Each guest room is
special. You can have Christmas year-
round in the Christmas Room, see all the
treasures in Papaw's Treasure Room,
sleep in Grandma's antique feather bed,

or lounge in bows and lace in the lovely
Jo-lia-Reneé Room.

Hosts: Jeanie and Ray Sweet
Rooms: 4 (SB)
Continental Breakfast and Evening Snack
Credit Cards: none
Notes: 2, 4, 5, 7

circa 1893

Queen Anne Inn

SOUTH BEND

Queen Anne Inn

420 W. Washington, 46601
(219) 234-5959; (800) 582-2379;
FAX (219) 234-4324
E-mail: queenann@michiana.org
Web site: http://business.michiana.org/queenann

An 1893 Victorian house with antiques,
original Frank Lloyd Wright bookcases,
silk cloth wall covering, and beautiful tiger
oak staircase. Abundant breakfast, afternoon tea, and snacks provided. Near
downtown, Notre Dame, local attractions,
and good restaurants. Relax and relive
earlier days. Step back into the past.

Hosts: Bob and Pauline Medhurst
Rooms: 6 (PB) $70-105
Full Breakfast
Credit Cards: A, B, C
Notes: 2, 5, 7, 8, 10, 11, 12

NOTES: Credit cards accepted: A Master Card; B Visa; C American Express; D Discover; E Diners
Club; F Other; 2 Personal checks accepted; 3 Lunch available; 4 Dinner available; 5 Open all year; 6 Pets

TIPPECANOE

Bessinger's Hillfarm Wildlife Refuge B&B

4588 State Road 110, 46570
(219) 223-3288

This cozy log home overlooks 265 acres of rolling hills, woods, pasture fields, and marsh with 31 islands. It is ideal for geese and deer year-round. This farm features hiking trails with beautiful views, picnic areas, and benches tucked away in a quiet area. Varied seasons make it possible to canoe, swim, fish, bird-watch, hike, and cross-country ski. Start with a country breakfast and be ready for an unforgettable table experience.

Hosts: Wayne and Betty Bessinger
Rooms: 3 (PB) $69.90
Full Breakfast
Credit Cards: none
Notes: 2, 5, 9

WARSAW

White Hill Inn

2513 E. Center Street, 46580
(219) 269-6933; FAX (219) 268-1936

This restored English Tudor mansion is situated on the highest point in Warsaw. Surrounded by whispering trees, the Inn is a retreat into the elegance of yesteryear.

Only minutes from fine dining, shopping, lake recreation, and the business community. The accommodations include telephones, voice mail, laptop computer hook-ups, TVs, private baths, and desks. Full breakfast is served on the porch. The suite has a double-wide Jacuzzi.

Hosts: Carm and Zoyla Henderson
Rooms: 8 (PB) $70-120
Full Breakfast
Credit Cards: A, B, C, D, E
Notes: 2, 5, 6, 7, 8, 9, 10, 11, 12

WEST BADEN SPRINGS

E.B. Rhodes House Bed and Breakfast

Box 7, 47469-0007
(812) 936-7378; (800) 786-5176

Relax in the homey luxury of an 1890s Victorian home fill with beautiful carved wood and stained glass. Rock on one of the wraparound porches and enjoy the peaceful view of the town park. Enjoy Hoosier hospitality with a home-grown breakfast. Opportunity abounds for historians, sports buffs and antique enthusiasts. Carriage house available, with full bath and fireplace.

Hosts: Marlene and Frank Sipes
Rooms: 3 (PB) $40-60
Full Breakfast (guests' preference)
Credit Cards: A, B, D
Notes: 5, 6 (housed separately), 7, 8, 9, 10, 11

---

welcome; 7 Children welcome; 8 Tennis nearby; 9 Swimming nearby; 10 Golf nearby; 11 Skiing nearby; 12 May be booked through travel agent.

IOWA

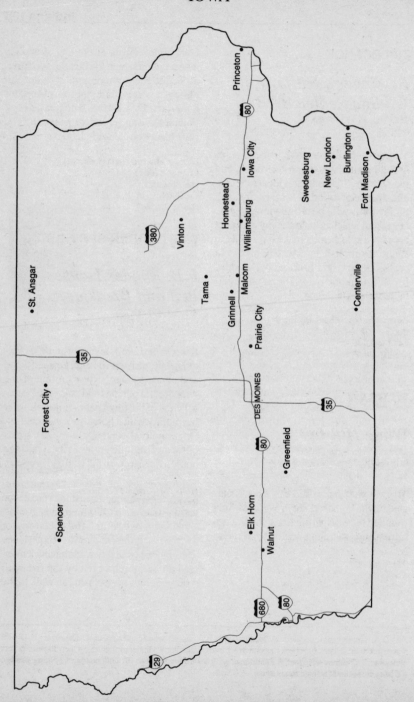

Iowa

BURLINGTON

Lakeview Bed and Breakfast

11351 60th Street, 52601
(319) 752-8735; (800) 753-8735;
FAX (319) 752-5126

Built from the ruins of the county's third-oldest home, this elegant country home stands where stagecoach passengers once slept. Now your retreat to Lakeview is a mix of the old and the new on thirty acres of magnificent country charm. The house features crystal chandeliers, antiques, collectibles, and a circular staircase. Outdoors your can enjoy a swim in our pool; fishing in our three-acre lake stocked with catfish, bass, crappie, and bluegill; or making friends with our family of miniature horses. Guests can take advantage of our large video library of noted Christian speakers. A video studio is available for recording and small conferences.

Hosts: Jack and Linda Rowley
Rooms: 4 (PB) $45-60
Full Breakfast
Credit Cards: A, B
Notes: 2, 5, 7 (limited), 8, 9, 10, 12

The Schramm House Bed and Breakfast

The Schramm House Bed and Breakfast

616 Columbia Street, 52601
(319) 754-0373; (800) 683-7117;
FAX (319) 754-0373

Step into the past when you enter this restored 1870s Victorian in the heart of the Burlington historic district. Unique architecture and antique furnishings create the mood of an era past. Three guest rooms, all with private baths, offer queen-size or twin beds, quilts, and more. Experience Burlington hospitality while having lemonade on the porch or tea by the fire with your gracious hosts. You can walk to the

---

NOTES: Credit cards accepted: A Master Card; B Visa; C American Express; D Discover; E Diners Club; F Other; 2 Personal checks accepted; 3 Lunch available; 4 Dinner available; 5 Open all year; 6 Pets welcome; 7 Children welcome; 8 Tennis nearby; 9 Swimming nearby; 10 Golf nearby; 11 Skiing nearby; 12 May be booked through travel agent.

Mississippi River, antique shops, restaurants, etc.

Hosts: Sandy and Bruce Morrison
Rooms: 3 (PB) $65-85
Full Breakfast
Credit Cards: A, B, C, D
Notes: 2, 5, 7, 8, 9, 10, 12

CENTERVILLE

One of a Kind

314 W. State, 52544
(515) 437-4540 (voice and FAX)

One of a Kind is a stately, three-story brick home built in 1867 and situated in one of Iowa's delightful small communities. You are within walking distance of antique shops, the town square, the city park with tennis courts, the swimming pool, etc. A twelve-minute drive to Iowa's largest lake. A tearoom and gift shop with handcrafts by local artists affords many one-of-a-kind decorative or gift items.

Hosts: Jack and Joyce Stufflebeem
Rooms: 5 (2PB; 3SB) $35-60
Full Breakfast
Credit Cards: A, B, C, D
Notes: 2, 3, 4, 5, 8, 9, 10, 11, 12

DAVENPORT (PRINCETON)

The Woodlands Bed and Breakfast

PO Box 127, **Princeton**, 52768
(800) 257-3177

The Woodlands Bed and Breakfast is a secluded woodland escape that can be as private or social as you wish. The Woodlands Bed and Breakfast is nestled among pines on twenty-six acres of forest and meadows in a private wildlife refuge. Guests delight in an elegant breakfast by the swimming pool or by a cozy fireplace, while viewing the outdoor wildlife activity. The Woodlands is the perfect setting for intimate weddings!

Hosts: The Wallace Family
Rooms: 2 (PB) $60-115
Full Breakfast
Credit Cards: none
Notes: 2, 3, 4, 5, 6 (limited), 7, 8, 9, 10, 11, 12

ELK HORN

Joy's Morning Glory Bed and Breakfast

4308 Main Street, Box 12, 51531
(712) 764-5631; (888) 764-5631

Be special guests in our beautiful, refurbished 1912 home. As our guest, you will be greeted by an abundant array of flowers that line our walkways. Inside, your choice of floral-decorated bedrooms awaits you. Breakfast is prepared on Joy's antique cookstove and served in the dining room, on the front porch, or in the flower-filled backyard. Elk Horn community is home to the largest rural Danish settlement in the United States. The town has a working windmill and is home to the National Danish Immigrant Museum and the Tivoli Festival.

Hosts: Merle and Joy Petersen
Rooms: 3 (SB) $50
Full Breakfast
Credit Cards: none
Notes: 2, 7 (over 10), 8, 9, 10

NOTES: Credit cards accepted: A Master Card; B Visa; C American Express; D Discover; E Diners Club; F Other; 2 Personal checks accepted; 3 Lunch available; 4 Dinner available; 5 Open all year; 6 Pets

1897 Victorian House Bed and Breakfast

FOREST CITY

1897 Victorian House Bed and Breakfast

306 S. Clark Street, 50436
(515) 582-3613

As a guest in this turn-of-the-century Queen Anne Victorian home, you may choose from four beautifully decorated bedrooms, each with private bath. Breakfast, included in your rate, is served in our dining room, and we specialize in good, homemade food. A Victorian antique shop and tearoom are two blocks away. Play our 1923 baby grand player piano, play croquet, and relax in Forest City, a quiet yet progressive rural community.

Hosts: Richard and Doris Johnson
Rooms: 4 (PB) $60-90
Full Breakfast
Credit Cards: A, B
Notes: 2, 3 and 4 (by reservation), 5, 9, 10, 12

FORT MADISON

Kingsley Inn

707 Avenue H, 52627
(319) 372-7074; (800) 441-2327;
FAX (319) 372-7096

Experience complete relaxation in 1860s Victorian luxury. Fourteen spacious rooms are furnished in period antiques with today's modern comforts. Awaken to the aroma of "Kingsley Blend" coffee and enjoy a specialty breakfast in the elegant Morning Room. Stroll to a replica of an 1808 fort, museum, parks, shops, Catfish Bend Casino, and antique malls. Located just fifteen minutes from historic Nauvoo, Illinois. You may treat yourselves to a unique lunch or dinner at Alpha's on the Riverfront, right off our lobby. Private baths (some whirlpools), CATV, AC, and telephones are available. Kingsley Inn is a nonsmoking facility.

Hostess: Nannette Evans
Rooms: 14 (PB) $70-115
Continental Plus Breakfast
Credit Cards: A, B, C, D, E
Notes: 2, 3, 4, 5, 7 (limited), 9, 10, 12

GREENFIELD

Brass Lantern

2446 State Highway 92, 50849
(515) 743-2031; (888) 743-2031;
FAX (515) 343-7500
E-mail: info@brasslantern.com
Web site: www.brasslantern.com

Enjoy quality time together! The Brass Lantern offers a private guest house with a forty-foot heated pool on twenty peaceful acres. Located near the bridges of Madison County. There is plenty of room for year-round family fun and relaxation—or it can be the perfect retreat to renew relationships, regain perspectives, and relieve stress. Spacious rooms with luxury amenities overlook the pool and adjoin a fully furnished guest kitchen. The family suite sleeps six. Guests may enjoy breakfast at poolside. Lakes, a country zoo, an

welcome; 7 Children welcome; 8 Tennis nearby; 9 Swimming nearby; 10 Golf nearby; 11 Skiing nearby; 12 May be booked through travel agent.

Brass Lantern

antique air museum, fishing, golf, and antiquing are found nearby. Gift certificates are offered. The whole house is available for rental.

Hosts: Terry and Margie Moore
Rooms: 2 (PB) $95-145
Full Breakfast
Credit Cards: none
Notes: 2, 5, 6 (restricted), 7, 9 (on site), 10, 12

GRINNELL

Carriage House Bed and Breakfast

1133 Broad Street, 50112
(515) 236-7520

Beautiful Queen Anne-style Victorian home with relaxing wicker furniture and a swing seat on the front porch. Several fireplaces to be enjoyed in the wintertime. Gourmet breakfast with fresh fruit, quiche, and Irish soda bread fresh from the griddle. Local shopping, nearby lake and hiking, excellent restaurants. One block

from Grinnell College, one hour from Des Moines and Iowa City. Member of Iowa Bed and Breakfast Innkeepers Association, Iowa Lodging Association, and Grinnell Area Chamber of Commerce.

Hosts: Ray and Dorothy Spriggs
Rooms: 5 (3PB; 2SB) $45-60
Full Breakfast
Credit Cards: none
Notes: 2, 5, 8, 9, 10, 11, 12

Clayton Farms Bed and Breakfast

621 Newburg Road, 50112
(515) 236-3011

Clayton Farms Bed and Breakfast is an extra nice contemporary farm home on a 320-acre livestock and grain operation. Guests may enjoy fishing and boating on the farm pond, with a place for campfires in season. You may use the family room with fireplace, TV, VCR, library of movies, and kitchenette stocked with beverages and snacks. A family-style country breakfast is served. Group packages for pheasant hunters and hunters of antiques and collectibles. Seven miles from Grinnell College; one hour from Des Moines, Iowa City, and Cedar Rapids; forty-five minutes from the Amana Colonies; twenty miles from casino. The accommodations are air-conditioned. Smoking is restricted to outdoors. State licensed and inspected. Brochures are available—specify general, hunting, or antiquing; request a brochure for hunting rates.

Hosts: Ron and Judie Clayton
Rooms: 3 (1PB; 2SB) $57.75-63
Full Breakfast
Credit Cards: A, B, C
Notes: 2, 7, 8, 9, 10, 11

Clayton Farms Bed and Breakfast

HOMESTEAD (AMANA COLONIES)

Die Heimat Country Inn

4430 V Street, 52236
(319) 622-3937

Die Heimat, "the home place," has nineteen rooms furnished with Amana walnut and cherry furniture, televisions, and air-conditioning. Amana walnut canopy beds are the specialty of this—the oldest and largest—bed and breakfast in the Colonies. A nature trail, wineries, woolen mills, and restaurants are all nearby.

Hosts: Jacki and Warren Lock
Rooms: 19 (PB) $47-70
Full Breakfast
Credit Cards: A, B, D
Notes: 2 (preferred), 5, 6, 7, 8, 9, 10

IOWA CITY

2 Bella Vista Place Bed and Breakfast

2 Bella Vista Place, 52245
(319) 338-4129

Daissy Owen has furnished her lovely, air-conditioned, 1920s home with antiques and artifacts she has acquired on her travels in Europe and Latin America. The home is conveniently located on the city's historical north side with a beautiful view of the Iowa River. The Hoover Library, the Amana Colonies, and the Amish center of Kalona are all nearby. A full breakfast, with Daissy's famous coffee, is served in the dining room's unique setting each morning. Daissy is fluent in Spanish and speaks some French. From I-80, take Dubuque Street Exit 244, turn left on Brown Street, then first left on Linn Street; it is one block to #2 Bella Vista Place Bed and Breakfast.

Hostess: Daissy P. Owen
Rooms: 4 (2PB; 2SB) $55-95
Full Breakfast
Credit Cards: none
Notes: 2, 5, 8, 9, 12

welcome; 7 Children welcome; 8 Tennis nearby; 9 Swimming nearby; 10 Golf nearby; 11 Skiing nearby; 12 May be booked through travel agent.

Haverkamps' Linn Street Homestay

Haverkamps' Linn Street Homestay Bed and Breakfast

619 N. Linn Street, 52245-1934
(319) 337-4363; FAX (319) 354-7057

Enjoy the warmth and hospitality in our 1908 Edwardian home filled with heirlooms and collectibles. Only a short walk to downtown Iowa City and the University of Iowa main campus, and a short drive to the Hoover Library in West Branch, to the Amish in Kalona, and to seven Amana Colonies.

Hosts: Clarence and Dorothy Haverkamp
Rooms: 3 (SB) $35-45
Full Breakfast
Credit Cards: none
Notes: 2, 5, 7, 8, 9, 12

MALCOM

Pleasant Country B&B

4386 110th Street, 50157
(515) 528-4925

Eugene and Mary Lou Mann are a third-generation farm family, living in their home which was built in 1896. It is filled with antiques and country deco. The home is

a working farm; tours are available. Enjoy a full country breakfast with homemade specialties. We have a pond for fishing and pheasant hunting in season. Rest and relax in the quietness of the countryside.

Hosts: Mary Lou and Eugene Mann
Rooms: 4 (SB) $50-55
Full Breakfast
Credit Cards: none
Notes: 2, 5, 7, 8, 9, 10, 11, 12

Old Brick Bed and Breakfast

NEW LONDON

Old Brick Bed and Breakfast

2759 Old Highway 34, 52645
(319) 367-5403

This 1860s Italianate-style brick farmhouse, comfortably furnished with family pieces, beckons guests with welcome candles in each window. Our working grain farm offers an opportunity to view current farming techniques, equipment, and specialty crops. Enjoy peaceful surroundings, walk down a country road, visit area antique shops, sit on one of the porches, or relax in spacious guest rooms with queen-size beds and private baths.

NOTES: Credit cards accepted: A Master Card; B Visa; C American Express; D Discover; E Diners Club; F Other; 2 Personal checks accepted; 3 Lunch available; 4 Dinner available; 5 Open all year; 6 Pets

A full breakfast and arrival refreshments are served.

Hosts: Jerry and Caroline Lehman
Rooms: 2 (PB) $50
Full Breakfast
Credit Cards: none
Notes: 2, 4, 5, 7, 8, 9, 10

The Country Connection Bed and Breakfast

PRAIRIE CITY

The Country Connection Bed and Breakfast

9737 W. 93rd Street S., 50228-8306
(515) 994-2023

Experience the friendly atmosphere of a working farm community surrounded by the tranquillity of beautiful crop land. The Country Connection Bed and Breakfast is a turn-of-the-century farm home with period furnishings, blended with privacy, charm, and hospitality. A hearty breakfast is served on the cheerful sunporch or in the formal dining room. Guests are treated to a complimentary bedtime snack, homemade ice cream and cookies. Near Pella Tulip Time and Walnut Creek Wildlife Refuge, twenty miles east of Des Moines, three and a half miles southeast of Prairie City. Open May-November.

Hostess: Alice A. Foreman
Rooms: 2 (SB); $50-60
Full Breakfast
Credit Cards: A, B
Notes: 2, 7, 9, 10, 12

ST. ANSGAR

Blue Belle Inn

513 W. Fourth Street, PO Box 205, 50472
(515) 736-2225

Rediscover the romance of the 1890s while enjoying the comfort and convenience of the 1990s in one of six distinctively decorated guest rooms at the Blue Belle Inn. The festive Victorian "painted lady" features AC, fireplaces, and Jacuzzis. Lofty tin ceilings, gleaming maple woodwork, stained glass, and crystal chandeliers in bay and curved window pockets create a shimmering interplay of light and color. Enjoy breakfast on the balcony or gourmet dining by candlelight.

Hostess: Sherrie C. Hansen
Rooms: 6 (5PB; 1SB) $50-130
Full Breakfast
Credit Cards: A, B, C, D
Notes: 2, 3, 4, 5, 7, 9, 10, 12

SPENCER

Hannah Marie Country Inn

4070 Highway 71, 51301
(712) 262-1286; (800) 972-1286;
FAX (712) 262-3294
Web site: http://www.nwiowabb.com/hannah.htm

Journey here. The romance of country is enjoyed in this pretty place. Themed guest

welcome; 7 Children welcome; 8 Tennis nearby; 9 Swimming nearby; 10 Golf nearby; 11 Skiing nearby; 12 May be booked through travel agent.

Hannah Marie Country Inn

rooms, loved and comfortable, are very much romantic places with in-room double whirlpools in alcoves, private commodes, queen-size featherbeds, down comforters, softened water, and air-conditioning. Candlelit full breakfasts—or request a light breakfast basket in your room, on the veranda, or under the apple trees. Parasol stroll among the fragrant herbs, vibrant wildflowers, and vegetables. Candlelit dinners are available on request. Nurture your spirit here. *Come*.

Hostess: Mary Nichols
Rooms: 6 (PB) $77-105
Full Breakfast
Credit Cards: A, B, D
Notes: 2, 3, 4, 5, 7, 8, 9, 10, 12 (10%)

SWEDESBURG

The Carlson House

105 Parks Street, PO Box 86, 52652
(319) 254-2451; FAX (319) 254-8809

Experience a touch of Sweden in this stylish home in a Swedish-American country village. Guests enjoy comfortable rooms with queen-size beds and private baths (one with a whirlpool tub); a full Swedish breakfast; a cheerful sitting room for re-laxation, reading and television; and a new whirlpool hot tub on our deck. Favorite pastimes here include browsing in the books, chatting on the porches, strolling through the local Swedish immigrant villages, and visiting the nearby Swedish-American Museum.

Hosts: Ned and Ruth Ratekin
Rooms: 3 (2PB; 1SB) $50
Full Breakfast
Credit Cards: A, B
Notes: 2, 5

TAMA

Hummingbird Haven Bed and Breakfast

1201 Harding Street, 52339
(515) 484-2022

We hope you will join us at Hummingbird Haven and get a taste of Central Iowa's hospitality. The B&B offers two guest rooms with a large shared bath. Guests have use of the home, laundry services are available, and the home has central air and heat. Tama's central location makes our B&B a perfect home base for seeing many of Iowa's attractions. Ten minutes from Tama County Museum and Mesquaki Bingo and Casino; thirty minutes from Mashalltown, County Lake with water sports, Opera House in Brooklyn, and Grinnell College and Museum. One hour from many more attractions. Please, no pets or smoking.

Hostess: Bernita Thomsen
Rooms: 2 (SB) $38-50
Full Breakfast
Credit Cards: A, B
Notes: 2, 3, 4, 5, 7, 9, 10

NOTES: Credit cards accepted: A Master Card; B Visa; C American Express; D Discover; E Diners Club; F Other; 2 Personal checks accepted; 3 Lunch available; 4 Dinner available; 5 Open all year; 6 Pets

VINTON

The Lion and the Lamb Bed and Breakfast

913 2nd Avenue, 52349
(319) 472-5086 (voice and FAX);
(800) 808-LAMB (5262)
E-mail: LionLambBB@aol.com
Web site: http://members.aol.com/lionlambbb/
bnb.htm

Located along the Cedar River, this small town whispers of a time gone by when Victorian opulence was at its peak. Vinton boasts many turn-of-the-century homes. Experience elegant accommodations in this 1892 Queen Anne mansion. Each guest room features a queen-size bed, TV, overhead fan and AC. Call for a free color brochure and information on things to do in the area.

Hosts: Richard and Rachel Waterbury
Rooms: 4 (2PB; 2SB) $65-85
Full Breakfast
Credit Cards: A, B, D
Notes: 2, 5, 7, 8, 9, 10, 11 (cross-country), 12

WALNUT

Antique City Inn Bed and Breakfast

400 Antique City Drive, PO Box 584, 51577
(712) 784-3722

This 1911 Victorian home has been restored and furnished to its original state. Enjoy a nostalgic experience combining simplicity of life, the craftsmanship of yesterday, quiet living, and small-town hospitality. The inn is located one block from malls and stores that feature 250 antique dealers. The home has beautiful woods, a dumbwaiter icebox, French doors, and a wraparound porch. We offer a handicap-accessible room.

Hostess: Sylvia Reddie
Rooms: 6 (2PB; 4SB) $42.40-51.94
Full Breakfast
Credit Cards: A, B, C, D
Notes: 2, 3, 4, 5

Antique City Inn

Clark's Country Inn Bed and Breakfast

701 Walnut Street, PO Box 533, 51577
(712) 784-3010

Iowa's antique capital, one mile south of I-80 between Omaha and Des Moines. Six malls, individual shops, more than two hundred dealers, open all year. Clark's Country Inn is a 1912 two-story home with oak interior, antiques, newly remodeled guest rooms, private baths, king/queen beds, central air, and full breakfast. Mastercard/Visa deposit required. No smoking.

Host: Ron and Mary Lou Clark
Rooms: 3 (PB) $52
Full Breakfast
Credit Cards: A, B
Notes: 2, 5, 7 (over 12), 8, 9, 10, 12

welcome; 7 Children welcome; 8 Tennis nearby; 9 Swimming nearby; 10 Golf nearby; 11 Skiing nearby; 12 May be booked through travel agent.

WILLIAMSBURG

Lucille's Bed and Breakfast

2835 225th Street, 52361
(319) 668-1185

Enjoy the charm of our scenic country Tudor home. Guests may want to relax in our spacious yard or grill on our patios. Croquet, anyone? Flowers and shrubs enhance the area. Enjoy the comfort of our air-conditioned home. Our cozy fireplace will warm any chilly, snowy evening. Care for popcorn? Piano and organ available for music lovers. Sheephead card game and cribbage instructions offered. We will request the songbirds to greet you in the morning. Watch the goldfinch at their feeders. Children welcome. Smoking outside only, please. No pets, please. Full refund with twenty-four hours' notice. Member of Iowa Bed and Breakfast Innkeepers Association and Iowa Lodging Association.

Hosts: Dale and Lucille Bell
Full Breakfast

NOTES: Credit cards accepted: A Master Card; B Visa; C American Express; D Discover; E Diners Club; F Other; 2 Personal checks accepted; 3 Lunch available; 4 Dinner available; 5 Open all year; 6 Pets

Kansas

ABILENE

Victorian Reflections Bed and Breakfast

820 NW Third Street, 67410
(785) 263-7774; (800) 580-0948
E-mail: dianamaemc@aol.com

Enjoy the Victorian splendor of one of Abilene's finest historic homes. Victorian Reflections is located on Third Street in the historic Hurd House. Relax in the parlors or on one of the many porches. The city park, pool, and tennis courts are adjacent to the home, which is within walking distance of Abilene's many attractions.

Hosts: Don and Diana McBride
Rooms: 4 (PB) $55-75
Full Breakfast
Credit Cards: A, B
Notes: 2, 5, 8, 9, 12

ELK FALLS

The Sherman House

Box 15, 67345
(316) 329-4425
Web site: http://www.fn.net/~howell/towns/
elkfalls.html

A popular stop for passenger trains from 1879 to 1890, the Sherman House has been lovingly restored as a private guest house offering visitors a little unhurried time in this unusual rural community. Guests may visit in the studio of their hosts—professional potters for more than twenty years—and explore the waterfalls, floral gardens, unique restaurants, and historic churches, or just enjoy the peace and quiet. Large, comfortable rooms. A perfect retreat for couples, families, or small groups.

Hosts: Steve and Jane Fry
Rooms: 2 (PB) $48
Full Breakfast
Credit Cards: none
Notes: 2, 5, 7

GREAT BEND

Peaceful Acres Bed and Breakfast

Route 5, Box 153, 67530
(316) 793-7527

Enjoy a minifarm and sprawling, tree-shaded old farmhouse furnished with some antiques. If you like peace and quiet, chickens, calves, guineas, kittens in the springs, and old-fashioned hospitality, you need to come and visit us. Breakfast will

welcome; 7 Children welcome; 8 Tennis nearby; 9 Swimming nearby; 10 Golf nearby; 11 Skiing nearby; 12 May be booked through travel agent.

KANSAS

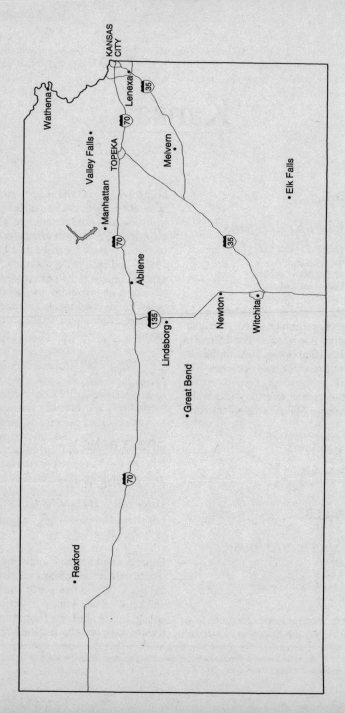

be fixed from homegrown products. We are near historical areas—Sante Fe Trail, Ft. Larned, Cheyenne Bottoms—and to the zoo and tennis courts.

Hosts: Dale and Doris Nitzel
Rooms: 3 (1 PB; 2 SB) $30
Full Breakfast
Credit Cards: none
Notes: 2, 3, 4, 5, 7, 8, 9, 10, 12

LINDSBORG

Swedish Country Inn

112 W. Lincoln, 67456
(913) 227-2985; (800) 231-0266;
FAX (913) 227-2795

Lindsborg is a lovely Swedish community in central Kansas. The furnishings in the Inn were imported from Sweden. Handstitched quilts top our Swedish pine beds. Bicycles, tandem and individual, are avail-

Swedish Country Inn

able. The Inn is within walking distance of many quaint shops and restaurants. For a unique experience, try our Inn for a "touch of Sweden in the Heartland."

Hostess: Becky Anderson
Rooms: 19 (PB) $49.50-75
Full Scandinavian Buffet Breakfast
Credit Cards: A, B, C, D
Notes: 2, 5, 7, 8, 10, 12

MANHATTAN

Casement Inn Christian Bed and Breakfast

1905 Casement Road, 66502-4932
(785) 776-6037

This home has been warmly called the "Casement Inn" for numerous years by friends and family. It has been a gathering place for reunions, Kansas State University events, and frequent guests. From time to time it has offered safety, renewal, and a place of reflection for those in crisis. For your relaxation and privacy, you may read, listen to tapes, or exercise on the nearby walking trail. You also can take a scenic drive to our beautiful Tuttle Creek Park. Casement is located on the northeastern side of Manhattan. The Kansas State University campus and football stadium are within a short distance. There are numerous restaurants and shopping establishments nearby.

Hostess: Jean Akin
Rooms: 1 suite (PB) $48-60
Continental Breakfast
Credit Cards: none
Notes: 2, 5

NOTES: Credit cards accepted: A Master Card; B Visa; C American Express; D Discover; E Diners Club; F Other; 2 Personal checks accepted; 3 Lunch available; 4 Dinner available; 5 Open all year; 6 Pets welcome; 7 Children welcome; 8 Tennis nearby; 9 Swimming nearby; 10 Golf nearby; 11 Skiing nearby; 12 May be booked through travel agent.

Schoolhouse Inn

MELVERN

Schoolhouse Inn

122 SE. Beck, 66510
(913) 549-3473

The Schoolhouse Inn is a two-story, limestone building built in 1870. It sits on a one-and-a-half-acre lawn. In 1986 it was entered in "Kansas Historic Places." The inn is a place you need to come visit. Guests can visit in a parlor with antique furniture or sit around a large table in the dining room and enjoy playing games. Four large bedrooms are upstairs with antiques and contemporary furnishings where guests can relax while reading a good book or looking at magazines. Enjoy this bed and breakfast for celebrating your anniversary or just a quiet getaway to our small town of Melvern. The Schoolhouse Inn is a member of the Kansas Bed & Breakfast Association.

Hosts: Rudy and Alice White
Rooms: 4 (2PB; 2SB) $50-60
Full Breakfast
Credit Cards: A, B
Notes: 2, 5, 7, 9

NEWTON

The Old Parsonage Bed and Breakfast

330 East Fourth Street, 67114
(316) 283-6808

Located in Newton's oldest neighborhood, this charming home once served as the parsonage for First Mennonite Church. It features a cozy yet spacious atmosphere filled with antiques and family heirlooms. The Old Parsonage is a short walk from the historical Warkentin House and Warkentin Mill, which are listed on the National Register of Historic Places. Two miles from Bethel College. Dine in one of Newton's fine ethnic eateries, or browse quaint antique and craft shops.

Hosts: Karl and Betty Friesen
Rooms: 3 (1PB; 2SB) $48
Continental Breakfast
Credit Cards: A, B
Notes: 2, 5, 7

REXFORD

The Carousel Cottage

310 Kansas Street, PO Box 87, 67753
(913) 687-3600

Enjoy the peace and quiet of northwestern Kansas in this quaint two-bedroom cottage filled with antiques and crystal chandeliers. The master bedroom has a king-size brass headboard and an antique floral carpet from an historical opera house. The living room is furnished with a television/VCR and plenty of good books to browse. Adjacent to the Shepherd's Staff Conference Center, which offers accom-

---

NOTES: Credit cards accepted: A Master Card; B Visa; C American Express; D Discover; E Diners Club; F Other; 2 Personal checks accepted; 3 Lunch available; 4 Dinner available; 5 Open all year; 6 Pets

modations for any size group. On Highway 83, twenty miles north of I-70.

Hostess: Nancy Dahl
Rooms: 2 (SB) $55-70
Continental Breakfast
Credit Cards: none
Notes: 2, 5, 7

VALLEY FALLS

The Barn
Bed and Breakfast Inn

14910 Bluemound Road, 66088
(913) 945-3225; (800) 869-7717;
FAX (913) 945-3226

In the rolling hills of northeast Kansas, this 101-year-old barn has been converted into a bed and breakfast. Sitting high on a hill with a beautiful view, it has a large indoor heated pool, fitness room, three living rooms, and king or queen beds in all rooms. We serve you supper, as well as a full breakfast, and have three large meeting rooms available.

Hosts: Tom and Marcella Ryan
Rooms: 20 (PB) $83-93
Full Breakfast and Supper
Credit Cards: A, B, C, D
Notes: 2, 3, 4, 5, 7, 8, 9, 10, 12

WATHENA

Carousel
Bed and Breakfast

Route 1, Box 124, 66090
(913) 989-3537; (800) 627-8115

The Carousel Bed and Breakfast, an early-1900s two-story Victorian house, sits atop a hill overlooking the beautiful countryside of glacial hills, bluffs, and forests of Doniphan County, Kansas. The house is wallpapered throughout. Four sets of bay windows with lace curtains, area rugs, and period antiques reflect the elegant Victorian style. A large front porch overlooks beautiful terraced lawns. Personalized decor in each guest room.

Hosts: Jack and Betty Price
Rooms: 3 (1PB; 2SB) $45-65
Full Breakfast
Credit Cards: A, B
Notes: 2, 5, 7, 9, 10, 11

WICHITA

The Castle Inn Riverside

1155 N. River Boulevard, 67203
(316) 263-9300; (800) 580-1131
FAX (316) 263-4998

The Castle Inn Riverside, the historic Campbell Castle, was built in 1888 by Col. Burton Harvey Campbell from blueprints of an original Scottish castle. This small luxury inn features fourteen uniquely appointed guest rooms, each with a distinctive theme. Amenities include Jacuzzi tubs for two (six rooms), fireplaces (twelve rooms), full gourmet breakfast, complimentary wine and hors d'oeuvres, and an assortment of homemade desserts and gourmet coffees served each evening.

Hosts: Terry and Paula Lowry
Rooms: 14 (14) $125-250
Full Breakfast
Credit Cards: A, B, D
Notes: 2, 5, 7 (over 10), 8, 10

---

welcome; 7 Children welcome; 8 Tennis nearby; 9 Swimming nearby; 10 Golf nearby; 11 Skiing nearby; 12 May be booked through travel agent.

KENTUCKY

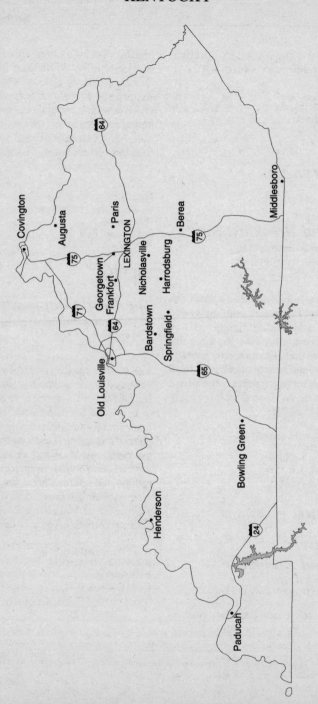

Kentucky

AUGUSTA

Augusta White House Inn Bed and Breakfast

307 Main Street, 41002-1038
(606) 756-2004; FAX (606) 756-2004

A beautifully restored, two-story brick structure (c. 1830) retaining its early Victorian-era style and elegance, coupled with true Southern hospitality. Comfortable rooms with flowered wallpaper and high crown molded ceilings as a reminder of yesteryear, but with modern convenience.

Hostess: R. C. Spencer
Rooms: 5 (2PB; 3SB) $59-79
Full Breakfast
Credit Cards: A, B, C, D
Notes: 8, 9, 10

BARDSTOWN

Beautiful Dreamer Bed and Breakfast

440 E. Stephen Foster Avenue, 40004
(502) 348-4004, (800) 811-8312

Beautiful Dreamer Bed and Breakfast is a Federal-design home in the historic district of Bardstown. Guest rooms are fully air-conditioned. The home features cherry furniture and antiques. All rooms are available with queen-size beds: Beautiful Dreamer (double Jacuzzi), Stephen Foster (handicap-accessible), and Captain's (fireplace, single Jacuzzi). Enjoy a hearty breakfast; then relax on our porches with a breathtaking view of my Old Kentucky Home. Come, and make your own beautiful dreams!

Hosts: Dan and Lynell Ginter
Rooms: 3 (PB) $79-99
Full Breakfast
Credit Cards: A, B
Notes: 2, 5, 7 (over 8), 8, 9, 10, 12

Jailer's Inn

111 W. Stephen Foster Avenue, 40004
(502) 348-5551; (800) 948-5551;
FAX (502) 349-1837

We pamper our "prisoners!" Come "spend time" in our jail and unlock a wonderful adventure in history. Large, spacious rooms, beautifully decorated in antiques and heirlooms. All rooms have private baths, so "escape" to our Victorian, Colonial, Library, Garden, or 1819 rooms. The 1819 and Colonial rooms have double

---

NOTES: Credit cards accepted: A Master Card; B Visa; C American Express; D Discover; E Diners Club; F Other; 2 Personal checks accepted; 3 Lunch available; 4 Dinner available; 5 Open all year; 6 Pets welcome; 7 Children welcome; 8 Tennis nearby; 9 Swimming nearby; 10 Golf nearby; 11 Skiing nearby; 12 May be booked through travel agent.

Jacuzzis. Delicious full breakfast served in lovely courtyard in the summertime. Located in the center of Historic Bardstown. Rated by AAA, Mobil Oil, American B&B Association. The Jailer's Inn is a "captivating experience."

Host: Paul McCoy
Rooms: 6 (PB) $65-105
Full Breakfast
Credit Cards: A, B, C, D
Notes: 2, 7, 8, 9, 10, 12

Kenmore Farms Bed and Breakfast

1050 Bloomfield Road, 40004
(502) 348-8023; (800) 831-6159

Drop your hurried ways and enjoy the charm and warmth of days gone by. This beautifully restored 1860s Victorian home features antiques, Oriental rugs, gleaming poplar floors, and a cherry stairway. Air-conditioned guest rooms are furnished with queen-size poster or Lincoln beds and lovely linens, including period pieces. Large, private baths; spacious vanities. A hearty country breakfast is served—all home-cooked. The decor and our brand

Kenmore Farms Bed and Breakfast

of hospitality create a relaxing and enjoyable atmosphere. AAA-approved.

Hosts: Dorothy and Bernie Keene
Rooms: 4 (PB) $80-90
Full Breakfast
Credit Cards: none
Notes: 2, 5, 7 (over 12), 8, 9, 10

Cabin Fever

BEREA

Cabin Fever

112 Adams Street, 40403
(606) 986-9075 (voice and FAX)
E-mail: jenrose@mis.net
Web site: http://www.bereaonline.com.jrose

Located in the folk arts and crafts capital of Kentucky, our home features hand-hewn log construction and hardwood floors. The Martin Room has a pecan bedroom suite with a queen bed covered with a handmade quilt, tapestries by Korean artisans, and private bath. The Gallery Room features our artwork and is decorated in a more modern style. Behind the house is a smaller cabin, built in 1819, featuring antique school furnishings and a rope bed. Guests can walk west to Old Town, where craftsmen are always at work, and east to Berea College.

Hosts: Alfredo Escobar and Jennifer Rose Escobar
Rooms: 2 (1PB; 1SB) $50-75
Full Breakfast
Notes: 2, 3, 4, 5, 7, 8, 9 (seasonal), 10

BOWLING GREEN

Alpine Lodge

5310 Morgantown Road, 42101-8201
(502) 843-4846; (888) 444-3791-6293

Alpine Lodge is a spacious, Swiss chalet-style home with more than six thousand square feet. It is located on eleven-and-a-half acres. The furnishings are mostly antiques. A typical southern breakfast of eggs, sausage, biscuits, gravy, fried apples, grits, coffee cake, coffee, and orange juice starts your day. There are lovely grounds and nature trails to stroll through. We also have a swimming pool, gazebo, and outdoor spa. All the rooms have phones and cable televisions (three movie channels). The lodge is near many popular attractions. Your hosts are retired musicians who might be persuaded to play something for the guests.

Hosts: Dr. and Mrs. David Livingston
Rooms: 5 (3PB; 2SB) $45-65
Full Breakfast
Credit Cards: none
Notes: 2, 3, 4, 5, 6, 7, 9, 10, 12

COVINGTON

Licking-Riverside Historic Bed and Breakfast

516 Garrard Street, 41011
(606) 291-0191; (800) 483-7822;
FAX (606) 291-0939

This is an historic home in the historic district along the Licking River. Accommodations include the famous Jacuzzi suite with river view, Victorian decor, fireplace, sitting area, TV/VCR; and deluxe queen rooms with private baths. A courtyard with decks overlooks a wooded area with river frontage. Enjoy a short walk to the Ohio River and get a marvelous view of the Cincinnati skyline. Many year-round activities are nearby, as well as our beautiful riverfront. Packages include Reds, Bengals, and the Arts!

Hostess: Lynda L. Freeman
Rooms: 3 (PB) $89-149
Continental Breakfast
Credit Cards: A, B, C, D
Notes: 2, 5, 7, 8, 9, 10, 12

FRANKFORT

The Patton Lane Bed and Breakfast

414 Conway Street, 40601
(502) 223-9839; FAX (502) 875-6459

Situated in historic downtown Frankfort, within walking distance of the state capital, Floral Clock, and Rebecca Ruth's Candies, and just a moment's drive from Daniel Boone's grave, Vietnam Veterans Memorial, and Kentucky Military Museum, just to name a few of the many points of interest in Frankfort. Conveniently located near I-64; Lexington and Louisville are less than an hour's drive away. Whether you are soaking up a little sun on the private terrace, having a cup of tea in the sunroom overlooking the perennial garden, or rocking on the screened-in porch, you are sure to feel the peace and charm of this wonderful home, which was built in the early 1900s.

Rooms: 4 (SB) $65
Full or Continental Breakfast
Credit Cards: A, B
Notes: 2, 5, 7, 8, 9, 10

welcome; 7 Children welcome; 8 Tennis nearby; 9 Swimming nearby; 10 Golf nearby; 11 Skiing nearby; 12 May be booked through travel agent.

GEORGETOWN

Pineapple Inn

645 S. Broadway, 40324
(502) 868-5453 (voice and FAX)

Located in beautiful, historic Georgetown, our Inn—built in 1876—is on the Historical Register. Furnished with antiques and beautifully decorated. Three private guest rooms are upstairs: the Country Room and Victorian Room, each with a full bed, and the Americana Room, with two full beds and one twin bed. Our Derby Room is on the main floor with a queen-sized canopy bed and hot tub in a private bath. Full breakfast is served in our Country French dining room. Relax in our large living room.

Hosts: Muriel and Les
Rooms: 4 (PB) $65-90
Full Breakfast
Credit Cards: A, B
Notes: 2, 5, 7, 8, 9, 10, 12

HARRODSBURG

Canaan Land Farm

700 Canaan Land Road, 40330
(606) 734-3984; (888) 734-3984
Web site: http://www.bbonline.com/ky/canaan

Step back in time to a house more than two hundred years old. Canaan Land B&B is a historic home, c.1795. Rooms feature antiques, collectibles, and feather beds. Full breakfast included, with true southern hospitality. This is a working sheep farm with lambing in spring and fall. Large swimming pool and hot tub. Your host is a shepherd/attorney, and your hostess is a handspinner/artist. The farm is secluded and peaceful. Close to Shaker

Village. An historic log cabin (c. 1815) has three additional rooms with private baths and two working fireplaces. This is a nonsmoking B&B.

Hosts: Theo and Fred Bee
Rooms: 7 (6PB;1SB) $75-125
Full Breakfast
Credit Cards: none
Notes: 2, 5, 7 (by arrangement), 8, 9 (onsite), 10, 12

HENDERSON

L&N Bed and Breakfast

327 N. Main Street, 42420
(502) 831-1100; FAX (502) 826-0075
E-mail: LNBB@aol.com
Web site: http://www.go-henderson.com/lnbb.htm

L&N is a two-story Victorian home featuring oaken floors, woodwork, stained glass, antique furnishings, and a convenient location in the heart of downtown Henderson, next door to a RR overpass. Four bedrooms are available, each with private bath, direct-dial telephone and cable TV. The John James Audubon Park and Museum is only three and a half miles away and is open year-round. Your innkeepers reside next door.

Hosts: Norris and Mary Elizabeth Priest
Rooms: 4 (PB) $75
Continental Breakfast
Credit Cards: none
Notes: 2, 5, 7, 8, 9, 10

LOUISVILLE

Ashton's Victorian Secret

1132 S. First Street, 40203
(502) 581-1914; (800) 449-4691, 0604

"Step inside and step back one hundred years in time" at this three-story, Victo-

---

NOTES: Credit cards accepted: A Master Card; B Visa; C American Express; D Discover; E Diners Club; F Other; 2 Personal checks accepted; 3 Lunch available; 4 Dinner available; 5 Open all year; 6 Pets

Ashton's Victorian Secret

rian brick mansion in historic Louisville. Recently restored to its former elegance, the hundred-year-old structure features spacious accommodations, high ceilings, and original woodwork. The Louisville area, rich in historic homes, also will tempt railbirds and would-be jockeys to make a pilgrimage to the famous Churchill Downs, Home of the Kentucky Derby.

Hosts: Nan and Steve Roosa
Rooms: 6 (2PB; 4SB) $58-89
Continental Breakfast
Credit Cards: none
Notes: 5, 7, 8, 9, 10, 11, 12

MIDDLESBORO

The RidgeRunner Bed and Breakfast

208 Arthur Heights, 40965
(606) 248-4299
Web site: http://www.bbonline.com/ky/
    ridgerunner

This 1891 Victorian home is furnished with authentic antiques and is nestled in the Cumberland Gap Mountains. A picturesque view is enjoyed from a sixty-foot front porch. You are treated like a special person in a relaxed, peaceful atmosphere. We are located only five minutes from Cumberland Gap National Historic Park, twelve miles from Pine Mountain State Park, and fifty miles from Knoxville, Tennessee.

Hostesses: Sue Richards and Irma Gall
Rooms: 4 (2PB; 2SB) $55-65
Full Breakfast
Credit Cards: none
Notes: 2, 5, 8, 9, 10, 12

The RidgeRunner Bed and Breakfast

NICHOLASVILLE

Sandusky House and O'Neal Log Cabin

1626 Delaney Ferry Road, 40356
(606) 223-4730

A tree-lined drive to the Sandusky House is just a prelude to a wonderful visit to the Bluegrass. A quiet, ten-acre country setting amid horse farms yet close to downtown Lexington, Horse Park, and Shakertown. The Greek Revival Sandusky House was built circa 1850 from bricks fired on the farm. A one-thousand-acre land grant from Patrick Henry, governor of Virginia, in 1780 was given to soldiers who had

welcome; 7 Children welcome; 8 Tennis nearby; 9 Swimming nearby; 10 Golf nearby; 11 Skiing nearby; 12 May be booked through travel agent.

fought in the American Revolution. In addtition to the Sandusky House, we have an 1820s, reconstructed, two-story, two-bedroom log cabin with full kitchen and whirlpool bath. The cabin has a large stone fireplace and AC, and is located in a wooded area close to the main house. An ideal getaway for the entire family! Please call for a brochure.

Hosts: Jim and Linda Humphrey
Rooms: 3 (PB) $69-75 main house, $85-95 cabin
Full Breakfast (Continental Plus in Cabin)
Credit Cards: A, B
Notes: 2, 5, 7 (over 12 in main house; all in cabin)

PADUCAH

The 1857's Bed and Breakfast

127 Market House Square, PO Box 7771, 42002-7771
(502) 444-3960; (800) 264-5607
FAX (502) 444-6751

The 1857's Bed and Breakfast is in the center of Paducah's historic downtown on Market House Square. The three-story building was built in 1857 and is on the National Register of Historic Places. The first floor is Cynthia's Ristorante. Second-floor guest rooms have been renovated in Victorian style. Period furnishings abound. On the third floor, guests may enjoy the game room with a view of the Ohio River. The game room features an elegant mahogany billiards table. A hot tub is on the second-floor outside deck. Advance reservations advised.

Hostess: Deborah Bohnert
Rooms: 3 (1PB; 2SB) $65-85
Continental Plus Breakfast
Credit Cards: A, B
Notes: 2, 5, 8, 9, 10, 11, 12

Ehrhardt's Bed and Breakfast

285 Springwell Lane, 42001
(502) 554-0644

Our brick colonial ranch home is located one mile off I-24, which is noted for its lovely scenery. We hope to make you feel at home in our antique-filled bedrooms and the cozy den with its fireplace. Nearby are the beautiful Kentucky and Barkley lakes and the famous Land Between the Lakes area.

Hosts: Eileen and Phil Ehrhardt
Rooms: 2 (SB) $45
Full Breakfast
Credit Cards: none
Notes: 2, 7 (over 6), 8, 9, 10

Farley Place Bed and Breakfast

Farley Place Bed and Breakfast

166 Farley Place, 42003
(502) 442-2488

Farley Place Bed and Breakfast is one of the finer Victorian homes in Paducah that dates back to the early to mid-1800s. Surrounded by a white picket fence, Farley Place dominates the block on a quiet side street. Farley Place is furnished in period antiques. It is on the National Register of

Historical Homes and is located one and a half miles from downtown Paducah.

Hosts: Bernice and Harold Jones (minister)
Rooms: 3 (1PB; 2SB) $55-85
Full Breakfast
Credit Cards: A, B, D
Notes: 2, 5, 6, 7, 8, 9, 10, 12

Trinity Hills Farm Bed and Breakfast Home —Stained-Glass Studio

10455 Old Lovelaceville Road, 42001
(502) 488-3999; (800) 488-3998

This seventeen-acre country retreat offers exceptional service and accommodations. Designed for romantic getaways or family gatherings. Handicap access is provided. Stained-glass windows, vaulted ceilings, fireplaces, spacious commons areas, and suites with whirlpool or private spa. Outdoors, guests may fishing, boating, birdwatching, hiking, visiting the farm animals and peacocks, or relaxing in the large spa near our water gardens. No smoking.

Hosts: Mike and Ann Driver
Rooms: 5 (PB) $60 (2 suites, $70-90)
Full Country or Gourmet Breakfast
Credit Cards: A, B, D
Notes: 2, 5, 6 (with prior notice), 7, 12

Trinity Hills Farm

PARIS

Rosedale B&B

1917 Cypress Street, 40361
(606) 987-1845; (800) 644-1862
Web sites: http://www.cre8IV.com/rosedale.html
　　　http://www.parisky.com

Nestled on three secluded acres, complete with flower and herb gardens, benches, a hammock, and lawn games. The fourteen-room, 1862 Italianate brick home is furnished with comfortable antiques. Guests are welcome to peruse the shelves of the mahogany library with its cozy fireplace. The screened porch, which overlooks some of the gardens, is a picturesque setting for breakfast, reading, and relaxing. Rosedale is located less than twenty miles from I-64 and I-75, eighteen miles northeast of Lexington in the heart of Bluegrass thoroughbred horse country. Paris and the surrounding area offer outstanding antique shopping and a number of specialty shops. The Kentucky Horse Park is fifteen minutes away; Keeneland Race Course, Rupp Arena, and the University of Kentucky are less than thirty minutes away.

Hosts: Katie and Jim Haag
Rooms: 4 (2PB; 2SB) $65-85
Full Breakfast
Credit Cards: A, B
Notes: 2, 5, 7 (12 and up), 8, 10

SPRINGFIELD

Maple Hill Manor

2941 Perryville Road, 40069
(606) 336-3075; (800) 886-7546

Listed on the National Register of Historic Places, Maple Hill Manor is surrounded by fourteen tranquil acres in the scenic

---

welcome; 7 Children welcome; 8 Tennis nearby; 9 Swimming nearby; 10 Golf nearby; 11 Skiing nearby; 12 May be booked through travel agent.

Bluegrass region. It took three years to build, circa 1851, and has ten-foot doors, thirteen-and-a-half-foot ceilings, nine-foot windows, a cherry spiral staircase, stenciling in the foyer, three brass and crystal chandeliers, and nine fireplaces. The honeymoon hideaway has a canopy bed and Jacuzzi. Ask about our murder mystery packages. Maple Hill is one hour from Louisville and Lexington. No smoking.

Hosts: Bob and Kay Carroll
Rooms: 7 (PB) $65-90
Full Breakfast
Credit Cards: A, B
Notes: 2, 5, 7, 8, 9, 10, 12

WILMORE

Scott Station Inn

305 E. Main Street, 40390
(606) 858-0121

The Scott Station Inn, a late 1800s country farmhouse, was beautifully refurbished

Scott Station Inn

in 1990. The inn has kept the charm and gracious air of an old Kentucky home. Each room has its own decorative theme reflecting the beauty of the state. The green shutters and white picket fence add just the right finishing touch.

Hosts: Ruth and Ian Yorston
Rooms: 6 (4PB; 2SB) $39.95-49.95
Full Breakfast
Credit Cards: A, B, D
Notes: 2, 5, 7, 10, 12

NOTES: Credit cards accepted: A Master Card; B Visa; C American Express; D Discover; E Diners Club; F Other; 2 Personal checks accepted; 3 Lunch available; 4 Dinner available; 5 Open all year; 6 Pets

Louisiana

CARENCRO/LAFAYETTE

La Maison de Compagne, Lafayette, Bed and Breakfast

825 Kidder Road, **Carencro** 70520
(318) 896-6529; (800) 895-0235;
FAX (318) 896-1494

This beautiful country Victorian home (circa 1871) with nine acres of quiet countryside is easily accessible from I-10 and I-49. A pool is available for guests to use in season. Children 12 and older are accepted. Alcoholic beverages are prohibited on premises; smoking is permitted outdoors only. We are located five minutes from three of the area's best-known Cajun restaurants. Antiques are placed throughout the home, which is occupied by the owners. Attractions within a thirty-mile radius include antebellum homes, churches, fishing, boating, golf, swamp tours, gardens, museums, festivals, food, Cajun music, and fun—all here in the heart of Cajun country.

Hosts: Joeann and Fred McLemore
Rooms: 4 (PB) $95-135
Full Breakfast
Credit Cards: A, B, C, D
Notes: 2, 5, 9 (on premises), 12

NEW ORLEANS

Bougainvillea House

841 Bourbon Street, 70116
(504) 525-3983

Antique ambience in the heart of the French Quarter—riverboats, gambling, antique stores, and famous restaurants. Central air/heat, private telephones, balconies, patios, cable TV. Walk to everything: aquarium, the Mississippi River, and more. Off street parking available.

Hostess: Flo Cairo
Rooms: 3 (PB) $90-250
Continental Breakfast
Credit Cards: B, C
Notes: 5, 10, 12

The Dusty Mansion

2231 Gen. Pershing, 70115
(504) 895-4576; FAX (504) 891-0049

Charming turn-of-the-century home, cozy and affordable. Sundeck, game room, hot tub. Close to St. Charles Avenue Street Car; easy access to French Quarter, Aquarium, Zoo, and Botanical Gardens.

Hostess: Cynthia Tomlin Riggs
Rooms: 4 (2PB; 2SB) $50-75
Continental Breakfast
Credit Cards: A, B, C, D
Notes: 2, 5, 7, 8, 10, 12

---

welcome; 7 Children welcome; 8 Tennis nearby; 9 Swimming nearby; 10 Golf nearby; 11 Skiing nearby; 12 May be booked through travel agent.

LOUISIANA

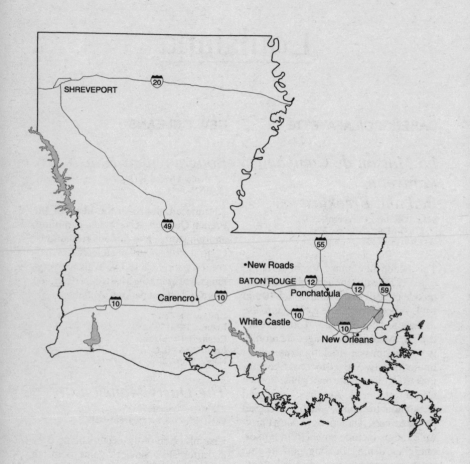

Essem's House— a.k.a. "New Orleans First Bed and Breakfast"

3660 Gentilly Boulevard, 70122
(504) 947-3401; (888) 240-0070;
FAX (504) 838-0140
E-mail: smb@neworleansbandb.com
Web site: http://www.neworleansbandb.com

Tree-shaded boulevards, direct transport to French Quarter (fifteen to twenty minutes), safe, convenient area of stable family homes. This ten-room brick home has three bedrooms, one king with private bath, two doubles with a shared bath. Separate cottage efficiency (one king or two singles with private bath). Guests enjoy the solarium, the living room, and the back garden.

Hostess: Sarah-Margaret Brown
Rooms: 4 (2PB; 2SB) $65-85
Continental Breakfast
Credit Cards: A, B, C, D
Notes: 5, 8, 9, 10

The Prytania Inns

1415 Prytania Street, 70130
(504) 566-1515; FAX (504) 566-1518

Built in the 1850s as a private home with slave quarters, Prytania Inn was actually used as an inn at the turn of the century. Having undergone an award-winning restoration in 1984 with all its original, splendid architectural features intact, it is once again open to visitors appreciative of the authentic Old New Orleans atmosphere it evokes. Close by are the Prytania Inns II and III, both historic mansions in the romantic neoclassical plantation style and

The Prytania Inns

decorated comfortably with antiques. The recently renovated St. Vincent's, an old orphanage, also has guest rooms available. The inns are five minutes from the French Quarter by streetcar.

Hosts: Sally and Peter Schreiber
Rooms: average 20 per building; $30-69
Full Breakfast
Credit Cards: A, B, C, D, E
Notes: 2, 3, 5, 6, 7, 8, 9, 10

NEW ROADS

Pointe Coupee Bed and Breakfast

405 Richey Street, 70760
(504) 638-6254

An unforgettable atmosphere for all in search of the "hospitality of the old South." Circa 1835 Creole plantation home featured in *Country Victoria* magazine. National Register candidate, newly renovated in 1997. Located in the historic district just moments from downtown shops, restaurants, and twenty-three-mile trophy

---

NOTES: Credit cards accepted: A Master Card; B Visa; C American Express; D Discover; E Diners Club; F Other; 2 Personal checks accepted; 3 Lunch available; 4 Dinner available; 5 Open all year; 6 Pets welcome; 7 Children welcome; 8 Tennis nearby; 9 Swimming nearby; 10 Golf nearby; 11 Skiing nearby; 12 May be booked through travel agent.

bass lake. Guest rooms have private baths. Morning coffee and full southern breakfast. Wonderful galleries with rockers overlook bird and butterfly sanctuaries.

Hosts: Mr. and Mrs. J.B. McVea
Rooms: 2 (PB) $100
Full Breakfast
Credit Cards: A, B
Notes: 3, 4, 5, 9, 10, 12

PONCHATOULA

The Bella Rose Mansion

255 N. Eighth Street, 70454
(504) 386-3857 (voice and FAX)
Web site: http://cimarron.net/usa/la/bella/html

"When only the best will do." Bella Rose is on the National Historical Register in the heart of America's antique city and plantations. Thirty-five minutes from New Orleans International Airport and forty-five minutes from Baton Rouge. Romantic, heart-shaped Jacuzzi suites and unique rooms. Exquisite hand-carved mahogany, spiral staircase crowned with a stained-glass dome is the finest in the South. Guests enjoy a silver service breakfast of Eggs Benedict, Banana Foster crepes, mimosas, and New Orleans-blend coffee in a marble-walled solarium with a fountain of Bacchus. Georgian in style, the mansion consists of more than 12,000 square feet. An indoor terrazzo shuffleboard court, an extensive library, and a heated

Olympic-style swimming pool are only a few of the magnificent features that await you at the Bella Rose Mansion. Available for functions.

Hostess: Rose James
Rooms: 2 Jacuzzi suites + 4 rooms (PB)
Full Breakfast
Credit Cards: A, B
Notes: 5, 8, 9, 10, 12

WHITE CASTLE

Nottoway Plantation Home

PO Box 160, 70788-0160
(504) 545-2730; FAX (504) 545-8632
E-mail: nottoway@worldnet.att.net
Web site: http://www.louisianatravel.com/
   nottoway

Built in 1859 by John Randolph, a wealthy sugar cane planter, Nottoway is a neo-classical mansion. Nottoway is the largest remaining plantation home in the South. Its guest rooms are individually decorated with period furnishings. Wake up with juice, coffee, and homemade muffins served to your room. Full breakfast served downstairs.

Hostess: Cindy Hidalgo
Rooms: 13 (PB) $125-250
Full Breakfast
Credit Cards: A, B, C, D
Notes: 2, 3, 4, 5, 7, 8, 9, 10, 12

NOTES: Credit cards accepted: A Master Card; B Visa; C American Express; D Discover; E Diners Club; F Other; 2 Personal checks accepted; 3 Lunch available; 4 Dinner available; 5 Open all year; 6 Pets

Maine

BAILEY ISLAND

Captain York House B&B

PO Box 298, 04003
(207) 833-6224

Stay at a restored sea captain's house on Bailey Island. Spectacular view of the ocean, beautiful sunsets. Relax in a peaceful environment, yet close to Portland, Freeport, Brunswick, Bath, and Booth Bay Harbor. Quiet island living in midcoast Maine. Quaint fishing villages nearby.

Hosts: Alan and Jean Thornton
Rooms: 5 (3PB; 2SB) $72-100
Full Breakfast
Credit Cards: A, B
Notes: 2, 5, 7 (over 12), 10, 12

BAR HARBOR

The Atlantic Oakes By-the-Sea

PO Box 3, Eden Street, 04609
(207) 288-5801; (800) 33 MAINE;
FAX (207) 288-8402
Web site: http://barharbor.com/oakes.html

We have restored the Sir Harry Oakes mansion/summer cottage on our grounds.

This charming house was named *The Willows* after the willow trees on the entrance drive. About two hundred summer cottages were built in Bar Harbor from 1880 to 1890. *The Willows* was built in 1913, one of the last estates built. The large wooden hotels (now gone) were built from 1865 to 1885. No matter how large and ostentatious the summer homes were, they always were called "cottages." *The Willows* is located on the ground of the Atlantic Oakes By-the-Sea. There are four tennis courts and indoor and outdoor pools available for use by B&B guests.

Hosts: The Coughs
Rooms: 9 (PB) $65-250
Continental or Full Breakfast
Credit Cards: A, B, C
Notes: 5, 8, 9, 10, 12

Black Friar Inn

10 Summer Street, 04609-1424
(207) 288-5091; FAX (207) 288-4197

Black Friar Inn is a completely rebuilt and restored inn incorporating beautiful woodwork, mantels, windows, and bookcases from old mansions and churches on Mount Desert Island. Gourmet breakfast includes

welcome; 7 Children welcome; 8 Tennis nearby; 9 Swimming nearby; 10 Golf nearby; 11 Skiing nearby; 12 May be booked through travel agent.

MAINE

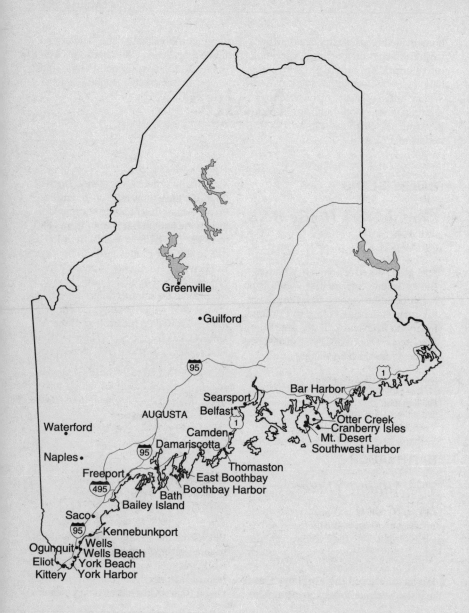

Greenville

• Guilford

95

Searsport
Belfast
AUGUSTA
Camden
Damariscotta
Waterford •
Naples •
Freeport
Bar Harbor
Otter Creek
Cranberry Isles
Mt. Desert
Southwest Harbor
1
Thomaston
East Boothbay
Boothbay Harbor
Bath
Bailey Island
495
Saco
95
Kennebunkport
Ogunquit
Wells
Wells Beach
Eliot
York Beach
Kittery
York Harbor

homemade breads, pastry, and muffins; fresh fruit; eggs du jour; etc. Afternoon refreshments are provided. All rooms have queen beds; the suite has a king bed. Within walking distance of the waterfront, restaurants, and shops, with ample parking available. Short drive to Acadia National Park.

Hosts: Perry and Sharon, Risley and Falke
Rooms: 7 (PB) $90-140
Full Breakfast
Credit Cards: A, B, D
Notes: 2, 5, 7 (over 11), 8, 9, 10, 11 (cross-country)

The Inn at Bay Ledge

The Inn at Bay Ledge

1385 Sand Point Road, 04609
(207) 288-4204; FAX (207) 288-5573

Dramatic and peaceful. Overlooking Frenchman's Bay at the top of an eighty-foot cliff with seventy-nine steps (and some benches along the way) leading to a private (Maine-stone) beach. Five miles to town center, two miles to Acadia National Park. Every room in the main house has an ocean view with the exception of one. Enjoy a dip in the pool, a sauna, a steam shower, or a book in the hammock overlooking the water. Eagles fly by. From the deck you watch seals and dolphins

eating their breakfast. The "added to a million times" early 1900s house has welcoming fireplaces, Oriental rugs, and rooms with featherbeds, antiques, designer linens, and down comforters.

Hosts: Jack and Jeani Ochtera
Rooms: 10 (PB) $135-250
Full Breakfast
Credit Cards: A, B
Notes: 2, 8, 9 (on site), 10

The Maples Inn

16 Roberts Avenue, 04609
(207) 288-3443; FAX (207) 288-0356
E-mail: maplesinn@acadia.net
Web site: http://www.acadia.net/maples

Built in the early 1900s, the Maples Inn is located on a quiet residential, tree-lined street. Guests will be away from Bar Harbor traffic, yet within walking distance of intimate restaurants and the surrounding sea. Reserve the White Birch Suite or the Red Oak room with its treehouse. Palates will be treated to the host's personal breakfast recipes, some of which have been featured in *Gourmet* and *Bon*

The Maples Inn

NOTES: Credit cards accepted: A Master Card; B Visa; C American Express; D Discover; E Diners Club; F Other; 2 Personal checks accepted; 3 Lunch available; 4 Dinner available; 5 Open all year; 6 Pets welcome; 7 Children welcome; 8 Tennis nearby; 9 Swimming nearby; 10 Golf nearby; 11 Skiing nearby; 12 May be booked through travel agent.

Appetit magazines. Classic tranquillity near Acadia National Park awaits you.

Hostess: Susan Sinclair
Rooms: 6 (PB) $60-150
Full Breakfast
Credit Cards: A, B, D
Notes: 2, 3 (picnic baskets), 8, 9, 10, 11

Stratford House Inn

45 Mt. Desert Street, 04609
(207) 288-5189

Built in 1900 by noted Boston book publisher Lewis A. Roberts, the Stratford House Inn is styled with the romantic charm of an English Tudor manor. It boasts ten beautifully decorated bedrooms. In the morning guests are treated to breakfast in the elegant dining room, replete with original period furnishings. After the day's events, find relaxation with a book in the library or interesting conversation on our large veranda, or try your hand at the grand piano in the music room. The inn is located within easy walking distance of the fine shops and restaurants of downtown Bar Harbor. Acadia National Park is but eight minutes by car.

Hosts: Norman and Barbara Moulton
Rooms: 10 (8PB; 2SB) $75-150
Continental Breakfast
Credit Cards: A, B
Notes: 2, 7, 8, 9, 10, 12

BATH

Fairhaven Inn

RR 2, Box 85, N. Bath Road, 04530
(207) 443-4391

Fairhaven Inn is a 1790 colonial nestled on the hillside overlooking the Kennebec

River. Guests have twenty acres of country sights and sounds to enjoy. Beaches, golf, and a maritime museum are nearby, plus cross-country ski trails and wood fire sites. A gourmet breakfast is served each morning, year-round. Candlelight dinners are available in winter.

Hosts: Dave and Susie Reed
Rooms: 8 (6PB; 2SB) $80-120
Full Breakfast
Credit Cards: A, B
Notes: 4 (weekend package), 5, 7 (by arrangement), 8, 9, 10, 11 (cross-country)

BELFAST

The Jeweled Turret Inn

40 Pearl Street, 04915
(207) 338-2304; (800) 696-2304
Web sites: http://www.maineguide.com/belfast/
jeweledturret
http://www.bbonline.com/me/jeweledturret

This grand representative of the Victorian era, built circa 1898, offers unique architectural features and is listed on the National Register of Historic Places. The Jeweled Turret Inn is named for the grand staircase that winds up the turret, which is lighted by stained- and leaded-glass panels with jewellike embellishments. Guests will find the rooms filled with Victoriana. Each guest room has its own bath. A gourmet breakfast is served each morning. Shops, restaurants, and the waterfront are a pleasant stroll away.

Hosts: Carl and Cathy Heffentrager
Rooms: 7 (PB) $75-95
Full Breakfast
Credit Cards: A, B
Notes: 2, 5, 8, 9, 10, 11, 12

Admiral's Quarters Inn

BOOTHBAY HARBOR

Admiral's Quarters Inn

71 Commercial Street, 04538
(207) 633-2474; FAX (207) 633-5904

Commanding an unsurpassed view of the harbor, this is a large old sea captain's house set on a knoll looking out to sea. Charming rooms, all with private entrances, baths, and individual decks, and decorated with a blend of white wicker and antiques. Ceiling fans cool several of the suites when sea breezes aren't working their magic. Each day begins with a hearty homemade breakfast that will fulfill any admiral's demands. "Way out of the ordinary . . . but not out of the way!"

Hosts: Les and Deb Hallstrom
Rooms: 6 (PB) $65-125
Full Hearty, Homemade Breakfast
Credit Cards: A, B, D
Notes: 2, 5, 8, 9, 10

Anchor Watch Bed and Breakfast

3 Eames Road, 04538
(207) 633-7565
E-mail: diane@lincoln.midcoast.com

Our seaside captain's house welcomes you to Boothbay Harbor. It is a short walk to

unique shops, fine dining, and scenic boat trips on your host's *Balmy Days Cruises*. A delicious breakfast is served each morning by the fireplace in the sunny breakfast nook by the sea. The comfortable guest rooms are decorated with quilts and stenciling and have private baths—one with a whirlpool tub, three with water-view balconies. You may enjoy late afternoon tea by the fire, watching the lobster boats returning, and beautiful sunsets from our private pier.

Hostess: Diane and Bob Campbell
Rooms: 4 (PB) $80-129
Full Breakfast
Credit Cards: A, B
Notes: 2, 5, 8, 9, 10, 12

Atlantic Ark Inn

64 Atlantic Avenue, 04538
(207) 633-5690
Web site: http://Atlanticarkinn.com

A quaint bed and breakfast inn offering lovely views of the harbor, a five-minute stroll from town. This hundred-year-old home offers a wraparound porch, balconies, antiques, Oriental rugs, floor-length drapes, poster beds, fresh flowers, and private baths—one with a Jacuzzi and another with a Greek tub. Each morning, celebrate the day with a delicious, full gourmet breakfast prepared with the freshest and purest of ingredients. Recommended in *Good Housekeeping* magazine as one of the best places to stay in Boothbay Harbor.

Hostess: Donna Piggott
Rooms: 6 (PB) $80-149
Full Breakfast
Credit Cards: A, B, C
Notes: 2, 7 (over 12), 8, 9, 10, 12

welcome; 7 Children welcome; 8 Tennis nearby; 9 Swimming nearby; 10 Golf nearby; 11 Skiing nearby; 12 May be booked through travel agent.

Five Gables Inn

Five Gables Inn

PO Box 335, Murray Hill Road, **East Boothbay**,
04544
(207) 633-4551; (800) 451-5048
Web site: http://www.maineguide.com/boothbay/
5gables

For more than a century, the Five Gables
Inn has perched on a garden-framed hillside overlooking Linekin Bay. The inn still
has a broad veranda with a hammock and
plenty of comfortable chairs, with a view
of lobster boats tugging at their moorings.
Completely renovated and restored to its
original Victorian charm. All the rooms
afford spectacular views of the bay. Five
rooms have working fireplaces.

Hosts: Mike and De Kennedy
Rooms: 15 (PB) $90-160
Full Breakfast
Credit Cards: A, B
Notes: 2, 8, 9, 10, 12

Harbour Towne Inn
on the Waterfront

71 Townsend Avenue, 04538
(207) 633-4300 (voice and FAX);
(800) 722-4240

Our refurbished Victorian inn retains turn-
of-the-century ambience while providing
all modern amenities. The colorful gardens and quiet, tree-shaded location

slopes right to the edge of the beautiful
New England harbor. Choose a room with
or without an outside deck for scenic
views, or a Carriage House room with waterfront decks. Our luxurious penthouse
is a modern and spacious home that sleeps
six in absolute luxury and privacy. No
smoking. No pets allowed.

Host: George Thomas
Rooms: 11 + penthouse (PB) $69-275
Deluxe Continental Breakfast
Credit Cards: A, B, C, D
Notes: 2, 5, 7 (well-behaved), 8, 9, 10, 11, 12

The Howard House

347 Townsend Avenue, 04538
(207) 633-3933; FAX (207) 633-6244

The unique chalet-type design features
beamed cathedral ceilings and sliding glass
patio doors with private balconies. Each
spacious room has cable TV, private bath,
and plush wall-to-wall carpeting. Early
America-style furnishings and appointments combine with natural wood walls
to provide luxurious accommodations with
a decidedly country feeling.

Hosts: The Farrins
Rooms: 14 (PB) $60-85
Full Breakfast
Credit Cards: none
Notes: 2, 8, 9, 10, 12

CAMDEN

Owl and Turtle Harbor
View Guest Rooms

PO Box 1265, 8 Bay View, 04843
(207) 236-9014

Two of the rooms immediately overlook
the harbor. AC, TV, electric heat, phone,

NOTES: Credit cards accepted: A Master Card; B Visa; C American Express; D Discover; E Diners
Club; F Other; 2 Personal checks accepted; 3 Lunch available; 4 Dinner available; 5 Open all year; 6 Pets

private bath, private parking. Breakfast served in your room. Downstairs is one of the state's best bookshops. Good restaurants and shops nearby. No smoking.

Hosts: The Conrads
Rooms: 3 (PB) $50-90
Continental Breakfast
Credit Cards: A, B, D
Notes: 5, 7, 8, 9, 10, 11, 12

CRANBERRY ISLES

The Red House

PO Box 164, Main Road, 04625
(207) 244-5297

Enjoy the breathtaking beauty of Maine while experiencing the relaxing, quiet atmosphere of The Red House, situated on a large saltwater inlet. Guests need only look outside for beautiful scenery and extraordinary ocean views. Six guest rooms, each distinctively decorated. Come share your hosts' island home and experience the tranquil peace of God's creation.

Hosts: John and Dorothy Towns
Rooms: 6 (3PB; 3SB) $50-80
Full Breakfast
Credit Cards: A, B
Notes: 2, 4, 7 (over 6), 9, 10 (off-island)

DAMARISCOTTA (WALPOLE)

Brannon-Bunker Inn

349B State Route 129, **Walpole**, 04573
(207) 563-5941; (800) 563-9225

Brannon-Bunker Inn is an intimate and relaxed country bed and breakfast situated only minutes from a sandy beach, lighthouse, and historic fort in Maine's midcoastal region. Located in a 1920s Cape, converted barn and carriage house, the guest rooms are furnished in themes that combine the charm of yesterday with the comforts of today. You'll find antique shops nearby.

Hosts: Jeanne and Joe Hovance
Rooms: 7 (5PB; 2SB) $60-70
Continental Plus Breakfast
Credit Cards: A, B, C
Notes: 2, 5, 7, 8, 9, 10, 12

ELIOT

The Farmstead

379 Goodwin Road, 03903
(207) 748-3145

Lovely country inn on three acres. Warm, friendly atmosphere exemplifies farm life

The Farmstead

welcome; 7 Children welcome; 8 Tennis nearby; 9 Swimming nearby; 10 Golf nearby; 11 Skiing nearby; 12 May be booked through travel agent.

of the late 1800s. Each Victorian-style guest room has a minirefrigerator and microwave for snacks or special diets. Breakfast may include blueberry pancakes or French toast, homemade syrup, fruit, and juice. Limited handicap access. Minutes from Kittery Factory Outlets, York beaches, and Portsmouth, historic sites. One hour from Boston.

Hosts: Meb and John Lippincott
Rooms: 6 (PB) $48-58
Full Breakfast
Credit Cards: A, B
Notes: 2, 5, 6, 7, 10, 12

FREEPORT

Captain Josiah Mitchell House Bed and Breakfast

188 Main Street, 04032
(207) 865-3289

Two blocks from L.L. Bean, this house is a few minutes' walk past centuries-old sea captains' homes and shady trees to more than 120 factory discount shops. After exploring, relax on our beautiful, peaceful veranda with antique wicker furniture and porch swing. State inspected and approved. Family owned and operated.

Hosts: Loretta and Alan Bradley
Rooms: 7 (PB) $68-85 (lower winter rates)
Full Breakfast
Credit Cards: A, B
Notes: 2, 5, 8, 9, 10, 11, 12

White Cedar Inn

178 Main Street, 04032
(207) 865-9099; (800) 853-1269
Web site: http://members.aol.com/bedandbrk/cedar

The White Cedar Inn is a historic inn located just two blocks north of L.L. Bean

and most of Freeport's luxury outlets. Our seven air-conditioned bedrooms, all with private baths, are spacious and furnished with antiques. We serve a full country breakfast each morning overlooking our beautifully landscaped grounds. A common room with a television and library is available to our guests. This is a nonsmoking Inn. The White Cedar Inn has a AAA three-diamond rating.

Hosts: Phil and Carla Kerber
Rooms: 7 (PB) $85-120
Full Breakfast
Credit Cards: A, B, C, D
Notes: 5, 8, 9, 10, 11, 12

GREENVILLE

Greenville Inn

PO Box 1194, Norris Street, 04441-1194
(207) 695-2206 (voice and FAX);
(888) 695-6000
E-mail: grlinn@moosehead.net
Web site: http://www.greenvilleinn.com

The Greenville Inn is a restored 1895 lumber baron's mansion situated on a hillside overlooking Moosehead Lake and the Squaw Mountains. A large, leaded-glass window decorated with a painted spruce tree, gaslights, embossed wall coverings, and carved fireplace mantles grace the home. A sumptuous continental breakfast buffet is included with the room price. In the evening, our restaurant is open to both guests and the public. The Greenville Inn is open year-round.

Hosts: Elfi, Susie and Michael Schnetzer
Rooms: 5 + 6 cottages + 1 suite (PB) $85-195
Continental Plus Buffet Breakfast
Credit Cards: A, B, D
Notes: 2, 4, 5, 7, 8, 9, 10, 11, 12

NOTES: Credit cards accepted: A Master Card; B Visa; C American Express; D Discover; E Diners Club; F Other; 2 Personal checks accepted; 3 Lunch available; 4 Dinner available; 5 Open all year; 6 Pets

GUILFORD

The Guilford Bed and Breakfast

PO Box 210, Elm and Prospect, 04443
(207) 876-3477; FAX (207) 876-3423

A lovely 1905 post-Victorian with a half-wrap porch situated high on a knoll within walking distance of town and shops. Enjoy a hearty breakfast of homemade pastries and muffins, buttermilk pancakes or red flannel hash with poached eggs in our dining room. In winter, enjoy tea by the fireplace in our library. Fish at Moosehead, hike the Appalachian Trail, or ski at Squaw Mountain.

Hosts: John and Pat Selicious
Rooms: 4-5 (2PB; 2SB) $50-60
Full Breakfast
Credit Cards: A, B
Notes: 2, 4, 5, 7 (over 12), 8, 9, 10, 11, 12

KENNEBUNKPORT

The Captain Lord Mansion

PO Box 800, 04046-0800
(207) 967-3141; FAX (207) 967-3172

The Captain Lord Mansion is an intimate, stylish luxury inn situated at the head of a sloping village green, overlooking the Kennebunk River. Built in 1812 as a private residence, the Inn is listed on the National Historic Register. The approximate acre of grounds include shaded lawns and brick-paved walkways lined with flowering trees and shrubs and beautiful flower gardens. The large, luxurious guest rooms are furnished with rich fabrics, original European paintings, romantic oversize four-poster canopy beds, excellent lighting, comfortable seating areas, and fine Federal period antiques. Yet they have modern comforts such as private baths with European-style, illuminated make-up mirrors and hair dryers, telephones, air-conditioning, and gas fireplaces. Six deluxe rooms overlook the Kennebunk River. One deluxe suite has a hydro-massage shower and double whirlpool. Christians, as well as your hosts and innkeepers, Bev Davis and husband Rick Litchfield and their staff are eager to make your visit enjoyable. We will be pleased to help map out guest itineraries for shopping, walking, biking, or driving. We also can point you to great restaurants, antique shops, and out-of-the-way sights.

Hosts: Bev Davis and Rick Litchfield
Rooms: 16 (PB) $149-375
Full Breakfast
Credit Cards: A, B, D
Notes: 2, 5, 8, 9, 10, 11 (cross-country)

The Inn on South Street

5 South Street, PO Box 478A, 04046
(207) 967-5151; (800) 963-5151

Now approaching its two-hundredth year, this stately Greek Revival house is in Kennebunkport's historic district. Located on a quiet street, the Inn is within walking distance of restaurants, shops, and the water. There are three beautifully decorated guest rooms and one luxury apartment/suite. Private baths, queen-size beds, fireplaces, a common room, afternoon refreshments, and early morning coffee are offered. Breakfast is always special and is served in the large country kitchen with

welcome; 7 Children welcome; 8 Tennis nearby; 9 Swimming nearby; 10 Golf nearby; 11 Skiing nearby; 12 May be booked through travel agent.

views of the river and ocean. Rated A⁺ and Excellent by ABBA.

Hosts: Eva and Jaques Downs
Rooms: 4 (PB) $105-225
Full Breakfast
Credit Cards: A, B
Notes: 2, 8, 9, 10, 12

Kennebunkport Inn

One Dock Square, PO Box 111, 04046
(207) 967-2621; (800) 248-2621;
FAX (207) 967-3705

Classic country inn located in the heart of Kennebunkport near shops and the historic district, beaches, boating, and golf. Originally a sea captain's home, the inn maintains its charm with antique furnishings, two elegant dining rooms, Victorian pub, and piano bar. Serving breakfast and dinner, May through October, the inn is recognized for its fine food. Rooms are available year-round.

Hosts: Rick and Martha Griffin
Rooms: 35 (PB) $69.50-229
Full Breakfast
Credit Cards: A, B, C
Notes: 2, 4, 5, 7, 8, 9, 10, 12

Maine Stay Inn and Cottages

34 Maine Street, PO Box 500, 04046
(207) 967-2117; (800) 950-2117;
FAX (207) 967-8757

A grand Victorian inn that exudes charm from its wraparound porch to its perennial flower garden and spacious lawn. The white clapboard house, built in 1860 and listed on the National Historic Register, and the adjoining cottages sit grandly in

Maine Stay Inn

Kennebunkport's historic district. The Maine Stay features a variety of delightful accommodations, all with private baths, color cable TV, and air-conditioning. Many rooms have fireplaces. A sumptuous full breakfast and afternoon tea are included. The Inn is an easy walk to the harbor, shops, galleries, and restaurants. AAA three-diamond- and Mobil three-star-rated.

Hosts: Lindsay and Carol Copelang
Rooms: 17 (PB) $85-225
Full Breakfast
Credit Cards: A, B
Notes: 5, 7, 8, 9, 10, 12

KITTERY

Enchanted Nights Bed and Breakfast

29 Wentworth Street, 03904-1720
(207) 439-1489
Web site: http://www.enchanted-nights-bandb.com

Affordable luxury seventy-five minutes north of Boston in coastal Maine. Fanciful and whimsical for the romantic at heart. French and Victorian furnishings with CATVs. Three minutes to historic Ports-

---

NOTES: Credit cards accepted: A Master Card; B Visa; C American Express; D Discover; E Diners Club; F Other; 2 Personal checks accepted; 3 Lunch available; 4 Dinner available; 5 Open all year; 6 Pets

mouth dining, dancing, concerts in the park, historic homes, theater, harbor cruises, cliff walks, scenic ocean drives, beaches, charming neighboring resorts, water park, and outlet malls. Whirlpool tub for two. Full breakfast, or $12 less, and enjoy a Portsmouth cafe. Pets welcome. No smoking indoors.

Hosts: Nancy Bogenberger and Peter Bogenberger
Rooms: 8 (6PB; 2SB) $47-180
Full Breakfast
Credit Cards: A, B, C, D
Notes: 2, 5, 6, 8, 9, 10, 12

LUBEC

Breakers By the Bay

37 Washington, 04652
(207) 733-2487

A two-hundred-year-old house with views of the bay, Campobello Island lighthouse, and Grand Manan Island. Private decks, three gas log fireplaces. Rooms have antique beds, chairs, hand-quilted bedspreads, hand-crocheted tablecloths. Rooms have private entrances, desks, TVs and refrigerators.

Hostess: E. M. Elg
Rooms: 5 (3PB; 2SB) $50-70
Full Breakfast
Credit Cards: none
Notes: 2, 10, 12

NAPLES

The Augustus Bove House

RR1, Box 501, 04055
(207) 693-6365

Historic Hotel Naples, visited in the '20s by Enrico Caruso and Joseph P. Kennedy of Boston. In the horse-and-buggy days, it was one of the first "summer hotels" in the area. Our central location and easy access places us within easy walking distance of causeway, restaurants, recreation, and shops. A four-season area of activity, Naples has something of interest for everyone. Our guest rooms have elegant yet homey furnishings and feature queen, twin and king beds. Most feature modern, private baths. Robes furnished. AC, TV, phones.

Hosts: Dave and Arlene Stetson
Rooms: 10 (8PB; 2SB) $59-139 (seasonal)
Full Breakfast
Credit Cards: A, B, C, D
Notes: 2, 5, 6, 7, 8, 9, 10, 11

Inn at Long Lake

Lakehouse Road, PO Box 806, 04055
(207) 693-6226; (800) 437-0328

Enjoy romantic elegance and turn-of-the-century charm at the Inn at Long Lake, nestled amid the pines and waterways of the lake region of western Maine. The inn has sixteen restored rooms with TV, air-conditioning, and private baths. Situated near the causeway, the inn is close to four-season activities and fine dining.

Hosts: Irene and Maynard Hincks
Rooms: 16 (PB) $149-225
Continental Breakfast
Credit Cards: A, B, D
Notes: 2, 7, 8, 9, 10, 11, 12

OGUNQUIT

The Terrace by the Sea

PO Box 831, 11 Wharf Lane, 03907
(207) 646-3232
Web site: http://www.terracebythesea.com

The Terrace by the Sea blends the elegance of our colonial inn and our deluxe motel

welcome; 7 Children welcome; 8 Tennis nearby; 9 Swimming nearby; 10 Golf nearby; 11 Skiing nearby; 12 May be booked through travel agent.

accommodations. Both offer spectacular ocean views in a peaceful, secluded setting across from the beach. All rooms have private baths, air-conditioning, telephones, color cable televisions, heat, refrigerators, and some efficiency kitchens. The Terrace by the Sea is within easy walking distance of the beautiful sandy beach, Marginal Way, shops, restaurants, and link to the trolleys. Come share the charm and hospitality of New England.

Hosts: John and Daryl Bullard
Rooms: 36 (PB) $46-160
Continental Breakfast
Credit Cards: none
Notes: 2, 4, 8, 9, 10

OTTER CREEK

Otter Creek Inn

Route 3, PO Box 9, 04665
(207) 288-5151; (800) 845-5852;
FAX (207) 288-0325

The Otter Creek Inn offers a variety of friendly, affordable, and convenient accommodations in a location from which to enjoy the beauty of Acadia National Park. Perfect for outdoor enthusiasts who enjoy hiking, bicycling, rock climbing, and horseback riding as well as travelers looking for a quiet setting to marvel at nature's wonders. Our six renovated guest rooms

have private baths, and there are two cabins with full kitchens and housekeeping facilities. Our large, two-bedroom apartment offers a full kitchen, living room, and dining area—ideal for two couples or a small family. We are open from May to October.

Rooms: 9 (PB) $60-125
Credit Cards: A, B, D
Continental Breakfast
Notes: 2, 6, 7

SACO

The Crown 'n' Anchor Inn

121 N. Street, PO Box 228, 04072
(207) 282-3829; (800) 561-8865;
FAX (207) 282-7495

Our North Street location places the Crown 'n' Anchor Inn at the hub of local attractions. Delight in this Greek Revival two-story house with ornate Victorian furnishings, period antiques, and many collectibles. Guests desiring to take time out from their busy schedules are invited to socialize in our parlor, curl up with a good book in our library, or just relax and enjoy the garden views from the comfort of our front porch. Just minutes from Kennebunkport, Wells, Ogunquit, Kittery, and more.

Host: John Barclay
Rooms: 6 (PB) $60-95
Full Breakfast
Credit Cards: A, B, C
Notes: 2, 5, 6, 7 (by arrangement), 8, 9, 10,
    11, 12

NOTES: Credit cards accepted: A Master Card; B Visa; C American Express; D Discover; E Diners Club; F Other; 2 Personal checks accepted; 3 Lunch available; 4 Dinner available; 5 Open all year; 6 Pets

SEARSPORT

Brass Lantern Inn

81 W. Main Street, PO Box 407, 04974
(207) 548-0150; (800) 691-0150;
FAX (207) 548-0304 (call first)
E-mail: brasslan@brasslan.sdi.astate.net

Nestled at the edge of the woods, this gracious Victorian inn, built in 1850 by a sea captain, overlooks Penobscot Bay. Features include an ornate tin ceiling in the dining room, where full breakfasts are served by candlelight. The Brass Lantern Inn is within walking distance of the ocean. Leave stress behind. Relax and unwind with us.

Hosts: Maggie and Dick Zieg
Rooms: 5 (PB) $65-85
Full Breakfast
Credit Cards: A, B
Notes: 2, 5, 7, 8, 9, 10, 11, 12

Thurston House Bed and Breakfast Inn

8 Elm Street, PO Box 686, 04974
(207) 548-2213; (800) 240-2213; call about FAX
E-mail: thurston@acadia.net

This beautiful colonial home, circa 1830, with ell and carriage house was built as a parsonage house for Stephen Thurston, uncle of Winslow Homer, who visited often. Now you can visit in a casual environment. The quiet village setting is steps away from Penobscot Marine Museum, beach park on Penobscot Bay, restaurants, churches, galleries, antiques, and more. Relax in one of our four guest rooms— one with a bay view, two that are great for

kids—and enjoy the "forget about lunch" breakfasts.

Hosts: Carl and Beverly Eppig
Rooms: 4 (2PB; 2SB) $50-65
Full Breakfast
Credit Cards: A, B, C
Notes: 2, 5, 7, 8, 9, 10, 11, 12

SOUTHWEST HARBOR

Island Watch Bed and Breakfast

73 Freeman Ridge Road, PO Box 1359, 04679-1359
(207) 244-7229

Wake to the rising sun over Cadillac Mountain and the majestic sea, high atop Freeman Ridge in the heart of Mount Desert Island. A fifteen-minute walk to Acadia National Park, five minutes to the village and harbor. A bird-watcher's paradise where wildlife abounds. Smoke-free. Private baths and hearty breakfasts.

Hostess: Maxine M. Clark
Rooms: 6 (PB) $75-85
Full Breakfast
Credit Cards: none
Notes: 2, 8, 9, 10

The Lambs Ear Inn

60 Clark Point Road, 04679
(207) 244-9828
Web site: http://www.acadia.net/lambsear

Our old Maine house was built in 1857. It is comfortable and scenic, away from the hustle and bustle. Private baths, comfortable beds with crisp, fresh linens. Enjoy the sparkling harbor views. Breakfast to remember. Come and be a part of this

welcome; 7 Children welcome; 8 Tennis nearby; 9 Swimming nearby; 10 Golf nearby; 11 Skiing nearby; 12 May be booked through travel agent.

The Lambs Ear Inn

special village and of Mt. Desert Island, surrounded by Acadia National Park.

Hostess: Elizabeth Hoke
Rooms: 8 (PB) $85-165
Full Breakfast
Credit Cards: A, B, C, D
Notes: 2, 8, 9, 10, 12

THOMASTON

Cap'n Frost Bed and Breakfast

241 Main Street, 04861
(207) 354-8217

Our 1840 Cape home is furnished with country antiques, some of which are for sale. If you are visiting our midcoastal area, we offer you a comfortable overnight stay, situated close to Mohegan Island and a two-hour drive to Acadia National Park. Reservations are helpful. Personal checks are accepted. All the guest rooms have private baths.

Hosts: Arlene and Harold Frost
Rooms: 3 (PB) $50-55
Full Breakfast
Credit Cards: none
Notes: 2

WATERFORD

Kedarburn Inn

Route 35, Box 61, 04088
(207) 583-6182; FAX (207) 583-6424
Web site: http://members.aol.com/kedar01/
index.html

Located in historic Waterford Village, a place to step back in time while you enjoy the comforts of today. Charming bedrooms decorated with warm country touches, including quilts handmade by Margaret, will add pleasure to your visit. Each day will start with a hearty breakfast. In the evening, one can relax and enjoy the elegant dinner that is served daily. Whether you come for outdoor activities or simply to enjoy the countryside, let us pamper you in our relaxed and friendly atmosphere.

Hosts: Margaret and Derek Gibson
Rooms: 7 (3PB; 4SB) $71-88
Full Breakfast
Credit Cards: A, B, C, D
Notes: 2, 4, 5, 6, 7, 9, 10, 11, 12

The Parsonage House Bed and Breakfast

Rice Road, PO Box 116, 04088
(207) 583-4115
E-mail: Parson@megalink.net

Built in 1870 for the Waterford Church, this restored historic home overlooks Waterford Village, Keoka Lake, and Mt. Tirem. The Parsonage House is located in a four-season area providing a variety of opportunities for the outdoor enthusiast. The Parsonage House is a haven of peace where Christ is honored. Double guest rooms are tastefully furnished.

NOTES: Credit cards accepted: A Master Card; B Visa; C American Express; D Discover; E Diners Club; F Other; 2 Personal checks accepted; 3 Lunch available; 4 Dinner available; 5 Open all year; 6 Pets

Weather permitting, we feature a full breakfast on the screened porch. Guests especially love our large New England farm kitchen and its wood-burning stove.

Hosts: Joe and Gail St. Hilaire
Rooms: 3 (1PB; 2SB) $70-85
Full Breakfast
Credit Cards: none
Notes: 2, 3, 5, 7, 9, 10, 11

WELLS (WELLS BEACH)

The Purple Sandpiper Guest House

1058 Post Road (Route 1), 04090
(207) 646-7990;
(800) 484-5040, Ext. 7990 (reservations)

Year-round bed and breakfast, just one mile from Wells Beach. All six rooms have private baths and entrances, color cable TV, and refrigerators. We also have an in-ground pool and barbecue area. In-season trolley service. Continental breakfast includes fresh-baked muffins, pastry, breads, cereal, juice, and coffee. Enjoy Wells' beaches, antique shops, and fine seafood restaurants. Conveniently located minutes from Kennebunkport, Ogunquit Village, York Harbor's lighthouse, and Kittery's shopping outlets.

Hosts: Stephen and Amy Beauregard
Rooms: 5 (PB); $45-75
Continental Breakfast
Credit Cards: A, B
Notes: 5, 7, 9

Sand Dollar Inn

50 Rachel Carson Lane, 04090
(207) 646-2346

Come, renew your spirit at our 1920s oceanfront beach house. The roll of the ocean waves, the smell of salt-air breezes, and the majesty of a starlit sky are simple creations of God accented by bountiful breakfasts and warm hospitality that will place you in a state of peace and tranquility. Join us in low season, as well, for a time of solitude, personal prayer and reflection. Small retreat groups welcomed.

Hosts: Bob and Carolyn Della Pietra
Rooms: 5 (3PB; 2SB) $85-145
Full Breakfast
Credit Cards: A, B
Notes: 2, 4 (occasionally), 5, 9, 10

Sand Dollar Inn

YORK BEACH

Homestead Inn Bed and Breakfast

PO Box 15, 03910
(207) 363-8952 (voice and FAX)

Friendly, quiet, homey—four rooms in a 1905 boardinghouse converted to our home in 1969. Panoramic view of ocean and shore hills. Walk to two beaches, shops, and Nubble Lighthouse. Great for small, adult groups. Living room fireplace.

Homestead Inn Bed and Breakfast

Breakfast served in barn-board dining room and outside on private sun deck.

Host: Dan Duffy
Rooms: 4 (SB) $54-64
Continental Plus Breakfast
Credit Cards: none
Notes: 2, 8, 9, 10, 12

YORK HARBOR

Bell Buoy
Bed and Breakfast

570 York Street, PO Box 445 (Route 1A), 03911
(207) 363-7264

At the Bell Buoy, there are no strangers, only friends who have never met. Located minutes from I-95 and U.S. 1, minutes from Kittery outlet malls, or a short walk to sandy beaches—or you may want to stroll the marginal way along the ocean shore just minutes away. Fireplace and cable TV. Homemade bread or muffins are served with breakfast in the dining room each morning or on the front porch.

Hosts: Wes and Kathie Cook
Rooms: 5 (3PB; 2SB) $60-85
Full Breakfast
Credit Cards: none
Notes: 2, 5, 7 (over 6), 9, 10

NOTES: Credit cards accepted: A Master Card; B Visa; C American Express; D Discover; E Diners Club; F Other; 2 Personal checks accepted; 3 Lunch available; 4 Dinner available; 5 Open all year; 6 Pets

Maryland

ALSO SEE LISTINGS UNDER DISTRICT OF COLUMBIA.

ANNAPOLIS

The Barn on Howard's Cove

500 Wilson Road, 21401
(410) 266-6840; FAX (410) 266-7293

The Barn on Howard's Cove welcomes you with warm hospitality to a converted 1850s horse barn overlooking a beautiful cove of the Severn River. You will be located just outside the hubbub of Annapolis and convenient to both Baltimore and Washington, DC. Begin the day with a choice of full breakfasts served in the dining area, on a sunny deck, or in a solarium—all overlooking the river. Our guests enjoy the beautiful gardens, rural setting, antiques, quilts, Oriental rugs, antiques, and the charming Noah's ark collection. Two guest bedrooms, each with a private bathrooms, await you. One room has a sleeping loft and private deck on the river. Both guest rooms overlook the river. Docking in deep water is provided. Canoes and a kayak are available for guests to use.

Hosts: Graham and Libbie Gutsche
Rooms: 2 (PB) $85-90
Full Breakfast
Credit Cards: none
Notes: 2, 5, 7, 8, 10, 12

Chesapeake Bed and Breakfast

408 Cranes Roost, 21401
(410) 757-7599 (voice and FAX)

Comfortable, English country town home nestled in a wooded community near Chesapeake Bay and Magothy River. Furnished in antiques, Orientals, and contemporaries. King, queen, single beds. Perfect for family vacation or couple's getaway. Guest space has private living room. Marked nature trail. Hostess was a local restaurant critic and can recommend dining options. Ten minutes from Annapolis, the U.S. Naval Academy, St. John's College, boating, and other marine adventures. Prefer two-night minimum.

Hostess: Carolyn Curtis
Rooms: 3 (1PB; 2SB) $70-90
Continental Breakfast
Credit Cards: none
Notes: 2, 5, 7, 8, 10

---

welcome; 7 Children welcome; 8 Tennis nearby; 9 Swimming nearby; 10 Golf nearby; 11 Skiing nearby; 12 May be booked through travel agent.

MARYLAND

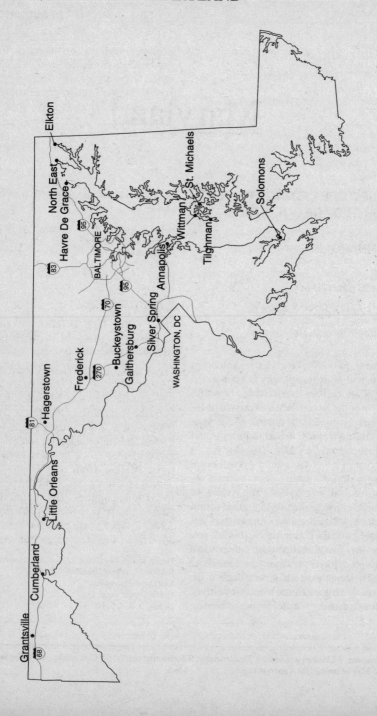

Chez Amis
Bed and Breakfast

85 East Street, 21401
(410) 263-6631; (888) 224-6455

Around 1900, Chez Amis "House of Friends" was a grocery store. Still evident are the original oak display cabinet, tin ceiling, and pine floors. One-half block from the capital, one block from the harbor, and minutes by foot from the naval academy. "European Country" decor with antiques and quilts. Four guest rooms with private baths. King and queen brass beds, TVs, central air-conditioning, terry robes, coffee service, and down comforters in every room. Don is a retired Army lawyer; Mickie a former DC tour guide. They welcome you with true "southern" Christian hospitality!

Hosts: Don and Mickie Deline
Rooms: 4 (PB) $75-95
Full Breakfast
Credit Cards: A, B
Notes: 2, 5, 12

The Flower Box—
A Bed and Breakfast

1601 St. Margaret's Road, 21401
(410) 757-3081

This charming ranch-style bed and breakfast home is only a short distance from historic downtown Annapolis. It is situated on three acres of old trees, gardens and seasonal flowers. A lovely breeze can be enjoyed on the porch or deck areas overlooking the pool. A full breakfast is served each morning in the dining room or,

weather permitting, on the porch. Each guest room is furnished lovingly with antiques, Oriental rugs, and family pictures. Your hosts invite you to share their many books as you relax and leave your burdens behind.

Hosts: John and Katherine Nolan
Rooms: 3 (2PB; 1SB) $80-90
Full Breakfast
Notes: 2, 5, 7, 8, 9, 10

CUMBERLAND

The Inn
at Walnut Bottom

120 Greene Street, 21502
(301) 777-0003; (800) 286-9718;
FAX (301) 777-8288

Classic country inn in downtown Cumberland consisting of twelve rooms and family suites, each with a telephone and color cable TV. Rooms are charmingly decorated with period reproductions and antique furniture. Afternoon refreshments and full breakfast included with lodging. Cozy parlor stocked with games and puzzles. Excellent restaurant on premises. The inn is within walking distance of the Western Maryland Scenic Railroad, the historical district, and several antique shops. Extraordinary hiking, biking, and sight-seeing close by. AAA-rated, three diamonds.

Hosts: Grant M. Irvin and Kirsten O. Hansen
Rooms: 10 + 2 suites (8PB; 4SB) $75-115
Full Breakfast
Credit Cards: A, B, C, D
Notes: 2, 3, 4, 5, 7, 9, 10, 11, 12

NOTES: Credit cards accepted: A Master Card; B Visa; C American Express; D Discover; E Diners Club; F Other; 2 Personal checks accepted; 3 Lunch available; 4 Dinner available; 5 Open all year; 6 Pets welcome; 7 Children welcome; 8 Tennis nearby; 9 Swimming nearby; 10 Golf nearby; 11 Skiing nearby; 12 May be booked through travel agent.

ELKTON

Garden Cottage at Sinking Springs Herb Farm

234 Blair Shore Road, 21921
(410) 398-5566

With an early plantation house, including a four-hundred-year-old sycamore, the garden cottage nestles at the edge of a meadow flanked by herb gardens and a historic barn with a gift shop. It has a sitting room with fireplace, bedroom, bath, air-conditioning, and electric heat. Freshly ground coffee and herbal teas are offered with the country breakfast. Longwood Gardens and Winterthur Museum are fifty minutes away. Historic Chesapeake City is nearby, with excellent restaurants. Sleeps three in two rooms. Third person pays only $25. Entrance at Elk Forest Road.

Hosts: Bill and Ann Stubbs
Rooms: 1 cottage (PB) $88
Full Breakfast
Credit Cards: A, B
Notes: 2, 5, 6, 7, 8, 10, 12

FREDERICK

Catoctin Inn

3613 Buckeystown Pike, PO Box 243,
   Buckeystown, 21717
(301) 874-5555; (800) 730-5550;
FAX (301) 874-2026
E-mail: catoctin@bigdog.fred.net
Web site: www.catoctininn.com

The Catoctin Inn is a memorable getaway and a business traveler's home away from home, located in the historic village of Buckeystown, south of Frederick. We offer sixteen antique-filled guest rooms, king beds, two-person whirlpool baths, fireplaces, color TV/VCRs (with free movies), phones with computer access, and an outdoor hot tub! Available for meetings and weddings. Ask about our two-night specials.

Hosts: Terry and Sarah MacGillivray
Rooms: 16 (PB) $85-150
Full Breakfast
Credit Cards: A, B, C, D, E
Notes: 2, 3 and 4 (on limited days), 5, 7, 8, 9, 10, 11, 12

Middle Plantation Inn

9549 Liberty Road, 21701-3246
(301) 898-7128
E-mail: BandB@MPInn.com
Web site: http://www.MPInn.com

From this charming inn built of stone and log, you can drive through horse country to the village of Mt. Pleasant. The inn is located several miles east of Frederick on twenty-six acres. Each guest room is furnished with antiques and has a private bath, air-conditioning, and television. The keeping room, a common room, features stained glass and a stone fireplace. Nearby you can find antique shops, museums, and a number of historic attractions. Middleton Plantation Inn is located within forty minutes of Gettysburg, Antietam Battlefield, and Harper's Ferry.

Hosts: Shirley and Dwight Mullican
Rooms: 4 (PB) $95-110
Continental Breakfast
Credit Cards: A, B
Notes: 2, 5, 8, 9, 10, 12

NOTES: Credit cards accepted: A Master Card; B Visa; C American Express; D Discover; E Diners Club; F Other; 2 Personal checks accepted; 3 Lunch available; 4 Dinner available; 5 Open all year; 6 Pets

GAITHERSBURG

Gaithersburg Hospitality Bed and Breakfast

18908 Chimney Place, 20879
(301) 977-7377

This luxury host home just off I-270 with all the amenities, including private parking, is located in the beautifully planned community of Montgomery Village, near churches, restaurants, and shops. It is ten minutes from a DC Metro station, and a convenient drive south to Washington, DC, and north to historic Gettysburg, Pennsylvania, and Harper's Ferry. This spacious bed and breakfast has two rooms with private baths; one has a queen bed. Also offered are a large, sunny third room with twin beds, and a fourth room with a single bed. Hosts delight in serving full, home-cooked breakfasts with your pleasure and comfort in mind.

Hosts: Suzanne and Joe Danilowicz
Rooms: 4 (2PB; 2SB) $50-60
Full Breakfast
Credit Cards: none
Notes: 2, 7, 8, 9, 10, 12

GRANTSVILLE

Walnut Ridge Bed and Breakfast

92 Main, 21536
(301) 895-4248

Experience country hospitality in our quiet, quaint, peaceful inn. We're located in western Maryland's Appalachian Mountains with Amish countryside, historical sites, local artisans, and year-round recreation, making this an attractive getaway.

Walnut Ridge is a restored farmhouse dating to 1864 with antiques, handmade quilts, and country collectibles. Fireplaces, wood-fired hot tub, garden gazebo, antique player piano, video library and country suite add to the charm. Hiking, fishing, boating, cross-country skiing, alpine and white-water rafting available. Antique and craft shops within walking distance, as well as our own gift shoppe. Easy to find right off I-68 Exit 19 into Grantsville. "We love to cater to our guests, helping them create wonderful, warm memories."

Hosts: Tim and Candy Fetterly
Rooms: 3 (PB) $60-85
Full Breakfast
Credit Cards: A, B, D
Notes: 2, 5, 7, 8, 9, 10, 11, 12

HAGERSTOWN

Lewrene Farm Bed and Breakfast

9738 Downsville Pike, 21740
(301) 582-1735

Enjoy our quiet, colonial country home on 125 acres near I-70 and I-81, a home

Lewrene Farm Bed and Breakfast

away from home for tourists, business-people, and families. We have ample room for family celebrations. You may sit by the fireplace or enjoy the great outdoors. Antietam Battlefield and Harper's Ferry are nearby; Washington, DC, and Baltimore are one and one half hours away. Quilts for sale.

Hosts: Irene and Lewis Lehman
Rooms: 6 (3PB; 3SB) $55-98
Full Breakfast
Credit Cards: A, B
Notes: 2, 5, 7, 8, 9, 10, 11

Sunday's Bed and Breakfast

39 Broadway, 21740
(301) 797-4331; (800) 221-4828

This elegant 1890 Queen Anne Victorian home is situated in the historic north end of Hagerstown. You may relax in any of the many public rooms and porches or explore the numerous historic attractions, antique shops, golf courses, museums, ski areas, and shopping outlets nearby. You'll experience special hospitality and many personal touches at Sunday's Bed and Breakfast. A full breakfast, afternoon tea and desserts, evening refreshments, fruit basket, fresh flowers, special toiletries, and late-night cordial and chocolate are just some of the offerings at Sunday's Bed and Breakfast. We are located less than ninety minutes from Baltimore and Washington, DC.

Host: Bob Ferrino
Rooms: 4 (PB) $75-110
Full Breakfast
Credit Cards: A, B, E
Notes: 2, 4, 5, 7 (12 and older), 8, 9, 10, 11, 12

Currier House

HAVRE DE GRACE

Currier House

800 S. Market Street, 21078
(410) 939-7886; (800) 827-2889
E-mail: janec@currier-bb.com
Web site: http://www.currier-bb.com

Casual comfort in the historic, residential district overlooking the Chesapeake Bay. One block to lighthouse, museums, and park. Fully renovated house dating from 1800. Four guest rooms, each with a queen bed and private bath. Central AC. Full "waterman's" breakfast might include sautéed oysters and Maryland stewed tomatoes (in season, of course).

Hosts: Jane and Paul Belbot
Rooms: 4 (PB) $85-95
Full Waterman's Breakfast
Credit Cards: A, B, C, D
Notes: 2, 5, 10, 12

LITTLE ORLEANS

Town Hill Hotel Bed and Breakfast

Beauty Spot of Maryland, 21766
(301) 478-2794

This unique bed and breakfast at the top of Town Hill Mountain is the first tourist

---

NOTES: Credit cards accepted: A Master Card; B Visa; C American Express; D Discover; E Diners Club; F Other; 2 Personal checks accepted; 3 Lunch available; 4 Dinner available; 5 Open all year; 6 Pets

hotel in Maryland. Located on scenic U.S. 40 along the Black-eyed Susan Trail, offering peace and quiet that will lift the heart and calm the soul. Closer than you think—two hours from Washington, Baltimore, and Pittsburgh.

Hosts: Dick and Florence Essers
Rooms: 8 (PB) $70-90; multiple-night discount
Full Breakfast
Credit Cards: none
Notes: 2, 4, 7, 9, 10, 11

NORTH EAST

Sandy Cove Ministries Hotel and Conference Center

60 Sandy Cove Road, 21901
(410) 287-5433; (800) 234-COVE (2683);
FAX (410) 287-3196
E-mail: cahouseal@aol.com

Enjoy the cozy warmth of our beautiful rooms and suites on the headwaters of the Chesapeake Bay. Savor a full breakfast in our main dining room overlooking the Bay. Get alone, get away, take time after a conference or come for a midweek break and escape to peace and comfort.

Hostess: Carol Houseal
Rooms: 152 (PB) $59-89
Full Breakfast
Credit Cards: A, B, D
Notes: 2, 4, 5, 7, 8, 9 (seasonal), 10

ST. MICHAELS

Kemp House Inn

412 Talbot Street, PO Box 638, 21663
(301) 745-2243

Built in 1807 by Col. Joseph Kemp, a commander in the War of 1812, this superbly crafted home is one of a collection of large Federal-period brick structures in St. Michaels. Each of the rooms are tastefully furnished with period decor. Cozy antique four-poster rope beds with patchwork quilts and down pillows, wingback chairs, low-light sconces, candles, and working fireplaces create an ambience of the early 19th century.

Hosts: Steve and Diane Cooper
Rooms: 8 (6PB; 2SB) $70-110
Continental Breakfast
Credit Cards: A, B, D
Notes: 2, 5, 7, 8, 9, 10, 12

Parsonage Inn

210 N. Talbot Street, 21663
(410) 745-5519; (800) 394-5519
E-mail: wworkman@ix.netcom.com
Web site: http://www.bestinns.net

This late Victorian, circa 1883, was lavishly restored in 1985 with seven guest rooms, private baths, and brass beds with Laura Ashley linens. Fireplaces in three rooms. The parlor and dining room are in the European tradition. Striking architecture! Two blocks to the maritime museum, shops, and restaurants. Mobil and AAA three-star ratings.

Host: Gayle Lutz
Rooms: 8 (PB) $100-160
Full Breakfast
Credit Cards: A, B
Notes: 2, 5, 7, 8, 10, 12

Wades Point Inn

PO Box 7, 21663
(410) 745-2500; FAX (410) 745-3443
E-mail: atwades@skipjack.bluecrab.org

For those seeking the serenity of the country and the splendor of the bay, we invite

welcome; 7 Children welcome; 8 Tennis nearby; 9 Swimming nearby; 10 Golf nearby; 11 Skiing nearby; 12 May be booked through travel agent.

you to charming Wades Point Inn, just a few miles from St. Michaels. Complemented by the ever-changing view of boats, birds, and water lapping the shoreline, our 120 acres of fields and woodlands, with a mile of walking or jogging trail, provide a peaceful setting for relaxation and recreation on Maryland's eastern shore. Closed January through March.

Hosts: Betsy and John Feiler
Rooms: 14 winter, 23 summer (16PB; 7SB)
   $95-195
Expanded Continental Breakfast
Credit Cards: A, B
Notes: 2, 8, 9, 10

SILVER SPRING

Varborg Bed and Breakfast

2620 Briggs Chaney Road, 20905-4508
(301) 384-2842; FAX (301) 384-4379
E-mail: rjohnson@nmaa.org

This suburban, colonial home in the countryside is convenient to Washington, DC, and Baltimore, just off Route 29 and close to Route 95. Three guest rooms with a shared bath are available. Your hosts will be happy to share their knowledge of excellent nearby restaurants. The specialty of Varborg Bed and Breakfast is our homemade bread.

Hosts: Bob and Pat Johnson
Rooms: 3 (SB) $50
Full Breakfast
Credit Cards: none
Notes: 2, 5, 7, 8, 9, 10

Webster House

SOLOMONS

Webster House— A Christian Bed and Breakfast

14364 Sedwick Avenue, PO Box 1607, 20688
(410) 326-0454; FAX (410) 326-5092
E-mail: webster@mail.ameritel.net

Rest and restoration are yours at this delightful Christian bed and breakfast in Solomons, a quaint community in southern Maryland. A reproduction of the old Webster House that stood on this property for 113 years was built to glorify God. Lovely gardens, a revitalizing hot tub, homemade delights served on our screened-in porch, and three charming guest rooms add a sense of peace that will touch your heart. Your hosts are looking forward to making your stay a wonderful memory. Gift certificates are available. Webster House is open to guests from April to November.

Hosts: Peter and Barbara Prentice
Rooms: 3 (2PB; 1SB) $85-110
Full Breakfast
Credit Cards: A, B
Notes: 2, 9, 10

NOTES: Credit cards accepted: A Master Card; B Visa; C American Express; D Discover; E Diners Club; F Other; 2 Personal checks accepted; 3 Lunch available; 4 Dinner available; 5 Open all year; 6 Pets

TILGHMAN

Harrison's Country Inn and Sportfishing Center, Inc.

21551 Chesapeake House Drive, PO Box 310, 21671
(410) 886-2121; FAX (410) 886-2599

We provide a relaxed atmosphere and feature a five-star restaurant, sportfishing fleet and guest rooms that overlook the picturesque Choptank River.

Hosts: Buddy and Bobbie Harrison
Rooms: 56 (PB) $85-95
No Breakfast
Credit Cards: A, B
Notes: 2, 3, 4, 5, 6, 7, 8, 9, 10

WITTMAN (ST. MICHAELS)

The Inn at Christmas Farm

8873 Tilghman Island Road, 21676
(410) 745-5312

Located just seven miles west of St. Michael's, our waterfront inn and farm (c.1830) contain a unique collection of historic buildings, including St. James Chapel (1893)—saved from destruction, moved to the farm, and restored as the Gabriel and Bell Tower suites. The inn is set back from Rte. 33 just past the general store in the small village of Wittman. The beauty of the Chesapeake and its wildlife bring visitors from afar. Enjoy the peaceful tranquillity; sit by our spring-fed pond (or swim, in warm weather!); walk along the shore. Bike into St. Michaels where the Chesapeake Bay Maritime Museum, antiques, seafood delicacies, and sights in the charming colonial town await. You may visit nearby Tilghman Island where the last sailing oyster fleet is harbored. We serve a full gourmet breakfast each morning, featuring our signature Christmas Farm quiche, on our enclosed farmhouse porch overlooking field, farm and woods. There you can observe our "toy" farm animals—peacocks, sheep, chickens, and miniature horses. Blue herons, ospreys, swans, ducks, and Canadian geese are also part of our special world.

Hosts: Paul Curtis and Sue Rockwell
Rooms: 4 (PB) $110-165
Full Breakfast
Credit Cards: A, B
Notes: 2, 5, 7, 8, 10

MASSACHUSETTS

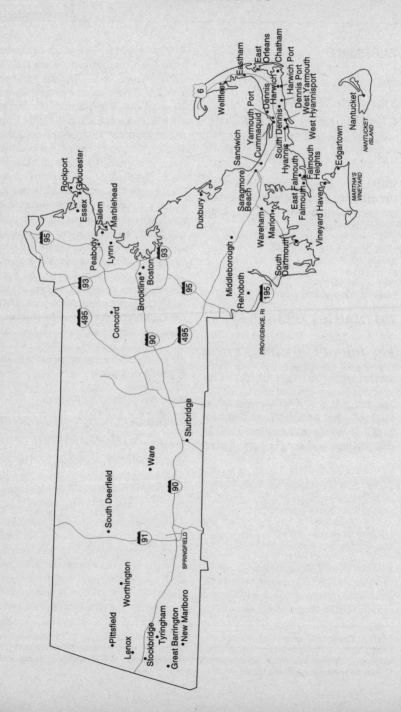

Massachusetts

American Country Collection of B&Bs

1353 Union Street, **Schenectady, NY**, 12308
(518) 370-4948; (800) 810-4948;
FAX (518) 393-1634

This reservation service provides reservations for eastern **New York**, western **Massachusetts**, and all of **Vermont**. One call does it all. Relax and unwind at any of our more than one hundred immaculate, personally inspected bed and breakfasts and country inns. Many include fireplace, Jacuzzi, and/or Modified American Plan. We have budget-minded to luxurious accommodations in urban, suburban, and rural locations. $50-200. Gift certificates available, and major credit cards accepted. Carol Matos, owner.

Bed & Breakfast Cape Cod

PO Box 341, 02672-0341
(508) 775-2772; (800) 686-5252;
FAX (508) 775-2884
E-mail: bedandb@capecod.net
Web site: http://www.oneweb.com/bbcc

Bed and Breakfast Cape Cod was developed in 1981 as a Capewide, year-round, personalized reservation service. The goal is to match the accommodation needs of guests with an extensive selection of historic sea captains' homes, country inns, and exquisitely restored houses. Many are located in secluded settings, near beaches and scenic bike paths. Hosts subscribe to the philosophy of B&B Cape Cod: providing guests with a feeling of a home away from home. Drawing on their extensive knowledge of the Cape, hosts gladly will provide tips on points of interest, shopping and off-the-beaten-path sightseeing. Clark Diehl, coordinator.

BOSTON

A B&B Agency of Boston (and Boston Harbor Bed and Breakfast)

47 Commercial Wharf, 02110
(617) 720-3540; (800) 248-9262;
FAX (617) 523-5761

Downtown Boston's largest selection of guest rooms in historic bed and breakfast homes, including Federal and Victorian town houses and beautifully restored 1840s waterfront lofts. Available nightly, weekly, monthly. Or choose from the lovely selection of fully furnished, private

---

NOTES: Credit cards accepted: A Master Card; B Visa; C American Express; D Discover; E Diners Club; F Other; 2 Personal checks accepted; 3 Lunch available; 4 Dinner available; 5 Open all year; 6 Pets welcome; 7 Children welcome; 8 Tennis nearby; 9 Swimming nearby; 10 Golf nearby; 11 Skiing nearby; 12 May be booked through travel agent.

studios, one- and two-bedroom condos, corporate suites and lofts with all amenities, including fully furnished kitchens, private baths (some with Jacuzzis), TVs, and phones. Exclusive locations include waterfront, Faneuil Hall/Quincy Market, North End, Back Bay, Beacon Hill, Copley Square, and Cambridge.

Hosts: Ferne Mintz
Rooms: 120 (80PB; 40SB) $65-120
Continental Breakfast
Credit Cards: A, B
Notes: 2, 5, 7, 12

Beacon Hill Bed and Breakfast

Beacon Hill Bed and Breakfast

27 Brimmer Street, 02108
(617) 523-7376

Three spacious bed-sitting rooms with queen beds, decorative fireplaces, and private baths. 1869 brick Victorian row house in picturesque, historically preserved, centrally located residential neighborhood with gas lights, brick sidewalks, front gardens and window boxes. Easy walk to tourist sites, shops, restaurants, subway, garage parking. Home-cooked, full breakfast. Luggage elevator.

Hostess: Susan Butterworth
Rooms: 3 (PB) $125-200 (seasonal)
Full Breakfast
Credit Cards: none
Notes: 2, 5, 7, 12

Greater Boston Hospitality

PO Box 1142, **Brookline** 02146
(617) 277-5430

Greater Boston Hospitality offers hundreds of Georgian, Federal, Victorian, and Brownstone private homes and condos throughout the greater Boston area. All include breakfast; many include parking. Most are located in historic areas. We provide on-call service to both business and pleasure travelers. Discounts available for longer stays. Wide range of accommodations from $50 to $125 a night. Call us and we will find the right place for you. Visit Boston as a native. Major credit cards accepted. Lauren Simonelli, owner.

CAPE COD

Liberty Hill Inn on Cape Cod

77 Main Street (Route 6A), **Yarmouth Port**, 02675
(508) 362-3976; (800) 821-3977
E-mail: libertyh@capecod.net
Web site: http://www.bbonline.com/ma/libertyhill

An elegant Cape Cod bed and breakfast, the Liberty Hill Inn welcomes travelers to historic Main Street in a seaside village.

NOTES: Credit cards accepted: A Master Card; B Visa; C American Express; D Discover; E Diners Club; F Other; 2 Personal checks accepted; 3 Lunch available; 4 Dinner available; 5 Open all year; 6 Pets

Liberty Hill Inn on Cape Cod

Meander country lanes to Cape Cod Bay and nature trails. Take a run on the beach. Stroll to village shops and first-class restaurants. Mobil three-star-rated. Special honeymoon packages. Cable TV, AC, canopy beds, luxurious double whirlpool, romantic fireplaces and gourmet breakfast. Its central location is ideal for exploring all of Cape Cod's attractions.

Hosts: Jack and Beth Flanagan
Rooms: 9 (PB) $85-185
Full Breakfast
Credit Cards: A, B, C
Notes: 2, 5, 7, 8, 9, 10, 12

CHATHAM (CAPE COD)

The Cranberry Inn at Chatham

359 Main Street, 02633
(508) 945-9232; (800) 332-4667;
FAX (508) 945-3769
Web site: http://www.capecod.com/cranberryinn

Welcoming Cape Cod visitors since 1830, the Cranberry Inn is ideally located in the heart of Chatham's picturesque historic district! Elegant yet relaxed, the Inn offers eighteen delightful guest rooms, each individually decorated with antique and reproduction furnishings. Rooms feature four-poster, brass, or canopy bed, private

bath, air-conditioning, telephone, and TV. Many rooms have fireplaces and balconies. Golfing, swimming, boating, and some of the finest shops and restaurants on the Cape are all nearby.

Hosts: Ray and Brenda Raffurty
Rooms: 18 (PB) $85-230, depending on season
Full Breakfast Buffet
Credit Cards: A, B, C, D
Notes: 2, 5, 7 (over 8), 8, 9, 10, 12

Old Harbor Inn

22 Old Harbor Road, 02633
(508) 945-4434; (800) 942-4434;
FAX (508) 945-7665

We feel our guests can speak better than ourselves. We'd like to share excerpts from the guest book: "what a lovely, great retreat," "a spectacular place to stay," "very special," "wonderful hosts," "it feels as though we are leaving good friends," "heavenly place," "all this and whales too!" "warm and cozy atmosphere," "relaxing nights," "good company," "excellent service," "delicious food," "absolutely charming," "a lovely, quiet inn," "made us feel at home," "we'll be back . . ."

Hosts: Judy and Ray Braz
Rooms: 8 (PB) $109-199
Deluxe (Healthy) Continental Breakfast
Credit Cards: A, B, C, D, E
Notes: 2, 5, 8, 9, 10, 12

CONCORD

Hawthorne Inn

462 Lexington Road, 01742
(978) 369-5610; FAX (978) 287-4949
Web site: http://www.concordmass.com

Beside the Battle Road the minutemen marched along in 1775 to face the British

---

welcome; 7 Children welcome; 8 Tennis nearby; 9 Swimming nearby; 10 Golf nearby; 11 Skiing nearby; 12 May be booked through travel agent.

regulars, the Hawthorne Inn was constructed circa 1870 on land once owned by Emerson, Hawthorne, and the Alcott family and surveyed by Thoreau. Amidst aged trees and bountiful gardens, this colourful Inn beckons the traveler to refresh the spirit in a winsome atmosphere abounding with original artworks, antique furnishings and archaic artifacts. With a copy of *Walden* or *Little Women* in hand, you can bask near the whispering fire or be led by the resident cat to a garden seat for a spot of tea.

Hosts: Gregory Burch and Marilyn Mudry
Rooms: 7 (PB) $110-220
Continental Plus Breakfast
Credit Cards: A, B, C, D
Notes: 2, 5, 7, 8, 9, 11

CUMMAQUID (CAPE COD)

The Acworth Inn

4352 Old King's Highway, PO Box 256, 02637
(508) 362-3330; (800) 362-6363;
FAX (508) 375-0304

The Acworth Inn is a romantic getaway nestled among the trees along the Old King's Highway, which winds through the historic, unspoiled north side of Cape Cod. Built in 1860, the Acworth Inn is a classic Cape house, completely renovated and outfitted with charming, hand-painted pieces and colorful fabrics. It features six bright and airy guest rooms, each with a private bath.

Hosts: Jack and Cheryl Ferrell
Rooms: 6 (PB) $75-95
Full Breakfast
Credit Cards: A, B, C, D
Notes: 2, 5, 8, 9, 10, 12

DEERFIELD-SOUTH

Deerfield's Yellow Gabled House

111 N. Main, 01373
(413) 665-4922

Located on the site of a historic battle of 1675 and one and a half miles from the crossroads of I-91, Route 116, and routes 5 and 10 is a picturesque house with gardens and three decorated bedchambers. Sitting room and library for reading and meeting your fellow travelers. Enjoy early morning coffee in the summer room.

Hostess: Edna J. Stahelek
Rooms: 3 (1PB; 2SB) $75-100
Full Breakfast
Credit Cards: none
Notes: 2, 5, 8, 9, 10, 11, 12

DENNIS (CAPE COD)

Isaiah Hall B&B Inn

PO Box 1007, 152 Whig Street, 02638
(508) 385-9928; (800) 236-0160;
FAX (508) 385-5879
E-mail: isaiah@capecod.net
Web site: http://www.virtualcapecod.com/market/
   isaiahhall

Enjoy country ambience and hospitality in the heart of Cape Cod. Tucked away on a quiet historic side street, this lovely 1857 farmhouse is within walking distance of the beach, restaurants, shops, and playhouse. Delightful gardens surround the Inn with country antiques, Oriental rugs, and quilts within. Rooms have private baths and air-conditioning, and most have queen-size beds. Some have balconies or fireplaces. Near biking, golf, and tennis. Rated AAA

NOTES: Credit cards accepted: A Master Card; B Visa; C American Express; D Discover; E Diners Club; F Other; 2 Personal checks accepted; 3 Lunch available; 4 Dinner available; 5 Open all year; 6 Pets

three diamonds and ABBA three-crown award.

Hostess: Marie Brophy
Rooms: 10 (PB) $85-149
Continental Breakfast
Credit Cards: A, B, C
Notes: 2, 7 (over 7), 12

DENNISPORT (CAPE COD)

The Rose Petal Bed and Breakfast

152 Sea Street, PO Box 974, 02639
(508) 398-8470
Web site: http://www.virtualcapecod.com/market/rosepetal

A picturesque, 1872 New England home, complete with picket fence, invites guests to share this historic, delightful seaside resort neighborhood. Stroll past century-old homes to a sandy beach. Home-baked pastries highlight a full breakfast. A comfortable parlor offers TV, piano, and reading. Enjoy queen-size beds, antiques, hand-stitched quilts, and spacious and bright baths. Convenient to all Cape Cod's attractions. Open all year. AAA three diamonds; ABBA three crowns.

Hosts: Gayle and Dan Kelly
Rooms: 3 (2PB; 1SB) $52-94
Full Breakfast
Credit Cards: A, B, C
Notes: 2, 5, 7, 8, 9, 10, 12

DUXBURY

The Winsor House Inn

390 Washington Street, 02332
(781) 934-0991; FAX (781) 934-5955

Built in 1803 by sea captain Nathaniel Winsor, this charming, antique-filled coun-

The Winsor House Inn

try inn is located thirty-five miles south of Boston in the quaint seaside village of Duxbury. The four cozy, sunlit bedrooms are complete with canopy beds and fireplaces. Casual dining in the English-style pub, gourmet dinner in the flower-filled Carriage House, romantic evening in the candlelit dining room. Rates are subject to change.

Hosts: Mr. and Mrs. David M. O'Connell
Rooms: 4 (PB) $130-210
Full Breakfast
Credit Cards: A, B, C, D
Notes: 2, 3 (seasonal), 4, 5, 7, 8, 9, 10, 12

EAST FALMOUTH (CAPE C0D)

The "Acorn" Country Bed and Breakfast

10 E. Harbor Drive, 02536
(508) 540-3518
E-mail: donc4@juno.com

We are country, close to beautiful beaches, ferries to islands, golf courses, great local seafood, casual or elegant dining. Full breakfast among handmade crafts and paintings. See our old-time Glenwood black cast iron cookstove. There is truly a relaxed atmosphere in our quiet residential area. We love our Lord Jesus. Our

welcome; 7 Children welcome; 8 Tennis nearby; 9 Swimming nearby; 10 Golf nearby; 11 Skiing nearby; 12 May be booked through travel agent.

bed and breakfast is small, therefore our rates are reasonable.

Hosts: Donald and Beverly Cruwys
Rooms: 2 (PB or SB) $80-120
Full Breakfast
Credit Cards: none
Notes: 2, 7 (2)

EAST ORLEANS (CAPE COD)

The Farmhouse at Nauset Beach

163 Beach Road, 02653
(508) 255-6654

Be our guest at an 1870 Greek Revival-style home with old-fashioned hospitality. A short walk to the beautiful sand dunes and surf of Nauset Beach (Atlantic Ocean). This historic farmhouse is situated on 1.6 acres, ninety feet from the road in a lovely, quiet residential area. Some ocean-view rooms. Open year-round. Close to many activities and fine restaurants. Begin the day with a lovely sunrise.

Hostess: Dot Standish
Rooms: 8 (PB) $52-105
Continental Breakfast
Credit Cards: A, B
Notes: 2, 5, 7 (over 5), 8, 9, 10, 12

Nauset House Inn

143 Beach Road, PO Box 774, 02643
(508) 255-2195
E-mail: jvessll@capecod.net
Web site: http://www.virtualcapecod.com/market/
    nausethouse

A real, old-fashioned, country inn farmhouse, circa 1810, is located on three acres with an apple orchard, one-half mile from Nauset Beach. A quiet, romantic getaway. Large common room with fireplace; brick-floored dining room where breakfast is served. Cozily furnished with antiques, eclectic—a true fantasy.

Hosts: Diane and Al Johnson; Cindy and John
    Vessella
Rooms: 14 (8PB; 6SB) $75-128
Full Breakfast
Credit Cards: A, B, D
Notes: 2, 8, 9, 10

Ship's Knees Inn

186 Beach Road, PO Box 756, 02643
(508) 255-1312; FAX (508) 240-1351

This 170-year-old restored sea captain's home is a three-minute walk to beautiful, sand-duned Nauset Beach. Inside the warm, lantern-lit doorways are nineteen

The Farmhouse at Nauset Beach

Ship's Knees Inn

rooms individually appointed with special colonial color schemes and authentic antiques. Some rooms feature authentic ship's knees, hand-painted trunks, old clipper ship models, braided rugs, and four-poster beds. Tennis and swimming are available on the premises. Three miles away, overlooking Orleans Cove, the Cove House property offers three rooms, a one-bedroom efficiency apartment, and two cottages.

Hosts: Jean and Ken Pitchford
Rooms: 22 + 1 efficiency + 2 cottages (PB) $50-110
Continental Breakfast
Credit Cards: A, B
Notes: 2, 5, 7 (Cove House), 8 and 9 (on premises), 10, 12

EASTHAM (CAPE COD)

The Over Look Inn, Cape Cod

3085 County Road, Route 6, 02642
(508) 255-1886; FAX (508) 240-0345
E-mail: stay@overlookinn.com
Web site: http://www.overlookinn.com

This Victorian mansion across from Cape Cod National Seashore offers Scottish hospitality. The Over Look Inn has ten antique-filled guest rooms with private baths. Guests enjoy the Victorian parlor, Winston Churchill Library, Hemingway Billiard Room, and Ann Hopper Dining Room for breakfast.

Hosts: The Aitchison Family
Rooms: 10 (PB) $95-145
Full Breakfast
Credit Cards: all
Notes: 2, 5, 7, 8, 9, 10, 12

EDGARTOWN —MARTHA'S VINEYARD

The Arbor Inn

PO Box 1228, 222 Upper Main Street, 02539
(508) 627-8137

This charming Victorian home originally was built on the island of Chappaquiddick and moved by barge to its present location. A short stroll to the village shops, fine restaurants, and bustling activity of the Edgartown harbor. The rooms are typically New England, furnished with antiques, and filled with the fragrance of fresh flowers. Central air-conditioning. Peggy gladly will direct you to unspoiled beaches, walking trails, fishing, and all the delights of Martha's Vineyard. A small, one-bedroom house is available on a weekly basis.

Hostess: Peggy Hall
Rooms: 10 (8PB; 2SB) $80-150
Continental Breakfast
Credit Cards: A, B
Notes: 2, 7 (over 12), 8, 9, 10, 12

Captain Dexter House of Edgartown

35 Pease's Point Way, PO Box 2798, 02539
(508) 627-7289; FAX (508) 627-3328 (May-Nov.)

Our historic inn offers both charm and hospitality. Enjoy beautiful gardens. Savor a home-baked breakfast and evening

welcome; 7 Children welcome; 8 Tennis nearby; 9 Swimming nearby; 10 Golf nearby; 11 Skiing nearby; 12 May be booked through travel agent.

aperitif. Relax in a lace-canopied, four-poster bed in a room with a working fireplace. Stroll to the harbor or town with its restaurants. Bike or walk to the beach. Let us make your vacation special!

Hosts: Rick Fenstemaker
Rooms: 11 (PB) $85-185
Continental Plus Breakfast
Credit Cards: A, B, C
Notes: 2, 8, 9, 10, 12

ESSEX

George Fuller House

148 Main Street, 01929
(508) 768-7766; (800) 477-0178
FAX (508) 768-6178
E-mail: rcameron@shore.net

Built in 1830, this handsome Federalist-style home retains its 19th-century charm, including Indian shutters and a captain's staircase. Three of the guest rooms have working fireplaces. Decorations include handmade quilts, braided rugs, and caned Boston rockers. A full breakfast might include such features as Cindy's French toast drizzled with brandy lemon butter. Gordon College and Gordon Conwall Seminary are close by.

Hosts: Cindy and Bob Cameron
Rooms: 7 (PB) $90-120
Full Breakfast
Credit Cards: A, B, C, D
Notes: 2, 5, 7, 8, 9, 10, 12

FALMOUTH (CAPE COD)

Bayberry Inn

226 Trotting Park Road, **East Falmouth**, 02536
(508) 540-2962

We are a small B&B catering especially to families (children of all ages) and even pets. Our two rooms are large, light and airy, and decorated in comfortable antiques and books. Each room has multiple beds and a private bath. Breakfast may be Belgian waffles or blueberry coffee cake and cheese omelets—served with linen, candles, and flowers.

Hosts: Joel and Anna Marie Peterson
Rooms: 2 (PB) $70 (off-season discount)
Full Breakfast
Credit Cards: none
Notes: 2, 5, 6, 7, 8, 9, 10, 12

Captain Tom Lawrence House

Captain Tom Lawrence House

75 Locust Street, 02540
(508) 540-1445; (800) 266-8139;
FAX (508) 457-1790

1861 whaling captain's residence in historic village close to beach, bikeway, ferries, bus station, ships, and restaurants. Explore entire Cape, Vineyard, and Plymouth by day trips. Six beautiful guest rooms have private baths and firm beds, some with canopies. Fully furnished, air-conditioned apartment with kitchenette sleeps two to four people. Antiques, Steinway piano, fireplace in sitting room. Homemade, delicious breakfasts include specialties from organic grain. German is spoken here. All rooms have central air-

---

NOTES: Credit cards accepted: A Master Card; B Visa; C American Express; D Discover; E Diners Club; F Other; 2 Personal checks accepted; 3 Lunch available; 4 Dinner available; 5 Open all year; 6 Pets

conditioning. No smoking! AAA- and Mobil-rated. Closed in January.

Hostess: Barbara Sabo-Feller
Rooms: 6 (PB) $85-140
Full Breakfast
Credit Cards: A, B
Notes: 2, 7, 8, 9, 10

The Inn at One Main Street

One Main Street, 02540
(508) 540-7469; (888) 281-6246
E-mail: onemain@capecod.net
Web site: www.bbonline.com/ma/onemain

The Inn at One Main Street is a decorative shingled 1892 Victorian with Queen Anne accents, an open front porch and a two-story turret, surrounded by a white picket fence and tastefully landscaped grounds. The inn is a most attractive introduction to the charming three-hundred-year-old village of Falmouth.

Hosts: Mari Zylinski and Karen Hart
Rooms: 6 (PB) $80-115
Full Breakfast
Credit Cards: A, B, C
Notes: 2, 5, 8, 9, 10

Inn on the Sound

313 Grand Avenue, 02540
(508) 457-9666; (800) 564-9668;
FAX (508) 457-9631

This oceanfront bed and breakfast offers ten spacious guest rooms, nine with water views, all with serene, casual, and comfortable beachhouse-style atmosphere. Enjoy the magnificent view from the forty-foot deck, sample the full gourmet breakfast, relax with a favorite book in front of the fireplace, or visit the many year-round

attractions from our ideally located inn. Walk to the Martha's Vineyard ferry. Bicycle rentals, great restaurants, and, of course, the beach. Reservations recommended, especially in the summer.

Hosts: Renee Ross and David Ross
Rooms: 10 (PB) $60-150
Full Breakfast
Credit Cards: A, B, C, D
Notes: 2, 5, 8, 9, 10, 12

The Palmer House Inn

81 Palmer Avenue, 02540
(508) 548-1230; (800) 472-2632;
FAX (508) 540-1878
E-mail: palmerhse@aol.com

Enjoy the warmth and charm of a Victorian home. Built in 1901, the inn with its adjacent guest house and romantic Cottage Suite is listed on the National Register of Historic Places. The stained-glass windows, rich, hand-rubbed woodwork, gleaming hardwood floors, and antique furnishings let the weary traveler step back in time to a more genteel era. Breakfast is a gourmet delight. All rooms have private baths; some have whirlpools.

Hosts: Ken and Joanne Baker
Rooms: 12 + cottage (PB) $78-199
Full Gourmet Breakfast
Credit Cards: A, B, C, D, E
Notes: 2 (deposit only), 5, 7 (10 and over), 8, 9, 10, 12

Village Green Inn

40 Main Street, 02540
(508) 548-5621; (800) 237-1119;
FAX (508) 457-5051
E-mail: CGI40@aol.com
Web site: http://www.sunsol.com/villagegreen

This gracious old 1804 Colonial-Victorian is ideally located on Falmouth's historic

welcome; 7 Children welcome; 8 Tennis nearby; 9 Swimming nearby; 10 Golf nearby; 11 Skiing nearby; 12 May be booked through travel agent.

Village Green Inn

village green. You can walk to fine shops and restaurants, or bike to beaches and picturesque Woods Hole along the Shining Sea Bike Path. Enjoy 19th-century charm and warm hospitality amidst elegant surroundings. Four lovely guest rooms and one romantic suite all have private baths and unique fireplaces (two are working). A full gourmet breakfast is served each morning, featuring delicious house specialties. Many thoughtful amenities are included. Air-conditioned.

Hosts: Diane and Don Crosby
Rooms: 5 (PB) $85-150
Full Breakfast
Credit Cards: A, B, C
Notes: 2 (deposit only), 5, 7 (12 and over), 8, 9, 10

FALMOUTH HEIGHTS (CAPE COD)

Grafton Inn

261 Grand Avenue S., 02540
(508) 540-8688; (800) 642-4069;
FAX (508) 540-1861

Oceanfront Victorian. Thirty steps to a sandy beach. Breathtaking views of Martha's Vineyard. Comfortable queen and king beds. Period antiques. A sumptuous, full breakfast is served at individual tables overlooking Nantucket Sound. AC/heat, CCTV. Thoughtful amenities. Fresh flowers, homemade chocolates. Evening wine and cheese. Beach chairs and towels. Eight-minute walk to island ferry. Restaurants one block away. AAA/Mobil three-star-rated.

Hosts: Liz and Rudy Cvitan
Rooms: 11 (PB) $95-169
Full Breakfast
Credit Cards: A, B, C, D
Notes: 2 (deposit only), 5, 8, 9, 10

The Moorings Lodge

207 Grand Avenue S., 02540
(508) 540-2370

Capt. Frank Spencer built this large, lovely Victorian home in 1905. It is directly across from a sandy beach with lifeguard safety, and it is within walking distance of good restaurants and the island ferry. Your homemade, buffet breakfast is served on a glassed-in porch overlooking the island, Martha's Vineyard. Your airy rooms with private baths add to your comfort. Call us home while you tour the Cape!

Hosts: Ernie and Shirley Benard
Rooms: 8 (PB) $75-110
Full Breakfast
Credit Cards: A, B
Notes: 2, 7, 8, 9, 10, 12

The Moorings Lodge

GLOUCESTER

Gray Manor

14 Atlantic Road, 01930
(978) 283-5409
Web site: http://www.cape-ann.com/gray-manor

Located on historic Cape Ann. A home away from home filled with New England hospitality. Only a three-minute walk to the beautiful, white, sandy Good Harbor Beach. All private baths, cable TV, AC, refrigerators; some have decks. Season rates: $58-64; off-season (5/1-6/21) and after Labor Day: $42-48. Kitchenettes—season: $450 weekly; off-season: $52-55. Includes continental breakfast and movies at night in the lounge. Gray Manor is furnished in charming modern decor with wall-to-wall carpeting and modern equipment.

Hostess: Madeline Gray
Rooms: 9 (PB) $42-450
Continental Breakfast
Credit Cards: A, B
Notes: 7, 8, 9

GT. BARRINGTON

Thornewood Inn

453 Stockbridge Road, 01230
(413) 528-3828; (800) 854-1008;
FAX (413) 528-3307
Web site: http://www.thornewood.com

Family owned and run, our inn is located in the beautiful Berkshire Hills. Our turn-of-the-century Dutch Colonial has twelve guest rooms, all with private baths, air-conditioning, and televisions. A full country breakfast is included. Spencer's, our restaurant, is open year-round. All major

credit cards accepted. Swimming pool. AAA- and Mobil-rated.

Hosts: David and Terry Thorne and Thorne
 Family
Rooms: 12 (PB) $65-195
Full Breakfast
Credit Cards: A, B, C, D, F
Notes: 2, 4, 5, 7, 8, 9, 10, 11, 12

HARWICH PORT (CAPE COD)

Augustus Snow House

528 Main Street, 02646
(508) 430-0528; (800) 320-0528;
FAX (508) 432-7995

A romantic Victorian mansion built in 1901, the Augustus Snow House remains one of Cape Cod's most breathtaking examples of Queen Anne Victorian architecture. Today, this turn-of-the-century home with its gabled dormers and wrap-around veranda is one of the Cape's most elegant and exclusive inns, catering to a small number of discerning guests. Five exquisite bedrooms with queen or king beds, private baths (some with Jacuzzis), fireplaces, and color TVs. A gourmet breakfast and afternoon refreshments are served. The private beach is just a three-minute stroll away.

Hosts: Joyce and Steve Roth
Rooms: 5 (PB) $105-160
Full Gourmet Breakfast
Credit Cards: A, B, C, D
Notes: 2, 3, 4, 5, 8, 9, 10, 12

Harbor Walk

6 Freeman Street, 02646
(508) 432-1675

This Victorian summer guest house was built in 1880 and is furnished with eclectic

---

welcome; 7 Children welcome; 8 Tennis nearby; 9 Swimming nearby; 10 Golf nearby; 11 Skiing nearby; 12 May be booked through travel agent.

charm. A few steps from the house will bring you into view of Wychmere Harbor and, further along, to one of the fine beaches of Nantucket Sound. The village of Harwich Port is only one-half mile from the inn and contains interesting shops and some of the finest restaurants on Cape Cod. Harbor Walk offers six comfortable rooms with twin or queen beds. An attractive garden and porch are available for sitting, lounging, and reading. Open May through October.

Hosts: Marilyn and Preston Barry
Rooms: 6 (4PB; 2SB) $60
Full Breakfast
Credit Cards: none
Notes: 2, 7, 8, 9, 10, 12

HYANNIS (CAPE C0D)

Sea Breeze Inn

397 Sea Street, 02601
(508) 771-7213; FAX (508) 862-0663
E-mail: seabreeze@capecod.net
Web site: http://www.capecod.net/seabreeze

Come to a Victorian Inn by the beach. Sea Breeze is a fourteen-room, quaint bed and breakfast. It is just a three-minute walk to the beach and twenty minutes to the island ferries. Restaurants, nightlife, shopping, golf, and tennis are within a ten-minute drive. Some of the guest rooms have ocean views. An expanded continental breakfast is served between 7:30 and 9:30 each morning. All rooms are air-conditioned.

Hostess: Patricia Gibney
Rooms: 14 (PB) $55-130
Expanded Continental Breakfast
Credit Cards: A, B, C, D
Notes: 5, 7, 8, 9, 10, 12

LENOX

Cornell Inn

203 Main Street, 01240
(413) 637-0562; (800) 637-0562;
FAX (413) 637-0927

We are a full-service Inn with a restaurant and pub. You may choose a cozy bedroom, a fully equipped suite with a fireplace and kitchen, or a four-poster with fireplace and Jacuzzi in our newly renovated, 200-year-old MacDonald House. Relax in our health spa with whirlpool, sauna, steam bath, and exercise equipment. You may dine by the fishpond or in our Japanese-style garden. The inn has facilities for intimate weddings, family reunions, and other events. Special packages are offered.

Host: Jack D'Elia
Rooms: 30 (PB) $59-195
Continental Plus Breakfast
Credit Cards: A, B, C, D, E
Notes: 2, 3, 4, 5, 7, 8, 9, 10, 11, 12

Garden Gables Inn

PO Box 52, 01240
(413) 637-0193; FAX (413) 637-4554
E-mail: gardeninn@aol.com

Garden Gables is a 220-year-old charming and quiet inn in historic Lenox on five wooded acres dotted with gardens. It features a seventy-two-foot swimming pool. Some guest rooms have fireplaces, and sitting rooms are furnished with antiques and a Steinway grand piano. All rooms have private baths and air-conditioning, and some rooms also have whirlpool tubs and private porches. Breakfast is included.

NOTES: Credit cards accepted: A Master Card; B Visa; C American Express; D Discover; E Diners Club; F Other; 2 Personal checks accepted; 3 Lunch available; 4 Dinner available; 5 Open all year; 6 Pets

In-room telephones are provided for guests. The famous Tanglewood festival is only one mile away. Restaurants are all within walking distance.

Hosts: Mario and Lynn Mekinda
Rooms: 18 (PB) $90-225
Full Breakfast
Credit Cards: A, B, C, D
Notes: 2, 5, 8, 9, 10, 11

Seven Hills Country Inn and Restaurant

40 Plunkett Street, 01240
(413) 637-0060; (800) 869-6518
FAX (413) 637-3651
Web site: http://www.SevenHillsInn.com

This is a lovely, twenty-seven-acre country property featuring beautiful terraced lawns and gardens, a huge swimming pool, two hard-surface tennis courts, banquet and meeting facilities, and an outstanding restaurant with wonderful and creative cuisine. Many guest rooms are furnished with antiques; all have private baths and air-conditioning. We offer a romantic spot and do weddings like no one else can. Seven Hills is a popular resort and vacation destination—but business travelers love us, too. Lodging/food packages and tie-in discounts are available. Located near Tanglewood, summer home of the Boston Symphony Orchestra, and Jacob's Pillow, featuring the world's finest dance troupes. Lose yourself in time and come visit us!

Hosts: Jim and Patricia Eder
Rooms: 52 (PB) $85-250
Full or Continental Breakfast (seasonal)
Credit Cards: A, B, C, D
Notes: 2, 4, 5, 6, 7, 8, 9, 10, 11, 12

Diamond District Breakfast Inn

LYNN

Diamond District Breakfast Inn

142 Ocean Street, 01902
(617) 599-4470; (800) 666-3076;
FAX (617) 599-5122

Architect-designed Georgian mansion in the historic "Diamond District," built in 1911. Gracious foyer and grand staircase, fireplace, living and dining room with ocean view, French doors to veranda overlooking the gardens, ocean. Guest rooms offer antiques, AC, TVs, phones, down comforters, some fireplaces and private baths. Three hundred feet off three-mile sandy beach for swimming, walking, jogging. Walk to restaurants. Home-cooked breakfast; vegetarian, lowfat available.

Hosts: Sandra and Jerry Caron
Rooms: 10 (6PB; 4SB) $80-195
Full Breakfast
Credit Cards: A, B, C, D, E
Notes: 5, 7, 9, 10, 12

MARBLEHEAD

Harborside House

23 Gregory Street, 01945-3241
(617) 631-1032
E-mail: swliving@shore.net

An 1850 colonial overlooks picturesque Marblehead Harbor, with water views

---

welcome; 7 Children welcome; 8 Tennis nearby; 9 Swimming nearby; 10 Golf nearby; 11 Skiing nearby; 12 May be booked through travel agent.

from the paneled living room. Guests enjoy our cozy fireplace, period dining room, sunny breakfast porch, and third-story deck. A generous breakfast includes juice, fresh fruit, home-baked goods, and cereals. Antique shops, gourmet restaurants, historic sites, and beaches are a pleasant stroll away. The owner is a professional dressmaker and nationally ranked competitive swimmer. Harborside House is a no-smoking bed and breakfast.

Hostess: Susan Livingston
Rooms: 2 (SB) $65-80
Expanded Continental Breakfast
Credit Cards: none
Notes: 2, 5, 7 (over 10), 8, 9

MARION

Pineywood Farm Bed and Breakfast

599 Front Street, PO Box 322, 02738
(508) 748-3925; (800) 858-8084
E-mail: gmcturk@capecod.net
Web site: http://www.virtualcities.com

Pineywood Farm is a charming, 1815 farmhouse with a carriage house. It has been completely restored, yet retains the warmth and ambience of a bygone era, complete with wide-plank, white pine floors; four working fireplaces; a large screened porch; and a "good morning" staircase. We offer spacious rooms with air-conditioning, cable TV, paddle fans, and private baths, overlooking a lovely perennial garden and private swimming pool. Pineywood Farm is located on a three-acre estate, one and a half miles from the Tabor Academy. The town beach is at the end of our street. The bed and breakfast is open year-round.

Hosts: Beverly and George McTurk
Rooms: 5 (3PB; 2SB) $85-100
Continental Breakfast
Credit Cards: A, B, C
Notes: 2, 5, 8, 9, 10

Pineywood Farm Bed and Breakfast

NANTUCKET

Martin House Inn

61 Centre Street, PO Box 743, 02554
(508) 228-0678; (508) 325-4798

In a stately 1803 mariner's home in Nantucket's historic district, a romantic sojourn awaits you. A glowing fire in a spacious, charming living/dining room; large, airy guest rooms—three with fireplaces—with authentic period pieces and four-poster beds; a lovely yard and veranda for peaceful summer afternoons. Our complimentary breakfast includes inn-baked breads and muffins, fresh fruit, and homemade granola.

Hosts: Cecilia and Channing Moore
Rooms: 13 (9PB; 4SB) $65-160
Expanded Continental Breakfast
Credit Cards: A, B, C
Notes: 2, 5, 7 (over 5), 8, 9, 10

NOTES: Credit cards accepted: A Master Card; B Visa; C American Express; D Discover; E Diners Club; F Other; 2 Personal checks accepted; 3 Lunch available; 4 Dinner available; 5 Open all year; 6 Pets

NEW MARLBOROUGH

Old Inn on the Green and Gedney Farm

Route 57, 01230
(413) 229-3131; (800) 286-3139
Web site: http://www.oldinn.com

This is a 1760 inn offering period guest rooms with private bath and a three-star restaurant (*Boston Globe*) with candlelit dining rooms and fireplace. Terrace dining is available. A turn-of-the-century, renovated barn features deluxe guest rooms and suites with granite fireplaces and whirlpools. Banquet facilities can be provided. The Old Inn on the Green is a superb wedding site.

Hosts: Leslie Miller and Brad Wagstaff
Rooms: 21(PB) $120-285
Continental Breakfast
Credit Cards: A, B, C
Notes: 2, 3 (seasonal), 4, 5, 7, 8, 9, 10, 11, 12

PEABODY

Joan's Bed and Breakfast

R210 Lynn Street, 01960
(508) 532-0191

Located twenty-five miles from Boston, ten miles from historic Salem, and twenty-five miles from quaint Rockport. We have wonderful restaurants in the area, two large shopping malls and a terrific summer theater. Enjoy our in-ground pool!

Hostess: Joan Hetherington
Rooms: 3 (1PB; 2SB) $50-60
Continental Plus Breakfast and Afternoon Tea
Credit Cards: none
Notes: 2, 5, 7, 9, 12

PITTSFIELD

The Barker House

456 Barker Road, 01201
(413) 499-6122 (voice and FAX)
E-mail: sdennis@aol.com

The Berkshires are in western Massachusetts near the New York border. We are forty-five minutes from Albany. This is a popular tourist area with "high" seasons being July and August (Tanglewood—home of Boston Symphony Orchestra) and October (fall foliage). With hiking and skiing, this is a four-season area with tons to do for singles, couples and families. Family friendly—an oddity in Berkshire inns. No minimums on the shared bathrooms—also very rare in these parts. Smoke-free.

Hosts: Steve and Marriann Dennis
Rooms: 3 (1PB; 2SB) $75-110
Continental Breakfast
Credit Cards: none
Notes: 2, 5, 6, 7, 8, 9, 10, 11

REHOBOTH
(NEAR PROVIDENCE, RI)

Gilbert's Tree Farm Bed and Breakfast

30 Spring Street, 02769
(508) 252-6416

Our 150-year-old home is special in all seasons. The in-ground pool refreshes weary travelers, and the quiet walks through our hundred acres give food for the soul. Guests also enjoy the horses.

welcome; 7 Children welcome; 8 Tennis nearby; 9 Swimming nearby; 10 Golf nearby; 11 Skiing nearby; 12 May be booked through travel agent.

One room has a fireplace. We praise God for being allowed to enjoy the beauty with others. No smoking inside the house.

Hosts: Jeanne Gilbert
Rooms: 3 (1PB, 2SB) $45-80
Full Breakfast
Credit Cards: none
Notes: 2, 5, 6 (horses only), 7, 8, 9, 10, 12

Perryville Inn B&B

Perryville Inn B&B

157 Perryville Road, 02769
(508) 252-9239; (800) 439-9239;
FAX (508) 252-9054

This 19th-century restored Victorian (listed on the National Register of Historic Places) is located on four and a half wooded acres featuring a quiet brook, millpond, stone walls, and shaded paths. Bicycles are available (including a tandem) to explore the unspoiled countryside. The inn overlooks an eighteen-hole public golf course. All rooms are furnished with antiques and accented with colorful handmade quilts. Nearby you will find antique shops, museums, Great Woods Performing Arts Center, fine seafood restaurants, and even an old-fashioned New England clambake, or arrange for a horse-drawn hayride or a hot-air balloon ride. Within an hour's drive of Boston, Plymouth,

Newport and Mystic; seven miles from Providence, Rhode Island.

Hosts: Tom and Betsy Charnecki
Rooms: 5 (PB) $65-85
Continental Breakfast
Credit Cards: A, B, C, D
Notes: 2, 5, 7, 8, 10, 12

ROCKPORT

The Inn on Cove Hill

37 Mt. Pleasant Street, 01966
(508) 546-2701; (888) 546-2701
Web page: http://www.cape-ann/covehill

A friendly atmosphere with the option of privacy is available in this painstakingly restored, 200-year-old Federal home in a perfect setting two blocks from the harbor and shops. Cozy bedrooms are meticulously appointed with antiques; some have canopy beds. Wake up to the aroma of hot muffins and enjoy breakfast at the umbrella tables in the pump garden.

Hosts: John and Marjorie Pratt
Rooms: 11 (9PB; 2SB) $48-104
Continental Breakfast
Credit Cards: A, B
Notes: 2, 9

Lantana Guest House

22 Broadway, 01966-1537
(508) 546-3535; (800) 291-3535

This intimate guest house in the heart of historic Rockport is close to Main Street, the T-Wharf, and the beaches. A large sundeck is reserved for guests, as well as color cable TV, games, magazines, books, a guest refrigerator, and ice service. AC in all the rooms. Nearby are golf, tennis,

NOTES: Credit cards accepted: A Master Card; B Visa; C American Express; D Discover; E Diners Club; F Other; 2 Personal checks accepted; 3 Lunch available; 4 Dinner available; 5 Open all year; 6 Pets

picnic areas, rocky bays, and inlets. Boston is an hour's drive. No smoking.

Hostess: Cynthia A. Sewell
Rooms: 7 (5PB; 2SB) $68-85
Continental Plus Breakfast
Credit Cards: A, B, D
Notes: 2, 5, 7, 8, 9, 10

Linden Tree Inn

Linden Tree Inn

26 King Street, 01966
(508) 546-2494; (800) 865-2122
E-mail: ltree@shore.net
Web site: http://www.shore.net/~ltree

Located on one of Rockport's many picturesque streets, the Inn is a haven for a restful, relaxing vacation. We are a leisurely eight-hundred-foot walk from the sandy beach, restaurants, art galleries, unique shops, and train station. Inside our Victorian-style home are fourteen individually decorated guest rooms, all with private baths. Guests enjoy the inn's formal living room, sunporch, bay and pond views from the cupola, spacious yard, and Dawn's "made from scratch" breakfast served buffet-style in the dining room.

Hosts: Dawn and Jon Cunningham
Rooms: 18 (PB) $72-109
Hearty Homemade Continental Breakfast
Credit Cards: A, B
Notes: 2, 5, 7, 8, 9, 10, 12

SAGAMORE BEACH (CAPE COD)

Widow's Walk

152 Clark Road, Box 605, 02562
(508) 888-0762

Located two hundred feet from beautiful Sagamore Beach on Cape Cod Bay, the Widow's Walk provides a soothing atmosphere that encourages you to relax and enjoy the magnificence of old Cape Cod. Bask in the sunshine by day, walk for miles on a quiet, sandy beach, or marvel over the romantic sunset on the Bay in the evening. Our Cape-style country home gives you that "homecoming feeling," with wide plank floors, three fireplaces, and an authentic widow's walk. Start your day with a delicious breakfast in our country kitchen or on the deck. Two beautiful bedrooms on the second floor share a bath and are separated by a "gathering room" with a fireplace. We also offer a fully equipped apartment with its own entrance on the ground level. No smoking.

Hosts: Meredith and Bill Chase
Rooms: 2 (2SB) $60-85
Full Breakfast
Credit Cards: none
Notes: 2, 5, 7, 8, 9, 10

SALEM

Amelia Payson House

16 Winter Street, 01970
(978) 744-8304
E-mail: aph@star.net
Web site: http://www.salemweb.com/biz/
    ameliapayson

Built in 1845, 16 Winter Street is one of Salem's finest examples of Greek Revival

---

welcome; 7 Children welcome; 8 Tennis nearby; 9 Swimming nearby; 10 Golf nearby; 11 Skiing nearby; 12 May be booked through travel agent.

architecture. Elegantly restored and beautifully decorated, each room is furnished with period antiques and warmed by a personal touch. Comfort amenities include private baths, air-conditioning, and cable TV. Located in the heart of Salem's historic district; a five-minute stroll finds downtown shopping, historic houses, museums, and Pickering Wharf's waterfront dining. The seaside towns of Rockport and Gloucester are a short drive up the coast; downtown Boston is only thirty minutes away by car or easily can be reached by train or bus. A color brochure is available. No smoking.

Hosts: Ada and Donald Roberts
Rooms: 4 (PB) $65-95
Continental Plus Breakfast
Credit Cards: A, B, C
Notes: 5, 9, 10

Amelia Payson House

The Salem Inn

7 Summer Street, 01970
(508) 741-0680; (800) 446-2995;
FAX (508) 744-8924
E-mail: saleminn@earthlink.net
Web site: http://www.salemweb.com/biz/saleminn

The Salem Inn is an upscale, thirty-one-room inn located in the heart of the downtown McIntire Historic District. The inn comprises two renovated and restored sea captains' homes on the National Register: the West House and the Curwen House. The ambience in this unique setting includes working fireplaces, canopy beds, antique furnishings, and period details, as well as the modern-day convenience of whirlpool baths, cable TV, telephones, in-room coffeemakers, and air-conditioning. This full-service inn features an excellent on site restaurant and a unique gift shop, The Enchanted Forest. Special packages! For a corporate meeting or special function, the perfect choice is the Salem Inn. The inn offers private, exclusive meeting space, full catering, parking on site, deluxe guest rooms, complete line of audiovisual equipment, FAX machine, and computer hookups. We supply the staff, service, and spirit for the most successful meeting and special occasion.

Hosts: Richard and Diane Pabich
Rooms: 33 (PB) $99-175
Continental Breakfast
Credit Cards: A, B, C, D, E
Notes: 2, 4, 5, 6, 7, 9, 10, 12

SANDWICH (CAPE COD)

Captain Ezra Nye House

152 Main Street, 02563
(508) 888-6142; (800) 388-CAPT;
FAX (508) 833-2897

Whether you come to enjoy summer on Cape Cod, a fall foliage trip, or a quiet winter vacation, the Captain Ezra Nye House is a great place to start. It is located sixty miles from Boston, twenty miles from Hyannis, and within walking distance of many noteworthy attractions,

---

NOTES: Credit cards accepted: A Master Card; B Visa; C American Express; D Discover; E Diners Club; F Other; 2 Personal checks accepted; 3 Lunch available; 4 Dinner available; 5 Open all year; 6 Pets

including Heritage Plantation, Sandwich Glass Museum, and the Cape Cod Canal. Award-winning "Readers Choice" named Best Bed and Breakfast, Upper Cape, by *Cape Cod Life* magazine for three years; named one of the Top Fifty Inns in America by *Inn Times*.

Hosts: Elaine and Harry Dickson
Rooms: 7 (PB) $85-110
Full Breakfast
Credit Cards: A, B, C, D
Notes: 2, 5, 7 (over 6), 8, 9, 10, 12

The Cranberry House Bed and Breakfast

50 Main Street, 02563
(508) 888-1281

The Cranberry House is a friendly place to stay on Cape Cod. A full breakfast is served in the dining room or on the deck. Relax in the den overlooking the beautifully landscaped yard. Hosts offer cable TV and complimentary soft drinks. Sandwich, the Cape's oldest town, has many shops, restaurants, museums, gardens, and beaches. The Cape Cod Canal has walking and biking trails. No smoking inside.

Hosts: John and Sara Connolly
Rooms: 4 (PB) $65-85
Full Breakfast
Credit Cards: none
Notes: 2 (and travelers checks), 5, 7 (over 10), 8, 9, 10

The Summer House

158 Main Street, 02563
(508) 888-4991; (800) 241-3609
E-mail: sumhouse@capecod.net

This exquisite 1835 Greek Revival home, featured in *Country Living* magazine, is located in the heart of historic Sandwich village. It features antiques; working fireplaces; hand-stitched quilts; flowers; large, sunny rooms; and English-style gardens. The Summer House is within strolling distance of dining, museums, shops, a pond, and the boardwalk to the beach. Guests are served bountiful breakfasts and afternoon tea in the garden. The home is open year-round.

Hosts: Marjorie and Kevin Huelsman
Rooms: 5 (PB) $65-95
Full Breakfast
Credit Cards: A, B, C, D
Notes: 2, 5, 7 (over 6), 8, 10, 12

SOUTH DARTMOUTH

The Little Red House

631 Elm Street, 02748
(508) 996-4554

The Little Red House is a charming gambrel colonial home located in the lovely coastal village of Padanaram. This home is beautifully furnished with country accents, antiques, lovely living room with fireplace, and luxuriously comfortable four-poster or brass-and-iron beds. A full homemade breakfast in the romantic, candlelit dining room is a delectable treat. Close to the harbor, beaches and historic sites; a short distance to New Bedford, Newport, Plymouth, Boston, and Cape Cod. The Martha's Vineyard ferry is just ten minutes away.

Hostess: Meryl Zwirblis
Rooms: 3 (1PB; 2SB) $55-75
Full Breakfast
Credit Cards: none
Notes: 2, 5, 9, 10, 12

welcome; 7 Children welcome; 8 Tennis nearby; 9 Swimming nearby; 10 Golf nearby; 11 Skiing nearby; 12 May be booked through travel agent.

Captain Nickerson Inn

SOUTH DENNIS (CAPE COD)

Captain Nickerson Inn

333 Main Street, 02660
(508) 398-5966; (800) 282-1619
FAX (508) 398-5966

Delightful Victorian sea captain's home on a bike path in the historic section of Dennis. Comfortable front porch is lined with white wicker rockers. Five guest rooms are decorated in period four-poster or white iron queen beds and Oriental or hand-woven rugs. Cozy terry robes and air-conditioning available in all rooms. Full breakfast served in the fireplaced dining room. Walk to Indian lands trail on the Bass River. Only a half mile from the Cape Cod Rail Bike twenty-two-plus-mile trail. Close to shops and good restaurants.

Hosts: Pat and Dave York
Rooms: 5 (3PB; 2SB) $65-95
Full Breakfast
Credit Cards: A, B, D
Notes: 2, 4 (weekends only), 5, 7, 9, 10, 12

STOCKBRIDGE

Arbor Rose B&B

8 Yale Hill Road, 01262
(413) 298-4744

A charming 1810 mill and farmhouse with flowing pond, gardens, antiques, home

baking, tranquillity, and smiles. Close to Stockbridge center, museums, restaurants, and Berkshire Theatre. Four-poster beds, fireplaces, gallery shop, and ski packages. No smoking. Families welcome.

Hostess: Christina Alsop
Rooms: 4 (PB) $65-155
Full Breakfast
Credit Cards: A, B, C
Notes: 2, 5, 7, 8, 9, 10, 11, 12

STURBRIDGE

The Colonel Ebenezer Crafts Inn

66 Fiske Hill Road, 01566
(508) 347-3313; (800) PUBLICK;
FAX (508) 347-5073
E-mail: phmkting@aol.com
Web site: http://www.publickhouse.com

The Colonel Ebenezer Crafts Inn, built in 1786 on the summit of Fiske Hill, offers a sensational panoramic view. Accommodations at the magnificently restored inn are enchanting and historically captivating. There are canopy beds, as well as poster beds. Relax by the pool or unwind in the sunroom, take afternoon tea, or simply enjoy sweeping views of the countryside.

Host: Albert Cournoyer
Rooms: 8 (PB) $79-145
Full Breakfast
Credit Cards: A, B, C, E
Notes: 3, 4, 5, 6 (limited), 7, 8, 9, 10, 11, 12

TYRINGHAM

The Golden Goose

123 Main Road, Box 336, 01264
(413) 243-3008

Warm, friendly, circa 1800 bed and breakfast nestled in a secluded valley. Near to

---

NOTES: Credit cards accepted: A Master Card; B Visa; C American Express; D Discover; E Diners Club; F Other; 2 Personal checks accepted; 3 Lunch available; 4 Dinner available; 5 Open all year; 6 Pets

Tanglewood, Stockbridge, skiing, and hiking. All homemade jams, applesauce, and biscuits, fresh fruit in season, and hot and cold cereals. Rooms are air-conditioned. Open all year.

Hosts: Lilja and Joe Rizzo
Rooms: 6 + apartment (4PB; 2SB) $80-125
Full Breakfast
Credit Cards: A, B, C
Notes: 2, 5, 7, 8, 9, 10, 11, 12

VINEYARD HAVEN (MARTHA'S VINEYARD)

Captain Dexter House of Vineyard Haven

92 Main Street, Box 2457, 02568
(508) 693-6564; FAX (508) 693-8448

Your perfect country inn! Built in 1840, the house has been meticulously restored and exquisitely furnished to reflect the charm of that period. You will be surrounded by flowers from our garden and pampered by innkeepers who believe in old-fashioned hospitality. The inn's eight romantic guest rooms are distinctively decorated. Several rooms have working fireplaces (as does the parlor) and four-

Captain Dexter House of Vineyard Haven

poster canopy beds. Stroll to town and harbor.

Hosts: Rick Fenstemaker
Rooms: 8 (PB) $55-195
Continental Plus Breakfast
Credit Cards: A, B, C
Notes: 2, 7, 8, 9, 10, 12

WARE (STURBRIDGE)

Antique 1880 Inn

14 Pleasant Street, 01082
(413) 967-7847

Built in 1876, this colonial-style inn has pumpkin and maple hardwood floors, beamed ceilings, six fireplaces, and antique furnishings. Afternoon tea is served by the fireplace; breakfast is served in the dining room or on the porch, weather permitting. It is a short, pretty country ride to historic Old Sturbridge Village and Old Deerfield Village. Hiking and fishing are nearby. Situated midway between Boston and the Berkshires. You will find the Antique 1880 Inn to be a very comfortable bed and breakfast.

Hostess: Margaret Skutnik
Rooms: 5 (2PB; 3SB) $40-65
Full Breakfast
Credit Cards: none
Notes: 2, 5, 8, 9, 10, 11, 12

WAREHAM

Mulberry Bed and Breakfast

257 High Street, 02571
(508) 295-0684; FAX (508) 291-2989

Mulberry Bed and Breakfast sits on a half-acre lot shaded by a majestic, seven-trunk

welcome; 7 Children welcome; 8 Tennis nearby; 9 Swimming nearby; 10 Golf nearby; 11 Skiing nearby; 12 May be booked through travel agent.

Mulberry Bed and Breakfast

mulberry tree. This Cape Cod-style home, built in 1847 by a blacksmith, offers three cozy guest rooms with two shared baths and a hearty, homemade breakfast. Mulberry is one mile from I-195 and I-495. The historic, picturesque cities of Boston, Newport, New Bedford, and Plymouth are within an hour's drive.

Hostess: Frances A. Murphy
Rooms: 3 (SB) $50-65
Full Breakfast
Credit Cards: A, B, C, D
Notes: 2, 5, 7, 8, 9, 10, 11 (cross-country), 12

WELLFLEET (CAPE COD)

The Inn at Duck Creeke

70 Main Street, Box 364, 02667
(508) 349-9333; FAX (508) 349-0234
E-mail: duckinn@capecod.net

Discover the unique blend of history and hospitality at the Inn at Duck Creeke. The Captain's House, built in the early 1800s, is one of the four buildings of traditional New England character that comprise the inn complex. Situated on a knoll on a woodsy five acres in Wellfleet's historic district, the inn has views of its duckpond, a tidal creek and salt marsh. Within the three lodging buildings are twenty-five rooms decorated to preserve the simple, antique charm. Most rooms have private

baths. The common room and screened porches are perfect for relaxing and lazy days. Our friendly, energetic staff work to make your stay a pleasant and memorable one. We welcome you with comfortable rooms, an informal continental breakfast, and warm hospitality. We are friendly, not fussy.

Hosts: Bob Morrill and Judy Pihl
Rooms: 25 (18PB; 7SB) $65-95
Continental Breakfast
Credit Cards: A, B, C
Notes: 4, 7, 8, 9, 10

The Inn at Duck Creeke

WEST YARMOUTH (CAPE COD)

The Manor House Bed and Breakfast

57 Maine Avenue, 02673
(508) 771-3433; (800) 9MANOR9
E-mail: manorhse@capecod.net
Web site: http://www.capecod.net/manorhouse

The Manor House is a lovely, 1920s, six-bedroom, Dutch Colonial bed and breakfast overlooking Lewis Bay. Each room has a private bath; all are decorated differently and named after special little touches of Cape Cod. We are ideally lo-

---

NOTES: Credit cards accepted: A Master Card; B Visa; C American Express; D Discover; E Diners Club; F Other; 2 Personal checks accepted; 3 Lunch available; 4 Dinner available; 5 Open all year; 6 Pets

The Manor House Bed and Breakfast

cated mid-Cape on the southern side, with easy access to virtually everything the Cape has to offer. We offer our guests a bountiful breakfast, afternoon tea and friendly hospitality.

Hosts: Rick and Liz Latshaw
Rooms: 6 (PB) $78-128
Full Breakfast
Credit Cards: A, B, C
Notes: 2, 5, 8, 9, 10, 12

WORTHINGTON

The Hill Gallery Bed and Breakfast

137 E. Windsor Road, 01098
(413) 238-5914
Web site: http://www.virtualcities.com

Relax in an artist/owner-designed, eight-room, multilevel home that was built to ensure privacy. We are secluded yet easily accessible, just more than two miles off Route 9. Our home showcases original artworks and pottery by Massachusetts artists. The two guest rooms have private baths (cots are available). An American breakfast is served each morning. Rates on request for a self-contained cottage.

Hosts: Ellen and Walter Korzec
Rooms: 3 (2PB; 1SB) $50-70 (10-percent
    discount Monday-Thursday)
Full Breakfast
Credit Cards: none
Notes: 2, 5, 7, 8, 9, 10, 11

welcome; 7 Children welcome; 8 Tennis nearby; 9 Swimming nearby; 10 Golf nearby; 11 Skiing nearby; 12 May be booked through travel agent.

MICHIGAN (UPPER PENINSULA)

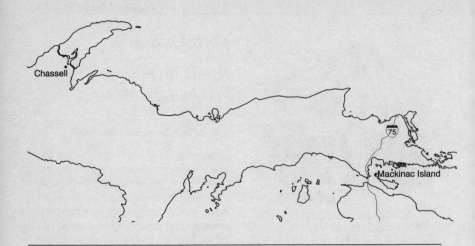

Chassell

75

Mackinac Island

MICHIGAN

Petoskey
Boyne City
•Bellaire
Traverse City

•Onekama
•Lake City

75

Ludington• •Scottville
•Pentwater
•Mears
•Shelby

•Bay City •Caro
•Alma
•Frankenmuth
•Clio

Owosso• FLINT
•Muskegon
Fruitport
Spring Lake
Grand GRAND •Lowell 69
Haven RAPIDS 75 94
196 96
•Holland LANSING
•Saugatuck 96
•Fennville •Charlotte
•Plainwell DETROIT
South Haven •Battle Creek 94 Romulus
94 Ypsilanti
St. Joseph 275
94 •Jonesville
Union Pier Coldwater• •Adrian
New Buffalo 69 75

69

69

Michigan

ADRIAN

Briaroaks Inn

2980 N. Adrian Highway, 49221
(517) 263-1659; (800) 308-7279

Come experience warm hospitality and elegant decor at our Williamsburg-style inn. Briaroaks sits nestled among century-old oak trees, overlooking picturesque Beaver Creek. The inn features three romantic guest rooms, two Jacuzzi suites with fireplaces and canopy beds. All guest rooms offer private baths, telephones, central air-conditioning, and televisions. In the morning, let your taste buds savor your full gourmet breakfast. AAA-approved.

We offer 20 percent off Jacuzzi suites, Sunday-Thursday.

Hosts: Connie and Dallas Marvin
Rooms: 3 (PB) $75-145
Full Gourmet Breakfast
Credit Cards: A, B
Notes: 2, 5, 8, 9, 10, 11, 12

ALMA

Saravilla B&B

633 N. State Street, 48801-1604
(517) 463-4078
Web site: http://www.laketolake.com

Enjoy the charm and original features of this 1894, eleven-thousand-square-foot

Saravilla Bed and Breakfast

NOTES: Credit cards accepted: A Master Card; B Visa; C American Express; D Discover; E Diners Club; F Other; 2 Personal checks accepted; 3 Lunch available; 4 Dinner available; 5 Open all year; 6 Pets welcome; 7 Children welcome; 8 Tennis nearby; 9 Swimming nearby; 10 Golf nearby; 11 Skiing nearby; 12 May be booked through travel agent.

Dutch Colonial home. You may enjoy the pool table, the fireplace in the library, and the hot tub in the sunroom. Guest rooms are spacious and quiet; several have fireplaces, and one has a whirlpool tub. A full breakfast is served each morning in the elegant turret dining room. The casino is twenty minutes away.

Hosts: Linda and Jon Darrow
Rooms: 7 (PB) $70-110
Full Breakfast
Credit Cards: A, B, D
Notes: 2, 5, 7, 8, 10, 12

BATTLE CREEK

Greencrest Manor

6174 Halbert Road, 49017
(616) 962-8633; FAX (616) 962-7254

To experience Greencrest Manor is to step back in time to a way of life that is rare today. From the moment you enter the iron gates, you will be mesmerized. This French Normandy mansion, situated on the highest elevation of St. Mary's Lake, is constructed of sandstone, slate, and copper. The three levels of formal gardens include fountains, stone walls, iron rails, and cut sandstone urns. The home is air-conditioned for your comfort. Greencrest Manor was the featured "Inn of the Month" in *Country Inns* magazine, August 1992, and was chosen as one of the magazine's top twelve inns in the nation for that year.

Hosts: Kathy and Tom Van Daff
Rooms: 8 (6PB; 2SB) $75-200
Continental Breakfast
Credit Cards: A, B, C, E
Notes: 2, 5, 8, 10

BAY CITY

Clements Inn

1712 Center Avenue, 48708-6122
(517) 894-4600; (800) 442-4605;
FAX (517) 895-8535

This 1886 Queen Anne-style Victorian home features six fireplaces, magnificent woodwork, oak staircase, amber-colored glass windows, working gas lamps, organ pipes, and two clawfoot tubs. Each of the six bedrooms includes cable television, VCR, telephone, private bath, and AC. Special features include in-room gas fireplaces, in-room whirlpool tubs, and the twelve-hundred-square foot Ballroom Suite, including fireplace, whirlpool, and furnished kitchen.

Hosts: Brian and Karen Hepp
Rooms: 6 (PB) $70-175
Continental Breakfast
Credit Cards: A, B, C, D, E
Notes: 2, 5, 7, 8, 10, 11, 12

BELLAIRE

Grand Victorian B&B Inn

402 N. Bridge Street, 49615
(616) 533-6111; (800) 336-3860;
FAX (616) 533-8197

This 1895 Victorian gingerbread mansion was built by lumber baron Henri Richardi. Listed on the National Register, the inn features antiques and three fireplaces, etched glass, exquisite woodwork, and wicker-filled front porch/balconies overlooking a park. Minutes to golf/skiing (Shanty/Schuss). Tandem town bike for shopping. Elegant breakfast experience. No smoking. Four rooms, each with private bath. Named among "Top Ten Affordable Luxury Inns" by *Country Inns*, 1997.

Hosts: George and Jill Watson
Rooms: 4 (PB) $95-125
Full Breakfast
Credit Cards: A, B, C
Notes: 2, 8, 9, 10, 11, 12

Deer Lake Bed and Breakfast

BOYNE CITY

Deer Lake Bed and Breakfast

00631 E. Deer Lake Road, 49712
(616) 582-9039; FAX (616) 582-5385
E-mail: info@deerlakebb.com
Web site: http://www.deerlakebb.com

Deer Lake is a contemporary waterfront bed and breakfast in a quiet country setting. Breakfast is served in the parlor at tables set with fine china and crystal, by candlelight. Guest rooms each have air-conditioning and individual heat. Between the home and the lake is a small pond that's perfect for a quick swim or a place to sit in the morning with a cup of coffee and

watch the countryside wake up. A jewelry class is available.

Hosts: Glenn and Shirley Piepenburg
Rooms: 5 (PB) $80-95
Full Breakfast
Credit Cards: A, B, D
Notes: 2, 5, 7, 8, 9, 10, 11, 12

CARO

Garden Gate Bed and Breakfast

315 Pearl Street, 48723
(517) 673-2696

Built with charm in the Cape Cod colonial style, it is a home designed for our guests. In summer, the yards are full of flowers. Our rooms are individually decorated and offer queen/king beds, cable TV, AC, and whirlpool tub. Honeymoon/anniversary suite. We offer state rates, as well.

Hostess: Evelyn L. White
Rooms: 4 (PB) $55-85
Full Breakfast
Credit Cards: A, B
Notes: 2, 5, 7, 8, 9, 10, 12

CHARLOTTE

Schatze Manor Bed and Breakfast

1281 W. Kinsel Highway, 48813
(517) 543-4170; (800) 425-2244

Come and enjoy quiet elegance in our Victorian Oak Suite with red Oriental soaking tub, or enjoy sleeping in the 1948 Chevy Woody Room, or feel like a celebrity and

welcome; 7 Children welcome; 8 Tennis nearby; 9 Swimming nearby; 10 Golf nearby; 11 Skiing nearby; 12 May be booked through travel agent.

relax in our Movie Star Room. All with private baths, distinctive hand-carved woodwork, unique decorating, full breakfast, evening dessert, and a nonsmoking atmosphere. Golf packages and dinner/theater packages available. Lansing is twenty miles away.

Hosts: Donna and Paul Dunning
Rooms: 3 (PB) $60-105
Full Breakfast
Credit Cards: A, B, C
Notes: 2, 5, 8, 9, 10

CHASSELL

Palosaari's Rolling Acres Bed and Breakfast

Route 1, Box 354, N. Entry Road, 49916
(906) 523-4947

Guests are welcome to visit the dairy barn during milking. We serve a full country breakfast. Walks to the lake are one way to unwind after visiting the many sights of our beautiful Keweenaw Peninsula.

Hosts: Evey and Cliff Palosaari
Rooms: 3 (SB) $45
Full Breakfast
Credit Cards: none
Notes: 2, 5, 7 (well-mannered), 9

Cinnamon Stick Bed and Breakfast

CLIO

Cinnamon Stick Bed and Breakfast

12364 N. Genesee Road, 48420
(810) 686-8391

Hospitality award-winning Cinnamon Stick is a unique country farm home sitting on fifty rolling acres in rural Genesee County. Guests may choose from five quaint bedrooms with charming country antiques and comfortable beds, great room with fieldstone fireplace, living room, dining room, patio flower garden area, walking trails and stocked fishing pond. One room has a Jacuzzi. Admire the Belgian draft horses kept on the farm. Time permitting, a wagon ride pulled by the mighty Belgians may be arranged in the summer, or perhaps a sleigh ride in the winter. Full country breakfast. Minutes from Clio

Palosaari's Rolling Acres Bed and Breakfast

NOTES: Credit cards accepted: A Master Card; B Visa; C American Express; D Discover; E Diners Club; F Other; 2 Personal checks accepted; 3 Lunch available; 4 Dinner available; 5 Open all year; 6 Pets

Amphitheater, Flint Crossroads Village/ Huckleberry Railroad, Genesee Bell River Boat, Frankenmuth, Birch Run Outlet Mall and Historic Chesaning. Open all year.

Hosts: Brian and Carol Powell
Rooms: 5 (4PB; 1SB) $60-80
Full Breakfast
Credit Cards: A, B
Notes: 2, 5, 7, 9, 10

COLDWATER

Batavia Inn

1824 W. Chicago Road, 49036
(517) 278-5146

This 1872 Italianate country inn has original massive woodwork, high ceilings, and restful charm. Seasonal decorations are a specialty. Christmas festival of trees. Located near recreation and discount shops. In-ground pool, cross-country skiing, and fifteen acres of wildlife trails. Horse stables. Guest pampering is the innkeepers' goal, with treats and homemade breakfast. Perfect for small retreats.

Host: Fred Marquardt
Rooms: 5 (PB) $64-110
Full Breakfast
Credit Cards: A, B, D
Notes: 2, 5, 8, 9, 11

FENNVILLE

The Kingsley House

626 W. Main Street, 49408
(616) 561-6425; FAX (616) 561-2593
E-mail: GaryKing@accn.org

This elegant Queen Anne Victorian was built by the prominent Kingsley family in 1886 and selected by *Inn Times* as one of the fifty best bed and breakfasts in America. Also featured in *Insider* magazine. Near Holland, Saugatuck, Allegan State Forest, sandy beaches, and cross-country skiing. Bicycles available, three rooms with whirlpool baths and fireplaces, and a getaway honeymoon suite. Enjoy beautiful surroundings and family antiques. Breakfast is in the formal dining room.

Hosts: Gary and Kari King
Rooms: 8 (PB) $80-165
Full and Continental Breakfasts
Credit Cards: A, B, C, D
Notes: 2, 4, 5, 8, 9, 10, 11, 12

The Kingsley House

Ridgeland

6875 126th Avenue, 49408
(616) 857-1633

Take a walk back in time to the turn of the century and experience a stay in one of the original guest homes of the Lakeshore area. We are a family-oriented bed and breakfast with antique furnishings. Located near the Saugatuck-Douglas area in a rural setting by Lake Michigan. See wildlife in its natural setting. Private bath and Jacuzzi. Nonsmoking.

Hosts: Carl and Michele Nicholson
Rooms: 3 (PB) $75-85
Full Breakfast
Credit Cards: A, B
Notes: 2, 5, 7, 9, 10, 11

welcome; 7 Children welcome; 8 Tennis nearby; 9 Swimming nearby; 10 Golf nearby; 11 Skiing nearby; 12 May be booked through travel agent.

FRANKENMUTH

Bavarian Town Bed and Breakfast

206 Beyerlein Street, 48734
(517) 652-8057

Beautifully decorated Cape Cod dwelling with central air-conditioning and private half baths in a peaceful, residential district of Michigan's most popular tourist town, just three blocks from Main Street. Bilingual hosts are descendants of original German settlers. Will serve as tour guides of the area, including historic St. Lorenz Lutheran Church. Color television with comfortable sitting area in each room. Shared kitchenette. Enjoy leisurely served full breakfasts with homemade, baked food. We share recipes and provide superb hospitality.

Hosts: Kathy and Louie Weiss
Rooms: 2 (private half baths, shared shower) $65-70
Full Breakfast
Credit Cards: none
Notes: 2, 5, 7, 8, 9, 10

Bed and Breakfast at the Pines

327 Ardussi Street, 48734
(517) 652-9019

Welcome to our clean, casual, comfortable ranch-style home located in a quiet neighborhood within walking distance of main tourist attractions and famous restaurants. Relax and enjoy reading or visiting with other guests in our "great room" overlooking our perennial garden and bird

Bed and Breakfast at the Pines

feeders. Guest rooms are individually furnished with double/twin beds, cotton sheets, terry robes and ceiling fans. Modified full breakfast of homemade breads, fresh seasonal fruits and specialty beverages. This is a smoke-free home, established in 1986.

Hosts: Richard and Donna Hodge
Rooms: 2 (1PB; 1SB) $50
Modified Full Breakfast
Credit Cards: none
Notes: 2, 5, 6, 7

GRAND HAVEN

Boyden House Inn

301 South 5th, 49417
(616) 846-3538
Web site: http://www.laketolake.com/sw/
grandhaven.html

Built in 1874, our charming Victorian inn is decorated with treasures from faraway places, antiques, and original art. Enjoy the comfort of air-conditioned rooms with private baths and two whirlpool baths. Some rooms feature fireplaces or balconies. Relax in our common room and veranda surrounded by a beautiful perennial garden. Full, homemade breakfast served in our lovely dining room. Within walking

NOTES: Credit cards accepted: A Master Card; B Visa; C American Express; D Discover; E Diners Club; F Other; 2 Personal checks accepted; 3 Lunch available; 4 Dinner available; 5 Open all year; 6 Pets

distance of boardwalk beaches, shopping, and restaurants.

Hosts: Corrie and Bernie Snoeyer
Rooms: 6 (PB) $65-110
Full Breakfast
Credit Cards: A, B, C, D
Notes: 2, 5, 7, 8, 9, 10, 11, 12

Village Park Bed and Breakfast

60 W. Park Street, **Fruitport**, 49415
(616) 865-6289; (800) 469-1118

Overlooking the welcoming waters of Spring Lake and Village Park, where guests can picnic, play tennis, or use the pedestrian bike paths and boat launch. Spring Lake has access to Lake Michigan. Relaxing common area with a fireplace; also, an exercise room with a sauna and an outdoor hot tub. Historic setting of Mineral Springs Health Resort, serving the Grand Haven-Muskegon areas. Hoffmaster Park with the Gillette Sand Dune Nature Center is nearby. We're located close to the Maranatha Bible Conference Center.

Hosts: John Hewett (and B&B angel, Virginia)
Rooms: 6 (PB) $60-90
Continental or Full Breakfast
Credit Cards: A, B
Notes: 2, 5, 7, 8, 9, 10, 11 (cross-country), 12

HOLLAND

Bonnie's Parsonage 1908 Bed and Breakfast

6 East 24th Street/Central Avenue, 49423
(616) 396-1316

Our lovely, historic parsonage was built in 1908 by one of Holland's early Dutch churches in order to call their first minister. Holland's first bed and breakfast opened in 1984. Since then, our guests' compliments have placed us on top of the list with Michigan's best lodging facilities! A delicious full breakfast is served in our formal dining room. Beautiful residential setting near Hope College. Saugatuck Resort is twelve miles away. Other attractions include antique shops, mall shops, bike/hike trails, and fine art shops. AAA-approved. Fodor's Best Upper Great Lakes.

Hostess: Bonnie McVoy-Verwys
Rooms: 2-3 (2PB; 2SB)
Full Breakfast
Credit Cards: none
Notes: 2, 5, 8, 9, 10, 11, 12

Dutch Colonial Inn

560 Central Avenue, 49423
(616) 396-3664; FAX (616) 396-0461

Relax and enjoy a gracious 1928 Dutch Colonial. Your hosts have elegantly decorated their home with family heirloom antiques and furnishings from the 1930s. Guests enjoy the cheery sunporch, honeymoon suites, fireplaces, and rooms with whirlpool tubs for two. Festive touches are everywhere during the Christmas holiday season. Nearby are Windmill Island, a wooden shoe factory, the Delftware factory, the tulip festival, Hope College, Michigan's finest beaches, bike paths, and cross-country ski trails. Corporate rates are available for business travelers.

Hosts: Barb, Jan, Bob and Pat
Rooms: 5 (PB) $75-150
Full Breakfast
Credit Cards: A, B, C, D
Notes: 2, 5, 8, 9, 10, 11, 12

---

welcome; 7 Children welcome; 8 Tennis nearby; 9 Swimming nearby; 10 Golf nearby; 11 Skiing nearby; 12 May be booked through travel agent.

North Shore Inn of Holland

686 North Shore Drive, 49424
(616) 394-9050

Water views, three-course gourmet breakfasts, and personalized service are hallmarks of the North Shore Inn. This elegantly restored 1920s lakeside B&B is in a tranquil setting, yet close to area attractions. The cozy bedrooms, decorated with quilts and antiques, feature private baths and king or queen beds. The North Shore Inn is open year-round. Relax in the wicker chaise on the screened porch in summer or enjoy the comfortable sofa in front of the fireplace in the winter time.

Hosts: Kurt and Beverly Van Genderen
Rooms: 3 (2PB; 1SB) $100-125
Full 3-Course Breakfast
Credit Cards: none
Notes: 2, 5, 8, 9, 10, 12

IONIA

Union Hill Inn Bed and Breakfast

306 Union Street, 48843
(616) 527-0955
Web site: http://www.laketolake.com

Elegant 1868 Italianate-style home that served as a former station for the underground railroad. The rooms are beautifully furnished with antiques. Enjoy the living area with fireplace, piano, porcelain village, and dolls. Flower beds surround this home noted for its expensive veranda and panoramic view. With all the beauty at Union Hill Inn, the greatest thing you

Union Hill Inn Bed and Breakfast

will experience is the love and peace that abide here.

Hosts: Tom and Mary Kay Moular
Rooms: 6 (1PB; 5SB) $50-75
Full Breakfast
Credit Cards: none
Notes: 2, 5, 7, 8, 10

JONESVILLE

The Munro House B&B

202 Maumee, 49250
(517) 849-9292; (800) 320-3792
Web site: www.getaway25mi.com/munro

This 1840 Greek Revival structure was built by George C. Munro, a brigadier general during the Civil War. Visitors can see the secret room used to hide runaway slaves as part of the underground railway. The seven cozy guest rooms, all with private baths, are furnished with period antiques, many with working fireplaces and Jacuzzis. Five common area rooms, including a library and breakfast room with open-hearth fireplace. Evening snack.

Hostess: Joyce Yarde
Rooms: 7 (PB) $75-150
Full Breakfast
Credit Cards: A, B, D
Notes: 2, 5, 7, 8, 9, 10, 11, 12

NOTES: Credit cards accepted: A Master Card; B Visa; C American Express; D Discover; E Diners Club; F Other; 2 Personal checks accepted; 3 Lunch available; 4 Dinner available; 5 Open all year; 6 Pets

LAKE CITY

Bed and Breakfast in the Pines

1940 Schneider Park Road, 49651
(616) 839-4876

A quaint chalet nestled among the pines on shimmering Sapphire Lake. Each bedroom has its own outside door leading to its own deck facing the lake. Enjoy our large fireplace and warm hospitality. Handicap ramp. Thirteen miles east of Cadillac. No alcohol, smoking, or pets. Enjoy downhill/cross-country skiing, fishing, swimming, hiking, biking, and boating. Two-week advance reservation only.

Hostess: Reggie Ray
Rooms: 2 (1PB; 1SB) $75-100
Full Breakfast
Credit Cards: none
Notes: 2, 5, 8, 9, 10, 11

LOWELL

McGee Homestead Bed and Breakfast

2534 Alden Nash NE, 49331
(616) 897-8142

Join us in the country! An 1880 farmhouse with a barn full of petting animals.

McGee Homestead Bed and Breakfast

Five acres surrounded by orchards, next to a golf course. Guests have a separate entrance to a living room with fireplace, parlor, and small kitchen, furnished with antiques. Big country breakfast.

Hosts: Bill and Ardie Barber
Rooms: 4 (4PB) $38-58
Full Breakfast
Credit Cards: A, B, C, D
Notes: 2, 7, 8, 9, 10, 11

LUDINGTON

Bed and Breakfast at Ludington

2458 S. Beaune Road, 49431
(616) 843-9768

For a relaxing change of pace, our B&B offers privacy and fresh air, and nature beckons your "child" at heart. Located in a beautiful little valley where a small Indian village once was. Now you can enjoy our shaded lawn, try out the tree swing, explore our little creek, join our frequent summer campfires, watch the sun set, or swim in Lake Michigan ten minutes away. Ask about our barn loft hideaway. A Jacuzzi is available during the winter months, air-conditioning in summer.

Hosts: Grace and Robert Schneider
Rooms: 3 (2PB; 1SB) $40-60
Credit Cards: none
Notes: 2, 5, 6, 7 (arrange in advance; extra charge),
    8, 9, 10, 11

Doll House Inn

709 E. Ludington Avenue, 49431
(616) 843-2286; (800) 275-4616

The Doll House Inn is a gracious 1900 American Foursquare with seven rooms,

welcome; 7 Children welcome; 8 Tennis nearby; 9 Swimming nearby; 10 Golf nearby; 11 Skiing nearby; 12 May be booked through travel agent.

including a bridal suite with whirlpool tub for two. Enclosed porch. We offer smoke- and pet-free adult accommodations. A full, heart-smart breakfast is served each morning. The home is air-conditioned. Corporate rates, bicycles, cross-country skiing, walk to beach and town, and special weekend and murder mystery packages in fall and winter. Transportation to and from car ferry/airport. Closed December 20-March 15.

Hosts: Barb and Joe Gerovac
Rooms: 7 (PB) $60-110
Full Breakfast
Credit Cards: A, B
Notes: 2, 8, 9, 10

The Inn at Ludington

701 E. Ludington Avenue, 49431
(616) 845-7055; (800) 845-9170
FAX (616) 845-0794

Enjoy the charm of the past with the comfort of today. No stuffy, hands-off museum atmosphere here—our vintage furnishings invite you to relax and feel at home. The bountiful breakfast will sustain you for a day of beachcombing, biking, or antiquing. In winter, cross-country skiing awaits at Ludington State Park. Looking for something different? Murder mysteries are a specialty. Make this your headquarters for a Ludington/Lake Michigan

adventure. Just look for the "painted lady" with the three-story turret. The Inn at Ludington is a nonsmoking home.

Hosts: Diane Shields and David Nemitz
Rooms: 6 (PB) $65-85
Full Buffet Breakfast
Credit Cards: A, B, C
Notes: 2, 3 (picnic), 5, 7, 8, 9, 10, 11, 12

Snyder's Shoreline Inn

903 W. Ludington Avenue, 49431
(616) 845-1261; FAX (616) 843-4441

Snyder's Shoreline Inn offers a beautiful location on the edge of town and tremendous views of Lake Michigan. Guests enjoy watching freighters, fishing boats, and spectacular Lake Michigan sunsets from private covered balconies. Sleep comfortably in our pleasant guestrooms, each one immaculate and individually decorated with a charm that reflects the owners' personal touch. Explore local antique shops and miles of nearby sandy beaches. The inn features in-room spas, quilts, and stenciled walls. Continental breakfast. Outdoor pool/spa. Smoke-free. No pets.

Hosts: Kate Whitaker and Angie Snyder
Rooms: 44 (PB) $65-229
Continental Breakfast
Credit Cards: A, B, C, D
Notes: 8, 9, 10

Snyder's Shoreline Inn

NOTES: Credit cards accepted: A Master Card; B Visa; C American Express; D Discover; E Diners Club; F Other; 2 Personal checks accepted; 3 Lunch available; 4 Dinner available; 5 Open all year; 6 Pets

MACKINAC ISLAND

Haan's 1830 Inn

PO Box 123, 49757
(906) 847-6244

The earliest Greek Revival home in the Northwest Territory, the completely restored inn is on the Michigan Historic Registry. It is in a quiet neighborhood three blocks around Haldiman Bay from the bustling 1800s downtown and Old Fort Mackinac. Adjacent to St. Anne's Church and gardens. Rooms are furnished with antiques. 19th-Century ambience of horse-drawn buggies and wagons. Closed late October to mid-May.

Hosts: Nancy and Nick Haan
Rooms: 7 (5PB; 2SB) $90-150
Deluxe Continental Breakfast
Credit Cards: none
Notes: 2, 7, 8, 9, 10

MEARS

The Dunes B&B

1618 N. Shore Drive, PO Box 53, Silver Lake, 49436-0053
(616) 873-5128; FAX (616) 873-0554
E-mail: lathers@oceana.net
Web site: http://www.webmaster@oceana.net

Located on scenic Silver Lake within an easy walk of the famous shifting sand dunes. Our bed and breakfast is casual and comfortable, with beautiful sunsets from our private lawn or deck. Close to golf course, bike trails, dune rides, and more. AC, TV, waterfront.

Hosts: Jan and Dale Lathers
Rooms: 3 (1PB; 2SB) $65-85
Full Breakfast
Credit Cards: A, B, C, D
Notes: 2, 5, 7, 9, 10, 11

MUSKEGON

Port City Victorian Inn

1259 Lakeshore Drive, 49441
(616) 759-0205 (voice and FAX); (800) 274-3574

An 1877 romantic Victorian getaway on the bluffs of Muskegon Lake. Minutes from Lake Michigan beaches, state parks, theaters, sports arena, and restaurants. Five bedrooms with private baths, two featuring suites with lake views and private double-whirlpools. Rooftop balcony, TV/VCR room with a view of the lake. The main floor is all common area for our guests' enjoyment. Includes two parlors—one with a fireplace—large dining room, sunroom, and music room with piano. All rooms have air-conditioning, cable TV, and phones. FAX and bicycles available.

Hosts: Fred and Barbara Schossau
Rooms: 5 (PB) $95-125
Full Breakfast
Credit Cards: A, B, C, D, E, F
Notes: 2, 5, 7, 8, 9, 10, 11, 12

NEW BUFFALO

Sans Souci Euro Inn

19265 S. Lakeside Road, 49117
(616) 756-3141; fax (616) 756-5511
E-mail: sans-souci@worldnet.att.net
Web site: http://www.laketolake.com/sans-souci

Sans Souci ("without a care") is far removed from the hustle of everyday life. Inside our gates, you will find silence and serenity. Lakeside cottages, honeymoon suites, vacation homes with whirlpools and fireplaces. Enjoy a fifty-acre nature retreat with private lake (fishing, swimming, or skating) and wondrous wildlife. Birder's paradise—spring and fall migration stopover. Fine dining, antiques, art galleries, golf courses nearby. Family reunions, small seminars welcome. AAA-approved. Chicago seventy miles.

Hosts: The Siewert Family
Rooms: 9 (PB) $98-185
Full Breakfast
Credit Cards: A, B, C, D
Notes: 2, 5, 6, 7, 8, 9, 10, 11 (cross-country), 12

Sans Souci Euro Inn

ONEKAMA

Lake Breeze House

5089 Main Street, 49675
(616) 889-4969

Our two-story frame house on Portage Lake is yours with a shared bath, living room, and breakfast room. Each room has its own special charm with family antiques. Come, relax, and enjoy our back porch and the sounds of the babbling creek. By reservation only. Boating and charter service available.

Hosts: Bill and Donna Erickson
Rooms: 3 (1P half B; 2SB) $55
Full Breakfast
Credit Cards: none
Notes: 2, 7, 8, 9, 10, 11

OWOSSO

R&R Ranch Bed and Breakfast

308 E. Hibbard Road, 48867
(517) 723-2553; FAX (517) 725-5392

A newly remodeled farmhouse from the 1900s, the ranch sits on 130 acres overlooking the Maple River Valley. A large concrete, circular drive with white board fences leads to stables of horses and cattle. The area's wildlife include deer, fox, rabbits, pheasant, quail, and songbirds. Observe and explore from the farm lane, river walk, or outside deck. Countrylike accents adorn the interior of the farmhouse, and guests are welcome to use the family parlor, garden, game room, and fireplace. Newly installed central air-conditioning adds to your comfort.

Hosts: Carl and Jeanne Rossman
Rooms: 3 (SB) $45
Continental Breakfast
Credit Cards: none
Notes: 2, 5, 6, 7, 10

PENTWATER

Historic Nickerson Inn

262 Lowell, PO Box 986, 49449
(616) 869-6731; FAX (616) 869-6151

The Historic Nickerson Inn has been serving guests with "special hospitality" since 1914. Our Inn was totally renovated in 1991. All our rooms have private baths and AC. We have two Jacuzzi suites with fireplaces and balconies overlooking Lake Michigan. Two short blocks to Lake Michigan beach, and three blocks to shopping district. New ownership. Open all year. Casual, fine dining in our eighty-seat restaurant. Excellent for retreats, workshops, and year-round recreation.

Hosts: Gretchen and Harry Shiparski
Rooms: 12 (PB) $90-190
Full Breakfast
Credit Cards: A, B, D
Notes: 2, 4, 5, 7 (12 and older), 9, 10, 11 (cross-country), 12

Pentwater "Victorian" Inn

180 E. Lowell, PO Box 98, 49449
(616) 869-5909; FAX (616) 869-7002
Web sites: http://www.travelassist.com/reg/
   mi103s.html
   http://www.laketolake.com/nw/pentwater.html

This beautiful Victorian inn, built in the 1800s, has an attractive gingerbread exterior and stained-glass windows that have been lovingly preserved. Located a short walk from the village shops, fine dining, and Lake Michigan Beach with its spectacular sunsets. This popular B&B inn provides comfort and hospitality, from the personal greeting by your hosts to the evening snack to the elegant three-course breakfast made all from scratch and served in the dining room. Each of the five bedrooms is tastefully decorated with British and American antiques the hosts collected

Pentwater "Victorian" Inn

while living in England. Three porches grace the Inn, and the back porch is enclosed with a hot tub room. No smoking.

Hosts: Quintus and Donna Renshaw
Rooms: 5 (PB) $65-95
Full Breakfast
Credit Cards: A, B
Notes: 2, 5, 7, 8, 9, 10, 11 (cross-country), 12

PETOSKEY

Terrace Inn

1549 Glendale, PO Box 266, 49770
(616) 347-2410; (800) 530-9898;
FAX (616) 347-2407

Located in the Victorian community of Bay View among four hundred-plus turn-of-the-century cottages. Bay View originated in 1875 as a summer retreat for the United Methodist Church. The Chautauqua programs continue to offer spectacular religious, cultural, and family activities. The Terrace Inn was built in 1910 and is furnished with original furniture and Victorian floral and lace. Each guest room is different in decor and each has a private bath. The dining room is open Saturday for dinner in the off-season (October-May), but offers dining six nights a week in summer. Enjoy our famous planked whitefish while viewing Lake Michigan sunsets from the spacious porch. Guests have use of private beach, tennis courts, bicycles and Bay View programs, including world-class concerts. The absence of TVs and telephones creates a peaceful, relaxing atmosphere.

Hosts: Tom and Denise Erhart
Rooms: 44 (PB) $44-99
Continental Plus Breakfast
Credit Cards: A, B, C
Notes: 2, 4, 5, 7, 8, 9, 10, 11, 12

welcome; 7 Children welcome; 8 Tennis nearby; 9 Swimming nearby; 10 Golf nearby; 11 Skiing nearby; 12 May be booked through travel agent.

PLAINWELL

The 1882 John Crispe House Bed and Breakfast

404 East Bridge Street, 49080-1802
(616) 685-1293

Enjoy museum-quality Victorian elegance on the Kalamazoo River just off U.S. 131 on Michigan 89. The house is close to some of western Michigan's finest gourmet dining, golf, skiing, and antique shops. AC. No smoking or alcohol. Gift certificates are available.

Hosts: Nancy E. Lefever and Joel T. Lefever
Rooms: 3 (PB) $75-110
Full Breakfast
Credit Cards: A, B
Notes: 2, 5, 7, 8, 10, 11

The 1882 John Crispe House

ROMULUS

Countryside Bed and Breakfast

32285 Sibley Road, 48174
(313) 753-4586; (800) 951-1245

Country hospitality awaits you at our Cape Cod home on a twenty-acre farm. Large, air-conditioned guest rooms have TV, fridge, microwave, phone, desk and snacks. You will enjoy strolling through gardens and wooded trails, or barbecue and relax in the gazebo. Near Detroit Metropolitan Airport (transportation available). Special package discount for nearby Greenfield Village. Parks, golfing, walleye fishing, and many other attractions close by.

Hostess: Veronica Laroy
Rooms: 2 (1PB; 2SB) $50-60
Full Breakfast
Credit Cards: none
Notes: 2, 5 (except October), 7, 8, 9, 10, 12

ST. JOSEPH

South Cliff Inn Bed and Breakfast

1900 Lakeshore Drive, 49085
(616) 983-4881; FAX (616) 983-7391

South Cliff Inn is a beautifully renovated bed and breakfast on a bluff overlooking Lake Michigan, in the quaint village of St. Joseph. The exterior of the inn is brick, much like an English cottage complete with a formal perennial garden and decks overlooking the lake. The interior of South Cliff is finished with custom-designed fur-

South Cliff Inn

NOTES: Credit cards accepted: A Master Card; B Visa; C American Express; D Discover; E Diners Club; F Other; 2 Personal checks accepted; 3 Lunch available; 4 Dinner available; 5 Open all year; 6 Pets

nishings and many antiques. Each of the seven beautifully appointed guest rooms has a private bath; several have fireplaces or whirlpool tubs or both; several have balconies overlooking the lake. The atmosphere of the inn is one of warmth and friendliness. The innkeeper is a retired chef, so get ready to enjoy the homemade breakfast every morning. South Cliff Inn has received the readers' choice award for Best Bed and Breakfast in Southwestern Michigan in 1994, 1995 and 1996. We strive to make your stay at South Cliff Inn a most enjoyable and relaxing time.

Hosts: Bill Swisher
Rooms: 7 (PB) $75-165
Full or Continental Breakfast
Credit Cards: A, B, C, D
Notes: 5, 8, 9, 10, 11, 12

Sherwood Forest Bed and Breakfast

SAUGATUCK

Sherwood Forest Bed and Breakfast

938 Center Street, PO Box 315, 49453
(800) 838-1246; FAX (616) 857-1996
Web site: http://www.virtualcities.com/ons/mi/s/
   mis4605.htm

Surrounded by woods, this beautiful Victorian-style home offers antique-furnished

guest rooms with private baths, cozy wing chairs, and Persian rugs. One room sports a spacious Jacuzzi, while the mural room has an oak-mantled fireplace. Guests may swim in the heated pool adorned with dolphins riding the ocean waves, or walk a half block to a Lake Michigan public beach to enjoy the spectacular sunsets. In winter, you can cross-country ski or hike along wooded paths. A separate cottage is available on request.

Hosts: Keith and Susan Charak
Rooms: 4 (PB)
Continental Breakfast
Credit Cards: A, B, D, E
Notes: 2, 7, 8, 9, 10, 12

Twin Gables Country Inn

900 Lake Street, PO Box 881, 49453
(616) 857-4346; (800) 231-2185;
FAX (616) 857-1092

Overlooking Kalamazoo Lake, the State Historic Inn has central air-conditioning throughout. Twin Gables features fourteen charming guest rooms with private baths, furnished in antiques and country decor. Cross-country skiers may relax in the large indoor hot tub and cozy up to a warm, crackling fireplace, while summer guests may take a refreshing dip in the outdoor pool and enjoy the glorious sunsets from the front veranda. Three separate one- and two-room cottages also are available.

Hosts: Michael and Denise Simcik
Rooms: 14 (PB) $68-98
Full Breakfast
Credit Cards: A, B, C, D
Notes: 2, 5, 7, 8, 9, 10, 11, 12

welcome; 7 Children welcome; 8 Tennis nearby; 9 Swimming nearby; 10 Golf nearby; 11 Skiing nearby; 12 May be booked through travel agent.

SCOTTVILLE

Eden Hill Bed and Breakfast

1483 E. Chauvez Road, 49454
(616) 757-2023; (888) 757-7570

Enjoy country, yet only twelve minutes from Ludington. Farmhouse more than one hundred years old, refurbished. Decorated country-style, it gives a relaxed, welcome feeling. House located high on a hill overlooking seventy-eight acres. Year-round comfort, cozy warmth for cross-country skiers. Family suite; children welcome. Full country breakfast. In-room TV, AC.

Hostess: Carla Craven
Rooms: 3 (PB) $65-77
Full Breakfast
Credit Cards: A, B

SHELBY

The Shepherd's Place Bed and Breakfast

2200 32nd Avenue, 49455
(616) 861-4298

Enjoy a peaceful retreat in a country atmosphere, near Lake Michigan beaches, dunes, fishing, golfing, and horseback riding. You may choose between our comfortable and cozy accommodations with queen-size bed or twin beds, both with private baths. Full breakfast is served in our dining room or porch overlooking a bird haven. No smoking allowed. Open May-October.

Hosts: Hans and Diane Oehring
Rooms: 2 (PB) $55-60
Full Breakfast
Credit Cards: none
Notes: 2, 9, 10

The Seymour House

SOUTH HAVEN

The Seymour House

1248 Blue Star Highway, 49090
(616) 227-3918; FAX (616) 227-3010

An 1862 Victorian mansion on eleven acres encourages relaxation with wide-open spaces, an acre pond for fishing, trails through the woods, and a garden patio. It's just minutes to popular Saugatuck/South Haven beaches, restaurants, galleries, horseback riding, golf, and orchards. Five individually decorated guest rooms with private baths, some with fireplaces or Jacuzzi. Gourmet breakfast. Log cabin with two bedrooms, fireplace. Central AC in cabin and bed and breakfast.

Hosts: Tom and Gwen Paton
Rooms: 5 (PB) $80-135
Full Breakfast
Credit Cards: A, B
Notes: 2, 5, 9, 10, 11, 12

SPRING LAKE

Seascape B&B

20009 Breton, 49456
(616) 842-8409

On private, sandy Lake Michigan Beach. All lakefront rooms. Relax and enjoy the

---

NOTES: Credit cards accepted: A Master Card; B Visa; C American Express; D Discover; E Diners Club; F Other; 2 Personal checks accepted; 3 Lunch available; 4 Dinner available; 5 Open all year; 6 Pets

warm hospitality and "country feeling" ambience of our nautical lakeshore home. Full homemade breakfast served in gathering room with fieldstone fireplace, porch or sundeck. All rooms offer panoramic view of lake and Grand Haven Harbor. Stroll or cross-country ski on dune land nature trails. Open year-round, offering a kaleidoscope of scenes with the changing of the seasons. Stay Sunday-Thursday and receive one night free.

Host: Susan Meyer
Rooms: 3 (PB) $79-150
Full Breakfast
Credit Cards: A, B
Notes: 2, 5, 8, 9, 10, 11

TRAVERSE CITY

Cider House Bed and Breakfast

5515 Barney Road, 49684
(616) 947-2833 (voice and FAX)
Web site: http://laketolake.com

Cider House Bed and Breakfast is a hilltop colonial overlooking an apple orchard, two-and-a-half miles from Transverse City. It offers four guest rooms, all with private baths. One bedroom walkout suite has a fireplace, full bath, and kitchen; sleeps four. Canopied pencil-post, white wicker and iron/brass beds are dressed in quilts and down comforters, piled high with feather pillows. A sumptuous breakfast is served each morning. Cable television available.

Hosts: Lynn and Shirley Boutwell
Rooms: 5 (PB) $75-120
Full Breakfast
Credit Cards: none
Notes: 2, 5, 8, 9, 10, 11

The Inn at Union Pier

UNION PIER

The Inn at Union Pier

9708 Berrien, PO Box 222, 49129
(616) 469-4700; FAX (616) 469-4720

Located just seventy-five minutes from Chicago and two hundred steps from the beach, the inn at Union Pier blends casual elegance with barefoot informality. You may choose from sixteen charming, spacious guest rooms. Most of them feature antique Swedish wood-burning fireplaces and porches overlooking the landscaped grounds. You may take one of the inn's bicycles out for a spin on a quiet country road, unwind in the outdoor hot tub and sauna, or enjoy Michigan wines and popcorn, which are served every evening in the inn's Great Room. A bountiful breakfast and afternoon refreshments are included every day. The Inn at Union Pier also hosts corporate retreats in a productive environment.

Hosts: Joyce Erickson Pitts and Mark Pitts
Rooms: 16 (PB) $125-195
Full Gourmet Breakfast
Credit Cards: A, B, D
Notes: 2, 5, 8, 9, 10, 11

welcome; 7 Children welcome; 8 Tennis nearby; 9 Swimming nearby; 10 Golf nearby; 11 Skiing nearby; 12 May be booked through travel agent.

YPSILANTI

The Parish House Inn

103 S. Huron Street, 48197
(313) 480-4800; (800) 480-4866;
FAX (313) 480-7472
E-mail: ParishInn@aol.com
Web site: http://www.innsandouts.com/property/
the_parish_house_inn

The Parish House Inn

This former parsonage of the First Congregational Church is a totally restored Queen Anne-style house. The nine guest rooms all have antique furniture, Victorian colors and wallpaper, yet offer guests all the modern conveniences. Awake to the aroma of freshly brewed coffee, baking breads, and sizzling bacon. The location is ideal for travelers on I-94 and U.S. 23 who are going to the University of Michigan, EMU, an area event, or a local business or industry.

Hostess: Mrs. Chris Mason
Rooms: 9 (PB) $75-125
Full Breakfast
Credit Cards: A, B, C, E
Notes: 2, 5, 8, 9, 10, 11, 12

Minnesota

ALBERT LEA

The Victorian Rose Inn

609 W. Fountain Street, 56007
(507) 373-7602; (800) 252-6558

Queen Anne Victorian home (1898) in virtually original condition, with fine woodwork, stained glass, gingerbread, antique light fixtures. Antique furnishings, down comforters. Spacious rooms, one with fireplace. Air-conditioned. A full breakfast is served each day. Business/extended-stay rates and gift certificates offered. Children by arrangement; no pets; no smoking.

Hosts: Darrel and Linda Roemmich
Rooms: 4 (PB) $40-80
Full Breakfast
Credit Cards: A, B
Notes: 2, 5, 7, 8, 10, 12

CANBY

Eaton's Victorian Rose

201 4th Street W., 56220
(507) 223-5474, (888) 212-7673;
FAX (507) 223-5474

Eaton's Victorian Rose is a romantic, restored late-1800s Queen Anne. Relax, read, or have a quiet conversation in many public rooms furnished with antiques, beautiful wallpapers, and accent pieces. Breakfast and homemade dessert served on a sunny porch or in the spacious dining room. Like going home to Grandma's.

Hostess: Flora Ann and Warren Hiese
Rooms: 3 (PB) $60-65
Full Breakfast
Credit Cards: A, B
Notes: 2, 3, 4, 5, 8, 9, 10, 11

CHASKA (MINNEAPOLIS)

Bluff Creek Inn

1161 Bluff Creek Drive, 55318
(612) 445-2735

Named as one of the top ten B&Bs in the Midwest by the *Chicago Tribune*. River bluff scenery. Elegant whirlpool/fireplace suites. Gourmet three-course breakfast. Only minutes from Mall of America, Chauhassen Dinner Theatre, Minnesota arboretum; adjacent to twenty miles of hiking, biking, skiing trails. Thirty minutes to downtown Minneapolis.

Hosts: Anne and Gary Delaney
Rooms: 5 (PB) $75-175
Full Breakfast
Credit Cards: A, B, C, D, E
Notes: 2, 5, 8, 9, 10, 11

---

welcome; 7 Children welcome; 8 Tennis nearby; 9 Swimming nearby; 10 Golf nearby; 11 Skiing nearby;
12 May be booked through travel agent.

MINNESOTA

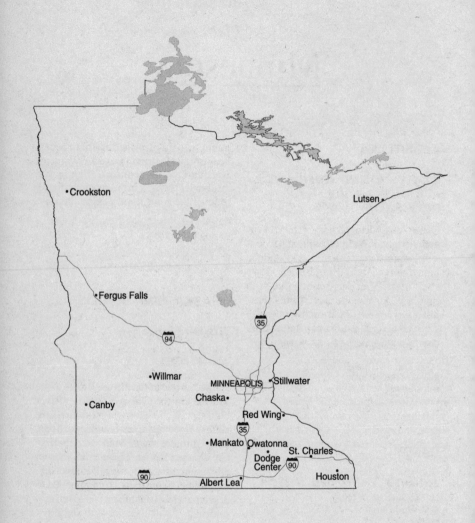

Elm Street Inn

CROOKSTON

Elm Street Inn
Bed and Breakfast

422 Elm Street, 56716
(218) 281-2343; (800) 568-4467;
FAX (218) 281-1756

The Elm Street Inn is a Georgian Revival (1910) home with antiques, hardwood floors, and stained and beveled glass. Guests enjoy the wicker-filled sunporch, old-fashioned beds, quilts, and fresh flowers—and the memorable full breakfast by candlelight. Bicycles are available, as is a limo to the casino. A community pool is next door. Children are permitted by arrangement. No pets. The Elm Street Inn is a no-smoking home.

Hosts: John and Sheryl Winters
Rooms: 4 (PB) $65
Full Breakfast
Credit Cards: A, B, C
Notes: 2, 5, 8, 9, 10, 12

DODGE CENTER

Pfeifer's Eden B&B

RR 1, Box 215, 55927
(507) 527-2021

An 1898 Victorian home with peaceful surroundings just a few miles from the historic town of Mantorville and twenty-five miles from the Mayo Clinic in Rochester. Many antique furnishings are yours to enjoy. Guests are intrigued by old-fashioned pastimes: playing the eight-foot pump organ, touring the world in stereographic cards, pedaling the player piano, or just relaxing on the open and screened porches on mild days, or by the fireplace in autumn and winter.

Hosts: Michael and Debra Pfeifer
Rooms: 4 (2 PB, 2SB) $45-55
Full Breakfast
Credit Cards: none
Notes: 2, 5, 7, 8, 9, 10, 11

FERGUS FALLS

Bakketopp Hus

RR 2, Box 187-A, 56537
(218) 739-2915; (800) 739-2915
Web site: http://vhost.telalink.net/~bbonline/mn/
bakketopp/index.html

Quiet, spacious lake home with vaulted ceilings, fireplaces, private spa, flower garden patio, and lakeside decks. Antique furnishings from family homestead; four-poster, draped, French canopy bed; and private baths. Here you can listen as loons call to each other across the lake in the still of dusk, witness the falling foliage splendor, relax by the crackling fire, or sink

---

NOTES: Credit cards accepted: A Master Card; B Visa; C American Express; D Discover; E Diners Club; F Other; 2 Personal checks accepted; 3 Lunch available; 4 Dinner available; 5 Open all year; 6 Pets welcome; 7 Children welcome; 8 Tennis nearby; 9 Swimming nearby; 10 Golf nearby; 11 Skiing nearby; 12 May be booked through travel agent.

into the warmth of the spa after a day of hiking or skiing. Near antique shops and Maplewood State Park. Ten minutes off I-94. Gift certificates available. Reservation with deposit.

Hosts: Dennis and Judy Nims
Rooms: 3 (PB) $65-95
Full Breakfast
Credit Cards: A, B, D
Notes: 2, 5, 8, 9, 10, 11

HOUSTON

Addie's Attic Bed and Breakfast

117 S. Jackson Street, PO Box 677, 55943
(507) 896-3010

Beautiful home, circa 1903. Cozy front parlor with curved glass window. Games, TV, player piano. Rooms are decorated and furnished with "attic finds." Hearty breakfast served in dining room. Near hiking, biking, cross-country ski trails, canoeing, antique shops. Weekday rates.

Hosts: Fred and Marilyn Huhn
Rooms: 3 (SB) $45-50
Full Country Breakfast
Credit Cards: none
Notes: 5, 8, 9, 10, 11

Addie's Attic

LUTSEN

Lindgren's Bed and Breakfast

County Road 35, PO Box 56, 55612-0056
(218) 663-7450

A 1920s log home in Superior National Forest on a walkable shoreline of Lake Superior. Knotty cedar interior decorated with wildlife trophies. Massive stone fireplaces, Finnish sauna, whirlpool, baby grand piano, and TVs/VCRs/CD. In center of area known for skiing, golf, stream and lake fishing, mountain biking, snowmobiling, horseback riding, skyride, alpine slide, fall colors, and Superior Hiking Trail. Near the Boundary Waters Canoe Area entry point. You'll enjoy the spacious, manicured grounds. Located one-half mile off Highway 61 on the Lake Superior Circle Tour.

Hostess: Shirley Lindgren
Rooms: 4 (PB) $85-125
Full Northwoods Country Breakfast
Credit Cards: A, B
Notes: 2, 5, 7 (over 12), 8, 9, 10, 11, 12

MANKATO

Butler House Bed and Breakfast

704 S. Broad Street, 56001
(507) 387-5055; FAX (507) 388-5462

This English-style (1905) mansion is elegantly furnished and includes a palatial porch, beautiful suites, canopy beds, whirlpool, fireplace, and private baths. Features include hand-painted murals,

---

NOTES: Credit cards accepted: A Master Card; B Visa; C American Express; D Discover; E Diners Club; F Other; 2 Personal checks accepted; 3 Lunch available; 4 Dinner available; 5 Open all year; 6 Pets

Butler House

Steinway grand, window seats, and a conference room. No smoking. Near state trail, civic center, biking, skiing, golfing, and antiquing. Come join us for an escape into a world of comfort and relaxation.

Hosts: Sharry and Ron Tschida
Rooms: 5 (PB) $55-115 (deposit required)
Full Breakfast, weekends; Continental, weekdays
Credit Cards: A, B, C
Notes: 2, 5, 9, 10, 11, 12

OWATONNA

The Northrop-Oftedahl House Bed and Breakfast

358 E. Main Street, 55060
(507) 451-4040; FAX (507) 451-2755

This 1898 Victorian with stained glass is three blocks from downtown. It has pleasant porches, grand piano, six-foot footed bathtub and souvenirs (antiques and collectibles from the estate). Northrop, family owned and operated, is one of twelve historical homes in the area, rich in local history, with an extensive reading library, backgammon, croquet, badminton, bocce, and more. Near hiking and biking trails, tennis, parks, and snowmobiling. Thirty-five miles to Mayo Clinic, fifty miles

to Mall of America. Special group rates for retreats. Bikers' bunks.

Hosts: Jean and Darrell Stewart/Gregory Northrop
Rooms: 5 (SB) $49-79.95
Continental or Full Breakfast
Credit Cards: none
Notes: 2, 3 and 4 (by reservations), 5, 6 (by arrangement), 7, 8, 9, 10, 11

RED WING

The Red Wing Blackbird

722 W. 5th Street, 55066
(612) 388-2292
E-mail: blackbird@pressenter.com
Web site: http://www.redwing.org

The Red Wing Blackbird Bed and Breakfast is a fine example of Queen Anne architecture, built in 1880. A charming three-season porch was added recently. The inn is located in the historic district, within walking distance of the Sheldon Theatre for the performing arts, downtown shopping and antique alley. The innkeepers look forward to sharing their Norwegian culture and musical talents.

Hosts: Lois and Paul Christenson
Rooms: 2 (PB) $90-135
Full Breakfast
Credit Cards: A, B
Notes: 2, 5, 8, 9, 10, 11

ST. CHARLES

Thoreson's Carriage House Bed and Breakfast

606 Wabasha Avenue, 55972
(507) 932-3479

Located near beautiful Whitewater State Park with its swimming, trails, and demonstrations by the park naturalist. We are

welcome; 7 Children welcome; 8 Tennis nearby; 9 Swimming nearby; 10 Golf nearby; 11 Skiing nearby; 12 May be booked through travel agent.

in Amish territory and minutes from the world-famous Mayo Clinic. Piano and organ are available for added enjoyment. Please write for free brochure.

Hostess: Moneta Thoreson
Rooms: 2 (SB) $40-45
Full Breakfast
Credit Cards: none
Notes: 2, 5, 7, 8, 9, 10

STILLWATER

The Ann Bean House

319 W. Pine Street, 55082
(612) 430-0355; (800) 933-0355

Welcome to our elegant Victorian bed and breakfast. It is the oldest surviving lumber baron's home in historic Stillwater, birthplace of Minnesota. Jacob Bean, co-founder of the Hersey, Bean and Brown lumber mill, purchased this towering, four-story mansion in 1880. The home still retains the finest in Victorian design: ornately carved oak fireplaces, shutters that fold into eighteen-inch-thick walls, and two stately towers with magnificent views of the St. Croix valley. Impressive, spacious guest rooms, each one distinctive.

Host: John Wubbels
Rooms: 5 (PB) $99-159
Full Breakfast
Credit Cards: A, B
Notes: 2, 5, 8, 10

James A. Mulvey Residence Inn

622 W. Churchill Street, 55082
(612) 430-8008; (800) 820-8008
Web site: http://www.cotn.com/bb

This is an enchanting place. Built in 1878 by lumberman James A. Mulvey, the Italianate residence and stone carriage house grace the most visited historic river town in the upper Midwest. Exclusively for you are the grand parlor, formal dining room, Victorian sunporch, and five fabulously decorated guest rooms filled with exquisite art and antiques. Four-course breakfast, double whirlpools, mountain bikes, fireplaces and air-conditioning. Welcome refreshments. Grace-filled service from innkeepers who care.

Hosts: Rev. Truett and Jill Lawson
Rooms: 5 (PB) $99-169
Full 4-Course Breakfast
Credit Cards: A, B, C, D
Notes: 2, 5, 8, 9, 10, 11, 12

WILLMAR

The Buchanan House Bed and Breakfast

725 SW 5th Street, 56201
(320) 235-7308; (800) 874-5534
Web site: http://www.thebuchananhousebandb
    .com

Gracious colonial-style home built in 1940. Four beautifully furnished bedrooms, all with queen-size beds and private baths. Guests are welcome to use our large, comfortable living room with fireplace to read by. Also available is a year-round gazebo with a fireplace surrounded by decks to relax on in nice weather and a hot tub kept in operation throughout the year. Gourmet breakfast. Golfing, fishing, swimming, boating, hiking, and trails nearby.

Hosts: Sharon and Ron Buchanan
Rooms: 4 (PB) $79-99
Full Breakfast
Credit Cards: A, B

NOTES: Credit cards accepted: A Master Card; B Visa; C American Express; D Discover; E Diners Club; F Other; 2 Personal checks accepted; 3 Lunch available; 4 Dinner available; 5 Open all year; 6 Pets

Mississippi

Natchez Trace Bed and Breakfast Reservation Service

PO Box 193, **Hampshire, TN**, 38461
(615) 285-2777; (800) 377-2770

This reservation service is unusual in that all the homes listed are close to the Natchez Trace, the delightful National Parkway running from Nashville, Tennessee, to Natchez, Mississippi. Kay Jones can help you plan your trip along the Trace, with homestays in interesting and historic homes along the way. Locations of homes include Ashland City, Columbia, FairView, Franklin, Hohenwald, and Nashville, **Tennessee**; Florence and Cherokee, **Alabama**; and Church Hill, Corinth, French Camp, Kosciusko, Lorman, Natchez, New Albany, Tupelo, and Vicksburg, **Mississippi**. Rates $60-125.

BELMONT

Belmont Hotel

121 Main Street, PO Box 140, 38827
(601) 454-7948

This Georgian-style hotel was built in 1924 and is the oldest hotel in operation in the state of Mississippi. All rooms downstairs are smoke-free, including the lobby and dining area. A complimentary continental breakfast is served daily in the dining room. Monday-Friday, breakfast will be put out at 6 AM; 6:30 AM on the weekend. Breakfast can be provided at an earlier time if needed. Ice machine available. Iron and ironing board on request. TVs in each room. Wake-up call offered. Portable phone can be arranged.

Hosts: Pat and Ron Deaton
Rooms: 16 (PB) $35-40
Continental Breakfast
Credit Cards: A, B, C
Notes: 5, 7, 8, 9, 11, 12

CORINTH

The Generals' Quarters

924 Fillmore Street, 38834
(601) 286-3325; FAX (601) 287-8188

The Generals' Quarters is a beautifully restored, Victorian home located in the historic district of the old Civil War town. The rooms are decorated with period antiques and contemporary pieces; and all rooms have private baths, cable TVs and telephones; the suite boasts a 140-year-old, four-poster canopy bed. There is a second-floor lounge with veranda, beautiful

welcome; 7 Children welcome; 8 Tennis nearby; 9 Swimming nearby; 10 Golf nearby; 11 Skiing nearby; 12 May be booked through travel agent.

MISSISSIPPI

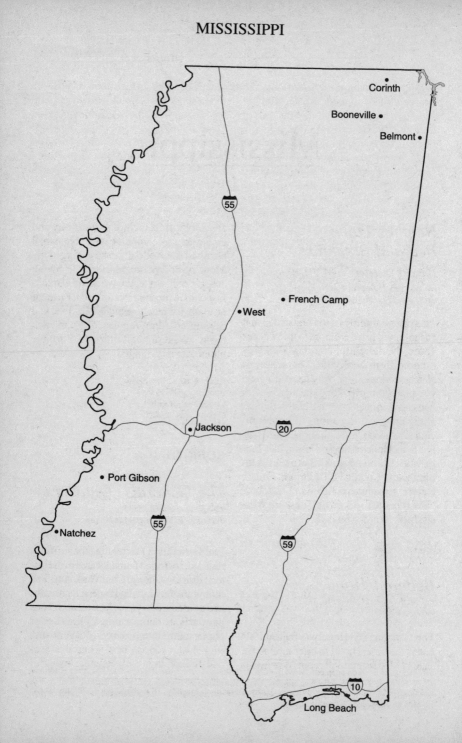

parlor and porch on the first floor, and lovely gardens to relax in after a day of sight-seeing, antiquing, playing golf, or touring the various Civil War sights in Corinth and the outlying areas. Our resident chef prepares a delicious full breakfast and evening snack. We are situated close to Shiloh National Military Park and the Tennessee-Tombigbee Waterway. The Generals' Quarters provides some of the best hospitality the South has to offer. The home is rated AAA three diamonds, ABBA three crowns.

Hosts: Luke Doehner and Charlotte Brandt
  Doehner
Rooms: 5 (PB) $75-90
Full Breakfast
Credit Cards: A, B, C, D
Notes: 5, 8, 9, 10, 12

French Camp Bed and Breakfast Inn

FRENCH CAMP

French Camp Bed and Breakfast Inn

1 Bluebird Lane, PO Box 120, 39745
(601) 547-6835; FAX (601) 547-6790

The inn is located on the historic Natchez Trace National Parkway, halfway between Jackson and Tupelo, Mississippi. It has been constructed from two restored, authentic hand-hewn log cabins, each more than a hundred years old. Indulge in southern cooking at its finest: fresh orange juice, "scratch" muffins, creamy grits, skillet-fried apples, fresh cheese, scrambled eggs, crisp slab bacon, and lean sausage, with two kinds of homemade bread and three kinds of homemade jellies. Life doesn't get any better!

Hosts: Ed and Sallie Williford
Rooms: 5 (PB) $60
Full Breakfast
Credit Cards: B
Notes: 2, 3, 4, 5, 6, 7, 8, 9, 12

Fairview Inn

JACKSON

Fairview Inn

734 Fairview Street, 39202
(601) 948-3429; (888) 948-1908;
FAX (601) 948-1203
E-mail: fairview@teclink.net
Web site: http://www.fairviewinn.com

The Fairview Inn is a Colonial Revival mansion listed on the National Historic Register. The inn offers elegant and comfortable ambience accented by fine fabrics and antiques in a historic neighborhood. Near churches, shopping, two colleges, and major medical complexes. AAA award,

NOTES: Credit cards accepted: A Master Card; B Visa; C American Express; D Discover; E Diners Club; F Other; 2 Personal checks accepted; 3 Lunch available; 4 Dinner available; 5 Open all year; 6 Pets welcome; 7 Children welcome; 8 Tennis nearby; 9 Swimming nearby; 10 Golf nearby; 11 Skiing nearby; 12 May be booked through travel agent.

four diamonds; "Top Inn of 1994" award by *Country Inns* magazine.

Hosts: Carol and Bill Simmons
Rooms: 8 (PB) $115-165
Full Breakfast
Credit Cards: A, B, C, D
Notes: 2, 4 (by reservation), 5, 8, 9, 10, 12

Red Creek Inn, Vineyard, and Racing Stable

LONG BEACH

Red Creek Inn, Vineyard, and Racing Stable

7416 Red Creek Road, 39560
(601) 452-3080; (800) 729-9670;
FAX (601) 452-4450

Raised French cottage built in 1899 by a retired Italian sea captain to entice his young bride away from her parents' home in New Orleans. Red Creek Inn, Vineyard, and Racing Stable is situated on eleven acres with ancient live oaks and fragrant magnolias, and delights itself in peaceful comforts. With a sixty-four-foot porch, including porch swings, our inn is furnished in antiques for our guests' enjoyment. New marble Jacuzzi in Victo-

rian Room. A ministerial discount of 10 percent is offered.

Hosts: Karl and "Toni" Mertz
Rooms: 7 (5PB; 2SB) $49-89
Continental Plus Breakfast
Credit Cards: none
Notes: 2, 3 and 4 (advance request), 5, 7, 9, 10, 12

NATCHEZ

The Bed and Breakfast Mansions of Natchez

PO Box 347, 200 State Street, 39121
(601) 446-6631; (800) 647-6742;
FAX (601) 446-8687

More than thirty magnificent B&B inns offer exquisite accommodations in pre-Civil War mansions, country plantations, and charming Victorian elegance. Historic Natchez, situated on high buffs that overlook the Mississippi River, offers visitors year-round tours of historic homes, horse-drawn carriage tours, plus the famous spring and fall pilgrimages featuring some of America's most splendid historic homes.

Hosts: Natchez Pilgrimage Tours
Rooms: More than 100 (PB) starting at $85
Full Southern Breakfast (at most inns)
Credit Cards: A, B, C, D
Notes: 2, 12

Dunleith

84 Homochitto, 39120
(601) 446-8500; (800) 433-2445

Dunlieth is listed on the National Register of Historic Places and is a national landmark. It is located on forty acres near downtown Natchez. Eleven rooms, three in main house and eight in courtyard wing. Full southern breakfast served in Poultry

Dunleith

House. All rooms have private baths and working fireplaces. No children. Reservations required.

Hosts: Nancy Gibbs and W.F. Heins
Rooms: 11 (PB) $85-130
Full Breakfast
Credit Cards: A, B, D, F
Notes: 8, 10

PORT GIBSON

Oak Square Plantation

1207 Church Street, 39150
(601) 437-4350; (800) 729-0240;
FAX (601) 437-5768

This restored antebellum mansion of the Old South is in the town Gen. U.S. Grant said was "too beautiful to burn." On the National Register of Historic Places, it has family heirloom antiques and canopied beds and is air-conditioned. Your hosts' families have been in Mississippi two hundred years. Christ is the Lord of this house. "But as for me and my house, we will serve the Lord" (Joshua 24:15). On U.S. Highway 61, adjacent to the Natchez Trace Parkway.

Hosts: Mr. and Mrs. William Lum
Rooms: 10-12 (PB) $85-95
Full Breakfast
Credit Cards: A, B, C, D
Notes: 2, 5, 7 (limited), 8, 9, 10

WEST

The Alexander House

210 Green Street, PO Box 187, 39192
(601) 967-2417; (800) 350-8034

Step inside the front door of the Alexander House Bed and Breakfast and go back in time to a more leisurely and gracious way of life. Victorian decor at its prettiest and country hospitality at its best are guaranteed to please your senses. Capt. Alexander, Dr. Joe, Ulrich, Annie, and Miss Bealle are all rooms waiting to cast their spell over those who visit. Day trips to historic or recreational areas may be charted or chartered. Located just three miles off I-55.

Hosts: Ruth Ray and Woody Dinstel
Rooms: 5 (3PB; 2SB) $65
Full Breakfast
Credit Cards: A, B, C, D
Notes: 2, 4, 5, 12

The Alexander House

welcome; 7 Children welcome; 8 Tennis nearby; 9 Swimming nearby; 10 Golf nearby; 11 Skiing nearby; 12 May be booked through travel agent.

MISSOURI

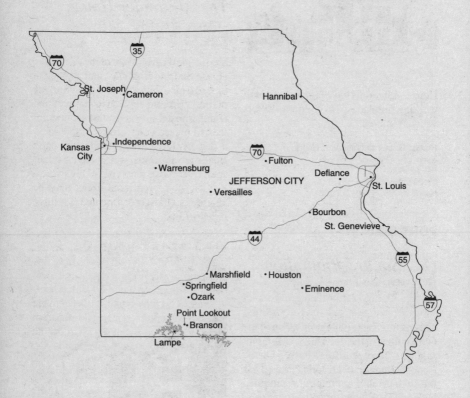

Missouri

BOONVILLE

Morgan Street Repose Bed and Breakfast

611 E. Morgan Street, 65233
(816) 882-7195; (800) 248-5061

1869 National Historic Registered Home delightfully restored for a romantic, gracious, hospitable stay. Heirlooms, antiques, books, games, and curiosities. Our extravagant breakfasts are formally served in one of three dining rooms or the Secret Garden. One block from antique/specialty shops, restaurants, and the Katy biking/hiking trail. Rental bikes available. Afternoon tea served.

Hostess: Doris Shenk
Rooms: 3 (PB) $65-95
Full Breakfast
Credit Cards: none
Notes: 2, 5, 7 (older), 12

Morgan Street Repose Bed and Breakfast

BOURBON

The Wildflower Inn

2739 Highway D, 65441
(573) 468-7975

Enjoy a bed and breakfast in the foothills of the Ozarks. Wake up to a private getaway in the heart of the Meramec River Valley. Two downstairs guest rooms, two upstairs, each opening onto a shared living and dining area. All rooms have private baths, color TVs, and peaceful view of the surrounding woods. Central heating and AC. Guests relax and visit in the spacious gathering room, or enjoy the fresh country air from a rocking chair on the front porch as Ozark wildlife parades by.

Hosts: Mary Lou and Jerry Hubble
Rooms: 4 (PB) $65-75
Full Breakfast
Credit Cards: A, B
Notes: 2, 5, 8, 9, 10

BRANSON

Annie's Place

PO Box 295, 65616
(417) 334-4720; (800) 695-1546

Near the end of a quiet road six miles east of Branson is a lovely, contemporary, An

---

NOTES: Credit cards accepted: A Master Card; B Visa; C American Express; D Discover; E Diners Club; F Other; 2 Personal checks accepted; 3 Lunch available; 4 Dinner available; 5 Open all year; 6 Pets welcome; 7 Children welcome; 8 Tennis nearby; 9 Swimming nearby; 10 Golf nearby; 11 Skiing nearby; 12 May be booked through travel agent.

A-frame private cottage. Queen-size beds, one on the main level and one in the loft bedroom. Main level bath includes a tub/shower. Spacious living area opens to a deck overlooking Lake Taneycomo. Hot tub on a private deck. Breakfast "fixin's" included. Easy access to all area attractions. Great trout fishing.

Hostess: Thelma Yeates
Rooms: cottage (PB) $65-95
Continental Breakfast
Credit Cards: A, B, D
Notes: 2, 5, 12

Cameron's Crag

PO Box 295, 65615
(417) 335-8134 (voice and FAX); (800) 933-8529
E-mail: mgcameron@aol.com

High on a bluff overlooking Lake Taneycomo and the valley, three miles south of Branson. Guests enjoy a spectacular view from a new, spacious, detached, private suite with whirlpool tub, kitchen, living-and-bedroom area. Two-room suite with indoor hot tub and private bath. A third room has a great view of the lake and a private hot tub on the deck. All rooms have king-size beds, hot tubs, private entrances, TV/VCRs, and a video library.

Hosts: Kay and Glen Cameron
Rooms: 3 (PB) $75-95
Full Breakfast
Credit Cards: A, B, C, D
Notes: 2, 5, 7, 8, 9, 10, 11, 12

Josie's Peaceful Getaway

HCR 1 Box 1104, 65616
(417) 338-2978, (800) 289-4125

Pristine, gorgeous lakefront scenery on Table Rock Lake where sunsets and moonlit nights lace the sky. Contemporary design featuring cathedral ceilings and stone fireplaces mingled with a Victorian flair. Cozy wood-burning fireplaces, lavish Jacuzzi spas, candlelight, and fresh flowers abound. Dine in luxury as you enjoy breakfast served on china and crystal. Celebrate your honeymoon or anniversary in style. Eight miles to Branson and music shows; five minutes to Silver Dollar City/Marina. Smoke-free environment.

Hosts: Bill and Jo Anne Coats
Rooms: 3 (PB) $60-110
Full and Continental Breakfast
Credit Cards: A, B, C, D
Notes: 2, 5, 7 (with restrictions), 9, 10, 12

Lakeshore Bed and Breakfast

HC#1 Box 935, 65616
(417) 338-2698 (voice and FAX)

A peaceful place on beautiful Table Rock Lake, two miles from Silver Dollar City. Great for family or church groups up to twelve people, also honeymoons and anniversaries. A contemporary home with boat dock and swim deck, covered patio with picnic table and grill, glider swing. Two units have private entrances, queen beds, hide-a-beds, coffee bars, refrigerators, microwaves, TVs, VCRs, A/C, and

Lakeshore Bed and Breakfast

private baths with showers; one has a whirlpool tub. One unit has a double bed and private bath. A nutritious, hearty breakfast.

Hostess: Gladys Lemley
Rooms: 3 (PB) $50-75
Full Breakfast
Credit Cards: none
Notes: 2, 5, 7, 8, 9, 10, 11, 12

Patchwork Quilt Bed and Breakfast

PO Box 126, 65615
(417) 334-7999

A comfy, rustic cedar home on four wooded acres in Branson, just five minutes from the Grand Palace and many other top music shows, attractions, and lakes. Private hot tub on the large porch, king-size bed, refrigerator, microwave, coffee pot, TV, VCR and tapes, telephone in your room. A big country breakfast is served each morning.

Hostess: Jewell Schroll
Rooms: 2-bedroom suite (PB) $45-75
Full Breakfast
Credit Cards: none
Notes: 2, 5, 6, 7, 8, 9, 10, 11 (water), 12

CAMERON

Cook's Country Cottage Bed and Breakfast

7880 NE Bacon Road, 64429
(816) 632-1776

Cook's Country Cottage is nestled in forty acres of beautiful hardwood trees beside a private lake. Private entrances and baths let you be as social or as private as you

choose. Escape today's stressful world in the peace and beauty our Lord has provided. You can walk in the woods, sit beside the lake, or rock on the porch while enjoying deer, Canada geese, wild turkey, and an abundance of songbirds to truly soothe the soul! We look forward to serving you.

Hosts: Don and Loura Cook
Rooms: 2 (PB) $50-75
Full Country Breakfast
Credit Cards: none
Notes: 2, 3, 4, 5, 8, 9, 10, 11

The Parsons House Bed and Breakfast

DEFIANCE

The Parsons House Bed and Breakfast

211 Lee Street, PO Box 38, 63341
(314) 798-2222; (800) 355-6878;
FAX (314) 798-2220

Stately 1842 Federalist home overlooks the Missouri River Valley. Listed in the Historic Survey, it features fireplaces, a large gathering room, and many antiques. For your enjoyment: a piano, organ, large library, porches, gardens and hot tub. Close by are the Katy Bicycle Trail, Daniel Boone Home, and Missouri wineries—yet downtown St. Louis is only thirty-five miles

welcome; 7 Children welcome; 8 Tennis nearby; 9 Swimming nearby; 10 Golf nearby; 11 Skiing nearby; 12 May be booked through travel agent.

away. A generous country breakfast is served in the gathering room by the fireplace in cool weather, on the porch or in the gardens in the summer.

Hosts: Al and Carol Keyes
Rooms: 3 (PB) $70-90
Full Breakfast
Credit Cards: A, B
Notes: 2, 5 (except Christmas), 7 (limited), 10

EMINENCE

Eminence Cottages

PO Box 548, 65466-0548
(573) 226-3500

Enchanting, informal cottages nestled on thirty acres await to welcome you to Ozark Mountain tranquillity; the perfect place to unwind after a day of fun! Our modern, fully equipped minihomes are cozy enough for a romantic getaway or roomy enough for the entire family. Canoe, tube, hike, golf, fish, horseback ride, sight-see or sit back and relax. You may take advantage of our weekday getaway packages for extra savings.

Hosts: Patti and Wes Tastad
Rooms: 9 (PB) $59-73.15
Full Breakfast
Credit Cards: A, B, D
Notes: 2, 3, 4, 6, 7, 8, 9, 10, 12

FULTON

Loganberry Inn

310 W. Seventh Street, 65251
(573) 642-9229
Web site: http://www.loganberryinn.com

Experience this turn-of-the-century Victorian bed and breakfast that hosted former prime minister Margaret Thatcher and Scotland Yard. The Loganberry Inn is located near Columbia, Hermann, Rocheport, Lake of the Ozarks, Jefferson City, and St. Louis. Located in historically rich Fulton, the inn is within strolling distance of several historic sites, including the Winston Churchill Memorial and Museum, Westminster College and William Woods University. Four U.S. presidents and several European heads of state have visited this unique town with its brick streets and quaint shops. The Loganberry Inn has private baths and a quiet, private atmosphere. The elegant and gracious surroundings are yet comfortable and uncluttered. The hosts are warm, gracious, and fun and they truly listen to you. Enjoy special pampering, such as Cathy's Special Recipe Chocolate Chip Cookies and milk at bedtime, or your own tea service brought up to your room.

Hosts: Carl and Cathy McGeorge
Rooms: 4 (PB) $65-85
Full Breakfast
Credit Cards: A, B, C
Notes: 2, 5, 8, 9, 10

Romancing the Past Bed and Breakfast

830 Court Street, 65251
(573) 592-1996
Web site: http://www.bbonline.com/mo/romance

An exceedingly beautiful Queen Anne Victorian home, circa 1868. Wraparound porch, winding staircase, Victorian antiques throughout and fireplaces in every room. Three beautifully decorated guest rooms with private baths and all the amenities ensure a delightful, romantic retreat. Hot tub. Delicious gourmet breakfast by

Romancing the Past Bed and Breakfast

candlelight in the formal dining room. All this in a spacious garden setting on a beautiful historic street.

Hosts: Jim and Reneé Yeager
Rooms: 3 (PB) $85-110
Full Breakfast
Credit Cards: A, B
Notes: 2, 3, 5, 7 (over 10), 8, 9, 10

HANNIBAL

Fifth Street Mansion Bed and Breakfast Inn

213 S. Fifth Street, 63401
(573) 221-0445; (800) 874-5661;
FAX (573) 221-3335

Built in 1858 in Italianate style by friends of Mark Twain. Antique furnishings complement the stained glass, ceramic fireplaces, and original gaslight fixtures of the house. Two parlors, dining room, and library with hand-grained walnut paneling, plus wraparound porches, provide space for conversation, reading, TV, and games. Walk to the Mark Twain historic district, shops, restaurants, and riverfront. The Fifth Street Mansion blends Victorian charm with plenty of old-fashioned hospitality.

The whole house is available for reunions and weddings.

Hosts: Mike and Donalene Andreotti
Rooms: 7 (PB) $65-90
Full Breakfast
Credit Cards: A, B, C, D
Notes: 2, 5, 7, 8, 9, 10, 12

HOUSTON

Windstone House Bed and Breakfast

539 Cleveland Road, 65483
(417) 967-2008

Windstone House is a large, two-story home with a spacious wraparound porch and balcony, sitting in the middle of more than eighty acres that provide a breathtaking view of the Ozarks countryside. The home has been tastefully furnished with a collection of antiques. In warm weather, breakfast is served on the balcony overlooking a spectacular panorama of meadows and woodland. If you are bent on unwinding, then this is the place for you.

Hostess: Barbara Kimes
Rooms: 3 (1PB; 2SB) $60
Full Breakfast
Credit Cards: none
Notes: 2, 5, 7 (over 12), 9, 10

INDEPENDENCE

The Mansion House

2121 S. Sterling Avenue, 64052
(816) 254-5416

The integrity of this beautiful, historic plantation home, which is very deserving, has been kept intact. Built in 1832, it boasts

welcome; 7 Children welcome; 8 Tennis nearby; 9 Swimming nearby; 10 Golf nearby; 11 Skiing nearby; 12 May be booked through travel agent.

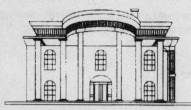

The Mansion House

many interesting stories connected with people and the Quantrills. This is one of Missouri's best-kept secrets. It comes with four exquisitely decorated Victorian bedrooms and baths, all with their own unique settings. You will find yourself surrounded with the elegance of a long-ago era, which is the harmony this home so richly deserves. You will wake up to a freshly cooked breakfast in our formal dining room.

Hosts: Dave and Paula Swayne
Rooms: 4 (PB) $85-125
Full Breakfast
Credit Cards: A, B
Notes: 2, 5, 8, 9

Woodstock Inn Bed and Breakfast

1212 W. Lexington, 64050
(816) 833-2233

Nestled within Independence's famous historical district, the Woodstock Inn is just a short stroll from all the sites you came to Independence to see! We have eleven warm and inviting rooms, each with a distinct personality and private bath. After a restful night's sleep, wake up to a piping hot cup of coffee and take a seat at our long oak dining table. Tempt your palate with our house specialty, gourmet Belgian waffles topped off with powdered sugar and smothered with specialty syrups or fresh fruit sauce. Our full breakfast is exactly what you need to start off a wonderful day of sight-seeing!

Hosts: Todd and Patricia Justice
Rooms: 11 (PB) $54-99
Full Breakfast
Credit Cards: A, B, C, D
Notes: 2, 5, 7, 12

KANSAS CITY

Bed and Breakfast Kansas City (Reservation Service)

PO Box 14781, Lenexa, KS 66285
(913) 888-3636

Accommodations are available in Kansas City, Weston, Liberty, Independence, and St. Joseph. Thirty-five inns and homestays range from circa 1845 to a contemporary Geodesic dome in the woods. Amenities include hot tubs, Jacuzzis, queen- and king-size beds, private baths, and full gourmet breakfasts. Prices range from $50 to $150. Major credit cards are welcome at the individual inns. Edwina Monroe, coordinator.

The Doanleigh Inn

217 E. 37th Street, 64111
(816) 753-2667; FAX (816) 531-5185

In the heart of the city, the Doanleigh Inn is ideally located between the famed Country Club Plaza and Hallmark Crown Center. Lovely European and American antiques enhance the Georgian architec-

---

NOTES: Credit cards accepted: A Master Card; B Visa; C American Express; D Discover; E Diners Club; F Other; 2 Personal checks accepted; 3 Lunch available; 4 Dinner available; 5 Open all year; 6 Pets

The Doanleigh Inn

ture of the inn. Wine and hors d'oeuvres await you each evening and a full gourmet breakfast is served each morning. Fireplaces and Jacuzzis provide the ultimate in relaxation. Other amenities include afternoon cookies, daily newspapers, free local calls and faxes, and in-room computer modem access.

Hosts: Cynthia Brogdon and Terry Maturo
Rooms: 5 (PB) $95-150
Full Breakfast
Credit Cards: A, B, C, D
Notes: 2, 5, 8, 9, 12

Hotel Savoy

219 W. 9th Street, 64105
(816) 842-3575 (voice and FAX);
(800) 729-6922

Kansas City's oldest and most historic hotel (c. 1888) is located in the heart of the convention and business district. The hotel offers beautifully appointed guest suites filled with antiques and personal amenities. Our breakfast has more than thirty-two items to choose from. Start your day with lobster bisque, smoked salmon with caviar, medallions of beef, or a light continental breakfast. A truly memorable

experience for your next business trip, special getaway, or catered event. The surrounding area has many places of historic value to visit that are within a few blocks' walk or just minutes by car.

Host: Larry Green
Rooms: 22 (PB) $79-150
Full Gourmet Breakfast
Credit Cards: A, B, C, D, E, F
Notes: 2, 3, 4, 5, 7, 8, 9, 10, 12

Hotel Savoy

Southmoreland on the Plaza

116 E. 46th Street, 64112
(816) 531-7979; FAX (816) 531-2407

Classic New England colonial mansion located between renowned Country Club Plaza (shopping/entertainment district) and the Nelson-Atkins and Kemper museums of art. Elegant B&B ambience with small hotel amenities. Rooms with private decks, fireplaces, or Jacuzzi baths. Special services for business travelers. Membership privileges at a plaza athletic club. Summer weekend "Kansas City-style" breakfast barbecues are our newest offerings for our guests. Mobil Travel Guide four-star winner since 1993. The only bed and

welcome; 7 Children welcome; 8 Tennis nearby; 9 Swimming nearby; 10 Golf nearby; 11 Skiing nearby;
12 May be booked through travel agent.

breakfast to receive the Midwest Travel Writers' "Gem of the Midwest" award.

Hostesses: Susan Moehl and Penni Johnson
Rooms: 12 (PB) $115-170
Full Breakfast
Credit Cards: A, B, C
Notes: 2, 5, 8, 9, 10, 12

LAMPE

Grandpa's Farm Bed and Breakfast

HC3, Box 476, 65681
(417) 779-5106; (800) 280-5106
FAX (417) 779-2050
Web site: http://iaswww.com/grandpa.html

A real old-time, 116-acre Ozark Mountain farm with plenty of friendly animal life. Luxurious Honeymoon Suite with spa, Red Bud Suite with large whirlpool tub, Dogwood Suite with kitchenette, and Mother Hen Room. Near Branson , Missouri, and Eureka Springs, Arkansas. Big, country breakfast served on screened-in porch. Secret hideout lofts for children.

Hosts: Keith and Pat Lamb
Rooms: 4 (PB) $65-85
Full Breakfast
Credit Cards: A, B, D
Notes: 2, 5, 7, 9, 12

MARSHFIELD

The Dickey House Bed and Breakfast Inn

331 S. Clay Street, 65706
(417) 468-3000; (800) 450-7444;
FAX (417) 859-5478
E-mail: wildor@aol.com
Web site: http://www.bbonline.com/mo/
    dickeyhouse

This mansion situated on one acre of park-like grounds is one of Missouri's finest bed

and breakfast inns. The Dickey House offers three antique-filled guest rooms with private baths, plus three spectacular suites with luxuriously appointed decor, double Jacuzzi, fireplace, and cable TV. The inn and dining room are enhanced by a display of fine American and European art and antiques. A gourmet breakfast is served in true Victorian style, amid fine china, silver, and crystal. The Dickey House Bed and Breakfast Inn has a four-diamond AAA rating.

Hosts: William and Dorothy Buesgen
Rooms: 7 (PB) $60-105
Full Breakfast
Credit Cards: A, B, D
Notes: 2, 5, 8, 9, 10, 12

NIXA

Wooden Horse Bed and Breakfast

1007 W. Sterling Court, 65714
(417) 724-8756; (800) 724-8756
Web site: http://www.nixa.com/chamber/
    woodenhorse

Our contemporary home, sprinkled with antiques, is located near city conveniences but is in the quiet country. The Rocking Horse Room has a bold queen bed and double rocker. The Carousel Room has a day bed with a trundle that lends to versatile arrangements amongst the floral decor. Near Springfield, only thirty minutes from Branson and Silver Dollar City.

Hosts: Larry and Valeta Hammar
Rooms: 2 (PB) $55-70
Full Breakfast
Credit Cards: none
Notes: 2, 5, 6, 8, 9, 10

NOTES: Credit cards accepted: A Master Card; B Visa; C American Express; D Discover; E Diners Club; F Other; 2 Personal checks accepted; 3 Lunch available; 4 Dinner available; 5 Open all year; 6 Pets

Dear's Rest Bed and Breakfast

OZARK

Dear's Rest B&B

1408 Capp Hill Ranch Road, 65721
(417) 581-3839; (800) 588-2262 (LUV2BNB);
FAX (417) 581-3839 (call first)
E-mail: info@dearsrest.com
Web site: http://www.dearsrest.com

Slip away from stress and relax surrounded by nature "with a view." Our Amish-built cedar home waits for "only you" (up to six), where hiking through the forest or stream snorkeling in clear, spring-fed Bull Creek are just part of the fun. The fireplace and homey antiques give Dear's Rest a peaceful feeling of bygone days. If antique shopping and Branson shows get too strenuous, try our hot tub "under the stars."

Hosts: Linda and Allan Schilter
Rooms: 1 suite (PB) $75
Full Country Breakfast
Credit Cards: A, B, D
Notes: 2, 5, 7, 9, 12

Smokey Hollow Lake Bed and Breakfast

880 Cash Spring Road, 65721
(417) 485-0286; (800) 485-0286

A country retreat nestled in 180 acres of Ozark hills and hollows between Branson and Springfield. Fish in our six-acre lake or try our canoe or paddleboat. Enjoy the birds, wildlife, creek, and pets. Accommodations in our private barn loft apartment include a whirlpool for two, kitchen, and two baths, done in a cozy country decor.

Hosts: Brenda and Richard Bilyeu
Rooms: 1 suite (PB) $85
Full Breakfast
Credit Cards: none
Notes: 2, 5, 7 (4 and up), 9, 10, 12

POINT LOOKOUT

Bird's Eye View

PO Box 1188, 65726
(417) 336-6551; (800) 933-8529;
FAX (417) 335-8134
E-mail: mgcameron@aol.com

A private, spacious suite in our unique, detached guest house. Spectacular bird's-eye view overlooking the lake and valley from your suite and private deck with spa. Private entrance, king-size bed, full kitchen with dining area, cable TV/VCR, shower, and deluxe whirlpool bath for two.

Hosts: Kay and Glen Cameron
Rooms: 1 (PB) $95
Full Breakfast
Credit Cards: A, B, C, D
Notes: 2, 5, 7, 8, 9, 10, 11

ST. GENEVIEVE

The Inn St. Gemme Beauvais

78 N. Main Street, 63670
(573) 883-5744

Jacuzzis, hors d'oeuvres, and private suites filled with antiques only serve to begin your

welcome; 7 Children welcome; 8 Tennis nearby; 9 Swimming nearby; 10 Golf nearby; 11 Skiing nearby; 12 May be booked through travel agent.

The Inn St. Gemme Beauvais

pampering stay in Missouri's oldest continually operating bed and breakfast. The romantic dining room with working fireplace is the perfect setting for an intimate breakfast. The inn has been redecorated and is within walking distance of many shops and historical sites. Packages available for that special occasion, as well as picnics to take on hiking trails.

Hostess: Janet Joggerst
Rooms: 7 (PB) $69-125
Full Breakfast
Credit Cards: A, B
Notes: 2, 3, 5, 7, 8, 9, 10

ST. JOSEPH

Harding House

219 N. 20th Street, 64501
(816) 232-7020 (voice and FAX)

Gracious turn-of-the-century home. Elegant, oak woodwork and pocket doors. Antiques and beveled, leaded-glass windows. Historic area near museums, churches, and antique shops. Four unique guest rooms. Eastlake has a romantic wood-burning fireplace and queen-size bed; the Blue Room has an antique water

lily quilt on the wall. Children welcome. Full breakfast with homemade pastry.

Hosts: Glen and Mary Harding
Rooms: 4 (2PB; 2SB) $45-65
Full Breakfast
Credit Cards: A, B, C, D
Notes: 2, 5, 7, 8, 10, 12

ST. LOUIS

The Gables

404 Darst Road, 63135
(314) 521-2080

A seven-gable English Tudor-style house in the historic "Old Town" section of Ferguson. Located two miles north of I-70, two miles south of I-270, four miles from the airport, close to a Metro station, and a few minutes from all St. Louis attractions. One master bedroom suite with queen bed and adjoining sitting room, two bedrooms with double beds. Outside, relax in the gazebo or by the fishpond.

Hosts: John and Claudine DuRall
Rooms: 3 (SB) $55-75
Gourmet Continental Breakfast
Credit Cards: none
Notes: 2, 5

Lafayette House

2156 Lafayette Avenue, 63104
(314) 772-4429; (800) 641-8965;
FAX (314) 664-2156
Web site: http://www.bbonline.com/mo/lafayette

This 1876 Queen Anne mansion is in historic Lafayette Square, only minutes from downtown St. Louis. Attend a baseball or football game; shop at historic Union Station; visit the St. Louis Arch, science center, and zoo; or simply stroll through lovely Lafayette Square Park. From the

---

NOTES: Credit cards accepted: A Master Card; B Visa; C American Express; D Discover; E Diners Club; F Other; 2 Personal checks accepted; 3 Lunch available; 4 Dinner available; 5 Open all year; 6 Pets

Lafayette House

moment you arrive, you'll be surrounded by this bed and breakfast's unique personality! Annalise will treat you to a full gourmet breakfast, which may include homemade breads, muffins, crab-stuffed quiche or Belgian waffles with warm blueberry compote. The house is furnished comfortably with antiques and traditional furniture. The suite on the third floor, accommodating six, has a private bath and kitchen. Maybe you'll prefer our Victorian Room with its fireplace and Jacuzzi for that romantic getaway. For business guests we offer FAX, in-room phones, flexible breakfast hours. ABBA inspected and approved. Resident cats!

Hosts: Annalise Millet and Nancy Buhr
Rooms: 6 (3PB; 3SB) $60-150
Full Breakfast
Credit Cards: A, B, C, D, E, F
Notes: 2, 5, 7, 8, 9, 10, 11, 12

SPRINGFIELD

Virginia Rose Bed and Breakfast

317 E. Glenwood, 65807
(417) 883-0693; (800) 345-1412

This two-story farmhouse, built in 1906, offers country hospitality right in town.

Situated in a tree-covered acre, our home is furnished with early-1900s antiques, quilts on queen-size beds, and rockers on the porch. Relax in the parlor with a book, puzzle, or game, or watch a movie on the TV/VCR. We are located only minutes from BASS Pro Outdoor World, restaurants, shopping, antique shops, and miniature golf, and only forty miles from Branson.

Hosts: Jackie and Virginia Buck
Rooms: 5 (PB) $50-100
Full Breakfast
Credit Cards: A, B, C, D
Notes: 2, 5, 7, 9, 10, 12

The Hilty Inn Bed and Breakfast

VERSAILLES

The Hilty Inn Bed and Breakfast

206 E. Jasper, 65084
(573) 378-2020; (800) 667-8093

A Victorian setting near the historic Morgan County Courthouse. We have a courtyard with outdoor dining, when weather permits. A place to get away from it all, relax and enjoy being catered to. It is a

welcome; 7 Children welcome; 8 Tennis nearby; 9 Swimming nearby; 10 Golf nearby; 11 Skiing nearby; 12 May be booked through travel agent.

fun place for reunions or for friends to meet and have good visits together.

Hostess: Doris Hilty
Rooms: 4 (PB) $55-95
Full or Continental Breakfast
Credit Cards: A, B, C
Notes: 2, 4, 5, 7 (inquire first), 10

WARRENSBURG

The Camel Crossing

210 E. Gay Street, 64093
(816) 429-2973
E-mail: camelx@internetland.net

Ride a magic carpet to this bed and breakfast that is homey in atmosphere but museumlike in its decor. Brass, copper, hand-tied carpets, and furnishings from the Far East will captivate your imaginations. An oasis for mind and body. If you come a stranger, you'll leave as a friend.

Hosts: Ed and Joyce Barnes
Rooms: 4 (2PB; 2SB) $55-65
Full Breakfast
Credit Cards: A, B
Notes: 2, 5, 7, 8, 9, 10

Montana

BOZEMAN

The Lehrkind Mansion Bed and Breakfast

719 N. Wallace Avenue, 59715
(406) 585-6932 (voice and FAX; call first);
(800) 992-6932
E-mail: lehrkindmansion@imt.net
Web site: http://www.imt.net/~lehrkindmansion/
    index.htm

Listed in the National Register and built in 1897, The Lehrkind Mansion offers one of Montana's finest examples of Victorian Queen Anne architecture. A spacious yard and gardens, porches, and the large cor-

The Lehrkind Mansion Bed and Breakfast

ner tower are among this three-story mansion's spectacular features. Victorian antiques are found throughout the mansion. The music parlor features Victrolas and a rare 1897 Regina music box—seven feet tall! Queen beds, comforters, and overstuffed chairs provide relaxation. A large hot tub will soak away the aches of an active day. The Lehrkind Mansion is just seven blocks from Bozeman's historic Main Street shopping district. A stay at the Lehrkind Mansion Bed and Breakfast is not just a room for the night—it's a memorable experience!

Hosts: Jon Gerster and Christopher Nixon
Rooms: 4 (3PB; 1SB) $65-155
Full Breakfast
Credit Cards: A, B, C, D
Notes: 2, 5, 8, 9, 10, 11, 12

Lindley House

202 Lindley Place, 59715
(406) 587-8403; (800) 787-8404
FAX (406) 582-8112
E-mail: lindley@avicom.net
Web site: http://www.avicom.net/lindley

A charming and distinctive Victorian manor house listed on the National Historic Register and located close to the downtown area, within walking distance of the university, theaters, fine restaurants, quaint shops, and galleries. The Lindley House

welcome; 7 Children welcome; 8 Tennis nearby; 9 Swimming nearby; 10 Golf nearby; 11 Skiing nearby; 12 May be booked through travel agent.

MONTANA

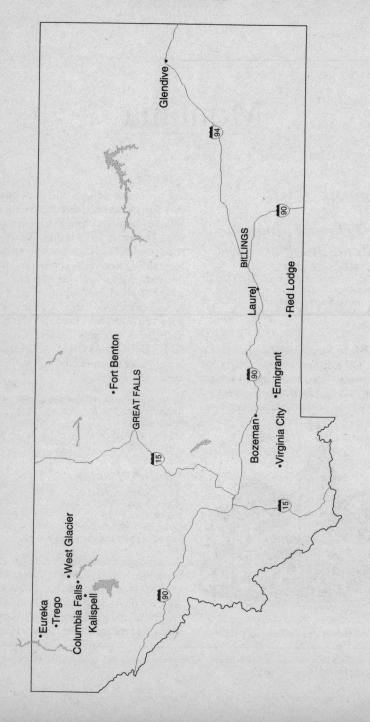

has undergone a complete restoration, with dramatic French wall coverings, antique beds, fireplaces, stained-glass windows and an enclosed English garden.

Hostess: Stephanie Volz
Rooms: 8 (6PB; 2SB) $90-250
Full Breakfast
Credit Cards: A, B
Notes: 2, 5, 8, 9, 10, 11, 12

Park View Inn Bed and Breakfast

COLUMBIA FALLS

Park View Inn Bed and Breakfast

PO Box 567, 59912
(406) 892-7275

Located in a small-town setting with views of Glacier National Park and our own city park across the street, with swimming pool, basketball court, and children's play area, as well as beautiful trees and picnic areas. We know you'll enjoy our two-story Victorian home with two suites and two luxury rooms, or one of our three cabins—espe-

cially our honeymoon cabin featuring Jacuzzi and four-poster bed.

Hosts: Jayne and Gary Hall
Rooms: 7 (3PB; 4SB) $45-110
Full Breakfast
Credit Cards: A, B
Notes: 5, 7, 8, 9, 10, 11

EMIGRANT (NEAR NORTH ENTRANCE, YELLOWSTONE)

Paradise Gateway B&B and Guest Log Cabin

PO Box 84, 59027
(406) 333-4063; (800) 541-4113
Web site: http://www.wtp.net/go/paradise

Paradise Gateway B&B, just minutes from Yellowstone National Park, offers quiet, charming, comfortable guest rooms in the shadow of the majestic Rocky Mountains. As day breaks, enjoy a country, gourmet breakfast by the banks of the Yellowstone River, a noted blue-ribbon trout stream. A "cowboy treat tray" is served in the afternoon. Enjoy summer and winter sports. Only entrance open to Yellowstone year-round. Call for reservations. Also, Emigrant Peak Log Cabin is located on twenty-eight acres of Yellowstone River frontage next to the bed and breakfast. Modern, two-bedroom cabin with laundry services and complete kitchen. Decorated in country charm. Extremely private. $150 a night. Member of Montana Bed and Breakfast Association.

Hosts: Pete and Carol Reed
Rooms: 4 (PB) $85-110; cabin $150
Full Breakfast in B&B; Continental in cabin
Credit Cards: A, B
Notes: 2, 5, 8, 9, 10, 11, 12

NOTES: Credit cards accepted: A Master Card; B Visa; C American Express; D Discover; E Diners Club; F Other; 2 Personal checks accepted; 3 Lunch available; 4 Dinner available; 5 Open all year; 6 Pets welcome; 7 Children welcome; 8 Tennis nearby; 9 Swimming nearby; 10 Golf nearby; 11 Skiing nearby; 12 May be booked through travel agent.

EUREKA

Huckleberry Hannah's Bed and Breakfast

3100 Sophie Lake Road, 59917
(888) 889-3381 toll-free
E-mail: huckhana@libby.org
Web site: http://www.libby.org/
    HuckleberryHannah

Nearly six thousand square feet of old-fashioned, country-sweet charm, it is the answer to vacationing in Montana. The B&B sits on fifty wooded acres bordering a trout-filled lake with glorious views of the Rockies. Depicts a quieter time in history when the pleasures of life represented a walk in the woods or moonlight swim. Or maybe a little early morning relaxation in a porch swing, sipping a fresh cup of coffee and watching the sun rise. The surrounding area is mostly public lands—perfect for hiking, biking, hunting, fishing, and swimming. Skier's dream. Comfortable, sunny rooms and home-cooked food. Owned and operated by the author of one of the Northwest's best-selling cookbooks. Ask about kids, pets, senior discounts! Local airport nearby.

Hosts: Jack and Deanna Doying
Rooms: 5 + lake cottage (PB) $55-90
Full Breakfast (Continental on request)
Credit Cards: A, B, D
Notes: 2, 3, 4, 5, 6 (some), 7, 8, 9, 11, 12

FORT BENTON

Long's Landing

1011 17th Street, 59442
(406) 622-3461

Forty minutes north of Great Falls, just off Highway 87, near the Missouri River in the birthplace of Montana. Three charming guest rooms await. Enjoy two museums, a golf course, Old Fort Park, river trips, and other points of interest. Open May 1 to November 1. No smoking.

Hostess: Amy Long
Rooms: 3 (1PB; 2SB) $45
Continental Breakfast
Credit Cards: none
Notes: 2, 7 (over 10), 8, 9, 10

GLENDIVE

The Hostetler House

113 N. Douglas Street, 59330
(406) 365-4505; (800) 965-8456
FAX (406) 365-8456

Two blocks from downtown shopping and restaurants, The Hostetler House is a charming, 1912 historic home with two comfortable guest rooms, sitting room, sunporch, deck, gazebo, and hot tub. Full gourmet breakfast is served on Grandma's china. On I-94 and the Yellowstone River, close to parks, swimming pool, tennis courts, golf course, antique shops, and churches. Craig and Dea invite you to "arrive as a guest and leave as a friend."

Hosts: Craig and Dea Hostetler
Rooms: 2 (SB) $50
Full Gourmet Breakfast
Credit Cards: A, B, D
Notes: 2, 5, 8, 9, 10, 11 (cross-country), 12

KALISPELL

Stillwater Inn

206 4th Avenue E., 59901-4539
(406) 755-7080; (800) 398-7024
E-mail: morison@in-tch.com

Relax in this lovely 1900 home decorated to fit the period, furnished with turn-of-

---

NOTES: Credit cards accepted: A Master Card; B Visa; C American Express; D Discover; E Diners Club; F Other; 2 Personal checks accepted; 3 Lunch available; 4 Dinner available; 5 Open all year; 6 Pets

the-century antiques. Four guest bedrooms, two with private baths. Walking distance to churches, shopping, dining, art galleries, antique shops, Woodland Park, and the Conrad Mansion. Short drive to Glacier National Park, Big Mountain skiing, six golf courses, excellent fishing, and hunting. Please, no smoking in the house.

Hosts: Pat and Jane Morison
Rooms: 4 (2PB; 2SB) $60-85
Full Gourmet Breakfast
Credit Cards: A, B
Notes: 2, 5, 7, 8, 9, 10, 11, 12

LAUREL

Riverside B&B

2231 Thiel Road, 59044
(406) 628-7890; (800) 768-1580
E-mail: RiversideBB@cwz.com

Just off I-90, fifteen minutes from Billings, on a main route to skiing and Yellowstone National Park. Fly-fish the Yellowstone from our backyard; soak away stress in the hot tub; llinger and llook at the llovable llamas; take a spin on our bicycle built for two; enjoy a peaceful sleep, a friendly visit, and a fantastic breakfast.

Hosts: Lynn and Nancy Perey
Rooms: 2 (PB) $65
Full Breakfast
Credit Cards: A, B, C
Notes: 2, 5, 7 (age restriction), 10, 11, 12

RED LODGE

Willows Inn

224 S. Platt Avenue, PO Box 886, 59068
(406) 446-3913

Nestled beneath the majestic Beartooth Mountains in a quaint historic town, this delightful turn-of-the-century Victorian, complete with picket fence and porch swing, awaits you. A light and airy atmosphere with warm, cheerful decor greets the happy wanderer. Five charming guest rooms, each unique, are in the main inn. Two delightfully nostalgic cottages with kitchen and laundry are also available. Home-baked pastries are a specialty. Videos, books, games, afternoon refreshments, and sun deck.

Hosts: Kerry, Carolyn, and Elven Boggio
Rooms: 5 + 2 cottages (3PB; 2SB) $55-80
Continental Plus Breakfast
Credit Cards: A, B, D
Notes: 2, 5, 7 (restricted), 8, 9, 10, 11, 12

TREGO

Tucker's Inn

PO Box 220, 59934
(406) 882-4200; (800) 500-3541;
FAX (406) 882-4201
E-mail: tuckrinn@libby.org
Web site: http://www.tuckersinn.com

A country inn with a guest ranch atmosphere. Executive rooms with two-person Jacuzzi tubs, log cabins that sleep ten with full kitchens, lodge, fabulous food, and friendly country folks. Nestled in the majestic Kootenai Mountains. Open year-round. Wilderness adventures include horseback riding, fly-fishing, white-water rafting, mountain biking, snowmobiling, downhill and cross-country skiing. The perfect getaway!

Hosts: Charles and Jan Tucker
Rooms: 2 + 4 cabins (PB) $120-135
Full Breakfast
Credit Cards: A, B, C, D
Notes: 2, 3, 4, 5, 7, 9, 10, 11, 12

welcome; 7 Children welcome; 8 Tennis nearby; 9 Swimming nearby; 10 Golf nearby; 11 Skiing nearby; 12 May be booked through travel agent.

Stonehouse Inn Bed and Breakfast

VIRGINIA CITY

Stonehouse Inn Bed and Breakfast

Box 205, 306 E. Idaho, 59755
(406) 843-5504; FAX (406) 843-5504
E-mail: roojake@aol.com

Located on a quiet street only blocks away from the historic section of Virginia City, this Victorian stone home is listed on the National Register of Historic Places. Brass beds and antiques in every room give the inn a romantic touch. Five bedrooms share two baths. Full breakfasts are served each morning, and smoking is allowed on our porches. Skiing, snowmobiling, golfing, hunting, and fly-fishing nearby.

Hosts: John and Linda Hamilton
Rooms: 5 (SB) $55
Full Breakfast
Credit Cards: A, B
Notes: 2, 4, 5, 7, 8, 10, 12

WEST GLACIER

Mountain Timbers Bed and Breakfast

PO Box 94, 59936
(406) 387-5830; (800) 841-3835;
FAX (406) 387-5835

Tucked in the heart of northwestern Montana stands Mountain Timbers, a magnificent, hand-hewn hideaway that provides wilderness, wildlife, and spectacular vistas into Glacier National Park. Inside the spacious lodge you'll find massive rock and stone fireplaces, comfortable sitting areas, a fully stocked library, and outstanding views from almost every window. Beyond the calm of our lodge stretch miles of high-country adventures—white-water rafting in the early summer run-off, fishing in clear mountain streams, horseback riding and hiking in Glacier, big-game hunting, or playing golf on one of the Flathead Valley's many championship courses. In the winter, we're renowned for our fifteen kilometers of groomed, private cross-country ski trails, with downhill skiing at the Big Mountain, located only twenty-five miles away.

Hosts: Dave and Betty Rudisill
Rooms: 7 (4PB; 3SB) $55-125
Full Breakfast
Credit Cards: A, B, C
Notes: 2, 5, 7, 9, 10, 11, 12

NOTES: Credit cards accepted: A Master Card; B Visa; C American Express; D Discover; E Diners Club; F Other; 2 Personal checks accepted; 3 Lunch available; 4 Dinner available; 5 Open all year; 6 Pets

Nebraska

BERWYN

1909 Heritage House at Berwyn

PO Box 196, 101 Curran, 68819
(308) 935-1136; (800) 758-8619

A warm welcome awaits you in this lovely three-story Victorian country home with air-conditioned rooms. Heritage House is located in central Nebraska on Highway 2, one of the most scenic highways in America. Enjoy a country breakfast served in an elegant dining room, country kitchen, sunroom, or the Garden Room. Relax in the therapy spa. Visit the country chaple and gift shop in Heritage House Park. Guests share refreshments in the Garden Room after 5 PM.

Hosts: Meriam and Dale Thomas
Rooms: 5 (1PB; 4SB) $60-90
Full Breakfast
Credit Cards: none
Notes: 2, 3, 4, 5, 8, 9, 10

CRETE

The Parson's House

638 Forest Avenue, 68333
(402) 826-2634

Enjoy warm hospitality in a restored four-square home built at the turn of the cen-

The Parson's House

tury, furnished with antiques and a modern whirlpool tub. Located near Doane College's beautiful campus. Breakfast is served in the formal dining room.

Hostess: Sandy Richardson
Rooms: 2 (SB) $45
Full Breakfast
Credit Cards: none
Notes: 2, 5, 8, 9

DANNEBROG

Nestle Inn-Dannebrog

209 E. Roger Welsch Avenue, PO Box 91, 68831
(308) 226-8252

Lovingly restored 1908 bungalow in the Danish capital of Nebraska with oak floors, library, and covered porch with swing for your pleasure. Have your first cup of coffee in the sunny breakfast nook

welcome; 7 Children welcome; 8 Tennis nearby; 9 Swimming nearby; 10 Golf nearby; 11 Skiing nearby; 12 May be booked through travel agent.

NEBRASKA

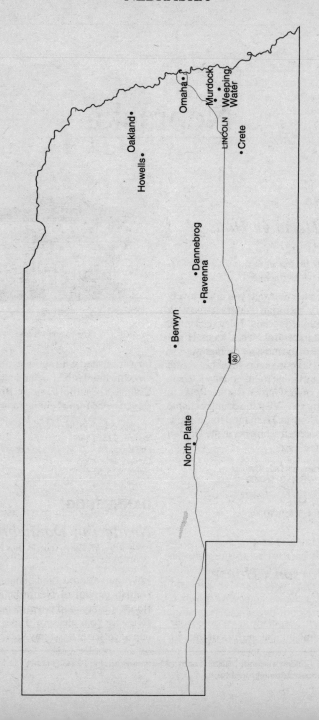

or lovely gazebo before you walk the short block to "Harriett's Danish" for a full breakfast. Nearby hike and bike trail and sand-green golf course. Enjoy the Danish Independence Day Festival in June and Danish Christmas Festival in December. Candlelight dinners by reservation.

Hosts: Gaylord and Judy Mickelsen
Rooms: 3 (SB) $50
Full Breakfast
Credit Cards: none
Notes: 4 (by reservation)

HOWELLS

Beran Bed and Breakfast

1604 Road 16, 68641-3043
(402) 986-1358

Enjoy the peace of the country in our grand, gabled farmhouse, among century-old cottonwoods and rock gardens. The house, built in 1905, has original furnishings. Gift shop features jellies and crafts.

Hosts: Emil and Nadine Beran
Rooms: 3 (SB) $45
Full Breakfast
Credit Cards: none
Notes: 2, 5, 6, 7

MURDOCK

The Farm House

32617 Church Road, 68407
(402) 867-2062

Built in 1896, The Farm House provides a glimpse back to country life of the past. The home is complete with expansive, ten-foot ceilings, wood floors, an oak spindle staircase, antiques, and even a front porch swing. Room decor and furnishings

The Farm House

throughout provide a feeling of comfortable, country elegance with many quilts and Pat Meierhenry's collection of angels. Air-conditioned. Half hour from Lincoln and Omaha.

Hosts: Mike and Pat Meierhenry
Rooms: 3 (1PB; 2SB) $35-45
Full Breakfast
Credit Cards: none
Notes: 2, 5, 6, 7, 8, 9, 10

NORTH PLATTE

Knoll's Country Inn

6132 S. Range Road, 69101
(308) 368-5634; (800) 337-4526
Web site: http://www.bbonline.com/ne/knolls

Knoll's Country Inn is a modern home in the country where it is peaceful and quiet. Take a walk and enjoy a beautiful sunset across the prairie. Relax in a whirlpool bathtub or under the stars in our outdoor spa. After a refreshing night's sleep, you will wake to the aroma of a home-cooked breakfast. Weather permitting, you can

NOTES: Credit cards accepted: A Master Card; B Visa; C American Express; D Discover; E Diners Club; F Other; 2 Personal checks accepted; 3 Lunch available; 4 Dinner available; 5 Open all year; 6 Pets welcome; 7 Children welcome; 8 Tennis nearby; 9 Swimming nearby; 10 Golf nearby; 11 Skiing nearby; 12 May be booked through travel agent.

take breakfast on the deck and enjoy the flower gardens and birds.

Hosts: Arlene and Robert Knoll
Rooms: 5 (1PB; 4SB) $60-75
Full Breakfast
Credit Cards: none
Notes: 2, 5, 7 (inquire first), 8, 9, 10, 11 (water)

OAKLAND

Benson Bed and Breakfast

402 N. Oakland Avenue, 68045
(402) 685-6051

Located in the center of a small town. Benson Bed and Breakfast is beautifully decorated and offers a breakfast you won't soon forget, served in the dining room with all its finery. Features include a large collection of soft-drink collectibles, a library full of books, a beautiful garden room to relax in, and a large whirlpool tub with color TV on the wall. All rooms are on the second level. Craft and gift shops are on the main floor. Three blocks west of Highway 77. No smoking.

Hosts: Stan and Norma Anderson
Rooms: 3 (SB) $50-55
Full, Elegant Breakfast
Credit Cards: none
Notes: 2, 5, 8, 9, 10, 12

OMAHA

The Jones'

1617 S. 90th Street, 68124
(402) 397-0721

Large, private residence with large deck and gazebo in the back. Fresh cinnamon rolls are served for breakfast. Your hosts' interests include golf, travel, needlework,

and meeting other people. Located five minutes from I-80.

Hosts: Don and Theo Jones
Rooms: 3 (1PB; 2SB) $25
Continental Breakfast
Credit Cards: none
Notes: 2, 5, 6, 7, 8

Offutt House

140 N. 39th Street, 68131
(402) 553-0951; FAX (402) 553-0704

This refined 1894 mansion has charmed bed and breakfast travelers for ten years. Enjoy the elegance of an earlier era combined with modern conveniences such as private baths, an Inn Fone telephone system, and fax availability. The house is centrally located in Omaha, ten minutes from downtown, shopping, and the airport.

Hosts: Janet and Paul Koenig
Rooms: 6 (PB) $65-105
Full Breakfast, weekends; Continental, Monday-Thursday
Continental Breakfast Mon.-Thurs.
Credit Cards: A, B, C, D
Notes: 2, 5, 6 (by prior approval), 7, 8, 10, 12

RAVENNA

Aunt Betty's Bed and Breakfast

804 Grand Avenue, 68869
(308) 452-3739; (800) 632-9114

Enjoy the peacefulness of a small, central Nebraska town while staying at Aunt Betty's three-story Victorian bed and breakfast. Four bedrooms furnished in antiques and decorated with attention to detail. Relax in the sitting room while awaiting a delicious, full breakfast includ-

---

NOTES: Credit cards accepted: A Master Card; B Visa; C American Express; D Discover; E Diners Club; F Other; 2 Personal checks accepted; 3 Lunch available; 4 Dinner available; 5 Open all year; 6 Pets

ing Aunt Betty's "Sticky Buns" and home-made goodies. Flower garden area with fishpond for relaxing. Accommodations for hunters in the hunter's loft. Antique shop is part of the bed and breakfast. Golf and tennis nearby. Half hour from I-80.

Hosts: Harvey and Betty Shrader
Rooms: 4 (SB) $45-55
Full Breakfast
Credit Cards: A, B
Notes: 2, 3, 4 (by appointment), 5, 7, 8, 9, 10

WEEPING WATER

Lauritzen's Danish-American Bed and Breakfast

1002 E. Eldora Avenue, 68463
(402) 267-3295

Enjoy quiet times in this late Victorian home decorated with American antiques and Danish keepsakes. Relax in the gazebo in the beautifully landscaped yard,

Lauritzen's Danish-American B&B

or treat yourself to the spa. Breakfast includes Danish and American specialties and gourmet coffee served on antique Danish dishes. While in Weeping Water, enjoy the small-town atmosphere and wonderful museums of early America, or visit Ken's farm, where you can get a feel for the crop and cattle operations or take a wildlife/nature tour. Thirty minutes from Omaha or Lincoln.

Hosts: Ken and Alice Lauritzen
Rooms: 2 (PB)
Full Breakfast
Credit Cards: A, B
Notes: 2, 4, 5, 9, 10, 11, 12

welcome; 7 Children welcome; 8 Tennis nearby; 9 Swimming nearby; 10 Golf nearby; 11 Skiing nearby; 12 May be booked through travel agent.

NEVADA

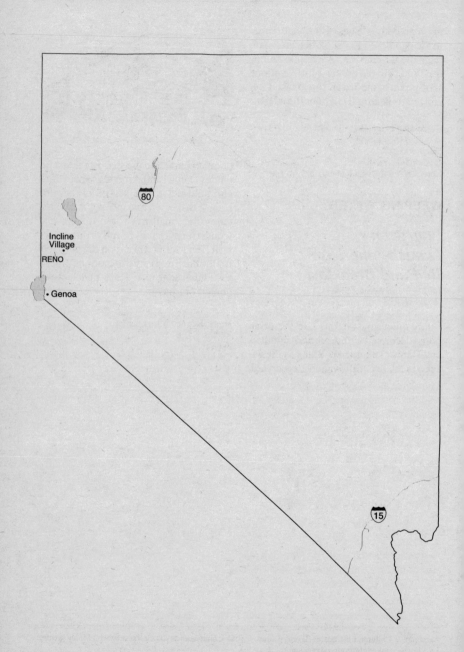

Incline
Village
·
RENO

· Genoa

80

15

Nevada

Mi Casa Su Casa
Bed and Breakfast
Reservation Service

PO Box 950, **Tempe, AZ,** 85280-0950
(602) 990-0682; (800) 456-0682 (reservations);
FAX (602) 990-3390
E-mail: ruthy2425@aol.com

Since 1981, we proudly have listed inspected, clean, comfortable homestays, inns, cottages and ranches in Arizona and the Southwest. We list about two hundred modest to luxurious, historic to contemporary B&Bs. In **Nevada**, we list Henderson and Las Vegas. Most rooms have private baths and range from $50 to $275, double-occupancy. Continental to gourmet breakfasts. A book with individual descriptions and pictures is available for $9.50. Ruth Young, coordinator.

GENOA

The Genoa House Inn

Box 141, 89411
(702) 782-7075

Historic Genoa is known as Nevada's oldest settlement. Snuggled by the Sierra foothills, it is a vision of the Old West, with a panoramic view of the lush Carson Valley and surrounding mountains. The authentic Victorian Inn, listed in the National Register, has been restored to the charm and tranquillity of an earlier time. Gracious accommodations are accented by antiques and collectibles. Refreshments are served when you arrive. Early in the morning, coffee is delivered to your door, followed by a full breakfast in your room or in the sunlit dining room. Local activities include soaring, ballooning, and bicycling. The old town invites you to a casual walk, touring old homes and buildings.

Hosts: Bob and Linda Sanfilippo
Rooms: 3 (PB) $105-130
Full Breakfast
Credit Cards: A, B, D
Notes: 2, 5, 6 and 7 (on approval), 8, 9, 10, 11, 12

The Genoa House Inn

INCLINE VILLAGE

Haus Bavaria

593 N. Dyer Circle, PO Box 9079, 89452
(702) 831-6122; (800) 731-6222;
FAX (702) 831-1238

This European-style residence in the heart of the Sierra Nevadas is within walking distance of Lake Tahoe. Each of the five guest rooms opens onto a balcony, offering lovely views of the mountains. Breakfast, prepared by your host Bick Hewitt, includes a selection of home-baked goodies, fruit, juices, freshly ground coffee, and teas. A private beach and swimming pool are available to guests. Ski at Diamond Peak, Mt. Rose, Heavenly Valley, and other nearby areas.

Host: Bick Hewitt
Rooms: 5 (PB) $155
Full Breakfast
Credit Cards: A, B, C, D
Notes: 2, 5, 8, 9, 10, 11, 12

NOTES: Credit cards accepted: A Master Card; B Visa; C American Express; D Discover; E Diners Club; F Other; 2 Personal checks accepted; 3 Lunch available; 4 Dinner available; 5 Open all year; 6 Pets

New Hampshire

ASHLAND

Glynn House Victorian Inn

43 Highland Street, 03217
(603) 968-3775; (800) 637-9599;
FAX (603) 968-3129

The Glynn House Inn is nestled among the lakes and mountains of New Hampshire. The inn is a fully restored Queen Anne Victorian. The eight rooms all have private baths and some have fireplaces and whirlpool tubs. A full breakfast is served. Easy access from I-93, Exit 24. A quiet, romantic escape where attention to detail is our hallmark.

Hosts: Karol and Betsy Paterman
Rooms: 8 (PB) $75-145
Full Breakfast
Credit Cards: A, B, C, D
Notes: 2, 5, 7 (over 10), 8, 9, 10, 11, 12

BRADFORD

Candlelite Inn Bed and Breakfast

5 Greenhouse Lane, 03221
(603) 938-5571

An 1897 country Victorian inn nestled on three acres in the Lake Sunapee Region.

Candlelite Inn Bed and Breakfast

We serve a full breakfast—down to dessert—in our Sun Room, which overlooks the pond. Relax on the gazebo porch while sipping lemonade on a lazy summer day, or curl up in the living room in front of the corner fireplace. Within minutes of skiing, hiking, antiquing, and restaurants. We are a nonsmoking inn.

Hosts: Les and Marilyn Gordon
Rooms: 6 (PB) $65-85
Full Breakfast
Credit Cards: A, B, C, D
Notes: 2, 5, 8, 9, 10, 11, 12

CAMPTON

Mountain Fare Inn

Mad River Road, PO Box 553, 03223
(603) 726-4283

Located in New Hampshire's White Mountains. A lovely 1840s village home

---

welcome; 7 Children welcome; 8 Tennis nearby; 9 Swimming nearby; 10 Golf nearby; 11 Skiing nearby; 12 May be booked through travel agent.

NEW HAMPSHIRE

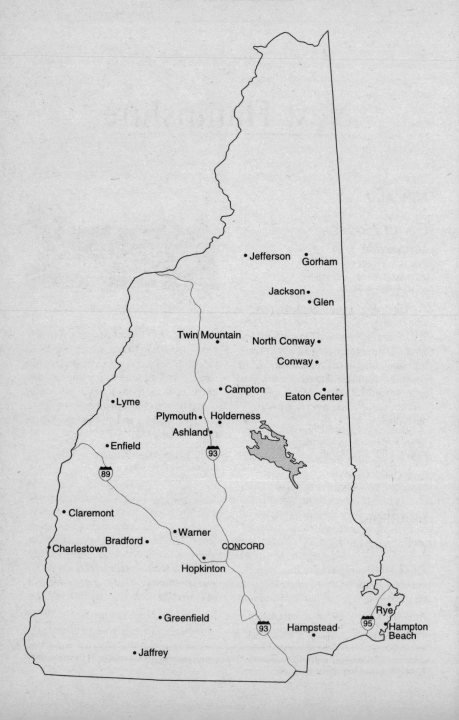

with the antiques, fabrics, and feel of country cottage living. Gardens in summer; foliage in fall; a true skier's lodge in winter. Accessible, peaceful, warm, friendly, affordable. Hearty breakfasts. Unspoiled beauty from Franconia Notch to Squam Lake. Four-season sports, soccer field, music, and theater. Features summer camps, including hiking, biking, and rock climbing, for families, adults, and children. Wonderful family vacationing.

MapleHedge Bed and Breakfast Inn

Hosts: Susan and Nick Preston
Rooms: 10 (8 PB; 2 SB) $65-95
Full Breakfast
Credit Cards: none
Notes: 2, 5, 7, 8, 9, 10, 11, 12

CHARLESTOWN

MapleHedge Bed and Breakfast Inn

355 Main Street, PO Box 638, 03603
(603) 826-5237 (voice and FAX); (800) 9-MAPLE-9
E-mail: debrine@fmis.net

Rather than just touring homes two and a half centuries old, make one your "home away from home" while visiting western New Hampshire or eastern Vermont. MapleHedge offers five distinctly different bedrooms with private baths and antiques chosen to complement the individual decor. It has very tastefully added all modern-day amenities such as central air-conditioning, fire sprinkler system, and queen beds. Enjoy a gourmet breakfast in the grand dining room of this magnificent home that is on the National Register and situated among two-hundred-year-old

maples and lovely gardens. Day trips show local attractions. A brochure will be sent on request. Highly rated by Mobil and ABBA.

Hosts: Joan and Dick DeBrine
Rooms: 5 (PB) $85-100
Full Three-Course Breakfast
Credit Cards: A, B
Notes: 2, 5, 7 (over 12), 8, 9, 10, 11, 12

CLAREMONT

Goddard Mansion Bed and Breakfast

25 Hillstead Road, 03743
(603) 543-0603; (800) 736-0603 (reservations);
FAX (603) 543-0001

Circa 1905, this mansion with adjacent garden tea house is set amid acres of lawns and gardens with panoramic mountain views. This beautifully restored English manor-style, eighteen-room mansion has expansive porches and ten uniquely decorated guest rooms. The living room has a fireplace and window seats for cuddling

---

NOTES: Credit cards accepted: A Master Card; B Visa; C American Express; D Discover; E Diners Club; F Other; 2 Personal checks accepted; 3 Lunch available; 4 Dinner available; 5 Open all year; 6 Pets welcome; 7 Children welcome; 8 Tennis nearby; 9 Swimming nearby; 10 Golf nearby; 11 Skiing nearby; 12 May be booked through travel agent.

up with a good book and enjoying a vintage baby grand piano. A 1939 Wurlitzer jukebox lights up a corner of the walnut-paneled dining room where a full, natural breakfast awaits guests each morning. Four-season activities, historic sites, cultural events, fun, and "fine" dining are nearby. The area is an antique buff's adventureland! Brochere available. Families welcome.

Hostess: Debbie Albee
Rooms: 10 (3PB; 7SB) $65-125
Full Breakfast
Credit Cards: A, B, C, D
Notes: 2, 5, 7, 8, 9, 10, 11

CONWAY

The Darby Field Inn and Restaurant

PO Box D, Bald Hill Road, 03818
(603) 447-2181; (800) 426-4147;
FAX (603) 447-5726
E-mail: marc@darbyfield.com
Web site: http://www.darbyfield.com

A peaceful 1826 bed and breakfast, the Darby Field Inn & Restaurant is in New Hampshire's scenic Mt. Washington Valley. It features prize-winning gardens, terrace swimming pool, cozy pub, massive stone fireplace, fine dining, and spectacular views of the White Mountains. Enjoy biking, hiking, canoeing, fishing, golfing, skiing, snowshoeing, or relaxing in the comfortable living room, curled up with a book. AAA-rated, three diamonds.

Hosts: Marc and Maria Donaldson
Rooms: 16 (14PB; 2SB) $80-160
Full Breakfast
Credit Cards: A, B
Notes: 2, 4, 5 (except April), 7, 9, 10, 11, 12

EATON CENTER (CONWAY)

The Inn at Crystal Lake

Route 153, 03832
(603) 447-2120; (800) 343-7336;
FAX (603) 447-3599
Web site: http://www.nettx.com/innatcrystallake/index.html

Unwind in the comforts of our 1884 Victorian inn, nestled in peaceful Eaton village, just six miles south of Conway. Tastefully decorated guest rooms are furnished with antiques. Begin each day with a full country breakfast in old-fashioned elegance at your own private table. A short drive down a country road will bring you to all the activities of the Mt. Washington Valley. Shopping, dining, and five major ski areas will keep you happily entertained, or just relax here and enjoy our historic village, beautiful Crystal Lake, and the hospitality of your hosts. Experience New England in a country inn.

Hosts: Richard and Janice Octeau
Rooms: 11 (PB) $70-100
Full Breakfast
Credit Cards: A, B, C, D, E
Notes: 2, 5, 7 (over 6), 8, 9, 10, 11, 12

ENFIELD

Boulder Cottage on Crystal Lake

RR 1 Box 257, 03748
(603) 632-7355

A turn-of-the-century Victorian cottage owned by our family for seventy-three years. Our home faces beautiful Crystal Lake, a small, private lake centrally located in the Dartmouth-Sunapee Region. We promise guests an unspoiled environment with classic views of the lake and mountains. Enjoy swimming, canoeing, boating, fishing, hiking, or just relaxing on our comfortable screened porch or sunny decks. Weekly rates can be arranged. Children welcome. Nonsmoking home.

Hosts: Barbara and Harry Reed
Rooms: 4 (2PB; 2SB) $45-65
Full Country Breakfast
Credit Cards: none
Notes: 2, 7, 9, 10, 12

Mary Keane House

Box 5, Lower Shaker Village, 03748
(603) 632-4241; (888) 239-2153

A late Victorian house in a historic Shaker village setting on Lake Mascoma. Light-filled, spacious one- and two-room suites furnished with period antiques, accented with old linens and a touch of whimsy. Large screened porch and balconies with a view of the lake. Swim or boat from our private beach, or hike the trails through Chosen Vale. Relax by the fire with a glass of wine or a mug of hot cider. Great breakfasts! Close to Dartmouth College in Hanover, many fine restaurants, museums, and cultural events. This is a non-smoking home.

Hosts: Sharon and David Carr
Rooms: 7 (PB) $85-125
Full Breakfast
Credit Cards: A, B, C
Notes: 2, 5, 6, 7, 9, 10, 11, 12

GLEN

Covered Bridge House

Route 302, PO Box 989, 03838
(603) 383-9109; (800) 232-9109

Feel at home in our cozy bed and breakfast on the Saco River next to a restored 1850s covered bridge. With just six guest rooms and a cozy living room, our inn offers a comfortable, informal atmosphere. Awaken to a hearty country breakfast. In warm weather, enjoy the beauty of the Saco River in our backyard—swim, tube, fish, or sunbathe on the rocks. Just minutes from Attitash, where in winter you can enjoy some of the best skiing in the East. AAA three diamonds.

Hosts: Dan and Nancy Wanek
Rooms: 6 (4PB; 2SB) $39-79
Full Breakfast
Credit Cards: A, B, C, D
Notes: 2, 5, 7, 9, 10, 11, 12

Libby House Bed and Breakfast

GORHAM

Libby House Bed and Breakfast

55 Main Street, Box 267, 03581
(603) 466-2271; (800) 453-0023;
FAX (603) 466-9494
E-mail: libbyhouse@worldnet.att.net

The Libby House Bed and Breakfast is a turn-of-the-century Victorian home located on the town common in Gorham. We offer three guest rooms, each with a

welcome; 7 Children welcome; 8 Tennis nearby; 9 Swimming nearby; 10 Golf nearby; 11 Skiing nearby; 12 May be booked through travel agent.

private bath, queen-size bed, and mountain view. The Northern White Mountains National Forest is only minutes away, with numerous outdoor activities that are available year-round. Gorham's many wonderful shops and restaurants are within easy walking distance of the Libby House Bed and Breakfast.

Hosts: Paul and Margaret Kuliga
Rooms: 3 (PB) $55-95
Full Breakfast
Credit Cards: A, B, C, D
Notes: 2, 5, 7, 8; 9, 10, 11, 12

GREENFIELD

The Greenfield Bed and Breakfast Inn

Village Center, Junct. Routes 136 and 31 N., 03047
(603) 547-6327; FAX (603) 547-2418
E-mail: innkeeper@thegreenfieldinn.mv.com
Web site: http://www.travelassist.com

Bob Hope and his wife Dolores have visited The Greenfield Bed and Breakfast Inn twice because it is a romance in Victorian splendor. The inn offers a sleep-six hayloft suite with a kitchen, a sleep-six cottage with a kitchen and three bathrooms, plus a sleep-two to -three suite with a kitchen. Breakfast is served each morning with crystal, china, and Mozart. The Inn is situated in a quiet valley surrounded by mountains and big veranda views. It is only ninety minutes from Boston or forty minutes from Manchester airports.

Hosts: Barbara and Vic Mangini
Rooms: 13 (10PB; 3SB) $49-139
Full Breakfast
Credit Cards: A, B
Notes: 2, 5, 7 (restrictions), 8, 9, 10, 11, 12

Stillmeadow Bed and Breakfast at Hampstead

HAMPSTEAD

Stillmeadow Bed and Breakfast at Hampstead

PO Box 565, 545 Main Street, 03841
(603) 329-8381

Historic 1850 home with five chimneys, three staircases, hardwood floors, Oriental rugs, and woodstoves. Set on rolling meadows adjacent to conservation trails. Single, doubles, and suites, all with private baths. Families are welcome, with amenities such as a fenced-in play yard and children's playroom. Easy commute to Manchester and Boston. Complimentary refreshments—and the cookie jar is always full! Formal dining/living rooms.

Hosts: Lori and Randy Offord
Rooms: 4½ (4PB) $60-90
Expanded Continental Breakfast
Credit Cards: A, B, C, D
Notes: 2, 5, 7, 8, 9, 10, 11, 12

HAMPTON BEACH

The Oceanside

365 Ocean Boulevard, 03842
(603) 926-3542; FAX (603) 926-3549
E-mail: oceansid@nh.ultranet.com
Web site: http://www.nh.ultranet.com/oceansid

The Oceanside overlooks the Atlantic Ocean and its beautiful, sandy beaches.

NOTES: Credit cards accepted: A Master Card; B Visa; C American Express; D Discover; E Diners Club; F Other; 2 Personal checks accepted; 3 Lunch available; 4 Dinner available; 5 Open all year; 6 Pets

The interior has been completely renovated and is immaculately maintained. All common areas as well as the guest bedrooms reflect the owners' special attention to detail. Each of the ten rooms is tastefully and individually decorated; many have period antiques, and all have private modern baths. You will find lofty ceilings, Oriental carpets, braided rugs, hand-screened wallpapers, and an eclectic mix of fine furnishings, paintings and prints add to the intimacy and ambience.

Hosts: Skip and Debbie Windemiller
Rooms: 10 (PB) $95-140
Continental Breakfast
Credit Cards: A, B, C, D
Notes: 9, 10

HOLDERNESS

The Inn on Golden Pond

PO Box 680, Route 3, 03245-0680
(603) 968-7269; FAX (603) 968-9226
E-mail: innongpelr.net

This 1879 colonial home is nestled on fifty wooded acres, offering guests a traditional New England setting where they can escape and enjoy the warm hospitality and personal service of the resident hosts. The guest rooms are individually decorated with braided rugs and country curtains and bedspreads. A hearty, home-cooked breakfast every morning features farm-fresh eggs, muffins, homemade bread, and hostess Bonnie Webb's most requested rhubarb jam.

Hosts: Bill and Bonnie Webb
Rooms: 8 (PB) $105-140
Full Breakfast
Credit Cards: A, B, C
Notes: 2, 5, 8, 9, 10, 11, 12

HOPKINTON

The Country Porch Bed and Breakfast

281 Moran Road, 03229
(603) 746-6391

Situated on fifteen peaceful acres of lawn, pasture, and forest, this B&B is a reproduction of an 18th-century colonial. Sit on the wraparound porch and gaze out over the meadow, bask in the sun, and then cool off in the pool. The comfortably appointed rooms have a Colonial, Amish, or Shaker theme and have king or twin beds. Summer and winter activities are plentiful and fine country dining is a short drive away. "Come and sit a spell." No smoking permitted.

Hosts: Tom and Wendy Solomon
Rooms: 3 (PB) $75-80
Full Breakfast
Credit Cards: A, B
Notes: 2, 5, 9, 10, 11

JACKSON

Ellis River House

Route 16, Box 656, 03846
(603) 383-9339; (800) 233-8309;
FAX (603) 383-4142
E-mail: innkeeper@erhinn.com
Web site: http://www.erhinn.com

Sample true New England hospitality at this enchanting, small hotel/country inn within a short stroll of the village. The House has eighteen comfortable king- and queen-size guest rooms decorated with Laura Ashley prints, some with fireplaces and two-person Jacuzzis, cable television, scenic balconies, and period antiques, all with

---

welcome; 7 Children welcome; 8 Tennis nearby; 9 Swimming nearby; 10 Golf nearby; 11 Skiing nearby; 12 May be booked through travel agent.

individually controlled heat and AC. Two-room and family suites, riverfront cottage, hot tub, sauna, and heated pool, sitting and game rooms, delightful sundeck overlooking the pristine Ellis River. Enjoy a full country breakfast each morning with homemade breads, or a delicious trout dinner. Afterward, relax with libations and billiards in the pub.

Hosts: Barry and Barbara Lubao
Rooms: 18 (PB) $79-229
Full Country Breakfast
Credit Cards: A, B, C, D, E
Notes: 2, 4, 5, 6 and 7 (limited), 8, 9, 10, 11, 12

JAFFREY

Benjamin Prescott Inn

433 Turnpike Road (Route 124), 03452
(603) 532-6637

The Benjamin Prescott Inn stands shaded by maple trees and surrounded by a working dairy farm. Inside, careful attention has been taken to see that the early American atmosphere has been preserved through the use of color and design. All guest rooms in the Inn have private baths,

complete with classic toiletries the discerning traveler has come to expect. After a hearty New England breakfast, you'll want to explore the "Currier & Ives corner" of New Hampshire.

Hosts: Jan and Barry Miller
Rooms: 9 (PB) $65-130
Full Breakfast
Credit Cards: A, B, C
Notes: 2, 5, 7 (over 10), 9, 10, 11, 12

JEFFERSON

Applebrook Bed and Breakfast

Route 115A, 03583-0178
(603) 586-7713; (800) 545-6504
E-mail: applebrk@aol.com
Web site: http://members.aol.com/applebrk

Taste our midsummer raspberries while enjoying spectacular mountain views. Applebrook is a comfortable, casual bed and breakfast in a large Victorian farmhouse with a peaceful, rural setting. After a restful night's sleep, you will enjoy a hearty breakfast before venturing out for

Applebrook Bed and Breakfast

NOTES: Credit cards accepted: A Master Card; B Visa; C American Express; D Discover; E Diners Club; F Other; 2 Personal checks accepted; 3 Lunch available; 4 Dinner available; 5 Open all year; 6 Pets

a day of hiking, fishing, antique hunting, golfing, swimming, or skiing. Near Santa's Village and Six-Gun City. Dormitory available for groups. Brochures available. Hot tub under the stars.

Hosts: Sandra Conley and Martin Kelly
Rooms: 14 + dormitory (7PB; 7SB) $50-75
Full Breakfast
Credit Cards: A, B
Notes: 2, 6, 7, 8, 9, 10, 11, 12

LYME

Alden Country Inn

Box 60, On the Common, 03768
(603) 795-2222; (800) 794-2296;
FAX (603) 795-9436

The Alden Country Inn offers its services New England-style in a classic country ambience. Our accommodations reflect the history of the inn and village. Our Tavern and Grille emphasize New England foods that are creative in recipe and presentation and healthy in portion. In total, the Alden Country Inn is a home-away-from-home. It is one you will want to experience again and again.

Host: Mickey Dowd
Rooms: 15 (PB) $105-160
Full Breakfast
Credit Cards: A, B, C, D, E, F
Notes: 2, 3, 4, 5, 7, 8, 9, 10, 11, 12

NEW IPSWICH

The Inn at New Ipswich

11 Porter Hill Road, PO Box 208, 03071
(603) 878-3711

Relax a while in a graceful 1790 colonial amid stone walls and fruit trees. With cozy fireplaces, front porch rockers, and large guest rooms furnished country-style, you'll feel right at home. Breakfasts are bountiful! Situated in New Hampshire's Monadnock Region, where activities abound: hiking, band concerts, antique auctions, maple sugaring, apple picking, unsurpassed autumn color, and cross-country and downhill skiing. No smoking. Children over eight welcome.

Hosts: Steve and Ginny Bankuti
Rooms: 6 (PB) $75
Full Breakfast
Credit Cards: A, B
Notes: 2, 5, 7 (over 8), 10, 11

The 1785 Inn

NORTH CONWAY

The 1785 Inn

3582 White Mountain Highway, PO Box 1785, 03860-1785
(603) 356-9025; (800) 421-1785;
FAX (603) 356-6081
E-mail: the1785inn@aol.com

A relaxing place to vacation any time of year. The Inn is famous for its views and food. Located at the Scenic Vista, popularized by the White Mountain School of Art, its famous scene of Mt. Washington is virtually unchanged from when the inn

welcome; 7 Children welcome; 8 Tennis nearby; 9 Swimming nearby; 10 Golf nearby; 11 Skiing nearby; 12 May be booked through travel agent.

was built more than two centuries ago. The homey atmosphere will make you feel right at home, and the food and service will make you eagerly await your return.

Hosts: Becky and Charlie Mallar
Rooms: 17 (12PB; 5SB) $59-169
Full Breakfast
Credit Cards: A, B, C, D, E
Notes: 2, 4, 5, 7, 8, 9, 10, 11, 12

Buttonwood Inn on Mt. Surprise

PO Box 1817, Mt. Surprise Road, 03860
(603) 356-2625; (800) 258-2625 (U.S.);
FAX (603) 356-3140
E-mail: button_w@moose.ncia.net
Web site: http://www.buttonwoodinn.com

Visit our secluded 1820s Cape on Mt. Surprise, two miles from North Conway village. Nine guest rooms allow us time to pamper you with personal service; one room has a gas fireplace. Stroll five acres of lawns and award-winning gardens. Swim in our pool, surrounded by on old granite barn foundation. Rock on the porch or sit in an Adirondack chair and see if you can spy a hummingbird. Hike or cross-country ski from our door. Our breakfasts are second to none.

Hosts: Peter and Claudia Needham
Rooms: 9 (5PB; 4SB) $70-150
Full Breakfast
Credit Cards: A, B, C, D
Notes: 2, 5, 7, 8, 9, 10, 11, 12

The Victorian Harvest Inn

28 Locust Lane (just off White Mountain
    Highway), 03860
(603) 356-3548; (800) 642-0749;
FAX (603) 356-8430

Nonsmokers, delight in your comfortable, elegant B&B home at the edge of quaint

North Conway village. Explore shoppes, outlets, and the AMC trails. Our 1850s multigabled Victorian has six large, comfy rooms with mountain views. Start your romantic adventure with a bounteous breakfast. Relax by the fire or snuggle with a literary treasure in our elegant library. Private baths, in-ground pool, and full AC. AAA three-diamond award. American Bed and Breakfast Association-rated "A," three crowns. Cross-country skiing from the door; downhill skiing nearby. We welcome all God's people.

Hosts: Linda and Robert Dahlberg
Rooms: 6 (4PB; 2SB in 4-person suite) $70-115
    (higher rates in foliage season)
Full Breakfast
Credit Cards: A, B, C, D
Notes: 2, 5, 7 (over 6), 8, 9, 10, 11, 12

Colonel Spencer Inn

PLYMOUTH

Colonel Spencer Inn

RR #1, Box 206, 03264
(603) 536-3438

A 1764 center-chimney colonial with antique furnishings, wide pine floorboards, hand-hewn beams, and Indian shutters. Seven antique-appointed bedrooms with private baths welcome guests. A full country breakfast is served in a fireplaced dining room. The inn is convenient to both lake and mountain attractions, at Exit 27 off I-93, one-half mile south on Route 3.

Hosts: Carolyn and Alan Hill
Rooms: 7 (PB) $45-65
Full Breakfast
Credit Cards: none
Notes: 2, 5, 7, 8, 9, 10, 11, 12

RYE

Rock Ledge Manor

1413 Ocean Boulevard, 03870
(603) 431-1413

Rock Ledge Manor was built between 1840 and 1880. The home overlooks the Atlantic at Concort Point. Owners Stan and Sandi Smith welcome you to their oceanfront bed and breakfast, where breakfast is a major event. The meal is served in a breakfast room with a view of the sea.

Hosts: Stanley and Sandi Smith
Rooms: 4 (PB; 2 share a shower) $70-90
Full Breakfast
Credit Cards: none
Notes: 2, 5, 7 (12 and older), 8, 9, 10, 11

TWIN MOUNTAIN

Northern Zermatt Inn and Motel

PO Box 83, Route 3 N., 03595
(603) 846-5533; (800) 535-3214;
FAX (603) 846-5664

Clean and charming guest rooms have private baths in this country inn, some with kitchenettes (fully equipped). CTV is available in the motel and cottages. The inn is near Mt. Washington, hiking and biking trails, fishing, skiing, golf, and tennis. Guests may enjoy the outdoor pool, picnic area, and ground playings. Relax in front of the fireplace, or play a game of cards in the living room. Children stay free. Welcome seniors!

Hosts: Thomas and Kandy Lee
Rooms: 17 (PB) $40-79
Continental Breakfast
Credit Cards: A, B, D
Notes: 2, 5, 7, 8, 9, 10, 11

WARNER

Jacob's Ladder Bed and Breakfast

69 E. Main Street, 03278
(603) 456-3494

Situated in the quaint village of Warner, Jacob's Ladder Bed and Breakfast is conveniently located between exits 8 and 9 off I-89. The early-1800s home is furnished predominantly with antiques, creating a tasteful country atmosphere. Cross-country ski and snowmobile trail are on site, with three downhill ski areas located within twenty miles. Lakes, mountains, covered bridges, arts and crafts, and other attractions are found nearby. Jacob's Ladder is a nonsmoking bed and breakfast.

Hosts: Deb and Marlon Baese
Rooms: 3 (1PB; 2SB) $50-60
Full Breakfast
Credit Cards: D
Notes: 2, 5, 7, 8, 9, 10, 11

---

welcome; 7 Children welcome; 8 Tennis nearby; 9 Swimming nearby; 10 Golf nearby; 11 Skiing nearby; 12 May be booked through travel agent.

NEW JERSEY

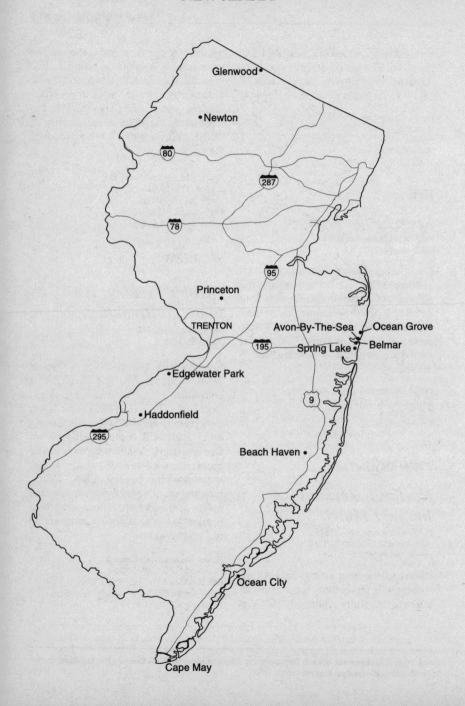

New Jersey

AVON-BY-THE-SEA

Cashelmara Inn

22 Lakeside Avenue, 07717
(732) 776-8727; (800) 821-2976;
FAX (732) 988-5819
E-mail: cashelmara@mo
Web site: http://www.belmar.com/cashelmara

And the views? Say "good morning" to
the Atlantic Ocean from almost every room
at the Cashelmara Inn. Come visit a landmark seaside mansion that has been tastefully restored as an Inn for all seasons. It
offers perhaps the finest unobstructed view
of the water you will find . . . anywhere!
Among the numerous fine accommodations are admission to the inn's Grand Victorian Movie Theater, antique furnishings,
private baths/Jacuzzis, full country breakfasts each morning, queen- or king-size
beds, gas log fireplaces, beach badges and
towels, cable television, air-conditioning,
free parking, and minirefrigerators for our
guests to use.

Host: Mary Wiernasz
Rooms: 14 (PB) $75-250
Full Breakfast
Credit Cards: A, B, D
Notes: 2, 5, 7, 8, 9, 10

BEACH HAVEN

Green Gables Inn and Restaurant

212 Centre Street, 08008
(609) 492-3553; FAX (609) 492-2507

Wake to the sound of seagulls and waves.
Start the day with an old-fashioned, home-
baked buffet breakfast (included in the
room price). Spend a lovely morning on
the beach, play tennis, have a gracious
lunch or tea, or explore the island's wildlife sanctuaries. Walk to shops, theaters,
concerts, the LBI Museum, galleries. Sunrises on the beach, sunsets on the bay.

Hosts: Rita and Adolfo de Martino
Rooms: 6 (2PB; 2SB) $95-135
Continental Breakfast
Credit Cards: A, B, C, D
Notes: 2, 3, 4, 5, 8, 9, 10

BELMAR

The Inn at the Shore

301 4th Avenue, 07719
(732) 681-3762; FAX (732) 280-1914
Web site: www.bbianj.com/innattheshore

The inn is located within sight of the Atlantic Ocean and Belmar's wide, beautiful

---

NOTES: Credit cards accepted: A Master Card; B Visa; C American Express; D Discover; E Diners
Club; F Other; 2 Personal checks accepted; 3 Lunch available; 4 Dinner available; 5 Open all year; 6 Pets
welcome; 7 Children welcome; 8 Tennis nearby; 9 Swimming nearby; 10 Golf nearby; 11 Skiing nearby;
12 May be booked through travel agent.

The Inn at the Shore

beaches and boardwalk, and just steps away from serene Silver Lake, home to the first flock of swans bred in America. Guests will enjoy the casual, Victorian-style ambience on our expansive wrap-around porch, where relaxing in a rocking chair takes you back to the seashore of days gone by. Visitors make themselves comfortable in our spacious common areas, including the cafe-style brick patio ready for barbecues or refreshing beverages after a day of reflection, our large living room with its lovely stone fireplace and state-of-the-art entertainment center, and the grand dining room and library, which are perfect for quiet moments of reading, writing, or just unwinding by our tranquil aquarium. We serve a bountiful, extended continental breakfast consisting of home-baked muffins, croissants, fresh fruits, cereals, juices, etc. Bikes, beach badges, air-conditioning available. The guest pantry has a refrigerator, microwave, dishes, etc. Available for family reunions, retreats and weddings. Sixty miles from Atlantic City, New York City, and Philadelphia; twenty miles from Six Flags Great Adventure Theme Park. Fifty percent off on the third night in our low season. We are child-friendly.

Hosts: Tom and Rosemary Volker
Rooms: 12 (3PB; 9SB) $55-125
Extended Continental Breakfast
Credit Cards: A, B, C
Notes: 2, 5, 7, 8, 9, 10, 11, 12

BEVERLY (EDGEWATER PARK)

Historic Whitebriar Bed and Breakfast

1029 Cooper Street, 08010
(609) 871-3859
Web site: http://www.virtualcities.com/ons/nj/w/
njw3501.htm

Historic Whitebriar is a German saltbox-style home that has been added on to many times since it was the home of John Fitch, Steam Ship Inventory 1787. The latest addition is an English Conservatory, built in Beverly, England, from a two-hundred-year-old design and shipped to Beverly just a few years ago. Breakfast is served in the Conservatory, overlooking the seasonal pool and spa. Whitebriar is a living history farm with animals to be tended, and guests are welcome to collect the eggs, brush the ponies, and pick the raspberries. Located thirty minutes from historic Philadelphia, three hours from Washington, and one and a half hours from the Big Apple, just off interstates.

Hostess: Carole Moore
Rooms: 2 + apartments (SB) $50-85
Full Breakfast
Credit Cards: none
Notes: 2, 5, 6, 7 (additional charge), 9

CAPE MAY

The Albert Stevens Inn

127 Myrtle Avenue, 08204
(609) 884-4717; (800) 890-CATS;
FAX (609) 884-8320
Web site: http://www.beachcomber.com

Built in 1898 by Dr. Albert G. Stevens as a wedding gift for his bride Bessie, the inn is just a ten-minute walk to the beach and two blocks from Victorian shopping. The guest rooms are furnished with antiques and have private baths and AC. A 102-degree, six-person Jacuzzi is scheduled privately for guests' comfort. Home of the original Cat's Garden Tea and Tour, the Albert Stevens Inn is known for its comfort, privacy, and gourmet breakfasts. Resident pet cats.

Hosts: Curt and Diane Diviney-Rangen
Rooms: 9 (PB) $90-165
Full Breakfast
Credit Cards: A, B, C, D
Notes: 2, 5, 7, 8, 9, 10, 12

Angel of the Sea

5-7 Trenton Avenue, 08204
(609) 884-3369; (800) 848-3369;
FAX (609) 884-3331
Web site: http://www.angelofthesea.com

Angel of the Sea Bed and Breakfast is a romantic Victorian mansion with ocean views, twenty-seven rooms with private baths, gourmet breakfasts, afternoon tea, wine and cheese, bikes. Rated as one of the top two bed and breakfasts in North America. A stay at the Angel will be an unforgettable experience filled with good friends, good food, and cherished memories that will last a lifetime.

Hosts: Gregg and Lorie Whissell
Rooms: 27 (PB) $95-285
Full Breakfast
Credit Cards: A, B
Notes: 2, 5, 8, 9, 10

Bedford Inn

805 Stockton Avenue, 08204
(609) 884-4158; FAX (609) 884-0533
Web site: http://www.beachcomber.com/capemay/
      Bbs/bedford.html

A fully restored Victorian bed and breakfast—romantic and elegant. All rooms and "honeymoon" suites are furnished with authentic antiques and have private baths, TVs, and air-conditioning; many with queen beds. Parlor with fireplace and two porches. Rates include gourmet breakfast and afternoon tea and treats, beach passes, beach chairs, and on site parking.

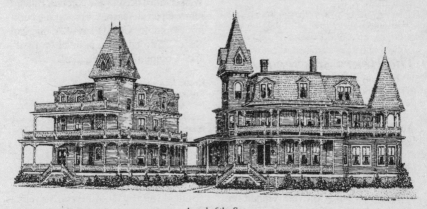

Angel of the Sea

Great location—very close to beach and town center.

Hosts: Alan and Cindy Schmucker
Rooms: 11 (PB) $90-195
Full Breakfast
Credit Cards: A, B, C
Notes: 8, 9, 10

Captain Mey's Inn

202 Ocean Street, 08204
(609) 884-7793

The inn is an 1890 Colonial Revival Victorian named after the Dutch explorer, Capt. Cornelius Mey. The Dutch heritage is evident from the Persian rugs on the tabletops to the Delft Blue china collection. The wraparound veranda is furnished with wicker furniture, hanging ferns, and Victorian wind curtains. A full breakfast is served by candlelight with classical music in the formal dining room; in the summer, breakfast is served on the veranda.

Hosts: George and Kathleen Blinn
Rooms: 7 (PB) $75-210
Full Breakfast
Credit Cards: A, B, C
Notes: 2, 7 (over 8), 8, 9, 10, 12 (off-season and midweek)

The Henry Sawyer Inn

722 Columbia Avenue, 08204-2332
(609) 884-5667; (800) 449-5667
Web site: http://www.beachcomber.com

An elegant 1877 Victorian bed and breakfast inn. All our spacious and airy rooms and suites have private baths, refrigerators, air-conditioners, TVs, and hair dryers. Some accommodations have other amenities, including a private veranda, fireplaces, whirlpool tub, and VCRs. All accommodations include a full breakfast and afternoon refreshments; the use of beach tags, towels, and chairs; private hot and cold beach showers; and off-street parking. A short walk to the Washington Street Mall, Washington Square stores, major antique shops, tennis courts, ocean promenade and beach, and fine restaurants.

Hostesses: Mary and Barbara Morris
Rooms: 5 (PB) $110-165
Full Breakfast
Credit Cards: D
Notes: 2, 5, 7 (10 and older), 8, 9, 10, 12

The Inn on Ocean

25 Ocean Street, 08204
(609) 884-7070; (800) 304-4477;
FAX (609) 884-1384
Web site: http://www.capenet.com/capemay/
   innocean

An intimate, elegant Victorian inn. Fanciful Second Empire style with an exuberant personality. Beautifully restored. King and queen beds. Private baths. Fireplaces. Fully air-conditioned. Full breakfasts. Wicker-filled ocean view porches. Billiard room. Open all seasons. Free on site parking available. Guests say: "A magical place!" "Second visit is as lovely as first!" and "Compliments to the chef!"

Hosts: Jack and Katha Davis
Rooms: 5 (PB) $99-195 (by season)
Full Breakfast
Credit Cards: A, B, C, D, E
Notes: 2, 5, 8, 9, 10, 12

John Wesley Inn

30 Gurney Street, 08204
(609) 884-1012

This is a Carpenter Gothic 1869 Victorian inn, exquisitely and romantically restored. Lace curtains and American antiques decorate each room. Guests are refreshed by the breeze-filled verandas and air-conditioned rooms and apartments. Centrally located in Cape May's primary historic district. The inn is located only a half block from the beach, with on site parking.

Hosts: John and Rita Tice
Rooms: 8 (6PB; 2SB) $95-165
Continental Breakfast
Credit Cards: none
Notes: 2, 5, 7, 8, 9, 10

The Kings Cottage

The Kings Cottage

9 Perry Street, 08204
(609) 884-0415

This three-story "Stick Style" Victorian Cottage is an exquisite example of the work done by noted architect Frank Furness. Taking full advantage of its location, the guest rooms, all with private baths, and the two wicker-filled verandas optimize the ocean views. The interior has been lovingly restored and furnished in true Victorian fashion to reflect the grandeur of that period. Antiques abound, especially in the parlor and formal dining room where a full

breakfast is served, utilizing fine china, crystal, and silver—all the trappings that make life that much more enjoyable. You may enjoy afternoon tea on the veranda or in the formal garden.

Hosts: Patricia and Tony Marino
Rooms: 9 (PB) $95-250
Full Breakfast
Credit Cards: A, B
Notes: 2 (deposit only), 5, 8, 9, 10, 12

The Mason Cottage

625 Columbia Avenue, 08204
(609) 884-3358; (800) 716-2766

Built in 1871 for a wealthy Philadelphia businessman, the inn is in the French Empire style. The Mason family purchased the house in 1945 and started welcoming guests in 1946. The curved, wood-shingle mansard roof was built by local shipyard carpenters. Restored original furniture remains in the house. The house endured the 1878 Cape May fire and several hurricanes. Honeymoon packages and gift certificates available. The inn is one block from the ocean. All rooms and suites are air-conditioned.

Hosts: Dave and Joan Mason
Rooms: 9 (PB) $95-265
Full Breakfast
Credit Cards: A, B, C
Notes: 2, 7 (over 12), 8, 9, 10, 12

The Mooring

801 Stockton Avenue, 08204
(609) 884-5425; FAX (609) 884-1357

Built in 1882, the Mooring is one of Cape May's original guest houses. Enjoy the comfortable elegance of this classic Second Empire inn, with its grand entrance

welcome; 7 Children welcome; 8 Tennis nearby; 9 Swimming nearby; 10 Golf nearby; 11 Skiing nearby; 12 May be booked through travel agent.

The Mooring

the spacious guest rooms—each of which has period furnishings, private bath, and ceiling fan; most have air-conditioning. A full breakfast and afternoon tea are served in the dining room at tables for two. The Mooring is a block from the beach, within easy walking distance of shops and restaurants. Free on site parking; low week-day rates off-season.

Hostess: Leslie Valenza
Rooms: 12 (PB) $75-165
Full Breakfast
Credit Cards: A, B
Notes: 2, 7 (over 5), 8, 9, 10, 12

The Queen Victoria®

102 Ocean Street, 08204
(609) 884-8702
E-mail: qvinn@aol.com
Web site: http://www.queen_victoria.com

The Queen Victoria includes three 19th-century homes that have been restored and furnished with antiques. There are two parlors, one with a fireplace and one with TV and games. Two dining rooms serve a hearty, country breakfast and afternoon tea. Special services include free bicycles, beach showers and towels, and turned-down beds with a special chocolate on your pillow. All rooms are air-conditioned

and have private baths, many with whirl-pool tubs.

Hosts: Joan and Dane Wells
Rooms: 23 (PB) $90-275
Full Breakfast
Credit Cards: A, B
Notes: 2, 5, 7, 8, 9, 10, 12

Sea Holly Bed and Breakfast

Sea Holly Bed and Breakfast

815 Stockton Avenue, 08204
(609) 884-6294; FAX (609) 884-5157

Located in the Victorian area of historic Cape May, the Sea Holly Inn is an elegant, three-story Gothic cottage with Italianate detailing. Rooms are furnished with authentic Renaissance Revival and Eastlake antiques. All rooms have private baths; some have ocean views. Guest rooms are airy and comfortable, each having AC for summer and central heating for a cozy winter stay. The Sea Holly is one block from the ocean, within walking distance of the Victorian Mall and restaurants.

Hostess: Christy Lacey-Igoe
Rooms: 8 (PB) $50-180
Full Breakfast
Credit Cards: A, B, C
Notes: 2 (deposit only), 5, 8, 9, 10, 12

NOTES: Credit cards accepted: A Master Card; B Visa; C American Express; D Discover; E Diners Club; F Other; 2 Personal checks accepted; 3 Lunch available; 4 Dinner available; 5 Open all year; 6 Pets

Windward House

24 Jackson Street, 08204
(609) 884-3368

An elegant Edwardian, seaside inn has an
entryway and staircase that are perhaps
the prettiest in town. Spacious, antique-
filled guest rooms have king and queen
beds, AC, and TVs. With three sun and
shade porches, cozy parlor fireplace, and
Christmas finery, the inn is located in the
historic district, a half block from the beach
and shopping mall. Rates include homemade breakfast, afternoon refreshments,
beach passes, and parking. Midweek discounts; off-season weekend packages.

Hosts: Sandy and Owen Miller
Rooms: 8 (PB) $85-179
Full Breakfast
Credit Cards: A, B
Notes: 2, 5, 7 (over 8), 8, 9, 10, 12

The Wooden Rabbit B&B

609 Hughes Street, 08204
(609) 884-7293; FAX (609) 898-0842
E-mail: wrabbit@bellatlantic.net

Charming country inn in the heart of Cape
May, surrounded by Victorian cottages.
Cool, shady street, the prettiest in Cape
May. Two blocks to beaches, one block
to shops and fine restaurants. Guest
rooms have AC, private baths and TVs,
and comfortably sleep two to four. Country decor with a relaxed family atmosphere. Delicious breakfasts, afternoon
tea. Three pet cats to fill your laps. Open
year-round. Families welcome.

Hostess: Debby Burow
Rooms: 4 (PB) $85-200
Full Breakfast
Credit Cards: A, B, D
Notes: 2, 5, 7, 8, 9, 10, 12

GLENWOOD

Apple Valley Inn

PO Box 302 (927 Route 517), 07418
(201) 764-3735; FAX (201) 764-1050

Elegant B&B in the Early American tradition. An 1831 colonial mansion. Pool,
trout stream, apple orchard, antique shop,
Old Grist Mill, skiing, water park, Appalachian Trail, West Point, Botanical Gardens, two state parks, and Hudson Valley
attractions within a short drive. Holidays.
Two-night minimum. Reduced rates for
six-plus-days. Special events weekends.

Hostess: Mitzi and John Durham
Rooms: 7 (2PB; 5SB) $70-90
Full Breakfast
Credit Cards: none
Notes: 2, 3 (picnic), 5, 7 (over 13), 8, 9 (on site), 10,
11, 12

HADDONFIELD

Queen Anne Inn

44 West End Avenue, 08033
(609) 428-2195; (800) 269-0014;
FAX (609) 354-1273
E-mail: QAInn@aol.com

This Victorian jewel in historic Haddonfield
is proud of its theatrical productions, symphony orchestra, museums, art center,
idyllic parks, dinosaur discovery, unique
shops, and restaurants. Take a carriage
ride or walking tour of period homes and
churches. Short train ride to Philadelphia.
Elegant surroundings with small hotel
amenities. "Hospitality, history, and home."

Hosts: Fred Chorpita and Nancy Lynn
Rooms: 8 (3PB; 5SB) $99-109
Full Gourmet Breakfast
Credit Cards: A, B, C, D
Notes: 2, 5, 8, 9, 10, 12

---

welcome; 7 Children welcome; 8 Tennis nearby; 9 Swimming nearby; 10 Golf nearby; 11 Skiing nearby;
12 May be booked through travel agent.

NEWTON

The Wooden Duck

140 Goodale Road, 07860
(201) 300-0395; FAX (201) 300-0141

The Wooden Duck is a secluded, seventeen-acre mini-estate about an hour's drive from New York City. Located on a country road in rural Sussex County, it is close to antiques, golf, the Delaware Water Gap, Waterloo Village, and winter sports. The rooms are spacious with private bath, TV, VCR, phone, and desk. Features include central air-conditioning, an in-ground pool, game room, and living room with see-through fireplaces. The home features antique furnishings and reproductions. Biking and hiking are at the doorstep with a thousand-acre state park across the street and a "Rails to Trails" (abandoned railway maintained for hiking and biking) running behind the property. Wildlife abounds in the area.

Hosts: Bob and Barbara Hadden
Rooms: 5 (PB) $100-120
Full Breakfast
Credit Cards: A, B, C, D
Notes: 2, 5, 8, 9, 10, 11

OCEAN CITY

Delancey Manor

869 Delancey Place, 08226
(609) 398-6147

Delancy Manor is a turn-of-the-century summer house just one hundred yards from a great beach and our 2.45-mile boardwalk. Summer fun is available for families and friends at "America's great-

est family resort." We have two breezy porches with ocean views. Guests can walk to restaurants, boardwalk fun, and the Tabernacle with its renowned speakers. The inn is located in a residential neighborhood in a dry town. Larger family rooms are available. Advance reservations are recommended.

Hosts: Stewart and Pam Heisler
Rooms: 4 (PB) $65-85
Morning Coffee (no breakfast)
Credit Cards: none
Notes: 2, 7, 8, 9, 10

Delancey Manor

Scarborough Inn

720 Ocean Avenue, 08226
(609) 399-1558; (800) 258-1558;
FAX (609) 399-4472
E-mail: cgbruno@earthlink.net
Web site: http://www.scarboroinn.com

The Scarborough Inn, invitingly adorned in colors of wedgewood, rose, and soft cream, lends its special character to the neighborhood where it stands, just one-and-a-half short blocks from the Atlantic Ocean. The Scarborough Inn affords visitors a vacation residence reminiscent of an old-fashioned European-style inn—small enough to be intimate, yet large enough to offer privacy. Featured in *Country Inns* magazine.

Hosts: Gus and Carol Bruno
Rooms: 23 (PB) $75-160
Continental Breakfast
Credit Cards: A, B, C, D
Notes: 7, 8, 9, 10, 12

OCEAN GROVE

Cordova

26 Webb Avenue, 07756
(973) 774-3084

Ocean Grove was founded as a religious retreat center at the turn of the century. This flavor has lasted in the quiet, peaceful atmosphere. Constant religious family programs, as well as popular music, are arranged in the Great Auditorium. The Cordova has "Old World" charm. Rooms are furnished with antiques. Friendliness, hospitality, cleanliness, and quiet, one block from the magnificent white-sand beach and boardwalk. The Cordova has been featured in *Ol' New Jersey* and listed in *New Jersey* magazine as one of the "seven best on the Jersey shore." Porches have an ocean view. Call about murder mystery and Tai Chi weekends. Midweek specials; also, seven nights for the price of five. Saturday night refreshments.

Hostess: Doris Chernik
Rooms: 18 + 2 cottages (5PB; 15SB) $45-95
Continental Breakfast
Credit Cards: none
Notes: 2, 7, 8, 9, 12

Pine Tree Inn

10 Main Avenue, 07756
(732) 775-3264; FAX (732) 775-2939

A small Victorian inn offering a quiet interlude for visitors to the Jersey shore—truly a bed and breakfast adhering to the charm of an earlier time. Enjoy breakfast each morning amidst midsummer ocean breezes on our front porch or sunny sideyard. A popular seaside resort since 1869, our village is a historic landmark. A commercial-free boardwalk and beautiful, uncrowded beaches await you.

Hostess: Karen Masen
Rooms: 12 (4PB; 7SB) $45-110
Continental Plus Breakfast
Credit Cards: A, B
Notes: 2, 5, 7 (12 and older), 8, 9, 10, 11

PRINCETON

Bed and Breakfast of Princeton

PO Box 571, 08542
(609) 924-3189; FAX (609) 921-6271
E-mail: bbop@compuserve.com

BBOP offers homestay accommodations in a small group of private homes. Some are within walking distance of the town center, while others are minutes away by automobile or public transportation. Most homes are nonsmoking. Rates begin at $50 single and $60 double occupancy, including a continental breakfast. There is a two-night minimum stay requirement. John Hurley, coordinator.

SPRING LAKE

Sea Crest by the Sea

19 Tuttle Avenue, 07762
(908) 449-9031; (800) 803-9031;
FAX (908) 974-0403
E-mail: jk@seacrestbythesea.com
Web site: http://www.seacrestbythesea.com

Your romantic fantasy escape. A Spring Lake bed and breakfast inn just for the

welcome; 7 Children welcome; 8 Tennis nearby; 9 Swimming nearby; 10 Golf nearby; 11 Skiing nearby; 12 May be booked through travel agent.

Sea Crest by the Sea

two of you. A lovingly restored 1885 Queen Anne Victorian for ladies and gentlemen on seaside holiday. Ocean views, open fireplaces, luxurious linens, featherbeds, antique-filled rooms, sumptuous breakfast, and afternoon tea. A *Gourmet Magazine* "top choice," one of *Country Inns Magazine's* "Top Inns." *Victoria Magazine* calls it "a perfect ocean refuge." John and Carol Kirby welcome you with old-fashioned hospitality to an atmosphere to soothe your weary body and soul.

Hosts: John and Carol Kirby
Rooms: 12 (PB) $145-259
Full Breakfast
Credit Cards: A, B, C
Notes: 5, 8, 9, 10, 12

Villa Park House

417 Ocean Road, 07762
(908) 449-3642
Web site: http://members.aol.com/villapk/
home.htm

It's like going to Grandma's house. Airy, sunny rooms with homemade quilts. Fresh, full breakfast—cooked as you order. Fresh-baked muffins and seasonal fruit dishes. Comfortable chairs for reading,

large front porch for relaxing, bicycles for traveling around town. Twenty years and we still love having company.

Hosts: Alice and David Bramhall
Rooms: 3 (PB) $90-110
Full Breakfast
Credit Cards: none
Notes: 2, 7, 8, 9, 10

White Lilac Inn

414 Central Avenue, 07762
(732) 449-0211
Web site: http://www.bbianj.com/whitelilac

We are in the shore region! The White Lilac Inn, circa 1888, with its triple-tiered porches, reflects the graciousness of a southern style that allows guests to relax and enjoy the simple life of an earlier time. Sit by the fire and enjoy friendly hospitality. Breakfast is full, leisurely, homemade, and served at tables for two in our Garden Room and enclosed porch. Discover the romance at the end of each day. Closed January 1 through February 10.

Host: Mari Kennelly Slocum
Rooms: 10 (8PB; 2SB) $89-159
Full Breakfast
Credit Cards: A, B, C, D
Notes: 2, 7 (14 and older), 8, 9, 10, 12

White Lilac Inn

NOTES: Credit cards accepted: A Master Card; B Visa; C American Express; D Discover; E Diners Club; F Other; 2 Personal checks accepted; 3 Lunch available; 4 Dinner available; 5 Open all year; 6 Pets

New Mexico

Mi Casa Su Casa B&B Reservation Service

PO Box 950, **Tempe, AZ,** 85280-0950
(602) 990-0682; (800) 456-0682 (reservations);
FAX (602) 990-3390
E-mail: ruthy2425@aol.com

Since 1981, we proudly have listed inspected, clean, comfortable homestays, inns, cottages and ranches in Arizona and the Southwest. We list about two hundred B&Bs, modest to luxurious, historic to contemporary. In **New Mexico**, we list Albuquerque, Algodones, Bernalillo, Chama, Chimayo, Corrales, Espanola, Lincoln, Las Cruces, Santa Fe, and Taos. Most rooms have private baths and range from $50 to $275, double-occupancy. Continental to gourmet breakfasts. A book with descriptions and pictures costs $9.50. Ruth Young, coordinator.

ALBUQUERQUE

Böttger Mansion B&B in Old Town

110 San Felipe NW, 87104
(505) 243-3639 (voice and FAX); (800) 758-3639

Walk to everything! Museums, galleries, fine restaurants, historic structures and sights, plus unlimited shopping. Experience a stay in an historic, elegant Victorian. Seven gracious bedrooms all have private baths; one has a Jacuzzi. Relax in shaded grass and marble courtyards, and enjoy our twenty-four-hour soda fountain and coffee/tea bar. Wake up each morning to a full specialty breakfast, and look forward to our evening social hour with wine and hors d'oeuvres.

Hostesses: Patsy Garcia and Jo Ivey
Rooms: 7 (PB) $89-149
Full Breakfast
Credit Cards: A, B, C, E
Notes: 2, 5, 7, 8, 9, 10, 11, 12

Enchanted Vista Bed and Breakfast

10700 Del Rey NE, 87122
(505) 823-1301

A southwestern villa on a one-acre estate, totally fenced for privacy with parking in the rear by a private entrance to all suites. The spacious suites with decks and verandas offer spectacular views. Continental breakfast is served at your convenience in your suite. Suites include microkitchens, perfect for extended stays. Enchanted Vista is located just twenty minutes from the airport and forty-five minutes from Santa Fe. Just

---

welcome; 7 Children welcome; 8 Tennis nearby; 9 Swimming nearby; 10 Golf nearby; 11 Skiing nearby; 12 May be booked through travel agent.

NEW MEXICO

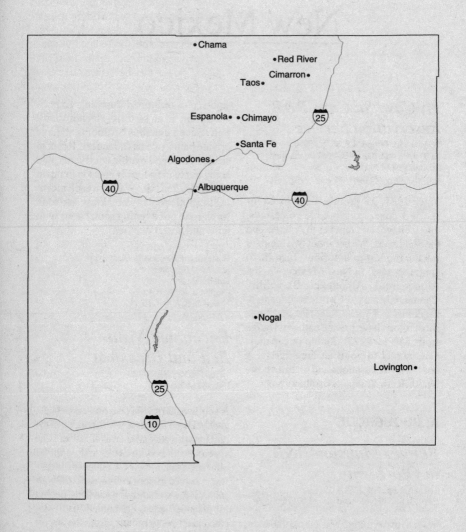

minutes from ski slopes, and only five minutes from the tram.

Hosts: Tillie and Al Gonzales
Rooms: 2 (PB) $62-74
Continental Breakfast
Credit Cards: none
Notes: 2, 3, 5, 6, 7, 8, 9, 10, 11, 12

Maggie's Raspberry Ranch

9817 Eldridge Road NW, 87114
(505) 897-1523; (800) 897-1523;
FAX (505) 897-1523

Maggie's Raspberry Ranch is a bed and breakfast for families in a country setting. Gather eggs from geese, chickens, and ducks. Feed the doves, rabbits, turtles, fish, and Callie the cat. Large pool, hot tub, an acre of trees and flowers, and, of course, raspberries! Garden-fresh full breakfasts. Pets welcome with a deposit.

Hostess: Maggie Lilly
Rooms: 5 (2PB; 3SB) $65-95
Full Breakfast
Credit Cards: B
Notes: 2, 5, 6, 7, 8, 9, 10, 11

ALGODONES/SANTA FE

Hacienda Vargas Bed and Breakfast Inn

PO Box 307, 1431 El Camino Real, 87001
(505) 867-9115
E-mail: hacvar@swcp.com
Web site: http://www.swcp.com/hacvar

Located on the historic El Camino Real, Hacienda Vargas occupies a site of historical significance in the saga of New Mexico. It has been a stagecoach stop, an Indian trading post, and a U.S. post office. During the renovation, great care was taken to preserve the original structure. The oldest part dates to the 1840s. The inn has two bedrooms and five suites with private entrances, baths, and fireplaces. Four suites have Jacuzzi tubs. A large barbecue area and hot tub are available for guests' enjoyment. A full country breakfast is served in the main dining room. The inn is conveniently located in the village of Algodones, approximately thirty minutes south of Santa Fe and fifteen minutes north of Albuquerque. The innkeepers are well-traveled former bankers who speak Spanish. Hacienda Vargas is AAA three-diamond-rated.

Hosts: Paul and Jule De Vargas
Rooms: 8 (PB) $69-139
Full Breakfast
Credit Cards: A, B
Notes: 5, 10, 11, 12

ARTESIA

Heritage Inn

209 W. Main Street, 88210
(505) 748-2552; (800) 594-7392;
FAX (505) 746-3407

New country/Victorian atmosphere will take you back in time and warm your heart and soul. Spacious rooms with private baths, room phones, color TVs, continental breakfast, computer modem hookups for business travelers and outside patio and deck for relaxation. Very secure second floor; downtown location convenient to

---

NOTES: Credit cards accepted: A Master Card; B Visa; C American Express; D Discover; E Diners Club; F Other; 2 Personal checks accepted; 3 Lunch available; 4 Dinner available; 5 Open all year; 6 Pets welcome; 7 Children welcome; 8 Tennis nearby; 9 Swimming nearby;   10 Golf nearby; 11 Skiing nearby; 12 May be booked through travel agent.

Heritage Inn

excellent restaurants. Smoke-free. No pets. AAA three-diamond-rated.

Hosts: James and Wanda Maupin
Rooms: 9 (PB) $55-60
Continental Breakfast
Credit Cards: A, B, C, D
Notes: 5

CHAMA

The Refuge Bed and Breakfast

PO Box 819, 87520
(505) 756-2136; (800) 566-4799

Impeccably adorned yet comfortable guest rooms, more than a thousand feet of screened and covered porches, and magnificent views of the 20,400-acre wildlife refuge directly across the river from this distinctive country inn. Relaxed atmosphere with horseshoe pits, outdoor fire pit, hiking, outdoor sports, and watchable wildlife. Sumptuous breakfasts and personal service and hospitality provide the finishing touches for a memorable retreat. Only six-tenths of a mile to the train.

Hosts: Jeff and Jackie Nettleton
Rooms: 5 (PB) $90-120
Full Gourmet Breakfast
Credit Cards: A, B
Notes: 2, 4, 5, 7, 11, 12

CHIMAYO

Hacienda Rancho De Chimayo

PO Box 11, 87522
(505) 351-2222; FAX (505) 351-4038

In August 1984, the Jaramillo family completed restoration of Hacienda Rancho de Chimayo, the family home of Epifanio and Adelaida Jaramillo. Built in the adobe tradition, the home has been renovated into seven lovely guest rooms. Each guest room opens into an enclosed courtyard, and within each room one can find turn-of-the-century antiques, a private bath, a quiet sitting area, and a fireplace. In the Old World tradition, a continental breakfast with pastry, fruit, fresh-squeezed orange juice, and coffee or tea awaits each guest in the morning.

Hostess: Delilah Brown
Rooms: 7 (PB) $62-105
Continental Breakfast
Credit Cards: A, B, C, D, E
Notes: 3, 4, 5, 7 (over 9), 11

CIMARRON

Casa del Gavilan Historic Inn

PO Box 518, Highway 21 S., 87714
(505) 376-2246; (800) GAVILAN

Casa del Gavilan is a place of the spirit where hawk and eagle soar. The secluded, turn-of-the-century adobe villa is nestled in the foothills of the Sangre de Cristo Mountains. Enjoy elegant hospitality and breathtaking views in a historic

---

NOTES: Credit cards accepted: A Master Card; B Visa; C American Express; D Discover; E Diners Club; F Other; 2 Personal checks accepted; 3 Lunch available; 4 Dinner available; 5 Open all year; 6 Pets

setting. The inn offers four guest rooms with private baths, plus a two-room suite. In the shadow of the Tooth of Time, the Casa is adjacent to Philmont Scout Ranch and the Santa Fe Trail. Villa Vidale recreation area, Kit Carson's home and several fine museums are located nearby. Eagle Nest Lake, Angel Fire and Red River ski resorts, and Taos are all within easy driving distance.

Hosts: Bob and Helen Hittle
Rooms: 5 (PB) $ 70-100
Full Breakfast
Credit Cards: A, B, C, D
Notes: 2, 5, 7, 12

ESPANOLA

The Inn of La Mesilla

Route 1, Box 368A, 87532
(505) 753-5368 (voice and FAX)

A beautiful Pueblo-style home, the Inn of La Mesilla is rural elegance in the heart of the Eight Northern Indian Pueblos. It is high on a hill with fabulous views. Quiet. Full breakfast and afternoon tea are served. Guests enjoy a Jacuzzi on a large redwood deck with views. Two rooms, both with private full bath, color television, and ceiling fans. Twenty-three miles to downtown Santa Fe. Two English springer spaniels, Pork Chop and Te-Bon! Baby grand piano in living room/great room/common room.

Hostess: Yolanda F. Hoemann (Pork Chop and Te-Bon)
Rooms: 2 (PB) $90
Full Breakfast
Credit Cards: none
Notes: 2, 5, 10, 11

LOVINGTON

Pyburn House Bed and Breakfast

203 N. 4th Street, 88260
(505) 396-3460; FAX (505) 396-7315

This folklore two-story rock house, built in 1935 by John Pyburn, is listed on the state and national registers of historic places. A very comfortable, down-home atmosphere. Each guest room has its special ambience and is furnished with lovely antiques, luxury linens, and thick towels, and has a plush bathroom. Amenities include cable TV/VCRs, full, queen and king beds, Jacuzzi, and bicycle built for two. Smoking is permitted on outside porches.

Hosts: Don and Sharon Ritchey
Rooms: 4 (PB) $55-95
Continental Breakfast
Credit Cards: A, B, D
Notes: 2, 5, 8, 9, 10

NOGAL

Monjeau Shadows

HC 67, Box 87, 88341
(505) 336-4191

Four-level Victorian farmhouse on ten acres of beautiful, landscaped grounds. Picnic area, nature trails. King and queen beds, honeymoon suite. Antiques. Just minutes from Lincoln National Park and White Mountain Wilderness. Fishing, cross-country skiing, fishing, and horseback riding. For fun or relaxation, enjoy Monjeau Shadows' year-round comfort.

Hosts: Billie and Gil Reidland
Rooms: 4 (PB) $65-100
Full Breakfast
Credit Cards: A, B, D
Notes: 2, 5, 8, 9, 10, 11

welcome; 7 Children welcome; 8 Tennis nearby; 9 Swimming nearby; 10 Golf nearby; 11 Skiing nearby; 12 May be booked through travel agent.

RED RIVER

Sundance Bed and Breakfast

1301 E. Highway 38, 87558
(505) 754-2321
E-mail: sundance@newmex.com
Web site: http://taoswebb.com/hotel/sundance

Enjoy Red River's cool summer weather and yellow aspen trees in the fall. When ski season comes, catch the chairlift in the middle of town! We have fantastic views of Red River from every room. Delight in the country decor; original artwork; hearty, home-style breakfasts; and charming personal service. Guest telephone, private baths, television/VCRs, Jacuzzi, fireplaces, washer/dryer, and more.

Hosts: John and Linda Hoag
Rooms: 4 (PB) $75-95
Full Breakfast
Credit Cards: A, B, C, D
Notes: 2, 5, 7, 8, 10, 11, 12

SANTA FE

El Paradero

220 W. Manhattan, 87501
(505) 988-1177

El Paradero is located on a quiet downtown side street, ideal for exploring the heart of historic Santa Fe. The owners have turned the old, adobe Spanish farmhouse into a warm and relaxing experience of true southwestern camaraderie and hospitality. The inn is furnished in the southwestern tradition with folk art and has an eccentric, rambling character typical of old adobe homes. Breakfasts are huge and special.

Hosts: Ouida MacGregor and Thom Allen
Rooms: 14 (10PB; 4SB) $75-135
Full Breakfast
Credit Cards: A, B
Notes: 2, 5, 6, 7, 8, 9, 10, 11, 12

TAOS

Orinda Bed and Breakfast

Box 4451, 81571
(505) 758-8581; (800) 847-1837;
FAX (505) 751-4895
E-mail: orinda@newmex.com
Web site: http://wwwtaosnet.com/orinda

A fifty-year-old adobe home. Dramatic pastoral setting on two acres. View of Taos Mountains, surrounded by elm and cottonwood trees. Decorated in southwestern design. Original art presented in rooms and common areas. *Kiva* fireplaces in suites. Quiet, on a private road, but only a fifteen-minute walk to galleries, plaza, and restaurants.

Hosts: Cary and George Pratt
Rooms: 4 (3PB; 1SB) $70-88
Full Breakfast
Credit Cards: A, B, C, D
Notes: 2, 5, 7, 8, 9, 10, 11, 12

Orinda Bed and Breakfast

NOTES: Credit cards accepted: A Master Card; B Visa; C American Express; D Discover; E Diners Club; F Other; 2 Personal checks accepted; 3 Lunch available; 4 Dinner available; 5 Open all year; 6 Pets

The Willows Inn Bed and Breakfast

412 Kit Carson Road, NDCBU 6560, 87571
(505) 758-2558; (800) 525-8267;
FAX (505) 758-5445
E-mail: willows@newmex.com
Web site: http://taoswebb.com/hotel/willows

The Willows Inn Bed and Breakfast

The Willows Inn is a B&B located on a secluded acre lot just a short walk from the Taos Plaza. Listed on the National Historic Registry, the property was the home and studio of E. Martin Hennings. Hennings was a member of the revered Taos Society of Artists, the group that established Taos as an artist colony in the 1920s. Scrumptious, full breakfasts are served family-style in the dining rooms. Guests enjoy homemade snacks and beverages in the late afternoon on the flagstone courtyard in summer or by the fire in the cooler seasons. Each guest room has smooth adobe walls with *kiva* fireplaces, open beam (*viga*) ceilings, and Douglas fir floors with various decor themes which highlight cultures significant to the Taos area. The grounds and courtyards form a parklike oasis with flowers, fountains, and two of America's largest living willow trees.

Hosts: Janet and Doug Camp
Rooms: 5 (PB) $95-130
Full Breakfast
Credit Cards: A, B
Notes: 2, 5, 7, 9, 10, 11, 12

welcome; 7 Children welcome; 8 Tennis nearby; 9 Swimming nearby; 10 Golf nearby; 11 Skiing nearby; 12 May be booked through travel agent.

NEW YORK

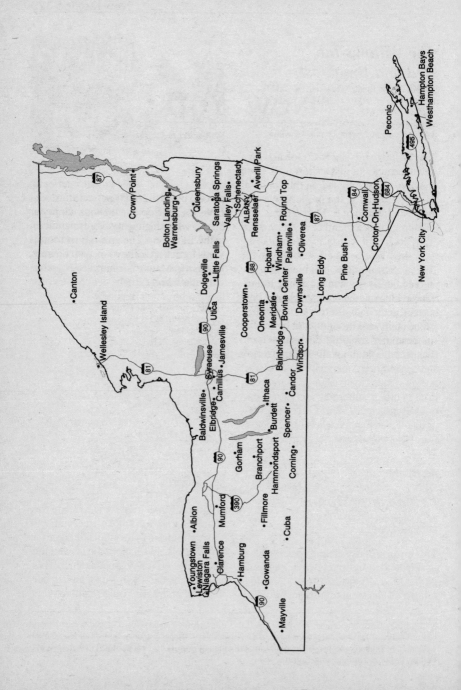

New York

American Country Collection of B&Bs

1353 Union Street, **Schenectady**, 12308
(518) 370-4948; (800) 810-4948;
FAX (518) 393-1634

This reservation service provides reservations for eastern **New York**, western **Massachusetts**, and all of **Vermont**. Just one call does it all. Relax and unwind at any of our more than one hundred immaculate, personally inspected B&Bs and country inns. Many include fireplace, Jacuzzi, and/or Modified American Plan. We have budget-minded to luxurious accommodations in urban, suburban, and rural locations. Rates are $50-200. Gift certificates available, and major credit cards accepted. Carol Matos, owner.

ALBION

Friendship Manor

349 S. Main Street, 14411
(716) 589-7973

This historic house, dating back to 1880, is surrounded by lovely roses, an herb garden, and lots of shade trees. A swimming pool and tennis courts are provided for your pleasure. The intimate interior is an artful blend of Victorian-style furnishings with antiques throughout. Enjoy a breakfast of muffins, breads, fruit, juice, coffee, or tea in the formal dining room, served buffet-style for your convenience. Friendship Manor is central to Niagara Falls, Buffalo, or Rochester. For traveling through or just a getaway.

Hosts: Jack and Marylin Baker
Rooms: 4 (1PB; 3SB) $55
Continental Plus Breakfast
Credit Cards: none
Notes: 2, 5, 7, 10

AVERILL PARK

Ananas Hus Bed and Breakfast

148 South Road, 12018
(518) 766-5035

The Tomlinsons invite you to share the beautiful, tranquil, smoke-free, and pet-free environment of their hillside home on thirty acres with a panoramic view of the Hudson River Valley. Ananas Hus serves breakfast by the fire in winter and, in fair weather, under the roofed patio. AC is

NOTES: Credit cards accepted: A Master Card; B Visa; C American Express; D Discover; E Diners Club; F Other; 2 Personal checks accepted; 3 Lunch available; 4 Dinner available; 5 Open all year; 6 Pets welcome; 7 Children welcome; 8 Tennis nearby; 9 Swimming nearby; 10 Golf nearby; 11 Skiing nearby; 12 May be booked through travel agent.

available. Ananas Hus is located eight-tenths of a mile off Route 43 on County Road 23 in West Stephenton, convenient to western Massachusetts and the Capitol District of New York State, which abounds with cultural, natural, historical, and sports attractions. Great downhill and cross-country skiing.

Hosts: Clyde H. Tomlinson Jr. and Thelma Olsen Tomlinson
Rooms: 3 (2PB; 1SB) $60-75
Full Homemade Breakfast
Credit Cards: C
Notes: 2, 5, 7 (over 12), 9, 10, 11, 12

BAINBRIDGE

Berry Hill Gardens Bed and Breakfast

242 Ward-Loomis Road, 13733
(607) 967-8745; (800) 497-8745;
FAX (607) 967-2227

This restored 1820s farmhouse on a hilltop is surrounded by extensive herb and perennial gardens and 180 acres where you can hike, swim, bird-watch, skate, cross-country ski, or sit on the wrap-around porch and watch nature parade. Our rooms are furnished with comfortable antiques. A ten-minute drive takes you to restaurants, golf, tennis, auctions, and antique centers. You can buy plants, dried flowers, and wreaths grown and hand-crafted on the farm to take home with you. Cooperstown and most local colleges are only forty-five minutes away. Three hours to New York City.

Hosts: Jean Fowler and Cecilio Rios
Rooms: 5 (1PB; 4SB) $60-70
Full Breakfast
Credit Cards: A, B, C
Notes: 2, 5, 7, 8, 9, 10, 11, 12

BALDWINSVILLE

Pandora's Getaway

83 Oswego Street, 13025
(315) 635-9571; (888) 638-8668
E-mail: PGetaway@worldnet.att.net

One-hundred-and-fifty-year-old Greek Revival in a quiet village setting minutes from all locations in Syracuse. Lots of antiques, collectibles, and country charm. Cozy fireplace in one bedroom and living room. Enjoy on the front porch or fireplace. Easy access to thruway, fairgrounds, SU and SUNY Oswego. Near all central New York locations.

Hostess: Sandy Wheeler
Rooms: 4 (3PB; 1SB) $60-85
Full Breakfast
Credit Cards: A, B, D
Notes: 2, 5, 7, 8, 9, 10, 11, 12

BOLTON LANDING

Hilltop Cottage Bed and Breakfast

6883 Lakeshore Drive, 12814-0186
(518) 644-2492

A clean, comfortable, renovated farmhouse near Lake George in the beautiful eastern Adirondack Mountains. Walk to beaches, restaurants, and marinas. Enjoy a quiet, home atmosphere with hearty breakfasts. In the summer, this is a busy resort area. Autumn offers foliage, hiking, and skiing. A wood-burning stove is used in winter. Brochure available.

Hosts: Anita Richards
Rooms: 4 (2PB; 2SB) $60-80
Full Breakfast
Credit Cards: A, B
Notes: 2, 7, 8, 9

NOTES: Credit cards accepted: A Master Card; B Visa; C American Express; D Discover; E Diners Club; F Other; 2 Personal checks accepted; 3 Lunch available; 4 Dinner available; 5 Open all year; 6 Pets

BOVINA CENTER

The Swallow's Nest Bed and Breakfast

Box 112, Bramley Mt. Road, 13740
(607) 832-4547

We are an 1850 farmhouse with four bedrooms and a large dining room where you are served a special breakfast. We have a large room available for seminars, workshops or just to relax in. There is hiking on our property and swimming on our pond. Nearby are horseback riding, fishing, hunting, golf, antiquing, and auctions. Or just sit under a tree or by the brook and unwind. We are nine miles from Delhi College and nineteen miles from Oneonta. Reservations are appreciated one week in advance with a 50-percent deposit. Three days' cancellation required. Check-in after 1 PM. Check-out by 11 AM is appreciated.

Hosts: Gunhilde and Walter Kuhnle
Rooms: 4 (1PB; 3SB) $65-70
Full Breakfast
Credit Cards: A, B
Notes: 2, 3, 4, 5, 7, 9, 10, 11

BRANCHPORT

Gone With the Wind Bed and Breakfast on Keuka Lake

453 W. Lake Road, 14418
(607) 868-4603

The name paints the picture—an 1887 stone Victorian on fourteen acres overlooking our quiet lake cove adorned by an inviting picnic gazebo. Feel the magic

Gone With the Wind Bed and Breakfast

of total relaxation and peace of mind in the solarium hot tub; gather your gifts of imagination on our pleasant nature trails; unlock your unique, God-given gifts to see your purpose accomplished. Fireplaces, delectable breakfasts, private beach and dock. Reserve "The Sequel," a log haven, for small retreats, business meetings, or gatherings. One hour south of Rochester in the New York Finger Lakes.

Hosts: Linda and Robert Lewis
Rooms: 6+; $75-125
Full Breakfast
Credit Cards: none
Notes: 2, 5, 8, 9, 10, 11

BURDETT

The Red House Country Inn

4586 Picnic Area Road, 14818-9716
(607) 546-8566; FAX (607) 546-4105 (call first)

Located in the thirteen-thousand-acre Finger Lakes National Forest. Twenty-eight miles of maintained hiking and cross-country ski trails. Six award-winning wineries are within ten minutes of the completely restored 1840s farmstead on five acres of groomed lawns and flower gardens. Enjoy beautifully appointed rooms, country

welcome; 7 Children welcome; 8 Tennis nearby; 9 Swimming nearby; 10 Golf nearby; 11 Skiing nearby; 12 May be booked through travel agent.

breakfasts, in-ground pool, and fully equipped kitchen. Twelve minutes from Ithaca, thirty from Corning.

Hostesses: Sandy Schmanke and Joan Martin
Rooms: 5 (SB) $49-89
Full Breakfast
Credit Cards: A, B, C, D
Notes: 2, 4 (November-April), 5, 7 (over 12), 8, 9 (on premises), 10, 11, 12

CAMILLUS

The Re Family B&B

4166 Split Rock Road, 13031
(315) 468-2039

One-hundred-year-old Early American farmhouse with log-style den, country kitchen, side deck for fair-weather breakfasts, forty-foot pool, lawns, two guest rooms with queen-size brass beds and orthopedic mattresses, and pedestal sink in each room. Next to garden-style bathroom with walk-in tile shower, vanity with double sinks, and full-mirrored back wall. One room has a full bed and captain's bed for two singles or children. Outdoor pool. Stress-free environment close to Syracuse.

Hosts: Joseph and Terry Re
Rooms: 2 (SB) $65-85
Continental Breakfast
Credit Cards: F
Notes: 2, 5, 7 (10 or older), 8, 9, 10, 11, 12

The Edge of Thyme Inn

CANDOR

The Edge of Thyme Inn Bed and Breakfast

6 Main Street, PO Box 48, 13743
(607) 659-5155

Featured in *Historic Inns of the Northeast*. Located in this quiet rural village is a large, gracious Georgian home. Leaded-glass, windowed porch, marble fireplaces, period sitting rooms, gardens, and pergola. Epicurean breakfast served in a genteel manner. Central to Cornell, Ithaca College, Corning, Elmira, Watkins Glen, and wineries. Gift shoppe. High tea is served by appointment.

Hosts: Eva Mae and Frank Musgrave
Rooms: 5 (3PB; 2SB) $65-125
Full Breakfast
Credit Cards: A, B
Notes: 2, 5, 7 (well-behaved), 8, 9, 10, 11 (cross-country), 12

CANTON

White Pillars Bed and Breakfast

395 Old State Road, 13630
(315) 386-2353

Experience classic antiquity and modern living in this beautifully renovated 1850s homestead. Room luxuries include whirlpool tub, marble floor, air-conditioning, cable TV, and expansive windows overlooking one hundred acres of meadows. This quiet, rural setting is located only six miles from Canton, the county seat and home of several colleges. Summer guests are invited to use the facilities of their hosts' seven-acre trout lake, twenty minutes

NOTES: Credit cards accepted: A Master Card; B Visa; C American Express; D Discover; E Diners Club; F Other; 2 Personal checks accepted; 3 Lunch available; 4 Dinner available; 5 Open all year; 6 Pets

White Pillars Bed and Breakfast

away, for swimming, canoeing, and fishing enjoyment.

Hosts: John and Donna Clark
Rooms: 4 (2PB; 2SB) $50-65
Full Breakfast
Credit Cards: A, B, C
Notes: 2, 5, 7, 8, 9, 10, 11, 12

CLARENCE

Asa Ransom House

10529 Main Street (Route 5), 14031
(716) 759-2315; FAX (716) 759-2791
E-mail: AsaRansom@aol.com,
innfo@asaransom.com

Warmth, comfort, and hospitality are our main attractions. Nine guest rooms have antique and period furnishings; seven have fireplaces. Many rooms have a porch or balcony. We also have a library, gift shop, and herb garden on a two-acre lot in the village. The original building housing the library, gift shop, and tap room dates to 1853, built by Asa Ransom. Closed in January.

Hosts: Robert Lenz; Judy Lenz
Rooms: 9 (PB) $95-145
Full Breakfast
Credit Cards: A, B, D
Notes: 2, 4, 7, 8, 9, 10

COOPERSTOWN

Berrywick II

RD 2, Box 486, 13326
(607) 547-2052

Located six miles from Cooperstown, home of the Baseball Hall of Fame, the Farmer's Museum, and the New York State Historical Association—Fenimore House and the Glimmerglass Opera House. All beautifully situated around nine-mile-long Otsego Lake. Berrywick II is a renovated 19th-Century farmhouse with separate entrance for guests to a converted, two-bedroom apartment. Queen, double, and twin rooms with kitchen/sitting room and bath perfectly suited for a couple of couples or families with well-behaved children. Sorry, no pets and no smoking.

Hosts: Helen and Jack Weber
Rooms: 3 (SB) (converted apartment) $75-85
Continental or Full Breakfast
Credit Cards: none
Notes: 2, 5, 7, 9, 10

CORNING

1865 White Birch Bed and Breakfast

69 E. First Street, 14830
(607) 962-6355

The White Birch, Victorian in structure but decorated in country, has been refurbished to show off its winding staircase, hardwood floors, and wall window in the dining room that overlooks the backyard. We are located in a residential area, two blocks from restored historic Market Street and

---

welcome; 7 Children welcome; 8 Tennis nearby; 9 Swimming nearby; 10 Golf nearby; 11 Skiing nearby; 12 May be booked through travel agent.

1865 White Birch Bed and Breakfast

six blocks from the Corning Museum of Glass. A warm fire during the colder months welcomes guests in the common room where TV and great conversation are available. A full gourmet breakfast is served each morning.

Hosts: Kathy and Joe Donahue
Rooms: 4 (2PB; 2SB) $65-80
Full Gourmet Breakfast
Credit Cards: A, B, C
Notes: 2, 5, 7, 8, 9, 10, 11 (cross-country)

Delevan House

188 Delevan Avenue, 14830
(607) 962-2347

This southern colonial house sits on a hill overlooking Corning. It is charming, graceful, and warm, in quiet surroundings. Delicious breakfast served from 8 to 9 AM. Check-in time 3 PM; check-out time 10:30 AM. Free transportation from airport. We are two minutes from Market Street and Glass Center by car. TV in all rooms. Very private. Enjoy a cool refreshment on the lovely screened-in porch.

Hostess: Mary M. De Pumpo
Rooms: 3 (1PB; 1½SB) $65-85
Full Breakfast
Credit Cards: none
Notes: 2, 5, 7 (over 10), 10, 11, 12

CORNWALL (WEST POINT)

Cromwell Manor Inn

Angola Road, 12518
(914) 534-7136
Web site: http://www.pojonews.com/enjoy/
cromwell

Built in 1820, Cromwell Manor Inn is a fully restored, romantic country estate. Set on seven landscaped acres overlooking a four-thousand-acre mountain forest preserve. The six thousand-square-foot manor is fully furnished with period antiques and fine furnishings. Enjoy breakfast on the veranda or in our country breakfast room, at your private table. A 1764 restored cottage for larger groups sleeps eight. Fifty-five minutes north of New York City, five miles from West Point. Fireplaces and romance. Visit nearby wineries, restorations, and Woodbury Commons; hike the majestic Hudson Valley.

Hosts: Dale and Brenda Ohara
Rooms: 13 (11PB; 2SB) $135-250
Full Breakfast
Credit Cards: A, B
Notes: 2, 5, 7 (over 7), 8, 9, 10, 11, 12

Cromwell Manor Inn

CROTON-ON-HUDSON

Alexander Hamilton House

49 Van Wyck Street, 10520
(914) 271-6737; FAX (914) 271-3927
E-mail: alexhmlths@aol.com

The Alexander Hamilton House, circa 1889, is a sprawling Victorian home on a

---

NOTES: Credit cards accepted: A Master Card; B Visa; C American Express; D Discover; E Diners Club; F Other; 2 Personal checks accepted; 3 Lunch available; 4 Dinner available; 5 Open all year; 6 Pets

cliff overlooking the Hudson. Many period antiques and collections. A queen bed suite has a fireplaced sitting room, two large rooms with queen beds (one with additional daybed), and a bridal chamber with king bed, Jacuzzi, entertainment center, marble fireplace, and skylights. The master suite has a queen bed, fireplace, picture windows, stained glass, entertainment center, Jacuzzi, skylight, and river views. A one-bedroom apartment with double bed, living room and kitchen, private bath, and separate entrance is available for longer stays. Attractions include West Point, Sleepy Hollow Restorations, Lyndhurst, Boscobel, Rockefeller mansion, hiking, biking, and sailing. New York City is less than an hour away. No smoking or pets. All rooms have AC, private baths, cable TVs, and phones. Off-street parking. Weekly and monthly rates available. Credit card guarantee required. Seven-day cancellation policy.

Hostesses: Barbara Notarius and Brenda Barta
Rooms: 7 (PB) $95-250
Full Breakfast
Credit Cards: A, B, C, D, E
Notes: 5, 7, 8, 9 (pool), 10, 11 (cross-country), 12

CROWN POINT

Crown Point Bed and Breakfast— The Wyman House

Route 9N, Main Street., PO Box 490, 12928
(518) 597-3651; FAX (518) 597-4451

An elegant "painted lady," Victorian manor house on five-and-a-half acres. The gracious interior is filled with period antiques. Each of five bed chambers is distinctively decorated and has its own ambience and

private bath. The house boasts woodwork panels of six types of wood. Outside are three porches and a fountain amidst blooming gardens. Homemade breakfast. Near Lake Champlain, the area has museums, historical sites, and antiques.

Hosts: Sandy and Hugh Johnson
Rooms: 5 (PB) $60-120
Continental Plus Breakfast
Credit Cards: A, B, C
Notes: 2, 5, 7, 8, 9, 10, 12

CUBA

Helen's Tourist Home

7 Maple Street, 14727
(716) 968-2200

Your hostess has been welcoming tourists to her comfortable, turn-of-the-century home for forty-three years. Located on a quiet residential street. Guests have the run of the house, including the large living room with TV. Coffee, a toaster, and a refrigerator always are available. Visit the Cuba Cheese Shop and historic Seneca Springs. A restaurant is just around the corner; a small shopping center nearby.

Hostess: Dora W. Wittmann
Rooms: 5 (1PB; 4SB) $25-40
Credit Cards: none
Notes: 2, 5, 7, 9, 10, 11

DOLGEVILLE

Adrianna Bed and Breakfast

44 Stewart Street, 13329
(315) 429-3249; (800) 335-4233

Adrianna Bed and Breakfast is located in a rural Little Falls area near I-90 Exit 29A.

welcome; 7 Children welcome; 8 Tennis nearby; 9 Swimming nearby; 10 Golf nearby; 11 Skiing nearby; 12 May be booked through travel agent.

The cozy residence blends antique and contemporary furnishings. It is convenient to Saratoga, Cooperstown, historic sites, and snowmobile, cross-country skiing, and hiking trails. Four guest rooms are offered, two with private baths. A full breakfast is served. Smoking is restricted. The home is air-conditioned.

Hostess: Adrianna Naizby
Rooms: 4 (2PB; 2SB) $55-65
Full Breakfast
Credit Cards: A, B
Notes: 2, 5, 6 (well-behaved), 7 (over 5), 9, 10, 11, 12

DOWNSVILLE

Adam's Farmhouse Bed and Breakfast

PO Box 18, Upper Main Street, 13755
(607) 363-2757

Catskill Mountains, on Route 206, Main Street, next to Papacton Reservoir and the east branch of the Delaware River. The best little bed and breakfast by a "dam site." Beautiful old farmhouse full of antiques. Surrounded by maple trees, babbling brook, lots of flowers and grass. Wicker-furnished porch is great for leisure time. Great village for canoeing, hiking, biking, swimming, fishing, hunting, and antiquing, near Cooperstown and Binghamton. Five guest rooms, two with private baths; gourmet breakfast. Picnic tables, grill, afternoon tea, cable TV, gift and antique store. Smoking restricted.

Hosts: Nancy and Harry Adams
Rooms: 5 (2PB; 3SB) $50-75
Full Breakfast
Credit Cards: D
Notes: 3, 4, 6, 7, 8, 9, 10, 12

FILLMORE

Just a "Plane" Bed and Breakfast

11152 Route 19-A, 14735
(716) 567-8338

Enjoy a relaxing, peaceful stay. Situated on the banks of the historic Genesee Valley Canal, the three-story Dutch Colonial home was constructed in 1926. Renovated in 1995, it has four guest rooms, each with a private bath. The "Plane" in the name refers to the scenic airplane rides, offered for an additional fee. Craig, a licensed commercial pilot, flies a Piper PA-22, which is hangared on the farm. In the morning, enjoy a full country breakfast in the dining room or sunroom.

Hosts: Audrey and Craig Smith
Rooms: 4 (PB) $55
Full Breakfast
Credit Cards: some

GORHAM

Gorham House Bed and Breakfast

PO Box 43, 4752 E. Swamp Road, 14461-0043
(716) 526-4402
E-mail: GORHAM.HOUSE@juno.com

A circa-1887, fourteen-room country colonial-style farmhouse decorated with family antiques is yours to enjoy in the heart of the Finger Lakes. Spacious, beautifully appointed guest rooms. In the kitchen you will find a large collection of advertising tins, while the eat-in pantry features framed Cream of Wheat advertisements from the early 1900s. Walk our five acres; explore

---

NOTES: Credit cards accepted: A Master Card; B Visa; C American Express; D Discover; E Diners Club; F Other; 2 Personal checks accepted; 3 Lunch available; 4 Dinner available; 5 Open all year; 6 Pets

the many different wildflowers, berry bushes, fruit trees and herbs. Relax on one of our three porches.

Hosts: Nancy and Al Rebmann
Rooms: 3 (1PB; 2SB) $65-95
Full Breakfast
Credit Cards: none
Notes: 2, 5, 7 (over 12), 8, 9, 10, 11, 12

GOWANDA

The Teepee

14396 Four Mile Level Road, 14070
(716) 532-2168

The Teepee is operated by full-blooded Seneca Indians on the Cattaraugus Indian Reservation. Max is of the Turtle Clan and Phyllis of the Wolf Clan. Tours of the reservation are available, as are tours of the nearby Amish community. Good base when visiting Niagara Falls.

Hosts: Max and Phyllis Lay
Rooms: 4 (SB) $50
Full Breakfast
Credit Cards: none
Notes: 2, 5, 7, 8, 9, 10, 11

HAMBURG

Sharon's Lake House Bed and Breakfast

4862 Lakeshore Road, 14075
(716) 627-7561

Built on the shore of Lake Erie. Rooms offer a magnificent view of the Buffalo city skyline and the Canadian border, only fifteen minutes west of the city. Rooms are new and beautifully decorated, with waterfront views. Food is prepared gourmet-

style. New hot tub room and widow's watch overlooking Lake Erie available. Reservations and a two-night minimum stay are required. We offer discounts every month—for example, one free night with a two-night stay.

Hosts: Sharon and Vince DiMaria
Rooms: 2 (1PB; 1SB) $100-110
Full Gourmet Breakfast
Credit Cards: none
Notes: 2, 3, 4, 5, 7 (by reservation), 9, 10, 11

The Blushing Rose Bed and Breakfast

HAMMONDSPORT

The Blushing Rose Bed and Breakfast

11 William Street, PO Box 201, 14840
(607) 569-3402; (800) 982-8818;
FAX (607) 569-3483

A pleasant hideaway for honeymooners, anniversary celebrators and other guests. Whether you spend your day driving, hiking, biking, or just plain relaxing, The Blushing Rose is the ideal safe haven in which to end your day—and a great place to start another, after enjoying a copious specialty breakfast. Open May 1 to December 31. Join us while rediscovering the

welcome; 7 Children welcome; 8 Tennis nearby; 9 Swimming nearby; 10 Golf nearby; 11 Skiing nearby; 12 May be booked through travel agent.

wonders of nature and, perhaps most important, the wonder of yourself!

Hosts: Ellen and Frank Laufersweiler
Rooms: 4 (PB) $75-95
Full Breakfast
Credit Cards: none
Notes: 2, 8, 9, 10

HAMPTON BAYS

House on the Water

Box 106, 11946
(516) 728-3560

Quiet waterfront residence in Hampton Bays surrounded by two acres of gardens on Shinnecock Bay. A pleasant neighborhood on a peninsula, good for jogging and walking. Two miles to ocean beaches, seven miles to Southampton. Kitchen facilities, bicycles, boats, lounges, and umbrellas. A full breakfast from 8 AM to noon is served on the terrace overlooking the water. Watch the boats and swans go by. Adults only. No pets. Rooms have water views and private baths and entrances. German, French, and Spanish are spoken.

Hostess: Mrs. Ute
Rooms: 3 (2PB; 1SB) $85-105 (seasonal)
Full Breakfast
Credit Cards: none
Notes: 2, 7 (over 12) 8, 9, 10, 12

HOBART

Breezy Acres Farm Bed and Breakfast

RD 1, Box 191, 13788
(607) 538-9338

For a respite from your busy, stressful lives, come visit us. We offer cozy accommo-dations with private baths in our circa-1830s farmhouse. You'll awaken refreshed to wonderful aromas from the kitchen. A full, homemade breakfast will be served to you while you plan your day. You could spend a week here leisurely exploring the museums, Howe Caverns, and the Baseball Hall of Fame—but leave some time every day to roam our three hundred acres, or to sit in a wicker swing on our old-fashioned, pillared porches, soaking in the views of meadows, pastures, and rolling hills. Or you can make use of golfing, tennis, fishing, and skiing facilities, all available nearby.

Hosts: Joyce and David Barber
Rooms: 3 (PB) $60-75
Full Homemade Breakfast
Credit Cards: A, B, C
Notes: 2, 5, 7 (some restrictions), 8, 9, 10, 11

ITHACA

Log Country Inn Bed and Breakfast of Ithaca

PO Box 581, 14851
(607) 589-4771; (800) 274-4771;
FAX (607) 589-6151
Web site: http://www.logtv.com/inn

Escape to the rustic charm of a log house at the edge of seven thousand acres of state forest in the Finger Lakes region. Modern accommodations provided in the spirit of international hospitality. Awaken to the sound of birds and explore the peaceful surroundings. Enjoy full Eastern European breakfasts with blintzes or Russian pancakes and comfortable rooms with private baths. Sauna and afternoon tea available during the fall and winter months. Easy

---

NOTES: Credit cards accepted: A Master Card; B Visa; C American Express; D Discover; E Diners Club; F Other; 2 Personal checks accepted; 3 Lunch available; 4 Dinner available; 5 Open all year; 6 Pets

access to hiking and cross-country trails. Families with children are welcome, and we will find a place for your pet. Our inn provides a perfect place for family reunions or spiritual retreats. Cornell University, Ithaca College, Corning Glass Center, wineries, and antique stores are close by. Your hostess is a biologist (former profession), and her husband Slawomir is a documentary filmmaker.

Hostess: Wanda Grunberg
Rooms: 5 (3PB; 2SB) $55-75
Full Breakfast
Credit Cards: A, B, C
Notes: 2, 5, 6, 7, 9, 11, 12

A Slice of Home

178 N. Main Street, **Spencer,** 14883
(607) 589-6073

Newly remodeled,150-year old farmhouse with four bedrooms. Country cooking with hearty breakfasts. Located in the Finger Lakes Winery area just twenty minutes from Ithaca and Watkins Glen. Hiking, tenting, bicycle tours, and cross-country skiing. Hospitality is our specialty.

Hostess: Beatrice Brownell
Rooms: 5 (PB) $45-150
Full Breakfast
Credit Cards: none
Notes: 2, 5, 6 (outside), 7, 8, 9, 10, 11, 12

LITTLE FALLS

The Master's House

189 Hilts Road, 13365
(315) 823-0498
E-mail: lritchie@ntcnet.com

John 14:1-4. Experience the warmth and charm of country life in this turn-of-the-century farmhouse situated on 170 acres. The Master's House offers guests breathtaking views in every direction. The Master's House is home to more than eighteen horses and features an art and pottery gallery. *We offer something for everyone in every season.* The home is situated in the heart of central New York State in the beautiful Mohawk Valley. Hiking, biking, fishing, boating, swimming, cross-country/downhill skiing, and snowmobiling are available. You will be staying within an hour and a half's drive of Syracuse, Albany, Cooperstown, Old Forge, and Speculator.

Hostess: Linda Ritchie
Rooms: 3 (1PB; 2SB) $85-90
Full Breakfast
Credit Cards: A, B, D
Notes: 2, 5, 7 (well-behaved, supervised), 8, 9, 10, 11

LONG EDDY

Rolling Marble Guest House

PO Box 33, 12760
(914) 887-6016

Stay right on the beautiful Delaware River in this charming, three-story Victorian with colorful details and wraparound porches. One hundred and nine years old and recently restored, the house is an elegant reminder of Long Eddy's historic past. Small and secluded. You will find this a marvelous place to hole up and do nothing, enjoy the river and the property, or explore the possibilities of many nearby activities. Casual comfort and a bountiful breakfast buffet are part of the magical

welcome; 7 Children welcome; 8 Tennis nearby; 9 Swimming nearby; 10 Golf nearby; 11 Skiing nearby; 12 May be booked through travel agent.

atmosphere created by innkeepers Karen and Peter.

Hosts: Karen Gibbons and Peter Reich
Rooms: 5 (SB) $70
Full Breakfast
Credit Cards: A, B
Notes: 2, 7, 9, 10

MARIDALE

The Old Stageline Stop Bed and Breakfast

PO Box 125, Turnpike Road, 13806
(607) 746-6856

This early-1900s farmhouse, once part of a dairy farm, is high on a hill overlooking the peaceful countryside. Comfortable rooms are decorated tastefully with country furnishings. Guests enjoy a variety of attractions, relaxing on the porch, and taking walks to absorb the beautiful views. A full breakfast and afternoon treats are served with pleasure. Delhi, Oneonta, and Hartwick colleges are nearby. The house is within a short drive of Cooperstown and many other attractions—antiques, fairs, auctions, and historic sites.

Hostess: Rose Rosino
Rooms: 4 (1PB; 3SB) $60-70
Full Breakfast
Credit Cards: A, B
Notes: 2, 5, 7 (over 6), 8, 10, 11 (20-25 miles)

MAYVILLE (CHAUTAUQUA)

The Village Inn Bed and Breakfast

111 S. Erie Street (Route 394), 14757
(716) 753-3583

Turn-of-the-century Victorian home located near the shores of lakes Chautauqua and Erie, three miles from Chautauqua Institution and less than a thirty-minute drive from Peek'n Peak and Cockaigne ski centers. We offer comfort in both single and double rooms in a home furnished with many antiques and trimmed in woodwork crafted by European artisians. In the morning, enjoy a breakfast of homemade waffles, nut kuchen, in-season fruit, coffee, and juice in our sunny breakfast room.

Host: Dean Hanby
Rooms: 3 (SB) $50-60
Full Breakfast
Credit Cards: C
Notes: 2, 5, 6, 7, 8, 9, 10, 11, 12

The Village Inn Bed and Breakfast

MUMFORD

The Genesee Country Inn

PO Box 340, 14511
(716) 538-2500; (800) NYSTAYS (reservations only); FAX (716) 538-4565

Classic, but cozy. Historic stone mill. Nine-room B&B inn with all private baths, some fireplaces, canopy beds, AC, and TV. Serenity and privacy just one mile from Genesee Country Village Museum and thirty minutes from downtown. Woods, waterfalls, and trout fishing on the property. Gourmet breakfasts. Recommended by AAA-3, Mobil-3, and Independent Innkeepers Association. No smoking. Pets in residence.

Hostess: Glenda Barcklow
Rooms: 9 (PB) $85-140
Full Breakfast
Credit Cards: A, B, C, D
Notes: 2, 5, 8, 9, 10, 11

NEW YORK CITY

Alma Mathews House

275 W. 11th Street, 10014
(212) 691-5931 or 5932; FAX (212) 727-9746

A pleasant but inexpensive guest house/conference center for persons in New York for nonprofit business. Located in a quiet corner of Greenwich Village, this splendid facility is offered as an act of stewardship by the Women's Division of the General Board of Global Ministries of the Methodist Church. It accommodates up to thirty-five persons overnight in nineteen rooms—twelve doubles, six singles, and one sofa-couch room. Ideal for meetings—two conference rooms, a common TV lounge, two formal parlors, plus laundry and kitchenette facilities. No meals are served; delicatessen arrangements can be made for groups. Handicap-accessible. Convenient to public transportation and neighborhood restaurants and shops.

Hosts: Alison A. Proft and Victor M. Fontanez
Rooms: 19 (3PB; 16SB) $45-90
Credit Cards: A, B
Notes: 2, 5

NIAGARA FALLS

The Cameo Inn

4710 Lower River Road, Route 18-F, **Lewiston**, 14092
(716) 745-3034
E-mail: cameoinn@juno.com
Web site: http://www.wnydirect.com/cameo

Imagine the ambience of our gracious Queen Anne Victorian authentically furnished with family heirlooms and period antiques, all with a breathtaking view of the Niagara River. Situated on an eighty-foot bluff, the inn offers the tranquillity of days past with the comforts of today. Three lovely guest rooms with shared or private bath are available, as well as our romantic "Riverview Suite." Breakfast is served at Cameo Manor (our other location) each morning. Smoke-free. No pets, please. Come and enjoy.

Hosts: Greg and Carolyn Fisher
Rooms: 4 (2PB; 2SB) $65-115
Full Breakfast
Credit Cards: A, B, D
Notes: 5, 7, 8, 9, 10, 11, 12

Cameo Manor North

3881 Lower River Road (Route 18-F), **Youngstown**, 14174
(716) 745-3034
E-mail: cameoinn@juno.com
Web site: http://www.wnydirect.com/cameo

Located just seven miles north of Niagara Falls, our English manor house is the perfect spot for that quiet getaway you have been dreaming about. Situated on three secluded acres, Cameo Manor North offers a great room with fireplaces, solarium, library, and an outdoor terrace for your enjoyment. Our beautifully appointed guest

welcome; 7 Children welcome; 8 Tennis nearby; 9 Swimming nearby; 10 Golf nearby; 11 Skiing nearby; 12 May be booked through travel agent.

rooms include suites with private sun rooms and cable television. A breakfast buffet is served daily.

Hosts: Greg and Carolyn Fisher
Rooms: 5 (3PB, 2SB) $65-130
Full Breakfast
Credit Cards: A, B, D
Notes: 5, 7, 8, 9, 10, 11, 12

The Country Club Inn

5170 Lewiston Road, **Lewiston**, 14092
(716) 285-4869 (voice and FAX)

Located just minutes from Niagara Falls, The Country Club Inn is a nonsmoking bed and breakfast. Three large and beautifully decorated guest rooms with private bath, queen-size bed, and cable TV. A great room with pool table leads to a covered patio overlooking the golf course. A full breakfast is served at our guests' convenience in our elegant dining room. Conveniently located near the NYS thruway and bridges to Canada.

Hosts: Barbara Ann and Norman Oliver
Rooms: 3 (PB) $75-90
Full Breakfast
Credit Cards: none
Notes: 2, 5, 7, 9, 10

Manchester House Bed and Breakfast

653 Main Street, 14301
(716) 285-5717; (800) 489-3009;
FAX (716) 282-2144

This brick-and-shingle residence was built in 1903 and used as a doctor's residence and office for many years. After extensive renovation, Manchester House opened as a bed and breakfast in 1991. Carl and Lis received a Niagara Falls beautification award for their work. Manchester House is within easy walking distance of the Falls, Aquarium, and Geological Museum. Off-street parking.

Hosts: Lis and Carl Slenk
Rooms: 3 (PB) $60-80
Full Breakfast
Credit Cards: A, B
Notes: 5, 7, 12

OLIVEREA

Slide Mt. Forest House

805 Oliverea Road, 12410
(914) 254-5365

Nestled in the Catskill Mountains State Park, our inn offers the flavor and charm

The Country Club Inn

of the old country. A 1900s farmstead with views of apple orchard lawns, towering evergreens, and gentle mountains. Come enjoy our beautiful country setting, superb lodging, fine dining, and chalet rentals. Family run for more than sixty years, we strive to give you a pleasant and enjoyable stay. German and continental cuisine, lounge, pool, tennis, hiking, fishing, and antiquing available for your pleasure.

Hosts: Ralph and Ursula Combe
Rooms: 21 (17PB; 4SB) $50-70
Full Breakfast
Credit Cards: A, B, D
Notes: 2, 3, 4, 7, 8, 9, 10, 11

ONEONTA

The Murphy House

33 Walnut Street, 13820
(607) 432-1367
E-mail: mmurphy@aol.com

Comfortable accommodations in the historic district of Oneonta, a small, rural city nestled among the hills of upstate New York. This 1920 bed and breakfast home is within walking distance of shops and restaurants. Tastefully prepared breakfasts and hospitality abound. Nearby attractions include college-based activities, national soccer and baseball halls of fame, the beauty of God's four seasons, and cultural events ranging from opera to dancing under the stars. Thirty minutes from Cooperstown, three and a half hours from New York City. Families welcome!

Hosts: Mike and Nancy Murphy
Rooms: 2 (PB) $65-85
Full Breakfast
Credit Cards: none
Notes: 2, 5, 7, 8, 9, 10, 11

PALENVILLE

The Kenmore Country Bed and Breakfast

HCR 1, Box 102, 12463
(518) 678-3494

This quaint country home was built in the late 1800s and is nestled at the bottom of Hunter Mountain. Spend the night in one of our three cozy bedrooms. Enjoy the day relaxing in the large living room or on the screened porch. Close to many attractions. The last operating "boarding house" on "boarding house row." Described by guests as "Greene County's best-kept secret."

Hosts: John and Lauren Hanzl
Rooms: 3 (1PB; 2SB) $50-68
Full Breakfast
Credit Cards: A, B, D
Notes: 5, 7, 9, 10, 11

PECONIC

Home Port Bed and Breakfast

2500 Peconic Lane, 11958
(516) 765-1435

Home Port is a lovely Victorian in the heart of wine country on the North Fork of Long Island. Built in 1876, it has three bedrooms with two shared baths. It features a full continental breakfast served in the dining room or on the front porch in season. One mile from Long Island Sound and Peconic Bay.

Hosts: Pat and Jack Combs
Rooms: 3 (SB) $70-85
Continental Breakfast
Credit Cards: none
Notes: 2, 5, 8, 9, 10

welcome; 7 Children welcome; 8 Tennis nearby; 9 Swimming nearby; 10 Golf nearby; 11 Skiing nearby; 12 May be booked through travel agent.

PINE BUSH

The Milton Bull House

1065 Route 302, 12566
(914) 361-4770

A traditional bed and breakfast. The historic house has nine rooms furnished with antiques. The house is Greek Revival in style. There are two large, airy guest rooms sharing a full bath. Located in the Hudson Valley, there are wonderful opportunities for hiking, rock climbing, shopping, and visits to nearby wineries and churches. Rates include an old-fashioned farm breakfast with home baking.

Hosts: Graham and Ellen Jamison
Rooms: 2 (1PB; 2SB) $64.35
Full Breakfast
Credit Cards: none
Notes: 2, 5, 8, 9, 10, 11

QUEENSBURY (ADIRONDACK AREA)

Crislip's Bed and Breakfast

693 Ridge Road, 12804-9717
(518) 793-6869

Located in the Adirondack area just minutes from Saratoga Springs and Lake George, this landmark Federal home provides spacious accommodations complete with period antiques, four-poster beds, and down comforters. The country breakfast menu features such items as buttermilk pancakes, scrambled eggs, and sausages. Your hosts invite you to relax on their porches and enjoy the beautiful mountain views of Vermont.

Hosts: Ned and Joyce Crislip
Rooms: 3 (PB) $65-75
Full Breakfast
Credit Cards: A, B
Notes: 2, 5, 6 (sometimes), 7, 8, 9, 10, 11, 12

RENSSELAER

Tibbitts House Inn

100 Columbia Turnpike, Routes 9 and 20, 12144
(518) 472-1348

Our inn is a 140-year-old restored farmhouse that has accepted guests for the past seventy years. My grandparents, the Tibbitts, became hosts to travelers then, and we have continued, introducing countless patrons to the pleasures of country living. Our grounds are spacious, tree-filled, and serene. Cheery wallpapers,

Tibbitts House Inn

NOTES: Credit cards accepted: A Master Card; B Visa; C American Express; D Discover; E Diners Club; F Other; 2 Personal checks accepted; 3 Lunch available; 4 Dinner available; 5 Open all year; 6 Pets

handcrafted quilts, and braided and rag rugs complement the guest rooms. Antiques are prevalent and become conversation pieces. Comfortable, cozy, and tranquil—that's Tibbitts House Inn. We are just one and a half miles from Albany, the state capital.

Hosts: Claire and Herb Rufleth
Rooms: 5 (1PB; 4SB) $56-80
Full or Continental Breakfast
Credit Cards: none
Notes: 2, 5, 7, 8, 9, 10

ROUND TOP (PURLING)

Tumblin' Falls House Bed and Breakfast

PO Box 281, 12473
(518) 622-3981 (voice and FAX)
E-mail: tfallsbb@francomm.com
Web site: http://www.thecatskills.com/tumble.htm

Nestled in the hamlet of Purling, where the clear, cool waters of the Shinglekill have drawn visitors since the early 1800s. Hidden among the trees, perched high atop a cliff, sits Tumblin' Falls House. Fall asleep to the soothing sounds of gentle waters. Wake up to a wonderful country breakfast served on the front porch overlooking the falls. In an area rich in history, Greene County offers an abundance of vacation activities for people of all ages: antiquing, bird-watching, hiking, fishing, skiing, and much, much more are nearby.

Hosts: Linda and Hugh Curry
Rooms: 5 (1PB; 4SB) $55-125; weekly rates
   available
Full Breakfast
Credit Cards: A, B, C
Notes: 2, 3, 4, 5, 6, 7, 9, 10, 11, 12

SARATOGA SPRINGS

The Lombardi Farm Bed and Breakfast

41 Locust Grove Road, 12866
(518) 587-2074 (voice and FAX)

Restored Victorian farmhouse just two miles from the center of Saratoga Springs. Newly decorated, private baths, AC, four-course gourmet breakfast, hot tub, and Jacuzzi. Near performing arts center, Skidmore College, National Museum of Racing, National Museum of Dance, mineral baths with massage, pools, lakes, golf, skiing, antiquing, track, and—at the ten-acre state park—bottle-feeding baby goats in the springtime.

Hosts: Dr. Vincent and Kathleen Lombardi
Rooms: 4 (PB) $100-130
Full Gourmet Breakfast
Credit Cards: none
Notes: 2, 5, 7, 8, 9, 10, 11, 12

Six Sisters B&B

149 Union Avenue, 12866
(518) 583-1173; FAX (518) 587-2470

An 1880 Victorian beckons with a relaxing veranda. Within walking distance of museums, city park, downtown, specialty shops, antiques, and restaurants. Spacious rooms, two with whirlpool tubs, three with porches, all with small refrigerators and TVs. King/queen beds. Home-cooked breakfast. Mineral bath and massage package, November-May. Recommended by *The NY Times* and *Gourmet*.

Hostess: Kate Benton
Rooms: 4 (PB) $70-150 (except racing season)
Full Breakfast
Credit Cards: A, B, C, D
Notes: 2, 5, 7 (over 8), 8, 9, 10, 11, 12

welcome; 7 Children welcome; 8 Tennis nearby; 9 Swimming nearby; 10 Golf nearby; 11 Skiing nearby; 12 May be booked through travel agent.

Giddings Garden Bed and Breakfast

SYRACUSE

Giddings Garden B&B

290 W. Seneca Turnpike, 13207
(315) 492-6389; (800) 377-3452

An early morning stroll through the luscious gardens, with the sounds of birds and waterfalls, enhances your appetite for breakfast. We are an upscale, historic B&B, circa 1810. Three rooms, all with exquisite baths with marble and mirrored walls. Queen poster beds, fireplaces, color cable TV, and air-conditioning. Choose your favorite mood: The Honey Room—romantic; The Executive—masculine; The Country Garden—flowery.

Hosts: Pat and Nancie Roberts
Rooms: 3 (3PB) $75-115
Full Gourmet Breakfast
Credit Cards: A, B, C, D
Notes: 2, 5, 7, 8, 9, 10, 11, 12

SYRACUSE AREA

Elaine's Bed and Breakfast Selections

Mailing address: 4987 Kingston Road, **Elbridge** 13060-9773
(315) 689-2082

Elaine's Bed and Breakfast Selections is a reservation service that lists bed and breakfasts in **New York State** in the following towns: Baldwinsville, Cincinnatus, Cleveland on Oneida Lake, DeWitt, Durhamville, Edmeston (Cooperstown), Elbridge, Fayetteville, Geneva, Glen Haven, Gorham, Groton, Homer, Jamesville, Lafayette, Liverpool, Lyons, Marathon (located near Binghamton and Ithaca), Marcellus, Minoa, Naples, Ovid, Owasco Lake, Port Ontario, Rome, Sheldrake-on-Cayuga, Skaneateles, Sodus Bay (on Lake Ontario), South Otselic, Spencer, Syracuse, Tully, Vernon, and Vesper. A descriptive catalog is available for $3 *cash* and a self-addressed, stamped (64 cents' postage) #10 envelope. Elaine N. Samuels, coordinator.

High Meadows Bed and Breakfast

3740 Eager Road, **Jamesville**, 13078
(315) 492-3517
E-mail: nmentz1@aol.com

Enjoy country hospitality at High Meadows, high in the hills ten miles south of Syracuse. We have two guest rooms with a shared bath, a private suite, and a furnished bedroom apartment. Enjoy a plant-filled solarium and wraparound deck with a magnificent fifty-mile view. A continental breakfast featuring fresh fruit, muffins, and homemade jams can be served on the deck, weather permitting. Explore scenic, lush central New York with its many lakes, nature centers, and vineyards.

Hosts: Al and Nancy Mentz
Rooms: 3 + furnished apartment (2PB; 2SB) $55-90
Continental Breakfast
Credit Cards: none
Notes: 2, 5, 7, 9, 10, 11, 12

NOTES: Credit cards accepted: A Master Card; B Visa; C American Express; D Discover; E Diners Club; F Other; 2 Personal checks accepted; 3 Lunch available; 4 Dinner available; 5 Open all year; 6 Pets

UTICA

The Iris Stonehouse Bed and Breakfast

16 Derbyshire Place, 13501-4706
(315) 732-6720; (800) 446-1456;
FAX (315) 732-6854
E-mail: royshirleykilgore@juno.com

Enjoy city charm close to everything, three miles south of I-90, Exit 31. This stone Tudor house has leaded-glass windows that add charm to the eclectic decor of the four guest rooms. A sitting room for guests offers a comfortable area for relaxing, reading, watching television, or just socializing in a smoke-free atmosphere. The Iris Stonehouse has central air-conditioning.

Hosts: Shirley and Roy Kilgore
Rooms: 4 (2PB; 2SB) $50-80
Full Breakfast
Credit Cards: A, B, C, D
Notes: 2, 5, 8, 10, 12

VALLEY FALLS

Maggie Towne's Bed and Breakfast

351 Phillips Road, 12185
(518) 663-8369; (518) 686-7331

This lovely old colonial home is located amid beautiful lawns and trees. Guests may enjoy a cup of tea or glass of wine before the huge fireplace in the family room. Use the music room or curl up with a book on the screened-in porch. Mornings, your host serves home-baked goodies. She gladly will prepare a lunch for you to take on tour or enjoy at the house.

It's twenty miles to historic Bennington, Vermont, and thirty to Saratoga.

Hostess: Margaret D. Towne
Rooms: 3 (SB) $45
Full Breakfast
Credit Cards: none
Notes: 2, 3, 5, 6 (sometimes), 7, 8, 9, 10, 11

WARRENSBURG

White House Lodge

53 Main Street, 12885
(518) 623-3640

An 1847 Victorian home in the heart of the queen village of the Adirondacks, an antiquer's paradise. The Lodge is furnished with many Victorian antiques that send you back in time. Five minutes to Lake George, Fort William Henry, and Great Escape. Walk to restaurants and shopping. Enjoy the air-conditioned television lounge for guests only. Wicker rockers and chairs on front porch. Window and Casablanca fans.

Hosts: Jim and Ruth Gibson
Rooms: 3 (SB) $85 (double bed)
Continental Breakfast
Credit Cards: A, B
Notes: 5, 7 (over 7), 9, 10, 11

WELLESLEY ISLAND

Hart House

PO Box 70, 13640
(315) 482-LOVE (5683) (voice and FAX);
(888) 481-5683
Web site: http://www.1000islands.com/hart

Hart House, a grand cottage before Boldt Castle, features four exquisite guest suites with canopy beds, decorator sheeting,

welcome; 7 Children welcome; 8 Tennis nearby; 9 Swimming nearby; 10 Golf nearby; 11 Skiing nearby; 12 May be booked through travel agent.

whirlpools, fine antiques, and a whisper-quiet peace for your restorations of body, mind, and spirit. A five-course, candle-light breakfast perfectly begins your day in the wonderful 1,000 Islands. The home is only a five-minute drive from I-81 and the Canadian border. We are redefining the term "hospitality."

Hosts: Rev. Dudley and Kathy Danielson
Rooms: 4 (PB) $115-175
Full Five-Course, Gourmet Breakfast
Credit Cards: A, B
Notes: 2, 5, 7, 8, 9, 10, 11, 12

WESTHAMPTON BEACH

1880 House
Bed and Breakfast

2 Seafield Lane, PO Box 648, 11978
(516) 288-1559; (800) 346-3290;
FAX (516) 288-7696
Web site: http://getawaysmag.com

The Seafield House is a hidden, hundred-year-old country retreat perfect for a romantic hideaway, a weekend of privacy, or just a change of pace from city life. Only ninety minutes from Manhattan, Seafield House is ideally situated on Westhampton Beach's exclusive Seafield Lane. The estate includes a swimming pool and tennis court and is a short, brisk walk from the ocean beach. The area offers outstanding restaurants, shops, and opportunities for antique hunting. Indoor tennis, Guerney's International Health Spa, and Montauk Point are nearby.

Hostess: Elsie Collins
Rooms: 3 suites (PB) $100-195
Full Breakfast
Credit Cards: A, B, C
Notes: 5, 8, 9, 10, 12

Ballycove

7 Cox Cove Road, 11978
(516) 288-6774

Ballycove is a quiet, relaxed bed and breakfast overlooking Quantuck Bay. We are part of the "Hamptons," Long Island. We are a short walk from a charming village and a beautiful Atlantic Ocean beach. Two beautiful, large rooms with private baths and TVs. One room with whirlpool private bath, couch, refrigerator, table and chairs. The other overlooks a sixty-foot pool with wonderful landscaping. The home is air-conditioned.

Hostess: Phyllis Noonan
Rooms: 4 (2PB; 2SB)
Full or Continental Breakfast
Credit Cards: none
Notes: 2, 5, 7, 8, 10, 12

WINDHAM

Country Suite
Bed and Breakfast

PO Box 700, 12496
(518) 734-4079

Lovely one-hundred-year-old farmhouse furnished with family heirlooms and antiques, nestled in the Catskill Mountains on ten and a half acres. Renovated by current owners to accommodate guests seeking the quiet charm and ambience of country life and relaxation. Open year-round for those who need "to get away."

Hostesses: Sondra Clark and Lorraine Seidel
Rooms: 7 (5PB; 2SB) $75-139
Full Breakfast
Credit Cards: C
Notes: 2, 5, 7 (well-behaved), 8, 9, 10, 11, 12

NOTES: Credit cards accepted: A Master Card; B Visa; C American Express; D Discover; E Diners Club; F Other; 2 Personal checks accepted; 3 Lunch available; 4 Dinner available; 5 Open all year; 6 Pets

WINDSOR

Country Haven Bed and Breakfast

66 Garrett Road, 13865
(607) 655-1204 (voice and FAX)
E-mail: CntryHaven@aol.com

A restored 1800s farmhouse in a quiet country setting on 350 acres. A haven for today's weary traveler and a weekend hideaway where warm hospitality awaits. Gift shop with food co-op. One mile from Route 17 E., Exit 78, twelve miles east of Binghamton, seven miles from Route 81.

Hostess: Rita Saunders
Rooms: 4 (2PB; 2SB) $45-55
Full Breakfast
Credit Cards: A, B, D
Notes: 2, 5, 7, 9, 10

YOUNGSTOWN

The Mill Glen Inn

1102 Pletcher Road., 14174
(716) 754-4085
E-mail: millgleninn@wzrd.com

You will enjoy a relaxing stay in a quiet country home with fresh flowers and early

The Mill Glen Inn

morning trays in each guest room. Breakfast is served in the Wagner Dining Room or, in season, on the covered porch with a view of our lovely gardens. Our renovated farmhouse was built in 1886 and has been designated an historic property by the Town of Lewiston's Historic Society. Great shopping and restaurants nearby.

Hosts: Peter and Milly Brass
Rooms: 3 (1PB; 2SB) $45-65
Continental Plus Breakfast
Credit Cards: none
Notes: 2, 5, 7, 8, 9, 10, 11, 12

---

welcome; 7 Children welcome; 8 Tennis nearby; 9 Swimming nearby; 10 Golf nearby; 11 Skiing nearby; 12 May be booked through travel agent.

NORTH CAROLINA

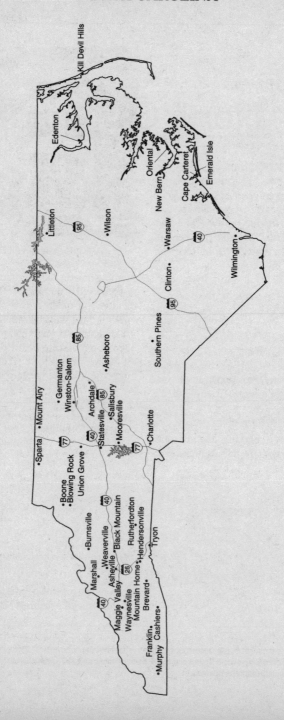

North Carolina

ASHEBORO

The Doctor's Inn

716 S. Park Street, 27203
(910) 625-4916; (910) 625-4822

The Doctor's Inn is a home filled with antiques. It offers its guests the utmost in personal accommodations. Amenities include a gourmet breakfast served on fine china and silver, fresh flowers, terry cloth robes and slippers, and ice cream parfaits. Nearby are more than sixty potteries and the North Carolina Zoo (five miles).

Hosts: Marion and Beth Griffin
Rooms: 2 (1PB; 1SB) $95
Full Breakfast
Credit Cards: none
Notes: 2, 5, 8, 9, 10

The Doctor's Inn

ASHEVILLE

Albemarle Inn

86 Edgemont Road, 28801
(704) 255-0027; (800) 621-7435

A distinguished Greek Revival mansion with an exquisitely carved oak staircase, balcony, paneling, and high ceilings. Located in a beautiful residential area. On the National Register of Historic Places. Spacious, tastefully decorated, comfortable guest rooms with TVs, telephones, AC, and private baths with clawfoot tubs and showers. Delicious full breakfast served in our dining room and on the sunporch. Swimming pool. Unmatched hospitality. AAA three-diamond-rated.

Hosts: Kathy and Dick Hemes
Rooms: 11 (PB) $95-150
Full Breakfast
Credit Cards: A, B, D
Notes: 2, 5, 7 (over 13), 8, 9, 10, 12

Cairn Brae

217 Patton Mountain Road, 28804
(704) 252-9219

A mountain retreat on three secluded acres above Asheville features beautiful views,

---

NOTES: Credit cards accepted: A Master Card; B Visa; C American Express; D Discover; E Diners Club; F Other; 2 Personal checks accepted; 3 Lunch available; 4 Dinner available; 5 Open all year; 6 Pets welcome; 7 Children welcome; 8 Tennis nearby; 9 Swimming nearby; 10 Golf nearby; 11 Skiing nearby; 12 May be booked through travel agent.

walking trails, and a large terrace overlooking Beaver Dam Valley. Homemade full breakfast. Quiet, away from traffic, and only minutes from downtown. Open April through November.

Hosts: Millie and Ed Adams
Rooms: 3 (PB) $95-110
Full Breakfast
Credit Cards: A, B
Notes: 2, 3, 7 (over 10), 8, 9, 10

Dry Ridge Inn

Dry Ridge Inn

26 Brown Street, **Weaverville**, 28787
(704) 658-3899; (800) 839-3899
E-mail: dryridgeinn@msn.com

This casually elegant bed and breakfast is quietly removed, ten minutes north of Asheville's many attractions. Country-style antiques and contemporary art enhance the unique 1800s village farmhouse. A full breakfast is served with individual seating. Relax in our outdoor spa or with quality, spiritual reading after enjoying a day of mountain adventure.

Hosts: Paul and Mary Lou Gibson
Rooms: 7 (PB) $85-120
Full Breakfast
Credit Cards: A, B, C, D
Notes: 2, 5, 7, 9, 10, 11, 12

Old Reynolds Mansion

100 Reynolds Heights, 28804
(704) 254-0496

An antebellum mansion in a country setting. This elegant, restored inn has mountain views from all rooms, huge verandas, wood-burning fireplaces, swimming pool, and AC. A continental breakfast and evening beverage are served. Listed on the National Register of Historic Places. Come see history brought back to life.

Hosts: Fred and Helen Faber
Rooms: 11 (9PB; 2SB)
Continental Breakfast
Credit Cards: none
Notes: 2, 8, 9, 10, 11

Reed House

119 Dodge Street, 28803
(704) 274-1604

This comfortable Queen Anne Victorian with rocking chairs and swings on the porch also has a rocking chair in every room. Breakfast features homemade muffins, rolls, and jams and is served on the porch. Listed on the National Register of Historic Places; near Biltmore Estate. Open May 1 through November 1.

Hostess: Marge Turcot
Rooms: 3 (1PB; 2SB) + 2-BR cottage $50-95
Continental Breakfast
Credit Cards: A, B
Notes: 2, 7, 8, 9, 10, 11

BLACK MOUNTAIN

Friendship Lodge

PO Box 877, 28711
(704) 669-9294 (summer);
(813) 895-4964 (mid-November to mid-May)

A cozy haven in Ridgecrest, within walking distance of the Baptist Conference

Center. We are only five minutes' driving time from Montreat, Christmount, and the Blue Ridge Assembly YMCA Center. Friendship Lodge has ten comfortable guest rooms, most of which offer two double beds. A full breakfast is included in the price. We can accommodate up to twenty-four people. The Lodge is open from Memorial Day weekend until mid-November.

Hosts: Bob and Sarah LaBrant
Rooms: 10 (8PB; 2SB) $50-55
Full Breakfast
Credit Cards: none
Notes: 2, 7, 8, 9, 10

The Inn at Ragged Gardens

BLOWING ROCK

The Inn at Ragged Gardens

203 Sunset Drive, 28605
(704) 295-9703
E-mail: Ragged-Gardens.INN@BlowingRock.com
Web site: http://Raged-Gardens.com

Surrounded by an acre of formal and "ragged" gardens, our 1900s manor-style house offers an enchanting hideaway in the heart of the village of Blowing Rock. Each of our eight guest rooms is complete with a ceiling fan, goose-down comforters and pillows, and a whirlpool bath, complemented by a beautiful breakfast. We look forward to welcoming everyone into our hundred-year-old home filled with God's presence.

Hosts: Lee and Jama Hyett
Rooms: 8 (PB) $105-150
Full Breakfast
Credit Cards: A, B
Notes: 2, 5, 7 (over 12), 8, 9, 10, 11, 12

BOONE

The Gragg House

Kalmia Acres, 210 Ridge Point Drive, 28607
(704) 264-7289

Located ten minutes from the beautiful Blue Ridge Parkway and blessed with mountain views, The Gragg House opens to a lush landscape of native wildflowers and rhododendron. Bird songs are nearly the only sound to break the silence of this secluded getaway. Hospitality at the Gragg House is an important supplement to the home's glorious setting. Your hosts like to offer friendly small touches without imposing too much activity or attention on guests who would rather be alone. A sumptuous breakfast can always truly be the unexpected.

Hosts: Judy and Robert Gragg
Rooms: 3 (1PB; 2SB) $75-95
Full Gourmet Breakfast
Credit Cards: none
Notes: 2, 5, 7 (by prior arrangement), 8, 9, 10, 11, 12

welcome; 7 Children welcome; 8 Tennis nearby; 9 Swimming nearby; 10 Golf nearby; 11 Skiing nearby; 12 May be booked through travel agent.

BREVARD

The Red House Inn Bed and Breakfast

412 Probart Street, 28712
(704) 884-9349

The Red House was built in 1851 and has served as a trading post, a railroad station, the county's first courthouse, and the first post office. It has been lovingly restored and is now open to the public. Charmingly furnished with turn-of-the-century antiques. Convenient to the Blue Ridge Parkway, Brevard Music Center, and Asheville's Biltmore Estate. Closed January through March.

Hostess: Lynne Ong
Rooms: 7 (5PB; 2SB) $45-79
Full Breakfast
Credit Cards: A, B
Notes: 2, 5, 8, 9, 10, 12

The Red House Inn

Womble Inn

301 W. Main Street, 28712
(704) 884-4770

Relax in a welcoming, comfortable atmosphere. Each guest room is especially furnished in antiques and decorated to make you feel cared for. All guest rooms have private baths and air-conditioning. Your breakfast will be served to you on a silver tray, or you may prefer to be seated in the dining room. The inn is one-half mile from the exciting Brevard Music Center.

Hosts: Beth and Steve Womble
Rooms: 6 (PB) $62
Continental Breakfast
Credit Cards: A, B, D
Notes: 2, 3, 4 (Thursday/Friday), 5, 7, 8, 9, 10

BURNSVILLE

A Little Bit of Heaven

937 Bear Wallow Road, 28714
(704) 675-5379; FAX (704) 675-0364

Get away from the day-to-day routine for a while and enjoy "A Little Bit of Heaven." This charming home offers spectacular mountain views all around. Guest rooms are beautifully decorated and furnished with queen or twin beds and private baths. While guests visit, they can enjoy an abundance of activities in the area or just relax around the house and be pampered by the warm hospitality of their hosts.

Hosts: John and Shelley Johnson
Rooms: 4 (PB) $65-85
Full Breakfast
Credit Cards: A, B
Notes: 2, 5, 7, 8, 9, 10, 11

Nu Wray Inn

Town Square, PO Box 156, 28714
(704) 682-2329; FAX (704) 682-2661

Historic country inn since 1833. Nestled in the Blue Ridge Mountains in a quaint town square setting, thirty miles northeast of Asheville. Close to Mt. Mitchell, Blue Ridge Parkway, Grandfather Mountain, antiques, golf, crafts, hiking, and fishing—

NOTES: Credit cards accepted: A Master Card; B Visa; C American Express; D Discover; E Diners Club; F Other; 2 Personal checks accepted; 3 Lunch available; 4 Dinner available; 5 Open all year; 6 Pets

or relax on the porch. Hearty breakfast, afternoon refreshments; our nationally famous family-style dinners are available.

Hosts: Doug and Barb Brown
Rooms: 26 (22PB; 4SB) $75-110
Full Country Breakfast
Credit Cards: A, B, C, D
Notes: 2, 4, 5, 7, 8, 9, 10, 11, 12

CAPE CARTERET

Harborlight Guest House

332 Live Oak Drive, 28584
(919) 393-6868 (voice and FAX);
(800) 624-VIEW

The Harborlight, located on the central North Carolina coast, is situated on a peninsula; thus, all suites offer panoramic water views. All suites also offer private entrances and private baths; luxury suites feature two-person Jacuzzis, fireplaces, and in-room breakfast. The guest house is minutes from area beaches, secluded island excursions, and the outdoor drama "Worthy is the Lamb"—a passion play that depicts the life of Christ.

Hosts: Bobby and Anita Gill
Rooms: 9 (PB) $75-175
Full Breakfast
Credit Cards: A, B, C
Notes: 5, 8, 9, 10

CASHIERS

Millstone Inn

Highway 64 W., PO Box 949, 28717
(704) 743-2737; (888) 645-5786;
FAX (704) 743-0208

Selected by *Country Inns* magazine as one of the best twelve inns, Millstone Inn

has breathtaking views of the Nantahala forest. The exposed beams are complemented by the carefully selected antiques and artwork. Enjoy a gourmet breakfast in our glass-enclosed dining room overlooking Whiteside Mountain. Located at 3,500 feet, it's always cool for a hike to the nearby Silver Slip Falls—or enjoy the nearby golf, tennis, restaurants, and antique shops.

Hosts: Paul and Patricia Collins
Rooms: 11 (PB) $84-154
Full Breakfast
Credit Cards: A, B, C, D
Notes: 2, 8, 9, 10, 11, 12

The Elizabeth Bed and Breakfast

CHARLOTTE

The Elizabeth Bed and Breakfast

2145 E. 5th Street, 28204
(704) 358-1368

This 1923 lavender "lady" is located in historic Elizabeth, second-oldest neighborhood in Charlotte. European country-style rooms are beautifully appointed with antiques, ceiling fans, decorator linens, and unique collections. All rooms have central air and private baths; some have TV

welcome; 7 Children welcome; 8 Tennis nearby; 9 Swimming nearby; 10 Golf nearby; 11 Skiing nearby; 12 May be booked through travel agent.

and phones. Enjoy a generous full or continental breakfast, then relax in our garden courtyard, complete with a charming gazebo, or stroll beneath giant oak trees to convenient restaurants and shopping. Nearby attractions include the Mint Museum of Art, Blumenthal Performing Arts Center, Discovery Place, and professional sporting events.

Hostess: Joan Mastny
Rooms: 4 (PB) $69-89
Full or Continental Breakfast
Credit Cards: A, B
Notes: 2, 5, 9, 12

The Homeplace Bed and Breakfast

5901 Sardis Road, 28270
(704) 365-1936; FAX (704) 366-2729

This restored 1902 country Victorian with wraparound porch and tin roof is nestled among two and one half wooded acres. Secluded "cottage-style" gardens with a gazebo, brick walkways, and a 1930s log barn further enhance this nostalgic oasis in southeast Charlotte. Experienced innkeepers offer a full breakfast. Opened in

The Homeplace Bed and Breakfast

1984, the Homeplace is a "reflection of the true bed and breakfast."

Hosts: Peggy and Frank Dearien
Rooms: 3 (PB) $105-135
Full Breakfast
Credit Cards: A, B, C
Notes: 2, 5, 7 (over 10), 12

Victorian Villa

10925 Windy Grove Road, 28208
(704) 394-5545

A beautifully restored Victorian home located on Lake Wylie. Victorian Villa has four fireplaces, stained-glass windows, a relaxing sunporch, and a gazebo. Unwind by the pool and Jacuzzi, drop a fishing line in by the dock, or enjoy a breathtaking sunset overlooking the lake. Gracious guest rooms and suites decorated with 18th-century antiques, each designed with your comfort in mind. Conveniently located to the airport, coliseum, Panther stadium, convention center, and Carowinds; easily accessible to interstates.

Hosts: Chan, Nancy and Amy Thompson
Rooms: 6 (4PB; 2SB) $89-199
Full Breakfast
Credit Cards: A, B, C
Notes: 2, 5, 7 (12 and older), 9

CLINTON

The Shield House Inn

216 Sampson Street, 28328
(910) 592-2634; (800) 462-9817;
FAX (910) 592-2929

The Shield House Inn consists of two estates. The Shield House, circa 1916, is reminiscent of *Gone With the Wind.*

Courthouse Inn, circa 1818, is a charmingly restored courthouse that once was described as "the most glorious courthouse in North Carolina." Both are listed on the National Register of Historic Places and have spacious rooms, Victorian antiques, wraparound porches, and rockers for your enjoyment.

Hosts: Anita Green and Juanita McLamb
Rooms: 6 (PB) $55-100
Full Breakfast
Credit Cards: A, B, C, D, E
Notes: 2, 5, 7 and 10 (by prior arrangement), 8, 12

Captain's Quarters Inn

EDENTON

Albemarle House

204 W. Queen Street, 27932
(919) 482-8204

Enjoy welcoming refreshments on the porch or in the parlor of our circa-1900 country Victorian home. Located in Edenton's historic district, we are just two blocks from the Albemarle Sound. Our air-conditioned home is furnished with antiques and reproductions, stenciling, artwork, quilts, and collections. The three spacious guest rooms are complete with queen beds, TVs, and private baths. A family suite is available. Coffee awaits outside your door each morning. An elegant full breakfast is served by candlelight. Bicycles and sailing cruises are offered to guests.

Hosts: Marijane and Reuel Schappel
Rooms: 4 (PB) $75
Full Breakfast
Credit Cards: A, B
Notes: 2, 5, 7 (over 10), 8, 9, 10

Captain's Quarters Inn

202 W. Queen Street, 27932
(919) 482-8945; (800) 482-8945

The Captain's Quarters Inn is a seventeen-room, circa-1907 home in the Edenton historic district with a sixty-five-foot wraparound front porch (swings and rockers). Eight charming bedrooms are offered with modern, private baths (seven have queen beds, two twin beds). We serve plenty of gourmet food, including welcome refreshments, continental breakfast, and a full three-course breakfast, as well as a gourmet dinner on weekends. Sailing is offered in the spring, summer, and fall months; mystery weekends are staged in the fall, winter, and spring. Bicycles are available for our guests to use. We are located within walking distance of the waterfront, visitors center, quaint shops, and fine restaurants.

Hosts: Bill and Phyllis Pepper
Rooms: 8 (PB) $80-95
Full and Continental Breakfast
Credit Cards: A, B
Notes: 2, 4, 5, 7 (8 and older), 8, 9, 10, 12

welcome; 7 Children welcome; 8 Tennis nearby; 9 Swimming nearby; 10 Golf nearby; 11 Skiing nearby; 12 May be booked through travel agent.

The Lords Proprietors' Inn

300 N. Broad Street, 27932
(919) 482-3641; FAX (919) 482-2432
E-mail: reserv@lordspropedenton.com
Web site: http://lordspropedenton.com

Historic Edenton's finest lodging since 1982. Twenty spacious and beautifully decorated rooms. Chef Kevin Yokley offers guests the opportunity to partake in northeastern North Carolina's best dining, Tuesday through Saturday evenings. Full breakfast each morning.

Hosts: Arch and Jane Edwards
Rooms: 20 (PB) $185-235 (MAP, Tuesday-
    Saturday; includes dinner)
Full Breakfast
Credit Cards: none
Notes: 4, 5, 7, 8, 9, 10, 12

Trestle House Inn at Willow Tree Farm

632 Soundside Road, 27932
(919) 482-2282; (800) 645-8466;
FAX (919) 482-7003
E-mail: thinn@coastalnet.com
Web site: www.edenton.com/trestlehouse

A bed and breakfast on a wildlife refuge surrounded on three sides by water in historic Edenton. Birding, canoeing, biking, hiking, touring, sight-seeing, and relaxing are our guests' favorite activities. Edenton was the original colonial capital of North Carolina.

Hosts: Peter L. Bogus and Wendy S. Jewett
Rooms: 5 (PB) $80-100
Full Breakfast
Credit Cards: A, B, C
Notes: 2, 5, 7, 8, 9, 10, 12

EMERALD ISLE

Emerald Isle Inn And B&B by the Sea

502 Ocean Drive, 28594
(919) 354-3222 (voice and FAX)

Located at the ocean, this jewel of a Crystal Coast inn is truly a treasure to be discovered. A peaceful haven to all who seek a quiet, restful, and sun-filled getaway. Your stay includes a full gourmet breakfast with freshly ground coffee and other tempting samplings. Suites include Victorian, French country, tropical, and our new luxury suite. New Oceanview king bed suite, porch rockers. All suites have private entrances and bathrooms. Swings and porches with ocean and sound views add to your enjoyment. With direct beach access, you are only steps away from discovering the gentle shoreline treasures. We are only minutes from antiquing, fine restaurants, historic sites and the outdoor drama passion play "Worthy is the Lamb." Come to your home away from home for a visit you'll always remember!

Host: Marilyn Detwiller
Rooms: 4 (PB) $75-115
Full Breakfast
Credit Cards: A, B
Notes: 2, 5, 7, 8, 9, 10

FRANKLIN

Heritage Inn

43 Heritage Hollow Drive, 28734
(704) 524-4150; (888) 524-4150
E-mail: heritage@dnet.net
Web site: http://www.intertekweb.com/heritage

Southern hospitality awaits you at this tin-roofed country inn. Each of the immacu-

---

NOTES: Credit cards accepted: A Master Card; B Visa; C American Express; D Discover; E Diners Club; F Other; 2 Personal checks accepted; 3 Lunch available; 4 Dinner available; 5 Open all year; 6 Pets

Heritage Inn

late, tastefully furnished bedrooms has its own bath, entrance and porch. Located in a quiet, in-town, private village close to everything. Relax in the veranda's rockers while listening to the cascading waterfall. The inn is a perfect place to enjoy the beauty and serenity of the Smoky Mountains. AAA- and Mobil-approved.

Hostess: Sally Wade
Rooms: 6 + apartment (PB) $65-75
Full or Continental Breakfast
Credit Cards: A, B
Notes: 5, 8, 9, 10, 11

Lullwater Retreat

88 Lullwater Road, 28734
(704) 524-6532; FAX (704) 369-7879
E-mail: rsmithlw@dnet.net

The 120-year-old farmhouse and cabins are located on a river and creek in a peaceful mountain cove. Hiking trails, river swimming, tubing, and other activities are on the premises. A retreat center for church groups and family reunions. Guests cook their own meals or visit nearby restaurants. Chapel, rocking chairs, wonderful views, and games. Christian videos and reading materials are supplied.

Hosts: Robert and Virginia Smith
Rooms: 10 (5PB; 5SB) $39-50
Self-serve Breakfast
Credit Cards: none
Notes: 2, 5, 7, 9, 10, 11, 12

HENDERSONVILLE

Apple Inn

1005 White Pine Drive, 28739
(704) 693-0107; (800) 615-6611

There's no place like home—unless it's the Apple Inn! Only two miles from downtown Hendersonville, the Inn is situated on three acres featuring charmingly comfortable rooms, each with modern private baths that await your arrival. Delicious home-cooked breakfasts, fresh flowers, and antiques complement the ambience of this turn-of-the-century home. Enjoy billards, tennis, swimming, hiking, antiquing, bird-watching, or just plain relaxing. Create tomorrow's memories amidst yesterday's charm!

Hosts: Bob and Pam Hedstrom
Rooms: 5 + cottage (PB) $79-89
Full Breakfast
Credit Cards: A, B
Notes: 2, 5, 7, 8, 9, 10, 11, 12

Apple Inn

The Claddagh Inn

755 N. Main Street, 28792
(704) 697-7778; (800) 225-4700;
FAX (704) 697-8664

The Claddagh Inn, Hendersonville's first bed and breakfast, is located just two blocks from the beautiful Main Street

welcome; 7 Children welcome; 8 Tennis nearby; 9 Swimming nearby; 10 Golf nearby; 11 Skiing nearby; 12 May be booked through travel agent.

Promenade. All guest rooms have private baths, telephones, air-conditioning, and TVs. Guests awaken to a full country Irish breakfast, relax in the library and parlor with an evening sherry or just enjoy the charm of rocking on the veranda. Listed on the National Register of Historic Places. AAA-approved. Group catering available for parties and meetings.

Hosts: August, Geraldine and Maryann Emanuele
Rooms: 14 (PB) $79-120
Full Breakfast
Credit Cards: A, B, C, D, E
Notes: 2, 5, 7, 8, 9, 10, 12

The Waverly Inn

783 N. Main, 28792
(704) 693-9193; (800) 537-8195;
FAX (704) 692-1010
E-mail: waverlyinn@ioa.com
Web site: http://www.waverly.com

Listed on the National Register, this is the oldest inn in Hendersonville. Recently renovated, there is something for everyone including claw-foot tubs, king and queen canopy beds, a suite, telephones, rocking chairs, and sitting rooms. All rooms have private baths. Enjoy our complimentary soft drinks and fresh-baked goods. Walk to exceptional restaurants, antique stores, and shopping. Biltmore Estate, the Blue Ridge Parkway, and Connemara are nearby. Full country breakfast included in rates. Rated as one of 1993's top ten bed and breakfasts in the U.S. by *INNovations*.

Hosts: John and Diane Sheiry, Darla Olmstead
Rooms: 14 (PB) $79-185
Full Breakfast
Credit Cards: A, B, C, D
Notes: 2, 5, 7, 8, 9, 10, 12

HIGH POINT

The Bouldin House

4332 Archdale Road, 27263
(910) 431-4909; (800) 739-1816;
FAX (910) 431-4914
E-mail: lmiller582@aol.com
Web site: http://www.bbonline.com/nc/bouldin

Our finely crafted and lovingly restored, historic bed and breakfast sits on three acres of a former tobacco farm. Quiet, country atmosphere; casual and relaxed, yet elegant. Warmly decorated rooms combine old and new, each with spacious, modern, private baths. Awaken to early morning coffee/tea service. Follow the aroma of our generous, home-cooked breakfast to the oak-paneled dining room. America's largest concentration of furniture showrooms are only minutes away. Come, indulge yourself.

Hosts: Ann and Larry Miller
Rooms: 4 (PB) $85-95
Full Gourmet Breakfast
Credit Cards: A, B, D
Notes: 2, 5, 8, 10, 12

KILL DEVIL HILLS

Cherokee Inn

500 N. Virginia Dare Trail, 27948
(919) 441-6127; (800) 554-2764;
FAX (919) 441-1072

Our beach house, located at Nags Head Beach on the Outer Banks of North Carolina, is six hundred feet from the ocean. Fine food, history, sports, and adventure galore. We welcome you for a restful, active, or romantic getaway. Enjoy the cy-

NOTES: Credit cards accepted: A Master Card; B Visa; C American Express; D Discover; E Diners Club; F Other; 2 Personal checks accepted; 3 Lunch available; 4 Dinner available; 5 Open all year; 6 Pets

press walls, white ruffled curtains, and wraparound porch.

Hosts: Bob and Kaye Combs
Rooms: 6 (PB) $75-105
Continental Breakfast
Credit Cards: A, B, C
Notes: 2, 9, 12

LITTLETON (LAKE GASTON)

Littleton's Maplewood Manor Bed and Breakfast

120 College Street, PO Box 1165, 27850
(919) 586-4682

A small hometown B&B offering you a nice, clean, spacious room with king or twin beds, shared bath, and full breakfast. There are books, games, videos, CDs, and tapes. There will be tea in the afternoon, wine and crackers in the evening. The grounds are parklike; benches and chairs are placed around for guests to use. The screened porch is a great place for relaxation. Multinight and multiroom discounts.

Hosts: Helen and Alan Burtchell
Rooms: 2 (SB) $55-60
Full Breakfast
Credit Cards: A, B
Notes: 5, 9, 10

MAGGIE VALLEY

Smokey Shadows Lodge

PO Box 444, Ski Mt. Road, 28751
(704) 926-0001

Very warm and friendly mountaintop lodge. The view is wonderful! We host candlelight dinners, rustic and wonderful family reunions, weddings, church and youth events. Only two miles to the ski slope. You can rent the whole lodge and

use the kitchen. Dinner available for $16.50. No smoking.

Hosts: Bud and Ginger Shinn and Family
Rooms: 11 (PB) $70-100
Continental Breakfast
Credit Cards: A, B
Notes: 2, 3, 4, 5, 7, 8, 10, 11, 12

MARSHALL

Marshall House Bed and Breakfast

5 Hill Street, PO Box 865, 28753
(704) 649-9205; FAX (704) 649-2999

Built in 1903, the inn overlooks the peaceful town of Marshall and the French Broad River. This country inn, listed on the National Historic Register, is decorated with fancy chandeliers, antiques, and pictures. Four fireplaces, formal dining room, parlor, and upstairs TV/reading room. Enjoy storytelling about the house, the town, the people, and the history. Loving house pets, the toot of a train, and good service make your visit a unique experience.

Hosts: Ruth and Jim Boylan
Rooms: 9 (2PB; 7SB) $39.50-75
Continental Plus Breakfast
Credit Cards: A, B, C, D, E
Notes: 3, 4, 5, 6, 7, 9, 10, 11, 12

MOORESVILLE (LAKE NORMAN)

Spring Run Bed and Breakfast

172 Spring Run, Lake Norman, 28117
(704) 664-6686

Enjoy an award-winning, three-course, gourmet breakfast at this home on Lake

---

welcome; 7 Children welcome; 8 Tennis nearby; 9 Swimming nearby; 10 Golf nearby; 11 Skiing nearby; 12 May be booked through travel agent.

Norman, which hosts many great lakeside eateries. Each guest room has a private bath, cable TV and free movie channel. Amenities include an exercise room with game table, paddle boat, lake swimming, boat hook-up at the pier, and fishing. Enjoy a round of golf at the course across the street. We are twenty-five minutes north of Charlotte, twenty minutes south of I-40. Spring Run Bed and Breakfast has been awarded three diamonds from the AAA, and for six years in a row has earned a perfect score from the BOH.

Hostess: Mary Farley
Rooms: 2 (PB) $95
Full Gourmet Breakfast
Credit Cards: A, B
Notes: 2, 5, 8, 9, 10, 12

MOUNTAIN HOME

Mountain Home Bed and Breakfast

PO Box 234, 28758
(704) 697-9090; (800) 397-0066;
FAX (704) 698-2477

Between Asheville and Hendersonville, near the airport. Antiques and Oriental-style rugs grace this English-style home. Large, marble porch and rocking chairs to relax the day or night away. Cable TV and phones in rooms. Some rooms have private entrance. Full candlelight break-

Mountain Home Bed and Breakfast

fast. Convenient to Biltmore Estate (on its preferred lodging list), Chimney Rock, Pisgah National Forest, Carl Sandburg Home, and much more. Wheelchair ramp to front and one room.

Hosts: Judy Brown and Pat Scoggins
Rooms: 7 (PB) $85-180
Full Breakfast
Credit Cards: A, B
Notes: 2, 5, 8, 10, 12

MT. AIRY

The Merritt House Bed and Breakfast

618 N. Main Street, 27030
(910) 786-2174; (800) 290-6290;
FAX (910) 786-2174
E-mail: dmac2895@advi.net
Web site: http://www.bbonline.com/nc/ncbbi

The Merritt House, completed in 1901, is in the downtown historic district. The house consists of twelve rooms decorated with local and family antiques. The smokehouse spa room is featured. Come and see where Andy Griffith was born and raised. You can find our home page at www.bbonline.com/nc/ncbbi; look for us under the Piedmont Central.

Hosts: Rich and Pat Mangels
Rooms: 4 (PB) $65-90
Full Breakfast
Credit Cards: A, B
Notes: 2, 5, 7, 10

MURPHY

Park Place B&B

100 Hill Street, 28906
(704) 837-8842

Welcome to your home away from home! For your comfort, Park Place—a two-

---

NOTES: Credit cards accepted: A Master Card; B Visa; C American Express; D Discover; E Diners Club; F Other; 2 Personal checks accepted; 3 Lunch available; 4 Dinner available; 5 Open all year; 6 Pets

story clapboard/brick house, circa 1900—offers three well-appointed guest rooms and serves a full gourmet breakfast. Hosts Rikki and Neil greatly enjoy sharing with guests the home's congenial atmosphere and its eclectic decor of family treasures, antiques, collectibles, and hand-knotted Oriental rugs. While relaxing on the screened, treetop-level porch, guests love shooting the breeze or just rocking the time away. *Willkommen—Wir sprechen Deutsch!*

Hosts: Rikki and Neil Wocell
Rooms: 3 (PB) $60-70
Full Breakfast
Credit Cards: none
Notes: 2, 5, 8, 9, 10

NEW BERN

The Aerie Inn

509 Pollock Street, 28562
(919) 636-5553 (voice and FAX); (800) 849-5553

Just one block from the Tryon Palace in the heart of the historic district, the Aerie offers the closest accommodations to all of New Bern's historic attractions. The Victorian inn is furnished with antiques and reproductions, yet each of the seven individually decorated guest rooms has a modern private bathroom, telephone, and color TV. Complimentary beverages are offered throughout your stay, and generous breakfasts await you each morning, served in the dining room.

Hosts: Howard and Dee Smith
Rooms: 7 (PB) $79-99
Full Breakfast
Credit Cards: A, B, C, D
Notes: 2, 5, 7, 8, 9, 10, 12

Howard House Victorian Bed and Breakfast

Howard House Victorian Bed and Breakfast

207 Pollock Street, 28560
(919) 514-6709; (800) 705-5261;
FAX (919) 514-6710
E-mail: howardhouse@coastalnet.com

Step back in time to a more gracious and elegant era by staying in this 1890 Victorian-style bed and breakfast. Located in the downtown historic district of New Bern, the Howard House is within walking distance of the riverfront, a variety of restaurants, historic homes, and sites like Tryon Place and specialty shops. The Wynns offer desserts, refreshments, and good conversation on the front porch or in the parlor as you return from a busy day around town. A bountiful breakfast is served each morning in the formal dining room. We await your arrival. . . .

Hosts: Steven and Kimberly Wynn
Rooms: 3 (PB) $85-95
Full Breakfast
Credit Cards: A, B, C, D
Notes: 2, 5, 9, 10

welcome; 7 Children welcome; 8 Tennis nearby; 9 Swimming nearby; 10 Golf nearby; 11 Skiing nearby; 12 May be booked through travel agent.

Magnolia House of New Bern

315 George Street, 28560
(916) 633-9488 (voice and FAX); (800) 601-9488

We invite you to romance yourselves with a stay at New Bern's Magnolia House. You may choose from three uniquely decorated guest rooms, each with private bath. Located two doors from Tryon Place, once home to the royal governor of North Carolina, you will find Magnolia House centrally located in the heart of the historic district. Fine restaurants, quaint shops, museums, and antiquing are within walking distance. Magnolia House is furnished with local estate antiques and family pieces. A full breakfast is served at your convenience. You may choose to have it served under the magnolia tree for which the inn is named. Honeymoon and anniversary packages are our specialties. Gift certificates are available.

Hosts: Kim and John Trudo
Rooms: 3 (PB) $90-100
Full Breakfast
Credit Cards: A, B, C, D
Notes: 2, 5, 7 (over 8), 10, 12

ORIENTAL

The Tar Heel Inn

PO Box 176, 28571
(919) 249-1078

The Tar Heel Inn is more than one hundred years old and has been restored to capture the atmosphere of an English country inn. Guest rooms have four-poster or canopy king and queen beds. Patios and bicycles are for guests' use. Five churches are within walking distance. Tennis, fishing, and golf are nearby. This quiet fishing village is known as the sailing capital of the Carolinas. Sailing cruises can be arranged, and there are great restaurants. Smoking on porch and patios only. Three-diamond AAA rating.

Hosts: Shawna and Robert Hyde
Rooms: 8 (PB) $70-90
Full Breakfast
Credit Cards: A, B, D
Notes: 2, 5, 7 (by arrangement), 8, 9, 10, 12

The Tar Heel Inn

RUTHERFORDTON

Carrier Houses Bed and Breakfast

415-423 N. Main, 28139
(704) 287-4222

Tinner-carpenter Garland Carrier came to Rutherfordton in the 1800s seeking a better climate for his asthma. Two of the five known homes he built are side-by-side on Main Street. The Carrier-McBrayer House has three bedrooms and is the residence of the owners. The Carrier-Ward House has five bedrooms, a sitting/reception room, a fully equipped kitchen, and a large dining room. The Carrier-Ward

---

NOTES: Credit cards accepted: A Master Card; B Visa; C American Express; D Discover; E Diners Club; F Other; 2 Personal checks accepted; 3 Lunch available; 4 Dinner available; 5 Open all year; 6 Pets

House is available for meetings, receptions, anniversaries, reunions, and other formal gatherings, as well as guest quarters. Authentic Victorian-style decor and antique furnishings. Two rooms have feather mattresses. Phone in each room, fireplaces. Private TV available on request.

Hosts: Boyce and Barbara Hodge
Rooms: 8 (PB) $60
Continental Plus Breakfast

SALISBURY

Rowan Oak House

208 S. Fulton Street, 28144-4845
(704) 633-2086; (800) 786-0437;
FAX (704) 633-2084
Web site: http://www.bbonline.com/nc/rowanoak

An elegant high Victorian located in the historic district. Stained and leaded glass, seven fireplaces, wraparound porch, and gardens adorn this one-hundred-year-old mansion. Each of four bedrooms is lavishly furnished with antiques, sitting area, desk, phone, duvet with down comforter, reading lights, fruit, and flowers. All have private baths (one with double Jacuzzi). Central AC and heat. Color TV, books, magazines, and board games are in upstairs parlor. Smoking limited. Full gourmet breakfast served. Close to furniture shopping and Charlotte Motor Speedway. Walking distance to downtown churches, antique shopping, historic buildings, and fine restaurants.

Hosts: Barbara and Les Coombs
Rooms: 4 (PB) $85-125
Full Breakfast
Credit Cards: A, B, C, D
Notes: 2, 5, 7 (over 12), 8, 9, 10, 12

Knollwood House

SOUTHERN PINES

Knollwood House

1495 W. Connecticut Avenue, 28387
(910) 692-9390; FAX (910) 692-0609

The English manor house stands among five acres of longleaf pines, dogwoods, azaleas, towering holly trees, and forty-foot magnolias. From a terrace where Glenn Miller's orchestra once gave a concert, Knollwood's lawns roll down to the fifteenth fairway of a famous golf course. Furnished with late-18th-century/early-19th-century antiques, both suites and guest rooms are available. Special golf package rates are available on request.

Hosts: Dick and Mimi Beatty
Rooms: 6 (PB) $80-150
Full Breakfast
Credit Cards: A, B
Notes: 2, 5, 7 (over 10), 8, 9, 10, 12

SPARTA

Turby Villa
Bed and Breakfast

2072 NC Highway 18 N., 28675
(910) 372-8490

At three thousand feet, this contemporary two-story home is the centerpiece of a

welcome; 7 Children welcome; 8 Tennis nearby; 9 Swimming nearby; 10 Golf nearby; 11 Skiing nearby; 12 May be booked through travel agent.

twenty-acre farm located two miles from town. The house is surrounded by an acre of trees and manicured lawn with a lovely view of the Blue Ridge Mountains. Breakfast is served on the enclosed porch with white wicker furnishings or in the formal dining room with Early American furnishings. Mrs. Mimi Turbiville takes justifiable pride in her attractive, well-maintained bed and breakfast.

Hostess: Maybelline R. Turbiville
Rooms: 3 (PB) $35 single, $50 couple
Full Breakfast
Credit Cards: none
Notes: 2, 5, 7, 8, 10

STATESVILLE

Cedar Hill Farm

778 Elmwood Road, 28677
(704) 873-4332; (800) 948-4423

An 1840 farmhouse and private cottages on a thirty-two-acre sheep farm in the rolling hills of North Carolina. Antique furnishings, air-conditioning, cable TV, and phones in rooms. After your full country breakfast, swim, play badminton, or relax in a porch rocker or hammock. For a

Cedar Hill Farm

busier day, visit two lovely towns with historic districts, Old Salem, or two larger cities in a forty-five-mile radius. Convenient to restaurants, shopping, and three interstate highways.

Hosts: Brenda and Jim Vernon
Rooms: 3 (PB) $60-95
Full Breakfast
Credit Cards: A, B
Notes: 2, 5, 6 (limited), 7, 9, 10, 12

Madelyn's in the Grove

PO Box 298, 1836 West Memorial Highway,
Union Grove, 28689
(704) 539-4151; (800) 948-4473;
FAX (704) 539-4080
E-mail: madelyns@yadtel.com

Listen to the birds and unwind. We have moved our B&B to Union Grove, only fifteen minutes north of Statesville and I-40, and only two minutes from I-77, Exit 65. There are many things to see and do. After a fun-filled day, come back and have cheese and crackers and a glass of lemonade. Sit on one of the porches or the gazebo, watch the stars, and be glad you are at Madelyn's in the Grove. Personal checks preferred.

Hosts: Madelyn and John Hill
Rooms: 5 (PB) $75-135
Full Breakfast
Credit Cards: A, B, C
Notes: 2, 5, 7, 10, 12

TRYON

The Fox Trot Inn

PO Box 1561, 28782
(704) 859-9706

This lovingly restored residence, circa 1915, is situated on six wooded acres

The Fox Trot Inn

within the city limits of Tryon. It is convenient to everything, yet secluded with a quietly elegant atmosphere. Guests are treated to a full gourmet breakfast; heated swimming pool; and fully furnished guest house with two bedrooms, kitchen, living room, fireplace, deck, and mountain views. Two of the guest rooms have sitting rooms. The inn and guest house are fully air-conditioned.

Host: Wim Woody
Rooms: 4 (PB) $80-125; guest house $550 weekly
Full Breakfast
Credit Cards: none
Notes: 2, 5, 6 (in guest house), 7, 8, 9, 10, 12

WARSAW

The Squire's Vintage Inn

748 NC Highways 24 and 50, 28398
(910) 296-1831 (voice and FAX)

"Your Inn for Something Special." Our rural setting adds to the privacy and relaxed atmosphere for a feeling of "getting away from it all." After a restful night's sleep, you can walk on brick sidewalks and rustic paths flanked by tall pines and towering oaks. Adjacent is the famous Country Squire Restaurant. Weekend package available. Take Exit 364 from

I-40. The inn is rated by AAA and Mobil Travel Guide.

Hostess: Iris Lennon
Rooms: 12 + cottage (PB) $52-100
Continental Breakfast
Credit Cards: A, B, C, E
Notes: 2, 3, 4, 5, 7, 10, 12

WAYNESVILLE

Wynne's Creekside Lodge

152 Bunny Run Lane, 28786
(704) 926-8300; (800) 849-4387;
FAX (704) 926-0888
E-mail: righton@primeline.com

Situated on trout-stocked Jonathan Creek in the scenic western North Carolina mountains, Wynne's Creekside Lodge lies on two and a half country acres five minutes outside Maggie Valley. The 1926 two-story farmhouse recently was raised and set upon a wood and stone contemporary addition. Six-person outdoor Jacuzzi, mountain bike rentals, and fishing. Breakfast includes homemade bread, jams, pastry; complimentary cappuccino or refreshments. Christian atmosphere. Church staff retreats welcome.

Hosts: Les and Gail Wynne
Rooms: 4 (PB) $55-65
Full Breakfast
Credit Cards: A, B
Notes: 2, 5, 7 (over 6), 8, 9, 10, 11

WILMINGTON

The Curran House

312 S. Third Street, 28401
(910) 763-6603; (800) 763-6603
FAX (910) 763-5116

The house is in historic downtown Wilmington, three blocks from the Cape Fear

welcome; 7 Children welcome; 8 Tennis nearby; 9 Swimming nearby; 10 Golf nearby; 11 Skiing nearby; 12 May be booked through travel agent.

River and fifteen minutes from Atlantic beaches. King and queen rooms, each uniquely decorated, with guest robes, hair dryers, cable TV/VCRs, telephones, and private baths. Within walking distance of great restaurants, antique shopping, museums, and carriage and riverboat rides.

Hosts: Vickie and Greg Stringer
Rooms: 3 (PB) $75-100
Full Breakfast
Credit Cards: A, B
Notes: 2, 5, 7 (12 and older), 8, 9, 10, 12

Taylor House Inn

14 N. Seventh Street, 28401
(910) 763-7581; (800) 382-9982

Located in the downtown historic district just blocks from the Cape Fear River. A haven of warm southern hospitality and thoughtfulness. The five bedrooms are filled with period antiques, fresh flowers and beautiful linens. A full gourmet breakfast is served in the formal dining room by candlelight. A slice of heaven—be pampered and enjoy the Cape Fear area.

Hosts: Karen and Scott Clark
Rooms: 5 (PB) $95-110
Full Gourmet Breakfast
Credit Cards: A, B, C
Notes: 2, 5, 8, 9, 10

WILSON

Miss Betty's Bed and Breakfast Inn

600 W. Nash Street, 27893-3045
(919) 243-4447; (800) 258-2058;
FAX (919) 243-4447

Selected as one of the "best places to stay in the South," Miss Betty's is ideally located midway between Maine and Florida along the main north-south route,

Miss Betty's B&B Inn

I-95. Comprised of three beautifully restored structures in the downtown historic section, the National Registered Davis-Whitehead-Harriss House (circa 1858), the adjacent Riley House (circa 1900), and Rosebud (circa 1942) have recaptured the elegance and style of quiet Victorian charm, but with modern-day conveniences. Guests can browse for antiques in the inn or visit numerous antique shops that give Wilson the title "Antique Capital of North Carolina." A quiet eastern North Carolina town famous for its barbecue, Wilson also has four beautiful golf courses and numerous tennis courts. Accommodations include three king suites.

Hosts: Betty and Fred Spitz
Rooms: 10 (PB) $60-85
Full Breakfast
Credit Cards: A, B, C, D, E
Notes: 2, 5, 8, 9, 10

WINSTON-SALEM

Lady Anne's Victorian Bed and Breakfast

612 Summit Street, 27101
(910) 724-1074

Warm, southern hospitality surrounds you in this 1890 Victorian home, listed on the

---

National Register of Historic Places. An aura of romance touches each suite or room. All are individually decorated with period antiques, treasures, and modern luxuries. Some rooms have two-person whirlpools, cable TVs, HBO, stereos, telephones, coffee, refrigerators, private entrances, and balconies. An evening dessert and full breakfast are served. Lady Anne's is ideally located near downtown attractions, performances, restaurants, shops, and Old Salem Historic Village. Smoking only on the porch!

Hostess: Shelley Kirby
Rooms: 4 (PB) $55-165
Full Breakfast
Credit Cards: A, B, C
Notes: 5, 8, 9, 10

MeadowHaven Bed and Breakfast

NC Highway 8, PO Box 222, **Germanton**, 27019-0222
(910) 593-3996; FAX (910) 593-3138

A contemporary retreat on twenty-five country acres along Sauratown Mountain in the Blue Ridge foothills. MeadowHaven offers a choice of romantic rooms, a new log cabin with mountain view, or a mountaintop cottage with two bedrooms. All provide private luxury baths, TV/VCRs with movies, hair dryers, and plush bathrobes. "Luv tubs" for two, fireplace, spa, and sauna available. Heated indoor pool, hot tubs, game room, fishing pond, pedal boats, gazebo, and more are on the property. Convenient to Hanging Rock and Pilot Mountain state parks, Old Salem, and the Dan River. Plan a "Lovebirds' Retreat" to MeadowHaven!

Hosts: Samuel and Darlene Fain
Rooms: 5 including cabin and cottage (PB) $80-175
Full Breakfast
Credit Cards: A, B, C, D
Notes: 2, 5, 8, 9, 10, 12

MeadowHaven Bed and Breakfast

---

welcome; 7 Children welcome; 8 Tennis nearby; 9 Swimming nearby; 10 Golf nearby; 11 Skiing nearby; 12 May be booked through travel agent.

NORTH DAKOTA

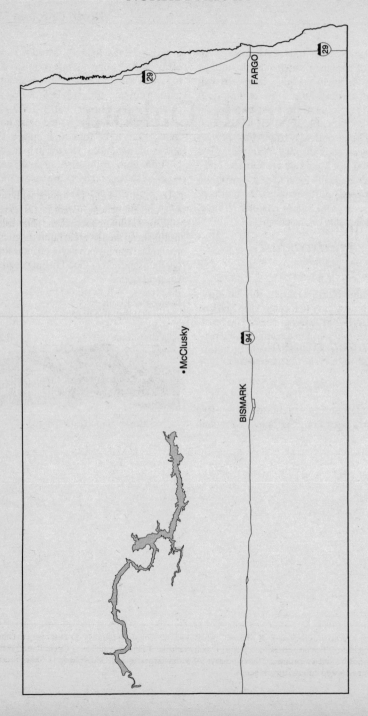

North Dakota

McCLUSKY

Midstate Bed and Breakfast

Route 3, Box 28, 58463
(701) 363-2520 (voice and FAX)

In central North Dakota, this country home is very easy to locate: Mile Marker 232 on ND 200. Built in 1980. The guest entrance takes you to a complete and private lower level containing your bedroom and bath, plus a large TV lounge with fireplace and kitchenette. Breakfast is served in the formal dining room or the plant-filled atrium. In an area of great hunting; guests are allowed hunting privileges on more than four thousand acres. Good fishing nearby. Air-conditioned.

Hostess: Grace Faul
Rooms: 4 (1PB, 3SB) $30-35
Full Breakfast
Credit Cards: none
Notes: 2, 3, 4, 5, 6 (conditional), 7, 8, 9

NOTES: Credit cards accepted: A Master Card; B Visa; C American Express; D Discover; E Diners Club; F Other; 2 Personal checks accepted; 3 Lunch available; 4 Dinner available; 5 Open all year; 6 Pets welcome; 7 Children welcome; 8 Tennis nearby; 9 Swimming nearby; 10 Golf nearby; 11 Skiing nearby; 12 May be booked through travel agent.

OHIO

Ohio

BEACH CITY

Herb Nest
Bed and Breakfast
13642 Navarre Road SW, 44608
(330) 359-5087

Two guest rooms await you in our one-hundred-year-old home. A complimentary continental breakfast is served at your request. Your large bedroom has a deck with private entrance and a large, antique double bed. Victorian antiques and country reproductions furnish the home. Relax on the porch, deck, flagstone patio, or herb terrace. During cooler times, you may want to spend your evening in the family room, where a warm fire will be burning. Special celebration arrangements for birthdays, anniversaries, honeymoons, reunions, showers, and other events can be provided for an additional fee. Gift certificates are available.

Hosts: Walt and Sue Helline
Rooms: 2 (SB) $45-55
Continental Breakfast
Credit Cards: none
Notes: 2, 5, 7, 9, 10, 12

BERLIN

Berlin House
Bed and Breakfast
4460 SR 39, 44610
(330) 674-1140

Berlin House is a quiet and peaceful bed and breakfast on the east edge of Berlin village, in the heart of the world's largest Amish community. It is convenient to all area attractions and Amish-cooking restaurants. Our delicious continental breakfast features homemade bread and granola and locally made Swiss cheese. Guests stay in three rooms with king or queen beds; a cozy living room with gas fireplace, kitchen, and dining area are provided. Relaxing outdoor patio and backyard. A/C; no smoking. Rent one room or the whole house—nightly or weekly. Your hosts are Amish-Mennonite.

Hosts: David and Erma Troyer, Karen Zook, and Wilma Dveck
Rooms: 3 (1PB; 2SB) $39-89
Continental Breakfast
Credit Cards: A, B
Notes: 2, 5, 7

NOTES: Credit cards accepted: A Master Card; B Visa; C American Express; D Discover; E Diners Club; F Other; 2 Personal checks accepted; 3 Lunch available; 4 Dinner available; 5 Open all year; 6 Pets welcome; 7 Children welcome; 8 Tennis nearby; 9 Swimming nearby; 10 Golf nearby; 11 Skiing nearby; 12 May be booked through travel agent.

Donna's Premier Lodging Bed and Breakfast

PO Box 307, East Street, 44610
(330) 893-3068
E-mail: info@donnasb-b.com
Web site: http://www.donnasb-b.com

Prepare yourself for pure luxury right in the heart of Ohio's Amish country as you recline in hickory rockers and watch the wildlife from the front porch of a log cabin. Couples in love can relax in a heart-shaped waterfall Jacuzzi while the fireplace warms an elegant chalet, or snuggle under warm covers and await the delivery of a scrumptious breakfast to the cottage. Families staying in a bed and breakfast room can walk to more than twenty-five gift and craft shops in the village of Berlin.

Hosts: Johannes and Donna Marie Schlabach
Rooms: 6 + cabin, cottages, chalets (PB) $45-225
Inquire about breakfast plan
Credit Cards: A, B, D
Notes: 2, 5, 7, 8, 9, 10, 12

Main Street Bed and Breakfast

4895 State Route 39 and U.S. 62, 44610
(330) 893-1300; (888) 648-1300;
FAX (330) 893-2100

In the heart of Berlin shops. Featuring three newly remodeled luxury rooms with waterfall Jacuzzi, queen-size beds, private baths, satellite TV, kitchenettes, and authentic Amish-crafted furniture and quilts. Full breakfast at local restaurant.

Hosts: Elvin and Laura Coblentz
Rooms: 3 (PB) $75-105
Full Menu Breakfast
Credit Cards: A, B, D
Notes: 2, 5, 7, 12

The Oaks

4752 U.S. 62, PO Box 421, 44610
(330) 893-3061; FAX (330) 893-2926

Nestled in the small town of Berlin in picturesque Holmes County, the Oaks Bed and Breakfast is "your home away from home." Three rooms, including a lofted master suite with skylights, whirlpool, and its own sitting room—a total private getaway! Relax on the screened porch or deck surrounded by large oak trees, or stroll uptown to craft shops, furniture stores, and eating establishments. Fully air-conditioned and smoke free.

Hosts: Duane and Carol Miller
Rooms: 3 (PB) $65-95 (seasonal)
Continental Breakfast
Credit Cards: A, B, D
Notes: 2, 5, 7, 8, 9, 10, 12

BLUE ROCK

McNutt Farm II Outdoorsman Lodge

6120 Cutler Lake Road, 43720
(614) 674-4555

Country bed and breakfast in rustic quarters on a working farm in the quiet of the Blue Rock hill country. Only eleven miles from I-70, thirty-five miles from I-77, and sixty miles from I-71. Guests enjoy their own private kitchen, living room with fireplace or wood-burner, private bath, porch with swing, and beautiful view with forests and pastured livestock. Choose the log cabin or the carriage house. For those who want more than an overnight stay, please ask about our log cabin by the week or weekend. A cellar house cabin (somewhat primitive) is also available. Sleep to the sounds of whippoorwills and tree frogs.

NOTES: Credit cards accepted: A Master Card; B Visa; C American Express; D Discover; E Diners Club; F Other; 2 Personal checks accepted; 3 Lunch available; 4 Dinner available; 5 Open all year; 6 Pets

Awake to the crowing rooster and the wild turkey calling; sometimes the bleating of a newborn fawn can be heard. We welcome you by reservation and deposit.

Hosts: Don R. and Patty L. McNutt
Rooms: 2 suites (PB) $40-100
Continental Breakfast
Credit Cards: none
Notes: 2 (deposit, cash for balance), 5, 6 and 7 (prearranged), 9, 10

BOWLING GREEN

Pine Ridge
Bed and Breakfast

14543 Sand Ridge Road, 43402
(419) 352-2064

Pine Ridge offers comfortable accommodations and warm hospitality in a Victorian-style farmhouse dating from 1878. Two guest rooms and bath on the second floor overlook woods, well-kept lawn and gardens, and fertile farms. Breakfast is served in the spacious living/dining room or sunny porch, and often includes homemade breads or coffee cakes and fruits from the orchard or garden.

Hosts: Bill and Sue Rock
Rooms: 2 (SB) $35-50
Full Breakfast
Credit Cards: none
Notes: 2, 7

CALDWELL

The Harkins House Inn

715 West Street (on I-77), 43724
(614) 732-7347

Come spend an enchanted evening in this immaculately restored home. Built in 1905 by an influential family of the area, ancestors of the proprietors. The inn features bountiful original woodwork with oak and heart pine flooring, and a stately library with fireplace and French doors. Enjoy your stay in one of our rooms with air-conditioning and cable. Then savor breakfast in the formal dining room. Caldwell is only twenty-five minutes between Cambridge and Marietta.

Hosts: Jeff and Stacey Lucas
Rooms: 2 (PB) $53-65
Full Breakfast
Credit Cards: A, B, C
Notes: 2, 5, 7, 8, 9, 10

CAMDEN

Pleasant Valley
Bed and Breakfast

7343 Pleasant Valley Road, 45311
(937) 787-3800

Welcome to our very country bed and breakfast home. This huge Victorian brick is a centerhall design. The home is garnished with lovely woodwork, fireplaces and screened porches for your enjoyment. We have a billiard room, white-sand volleyball court, and a big bark barn with deck that overlooks a pond. Pleasant Valley will host your private party or dinner. We

Pleasant Valley Bed and Breakfast

welcome; 7 Children welcome; 8 Tennis nearby; 9 Swimming nearby; 10 Golf nearby; 11 Skiing nearby; 12 May be booked through travel agent.

also do luncheons, retirement gatherings, family reunions, home weddings, and barn weddings for our guests.

Hosts: Tim and Peg Lowman
Rooms: 4 (2PB; 2SB) $50-60
Full Breakfast
Credit Cards: none
Notes: 2, 3, 4, 6, 7, 8, 9, 10, 11 (water)

CHARM

Guggisberg Swiss Inn

5025 State Route 557, PO Box 1, 44617
(330) 893-3600

New quaint, peaceful little inn nestled snuggly in the hills of the world's largest Amish settlement. Close to shops and attractions. Each room has two double beds with all the comforts of home; local TV channels plus HBO, TNT, etc. Enjoy a horse-drawn carriage or sleigh ride (seasonal, small additional charge), or sit outside and watch the farmers work their fields. Enjoy visiting with other guests in front of the lobby fireplace. Swiss breakfast includes cheese, meat, bread, cereal, fruit, Danish, coffee, and orange juice.

Hosts: Eric and Julia Guggisberg
Rooms: 24 (PB) $79-129
Credit Cards: A, B, D
Notes: 2, 5, 7, 8, 9, 10, 11

CIRCLEVILLE

The Castle Inn

610 S. Court Street, 43113
(614) 477-3986; (800) 477-3986

The Castle Inn, an elegant turn-of-the-century mansion, offers the warmth of a bed and breakfast with the privacy of an inn. This lavish castle was built in 1899 by Samuel Ruggles as a wedding present for his new bride. The architecture of this home is reminiscent of the old manor homes and castles of England, from which many of the original antiques were acquired. We have carefully restored the original enchantment of the home, while offering many of the modern conveniences of today. Numerous stained- and leaded-glass windows abound throughout the house. The stained-glass window at the head of the stairway is especially fine and features "The Four Seasons."

Hosts: Jason and Susan Anderson
Rooms: 6 (PB) $79-190
Continental Breakfast, weekday; Full Breakfast, weekend
Credit Cards: A, B, D
Notes: 2, 5, 9, 10, 12

The Castle Inn

CLEVELAND

Franklin Circle Inn

2826 Franklin Boulevard, 44113
(216) 241-1365

A large Queen Anne Victorian located in a historical area of Cleveland called Ohio City. Minutes from downtown Cleveland and Lake Erie. Excellent restaurants and museums nearby. Fifteen minutes from University Circle.

Hosts: Clark and Phyllis Gerber
Rooms: 8 (PB) $125-150
Continental Breakfast
Credit Cards: A, B
Notes: 2, 5, 7, 9, 12

Shamrock Bed and Breakfast

COLUMBUS

Shamrock Bed and Breakfast

5657 Sunbury Road, 43230-1147
(614) 337-9849

The Shamrock Bed and Breakfast is a half mile from I-270, close to the airport and fifteen minutes from downtown. The B&B is handicap-accessible and is all on one floor. One and a quarter acres of landscaped gardens, trees, patio, and arbor. Choose from the large library of books, videos, and CDs or just relax in front of the fireplace. Easy access to activities such as the Polaris Amphitheater, shopping, parks, gardens, galleries, and the country. AC. Smoking rooms available.

Host: Tom L. McLaughlin
Rooms: 2 (PB) $50-60 (discount for 3 or more days)
Full Irish Breakfast With Menu
Credit Cards: none
Notes: 2, 3, 5, 7, 8, 9, 10, 11

COSHOCTON

Apple Butter Inn

455 Hill Street, Roscoe Village, 43812
(614) 622-1329; (888) 279-0247;
FAX (614) 622-1946
Web site: http://members.tripod.com./
    ~AppleButter/attract.html

The Apple Butter Inn is located less than a block from the shops of Roscoe Village, with easy access for walkers and convenient parking in the rear. The inn features Greek Revival architecture with lazy-day rockers on the front porch overlooking this restored 1830s canal village. The landscaping is beautifully accented by brick and sandstone.

Host: Curt Crouso
Rooms: 6(PB) $69-125
Full Breakfast
Credit Cards: A, B, C, D
Notes: 2, 5, 6, 7, 9, 10, 12

DAYTON

Candlewick Bed and Breakfast

4991 Bath Road, 45424
(937) 233-9297

This tranquil Dutch Colonial home sits atop a hill on five rolling acres. George, a retired engineer, and Nancy, a retired schoolteacher, invite you to spend a peaceful night in comfortable rooms containing a blend of antiques and colonial and country furnishings. Full breakfast includes fresh fruit and juice, choice homemade pastries, and freshly brewed coffee. Weather permitting, enjoy breakfast on the screened porch overlooking a large pond often visited by

welcome; 7 Children welcome; 8 Tennis nearby; 9 Swimming nearby; 10 Golf nearby; 11 Skiing nearby; 12 May be booked through travel agent.

wild ducks and geese. Convenient to the Air Force Museum and major universities, Candlewick is a perfect retreat for either business or pleasure.

Hosts: George and Nancy Thompson
Rooms: 2 (SB) $55-60
Full Breakfast
Credit Cards: none
Notes: 2, 5

DEFIANCE

Sanctuary Ministries

20277 Schick Road, 43512
(419) 658-2069

Sanctuary Ministries is a quiet getaway in a Christian atmosphere. A two-story, cedar-sided home with air-conditioning, a six-acre lake, a pond, and five acres of woods make for a peaceful getaway. This is a favorite fishing hole for many with row boat and canoe. Picnicking and bird-watching from porch swings add to the tranquil atmosphere.

Hosts: Emil and Barbara Schoch
Rooms: 2 (SB) $35-50
Full Breakfast
Credit Cards: none
Notes: 2, 5, 7, 9, 10

DELLROY

Candleglow Bed and Breakfast

4247 Roswell Road SW, 44620
(330) 735-2407

Today's comfort in yesterday's Victorian atmosphere. Romantic, casual elegance. Three spacious guest rooms with king or queen beds. Private baths with claw-foot

or whirlpool tubs. Full breakfast, afternoon tea, and snack in room. Atwood Lake Resort Area. Swimming, boating, hiking, horseback riding, tennis, golf, and antique shops are all close by.

Hostess: Audrey Genova
Rooms: 3 (PB) $90 (summer; call for winter rates)
Full Breakfast
Credit Cards: none
Notes: 2, 5, 8, 9, 10

Mowrey's Welcome Home B&B

DOVER

Mowrey's Welcome Home Bed and Breakfast

4489 Dover-Zoar Road NE, 44622
(330) 343-4690

Hills, 120 species of native trees, and country hospitality provide the setting for this inviting home, modern in design and comfort, but traditional in ambiance. Explore woods and creek, or enjoy views from the porches. Converse or read from hundreds of books throughout the house. Guests are treated like favorite cousins and invited to play the grand piano, parlor organ, or old Victrola. Antique furnishings,

---

fireplaces, and family handiwork add to the welcome feel of home.

Hosts: Paul and Lola Mowrey
Rooms: 3 (2PB; 1SB) $45-75
Full Breakfast
Credit Cards: none
Notes: 2, 5, 7 (over 9), 8, 9, 10, 12

Olde World Bed and Breakfast

2982 State Route 516, 44622
(330) 343-1333; (800) 447-1273

Welcome to the 1880s. Our restored Victorian-style farmhouse nestled among the hills of Tuscarawas Valley is your escape from it all. Only one mile from I-77, we are centrally located to Amish country and historic sites. Five suites are uniquely decorated to include Victorian, Parisian, Oriental, Alpine, and Mediterranean flavors. The parlor is equipped with game table and TV; the hot tub and veranda are always available to guests. Complete packages are available, including romantic getaways and special winter rates.

Hostess: Jonna Sigrist
Rooms: 5 (PB) $55-85
Full Breakfast
Credit Cards: A, B, D
Notes: 2, 3, 5, 9, 10, 12

FREDERICKSBURG

Gilead's Balm Manor Bed and Breakfast

8690 CR 201, 44627
(330) 695-3881

Nestled among the Amish farms of Holmes County, fourteen minutes north of Berlin, Ohio, you will find five landscaped acres of Amish country elegance. We have added four luxurious and spacious suites with twelve-foot ceilings to our manor house. Each suite includes two-person Jacuzzi, fireplace/gas logs, kitchen, private bath, satellite TV, air-conditioner, and double French doors with round-top windows overlooking our two-and-a-half-acre lake. Just minutes from shops and restaurants. Our guests say it's like experiencing the luxurious accommodations of an estate in Europe overlooking a lake. Hosts David and Sara Mae Stutzman are both from Amish and Mennonite backgrounds.

Hosts: David A. and Sara Mae Stutzman
Rooms: 4 (PB) $125-175
Continental Breakfast
Credit Cards: A, B, C, D
Notes: 2, 5, 7, 8, 9, 10, 12

GEORGETOWN

Bailey House Bed and Breakfast

112 N. Water Street, 45121
(937) 378-3087

The Bailey House is on the National Register of Historic Places. The three-story Greek Revival home is furnished in antiques and features three bedrooms with washstands and antique beds. The Bailey House is a half block from U.S. Grant's boyhood home; private tours are available.

Hostesses: Nancy Purdy and Jane Sininger
Rooms: 4 (SB) $55
Full Breakfast
Credit Cards: none
Notes: 2, 5, 6, 7, 8, 9, 10

welcome; 7 Children welcome; 8 Tennis nearby; 9 Swimming nearby; 10 Golf nearby; 11 Skiing nearby; 12 May be booked through travel agent.

GERMANTOWN

Gunckel Heritage Bed and Breakfast

33 W. Market Street, 45327-1353
(937) 855-3508

Located in the heart of the Gunckel Town Plat historic district, our bed and breakfast is a Federal-style brick home with Victorian influences. It features a front-to-back foyer with its grand staircase. The six fireplaces, beautiful woodwork, and original interior shutters add to the ambience. Enjoy a full breakfast by candlelight in our elegant dining room, on the covered balcony, or on the porch furnished in wicker, weather permitting. We like to spoil our guests with complimentary refreshments and access to our ice cream sundae bar. The rooms are decorated in period antiques, with romantically furnished bed chambers. Antiquing, museums, parks, covered bridges, bike trails, and a nature center are all nearby. Ten-percent dinner coupon at the famous Florentine Hotel, two doors east.

Hosts: Bonnie Gunckel-Koogle and Lynn Edward Koogle
Rooms: 4 (3PB; 1SB) $65-75
Full Breakfast
Credit Cards: A, B, D
Notes: 2, 5, 7, 8, 9, 10, 12

GREENVILLE

The Waring House

304 W. Third Street, 45331
(937) 548-2682; FAX (937) 548-3448

The Waring House is an 1869 Victorian home restored to reflect the elegance of this romantic era. The ten-room Italianate home includes a double parlor, library, four bedrooms and guest bath, formal dining room, and kitchen, along with a lovely garden and in-ground pool. Your hosts individualize the accommodations to ensure a memorable stay for every guest. A highlight of your visit will include a home-cooked breakfast, which will be served in the formal dining room.

Hosts: Mike and Judy Miller
Rooms: 3 (SB) $50
Full Breakfast
Credit Cards: D
Notes: 2, 5, 7, 8, 9, 10

HAMILTON

Eaton Hill Bed and Breakfast

1951 Eaton Road, 45013
(513) 856-9552

Eaton Hill Bed and Breakfast has a country feel, although it is officially part of Hamilton. The white colonial home is surrounded by fields, trees, and flower beds. It is only ten miles from the Miami University campus and conveniently situated for parents, guests, and friends of the university and Butler County residents. Three bedrooms with shared bath will provide you with a quiet night's rest amid antique furnishings. Children are welcome ($10 each). A portable crib and high chair are available.

Hostess: Mrs. Pauline K. Zink
Rooms: 3 (SB) $55
Full Breakfast
Credit Cards: none
Notes: 2, 5, 6 (caged), 7, 8, 9, 10

NOTES: Credit cards accepted: A Master Card; B Visa; C American Express; D Discover; E Diners Club; F Other; 2 Personal checks accepted; 3 Lunch available; 4 Dinner available; 5 Open all year; 6 Pets

HOLMES COUNTY (AMISH COUNTRY)

Bigham House of Holmes County

151 S. Washington Street, **Millersburg**, 44654
(800) 689-6950
Web site: http://bbonline.com/bighamhs

A bed and breakfast and English tearoom located in a quiet village in the heart of Amish country, Holmes County, Ohio. Step back in time as you enter our 19th-century home, which is elegantly decorated in grand Victorian style. With your choice of four exquisite guest rooms and an extraordinary suite, indulge yourself in luxurious amenities that make each room unique. For a delightful afternoon away from the hustle of the world, treat yourself to an authentic English tea. Savor the warmth and hospitality, served with a cup of hot English tea by our own British gentleman. For a truly memorable getaway, ring the Ellises.

Hosts: Winnie and John Ellis
Rooms: 5 (PB) $60-110
Full Breakfast
Credit Cards: A, B, D
Notes: 2, 5, 7, 8, 9, 10, 12

LAKESIDE

Idlewyld Bed and Breakfast

350 Walnut, 43440
(419) 798-4198

Idlewyld has a homey ambience in which guests can relax and enjoy the tranquil beauty, friendly atmosphere and timeless charm of 19th-century Lakeside. The home has a large wraparound porch where guests can relax in comfort on Amish rockers. Rooms are clean, comfortable and tastefully decorated; many amenities and pleasant surprises await guests. There is an abundance of hospitality and country charm. Nowhere is it possible to find a breakfast equal to that served at Idlewyld—we are fussy about what we serve, and it shows. Lakeside is a special place; lively activity coexists with spiritual calm. Spiritual, cultural, intellectual and physical programs foster traditional Christian and family values.

Hosts: Dan and Joan Barris
Rooms: 15 (5PB; 10SB) $40-60
English Sideboard Breakfast
Credit Cards: A, B, D
Notes: 2, 7, 8, 9, 10

MESOPOTAMIA

Old Stone House Bed and Breakfast

8505 State Route 534, Box 177, 44439
(216) 693-4186

Wake your fondest memories in this setting from the past, built circa 1830 from sandstone used in northeastern Ohio's landmark buildings. Guests are intrigued by the oversize windowsills and immense walls of this architectural curiosity. Immerse yourself in the quaint life of the Amish and village commons built by Connecticut settlers as part of Ohio's Western Reserve. Retreat to our country room with fireplace and indulge in natural beauty. Private dining in Amish home, buggy ride, historic tours available. Three suites (two hydrotherapy whirlpools), sitting areas

welcome; 7 Children welcome; 8 Tennis nearby; 9 Swimming nearby; 10 Golf nearby; 11 Skiing nearby; 12 May be booked through travel agent.

overlooking rolling countryside. Children
welcome; no smoking; pet B&B $8/night;
evening snack and beverage. Forty-one
miles east of Cleveland.

Hosts: Samuel and Darcy Miller
Rooms: 3 (PB) $75
Full Breakfast
Credit Cards: none
Notes: 6, 7

MILAN

Gastier Farm Bed and Breakfast

1902 Strecker Road, 44846
(419) 499-2985

The farm homestead has been in the family for more than a hundred years. Now
the farmhouse is available for sharing with
travelers. Located two miles west of the
Ohio Turnpike, Exit 7, next to the Norfolk Southern Railroad between Toledo
and Cleveland. No pets or smoking.
Reservations required.

Hosts: Ted and Donna Gastier
Rooms: 3 (SB) $50
Continental Breakfast
Credit Cards: A, B
Notes: 2, 5, 7, 8, 9, 10

Gastier Farm Bed and Breakfast

MILLERSBURG

Indiantree Farm Bed and Breakfast

5488 State Route 515, 44654
(330) 893-2497

Peaceful lodging in a guest house on a picturesque hilltop farm in the heart of Amish
country, a mile from Walnut Creek. Large
front porch, farming with horses, hiking
trails. Apartments with kitchen and bath,
for the price of a room. An oasis where
time slows and the mood is conversation,
not television.

Host: Larry D. Miller
Rooms: 3 (PB) $60-75
Continental Breakfast
Credit Cards: none
Notes: 2, 5, 11

NEW BEDFORD

Valley View Inn of New Bedford

32327 State Route 643, 43824
(330) 897-3232; (800) 331-VIEW (8439);
FAX (330) 897-0636
Web site: http://www.ez-page.com/valleyview

The panoramic view from the back of the
inn is nothing short of breathtaking and is
enhanced only by the changing seasons.
Guests can enjoy the cozy fireplace in the
living room or relax in the family room.
While there are no TVs to interrupt the
serenity of the area, a player piano, check-
ers, ping-pong table, chess, or a comfortable Lazy Boy chair await you. Enjoy surrounding fields, farms and wildlife; stroll
down paths to our thirty-five acres of
woods; feed the pond fish or offer an apple

NOTES: Credit cards accepted: A Master Card; B Visa; C American Express; D Discover; E Diners
Club; F Other; 2 Personal checks accepted; 3 Lunch available; 4 Dinner available; 5 Open all year; 6 Pets

to one of the resident draft horses. Located in the midst of Amish country and our service is to God's people. No smoking. Handicap-accessible.

Hosts: Dan and Nancy Lembke
Rooms: 10 (PB) $75-105
Full Breakfast (Continental on Sunday)
Credit Cards: A, B
Notes: 2, 5, 7 (13 and older), 10

NEW RICHMOND

Hollyhock Bed and Breakfast

1610 N. Altman Road, 45157
(513) 553-7042

Country. Private suite with sitting room. Gourmet ($85/night) or continental ($60/night). Nearby are a fishing lake, Grants birthplace, River Downs races, and Woodland Mound Golf Course. Twenty minutes to Cincinnati. Square dancing, wedding chapel, horticultural gardens. Fine antiques available for purchase.

Hostess: Evelyn Cutter
Rooms: 1 (PB) $60-85
Full or Continental Breakfast
Credit Cards: none
Notes: 2, 3, 4, 5, 8, 9, 10, 12

PLAIN CITY

Yoder's Bed and Breakfast

8144 Cemetery Pike, 43064
(614) 873-4489

Located on a 107-acre farm northwest of Columbus. Big Darby Creek runs along the frontyard. Excellent bird-watching. Within minutes of Amish restaurants, gift shops, cheese house, Amish furniture store,

bookstores, and antique shops. King and queen beds, air-conditioning. No smoking or pets.

Hosts: Claribel and Loyd Yoder
Rooms: 4 (1PB; 3SB) $55-68
Full Breakfast
Credit Cards: none
Notes: 2, 5, 9, 10

RIPLEY

The Baird House Bed and Breakfast

201 N. Second Street, 45167
(937) 392-4918

On the Historic Register, built in 1825 five hundred feet from the Ohio River on scenic State Route 52, fifty miles east of Cinncinnati. Three porches, swings, rockers, beautiful sunsets, large historical area, museums, parks, and battle site areas nearby. Nine churches (several within walking distance), off-street parking. Large parlor and library. Books, games, music, good food, snacks, and warm hospitality. His and her bicycles.

Hosts: Glenn and Patricia Kittles
Rooms: 3 (2PB; 1SB) $95-150
Full Breakfast
Credit Cards: none
Notes: 2, 8, 10

SANDUSKY

The 1890 Queen Anne Bed and Breakfast

714 Wayne Street, 44870
(419) 626-0391

Spacious accommodations with charm and elegance await guests at the 1890 Queen

---

Anne B&B in downtown Sandusky. Built of native limestone, this 108-year-old Victorian home lends ambience and romance for its guests. Three large air-conditioned rooms offer tranquil luxury for relaxation. Beauty abounds in the regal outdoors as viewed from a screened-in porch, where continental plus breakfasts are enjoyed. Easy access abounds to beaches, Lake Erie island boat trips, Cedar Point, shopping, and other recreational opportunities. Brochure available upon request.

Host: Dr. Bob Kromer
Rooms: 3 (PB) $90
Continental Breakfast
Credit Cards: A, B, D
Notes: 2, 5, 8, 9, 10

Sunset Bay Bed and Breakfast

1102 W. Drive (Bay View Village), 44870
(419) 684-7394
E-mail: sunsetbay@kellnet.com
Web site: http://www.adkey.com/sunsetbay

Enjoy the serenity of a village waterfront home within a variety of area attractions such as Cedar Point and the Lake Erie islands. We can accommodate watercraft with dockage within a few feet of your suite. The bay is a perfect cove for water-skiing, jet-skiing or boating enthusiasts. Biking, walking, and rollerblading are favorite pastimes around the village. Decorated in modern nautical decor with knotty pine surroundings. An air-conditioned, oversize penthouse suite with queen bed, two-person Jacuzzi, and sixteen feet of windows overlooks the bay. A TV, VCR, refrigerator filled with soft drinks, coffeemaker, and radio with cassettes are a few of the amenities. You will be spell-

bound by the sunsets and star-filled nights from your suite or on the lighted deck. Sleep in or catch the early morning calm of the bay. Most important, arrive in time to see the spectacular sunset! Brochures for area attractions, ferries and tours available. Christian establishment.

Hosts: Jennifer and Jim Schmidutz
Rooms: 2 (PB) $100-140
Full Breakfast
Credit Cards: none
Notes: 2, 5, 8, 9, 10, 11, 12

Wagner's 1844 Inn

230 E. Washington Street, 44870
(419) 626-1726; FAX (419) 626-8465

Located in the historic district in an 1844 Victorian home. All rooms have private baths, queen beds and air-conditioning. Within walking distance of the bay, parks, museums, tennis courts, swimming pool, and ferries to Cedar Point and Lake Erie Islands.

Hosts: Walt and Barb Wagner
Rooms: 3 (PB) $70-100
Continental Breakfast
Credit Cards: A, B, D
Notes: 5, 6, 8, 9, 10

Wagner's 1844 Inn

SHELBY

Bethel Bed and Breakfast

4885 State Route 39, **Crestline**, 44827
(419) 347-3054; (419) 347-8377
E-mail: spry641365@aol.com

A Christian atmosphere on six acres in farm country. We have a half-acre stocked pond, sand volleyball pit, horseshoe pits, herb and vegetable gardens, flower beds, fruit trees, sitting porches, and Watchman Nee book room. Common living room with piano, board games, magazines, and door to deck outside. Located between Shelby and Tiro on State Route 39. Call for brochure.

Hostess: Sue Pry
Rooms: 3 (1PB; 2SB)
Continental Plus Breakfast
Credit Cards: None
Notes: 2, 3, 4, 5, 7 (call first), 8, 9, 10, 11, 12

SIDNEY

GreatStone Castle

429 N. Ohio Avenue, 45365
(937) 498-4728; FAX (937) 498-9950

GreatStone Castle, registered with the National Historical Society, is a hundred-year-old mansion on two beautiful acres. The castle is constructed of eighteen-inch limestone with three turrets and is finished with rare, imported hardwood. Antique furniture, fireplaces, and fine furnishings help complete the elegant setting. A deluxe continental breakfast is served in the conservatory.

Hosts: Frederick and Victoria Keller
Rooms: 5 (3PB; 2SB) $75-95
Deluxe Continental Breakfast
Credit Cards: A, B, C
Notes: 2, 5, 6, 10, 12

STRASBURG

Ellis's Bed and Breakfast

104 Fourth Street SW, 44680
(330) 878-7863

Our turn-of-the-century home is comfortably furnished for your "home away from home." A big-screen TV in the sunken living room and a secluded patio are for your relaxation. A tasty, complete breakfast, different each morning, is served in the dining room using our best china, silver, etc. We are conveniently located for Zoar, Amish country, Dover/New Philadelphia, and Canton. Antiques, flea markets, gift shops, and restaurants abound. No smoking, please.

Hosts: Tom and Grace Ellis
Rooms: 3 (SB) $35-50
Full Breakfast
Credit Cards: none
Notes: 2, 5, 7

SUGARCREEK

Breitenbach Bed and Breakfast

307 Dover Road, 44681
(330) 343-3603; (800) THE WINE

Splendid accommodations in a quaint Swiss village in the heart of Amish country. This home is artistically furnished with

Breitenbach Bed and Breakfast

welcome; 7 Children welcome; 8 Tennis nearby; 9 Swimming nearby; 10 Golf nearby; 11 Skiing nearby; 12 May be booked through travel agent.

a mixture of antiques, ethnic treasures, and local arts and crafts. Nearby Amish restaurants, cheese houses, flea markets, antique malls, and quilt and craft shops. Evening refreshments and a full gourmet breakfast.

Hostess: Deanna Bear
Rooms: 4 (PB) $65-85
Full Breakfast
Credit Cards: A, B, C
Notes: 2, 5, 8, 10

Marbeyo
Bed and Breakfast

2370 CR 144, 44681
(330) 852-4533; FAX (330) 852-3605

Hosted by an Amish/Mennonite family, nestled in the heart of the Amish country in eastern Holmes County. Three bedrooms, private baths, AC. Relax in the quiet country; take leisurely walks on the farm; see the animals. Enjoy a delicious breakfast at your convenience.

Hosts: Mark and Betty Yoder
Rooms: 3 (PB) $55-75
Full Breakfast
Credit Cards: A, B
Notes: 2, 5, 7, 10

SUGAR GROVE

Hickory Bend
Bed and Breakfast

7541 Dupler Road SE, 43155
(614) 746-8381
E-mail: ppeery@ohiolinks.com

Nestled in the Hocking Hills of southeastern Ohio on ten wooded acres. "So peaceful, we got to go out to watch *the car* go

by on Sunday afternoon," says Pat. Patty is a spinner and weaver. The cozy, private room is outside the home in the midst of dogwood, poplar, and oak trees. Guests come for breakfast and conversation. Heated in the winter and cooled in the summer. Write for brochure.

Hosts: Pat and Patty Peery
Rooms: 1 (PB) $50
Full Breakfast
Credit Cards: none
Notes: 2, 8, 9, 10

Fort Ball Bed and Breakfast

TIFFIN

Fort Ball
Bed and Breakfast

25 Adams Street, 44883
(419) 447-0776; (888) 447-0776;
FAX (419) 447-3499

Our restored Queen Anne Revival house was built in 1894 by John King for his fam-

---

NOTES: Credit cards accepted: A Master Card; B Visa; C American Express; D Discover; E Diners Club; F Other; 2 Personal checks accepted; 3 Lunch available; 4 Dinner available; 5 Open all year; 6 Pets

ily. King was the master builder who constructed the Tiffin Court House and College Hall at Heidelberg College. The whole house is arranged for guests' enjoyment. Relax in the family room with television/VCR or the formal parlor with a book or an old issue of *National Geographic*.

Hosts: Charles and Lenora Livingston
Rooms: 4 (2PB; 2SB) $55-85
Full Breakfast
Credit Cards: A, B, D
Notes: 2, 5, 7, 10

TIPP CITY

The Willowtree Inn

1900 W. State Route 571, 45371
(937) 667-2957; FAX (937) 667-2416

Nestled on five country acres and surrounded by broad, rolling fields, the Willowtree Inn is the perfect getaway for weary travelers. An ancient willow tree drowses by a springfed pond while ducks lazily paddle past. It's a wonderful place to relax, kick your shoes off, and enjoy good, old-fashioned hospitality. Built in 1830, our six-thousand-square-foot historic estate has been fully restored. The original wide plank, ash floors and built-in bookshelves add special elegance to the front parlor, where our guests enjoy gathering in the evening for complimentary refreshments.

Hosts: Jolene and Chuck Sell
Rooms: 4 (3PB; 1SB) $65-85
Full Breakfast
Credit Cards: A, B
Notes: 2, 5, 6, 7, 9, 10, 12

TOLEDO

The Nightingale House

525 S. Wheeling Street, 43616
(419) 698-2263 (voice and FAX)

The Nightingale House is an elegant Victorian farmhouse, built in 1877. It has been lovingly restored and is opulently furnished with period antiques. The Nightingale House is located just three miles from downtown Toledo in a lovely suburban neighborhood. Maumee Bay State Park on Lake Erie and the Ottawa National Wildlife Refuge are just minutes away, as are all area Toledo attractions. A full breakfast is provided.

Hosts: Randall Schnee, Denise McCroskey, and
    Miriam Patznick
Rooms: 4 (PB) $79-99
Full Breakfast
Credit Cards: A, B, C, D
Notes: 2, 3, 4, 5, 8, 9, 10, 12

WAKEMAN

Melrose Farm Bed and Breakfast

727 Vesta Road, 44889
(419) 929-1867 (voice and FAX)
E-mail: melrose@accnorwalk.com

Halfway between Ashland and Oberlin, Melrose Farm is a peaceful country retreat. Each of the three lovely guest rooms in the 125-year-old brick house has a private bath. Guests enjoy the tennis court, stocked pond, perennial gardens, and quiet rural setting. Thirty miles from Cedar Point, an hour's drive from Cleveland

welcome; 7 Children welcome; 8 Tennis nearby; 9 Swimming nearby; 10 Golf nearby; 11 Skiing nearby; 12 May be booked through travel agent.

or Toledo, two hours from Columbus. Air-conditioned comfort; old-fashioned, relaxed hospitality. Special Monday-Thursday rates for a multinight stay.

Hosts: Abe and Eleanor Klassen
Rooms: 3 (PB) $75
Full Breakfast
Credit Cards: none
Notes: 2, 3, 5, 7, 8 (on site), 9, 10

Hasseman House Inn

WILMOT

Hasseman House Inn

925 U.S. 62, PO Box 215, 44689
(330) 359-7904; FAX (330) 359-7159

Situated at the door to Ohio's Amish country. This charming and warm, early-1900s Victorian inn invites you to unpack your bags and relax. Furnished with antiques, the Hasseman House Inn is indeed a step back into a bygone era. The inn features four cozy rooms complete with private baths and air-conditioning. You will fall in love with the intricate woodwork and original stained glass. Walk-ins are welcome!

Hosts: Milo and Kathryn Miller
Rooms: 4 (PB) $69-110
Full Breakfast
Credit Cards: A, B, D
Notes: 2, 5, 9, 10

Raber's Tri-County View Bed and Breakfast

PO Box 155, 44689
(330) 359-5189

Located in the world's largest Amish settlement, with lots of rolling hills and fields all around. Each room has its own unique, peaceful atmosphere and decor, with private bath, queen-size bed, central heating and air, microwave, refrigerator, and coffeepot. From a garden swing, you can relax and enjoy the view of three different counties. No smoking inside. One mile from Wilmot, ten miles from Berlin, Walnut Creek, and Kidron in Amish country. Lots of quilts, antiques, and craft shops, cheese houses, furniture stores, and the best restaurants in the state.

Hosts: Ed and Esther Raber
Rooms: 3 (PB) $55-85
Full Breakfast
Credit Cards: A, B
Notes: 2, 5, 7, 8, 9, 10

WOOSTER

Historic Overholt House Bed and Breakfast

1473 Beall Avenue, 44691
(330) 263-6300; (800) 992-0643;
FAX (330) 263-9378

This elegantly decorated, "Stick-Style Victorian" historic home with a rare, solid walnut "flying staircase" is located at the gateway to Amish country, adjacent to the College of Wooster. Within walking distance of the Ohio Light Opera. Romantic candlelight and mystery dinners are available November through April. Executive candlelight breakfast, hot tub, Christmas

---

NOTES: Credit cards accepted: A Master Card; B Visa; C American Express; D Discover; E Diners Club; F Other; 2 Personal checks accepted; 3 Lunch available; 4 Dinner available; 5 Open all year; 6 Pets

parlor, two fireplaces and a parklike setting are other fine features.

Hostesses: Sandy Pohalski and Bobbie Walton
Rooms: 5 (PB) $65-70
Continental
Credit Cards: A, B, C, D
Notes: 2, 5, 7, 8, 9, 10

Millennium Classic Bed and Breakfast

1626 Beall Avenue, 44691
(330) 264-6005; (800) 937-4199;
FAX (330) 264-5008

Millennium Classic Bed and Breakfast is centrally located right in the heart of Wooster. Close to the College of Wooster, hospital, shopping mall, restaurants, and grocery store. A post-Victorian exterior, with a traditional, classic theme in the interior. Lots of decks, porches, quiet sitting areas, and shade trees. A friendly, homelike atmosphere.

Innkeeper: John Byler
Rooms: 5 (3PB; 2SB) $55-95
Extended Continental Breakfast
Credit Cards: A, B, C, D
Notes: 2, 5, 7, 8, 9, 10, 12

welcome; 7 Children welcome; 8 Tennis nearby; 9 Swimming nearby; 10 Golf nearby; 11 Skiing nearby; 12 May be booked through travel agent.

OKLAHOMA

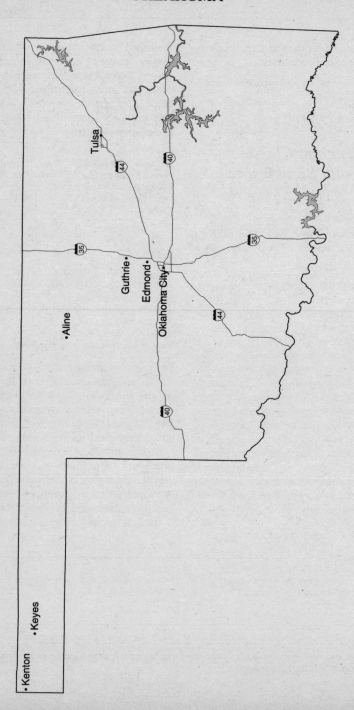

Oklahoma

ALINE

Heritage Manor

RR 3, Box 33, 73716
(405) 463-2566; (405) 463-2563; (800) 295-2563

Heritage Manor is a country getaway on eighty acres that was settled in the 1893 Land Run in northwest Oklahoma. Two prestatehood homes have been joined together and restored by innkeepers using a Victorian theme. Enjoy beautiful sunrises, sunsets, stargazing from the rooftop deck, relaxing in the hot tub and reading a book from the five-thousand-volume library. Ostriches, donkeys, and Scottish Highland cattle roam a fenced area. Close to Selenite Crystal digging area and several other attractions.

Hosts: A.J. and Carolyn Rexroat
Rooms: 4 (1 PB; 3SB) $50-150
Full Breakfast
Credit Cards: none
Notes: 2, 3 and 4 (by reservation), 5, 6 and 7 (by arrangement), 9, 10 (30 miles)

EDMOND

The Arcadian Inn

328 E. First Street, 73034
(405) 348-6347; (800) 299-6347;
FAX (405) 348-8100
E-mail: ArcadianInn@juno.com
Web site: http://bbonline.com/ok/arcadian

With angels watching over you, you are ministered peace and relaxation. The inn is a step back in time to the era of Christian love, hospitality, and family values. The historical home of Dr. Ruhl, the inn has five luxurious Victorian guest rooms with tubs, fireplaces, canopy beds, and sunrooms. A sumptuous homemade breakfast is served in the sunny dining room beneath cherub paintings. Perfect for romantic getaways, business travelers, or family gatherings. Jacuzzi, outdoor spa.

Hosts: Gary and Martha Hall
Rooms: 7 (PB) $75-150
Full Breakfast
Credit Cards: A, B, C, D
Notes: 2, 5, 8, 9, 10, 12

NOTES: Credit cards accepted: A Master Card; B Visa; C American Express; D Discover; E Diners Club; F Other; 2 Personal checks accepted; 3 Lunch available; 4 Dinner available; 5 Open all year; 6 Pets welcome; 7 Children welcome; 8 Tennis nearby; 9 Swimming nearby; 10 Golf nearby; 11 Skiing nearby; 12 May be booked through travel agent.

Victorian Rose Bed and Breakfast

GUTHRIE

Victorian Rose Bed and Breakfast

415 E. Cleveland, 73044
(405) 282-3928

The hundred-year-old Queen Anne home, built in 1894, mixes the charm of the past with the comforts of the present. Located on a brick street, it features a wraparound porch with gingerbread accents, with a porch swing and garden area. Lovely restoration with quality workmanship, displayed with beautiful oak floors, exquisite original beveled windows, gleaming brass light fixtures, and antiques. Three blocks from historic downtown (the largest urban historical district in the U.S.). Three beautiful Victorian guest rooms offer queen beds and private baths. Full, complimentary gourmet breakfast. Family rates and gift certificates available.

Hosts: Linda and Foy Shahan
Rooms: 3 (PB) $74-84
Full Gourmet Breakfast
Credit Cards: A, B, D
Notes: 2, 5, 7, 8, 9, 10, 12

KENTON

Black Mesa Bed and Breakfast

PO Box 81, 73946
(405) 261-7443; (800) 866-3009;
FAX (405) 261-7443

Located two miles north of Kenton at the foot of the Black Mesa, this 1910 rock ranch house boasts the best in country hospitality. Whether hiking, rock hounding, fishing, hunting, birding, or escaping the routine, rest in a double-occupancy or family suite (sleeps eight) at Black Mesa Bed and Breakfast.

Hosts: Monty Joe and Vicki Roberts
Rooms: 2 (PB)
Full Breakfast
Credit Cards: A, B, D
Notes: 2, 3, 4, 5, 6, 7, 10

KEYES

Cattle Country Inn

HCR 1, Box 34, 73947
(405) 543-6458

We are truly country located. If you like wide-open spaces where you can see for miles and not be in hearing distance of any highway traffic, come stay with us. Located in the panhandle between Guymon and Boise City, the inn is a nice stopping place on the way to or from the Rockies. Come experience the hospitality and hearty cookin' served up by your host in the beautiful, spacious, and very modern ranch-style home. Located thirty-eight miles west of Guymon on Highway 64, then eight and a half miles south on dirt roads. Cimarron County, the last county

---

NOTES: Credit cards accepted: A Master Card; B Visa; C American Express; D Discover; E Diners Club; F Other; 2 Personal checks accepted; 3 Lunch available; 4 Dinner available; 5 Open all year; 6 Pets

west, has many points of interest, as well as plenty of good prairie dog and pheasant hunting.

Hosts: Lane and Karen Sparkman
Rooms: 6 (1PB; 5SB) $55
Full Breakfast
Credit Cards: A, B, C
Notes: 2, 5, 7

OKLAHOMA CITY

The Grandison at Maney Park

1200 N. Shartel, 73103
(405) 232-8778; (800) 240-4667;
FAX (405) 232-5039

Nine bedrooms featuring antique furnishings, queen- and king-size beds, private baths with double Jacuzzi and shower, gas fireplaces. Built in 1904 and moved to its present location in 1909, the home features carved mahogany woodwork, massive entry with curved staircase, original stained-glass and brass fixtures—charming details at every turn. We offer both romantic getaways and executive services. Television and phone are available in

rooms on request. Refreshment bar, work-out room, and gift shop.

Hosts: Claudia and Bob Wright
Rooms: 9 (PB) $65-150
Full Breakfast weekends, Continental weekdays
Credit Cards: A, B, C, D
Notes: 2, 5, 6, 7, 12

TULSA

The Hideaway Bed and Breakfast

6130 W. 39th Street S., 74107-4818
(918) 445-2838

The perfect place for that much-needed getaway. Relax with morning coffee or have a quiet evening under the stars on your private deck. Bring along your favorite movie and spend a cozy romantic night in the privacy of your guest room. Come and let us pamper you. We'd love to have you as our guests.

Hosts: Mark and Pam Hollie
Rooms: 1 (PB) $80-135
Full Breakfast (optional)
Credit Cards: none
Notes: 2, 5

OREGON

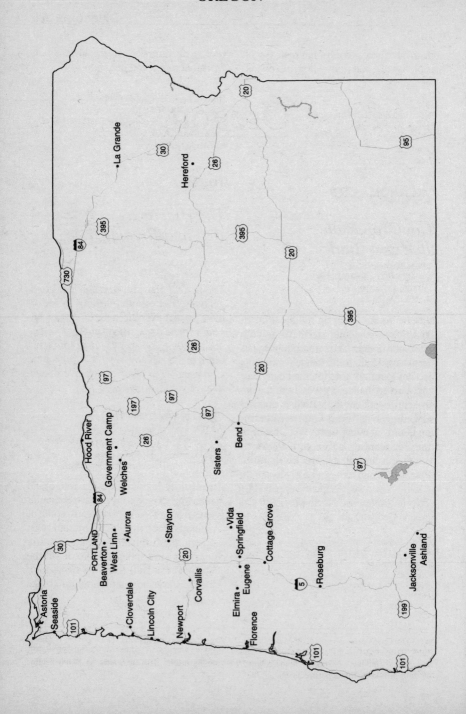

Oregon

ASHLAND

Cowslip's Belle
Bed and Breakfast

159 N. Main Street, 97520
(541) 488-2901; (800) 888-6819;
FAX (541) 482-6138
E-mail: stag@cowslip.com
Web site: http://www.cowslip.com/cowslip

Teddy bears, chocolate truffles, cozy down comforters, and scrumptious breakfasts. Cowslip's Belle Bed and Breakfast is a delightful 1913 Craftsman bungalow and carriage house in the heart of the historic district. Cowslip's Belle is a nationally recognized award winner, featured in *McCall's* as one of the "Most Charming Inns in America" and among *Country Accents* magazine's "Northwest Best Places," "The Best Places to Kiss in the Pacific Northwest," and "Weekends for Two in the Pacific Northwest—50 Romantic Getaways."

Hosts: Jon and Carmen Reinhardt
Rooms: 4 (PB) $95-130
Full Breakfast
Credit Cards: A, B
Notes: 2, 5, 8, 9, 10, 11, 12

Mt. Ashland Inn

Mt. Ashland Inn

550 Mt. Ashland Ski Road, 97520
(541) 482-8707 (voice and FAX); (800) 830-8707
E-mail: mtashinn@teleport.com
Web site: http://www.mtashlandinn.com

Beautifully handcrafted log lodge and sauna/spa terrace command spectacular views from a mountain ridge just south of Ashland. Rock fireplace, Oriental rugs, and antique furnishings create a warm, luxurious atmosphere. Hike or ski the Pacific Crest Trail from the front door. Quality snowshoes and mountain bikes

---

NOTES: Credit cards accepted: A Master Card; B Visa; C American Express; D Discover; E Diners Club; F Other; 2 Personal checks accepted; 3 Lunch available; 4 Dinner available; 5 Open all year; 6 Pets welcome; 7 Children welcome; 8 Tennis nearby; 9 Swimming nearby; 10 Golf nearby; 11 Skiing nearby; 12 May be booked through travel agent.

available at no charge. "A magical mountain retreat," says *Country Home*. Three stars, Northwest Best Places. AAA, Mobil. "A retreat for all seasons . . . promises renewal, relaxation, and adventure!" says *Country Living* magazine.

Hosts: Chuck and Laurel Biegert
Rooms: 5 (PB) $76-180
Full Breakfast
Credit Cards: A, B, C, D
Notes: 2, 5, 8, 9, 10, 11, 12

The Redwing Bed and Breakfast

115 N. Main Street, 97520
(541) 482-1807; (800) 461-6743;
FAX (541) 488-1433

The Redwing, nestled in Ashland's charming historic district, is a 1911 Craftsman home with its original lighting fixtures, beautiful wood, and comfortable decor. Each of our inviting guest rooms features queen-size beds and private bath. Located one city block from the Shakespeare Festival, Lithia Park, restaurants, and gift shops. Downhill and cross-country skiing, river rafting, and fishing are nearby. See the July 1994 *Bon Appetit*.

Hosts: Mike and Judi Cook
Rooms: 3 (PB) $70-125
Full Breakfast
Credit Cards: A, B, D
Notes: 2, 5, 8, 9, 10, 11

ASTORIA

Columbia River Inn Bed and Breakfast

1681 Franklin Avenue, 97103
(503) 325-5044; (800) 953-5044

Columbia River Inn is charming in every way. Built in 1870, this beautiful "painted

Columbia River Inn Bed and Breakfast

lady" Victorian has a gazebo for weddings and parties in the beautifully landscaped garden. Come see the "stairway to the stars," a unique terraced garden view of the celebrated Columbia River. The inn offers four elegantly furnished rooms, one with a working fireplace and Jacuzzi tub. Beautiful side garden added, with cobblestone sidewalk. My specialty is hospitality—"Home is where the heart is. . .". Guests may use off-street parking.

Hostess: Karen N. Nelson
Rooms: 4 (PB) $75-125
Full Breakfast
Credit Cards: A, B
Notes: 2, 5, 7 (6 and older), 9, 10

Grandview Bed and Breakfast

1574 Grand Avenue, 97103
(503) 325-5555; (800) 488-3250
Web sites: http://www.virtualcities.com/ons/or/a/ ora3501.htm
http://www.cdiguide.com/OR/503/a_bed/ grandvie.html

Antiques and white wicker furnishings grace this Victorian home, born in 1896. Ivy and alders grow profusely on the west side, sheltering birds and birdhouses.

Most rooms have birdcages for decoration. Some rooms overlook the Columbia River. Breakfast, served in the tower of the bullet turret, may include smoked salmon, cream cheese, and bagels. Astoria was established in 1811. Fur trading, then salmon and logging gave this town its start.

Hostess: Charlene Maxwell
Rooms: 9 (7PB; 2SB) $45-96
Full Breakfast
Credit Cards: A, B, D
Notes: 5, 7 (over 8), 8, 9, 10

Inn-Chanted Bed and Breakfast

707 8th Street, 97103
(503) 325-5223; (800) 455-7018

The historic Fulton House, built in 1883, is beautifully decorated with silk brocade wallpaper, crystal chandeliers, and ornately painted medallions and columns. Guest rooms have magnificent views of the Columbia River, private baths, queen beds, and TVs. Full gourmet breakfasts. Dolls and trains displayed. Walk to historic buildings, town, and antique shops.

Hosts: Richard and Dixie Swart
Rooms: 3 (PB) $70-100
Full Breakfast
Credit Cards: A, B, C, D
Notes: 2, 5, 7, 8, 12

AURORA

The Inn at Aurora

15109 NE 2nd Street, 97002
(503) 678-1932; FAX (503) 678-1342

Designed and furnished to reflect the simplicity of the Old Aurora Colony, this new home is located in the National Historic District near the Ox Barn Museum and

The Inn at Aurora

numerous antique shops. Handcrafted items by local artists are available. Seasonal fresh fruits, berries, nuts, and vegetables are treasures of this area, as are unique places to dine. Champoeg State Park by the Willamette River and Silver Falls State Park are nearby for hiking and biking. All rooms have king beds, AC, cable TVs, phones, and refrigerators. The suite is hearthside with a spa tub. Upper room balconies offer pleasant views of Aurora and the natural landscape.

Hostess: Elizabeth Heininge
Rooms: 4 (PB) $75-125
Full Breakfast
Credit Cards: A, B
Notes: 5, 6 (by prior arrangement), 7, 10, 12

BEAVERTON

The Yankee Tinker Bed and Breakfast

5480 SW 183rd Avenue, 97007
(503) 649-0932; (800) 846-5372;
FAX (503) 649-0932
E-mail: yankeetb7b@aol.com
Web site: http://www.yankeetinker.com

Easy access to Beaverton, Hillsboro business, ten miles west of Portland in Washington County wine country. Comfortable

welcome; 7 Children welcome; 8 Tennis nearby; 9 Swimming nearby; 10 Golf nearby; 11 Skiing nearby; 12 May be booked through travel agent.

home operating as a B&B since 1988, filled with heirlooms, antiques, quilts, and flowers. Private yard/gardens. Spacious deck. Quiet retreat, perfect for a day or week. Fireplace in guest sitting room. AC. Acclaimed breakfasts, timed and scaled to meet your needs, utilize the abundant variety of locally grown fruits and berries. Featured in *Hidden Oregon*.

Hosts: Jan and Ralph Wadleigh
Rooms: 3 (2PB; 1SB) $65-75
Full Breakfast
Credit Cards: A, B, C, D, E
Notes: 2, 5, 9, 10, 12

BEND

Gazebo Bed and Breakfast
21679 Obsidian Avenue, 97702
(541) 389-7202

Come visit our country home with a panoramic view of the Cascades from Mt. Hood to Mt. Bachelor. Relax among our antique furnishings or in the rock garden and gazebo. Enjoy nearby skiing, hiking, fishing, rafting, and the best golfing in Oregon. Minutes from town. Family-style breakfast. Smoking outdoors only.

Hosts: Gale and Helen Estergreen
Rooms: 2 (1PB; 1SB) $50-60
Full Breakfast
Credit Cards: none
Notes: 2, 5, 7, 9, 10, 11

CLOVERDALE

Sandlake Country Inn
8505 Galloway Road, 97112
(503) 965-6745

Sshhh. . . . We're a secret hideaway on the awesome Oregon coast—a private,

peaceful place for making memories. This 1894 shipwreck-timbered farmhouse on the Oregon Historic Registry is tucked into a bower of old roses. You will find hummingbirds, Mozart, cookies at midnight, marble fireplaces, whirlpool baths for two, a honeymoon cottage, breakfast en suite, vintage movies, close-captioned television, "green" rooms. . . . Sandlake Country Inn is a nonsmoking home. We are wheelchair accessible.

Hosts: Femke and David Durham
Rooms: 4 (PB) $80-125
Full Breakfast
Credit Cards: A, B, D
Notes: 2, 5, 12

CORVALLIS

Abed and Breakfast at Spark's Hearth
2515 SW 45th Street, 97333
(541) 757-7321; FAX (541) 753-4332
E-mail: abed@proaxis.com

Critque passing golfers from our back deck or spoil yourself in the outdoor spa—we furnish plush body towels and robes; you bring a suit. Visit on red velvet Victorian furnishings and Oriental carpets in the living room, or crash in comfort in the television/reading room. Sleep in country quiet on a king bed in a king-size bedroom. Awake to a full breakfast including fresh fruit compote, a hot entrée, and homemade pie, served on china and crystal. Life is good!

Hosts: Neoma and Herb Sparks
Rooms: 4 (2PB; 2SB) $68-82
Full Breakfast
Credit Cards: A, B, C, D, E
Notes: 2, 5, 7 (over 8), 8, 9, 10, 12

NOTES: Credit cards accepted: A Master Card; B Visa; C American Express; D Discover; E Diners Club; F Other; 2 Personal checks accepted; 3 Lunch available; 4 Dinner available; 5 Open all year; 6 Pets

COTTAGE GROVE

Apple Inn
Bed and Breakfast

30697 Kenady Lane, 97424
(541) 942-2393; (800) 942-2393;
FAX (541) 767-0402
E-mail: appleinn@pond.net
Web site: http://www.pond.net/~bnbassoc/
appleinn.html

Lovely country home snuggled in our 190-acre forest and tree farm. Close to I-5 and Cottage Grove with covered bridges, antiques, golf, and lakes. Two rooms with private baths charmingly decorated in country and antiques, comfortable beds, view, TV/VCR, phone, luxury hot tub. Featured in the Sunday *Oregonian* travel section. Homemade breakfast plus snacks. Smoking outside, children by arrangement. Cookbook available. Privacy and pampering. Be our guests!

Hosts: Harry and Kathe McIntire
Rooms: 2 (PB) $65-85
Full Breakfast
Credit Cards: D
Notes: 2, 5, 7, 8, 9, 10

ELMIRA

McGillivray's Log Home
Bed and Breakfast

88680 Evers Road, 97437
(541) 935-3564

Fourteen miles west of Eugene, on the way to the coast, you will find the best of yesterday and the comforts of today. King beds, air-conditioning, and quiet. Old-fashioned breakfasts usually are prepared on an antique, wood-burning cookstove.

McGillivray's Log Home

This built-from-scratch 1982 log home is near Fern Ridge Lake.

Hostess: Evelyn R. McGillivray
Rooms: 2 (PB) $70-80
Continental Breakfast
Credit Cards: A, B
Notes: 2, 5

EUGENE

Camille's
Bed and Breakfast

3277 Onyx Place, 97405
(541) 344-9576; FAX (541) 345-9970

A '60s contemporary home in a quiet, woodsy neighborhood furnished with American country antiques. Rooms have wonderfully comfortable queen beds, with work space. Cozy guest sitting room with phone and TV. Healthy breakfast. Just more than a mile south of the University of Oregon; downtown is minutes away. Bike path and park with major jogging path nearby. Excellent restaurant in walking distance. Hour's drive to Oregon coast.

Hosts: Bill and Camille Kievith
Rooms: 2 (1PB; 1SB) $55-70
Full Breakfast
Credit Cards: none
Notes: 2, 5, 8, 9, 10

---

welcome; 7 Children welcome; 8 Tennis nearby; 9 Swimming nearby; 10 Golf nearby; 11 Skiing nearby; 12 May be booked through travel agent.

The Campbell House—
A City Inn

252 Pearl Street, 97401
(541) 343-1119; (800) 264-2519;
FAX (541) 343-2258
E-mail: campbellhouse@campbellhouse.com
Web site: http://www.campbellhouse.com

Splendor and romance in the tradition of a fine European hotel. Each of the elegant rooms features private bath, TV/VCR, telephone, and robes. Selected rooms feature a four-poster bed, fireplace, and jetted or claw-foot tub. Take pleasure from the Old World ambience of the parlor and library with a fine selection of books and videos. Walking distance to restaurants, theaters, museums, and shops. Two blocks from nine miles of riverside bike paths and jogging trails.

Hostess: Myra Plant
Rooms: 12 (PB) $80-275
Full Breakfast
Credit Cards: A, B, C, D
Notes: 5, 7, 8, 9, 10, 12

Kjaer's House
in the Woods

814 Lorane Highway, 97405
(541) 343-3234

This 1910 Craftsman home in a parklike setting provides urban convenience and suburban tranquillity. The grounds have both wildflowers and landscaped shrubs, colorful in the spring but peaceful throughout the year; wildlife is abundant. The home is furnished with antiques, Oriental carpets, a square rosewood grand piano, an extensive music library, and a plate collection. A full breakfast is served, featuring local cheeses, nuts, and fruits. In operation since 1984, this B&B is inspected by the Eugene Area B&B Association and the Oregon B&B Guild. Hosts are long-time Eugene residents who take pleasure in sharing their knowledge of the area with guests.

Hosts: Eunice and George Kjaer
Rooms: 2 (PB) $65-75
Full Breakfast
Credit Cards: none
Notes: 2, 5, 7, 8, 9, 10, 12

FLORENCE

Betty's Barn Home
Bed and Breakfast

05659 Canary Road, 97439
(541) 997-2764

"Country on the Coast." Back to the real thing in the bed and breakfast experience. Quiet, peaceful surroundings. Tall trees, green lawns, beautiful landscaping. Located amid Oregon's National Recreation Area, just a quarter mile from our famous Jessie M. Honeyman State Park. Boating, swimming.

Host: (Betty) Marion E. Westfall
Rooms: 2 (SB) $55-65
Full Breakfast
Credit Cards: none
Notes: 2, 5, 7 (6 and older), 8, 9, 10, 11 (water)

HEREFORD

Fort Reading
Bed and Breakfast

HCR 86, Box 140, 97837
(541) 446-3478 (voice and FAX); (800) 573-4285

We are a working cattle ranch forty miles southwest of Baker City, in the Burnt River

---

NOTES: Credit cards accepted: A Master Card; B Visa; C American Express; D Discover; E Diners Club; F Other; 2 Personal checks accepted; 3 Lunch available; 4 Dinner available; 5 Open all year; 6 Pets

Fort Reading Bed and Breakfast

Valley. While you're with us, enjoy a stroll around the ranch, the country charm of your own two-bedroom cottage, and a ranch-style breakfast in the ranch house breakfast room. Squirrel, deer, and elk hunts can be arranged. There are streams and a lake nearby for fishing. No smoking. Open April through September.

Hosts: Daryl and Barbara Hawes
Rooms: 2 (SB) $45-75
Full Ranch-Style Breakfast
Credit Cards: none
Notes: 2, 3, 4, 6, 7

HOOD RIVER

The Upper Rooms on Avalon Bed and Breakfast

3444 Avalon Drive, 97031
(541) 386-2560; (888) 386-3941
E-mail: upperrooms@moriah.com

Down-home charm in our renovated Avalon farmhouse on the Heights in Hood River. Minutes from skiing, windsurfing, and other outdoor recreation. Cozy neighborhood with little traffic noise, yet just bordering the city limits. Deck and large upstairs bedrooms with views of Mt.

Adams. Relaxed, friendly atmosphere. Family-style breakfast. Barbeque available. Reasonable rates.

Hosts: Jim and Dorothy Tollen
Rooms: 2 (SB) $65
Full Breakfast
Credit Cards: A, B, D
Notes: 5, 7, 8, 9, 10, 11, 12

JACKSONVILLE

The Touvelle House

PO Box 1891, 97530
(541) 899-8938; (800) 846-8442;
FAX (541) 899-3992
E-mail: touvelle@wave.net
Web site: http://www.wave.net/upg/touvelle

Stately 1916 Craftsman, five thousand square feet, on two acres. Beautiful gardens, heated pool, and spa. Full three-course breakfast on fine china and antique crystal and silver. Relax in summer on our spacious verandas with a cool raspberry lemonade. In winter, cozy up to our massive stone fireplace with hot apple cider. Come, be pampered like travelers from yesteryear. City close and country quiet.

Hosts: Carolee and Dennis Casey
Rooms: 6 (PB) $75-105 (seasonal)
Full Breakfast
Credit Cards: A, B, C, D, E
Notes: 2, 5, 7 (over 12), 9 (on site), 10, 11, 12

LA GRANDE

Stang Manor Inn

1612 Walnut, 97850
(541) 963-2400 (voice and FAX); (888) 286-9463
E-mail: stang@eoni.com
Web site: http://www.eoni.com/stang

Capturing the romance and elegance of a former era, Stang Manor Inn is a lovingly

welcome; 7 Children welcome; 8 Tennis nearby; 9 Swimming nearby; 10 Golf nearby; 11 Skiing nearby; 12 May be booked through travel agent.

Stang Manor Inn

preserved, Georgian colonial home that beckons even the casual traveler to bask in its comfort and hospitality. One of the rooms adjoins a balcony overlooking the rose garden. The suite features a large fireplace in its comfortable sitting room. Extraordinary woodwork throughout the house serves as a reminder that the first owner, August Stang, spared no expense to make this 1920s mansion a masterpiece. Your full breakfast in the formal dining room will sparkle with silver, crystal, candles, and conversation.

Hosts: Margie and Pat McClure
Rooms: 4 (PB) $70-90
Full Breakfast
Credit Cards: A, B
Notes: 2, 5, 9, 10, 11, 12

LINCOLN CITY

Brey House
"Ocean View"
Bed and Breakfast Inn
3725 NW Keel Avenue, 97367
(541) 994-7123

The ocean awaits you just across the street. Enjoy whale watching, storm watching, or just beachcombing. We are conveniently located a short walking dis-

tance from local restaurants and retail shops. Guests have four beautiful rooms to choose from, all with private baths and queen beds. Flannel sheets and electric blankets are in all the guest rooms. Enjoy Milt and Shirley's talked-about breakfast. Brey House is a three-story, Cape Cod-style home.

Hosts: Milt and Shirley Brey
Rooms: 4 (PB) $70-135
Full Breakfast
Credit Cards: A, B, D
Notes: 2, 5, 9, 10, 12

Pacific Rest Bed and Breakfast

Pacific Rest
Bed and Breakfast
1611 NE 11th Street, 97367
(541) 994-2337; (888) 405-7378

Newer home on hillside within walking distance of shops, restaurants, lake and beach. Offering large suites, private baths, covered private decks, and large gathering room for visiting and relaxing. Family operated with gracious hospitality and personal service. Christian counseling available. Books for inspiration and enjoyment. Small pets and children welcome. Partial ocean and mountain views. One unit sleeps five; the other unit sleeps three. A full gourmet breakfast and evening homemade dessert are served.

Hosts: Ray and Judy Waetjen
Rooms: 2 (PB) $75-85
Full Breakfast
Credit Cards: none
Notes: 2, 5, 6, 7, 9, 10, 12

MT. HOOD AREA

Falcon's Crest Inn

87287 Government Camp Loop Highway, PO Box
   185, **Government Camp**, 97028
(503) 272-3403; (800) 624-7384;
FAX (503) 272-3454

Falcon's Crest Inn is a beautiful mountain lodge/chalet-style house, architecturally designed to fit into the quiet natural forest and majestic setting of Oregon's Cascade Mountains. Conveniently located at the intersection of Highway 26 and the Government Camp Loop Highway, the inn is within walking distance of Ski Bowl, a year-round playground featuring downhill skiing in the winter and the Alpine Slide in the summer! The inn has five suites, all with private baths. Each guest room is individually decorated with interesting and unique collectibles and beautiful views of the mountains and forests. Telephones are available for guests to use in each suite. Smoking is restricted. A fine-dining restaurant is located on the premises. Ski packages are available! Multiple-night discounts are offered.

Hosts: B.J. and Melody Johnson
Rooms: 5 (PB) $95-179
Full Breakfast
Credit Cards: A, B, C, D
Notes: 2, 4, 5, 8, 9, 10, 11, 12

Old Welches Inn
Bed and Breakfast

26401 E. Welches Road, **Welches**, 97067
(503) 622-3754; FAX (503) 622-5370
Web site: http://www.innsandouts.com/property/
   old_welches_inn.html

Enjoy casual elegance in a riverside retreat. The inn is the oldest building on the W-SW side of Mt. Hood. Lots of private places to sit and enjoy the scenery of the surrounding mountains.

Hosts: Judith and Ted Mondun
Rooms: 5, including cottage (2PB; 3SB) $75-130
Full Breakfast
Credit Cards: A, B, C, D
Notes: 2, 5, 6 and 7 (in cottage), 8, 9, 10, 11, 12

Old Welches Inn Bed and Breakfast

NEWPORT

Oar House
Bed and Breakfast

520 SW 2nd Street, 97365
(541) 265-9571; (800) 252-2358

A Lincoln County historic landmark built in 1900, renovated and expanded in 1993.

welcome; 7 Children welcome; 8 Tennis nearby; 9 Swimming nearby; 10 Golf nearby; 11 Skiing nearby;
12 May be booked through travel agent.

Centrally located in the picturesque Nye Beach area. Lighthouse tower provides 360-degree views of the ocean, local lighthouses, mountains, romantic sunsets, whales, and winter storms. Commodious guest common areas. Art, books, periodicals, daily newspapers. Unique guest rooms with ocean view and queen beds. *Gourmet*-inspired breakfast. The deck is sheltered from the wind. Off-street parking is provided.

Hostess: Jan LeBrun
Rooms: 5 (PB) $90-120
Full Breakfast
Credit Cards: A, B, D
Notes: 2, 5, 8, 9, 10

ROSEBURG

Hokanson's Guest House

848 SE Jackson; 97470
(541) 672-2632; FAX (541) 440-1996

Gracefully standing on land once owned by Roseburg's founding father Aaron Rose, the Guest House was built in 1852 in the Gothic Revival style. The Guest House is Roseburg's only B&B on the National Register of Historic Places. The two guest rooms, featuring Victorian decor, have private baths and claw-foot tubs. Breakfast is always a three-course affair. Conveniently located one block from downtown, Hokanson's Guest House is beautifully landscaped with lovely lawns, flower gardens, and even a pond for your aesthetic pleasure.

Hostess: John and Victoria Hokanson
Rooms: 2 (PB) $75-95
Full Breakfast
Credit Cards: A, B
Notes: 2, 5, 8, 9, 10

SEASIDE

10th Avenue Inn Bed and Breakfast

125 10th Avenue, 97138
(503) 738-0643 (voice and FAX); (800) 569-1114

Enjoy this ocean-view home just steps from the beach and a short walk along the promenade from restaurants and shopping. Light, airy guest rooms are decorated in soft colors and sprinkled in antiques, and include TVs. Experience the right balance of personal and private. A full breakfast is served. No smoking or pets. A separate cottage sleeps seven.

Hosts: Francie and Vern Starkey
Rooms: 4 (PB) $55-70
Full Breakfast
Credit Cards: A, B, C, D
Notes: 2, 5, 7 (over 9), 8, 9, 10

Sand Dollar Bed and Breakfast

Sand Dollar Bed and Breakfast

606 N. Holladay Drive, 97138
(503) 738-3491; (800) 738-3491

Historic Craftsman bungalow includes two upstairs bedrooms with private baths and comfy beds—or you may prefer our cottage with its spectacular view and full

---

NOTES: Credit cards accepted: A Master Card; B Visa; C American Express; D Discover; E Diners Club; F Other; 2 Personal checks accepted; 3 Lunch available; 4 Dinner available; 5 Open all year; 6 Pets

kitchen. Children are always welcome. Only a short walk to the beach, shops, or restaurants. Your hosts are a retired minister and his wife. The Sand Dollar is a no-smoking bed and breakfast.

Hosts: Bob and Nita Hempfling
Rooms: 3 (PB) $55-100
Full Breakfast
Credit Cards: A, B, C, D
Notes: 2 ,5 ,7, 8, 9, 10, 12

SISTERS

Conklin's Guest House

69013 Camp Polk Road, 97759
(541) 549-0123; (800) 549-4262;
FAX (541) 549-4481

Conklin's Guest House is surrounded by a sprawling meadow with a panoramic backdrop of snowcapped peaks. Rich in history, the near-century-old homesite gives evidence that early settlers chose the most beautiful sites first! Modern conveniences and attention to detail ensure a comfortable and restful stay. The house offers guests a truly peaceful environment within walking distance of the bustling shops and restaurants of Sisters. Guests are welcome to use the barbecue, swimming pool, and laundry facilities, and otherwise to *be at home!* The ponds are stocked with trout for catch-and-release fishing. The Sisters area has something for everyone, from rafting and rock climbing to dining and shopping and much more, all the time!

Hosts: Marie and Frank Conklin
Rooms: 5 (PB) $90-110
Full Breakfast
Credit Cards: none
Notes: 2, 5, 7 (over 5), 8, 9 (heated pool on B&B grounds), 10, 11

McKenzie View

SPRINGFIELD/EUGENE

McKenzie View— "A Riverside Bed and Breakfast"

34922 McKenzie View Drive, 97478
(541) 726-3887; (888) MCKVIEW (625-8439);
FAX (541) 726-6968
E-mail: mckenzieview@worldnet.att.net
Web site: http://design-web.com/mckenzieview/

Spacious country home on six acres of wooded, riverfront property only fifteen minutes from town and the University of Oregon. Richly appointed guest rooms include comfortable seating areas, many antiques, private baths, and other fine amenities. Picture window views of the

welcome; 7 Children welcome; 8 Tennis nearby; 9 Swimming nearby; 10 Golf nearby; 11 Skiing nearby; 12 May be booked through travel agent.

river and perennial gardens can be enjoyed throughout the house. Fish from the river's edge, rest in a hammock, or relax in front of a fire. McKenzie View's natural beauty will captivate and enchant you.

Hosts: Scott and Roberta Bolling
Rooms: 4 (PB) $85-215
Full Breakfast
Credit Cards: A, B
Notes: 2, 5, 8, 9

STAYTON

Gardner House Bed and Breakfast

633 N. Third Avenue, 97383
(503) 769-6331

Well House Suite! This extraordinary suite has coordinated decor, a separate entrance, kitchen, dining room, large bath, sitting room, queen bed, telephone, CATV, and VCR. The Madonna Room is in the main house and has much the same features as the Well House Suite. The dining room is on the same floor in a glassed-in porch. A bright room on any day.

Host: Richard Jungwirth
Rooms: 4 (3PB; 1SB) $55-75
Full Breakfast
Credit Cards: A, B, C, D, E, F
Notes: 2, 3, 4, 5, 6, 7, 8, 9, 10, 11, 12

WELCHES (MT. HOOD AREA)

Doublegate Inn B&B

26711 E. Welches Road, 97067
(503) 622-4859 (voice and FAX)

The house has been a landmark since it was built in the 1920s. Commonly referred to as "the house with the rock wall," located one block from a golf course, the B&B sits atop a cedar-treed knoll with a view of the Salmon River. The beautifully decorated inn, filled with crafts and antiques, features four distinctly styled guest rooms, some with spa tubs. Quietly yet conveniently located near the many diverse activities found on and around scenic Mt. Hood. Be spoiled and refreshed and find the romance in "God's Country" just off the Oregon Trail! Sumptuous "no lunch" breakfasts served "en suite" on the deck or at fireside in the dining room.

Hosts: Gary and Charlene Poston
Rooms: 4 (PB) $80-115
Full Breakfast
Credit Cards: none
Notes: 2, 5, 7 (over 12), 8, 9, 10, 11

WEST LINN

Swift Shore Chalet

1190 Swift Shore Circle, 97068
(503) 650-3853; FAX (503) 656-2105

The perfect getaway . . . a place to relax in the quiet surroundings of a beautiful home, surrounded by a panoramic view of green hillsides, a garden filled with fragrant flowers, and the songs of birds. A full breakfast is beautifully served on the deck or in the dining room. Specialties include Mandarin orange scones, raspberry cream cheese coffee cake, Belgian waffles, Dutch oven pancakes, and Pacific crab quiche. Be pampered and served with quiet attention to detail. Minutes from downtown Portland and scenic beauties. A wonderful setting for families.

Hosts: Nancy and Horace Duke
Rooms: 2 (1PB; 1SB) $80
Full Breakfast
Credit Cards: none
Notes: 5, 7, 10

NOTES: Credit cards accepted: A Master Card; B Visa; C American Express; D Discover; E Diners Club; F Other; 2 Personal checks accepted; 3 Lunch available; 4 Dinner available; 5 Open all year; 6 Pets

Pennsylvania

A Bed and Breakfast Connection/Bed and Breakfast of Philadelphia

PO Box 21, **Devon**, 19333
(610) 687-3565; (800) 448-3619;
FAX (610) 995-9524
E-mail: bnb@bnbphiladelphia.com
Web site: http://www.bnbphiladelphia.com

From elegant town houses in historic **Center City Philadelphia** to a manor house in scenic **Bucks County**; from an elegant home-within-a-barn in the **suburbs** to charming Victorian inns in **York**, A Bed and Breakfast Connection/Bed and Breakfast of Philadelphia offers a wide variety of styles and locations in its scores of inspected homes, guest houses and inns. For example, choose from accommodations just three blocks from "America's most historic square mile," **Independence National Historical Park**; or within easy distance of **Valley Forge Park**; or in the heart of the **Brandywine Valley** area with its magnificent historic estates and museums. Stay on a working farm in the Amish country of **Lancaster County**. Our accommodations range in price from $30 to $200 per night; we offer houses with one guest room and inns with many rooms. We cover seven counties in the southeastern corner of Pennsylvania. Mary Alice Hamilton and Peggy Gregg, co-owners. Major credit cards accepted.

Rest and Repast Bed and Breakfast Reservations

PO Box 126, **Pine Grove Mills**, 16868
(814) 238-1484; (814) 861-6566;
FAX (814) 234-9890
Web site: http://iul.com/business/bnbinpa

Since 1982, Rest and Repast has represented inspected bed and breakfasts in central Pennsylvania, including the Penn State University area, plus a fine selection of statewide inns. The sixty-plus properties include scenic farms near famous fly-fishing streams, estates on the National Register, private apartments, cottages, and lodges, as well as a variety of contemporary homes. Several sites are appropriate for small wedding receptions, family reunions, and corporate retreats. Visit our Web site for a more complete list and additional details on many of the properties represented. The 140 rooms vary widely, with private or shared baths; $55-100, double occupancy; corporate and long-term rates available. Deposit required, cash or check only. Free brochure.

---

welcome; 7 Children welcome; 8 Tennis nearby; 9 Swimming nearby; 10 Golf nearby; 11 Skiing nearby; 12 May be booked through travel agent.

PENNSYLVANIA

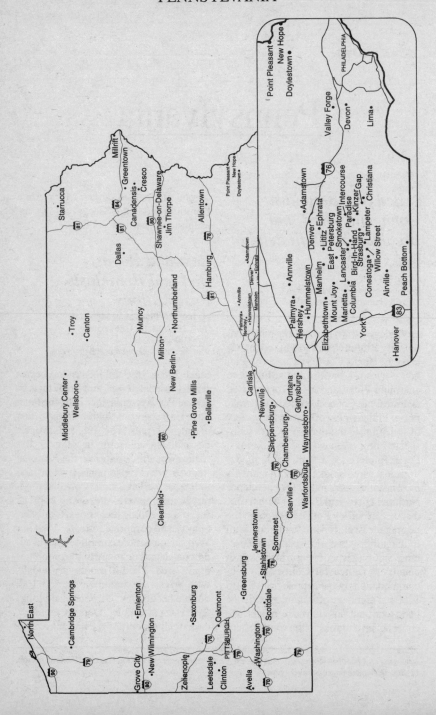

ADAMSTOWN

Adamstown Inns

62 W. Main Street, 19501-0938
(717) 484-0800; (800) 594-4808

Experience simple elegance in two Victorian homes resplendent with leaded-glass windows and door, magnificent chestnut woodwork, and Oriental rugs. All seven guest rooms are decorated with family heirlooms, handmade quilts, lace curtains, and many distinctive touches. Accommodations range from antique to king beds. Five rooms have Jacuzzis for two, and three rooms feature gas fireplaces. The inns are located in a small town brimming with antique dealers and only minutes from Reading and Lancaster.

Hosts: Tom and Wanda Berman
Rooms: 7 (PB) $70-135
Continental Plus Breakfast
Credit Cards: A, B, D
Notes: 2, 5, 8, 9, 10, 12

AIRVILLE

Spring House

1264 Muddy Creek Forks Road, 17302
(717) 927-6906

Built in 1798 of warm fieldstone, Spring House in the Pennsylvania Dutch area is a fine example of colonial architecture with original stenciling that overlooks a river valley. Now on the National Register of Historic Places, the Spring House has welcomed guests from around the world who seek a historic setting, tranquillity, antiques, and access to Amish country and Gettysburg, with a scenic railroad soon to be open to the public. Regional breakfast specialties and Amish cheeses welcome you. Country luxuries abound: featherbeds and woodstoves in the winter, large porch with swing for summer breezes. Also, creek swimming, hiking and biking trails, with horseback riding nearby. Location for the Tim Allen movie *For Richer or Poorer*; several actors stayed here.

Hosts: Ray Constance Hearne and Michael Schuster
Rooms: 4 (3PB; 1SB) $60-95
Full Breakfast
Credit Cards: none
Notes: 2, 5, 7, 9, 10, 11, 12

ALLENTOWN

Brennans Bed and Breakfast

3827 Linden Street, 18104
(610) 395-0869

We have three rooms available with private bathrooms. Located in a suburban area with nearby parks and restaurants available. Your home away from home.

Hosts: Lois and Edward J. Brennan
Rooms: 3 (PB) $35-40
Full Breakfast
Credit Cards: none
Notes: 2, 6 (check with proprietors), 7, 8, 9, 10

ANNVILLE

Swatara Creek Inn

Box 692, RD 2, 17003
(717) 865-3259

1860s Victorian mansion situated on four acres in the peaceful country. All rooms have private baths, canopied queen-size

---

NOTES: Credit cards accepted: A Master Card; B Visa; C American Express; D Discover; E Diners Club; F Other; 2 Personal checks accepted; 3 Lunch available; 4 Dinner available; 5 Open all year; 6 Pets welcome; 7 Children welcome; 8 Tennis nearby; 9 Swimming nearby; 10 Golf nearby; 11 Skiing nearby; 12 May be booked through travel agent.

Swatara Creek Inn

beds, and air-conditioning, and include a full breakfast. Sitting room, dining room, and gift shop on the first floor. Wheelchair-accessible. Close to Hershey, Mt. Hope Winery, Mt. Gretna, Reading outlets, and the Lancaster Amish area. Also near many historical sites: Cornwall Mines, Ephrata Cloisters, Gettysburg, etc. No smoking inside the house.

Hosts: Dick and Jeannette Hess
Rooms: 10 (PB) $55-80
Full Breakfast
Credit Cards: A, B, C, D, E
Notes: 2, 5, 7, 8, 9, 10, 12

AVELLA

Weatherbury Farm

1061 Sugar Run Road, 15312
(412) 587-3763; FAX (412) 587-0125

Award-winning bed and breakfast on working farm—meadows, gardens, cows, sheep, and tranquillity! Guest rooms, located in the 1870s farmhouse and summer kitchen, and suites in the livery stable are lovingly furnished with country charm; each has a private bath and air-conditioning. Heated pool. Bountiful farm breakfast. Visit our blacksmith shop. Great hiking, biking, boating, and fishing

nearby. Visit Meadowcroft Museum of Rural Life, historic southwest Pennsylvania, and Pittsburgh. Children welcome.

Hosts: Dale, Marcy, and Nigel Tudor
Rooms: 8 (PB) $65-95
Full, Bountiful Farm Breakfast
Credit Cards: A, B, C, D
Notes: 2, 5, 7, 8, 9, 10, 12

BELLEVILLE

Twin Oaks
Bed and Breakfast

73 S. Dryhouse Road, 17004
(717) 935-2026

In the heart of the Kishacoquillas Valley only thirty minutes from Penn State. Norman and Sarah welcome their guests to a new facility with clean, spacious rooms. In a quiet country setting with a panoramic view of Stone and Jacks mountains. A full breakfast is served. Children are welcome. Open all year.

Hosts: J. Norman and Sarah Glick
Rooms: 4 (1PB; 3SB) $40-50
Full Breakfast
Credit Cards: none
Notes: 2, 5, 7, 12

BIRD-IN-HAND

The Village Inn
of Bird-in-Hand

2695 Old Philadelphia Pike, PO Box 253, 17505
(717) 293-8369; (800) 914-2473;
FAX (717) 768-1117
E-mail: Smucker@Bird-in-Hand.com
Web site: http://www.herby.com/lanco/Smucker/
    Bird-in-Hand.html

Listed on the National Historic Register, our inn is located on Route 340, five miles

---

NOTES: Credit cards accepted: A Master Card; B Visa; C American Express; D Discover; E Diners Club; F Other; 2 Personal checks accepted; 3 Lunch available; 4 Dinner available; 5 Open all year; 6 Pets

east of Lancaster in the heart of the Pennsylvania Dutch country. Each room features its own private bath and includes a continental plus breakfast, free use of indoor and outdoor pools and tennis courts located within walking distance, and a complimentary two-hour tour of the surrounding Amish farmlands. Reservations suggested. Package available.

Hosts: Richmond and Janice Young
Rooms: 11 (PB) $79-139
Continental Plus Breakfast
Credit Cards: A, B, C, D
Notes: 2, 5, 8, 9, 10, 12

Bethany Guest House

CAMBRIDGE SPRINGS

Bethany Guest House

325 S. Main Street, 16403
(814) 398-2046; (800) 777-2046

Enjoy the luxury of an 1876 Italianate home built in a Victorian resort known worldwide for its healing waters. This home, on the National Register of Historic Places, has been restored and decorated with period furnishings. No phones or TV. Parlor, drawing room, Greek Revival dining room, and library. The Covenant Room

features a double whirlpool tub. Located near Lake Erie, wildlife refuges, bicycle trails, amusement parks, Edinboro University, and Allegheny College. Close to Erie, Edinboro, and Meadville. Clergy discount and gift certificates available.

Hosts: Dave and Katie White
Rooms: 4 (PB) $35-60
Full Breakfast
Credit Cards: A, B
Notes: 2, 5, 7, 8, 9, 10, 11

CANADENSIS

Brookview Manor Bed and Breakfast Inn

RR 1, Box 365, 18325
(717) 595-2451; (800) 585-7974;
FAX (717) 595-5065

Situated on four picturesque acres, the inn offers the traveler an ideal retreat from the workaday world. Enjoy the simple pleasures of hiking trails or a cozy glider on a spacious wraparound porch. Each room offers a panoramic view of the forest, mountains, and stream; all have private baths. Breakfast is served in our cheery dining room and includes fruits, juices, fresh muffins, and a hearty entrée.

Hostess: Mary Anne Buckley
Rooms: 10 (PB) $100-150
Full Breakfast
Credit Cards: A, B, C, D, E
Notes: 2, 5, 7 (over 12), 8, 9, 10, 11, 12

Dreamy Acres

PO Box 7, 18325-0007
(717) 595-7115

Esther and Bill Pickett started Dreamy Acres as a bed and breakfast inn in 1959, doing bed and breakfast before it was in

welcome; 7 Children welcome; 8 Tennis nearby; 9 Swimming nearby; 10 Golf nearby; 11 Skiing nearby; 12 May be booked through travel agent.

style. Situated on three acres with a stream and a pond, Dreamy Acres is in the heart of the Pocono Mountains vacationland, close to stores, churches, gift shops, and recreational facilities. Guest rooms have air-conditioning and color cable TV, and some have VCRs.

Hosts: Esther and Bill Pickett
Rooms: 6 (4PB; 2SB) $38-55
Expanded Continental Breakfast
Credit Cards: none
Notes: 2, 5, 8, 9, 10, 11

CANTON

M-mm Good Bed and Breakfast

RD 1, Box 71, 17724
(717) 673-8153

Located along Route 414, three miles east of Canton, in a quiet country setting in the center of the Endless Mountains. Enjoy clean, comfortable rooms and a full breakfast including homemade muffins or sticky buns. Picnic tables under maple trees. Hiking and fishing close by.

Hosts: Melvin and Irene Good
Rooms: 3 (SB)
Full Breakfast
Credit Cards: None
Notes: 2, 5, 7

CARLISLE

Line Limousin Farmhouse Bed and Breakfast

2070 Ritner Highway, 17013
(717) 243-1281

Relax and unwind in an 1864 brick-and-stone farmhouse on one hundred acres, two miles off I-81, Exit 12. French Limousin cattle are raised here. Enjoy antiques, including a player piano, and the use of a golf driving range. Join us for worship at our historic First Presbyterian Church. Two rooms having comfortable king beds and private baths; two rooms share a bath. Nonsmokers, please.

Hosts: Bob and Joan Line
Rooms: 4 (2PB; 2SB) $68.90-79.50
Full Breakfast
Credit Cards: none
Notes: 2, 5, 7 (over 8), 10

Pheasant Field Bed and Breakfast

Pheasant Field Bed and Breakfast

150 Hickorytown Road, 17013
(717) 258-0717 (voice and FAX)
E-mail: pheasant@pa.net
Web site: http://www.pa.net/pheasant

Stay in this lovely old brick farmhouse set in quiet country surroundings. Wake up to a full country breakfast including fresh bread or muffins, fresh fruit, a hot entrée, and plenty of hot coffee. After a game of tennis or a hike on the Appalachian Trail, relax in the family room or living room and help yourself to a homemade cookie (or two). Feel free to bring your horse—we offer overnight boarding, when space is available. Collector car shows, antiquing, and fly-fishing are nearby. Smoking is permitted outside. We can make arrangements for your pets at local kennels. AAA three-diamond rating. "Come home to the country."

Hosts: Dee Fegan and Chuck DeMarco
Rooms: 4 (2PB; 2SB) $65-105
Full Breakfast
Credit Cards: A, B, C
Notes: 2, 5, 7, 8 on site, 9, 10, 11, 12

CHAMBERSBURG

Falling Spring Inn

1838 Falling Spring Road, 17201
(717) 267-3654; FAX (717) 267-2584

Enjoy country living only two miles from I-81, Exit 6, and Route 30, on a working farm with animals and Falling Spring, a nationally renowned, freshwater trout stream. A large pond, lawns, meadows, ducks, and birds all make a pleasant stay. Historic Gettysburg is only twenty-five miles away. Relax in our air-conditioned rooms with queen beds. One room with spa. One room wheelchair-accessible.

Hosts: Adin and Janet Frey
Rooms: 5 (PB) $49-89
Full Breakfast
Credit Cards: A, B
Notes: 2, 5, 7, 8, 9, 10, 11, 12

CHRISTIANA

Georgetown Bed and Breakfast

1222 Georgetown Road, 17509
(717) 786-4570

Once a miller's home, the original structure was converted to a B&B for the enjoyment of guests in a relaxing home away from home. Entrance to the house is by a brick walkway. The herb garden on the left lets guests smell the lavender and mint that are just two of the herbs used to garnish morning breakfasts. There is a choice of three bedrooms decorated with antiques and collectibles. Lancaster County Amish, a unique group of people who travel in horse-drawn carriages, pass in front of the Georgetown. Visit the local Strasburg Train Museum.

Hostess: Doris W. Woerth
Rooms: 3 (1PB; 2SB) $40-50
Full Breakfast
Credit Cards: none
Notes: 2, 5, 9, 10

Victorian Loft Bed and Breakfast

CLEARFIELD

Victorian Loft Bed and Breakfast

216 S. Front Street, 16830
(814) 765-4805; (800) 798-0456;
FAX (814) 765-9596
E-mail: pdurant@mail.csrlink.net
Web site: http://travelassist.com/reg/pa106s.html

An elegant 1894 Victorian riverfront home in the Clearfield historic district. Memorable breakfast, air-conditioning, skylights, balcony, private kitchen and dining, guest

welcome; 7 Children welcome; 8 Tennis nearby; 9 Swimming nearby; 10 Golf nearby; 11 Skiing nearby; 12 May be booked through travel agent.

entertainment center, family movies, and whirlpool bath. Weaving/sewing studio; spinning demonstrations by request. Hosts are Bible college graduates. Perfect stop on I-80—three miles off Exit 19 in rural west-central Pennsylvania. Also, completely equipped three-bedroom cabin on eight forested acres, located two miles from Parker Dam and Elliot state parks with swimming, fishing, boating, and numerous outdoor activities.

Hosts: Tim and Peggy Durant
Rooms: 4 + cabin (2PB; 2SB) $50-100
Full Breakfast
Credit Cards: A, B, C, D
Notes: 2, 5, 6 (call ahead), 7, 8, 9, 10, 11, 12

CLEARVILLE (BEDFORD)

Conifer Ridge Farm

RD 2, Box 202A, 15535
(814) 784-3342

Conifer Ridge Farm has 126 acres of woodland, pasture, Christmas trees, and crops. There is a one-acre pond with a pier for swimming, fishing, and boating. The home's rustic exterior opens to a spacious contemporary design of exceptional beauty. You'll feel its country character in the old barn beams and brick walls that collect the sun's warmth for solar heat. Located near Bedford, Bedford Village, Raystown Lake, and Rocky Gap State Park in Maryland.

Hosts: Dan and Myrtle Haldeman
Rooms: 2 + cabin (PB) $60
Full Breakfast
Credit Cards: none
Notes: 2, 4, 5, 7, 9, 10, 11

CLINTON (PITTSBURGH)

Country Road B&B

Moody Road, Box 265, 15026
(412) 899-2528; (412) 899-2528
E-mail: croadbb@pulsenet.com
Web site: http://www.bnb.lm.com

A peaceful, quiet farm setting just five miles from Greater Pittsburgh Airport, with pick-up service available, and twenty minutes from downtown. A restored one-hundred-year-old farmhouse with trout pond, in-ground pool, and screened-in front porch. Recently a cottage, once a springhouse, and two-hundred-year-old log cabin were restored and made available to guests. Golf course within walking distance, and air tours available in vintage Piper restored aircraft.

Hosts: Janice and David Cornell
Rooms: 4 (3PB; 1SB) $95-110
Full Breakfast
Credit Cards: A, B, D
Notes: 2, 5, 7, 10

COLUMBIA

The Columbian

360 Chestnut Street, 17512
(717) 684-5869; (800) 422-5869
E-mail: Bedandb@aol.com
Web site: http://user.aol.com/Bedandb

Circa 1897. Centrally located in the small historic river town of Columbia, the Columbian, a brick Colonial Revival mansion, features an ornate stained-glass window, magnificent tiered staircase, and unique wraparound porches. Large, air-conditioned rooms offer queen-size beds, private baths, and CATV. Suite with bal-

---

NOTES: Credit cards accepted: A Master Card; B Visa; C American Express; D Discover; E Diners Club; F Other; 2 Personal checks accepted; 3 Lunch available; 4 Dinner available; 5 Open all year; 6 Pets

The Columbian

cony and rooms with fireplaces available. Come relax and unwind in our lovely home and browse through the nearby antique shops, art galleries, outlets, and museums only a brief stroll away.

Hosts: Chris and Becky Will and Katie and Zach
Rooms: 5 (PB) $65-99
Full Breakfast
Credit Cards: A, B
Notes: 2, 5, 7, 8, 9, 10, 11

CRESCO

LaAnna Guest House

RR 2, Box 1051, 18326
(717) 676-4225; FAX (717) 676-4225

The 111-year-old Victorian is furnished with Victorian and Empire antiques and

LaAnna Guest House

has spacious rooms, quiet surroundings, and a trout pond. Walk to waterfalls, mountain views, and wildlife.

Hostess: Kay Swingle
Rooms: 4 (SB) $35-40
Continental Breakfast
Credit Cards: none
Notes: 2, 5, 7, 8, 9, 10, 11

DALLAS (WILKES-BARRE)

Ponda-Rowland Bed and Breakfast Inn

RR 1, Box 349, 18612
(717) 639-3245; (800) 854-3286;
FAX (717) 639-5531

Ponda-Rowland Bed and Breakfast Inn is a circa-1850 inn on a large, scenic farm in the Endless Mountains of Pennsylvania. King beds, private baths, AC, beamed ceilings, ceiling fans. Completely furnished with museum-quality country antiques. Mountain views, thirty-four-acre private wildlife sanctuary with trails, and ponds. Fishing, canoeing, ice-skating, tobogganing, hay rides, horses, sheep, goats, turkeys, pot-bellied pig, donkeys, and more to see, do, and touch. Refreshments afternoon and evening. Large stone fireplace. Breakfast by candlelight. Nearby are air tours, swimming, horseback riding, downhill skiing, and fine restaurants. Approved by AAA, ABBA, and Mobil.

Hosts: Jeanette and Cliff Rowland
Rooms: 6 (PB) $75-125
Full Breakfast
Credit Cards: A, B, C, D
Notes: 2, 5, 7, 10, 11, 12

welcome; 7 Children welcome; 8 Tennis nearby; 9 Swimming nearby; 10 Golf nearby; 11 Skiing nearby; 12 May be booked through travel agent.

DENVER

Cocalico Creek Bed and Breakfast

224 S. 4th Street, 17517
(717) 336-0271; (888) 208-7334

Situated in northern Lancaster County, the 1927 classic stone colonial offers casual elegance in a country setting. Four tastefully decorated bedrooms with queen beds and private baths; one room has a private balcony. AC for summer comfort; heated beds with down comforters for winter chills. Minutes from antiquing, outlet shopping, golf, and farmers markets. Explore the history, culture, and rural scenic beauty.

Hostess: Charlene Sweeney
Rooms: 4 (PB) $60-85
Full Breakfast
Credit Cards: A, B
Notes: 2, 5, 7, 9, 10

DOYLESTOWN

The Inn at Fordhook Farm

105 New Britain Road, 18901
(215) 345-1766; FAX (215) 345-1791

Long-time family home of W. Atlee Burpee, founder of the Burpee Seed Company, and his family. Nine major historic buildings constitute Fordhook Farm; three of these are used for the inn. There are sixty acres of meadows, woodlands, and gardens to explore.

Hostess: Carole Burpee
Rooms: 7 + 2-BR apartment and carriage house (5PB; 2SB) $100-200
Full Breakfast
Credit Cards: A, B, C
Notes: 2, 5, 7 (12 and older), 11 (cross-country)

EAST PETERSBURG

George Zahm House

6070 Main Street, 17520
(717) 569-6026

The George Zahm House, built in 1854, is a restored Federal period home in beautiful Lancaster County. The inn features three bedrooms with private baths and a first-floor suite that offers a sitting room, bedroom, and private bath. The inn has ten-foot ceilings throughout and is furnished with an eclectic collection of antiques. Breakfast is served in the dining room and features homemade muffins, breads, Belgian waffles, granolas, and seasonal fresh fruit.

Hosts: Robyn and Jeff Keeports and Robyn's mother Daneen
Rooms: 4 (PB) $65-85
Continental Plus Breakfast
Credit Cards: A, B
Notes: 2, 5, 7 (over 12), 8, 9, 10

ELIZABETHTOWN

West Ridge Guest House

1285 West Ridge Road, 17022
(717) 367-7783; FAX (717) 367-8468

Country estate setting midway between Harrisburg and Lancaster. Nine guest rooms, four in the main house, five in a guest house that offers complete privacy. Some have fireplaces, Jacuzzi tubs, decks; all rooms have phones, TVs, VCRs (movie library available), private baths. Full breakfast is served. Local attractions: Hershey Park, Lancaster County Amish community, outlet shopping, Gettysburg.

NOTES: Credit cards accepted: A Master Card; B Visa; C American Express; D Discover; E Diners Club; F Other; 2 Personal checks accepted; 3 Lunch available; 4 Dinner available; 5 Open all year; 6 Pets

West Ridge Guest House

Four-star-rated by the American Bed & Breakfast Association.

Hostess: Alice P. Heisey
Rooms: 9 (PB) $60-110
Full Breakfast
Credit Cards: A, B, C
Notes: 2, 5, 7, 8, 10, 12

EMLENTON

Whippletree Inn and Farm

RD 3, Box 285, Big Bend Road, 16373
(412) 867-9543

The inn is a restored, turn-of-the-century home on a cattle farm. The house, barns, and one hundred acres of pasture sit on a hill above the Allegheny River. A pleasant trail leads down to the river. Guests are welcome to use the half-mile racetrack for horses and carriages. Nearby are hiking, biking, canoeing, hunting, fishing, and golfing. Emlenton offers antique and craft shopping in the restored Old Mill. AC. Open May through October.

Hosts: Warren and Joey Simmons
Rooms: 4 (2PB; 2SB) $50-60
Full Breakfast
Credit Cards: B
Notes: 2, 7, 9, 10

EPHRATA

Historic Smithton Inn

900 W. Main Street, 17522
(717) 733-6094

Smithton, an American pre-Revolutionary Inn opened 235 years, has been fully restored. It is in Lancaster County, perhaps the most spiritually focused county in America and home of the Amish, Mennonite, and Brethren people. A romantic and picturesque place. Its big, square rooms are bright and sunny. Each room has its own working fireplace and can be candlelit during evening hours. There is a sitting area in each guest room with comfortable leather upholstered chairs, reading lamps, soft goose down pillows, and handmade Pennsylvania Dutch quilts. Smithton's Dahlia Gardens feature a striking display of blossoms grown from tubers that were all winners in American Dahlia Society competitions. Mannerly children and pets welcome; please make prior arrangements. Smoking prohibited.

Hostess: Dorthy R. Graybill
Rooms: 8 (PB) $75-175
Full Breakfast
Credit Cards: A, B, C
Notes: 2, 5, 6 and 7 (prior arrangement), 8, 9, 10, 12

Historic Smithton Inn

welcome; 7 Children welcome; 8 Tennis nearby; 9 Swimming nearby; 10 Golf nearby; 11 Skiing nearby; 12 May be booked through travel agent.

Martin House

The Inns at Doneckers

318-324 N. State Street, 17522
(717) 738-9502; FAX (717) 738-9504

Relax in country elegance in historic Lancaster County. Four inns of forty distinctive rooms, decorated in fine antiques, some fireplace/Jacuzzi suites. A few steps from the Doneckers Community, you'll find a thirty-six-year-old family-owned business consisting of an exceptional fashion store for the family and home, an award-winning gourmet restaurant, art/craft/quilt galleries and artists' studios, and a farmers market. Only minutes from antique and collectible markets. "An oasis of sophistication in PA Dutch Country"— *Country Inns* magazine.

Host: H. William Donecker
Rooms: 40 (38PB; 2SB) $59-185
Continental Breakfast
Credit Cards: A, B, C, D, E, F
Notes: 2, 3, 4, 5, 7, 8, 9, 10

Martin House

265 Ridge Avenue, 17522
(717) 733-6804; (888) 651-8418
E-mail: vmartin@prolog.net
Web site: http://www.martin-house.com

Located in Pennsylvania Dutch country, our contemporary home is set against a wooded area. There are antique markets, outlet malls, Hershey Park, historical places, and golf courses within a few miles. For your comfort: spacious rooms with king or queen beds and a private hot tub! A living room and large, sunny deck are available for guests to use. Discount for three nights or more.

Hosts: Moses and Vera Martin
Rooms: 3 (PB) $75-115
Full Breakfast
Credit Cards: A, B
Notes: 2, 5, 7, 9, 10

GETTYSBURG

The Brafferton Inn

44 York Street, 17325
(717) 337-3423

The Brafferton Inn is one of historic Gettysburg's gracious landmarks. The elegant 1786 fieldstone home, listed on the National Register of Historic Places, has been fully restored to include a private bath for each of the ten guest rooms. Featured in *Country Living*, the inn has exquisite antiques and original artistry throughout. The inn combines elegance and ease. Warm-colored Orientals, comfortable wing-backs, and a tall 1800 grandfather clock grace the living room. The dining room boasts a stunning folk art mural. Other surprising nooks and crannies, a deck, and an in-town garden provide guests with getaway spots. The spirit of an earlier time pervades.

Hosts: Jane and Sam Back
Rooms: 10 (PB) $80-125
Full Breakfast
Credit Cards: A, B, C, D
Notes: 2, 5, 7 (over 7), 8, 9, 10, 11, 12

The Doubleday Inn

104 Doubleday Avenue, 17325
(717) 334-9119
Web site: http://www.bbonline.com/pa/doubleday

Located directly on the Gettysburg battlefield, this beautifully restored colonial country inn enjoys splendid views of historic Gettysburg and the battlefield. Guests enjoy candlelit country breakfasts, afternoon refreshments, and the cozy comfort of a centrally air-conditioned inn surrounded by lovely antiques and Civil War memorabilia. Free presentations by battlefield historians on selected evenings.

Hosts: Charles and Ruth Anne Wilcox
Rooms: 9 (5PB; 4SB) $84-104
Full Breakfast
Credit Cards: A, B, D
Notes: 2, 5, 7 (8 and older), 8, 9, 10, 11, 12

Keystone Inn

231 Hanover Street, 17325
(717) 337-3888

The Keystone Inn is a large, brick Victorian home built in 1913. The high-ceilinged rooms are decorated with lace and flowers, and a handsome chestnut staircase rises to the third floor. The guest rooms are bright, cheerful, and air-conditioned. Each has a reading nook and writing desk.

Choose your own breakfast from our full breakfast menu. One suite available.

Hosts: Wilmer and Doris Martin
Rooms: 5 (PB) $69-109
Full Breakfast
Credit Cards: A, B, D
Notes: 2, 5, 7, 8, 9, 10, 11

GREENSBURG

Huntland Farm B&B

RD 9, Box 21, 15601
(412) 834-8483; FAX (412) 838-8253

Nestled in the foothills of the Allegheny Mountains, the one-hundred-acre Huntland Farm is three miles northeast of Greensburg. The house, built in 1848 and listed in *Historic Places in Western PA*, is furnished with antiques. A large living room as well as porches and gardens are available for guests' use. Four large, corner bedrooms make it comfortable for up to eight people. Nearby are many scenic and historical places, walking trails, hot-air ballooning, and shops.

Hosts: Robert and Elizabeth Weidlein
Rooms: 4 (SB) $60-85
Full Breakfast
Credit Cards: C
Notes: 2, 10, 11, 12

GREENTOWN

Hall's Inn

RR 1, Box 137, 18426
(717) 676-3429

Located on Route 390 in Promised Land State Park, Hall's Inn offers you clean and comfortable rooms with a serene atmosphere. Guests may relax on the wraparound porch and enjoy the tranquillity and

welcome; 7 Children welcome; 8 Tennis nearby; 9 Swimming nearby; 10 Golf nearby; 11 Skiing nearby; 12 May be booked through travel agent.

fresh mountain air while watching the deer. A beautiful lake with beach and picnicking are enjoyed. In winter, cross-country skiing and snowmobiling are popular, with hiking all year. An outside grill and picnic tables are available to our guests.

Hosts: John and Lois Hall
Rooms: 9 (2PB; 7SB) $50-60
Continental Breakfast
Credit Cards: A, B
Notes: 2, 5, 7, 9, 11

GROVE CITY

Snow Goose Inn

112 E. Main Street, 16127
(412) 458-4644; (800) 317-4644

The Snow Goose Inn is a large turn-of-the-century home, circa 1895, formerly a doctor's home. It has a large, wraparound front porch with an old-fashioned porch swing. Comfortable, air-conditioned guest rooms have private baths. Each is decorated with antiques and touches of country. A full breakfast is served, along with homemade muffins, home-baked breakfast rolls, etc.

Hosts: Orvil and Dorothy McMillen
Rooms: 4 (PB) $65
Full Breakfast
Credit Cards: A, B
Notes: 2, 5, 7, 8, 9, 10, 11, 12

HAMBURG

Come Aside Inn

800 Schappell Toad, 19526
(610) 562-9293

Located conveniently off Interstate 78, our country home provides a tranquil respite. A wicker swing on the front porch invites you to "come aside and rest awhile," while winter brings the relaxing glow of the fireplace. A candlelit, expanded continental breakfast is served in the open-beamed dining room.

Hosts: Bob and Loretta Miller
Rooms: 3 (1PB; 2SB) $50-65
Continental Plus Breakfast
Credit Cards: F
Notes: 2, 5, 8, 9, 10, 11

HANOVER

Beechmont Inn

315 Broadway, 17331
(717) 632-3013; (800) 553-7009

Elegant, 1834 Federal Inn with seven guest rooms, all with private baths. Fireplaces, AC, afternoon refreshments, and gourmet breakfasts. One large suite has a private whirlpool tub and canopy beds. Gettysburg battlefield, Lake Marburg, golf, and great antiquing are nearby. Convenient location for visits to Hershey, York, or Lancaster. Weekend and golf packages and romantic honeymoon or anniversary packages are offered. Picnic baskets are available. Great area for biking and hiking. AAA- and Mobil-approved.

Hosts: William and Susan Day
Rooms: 7 (PB) $80-135
Full Breakfast
Credit Cards: A, B, C, D
Notes: 2, 3, 5, 8, 9, 10, 11, 12

HERSHEY

Mottern's B&B

28 E. Main Street, **Hummelstown**, 17036
(717) 566-3840; FAX (717) 566-3780

Enjoy small-town hospitality five minutes from Hershey Park. This private "suite"

---

in our restored 1860s home could be your "home away from home" with its old-house charm, modernized for the '90s. It overlooks beautifully landscaped gardens and is accented with antiques, reproductions and homemade quilts. It includes a living room (sofa bed), bedroom (queen-size bed), dining room, kitchen, private bath, cable TV, and central air. Private off-street parking is available for guests. No smoking. The bed and breakfast is convenient to Harrisburg, Lancaster, Gettysburg, and Reading.

Hosts: Jeffrey and Susan Mottern, Debbie Ness
Rooms: 1 suite sleeps up to 5 (PB) $85-100 (additional $10 per person over 5 years)
Continental Breakfast
Credit Cards: A, B
Notes: 2, 5, 7, 8, 9, 10, 11

Pinehurst Inn
Bed and Breakfast

50 Northeast Drive, 17033
(717) 533-2603; (800) 743-9140;
FAX (717) 534-2639

Spacious brick home surrounded by lawns and countryside. There is a warm, welcoming, many-windowed living room and old-fashioned porch swing. All this is within walking distance of all Hershey attractions: Hershey Museums, Rose Gardens, Hershey Park, and Chocolate World. Less than one hour's drive to Gettysburg and Lancaster County. Each room welcomes you with a queen-size bed and a Hershey Kiss on each pillow.

Hosts: Roger and Phyllis Ingold
Rooms: 15 (2PB; 13SB) $45-75
Complete Breakfast
Credit Cards: A, B
Notes: 2, 5, 7, 8, 9, 10, 12

Shepherd's Acres
Bed and Breakfast

RD 3, Box 370, **Palmyra** 17078
(717) 838-3899

Welcome to the Hershey-Lancaster area! You'll enjoy it more if you stay on our twenty-acre farmette overlooking the scenic Lebanon Valley. Our new, spacious Cape Cod home is filled with Margy's hand-sewn quilts and wall hangings, with some antique furniture accenting the "country theme," as well. The eat-in enclosed porch area is a great place to enjoy both beauty and tranquillity as you watch the sheep in the pasture or the deer in the fields.

Hosts: Jerry and Margy Allebach
Rooms: 3 (1PB; 2SB) $45-60
Full Breakfast
Credit Cards: none
Notes: 2, 5, 8, 9, 10, 11

HUMMELSTOWN

Nancy's Guest House

235 Hershey Road, 17036
(717) 566-9844

Comfort, hominess and privacy are what you find at our guest house. You are our only guests. Located two miles from Hershey Park, our second-floor, one-unit, nonsmoking apartment has a private entrance and a large deck. There are two bedrooms, a living room, a kitchen, and a bath with laundry. Color television and air-conditioning add to the comfort. Eat in or go out, choosing from fast food or fine dining. Traveler's checks or cash are accepted; checks limited. A ten-percent

welcome; 7 Children welcome; 8 Tennis nearby; 9 Swimming nearby; 10 Golf nearby; 11 Skiing nearby; 12 May be booked through travel agent.

discount for five nights or more. Three and a half miles from I-81 on Route 39.

Hosts: Marlin and Nancy Geesaman
Rooms: 2-room apartment (PB) $65-85
Credit Cards: none
Notes: 7, 8, 9, 10, 11

JENNERSTOWN

The Olde Stagecoach Bed and Breakfast

1760 Lincoln Highway, PO Box 337, 15547
(814) 629-7440; FAX (814) 629-9244

A renovated, two-hundred-year-old farmhouse that, during the 1700s and 1800s, was a stagecoach rest stop. It now has four lovely bedrooms decorated with antiques, adding country charm, each with its own private bath. Guests may relax in the Victorian-style common room. It is a place to stay in all four seasons, located on the historical Lincoln Highway. Nearby are the oldest professional summer theater, antique shops, golfing, outlet shopping, skiing, and cross-country skiing.

Hosts: Carol and George Neuhof
Rooms: 4 (PB) $65
Full Breakfast
Credit Cards: A, B
Notes: 2, 5, 10, 11

JIM THORPE

The Inn at Jim Thorpe

24 Broadway, 18229
(717) 325-2599; (800) 329-2599;
FAX (717) 325-9145

The inn rests in a unique and picturesque setting in the heart of historic Jim Thorpe. Elegant rooms are complete with private baths and color TVs/HBO, and are furnished with Victorian reproductions. Suites have fireplaces and whirlpools. Enjoy shopping, historic mansion and museum tours, mountain biking, and whitewater rafting—all right outside our doors!

Host: David Drury
Rooms: 29 (PB) $65-250
Continental Breakfast
Credit Cards: A, B, C, D, E
Notes: 3, 4, 5, 7, 9, 11, 12

KINZERS

Sycamore Haven Farm

35 S. Kinzer Road, 17535
(717) 442-4901

We have approximately forty milking cows and many young cattle and cats for children to enjoy. Our farmhouse has three guest rooms, all with double beds and one single. Cots and playpen. Fifteen miles east of Lancaster on Route 30.

Hosts: Charles and Janet Groff
Rooms: 3 (SB) $30-40
Continental Breakfast
Credit Cards: none
Notes: 2, 5, 6, 7, 8, 9, 10

LANCASTER

Australian Walkabout Inn Bed and Breakfast

837 Village Road, **Lampeter**, 17537
(717) 464-0707; FAX (717) 464-2501

This 1925 restored Mennonite farmhouse is in a village setting. It is landscaped with English and wildflower gardens and a lily pond. Wraparound porches, period antiques. Australian-born Richard serves an

---

NOTES: Credit cards accepted: A Master Card; B Visa; C American Express; D Discover; E Diners Club; F Other; 2 Personal checks accepted; 3 Lunch available; 4 Dinner available; 5 Open all year; 6 Pets

Australian Walkabout Inn

elegant, full candlelight breakfast and will help plot your course around the Amish countryside. Honeymoon and anniversary suites have fireplaces, queen canopy beds and Jacuzzis or hot tubs. No smoking.

Hosts: Richard and Margaret Mason
Rooms: 5 (PB) $99-149
Full Breakfast
Credit Cards: A, B, C, F
Notes: 2, 3, 4, 5, 7, 8, 9, 10, 12

Bed and Breakfast—The Manor

830 Village Road, 17602
(717) 464-9564

This cozy farmhouse is minutes from Lancaster's historical attractions. Guests delight in Mary Lou's homemade breakfasts featuring eggs Mornay, crepes, stratas, fruit cobblers, and homemade breads and jams. A swim in our pool and a nap under a tree are the perfect way to cap your day of touring. Dinner, an overnight stay, and a buggy ride with an Old Order Amish family can be arranged. Amish waitresses. Children welcome.

Hostesses: Jackie Curtis and Mary Paolini
Rooms: 6 (4PB; 2SB) $79-99
Full Buffet Breakfast
Credit Cards: A, B
Notes: 2, 5, 7, 8, 9

Country Living Inn

2406 Old Philadelphia Pike, 17602
(717) 295-7295
Web site: http://padutch.welcome.com/
   ctryliv.html

Just like "home!" Warm, inviting hospitality. Country decor with quilts on the full, queen, or king beds. New Shaker furniture, glider rockers, or sofas in the deluxe suite or queen rooms. Romantic suite with a whirlpool for two. Amish farms on the north and west sides. Coffee, tea, and hot chocolate served daily. Pastries served weekends (May through October) on the porch. The front porches have rockers and benches for visiting, relaxing, or watching Amish buggies go by.

Hosts: Bill and Judy Harnish
Rooms: 34 (PB) $43-130
Continental Breakfast
Credit Cards: A, B
Notes: 5, 10, 12

Country Living Inn

Flowers and Thyme Bed and Breakfast

238 Strasburg Pike, 17602
(717) 393-1460; FAX (717) 399-1986
Web site: http://members.aol.com/padutchbnb

Enjoy our rural ambience in a spacious brick B&B in the heart of Amish country.

welcome; 7 Children welcome; 8 Tennis nearby; 9 Swimming nearby; 10 Golf nearby; 11 Skiing nearby; 12 May be booked through travel agent.

We are bordered by farmlands, centrally located, five minutes from the outlets and Route 30. Rooms are furnished with queen beds, ceiling fans, antiques, quilts and wreaths. One room features a Jacuzzi. Lush perennial herb gardens surround our property. Bountiful breakfasts are served in the vaulted garden room. Amish dinners or personal tours can be arranged.

Hosts: Don and Ruth Harnish
Rooms: 3 (PB) $80-100
Full Breakfast
Credit Cards: A, B, C
Notes: 2, 5, 7 (over 12), 8, 9, 10

Gardens of Eden Bed and Breakfast

1894 Eden Road, 17601
(717) 393-5179; FAX (717) 393-7722

Victorian ironmaster's home built circa 1860 on the banks of the Conestoga River, three miles northeast of Lancaster. Antiques and family collections of quilts and coverlets fill the three guest rooms, all with private baths. The adjoining guest cottage (restored summer kitchen) features a walk-in fireplace, dining room, bedroom, and bath on the second floor. Marilyn's floral designs are featured and for sale. The three acres of gardens feature herbs, perennials, and wildflowers among the woodsy trails. Local attractions are personalized by a tour guide service and dinner in a young Amish couple's home. Canoe and rowboat available. Two bike trails pass the house.

Hosts: Marilyn Ebel and husband Bill
Rooms: 4 (PB) $85-130
Full Breakfast
Credit Cards: A, B
Notes: 2, 5, 7 (in guest house), 8, 9, 10, 12

The King's Cottage

The King's Cottage— A Bed and Breakfast Inn

1049 E. King Street, 17602
(717) 397-1017; (800) 747-8717;
FAX (717) 397-3447
Web site: http://www.innbook.com/~kings.html

Snuggled in the midst of historic Lancaster County, the King's Cottage is an oasis of ultimate comfort and amenities. This award-winning National Register Inn specializes in lavishly decorated rooms and personalized services. King- and queen-size beds, private baths with oversize tubs, and gourmet breakfasts. After visiting scenic Amish farmlands, touring historic sites, or quilt shopping, enjoy a gourmet treat in the fire-warmed library. Amish dinners arranged. Spanish spoken. AAA.

Hosts: Karen and Jim Owens
Rooms: 9 (PB) $100-175
Full Breakfast
Credit Cards: A, B, D
Notes: 2, 5, 8, 9, 10, 12

Lincoln Haus Inn

1687 Lincoln Highway E., 17602
(717) 392-9412
Web site: http://www.800padutch.com/
    linchaus.html

Lincoln Haus Inn is the only inn in Lancaster County with a distinctive hip roof. Furnished with antiques and rugs on gleaming, hardwood floors, with natural oak woodwork. I am a member of the Old Amish Church, serving family-style breakfast in a homey atmosphere. Located close to farmlands, malls, historic Lancaster; five minutes from Route 30 and the Pennsylvania Dutch Visitors' Bureau.

Hostess: Mary K. Zook
Rooms: 7 (PB) $53-80
Full Breakfast
Credit Cards: none
Notes: 2, 4, 5, 7, 8, 9, 10, 12

Meadowview Guest House

2169 New Holland Pike, 17601
(717) 299-4017

This Dutch Colonial home is located in the heart of the Pennsylvania Dutch Amish area. Three guest rooms and kitchen on the the second floor. There is a stove, refrigerator, sink, and dishes. A breakfast tray is put in the kitchen in the morning for each guest room. Close to many historic sites and to farmers and antique markets. Excellent restaurants and many attractions help guests enjoy the beautiful country. Personalized maps are provided.

Hosts: Edward and Sheila
Rooms: 3 (1PB; 2SB) $35-50
Continental Breakfast
Credit Cards: none
Notes: 2 (deposit only), 5, 7 (over 6) , 8, 9, 10, 12

New Life Homestead Bed and Breakfast

1400 E. King Street, 17602
(717) 396-8928; FAX (717) 396-0461
Web site: http://padutch.welcome.com/
    newlife.html

Located in the heart of Amish country. Close to all attractions. If you ever wanted

New Life Homestead

to know about the Amish and Mennonite people, this is where to learn. The home features antiques and heirlooms. Full breakfasts and evening refreshments are served. Your hosts are a Mennonite family with traditional family values. AC, private baths.

Hosts: Carol and Bill Giersch
Rooms: 3 (2PB; 1SB) $60-80
Full Family-Style Breakfast
Credit Cards: none
Notes: 2, 5, 7, 8, 9, 10, 12

O'Flaherty's Dingeldein House Bed and Breakfast

1105 E. King Street, 17602
(717) 293-1723; (800) 779-7765;
FAX (717) 293-1947

Enjoy genuine warmth and hospitality in the friendly atmosphere of our home. Our Dutch Colonial home is traditionally appointed for your comfort, with two fireplaces in the fall and winter and AC when needed to provide a restful, relaxing stay in beautiful Lancaster County. Conveniently located near downtown Lancaster attractions and just a short, scenic ride from the Amish farmland, outlet shopping, and antique area. Amish dining can be arranged. Personalized maps are prepared

welcome; 7 Children welcome; 8 Tennis nearby; 9 Swimming nearby; 10 Golf nearby; 11 Skiing nearby; 12 May be booked through travel agent.

for our guests. Our breakfast guarantees you won't go away hungry. The B&B is AAA-approved, three diamonds.

Hosts: Jack and Sue Flatley
Rooms: 4 (PB) $70-80
Full Breakfast
Credit Cards: A, B, D
Notes: 2, 5, 7, 8, 9, 10

Witmer's Tavern— Historic 1725 Inn and Museum

2014 Old Philadelphia Pike, 17602
(717) 299-5305

Witmer's Tavern is Lancaster's oldest and only pre-Revolutionary War inn still lodging travelers in the original building. Reflects rural and historic flavor of the area. Restored to the simple, authentic, pioneer style that was familiar to European immigrants who joined the Conestoga wagon trains being provisioned at the inn for the western and southern treks into the wilderness areas. Fresh flowers, working fireplaces, antique quilts, and antiques in all the romantic rooms. Pandora's Antique Shop is on the premises. Bird-in-Hand and Intercourse villages, other antique shops, and auctions just beyond. Valley Forge, Hershey, Gettysburg, Winterthur, Chadds Ford, and New Hope all within a ninety-minute drive. On the National Register of Historic Places, and a national landmark. Beautiful park across the street; Amish cow pasture in the rear.

Host: Brant Hartung
Rooms: 7 (2PB; 5SB) $60-90
Continental Plus Breakfast
Credit Cards: none
Notes: 2, 5, 8, 9, 10, 11, 12

Your Place Country Inn

2133 Lincoln Highway E., 17602
(717) 393-3413; FAX (717) 393-2889
E-mail: ypci@800padutch.com
Web site: http://www.800padutch.com/ypci.html

Charming country decor. Most furnishings made by Amish craftsmen. Two queen-size beds in each room. Deluxe rooms with refrigerators and country quilts. Front porch, elevator to second floor, handicap-accessible room. Restaurant/ lounge next door. Outlet shopping, great food, attractions, theaters—all just minutes away. We're close to it all.

Hostess: Trudy Carrington
Rooms: 125 (PB) $35-104 (seasonal)
Continental Breakfast
Credit Cards: A, B, C, D
Notes: 3, 4, 5, 7, 8, 9, 10, 12

LANCASTER COUNTY (PENNSYLVANIA DUTCH COUNTRY) (SEE ALSO—BIRD-IN-HAND, CHRISTIANA, COLUMBIA, DENVER, EAST PETERSBURG, ELIZABETHTOWN, EPHRATA, KINZERS, LANCASTER, MANHEIM, MARIETTA, MOUNT JOY, PARADISE, PEACH BOTTOM, AND SMOKETOWN)

The Apple Bin Inn Bed and Breakfast

2835 Willow Street Pike, **Willow Street**, 17584
(717) 464-5881; (800) 338-4296;
FAX (717) 464-1818
Web site: http://www.applebininn.com

Experience the hospitality and charm at one of the area's truly finest B&Bs. This 1865 home is nestled in the county's old-

---

NOTES: Credit cards accepted: A Master Card; B Visa; C American Express; D Discover; E Diners Club; F Other; 2 Personal checks accepted; 3 Lunch available; 4 Dinner available; 5 Open all year; 6 Pets

The Apple Bin Inn Bed and Breakfast

est village, three miles south of Lancaster. We offer distinctive country decor in a comfortable, relaxed setting. Enjoy the balcony, two-room suites, and patios. For a unique getaway, try our newly restored carriage house (two-story, with fireplace). Awaken to the aroma of a delicious homemade breakfast. AC, TV, phone in room. Fax available.

Hosts: Barry and Debbie Hershey
Rooms: 5 (PB) $95-150
Full Breakfast
Credit Cards: A, B, C
Notes: 2, 5, 8, 9, 10

Ben Mar Farm Bed and Breakfast

5721 Old Philadelphia Pike, **Gap**, 17527
(717) 768-3309

Come stay with us on our working dairy farm. We are located in the heart of the famous Amish country. You can experience quiet country life while staying in the large, beautifully decorated rooms of our two-hundred-year-old farmhouse. Our efficiency apartment is a favorite; it includes a full kitchen and queen and double beds with private bath. Enjoy a fresh continen-

tal breakfast brought to your room. The home is air-conditioned.

Hosts: Herb and Melanie Benner
Rooms: 3 (PB) $45-65
Continental Breakfast
Credit Cards: none
Notes: 2, 5, 7, 8, 9

Carriage Corner Bed and Breakfast

3705 E. Newport Road, PO Box 371, **Intercourse,** 17534-0371
(717) 768-3059; (800) 209-3059

"A comfortable bed, a hearty breakfast, a charming village, and friendly hosts" has been used to describe our B&B. We have five comfortable rooms with country decor, Amish quilt hangings, and private baths. Our bed and breakfast offers a relaxing country atmosphere with handcrafted touches of folk art and country. Rooms are air-conditioned. We are centered in the heart of beautiful farms and a culture that draws many to the nearby villages of Intercourse, Bird-in-Hand, and Strasburg. Amish dinners sometimes can be arranged. There is much to learn from these calm and gentle people.

Hosts: Mr. and Mrs. Gordon Schuit
Rooms: 5 (PB) $40-70
Full Breakfast
Credit Cards: A, B
Notes: 2, 5, 7, 12

The Inn at Hayward Heath

2048 Silver Lane, **Willow Street**, 17584
(717) 464-0994

Located in the gently rolling Lancaster County hills, our 1887 farmhouse has been beautifully restored to replicate colonial living. Reflect on America's past in our

welcome; 7 Children welcome; 8 Tennis nearby; 9 Swimming nearby; 10 Golf nearby; 11 Skiing nearby; 12 May be booked through travel agent.

Shaker-style room with queen canopy bed, or enjoy the romantic touch of our spacious country garden room with queen bed, sitting area, and attached private bath with two-person whirlpool. Our first-floor rose bedroom features a queen bed and a large private bath. A two-bedroom suite is available. Large living room for visiting, reading, or viewing TV. A sumptuous breakfast is served in the formal dining room. Close to historic areas; tourist attractions; outlet shopping malls; Amish farms; and craft, antique, and quilt shops.

Hosts: Joan and David Smith
Rooms: 4 (PB) $65-95
Full Breakfast
Credit Cards: A, B, D
Notes: 2, 5, 8, 10

The Inn at Hayward Heath

LIMA (BRANDYWINE VALLEY)

Hamanassett Bed and Breakfast

PO Box 129, 19037
(610) 459-3000 (voice and FAX)
E-mail: hamanasset@aol.com
Web sites: http://www.bbonline.com/pa/
    hamanassett/
    http://www.brandywinevalley.com

Enjoy an early-19th-century mansion on forty-eight secluded, peaceful acres of woodlands, gardens, and trails in the Brandywine Valley near Winterthur, Hagley, Nemours, Brandywine (Wyeth) museums, and Longwood Gardens. Well-appointed rooms have queens, doubles, twins, canopied king beds, private baths, TV and amenities. Beautiful Federalist living room and extensive library. Full country breakfast—sophisticated cuisine. Near tennis, golf, and excellent dining. An elegant, quiet, weekend escape along the U.S. Route 1 corridor and a world away. Two-night minimum. No smoking. Closed July 15-August 30.

Hostess: Mrs. Evelene Dohan
Rooms: 8 (6PB; 2SB) $90-125
Full Breakfast
Credit Cards: none
Notes: 2, 8, 10

LITITZ

Alden House Bed and Breakfast

62 E. Main Street, 17543
(717) 627-3363
E-mail: aldenbb@ptd.net

Fully restored 1850 Victorian/Colonial located in the heart of town's historic district. All local attractions and shops are a short walk. Home of the nation's oldest pretzel bakery. Spacious suites, central air-conditioning, off-street parking, and bicycle storage available. Antiques abound in this area, as well as handmade quilts. Enjoy our old-fashioned hospitality.

Hosts: Fletcher and Joy Coleman
Rooms: 5 (PB) $85-120
Full Breakfast
Credit Cards: A, B
Notes: 2, 5, 7 (over 10), 8, 9, 10

NOTES: Credit cards accepted: A Master Card; B Visa; C American Express; D Discover; E Diners Club; F Other; 2 Personal checks accepted; 3 Lunch available; 4 Dinner available; 5 Open all year; 6 Pets

The Inn at Mt. Hope

MANHEIM

The Inn at Mt. Hope

2232 E. Mt. Hope Road, 17545-0155
(717) 664-4708; (800) 664-4708;
FAX (717) 664-1006
E-mail: Info@InnAtMtHope.com
Web site: http://InnAtMtHope.com

The 19th-century stone house has not lost
its appeal over the years. The Inn at Mt.
Hope is a bed and breakfast inn restored
to its original simple charm. The rooms
are newly decorated and comfortable, creating a refuge from hectic 20th-century
lifestyles. Settle into the Parker Suite with
its fireplace, separate dressing room, and
bath; there is a special alcove with a built-
in bed for your child. Swing open the door
of Mary's Room with its charming view of
the grounds and a very special bath where
you can luxuriate in the claw-foot tub with
brass fixtures. You might prefer the informal charm of one of three under-the-eaves
rooms. The entire third floor is available
for larger groups. Enjoy the wide front
porch and four wooded acres. Historic
Mt. Hope Church, the Renaissance Faire,
Mt. Hope Winery, Quentin Riding Club,

Hershey Chocolate World and numerous
other attractions are nearby. Hearty
breakfast buffet.

Hosts: Joseph and Marilyn Fiedler
Rooms: 5 (2PB; 3SB) $60-110
Full Breakfast
Credit Cards: A, B
Notes: 2, 5, 7, 8, 9, 10, 11

Jonde Lane Farm

1103 Auction Road, 17545-9143
(717) 665-4231

John and Elaine Nissley and sons invite
you to share life on their hundred-acre
working dairy and poultry farm. Be a
spectator or a participant, or sit on the
back porch and enjoy the serenity. Four
guest rooms are offered in an 1859 farmhouse. You are welcome to join them at
their Mennonite church Sunday morning.
The Farm is thirty minutes from Hershey
and Amish country.

Hosts: Elaine and John Nissley
Rooms: 4 (SB) $45
Full Breakfast
Credit Cards: A, B
Notes: 2, 5, 7

Penn's Valley Farm and Inn

6182 Metzler Road, 17545
(717) 898-7386

Located on sixty-four acres of farmland is
our 1826 country cottage guest house. The
guest house sleeps up to seven people.
Private bath. Full breakfast is served in
the adjacent farmhouse dining room. One
Victorian room is available in the farmhouse, with a shared bath. The lodging is

welcome; 7 Children welcome; 8 Tennis nearby; 9 Swimming nearby; 10 Golf nearby; 11 Skiing nearby;
12 May be booked through travel agent.

centrally located between Amish country and Hershey Park.

Hosts: Mel and Gladys Metzler
Rooms: 2 (1PB; 1SB) $50-65
Full Breakfast
Credit Cards: A, B, C
Notes: 2, 5, 7

Wenger's Bed and Breakfast

571 Hossler Road, 17545
(717) 665-3862

Relax and enjoy your stay in the quiet countryside of Lancaster County. Our ranch-style house is within walking distance of our son's one-hundred-acre dairy farm. The spacious rooms will accommodate families. You can get a guided tour through the Amish farmland. Hershey (the chocolate town), Pennsylvania's state capital at Harrisburg, and the Gettysburg battlefield are all within one hour's drive.

Hosts: Arthur and Mary K. Wenger
Rooms: 2 (PB) $45-50
Full Breakfast
Credit Cards: none
Notes: 2, 5, 7

MARIETTA

Historic Linden House

606 E. Market Street, 17547-1808
(717) 426-4697; (800) 416-4697;
FAX (717) 426-4136

The Historic Linden House is a Federal-style home built in 1806 and listed on the National Historic Register. When built, it was considered one of the finest mansions in south-central Pennsylvania, costing $16,000–17,000 to build. Marietta is a charming town along the Susquehanna River which time has forgotten; forty-eight percent of its buildings are in the historic district. The home historically is known for its staircase, the longest original, preserved, continuous handrail staircase in Lancaster County. Guests enjoy queen beds and private baths. Fresh flowers in season. Spend a relaxing evening in the parlor by two crackling fireplaces (the house has sixteen fireplaces). Special packages and discounts available.

Hosts: Henry, Jeanene, and David Hill
Rooms: 4 (PB) $55
Full Breakfast
Credit Cards: A, B
Notes: 2, 5, 7

Vogt Farm Bed and Breakfast

1225 Colebrook Road, 17547
(717) 653-4810; (800) 854-0399;
FAX (717) 653-5288
E-mail: VOGTFARM@aol.com
Web site: http://www.patravel.org/members/
vogtfarm

Enjoy comfortable accommodations in our 1868 home on a twenty-six-acre cattle and sheep farm. You can enjoy the country and the quiet from one of our three porches. Each room is filled with our treasures—some old, some new—for your pleasure. We have been hosting guests from around the world for more than twenty years. We will be pleased to share maps and hints for touring beautiful Lancaster County. We are centrally located in Amish country between Harrisburg, Hershey, Lancaster, and York.

Hosts: Keith and Kathy Vogt
Rooms: 3 (1PB; 2SB) $65-99
Full Breakfast
Credit Cards: A, B, C, D, E
Notes: 2, 5, 7, 8, 9, 10, 12

NOTES: Credit cards accepted: A Master Card; B Visa; C American Express; D Discover; E Diners Club; F Other; 2 Personal checks accepted; 3 Lunch available; 4 Dinner available; 5 Open all year; 6 Pets

MILL RIFT

Bonny Bank Bungalow Bed and Breakfast

PO Box 481, 18340
(717) 491-2250

Let the rush of the rapids lull you to sleep in this cozy bungalow perched on the banks of the Upper Delaware National Scenic and Recreational River. Located on a dead-end road in a small town. Private entrance and private bath. TV available, if you can take your eyes off the view. River access for swimming and tubing (tubes available at no charge). Canoe/raft rentals and hiking on public lands nearby.

Hosts: Doug and Linda Hay
Rooms: 1 (PB) $50
Full Breakfast
Credit Cards: none
Notes: 2, 8, 9

MILTON

Pau-Lyn's Country Bed and Breakfast (A Restful Haven)

RD 3, Box 676, 17847
(717) 742-4110

The beautiful Susquehanna Valley of Central Pennsylvania is unique. Truly a variety of pleasant experiences await those who want to be in touch with God's handiwork and observe agriculture, scenic mountains, rivers, and valleys. Recreational activities abound. Guests experience "a restful haven" as the innkeepers provide nostalgic memories throughout the antique-furnished, 1850 Victorian brick house, two miles from I-80. Comfortable,

air-conditioned bedrooms add to the relaxing atmosphere.

Hosts: Paul and Evelyn Landis
Rooms: 7 (4PB; 3SB) $45-55
Full Breakfast
Credit Cards: none
Notes: 2, 5, 7, 8, 9, 10, 11, 12

MOUNT JOY

Cedar Hill Farm

305 Longenecker Road, 17552
(717) 653-4655

This 1817 stone farmhouse overlooks a peaceful stream and was the birthplace of the host. Stroll the acreage or relax on wicker rockers on the large front porch. Enjoy the singing of the birds and serene countryside. A winding staircase leads to the comfortable rooms, each with a private bath. Central AC. A room for honeymooners offers a private balcony. Breakfast is served by a walk-in fireplace. Located midway between the Lancaster and Hershey areas where farmers markets, antique shops, and good restaurants abound. Gift certificates for anniversary or holiday giving. Open all seasons.

Hosts: Russel and Gladys Swarr
Rooms: 5 (PB) $70-75
Continental Plus Breakfast
Credit Cards: A, B, C, D
Notes: 2, 5, 7, 8, 10

Green Acres Farm Bed and Breakfast

1382 Pinkerton Road, 17552
(717) 653-4028; FAX (717) 653-2840
Web site: http://www.800padutch.com/greenaf.html

Our 1830 farmhouse is furnished with antiques and offers a peaceful haven for your

Green Acres Farm Bed and Breakfast

getaway. The rooster, chickens, pigmy goats, lots of kittens, pony, and one thousand hogs provide a real farm atmosphere on this 160-acre grain farm. Children love the pony cart rides and the 8 x 10-foot playhouse, and everyone enjoys the trampoline and swings. We offer tour information about the Amish country and can arrange your dinner with an Amish family.

Hosts: Wayne and Yvonne Miller
Rooms: 7 (PB) $75
Full Breakfast
Credit Cards: A, B
Notes: 2, 5, 6, 7, 8, 9, 10

Hillside Farm Bed and Breakfast

607 Eby Chiques Road, 17552
(717) 653-6697; FAX (717) 653-5233
E-mail: hillside3@juno.com

Quiet, secluded 1863 brick farm homestead overlooking Chiques Creek, dam, and waterfall. Located ten miles west of downtown Lancaster and entirely surrounded by farmland. Comfortable, cozy, country furnishings include dairy antiques

and milk bottles. Close to Amish country, Hershey, antique shops, flea markets, auctions, wineries, and trails for hiking and biking. Bike trail maps available. Dinner arranged in advance with Amish. Strictly nonsmoking. Air-conditioned.

Hosts: Gary and Deb Lintner
Rooms: 5 (3PB; 2SB) $50-70
Full Country, Family-Style Breakfast
Credit Cards: A, B
Notes: 2, 5, 7 (10 and older), 8, 9, 10, 11, 12

MUNCY

The Bodine House Bed and Breakfast

307 South Main Street, 17756
(717) 546-8949

The Bodine House, featured in the December 1991 issue of *Colonial Homes* magazine, is located on tree-lined Main Street in the historic district. Built in 1805, the house has been authentically restored and is listed on the National Register of

Historic Places. Most furnishings are antiques. The center of Muncy, with its shops, restaurants, library, and churches, is just a short walk down the street. No smoking.

Hosts: David and Marie Louise Smith
Rooms: 4 (PB) $55-75; Carriage House (up to six guests) $125
Full Breakfast
Credit Cards: A, B, C, D
Notes: 2, 5, 7 (over 6), 8, 9, 10, 11, 12

NEW BERLIN

The Inn at Olde New Berlin

321 Market Street, 17855
(717) 966-0321; FAX (717) 966-9557
E-mail: nancy@newberlin-inn.com
Web site: http://www.newberlin-inn.com

"A luxurious base for indulging in a clutch of quiet pleasures" is *The Philadelphia Inquirer's* apt description of this elegantly appointed Victorian inn. The superb dining opportunities at Gabriel's Restaurant (on site) coupled with the antique-filled lodging accommodations provide romance and ambience. An upscale experience in a rural setting, only one hour north of Harrisburg. Guests relay that they depart feeling nurtured, relaxed, yet—most of all—inspired. Gifts, herb garden, air-conditioning. AAA- and Mobil-approved. Full line of Radko Christmas ornaments available at Gabriel's Gifts.

Hosts: John and Nancy Showers
Rooms: 9 (5PB; 4SB) $80-175
Full Breakfast
Credit Cards: A, B
Notes: 2, 3, 4, 5, 7, 8, 9, 10

NEW HOPE

Centre Bridge Inn

2998 N. River Road, Interstate Routes 32 & 263, 18938
(215) 862-9139; FAX (215) 862-3244

"The only thing we overlook is the Delaware River and Canal." Located in historic Bucks County, this romantic country inn offers its guests river views, canopy beds, full private baths, cable television, air-conditioning, and a continental breakfast in an authentic colonial decor. Enjoy our comfortable river-view guest lounge with fireplace, or our private house guest terrace, in season. A fine restaurant serving seasonal continental cuisine is found on the premises.

Host: Stephen R. Dugan
Rooms: 9 (PB) $80-150
Continental Breakfast
Credit Cards: A, B, C
Notes: 2, 4 (Sunday brunch), 5, 8, 9, 10

NEW WILMINGTON

Beechwood Inn

175 Beechwood Drive, 16142
(412) 946-2342

Beechwood Inn is a Civil War home with Victorian decor, offering three porches with lovely views. All the rooms enjoy private baths, queen beds, room keys, central air, and conversation areas. A common parlor is upstairs with cable TV, couch, and kitchen. A covered balcony stretches the width of the house and looks into our peaceful village park. Close to many shops and restaurants. Ten minutes

welcome; 7 Children welcome; 8 Tennis nearby; 9 Swimming nearby; 10 Golf nearby; 11 Skiing nearby; 12 May be booked through travel agent.

to routes 80, 60, 19, and 18. Full breakfast included. Nonsmoking.

Hosts: Tom and Jan Hartwell
Rooms: 3 (PB) $60
Full Breakfast
Credit Cards: A, B
Notes: 2, 5, 8, 9

Behm's Bed and Breakfast

Behm's Bed and Breakfast

166 Waugh Avenue, 16142
(412) 946-8641; (800) 932-3315

Located but one block from Westminster College campus, Behm's one-hundred-year-old B&B is comfortably furnished with family, primitive, and collected antiques. Located within walking distance of shops and restaurants, Behm's is surrounded by rural, Old Order Amish. Nationally recognized watercolorist Nancy Behm's gallery is on site. Lighted, off-street parking.

Hosts: Nancy and Robert Behm
Rooms: 4 (2PB; 2SB) $50-65
Full, Hearty Breakfast
Credit Cards: A, B
Notes: 2, 5, 7, 8, 9, 10, 11

NEWVILLE

Nature's Nook Farm

740 Shed Road, 17241
(717) 776-5619 (voice and FAX)

Located in a quiet, peaceful setting along the Blue Mountains. Warm Mennonite hospitality and clean, comfortable lodging await you. Enjoy freshly brewed garden tea and fresh fruit, in season. Homemade cinnamon rolls, muffins, and coffee cakes. Perennial flower garden. Close to Colonel Denning State Park with hiking trails, fishing, and swimming. Two hours to Lancaster, one hour to Harrisburg, and one and a half hours to Gettysburg and Hershey. Wheelchair-accessible.

Hosts: Don and Lois Leatherman
Rooms: 1 (PB) $50-58
Continental Breakfast
Credit Cards: none
Notes: 2, 5, 7 (8 and older), 8, 9, 10

NORTH EAST

Vineyard Bed and Breakfast

10757 Sidehill Road, 16428
(814) 725-8998; (888) 725-8998

Your hosts welcome you to the "Heart of Grape Country" on Lake Erie, surrounded by vineyards and orchards. Our turn-of-the-century farmhouse is quiet and peaceful, with rooms furnished with queen or king beds and tastefully decorated to complement our home.

Hosts: Clyde and Judy Burnham
Rooms: 4 (PB) $55-75
Full Breakfast
Credit Cards: A, B, C, D
Notes: 2, 5, 7, 9, 10, 11

NOTES: Credit cards accepted: A Master Card; B Visa; C American Express; D Discover; E Diners Club; F Other; 2 Personal checks accepted; 3 Lunch available; 4 Dinner available; 5 Open all year; 6 Pets

NORTHUMBERLAND

Campbell's Bed and Breakfast

707 Duke Street, 17857-1709
(717) 473-3276

Campbell's Bed and Breakfast is a country inn built in 1859. Three large bedrooms with queen-size beds await your occupancy. Enjoy a refreshing swim in the large, heated in-ground pool surrounded by the rose garden, or relax by the fire in the spacious living room during the cool months.

Hosts: Bob and Millie Campbell
Rooms: 3 (2PB; 1SB) $50-65
Full Breakfast
Credit Cards: A, B
Notes: 2, 5, 7 (call first), 8, 9 (on site), 10, 12

ORRTANNA

Hickory Bridge Farm

96 Hickory Bridge Road, 17353
(717) 642-5261
E-mail: hickory@mail.cvn.net
Web site: http://www.gettysburg.com/gcvb/hbf.htm

Only eight miles west of historical Gettysburg. Unique country dining and B&B. Cozy cottages with woodstoves and private baths located in secluded wooded settings along a stream. Lovely rooms available in the farmhouse with antiques, private baths, and whirlpool tubs. Full, farm breakfast served at the farmhouse, which was built in the late 1700s. Country dining offered on Fridays, Saturdays, and Sundays in a 130-year-old barn

with many antiques. Family owned and operated for more than fifteen years.

Hosts: Mary Lynn Martin
Rooms: 9 (PB) $79-89
Full Breakfast
Credit Cards: A, B, D
Notes: 2, 4 (weekends), 5, 8, 9, 10, 11

PARADISE

Maple Lane Farm Bed and Breakfast

505 Paradise Lane, 17562
(717) 687-7479

This two-hundred-acre, family-owned dairy farm is situated in the heart of Amish country with nearby quilt and craft shops, museums, farmers markets, antique shops, outlets, and auctions. The large front porch overlooks a spacious lawn, green meadows, and rolling hills with no busy highways. Pleasantly furnished rooms have quilts, crafts, canopy and poster beds, TVs, and air-conditioning. Victorian parlor for guest use. Breakfast served daily. Featured in several national magazines.

Hosts: Ed and Marion Rohrer
Rooms: 4 (2PB; 2SB) $45-58
Complimentary Breakfast
Credit Cards: none
Notes: 2, 5, 7, 8, 9, 10

Parson's Place Bed and Breakfast

37 Leacock Road, 17562
(717) 687-8529

Mid-1700s stone house with stone patio overlooking flower gardens and a picturesque road that was traveled by horse-drawn buggies to the Amish village-mecca

welcome; 7 Children welcome; 8 Tennis nearby; 9 Swimming nearby; 10 Golf nearby; 11 Skiing nearby; 12 May be booked through travel agent.

of Intercourse (tourist center of Lancaster County), three miles to the east. Share this charming home, furnished with country decor, with a former pastor and wife.

Hosts: Parson Bob and Margaret Bell
Rooms: 3 (2PB; 1SB) $50-70
Full Breakfast
Credit Cards: A, B
Notes: 2, 5

PEACH BOTTOM

Pleasant Grove Farm

368 Pilottown Road, 17563
(717) 548-3100

Located in beautiful, historic Lancaster County, this 160-acre dairy farm has been a family-run operation for 110 years, earning the title of Century Farm by the Pennsylvania Department of Agriculture. As a working farm, it provides guests the opportunity to experience daily life in a rural setting. Built in 1814, 1818, and 1820, the house once served as a country store and post office. Full country breakfast served by candlelight.

Hosts: Charles and Labertha Tindall
Rooms: 4 (SB) $45-60
Full Breakfast
Credit Cards: none
Notes: 2, 5, 7, 9

PITTSBURGH

The Inn at Oakmont

PO Box 103, **Oakmont**, 15139
(412) 828-0410; FAX (412) 828-1358
Web site: http://www.bnb.lm.com

Nestled in the historic village of Oakmont, we are next to Oakmont Country Club

and twenty minutes from Pittsburgh. Built in 1994, this meticulously designed bed and breakfast has become a mecca for the traveler seeking the service and charm of a more gracious era. All rooms include television, radio, telephone, and sleep machines. Some rooms have whirlpool tubs and fireplaces.

Hostess: Shelley Smith
Rooms: 8 (PB) $130-140
Full Breakfast
Credit Cards: A, B, C, D
Notes: 2, 5, 10, 11

Eagle Rock Lodge

POCONO MOUNTAINS
(SEE ALSO—CANADENSIS AND CRESCO)

Eagle Rock Lodge

PO Box 265, River Road, **Shawnee on Delaware**, 18356
(717) 421-2139

This century-old, eight-bedroom inn is located on ten and a half Delaware River acres adjacent to the scenic Delaware Water Gap National Recreation Area and the Pocono Mountains. Breakfast is served on an eighty-foot screened porch overlooking the river. Enjoy a step back in time

NOTES: Credit cards accepted: A Master Card; B Visa; C American Express; D Discover; E Diners Club; F Other; 2 Personal checks accepted; 3 Lunch available; 4 Dinner available; 5 Open all year; 6 Pets

to a more relaxed bygone era. Consider group rentals.

Hosts: Jane and Jim Cox
Rooms: 8 (1PB; 6SB) $60-95
Full Breakfast
Credit Cards: C
Notes: 2, 5, 7, 8, 9, 10, 11, 12

POINT PLEASANT (NEW HOPE)

Tattersall Inn

PO Box 569, Cafferty and River Road, 18950
(215) 297-8233; (800) 297-4988;
FAX (215) 297-5093
E-mail: NRHG17A@Prodigy.com
Web site: http://www.travelassist.com/reg/
  pa114s.html

This 18th-century, plastered, fieldstone home with broad porches and manicured lawns recalls the unhurried atmosphere of a bygone era. Enjoy the richly wainscoted entry hall, formal dining room with marble fireplace, and vintage phonographs. Step back in time when you enter the colonial common room with its beamed ceiling and walk-in fireplace. Spacious guest rooms, furnished with antiques. AC, private baths.

Hosts: Gerry and Herb Moss
Rooms: 6 (PB) $70-130
Full Breakfast
Credit Cards: A, B, C, D
Notes: 2, 5, 7, 8, 9, 12

SAXONBURG

The Main Stay
Bed and Breakfast

PO Box 507, 214 Main Street, 16056
(412) 352-9363
Web site: http://www.bnb.lm.com/mainstay.html

This 150-year-old country home is located in Saxonburg, in the heart of farm country

in southern Butler County, about thirty miles from Pittsburgh. It's a fine place to get away from the stress of everyday life or to spend the night en route east or west. Saxonburg is not a large place, but it boasts some fine shops to browse and an excellent restaurant to enjoy.

Hosts: Barbara and Ivan Franson
Rooms: 4 (PB) $60
Full Breakfast
Credit Cards: A, B, C
Notes: 2, 5, 7, 10

SCOTTDALE

Pine Wood Acres
Bed and Breakfast

Route 1, Box 634, 15683
(412) 887-5404

Experience gracious hospitality in our 1880 farmhouse. Enjoy the changes each season brings to the landscape of our tranquil country setting. Antiques, quilts, herb and perennial gardens, bountiful breakfasts, and afternoon tea. Near Wright's Fallingwater. Only ten miles south of I-70 at New Stanton.

Hosts: Ruth and James Horsch
Rooms: 3 (2PB; 1SB) $68.90-79.50
Full Breakfast
Credit Cards: some
Notes: 2, 5, 6, 7, 8, 9, 10, 11, 12

Zephyr Glen
Bed and Breakfast

205 Dexter Road, 15683
(412) 887-6577; FAX (412) 887-6177 (call first)

Our 1822 Federal-style Mennonite farmhouse is nestled on three wooded acres.

welcome; 7 Children welcome; 8 Tennis nearby; 9 Swimming nearby; 10 Golf nearby; 11 Skiing nearby; 12 May be booked through travel agent.

Zephyr Glen Bed and Breakfast

The house is filled with antiques, old quilts, and seasonal decorations. We feature caring Christian hospitality, warm country decor, afternoon tea, bed turn-down, and a hearty breakfast. Sit by the fireplace, rock on the wide porch, or stroll through herb, flower, and fruit gardens. Antiques, Fallingwater, hiking, biking, white-water, and historic sites are nearby. We'll help you find your favorite. Come and enjoy!

Hosts: Gil and Noreen McGurl
Rooms: 3 (PB) $70-75
Full Breakfast
Credit Cards: A, B, D
Notes: 2, 5, 7 (over 12), 8, 10, 11, 12

SEWICKLEY

The Whistlestop Bed and Breakfast

195 Broad Street, **Leetsdale**, 15056
(412) 251-0852
Web site: http://www.mountainsky.com

A quaint brick Victorian built in 1888 by the Harmonist Society, a Christian communal group similar to the Shakers. It features the "Upper Berth," a third-floor suite with a small kitchen and dining area, and the "Lower Berth" with a sofa bed and private entrance. Kids stay free with parents. Your hostess is well-known for her

country cooking, specializing in breads, muffins, pastries, and jams. Leetsdale is located on the Ohio River, twelve miles west of Pittsburgh (the airport is twenty minutes away) and close to the classic American village of Sewickley, where fine examples of historic architecture are well-maintained. The home is smoke-free.

Hosts: Steve and Joyce Smith
Rooms: 3 (PB) $60-70
Full Country Breakfast
Credit Cards: A, B, C, D
Notes: 2, 5, 7

Field and Pine Bed and Breakfast

SHIPPENSBURG

Field and Pine Bed and Breakfast

2155 Ritner Highway, 17257
(717) 776-7179
E-mail: fieldpine@aol.com
Web site: http://www.virtualcities.com

Surrounded by stately pine trees, Field and Pine is a family-owned B&B with the charm of an early-American stone house on an eighty-acre gentleman's farm. Built in 1790, the house has seven working fireplaces, original wide-pine floors, and stenciled walls. Bedrooms are furnished with antiques, quilts, and comforters. A gour-

---

NOTES: Credit cards accepted: A Master Card; B Visa; C American Express; D Discover; E Diners Club; F Other; 2 Personal checks accepted; 3 Lunch available; 4 Dinner available; 5 Open all year; 6 Pets

met breakfast is served in the formal dining room. Three miles from I-81, between Carlisle and Shippensburg.

Hosts: Allan and Mary Ellen Williams
Rooms: 3 (1PB; 2SB) $65-85
Full Breakfast
Credit Cards: A, B
Notes: 2, 5, 8, 9, 10, 11

SMOKETOWN

Homestead Lodging

184 East Brook Road (Route 896), 17576
(717) 393-6927; FAX (717) 393-1424

Welcome to Homestead Lodging in the heart of the Pennsylvania Dutch Amish farmlands. Listen to the clippity-clop of horses and buggies go by, or stroll down the lane to the scenic farmlands around us. Within walking distance of restaurants and minutes from farmers markets; quilt, antique, and craft shops; museums; and auctions. Tours available. This is a family-operated B&B with clean country rooms, each with private bath, cable color TV with remote/radio, refrigerator, AC, and heat. Microwave available.

Hosts: Robert and Lori Kepiro
Rooms: 5 (PB) $39-61
Continental Breakfast
Credit Cards: A, B, C, D
Notes: 2 (deposit only), 5, 7, 8, 9, 10, 12

Smoketown Motor Lodging and Carriage House B&B

190 East Brook Road, 17576
(717) 397-6944

Nestled on three beautiful acres of an original Amish homestead. Our guests call it

their "home away from home." Enjoy a walk down the lane to our Amish neighbors or by the stream to feed the ducks. Relax on our two patios or in our non-smoking lounge, or enjoy a game of tennis on our new court. Restaurants (one of them family-style) are within walking distance. Buggy rides, farmers and flea markets, and outlets are just a short distance away. Each room has full bath, AC, CATV, clock radio, and refrigerator.

Hosts: Don and Phyllis Ringuette
Rooms: 17 (PB) $40-80
Continental Breakfast
Credit Cards: A, B, C, D
Notes: 2, 5, 7, 8 (on premises), 9, 10, 12

SOMERSET

H.B.'s Cottage— A Bed and Breakfast

231 W. Church Street, 15501
(814) 443-1204

H.B.'s Cottage, an exclusive and elegant B&B located within the Borough of Somerset, is a stone-and-frame 1920s cottage with an oversize fireplace in the living room. It is furnished in the traditional manner with accent pieces from the overseas travels of the innkeepers—a retired

H.B.'s Cottage

naval officer and his wife—and collectible teddy bears from the hostess' extensive collection. The guest rooms are warmly and romantically decorated, and one has a private porch. Downhill and cross-country skiing, mountain biking, and tennis are specialties of the hosts. Located close to Seven Springs Mountain Resort, Fallingwater Hidden Valley Resort, biking and hiking trails, and white-water sports. Advance reservations are suggested.

Hosts: Hank and Phyllis Vogt
Rooms: 2 (PB) $60-75
Full Breakfast
Credit Cards: A, B
Notes: 2, 6 (limited), 8, 9, 10, 11

Quill Haven Country Inn

1519 N. Center Avenue, 15501
(814) 443-4514; FAX (814) 445-1376
E-mail: quill@surfshop.net
Web site: http://www.surfshop.net/users/quill/home.htm

Newly remodeled 1918 "gentleman's farmhouse" furnished with antiques and fine reproductions. Four uniquely decorated guest rooms, each with private bath, AC and TV. Common room with fireplace, sunroom where breakfast is served, and private deck with hot tub. Near Hidden Valley and Seven Springs ski resorts; Frank Lloyd Wright's Fallingwater; Youghiogheny Reservoir; Ohiopyle for hiking, biking, and white-water sports; outlet mall; state parks; golf courses; and antique shops. Located 1.2 miles from the Pennsylvania Turnpike, Exit 10.

Hosts: Rowland and Carol Miller
Rooms: 4 (PB) $75-95
Full Breakfast
Credit Cards: A, B
Notes: 2, 5, 7 (well-behaved), 8, 9, 10, 11

STAHLSTOWN

Thorn's Cottage

RD 1, Box 254, 15687
(412) 593-6429

Located in the historic Ligonier Valley area of the Laurel Mountains, seven miles from the Pennsylvania Turnpike, fifty miles east of Pittsburgh, the three-room cottage offers homey, woodland privacy. Relax on the sunporch or in the herb garden with its swing. Minutes to Fallingwater, white-water rafting, biking and hiking trails, and the quaint town of Ligonier with shops, dining, and amusement park. Breakfast at the cottage includes home-baked muffins and scones. Fully equipped kitchen.

Hosts: Larry and Beth Thorn
Rooms: 3-room cottage (PB) $55
Full Breakfast
Credit Cards: none
Notes: 2, 5, 7, 9, 10, 11

STARRUCCA

Nethercott Inn

Starrucca Creek Road, 18462
(717) 727-2211; FAX (717) 727-3811

This lovely, 1893 Victorian home is nestled in a small village in the Endless Mountains and furnished in country and antiques. All rooms have queen beds and private baths. Three-and-a-half hours from New York City and Philadelphia, eight from Toronto. "The Loft" sleeps eight and has a kitchen and two baths. Available for ski rentals, family reunions, etc.

Hosts: Charlotte and John Keyser
Rooms: 7 (PB) $75
Full Breakfast
Credit Cards: A, B, C, D
Notes: 2, 5, 7, 11, 12

NOTES: Credit cards accepted: A Master Card; B Visa; C American Express; D Discover; E Diners Club; F Other; 2 Personal checks accepted; 3 Lunch available; 4 Dinner available; 5 Open all year; 6 Pets

The Decoy Bed and Breakfast

STRASBURG

The Decoy Bed and Breakfast

958 Eisenberger Road, 17579
(717) 687-8585 (voice and FAX);
(800) 726-2287
E-mail: objoyful@lancnews.infi.net

This former Amish home is set in farmland with spectacular views and an informal atmosphere. Craft shops and attractions are nearby. We are part of an "inn to inn" tour. We host quilting seminars (yours or ours), a fabric store tour, family reunions, and church retreats. We can arrange dinner with an Amish family. Two cats in residence.

Hosts: Debby and Hap Joy
Rooms: 5 (PB) $60-70
Full Breakfast
Credit Cards: none
Notes: 2, 7, 8, 10, 12

TROY

Golden Oak Inn

196 Canton Street, 16947
(717) 297-4315; (800) 326-9834

Experience Victorian elegance in the heart of the Endless Mountains of northern Pennsylvania. The 1901 Queen Anne-style home is graced with Victorian decor, antiques, and heirlooms. It captures the history of the Civil War with a fine collection of artwork, memorabilia, artifacts, and a history library. Gourmet breakfasts prepared by Richard, a graduate of the Culinary Institute of America, are served amidst a romantic and relaxing atmosphere of candlelight and music. AAA-approved. Featured on the TV program "Breakfast on the Pennsylvania Road."

Hosts: Richard and Sharon Frank
Rooms: 4 (SB) $55-65
Candlelight Gourmet Breakfast
Credit Cards: A, B, D
Notes: 2, 5, 8, 9, 10, 11

VALLEY FORGE

Association of Bed and Breakfasts in Philadelphia, Valley Forge, and Brandywine

PO Box 562, 19481
(610) 783-7838; (800) 344-0123;
FAX (610) 783-7783
Web site: http://www.bnbassociation.com

There is a B&B for you!—whether business, vacation, getaways, or relocating.

welcome; 7 Children welcome; 8 Tennis nearby; 9 Swimming nearby; 10 Golf nearby; 11 Skiing nearby; 12 May be booked through travel agent.

Also serving **Bucks** and **Lancaster counties**. More than five hundred rooms are available in historic city/country inns, town houses, unhosted estate cottages, and suites. Family plan, Jacuzzi, fireplace, pool. Free brochure or descriptive directory ($3). Services include gift certificates, dinner reservations, weddings/special occasions/photography at unique bed and breakfasts, personal attention, gracious hospitality. No reservation fee. Featured in *Philadelphia Magazine*. Rate range: $35-135. Major credit cards accepted. Carolyn J. Williams, coordinator.

WARFORDSBURG

Buck Valley Ranch

Route 2, Box 1170, 17267
(717) 294-3759 (voice and FAX); (800) 294-3759
E-mail: buckvalleyranch@worldnet.att.net
Web site: http://.www.pafarmstay.com/
   buckvalleyranch

Located in the Appalachian Mountains of southern Pennsylvania's Fulton County. We are surrounded by two thousand acres of state game lands, which allows for hours of horseback riding. Experience the true peace and quiet of country life where you still can sit on the porch on a summer night and listen to whippoorwills. Meals are prepared from homegrown vegetables, homemade desserts, and local meats. Members of the Pennsylvania Farm Vacation Association. Rate includes all meals, lodging, and horseback riding for two people for two days and one night.

Hosts: Nadine and Leon Fox
Rooms: 4 (SB) $250
Full Breakfast
Credit Cards: A, B, D
Notes: 2, 3, 4, 5, 7, 8, 9 (on premises), 10, 11, 12

WASHINGTON

Rush House

810 E. Maiden Street, 15301
(412) 223-1890

Rush House is a one-hundred-year-old Victorian-style house built to accommodate Catfish Creek, which flows through a tunnel under the house. The bedrooms are decorated with antique pieces, and antique clocks abound throughout the house. A buffet breakfast is served each morning in the spacious dining room.

Hosts: Jim and Judy Wheeler
Rooms: 4 (PB) $75-110
Full Breakfast
Credit Cards: A, B
Notes: 2, 5, 8, 9

The Shepherd and Ewe Bed and Breakfast

WAYNESBORO

The Shepherd and Ewe Bed and Breakfast

11205 Country Club Road, 17268
(717) 762-8525; (888) 937-4393;
FAX (717) 762-5880

Renowned for its rich shepherding heritage, The Shepherd and Ewe extends that same nurturing tradition to its guests, who are invited to unwind in one of four guest

---

NOTES: Credit cards accepted: A Master Card; B Visa; C American Express; D Discover; E Diners Club; F Other; 2 Personal checks accepted; 3 Lunch available; 4 Dinner available; 5 Open all year; 6 Pets

rooms or the spacious master suite. Filled with Victoriana and lovingly restored and collected antiques, each room is clean and inviting. Full, hot country breakfast includes homemade pastries and fresh fruits of the season, with other delights. Located high atop lush acres of rolling farmland, the B&B is a short drive from Gettysburg and Mercersburg, Pennsylvania; Sharpsburg, Maryland; fine restaurants; state parks; hiking trails; art galleries; and antique shops.

Hosts: Twila and Robert Risser
Rooms: 5 (3PB; 2SB) $65-89
Full Country Breakfast
Credit Cards: A, B, C, D
Notes: 2, 5, 7, 8, 9, 10, 11

WELLSBORO

Kaltenbach's Bed and Breakfast

RD 6, Box 106A, Stony Fork Road (Kelsey Street), 16901
(717) 724-4954; (800) 722-4954
Web site: http://getawaysmag.com

This sprawling, country home with room for thirty-two guests offers visitors comfortable lodging, home-style breakfasts, and warm hospitality. Set on a seventy-two-acre farm, Kaltenbach's provides ample opportunity for walks through meadows, pastures, and forests; picnicking; and watching the sheep, pigs, rabbits, and wildlife. All-you-can-eat country breakfasts are served. Honeymoon suites have tub or Jacuzzi for two. Hunting and golf packages are available. Pennsylvania Grand Canyon. Hiking and biking on Pine Creek's all-new "Rail Trails," built on the old Conrail bed. Kaltenbach's was awarded a two-star rating in the Mobil Travel Guide for its accommodations and

hospitality. Professional Association of Innkeepers international inn member.

Host: Lee Kaltenbach
Rooms: 12 (9PB) $60-125
Full Breakfast
Credit Cards: A, B
Notes: 2, 3, 4, 5, 7, 8, 9, 10, 11

Wood's Rustic Inn Bed and Breakfast

Little Marsh Village, RR 2, Box 98A, **Middlebury Center**, 16935
(717) 376-3331

Relaxed, friendly atmosphere with beautiful flowers on a well-groomed, three-acre lawn. Clean, modern rooms with cable TV. Breakfast served in elegance on our lovely patio outside—weather permitting. Large, furnished porches. Golfing just ten minutes away. Near four lakes, all with swimming, camping, boating, and fishing. Great for bicycling, walking, sitting along the creeks and ponds, and enjoying our Belgian horses and wildlife on six hundred acres of land that is great for hunting. Near Pennsylvania Grand Canyon.

Hosts: Waldo and Olive Wood
Rooms: 3 (SB) $49
Full Country Breakfast
Credit Cards: none
Notes: 2, 7, 8, 9, 10

YORK

Friendship House Bed and Breakfast

728 E. Philadelphia Street, 17403
(717) 843-8299

An 1890s vintage town house located close to markets, shopping, and recreation. Spacious bedrooms with queen

---

welcome; 7 Children welcome; 8 Tennis nearby; 9 Swimming nearby; 10 Golf nearby; 11 Skiing nearby; 12 May be booked through travel agent.

beds. Property has a beautiful private yard with quaint gardens. Also has a three-car garage. A country breakfast is served most mornings. Free hostess gift.

Hostesses: Karen Maust and Becky Detwiler
Rooms: 3 (2PB; 1SB) $55-65
Full Breakfast
Credit Cards: none
Notes: 2, 5, 7, 8, 9, 10, 11

ZELIENOPLE

Benvenue Manor

160 Manor Drive, 16063
(412) 452-1710

"Benvenue," the original name of our 1816 stone manor home, means a "Good Wel-come." Guests enjoy a spectacular view, relax by the open fire, and feast on a gourmet breakfast. Four Victorian bedrooms are available, two with private baths, and a guest living room. You'll find gracious hospitality. High tea is served at 3 PM Tuesday and Thursday afternoons, and Saturday by special arrangement. We can host birthday parties and showers. Children are welcome. Benvenue Manor is located thirty-five minutes from downtown Pittsburgh.

Hostess: Margo Hogan and Family
Rooms: 4 (3PB) $55-100
Full Breakfast
Credit Cards: none
Notes: 2, 3, 4, 5, 7, 8, 9, 10

NOTES: Credit cards accepted: A Master Card; B Visa; C American Express; D Discover; E Diners Club; F Other; 2 Personal checks accepted; 3 Lunch available; 4 Dinner available; 5 Open all year; 6 Pets

Rhode Island

BLOCK ISLAND

The Barrington Inn

Corner of Beach and Ocean Avenues, PO Box 397, 02807
(401) 466-5510; FAX (401) 466-5880
Web site: http://www.ultranet.com/block-island/barrington

Known for its warmth and hospitality, The Barrington Inn is an 1886 farmhouse on a knoll overlooking the New Harbor area of Block Island. Six individually decorated guest rooms and two housekeeping apartments. A light breakfast is served. Amenities include two guest sitting rooms (one with TV), refrigerator, ceiling fans, comfortable beds, front porch, back deck, and afternoon beverages. No smoking.

Hosts: Joan and Howard Ballard
Rooms: 6 + 2 apartments (PB)
Continental Plus Breakfast
Credit Cards: A, B, D
Notes: 2, 7, 8, 9

Hotel Manisses and 1661 Inn

Spring Street, 02807
(401) 466-2421; (800) MANISSE;
FAX (401) 466-3162
E-mail: BIRESORTS@aol.com

Step into 19th-century yesteryear with a stay at our resort. Some rooms feature spectacular views of the Atlantic Ocean, decks, Jacuzzis and fireplaces. The award-winning dining room serves dinner every evening. Sample delicious selections from our varied menu as featured in *Gourmet* magazine.

Hosts: Joan and Justin Abrams, Rita and Steve Draper
Rooms: 47 (43PB; 4SB) $75-335
Full Breakfast
Credit Cards: A, B, C
Notes: 2, 3, 4, 5, 7, 8, 9, 12

The Rose Farm Inn

Roslyn Road, Box E, 02807
(401) 466-2053 (voice and FAX)

Experience the romance of the Victorian era. Treat yourself to a romantic room beautifully furnished with antiques and king- or queen-size canopy bed. Enjoy the peaceful tranquillity of the farm from shaded decks cooled by gentle ocean breezes. Gaze at the ocean from your window, or share a whirlpool bath for two. Awaken to a light buffet breakfast in a charming porch dining room with an ocean view. Bicycle rentals available. Children over twelve welcome.

Hostess: Judith B. Rose
Rooms: 19 (17PB; 2SB) $95-179
Continental Plus Breakfast
Credit Cards: A, B, C, D
Notes: 2, 7 (over 12), 8, 9

---

welcome; 7 Children welcome; 8 Tennis nearby; 9 Swimming nearby; 10 Golf nearby; 11 Skiing nearby; 12 May be booked through travel agent.

RHODE ISLAND

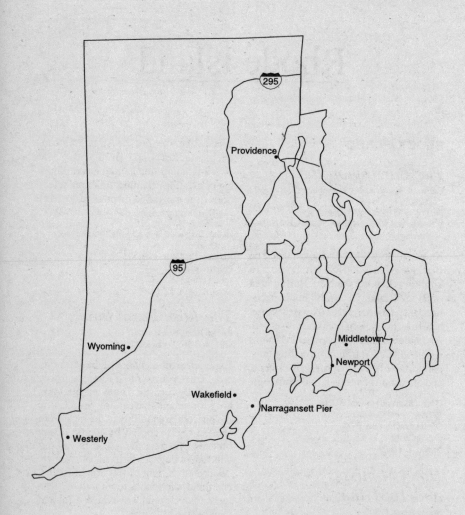

Providence

295

95

Wyoming

Middletown

Newport

Wakefield

Narragansett Pier

Westerly

Block Island

MIDDLETOWN

The Inn at Shadow Lawn

120 Miantonomi Avenue, 02842
(401) 847-0902; (800) 352-3750;
FAX (401) 848-6529
E-mail: randy@shadowlawn.com
Web site: http://www.shadowlawn.com

Stepping inside our historical 142-year-old mansion is like entering a grand Victorian painting. The doors open wide to a warm, old-fashioned ambience of French crystal chandeliers, pastel stained glass and classical music. Our eight spacious guest rooms have working fireplaces (some with kitchenettes) and are named for female Victorian writers. Just five minutes from beaches and downtown Newport. The Inn at Shadow Lane is ideal for weddings, receptions, conferences, meetings and retreats.

Hosts: Randy and Selma Fabricant
Rooms: 8 (PB) $55-155
Full Breakfast
Credit Cards: A, B, C, E, F
Notes: 5, 7, 8, 9, 10, 12

Lindsey's Guest House

6 James Street, 02842
(401) 846-9386

Walk to beaches and restaurants. Five minutes to Newport's famous mansions, Ocean Drive, Cliff Walk, boat and bus tours, and bird sanctuary. Quiet residential neighborhood with off-street parking. Large yard and deck with hostess available for information about events and discounts. Split-level, owner-occupied home

Lindsey's Guest House

with expanded continental breakfast. One room is wheelchair-accessible for twenty-eight-inch wheelchairs.

Hostess: Anne Lindsey
Rooms: 4 (2PB; 2SB) $45-85
Full Breakfast
Credit Cards: A, B
Notes: 2, 5, 7, 8, 9, 10, 12

NARRAGANSETT

1900 House

59 Kingstown Road, 02882
(401) 789-7971

Walk to the ocean at the end of our street, enjoy the sea breezes from our porch, luxuriate in a claw-foot tub, and slumber in a canopy bed. Awake to a full gourmet breakfast in this Victorian that will tantalize you with antiques, fanciful collections, and lovely gardens. There are color TVs in the rooms and a common guest refrigerator for chilled delights. Stay six nights and the seventh is *free*.

Hosts: Bill and Sandy Panzeri
Rooms: 3 (1PB; 2SB) $55-85
Full Breakfast
Credit Cards: none
Notes: 2, 5, 8, 9, 10, 12

NOTES: Credit cards accepted: A Master Card; B Visa; C American Express; D Discover; E Diners Club; F Other; 2 Personal checks accepted; 3 Lunch available; 4 Dinner available; 5 Open all year; 6 Pets welcome; 7 Children welcome; 8 Tennis nearby; 9 Swimming nearby; 10 Golf nearby; 11 Skiing nearby; 12 May be booked through travel agent.

NEWPORT

Admiral Benbow Inn

93 Pelham Street, 02840
(401) 848-8000; (800) 343-2863;
FAX (401) 848-8006
Web site: http://www.admiralsinns.com

Our inn was built in 1855 and is an easy
walk from world-class restaurants, night
life, art galleries, antique shops, historic
sites, and mansions. The inn has delightfully decorated rooms with brass beds and
fine antiques. A gourmet continental
breakfast is served in our common room.
It's not a museum or showcase but a welcoming inn with many returning guests.

Hostess: Cathy Darigan
Rooms: 15 (PB) $65-225
Continental Breakfast
Credit Cards: A, B, C, D
Notes: 8, 9, 10, 12

Admiral Farragut Inn

31 Clarke Street, 02840
(401) 848-8000; (800) 343-2863;
FAX (401) 848-8006
Web site: http://www.admiralsinns.com

Everywhere amid our guest rooms, keeping room, foyer, and halls are fresh inter-
pretations of colonial themes and even a
bit of whimsy to make your stay a delight.
A full breakfast is served in our guest
rooms. Our famed Newport Harbor, historic sites, mansions, shops, dining, and
night life are all just a walk away.

Host: Chris Leone
Rooms: 9 (PB) $65-175
Full Breakfast
Credit Cards: A, B, C, D
Notes: 5, 8, 9, 10, 11, 12

The Burbank Rose

111 Memorial Blvd. W., 02840
(401) 849-9457; (888) 297-5800

The Burbank Rose, built in 1850, is located in the historic downtown harborfront
area. Walk to everything in town. Close
to all attractions. Special off-season and
mid-week rates. Clean, comfortable
rooms with private baths and AC. Free
parking for our guests.

Hosts: Bonnie and John McNeely
Rooms: 4 (PB) $59-129
Full Breakfast
Credit Cards: C, D
Notes: 2, 5, 8, 9, 10, 11, 12

Cliffside Inn

2 Seaview Avenue, 02840
(401) 847-1811; (800) 845-1811;
FAX (401) 848-5850
E-mail: cliff@wsii.com
Web site: http://www.cliffsideinn.com

Nestled on a quiet neighborhood street just
steps away from the historic Cliff Walk,
the Inn displays the grandeur of a Victorian manor with the warmth and comfort
of a home. A full breakfast of homemade
muffins, granola, fresh fruit, and a hot
entrée such as eggs Benedict or whipped
cream-topped French toast is served each
morning in the spacious parlor. Fifteen
rooms, eleven with both fireplace and
double whirlpool. Coffee room service
from 7 to 9 AM. Full breakfast from 8 to
10 AM. Afternoon Victorian tea from 4:30
to 5:30 PM. Each room contains a telephone and private bath; some have working fireplaces and Jacuzzis or steam baths.
Smoking is permitted on the large front
veranda, furnished with wicker furniture

NOTES: Credit cards accepted: A Master Card; B Visa; C American Express; D Discover; E Diners
Club; F Other; 2 Personal checks accepted; 3 Lunch available; 4 Dinner available; 5 Open all year; 6 Pets

and covered with floral cushions. All rooms are air-conditioned.

Hosts: Stephen Nicolas
Rooms: 15 (PB) $175-325
Full Hot Gourmet Breakfast
Credit Cards: A, B, C, D, E
Notes: 2, 5, 8, 9, 10, 12

Halidon Hill Guest House

Halidon Avenue, 02840
(401) 847-8318

Georgian colonial home with large deck area and in-ground pool. Located near restaurants, shops, mansions, and yacht clubs. Spacious, beautifully decorated rooms with TV, phone, and small refrigerator. Full breakfast. Suites available.

Hosts: Helen and Paul Burke
Rooms: 2 + 2-bedroom apartment (PB) $55-150
Full Breakfast
Credit Cards: C, D, E
Notes: 7, 8, 9 (on site), 10

La Forge Cottage

96 Pelham Street, 02840-3130
(401) 847-4400 (voice and FAX)
E-mail: margotd@laforgecottage.com
Web site: http://www.laforgecottage.com

A Victorian bed and breakfast in the heart of Newport's Historic Hill area. Close to beaches and downtown. All rooms have private bath, TV, telephone, AC, refrigerator, and full-breakfast room service. French, German, and Spanish spoken. Reservations suggested. Minimum stay on weekends is two nights, on holidays three nights. No smoking.

Hosts: Louis and Margot Droual
Rooms: 10 (PB) $55-165
Full Breakfast
Credit Cards: A, B, C, D
Notes: 2, 5, 7, 8, 9, 10

The Willows of Newport

The Willows of Newport Romantic Inn and Garden

8 Willow Street, Historic Point, 02840-1927
(401) 846-5486
Web site: http://www.newportri.com/users/willows

Built in the 1700s, the inn exemplifies pre-Revolutionary charm and elegance. Be pampered with cut flowers, turned-down brass canopy beds, breakfast in bed, and AC. Stroll three blocks to downtown/waterfront, or enjoy our Secret Garden. Mobil three-star award; Best Garden Award, '94-'96; and ABBA award of excellence. Listed in *Best Places to Kiss*.

Hostess: Patricia "Pattie" Murphy
Rooms: 8 (PB) $98-198
Continental Breakfast
Credit Cards: none
Notes: 2, 5, 8, 9, 10, 12

PROVIDENCE

The Old Court Bed and Breakfast

144 Benefit Street, 02903
(401) 751-2002; FAX (401) 272-4830
E-mail: reserve@oldcourt.com
Web site: http://www.oldcourt.com

The Old Court Bed and Breakfast is filled with antique furniture, chandeliers, and memorabilia from the 19th century, with each room designed to reflect period tastes. All rooms have private baths, and the antique, Victorian beds are comfortable and spacious. Just a three-minute walk from the center of downtown Providence, near Brown University and Rhode Island School of Design.

Host: David Dolbashian
Rooms: 11 (PB) $85-250
Full Breakfast
Credit Cards: A, B, D
Notes: 2, 5, 8, 9, 12

State House Inn

43 Jewett Street, 02908
(401) 351-6111; FAX (401) 351-4261

Conveniently located minutes from downtown in a quiet and quaint neighborhood. The State House Inn offers business and vacation travelers privacy and personal service. Each guest room has a private bath and is decorated in Shaker or colonial furnishings. A hearty and healthy breakfast is served in our dining room.

Hosts: Frank and Monica Hopton
Rooms: 10 (PB) $89-119
Full Breakfast
Credit Cards: A, B, C, D
Notes: 5, 7, 8, 9, 10, 12

WAKEFIELD

Larchwood Inn

521 Main Street, 02879
(401) 783-5454; (800) 275-5450;
FAX (401) 783-1800

Watching over the main street of the quaint New England town for more than 160 years, this grand old house, surrounded by lawns and shaded by stately trees, dispenses hospitality and good food and spirits from early morning to late at night. Historic Newport, picturesque Mystic Seaport, salty Block Island, and Foxwoods Casino are a short ride away.

Hosts: Francis and Diann Browning
Rooms: 19 (11PB; 8SB) $50-110
Full Breakfast
Credit Cards: A, B, C, D, E
Notes: 2, 3, 4, 5, 6, 7, 8, 9, 10, 11, 12

Woody Hill Bed and Breakfast

WESTERLY

Woody Hill Bed and Breakfast

149 S. Woody Hill Road, 02891
(401) 322-0452

This colonial reproduction is set on a hilltop overlooking twenty acres of informal gardens, woods, and fields. Antiques, wide-board floors, handmade quilts, and fireplaces create an early-American atmosphere. Guests enjoy a full breakfast and the use of a secluded, forty-foot, in-ground pool. Close to Newport, Block Island, Mystic, and casino.

Hostess: Ellen L. Madison
Rooms: 4 (PB) $75-125
Full Breakfast
Credit Cards: none
Notes: 2, 5, 7, 8, 9, 10, 12

NOTES: Credit cards accepted: A Master Card; B Visa; C American Express; D Discover; E Diners Club; F Other; 2 Personal checks accepted; 3 Lunch available; 4 Dinner available; 5 Open all year; 6 Pets

WYOMING

Cookie Jar
Bed and Breakfast

64 Kingstown Road, 02898
(401) 539-2680; (800) 767-4262

The heart of our home, the living room, was built in 1732 as a blacksmith shop. Later, the forge was removed and a large granite fireplace was built by an American Indian stonemason. The original wood ceiling, hand-hewn beams, and granite walls remain today. The property was called the Perry Plantation—and yes, they had two slaves who lived above the blacksmith shop. We offer friendly, home-style living in a comfortable country setting. All rooms have a private bath, private sitting room, color TV, and air-conditioning. On Route 138 just off I-95.

Hosts: Dick and Madelein Sohl
Rooms: 3 (PB) $75
Full Breakfast
Credit Cards: none
Notes: 2, 5, 7, 8, 9, 10, 12

---

welcome; 7 Children welcome; 8 Tennis nearby; 9 Swimming nearby; 10 Golf nearby; 11 Skiing nearby; 12 May be booked through travel agent.

SOUTH CAROLINA

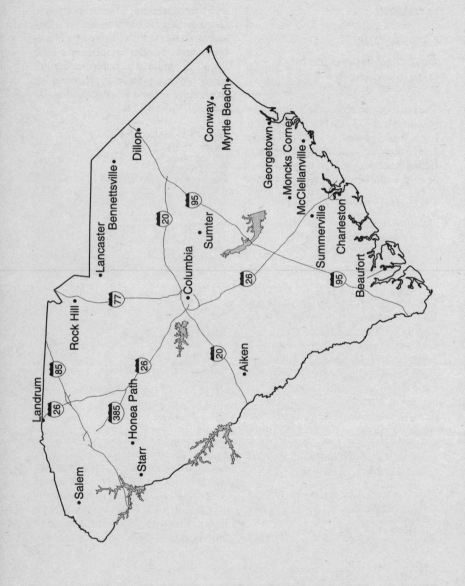

South Carolina

BEAUFORT

TwoSuns Inn
Bed and Breakfast

1705 Bay Street, 29902
(803) 522-1122; (800) 532-4244;
FAX (803) 522-1122
E-mail: twosuns@islc.net

Enjoy the charm of a small, resident host
B&B in a remarkably beautiful nationally
landmarked historic district about midway
between Charleston and Savannah—
complete with a panoramic bay-view veranda, individually appointed king or queen
guest rooms, an informal afternoon "Tea
and Toddy Hour," and sumptuous breakfasts. The setting is idyllic; the atmosphere
is casually elegant—a restored 1917 grand
home with modern baths and amenities
accented with collectibles and antiques.
Carrol and Ron are gracious.

Hosts: Carrol and Ron Kay
Rooms: 5 (PB) $105 and up
Full Breakfast
Credit Cards: A, B, C, D
Notes: 2, 5, 8, 9, 10, 12

The Breeden Inn and Carriage House

BENNETTSVILLE

The Breeden Inn
and Carriage House

404 E. Main Street, 29512
(803) 479-3665

Built in 1886, this romantic southern mansion is situated on two acres in Ben-
nettsville's historic district. Beautiful decor
and comfortable surroundings will capture
your interest and inspire your imagination.
The Breeden Inn is a haven for antique
lovers. Listed on the National Register of
Historic Places, the Inn is only twenty-five

NOTES: Credit cards accepted: A Master Card; B Visa; C American Express; D Discover; E Diners
Club; F Other; 2 Personal checks accepted; 3 Lunch available; 4 Dinner available; 5 Open all year; 6 Pets
welcome; 7 Children welcome; 8 Tennis nearby; 9 Swimming nearby; 10 Golf nearby; 11 Skiing nearby;
12 May be booked through travel agent.

minutes from I-95—a great halfway point between Florida and New York. Our porches and grounds—truly a southern tradition—can be enjoyed at both guest houses. Swings, rockers, wicker, cast iron, Adirondacks, and even ceiling fans await to play a part in helping you unwind. Curl up with a book under the old magnolia tree, sun by the pool—there's a comfy spot for everyone. Come—we have some peace, quiet, and comfort for you. No smoking. Owned and operated by a Christian family.

Hosts: Wesley and Bonnie Park
Rooms: 7 (PB) $65
Full Breakfast
Credit Cards: A, B, D
Notes: 2, 5, 7, 9, 10, 12

1837 Bed and Breakfast & Breakfast/Tearoom

CHARLESTON

1837 Bed
and Breakfast/Tearoom

126 Wentworth Street, 29401
(803) 723-7166 (Area Code 843 after March 1998)

Enjoy accommodations in a wealthy cotton planter's home and brick carriage house centrally located in Charleston's historic district. Canopied, poster, rice beds. Walk to boat tours, the old market, antique shops, restaurants, and main attractions. Near the Omni and College of Charleston. Full, gourmet breakfast is served in the formal dining room and includes sausage-and-grits casserole, raspberry French toast, ham frittata with Mornay sauce, and home-baked breads. The 1837 Tea Room serves afternoon tea to our guests and the public. Off-street parking. Special winter rates, December-February.

Hosts: Sherri Weaver and Richard Dunn
Rooms: 8 (PB) $69-135
Full Gourmet Breakfast
Credit Cards: A, B, C
Notes: 2, 5, 7 (7 and older), 8, 9, 10, 12

Ashley Inn B&B

201 Ashley Avenue, 29403
(803) 723-1848; (800) 581-6658;
FAX (803) 723-8007
(Area Code 843 after March 1998)

Stay in a stately, historic, circa-1835 home. So warm and hospitable, the Ashley Inn offers seven intimate bedrooms featuring canopy beds, private baths, fireplaces, and air-conditioning. Delicious breakfasts are served on a grand columned piazza overlooking a beautiful Charleston garden, or in the formal dining room. Relax with tea and cookies after touring nearby historic sites or enjoying the complimentary touring bicycles. The Ashly Inn offers simple elegance in a warm, friendly home noted for true southern hospitality.

Hosts: Sally and Bud Allen
Rooms: 7 (PB) $69-165
Full Breakfast
Credit Cards: A, B, C, D
Notes: 2, 5, 7 (over 12), 8, 9, 10, 12

NOTES: Credit cards accepted: A Master Card; B Visa; C American Express; D Discover; E Diners Club; F Other; 2 Personal checks accepted; 3 Lunch available; 4 Dinner available; 5 Open all year; 6 Pets

The Belvedere Bed and Breakfast

40 Rutledge Avenue, 29401
(803) 722-0973 (Area Code 843 after March 1998)

A late-1800s colonial mansion in the downtown historic district of Charleston on Colonial Lake. It has an 1800 Adam interior with mantels and woodwork. Three large bedrooms have antiques, Oriental rugs, and family collections. The Belvedere is within easy access of everything in the area. Closed December 1–February 15.

Hosts: David Spell and Rick Zender
Rooms: 3 (PB) $125-150
Continental Plus Breakfast
Credit Cards: none
Notes: 2, 7 (over 8), 8, 9, 10, 12

Cannonboro Inn

184 Ashley Avenue, 29403
(803) 723-8572; (800) 235-8039;
FAX (803) 723-8007
(Area Code 843 after March 1998)

This 1853 historic home offers six beautifully decorated bedrooms with antique four-poster and canopied beds. Cannonboro Inn is a place to be pampered, where you may sleep in until the aroma of sizzling sausage and home-baked biscuits lure you to a full breakfast on the columned piazza overlooking a Low Country garden and fountain. After breakfast, tour nearby historic sites on complimentary bicycles, and return to more pampering with afternoon sherry, tea, and sumptuous home-baked goods. Our private baths, off-street parking, color TV, and air-conditioning, along with that very special southern hospitality,

demonstrate this is what Charleston is all about!

Hosts: Sally and Bud Allen
Rooms: 6 (PB) $69-165
Full Breakfast
Credit Cards: A, B, C, D
Notes: 2, 5, 7 (over 12), 8, 9, 10, 12

Country Victorian Bed and Breakfast

105 Tradd Street, 29401-2422
(803) 577-0682 (Area Code 843 after March 1998)

Come relive the charm of the past. Relax in a rocker on the piazza of this historic home and watch the carriages go by. Walk to antique shops, churches, restaurants, art galleries, museums, and all historic points of interest. The house, built in 1820, is located in the historic district south of Broad. Rooms have private entrances and contain antique iron and brass beds, old quilts, antique oak and wicker furniture, and braided rugs over heart-of-pine floors. Homemade cookies will be waiting. Many extras! Featured in *Country Quilts Magazine*, fall 1997.

Hostess: Diane Deardurff Weed
Rooms: 2 (PB) $75-125
Continental Plus Breakfast
Credit Cards: none
Notes: 2, 5, 7 (over 10), 8, 9, 10, 11 (water)

King George IV Inn

32 George Street, 29401
(803) 723-9339; (888) 723-1667;
FAX (803) 723-7749
(Area Code 843 after March 1998)
Web site: http://www.bbonline.com/sc/kinggeorge

A two-hundred-year-old house in the heart of the historic district. The inn is Federal style, with three levels of Charleston side porches. Rooms have 10 x 12-foot

welcome; 7 Children welcome; 8 Tennis nearby; 9 Swimming nearby; 10 Golf nearby; 11 Skiing nearby; 12 May be booked through travel agent.

ceilings with decorative plaster moldings, wide-planked hardwood floors, old furnishings, and antiques. Private baths, parking, AC, TVs. One-minute walk to King Street, five minutes to the Market.

Hosts: Debra, Terry and Debbie
Rooms: 10 (8PB; 2SB) $75-149
Continental Plus Breakfast
Credit Cards: A, B
Notes: 2, 5, 7, 8, 9, 10, 12

The Kitchen House (Circa 1732)

126 Tradd Street, 29401
(803) 577-6362; FAX (803) 965-5615
(Area Code 843 after March 1998)

Nestled in the heart of the historic district, The Kitchen House is a totally restored 18th-century dwelling. You'll enjoy the southern hospitality, absolute privacy, fireplaces, and antiques. Private patio, colonial herb garden, fishpond, and fountain. Concierge service. The home has been featured in *Colonial Homes Magazine*, *The New York Times*, and *Best Places to Stay in the South*.

Hostess: Lois Evans
Rooms: 3 (PB) $125-195
Full Breakfast
Credit Cards: A, B
Notes: 2, 5, 7, 8, 9, 10, 12

Rutledge Victorian Inn

114 Rutledge Avenue, 29401
(803) 722-7551; (888) 722-7553;
FAX (803) 727-0065
(Area Code 843 after March 1998)
Web sites: http://www.bbonline.com/sc/rutledge
　　http://www.virtualcities.com
　　http://www.webpost.com/hia/listings/
　　rutledge.htm

Elegant Charleston home in downtown historic district. Century-old house with

Rutledge Victorian Inn

rare, decorative, Italianate architecture with beautiful ceiling moldings. Rooms have mahogany and oak fireplaces, twelve-foot ceilings, hardwood floors, tenfoot doors and windows, and antiques. Lovely, 120-foot porch with rocking chairs and joggling board overlooking the Park and Roman Columns, remains of the Confederate soldiers' reunion hall. Relaxed atmosphere, AC, parking, and TVs. Lovely formal dining rooms where complimentary continental plus breakfast is served. Five-to-twenty-minute walk to historic sites.

Hosts: Lyn, Norman, and Dave
Rooms: 11 (7PB; 4SB) $69-280
Continental Plus Breakfast
Credit Cards: A, B
Notes: 2, 5, 7 (12 and older), 8, 9, 10, 12

Two Meeting Street Inn

2 Meeting Street, 29401
(803) 723-7322 (Area Code 843 after March 1998)

Charleston's oldest and most elegant inn! Located at Battery Park in the historic district, this Queen Anne mansion delights its guests with English antiques and Tiffany windows. Nine spacious and beautifully

NOTES: Credit cards accepted: A Master Card; B Visa; C American Express; D Discover; E Diners Club; F Other; 2 Personal checks accepted; 3 Lunch available; 4 Dinner available; 5 Open all year; 6 Pets

appointed rooms await. Guests are served breakfast in the formal dining room or courtyard; afternoon tea is enjoyed on the veranda overlooking the harbor. The epitome of southern hospitality.

Hostess: Karen Spell Shaw
Rooms: 9 (PB) $145-235
Continental Breakfast
Credit Cards: none
Notes: 2, 8, 9, 10

Two Meeting Street Inn

Villa de La Fontaine Bed and Breakfast

138 Wentworth Street, 29401
(803) 577-7709 (Area Code 843 after March 1998)

Villa de La Fontaine is a columned Greek Revival mansion in the heart of the historic district. It was built in 1838 and boasts a three-quarter-acre garden with fountain and terraces. Restored to impeccable condition, it is furnished with museum-quality furniture and accessories. The hosts are retired ASID interior designers and have decorated the rooms with 18th-century American antiques. Several of the rooms feature canopied beds. Breakfast is prepared by a master chef who prides himself on serving a different menu every day.

Parking on the property, with seven-foot brick walls and iron gates! It is in the safest part of Charleston, near the College of Charleston. Minimum-stay requirements for weekends and holidays. The inn offers guests a choice between its four rooms and two suites.

Hosts: William Fontaine and Aubrey Hancock
Rooms: 4 (PB) $100-125
Full Breakfast
Credit Cards: none
Notes: 2, 5, 7 (12 and older), 8, 9, 10

COLUMBIA

Richland Street Bed and Breakfast

1425 Richland Street, 29201
(803) 779-7001; FAX (803) 256-3725

Richland Street Bed and Breakfast is a Victorian home located in the heart of Columbia's historic district within walking distance of tour homes, restaurants, and downtown shopping. Inside, you are greeted with a large gathering area, seven oversize guest rooms with private baths, and loads of hospitality. Each room has its own personality and is decorated with

Richland Street Bed and Breakfast

welcome; 7 Children welcome; 8 Tennis nearby; 9 Swimming nearby; 10 Golf nearby; 11 Skiing nearby; 12 May be booked through travel agent.

period antiques. The Bridal Suite with its whirlpool tub is especially inviting. You will enjoy the front porches with its gazebo and rockers. Special attention given to each guest includes a deluxe continental breakfast served in classic Victorian style. Rated four diamonds, American Auto Association.

Host: Naomi S. Perryman
Rooms: 8 (PB) $79-135
Deluxe Continental Breakfast
Credit Cards: A, B, C
Notes: 2 (in advance), 5

The Cypress Inn

CONWAY

The Cypress Inn

16 Elm Street, PO Box 495, 29528
(803) 248-8199; (800) 575-5307;
FAX (803) 248-0329
Web site: http://www.bbonline.com/sc/cypress

Coastal South Carolina is the location of this divine bed and breakfast where you'll find excellence in the little details, and it is never forgotten that this is where your memories are created. On the edge of the Waccamaw River overlooking a private marina, guests enjoy Jacuzzis, TVs, and phones with dataports for the business traveler. Morning breakfast is alive with delicious aromas and enthusiastic

voices. Days are spent bird-watching, taking ocean walks, exploring sculpture gardens, and much more.

Hosts: Jim and Carol Ruddick
Rooms: 12 (PB) $95-140
Full Breakfast
Credit Cards: A, B, C, E
Notes: 2, 5, 8, 9, 10, 12

DILLON

Magnolia Inn

601 E. Main Street, 29536
(803) 774-0679 (voice and FAX)

Warm hospitality and beautiful decor with antiques grace this century-old Greek Revival home located just two miles from Exit 190 on I-95. It's only sixty minutes from Myrtle Beach, forty minutes from Darlington Speedway.

Hosts: Eileen and Alan Kemp
Rooms: 4 (PB) $65
Full Breakfast
Credit Cards: A, B, C, D
Notes: 2, 5

GEORGETOWN

The Shaw House

613 Cypress Court, 29440
(803) 546-9663

The Shaw House is a spacious, two-story colonial home in a natural setting with a beautiful view overlooking miles of marshland—perfect for bird-watchers. Within walking distance of downtown and great restaurants on the waterfront. Rooms are large, with many antiques and private baths. Breakfast is served at our guests'

The Shaw House

convenience. Also included are nighttime chocolates on each pillow, turn-backs, and some loving extras. Guests always leave with a little gift like prayers, recipes, and/or jellies. Approved by AAA, Mobil, and ABBA.

Hosts: Mary and Joe Shaw
Rooms: 3 (PB) $50-65
Full Breakfast
Credit Cards: none
Notes: 2, 5, 7, 8, 9, 10

"Ship Wrights" Bed and Breakfast

609 Cypress Court, 29440
(803) 527-4475

Three-thousand-plus square feet of beautiful, quiet, clean home is yours to use when you stay. It's nautically attired and tastefully laced with family heirlooms. Guests say they feel like they just stayed at their best friend's home. The bedrooms and baths are beautiful and very comfortable. You'll never get "Grandma Eicker's Pancakes" anywhere else (the inn is famous for them). There's a great story behind the pancakes! The view from the large porch is breathtaking, perfect for bird-

watching. Five minutes from Ocean Beach. AAA-approved.

Hostess: Leatrice M. Wright
Rooms: 2 (PB) $60
Full Breakfast
Credit Cards: none
Notes: 2, 5, 7, 8, 9, 10

Winyah Bay Bed and Breakfast

403 Helena Street, 29440
(803) 546-9051; (800) 681-6176

Enjoy the breezes from the bay as you stroll down the longest private dock in the state. Relax on our small private island, watch the birds and boats, fish, crab, or sunbathe. Each room has a view of the bay. You have a private entrance, sitting area, and breakfast area. The cupboards and refrigerator are stocked, so your schedule is your own.

Hosts: Peggy, Diane, and Jason Wheeler
Rooms: 2 (PB) $65-100
Continental Plus Breakfast
Credit Cards: A, B
Notes: 5, 8, 9, 10, 11, 12

HONEA PATH

"Sugarfoot Castle"

211 S. Main Street, 29654
(864) 369-6565

Enormous trees umbrella this 19th-century brick Victorian home. Fresh flowers grace the fourteen-inch-thick-walled rooms furnished with family heirlooms. You can enjoy the living room's interesting collections or the library's comfy chairs, TV, VCR, books, fireplace, desk, and

welcome; 7 Children welcome; 8 Tennis nearby; 9 Swimming nearby; 10 Golf nearby; 11 Skiing nearby; 12 May be booked through travel agent.

game table. Upon arising, guests find coffee and juice outside their doors, followed by a breakfast of hot breads, cereal, fresh fruit, and beverages served by candlelight in the dining room. Rock away the world's cares on a screened porch overlooking peaceful grounds. AAA-approved.

Hosts: Gale and Cecil Evans
Rooms: 3 (PB) $59-85
Heavy Continental Breakfast
Credit Cards: A, B
Notes: 2, 5, 8, 9, 10

LANCASTER

Wade-Beckham House

3385 Great Falls Highway, 29720
(803) 285-1105

A pastoral setting for this 1800s plantation home offers serenity, spacious porches, heirloom family antiques and interesting historical artifacts. Guests may choose the Rose Room, Summer House Room or Wade Hampton Room, all located upstairs. Horses, cows, chickens, an old barn and an antique store are on the property. The home is listed on the National Register.

Hosts: Bill and Jan Duke
Rooms: 3 (PB) $75
Full Breakfast
Credit Cards: none
Notes: 2, 8, 10

LANDRUM

The Red Horse Inn

310 N. Campbell Road, 29356
(864) 895-4968; FAX (864) 895-4968

The Red Horse Inn is located on 190 acres in the foothills of the Blue Ridge Moun-

tains. Five Victorian cottages are luxuriously appointed. Each offers a kitchen, bathroom, bedroom, sleeping loft, living room with fireplace, deck or patio, color TV, and air-conditioning. Three have Jacuzzis. The sweeping mountain views, hiking trails, and peaceful countryside offer spiritual renewal.

Hosts: Mary and Roger Wolters
Rooms: 5 cottages (PB) $85
Continental Breakfast
Credit Cards: none
Notes: 2, 5, 6 (ask), 7, 8, 9, 10, 12

Laurel Hill Plantation

McCLELLANVILLE

Laurel Hill Plantation

PO Box 190, 8913 N. Highway 17, 29458
(803) 887-3708; (888) 887-3708
(Area Code 843 after March 1998)

A nature lover's delight! Laurel Hill faces the Atlantic Ocean. Wraparound porches provide spectacular views of creeks and marshes. The reconstructed house is furnished with antiques that reflect the Low Country lifestyle. A perfect blend of yesterday's nostalgia and today's comfort in a setting of unparalleled coastal vistas. Located on Highway 17, thirty miles north of Charleston, twenty-five miles south of

Georgetown, and sixty miles south of Myrtle Beach.

Hosts: Jackie and Lee Morrison
Rooms: 4 (PB) $85-95
Full Breakfast
Credit Cards: A, B, C, D, E
Notes: 2, 5, 7 (restricted), 9, 10, 12

MONCKS CORNER

Rice Hope Plantation Inn

206 Rice Hope Drive, 29416
(803) 761-4832; (800) 569-4038;
FAX (803) 761-1866
E-mail: doris@ricehope.com
Web site: ricehope.com

This nine-thousand-square-foot historic rice plantation is located on a bluff overlooking the Cooper River, forty miles from Charleston, with formal gardens, huge oak trees, and incredible sunsets. Step back in time and experience the relaxed atmosphere of an antebellum southern plantation. Rooms have comfortable seating and TVs, reproduction rice beds, and antique furnishings. Canoe, bicycles, tennis court, and whirlpool spa on premises.

Hostess: Doris Kasprak
Rooms: 5 (3PB; 2SB) $55-85
Continental Breakfast
Credit Cards: A, B, C
Notes: 2, 3, 4, 5, 7, 8, 9, 10, 12

MYRTLE BEACH

Serendipity—An Inn

407 - 71st Avenue N., 29572
(803) 449-5268; (800) 762-3229

An award-winning, Spanish-style inn—unique, elegant, and secluded—is just

Serendipity—An Inn

three hundred yards from the Atlantic beach. Guests may enjoy the heated pool and hot tub. Rooms are air-conditioned and have TVs, private baths, and refrigerators. More than seventy golf courses are nearby, as well as fishing, tennis, restaurants, theaters, and shopping. The inn is located near all the Myrtle Beach country music theaters. Ninety miles from historic Charleston.

Hosts: Terry and Sheila Johnson
Rooms: 14 (PB) $59-129
Continental Breakfast
Credit Cards: A, B, D
Notes: 7, 8, 9, 10, 12

ROCK HILL

East Main Guest House

600 E. Main Street, 29730
(803) 366-1161 (voice and FAX)

Located in the historic district and just twenty minutes from downtown Charlotte, North Carolina, this B&B offers guest rooms with queen-size beds, fireplaces, TVs, and phones. The honeymoon suite has stained-glass windows, canopy bed, and a whirlpool bath. A sitting/game room is provided, and a fax is available. A continental breakfast is served each morning

welcome; 7 Children welcome; 8 Tennis nearby; 9 Swimming nearby; 10 Golf nearby; 11 Skiing nearby; 12 May be booked through travel agent.

in the gracious dining room or, weather permitting, under the garden pergola. AAA three-diamond-rated.

Hosts: Melba and Jerry Peterson
Rooms: 3 (PB) $59-79
Expanded Continental Breakfast
Credit Cards: A, B
Notes: 2, 5, 8, 9, 10, 12

SALEM

Sunrise Farm Bed and Breakfast

325 Sunrise Drive, 29676
(864) 944-0121; (888) 991-0121;
FAX (864) 944-6195
E-mail: sfbb@bellsouth.net
Web site: http://www.bbonline.com/sc/sunrisefarm

This gracious 1890 Victorian farmhouse is set in the scenic foothills of the Blue Ridge Mountains. Surrounded by a seventy-four-acre cattle farm and located near waterfalls, nature trails, and mountain lakes. Well-decorated rooms in the main house, and two charming cottages with kitchens.

Hosts: Barbara and Ron Laughter
Rooms: 6 (PB) $70-100
Full Breakfast
Credit Cards: A, B
Notes: 2, 5, 6, 7, 9, 10, 12

STARR

The Gray House

111 Stone's Throw Avenue, 29684
(864) 352-6778; FAX (864) 352-6777

This turn-of-the-century home is the perfect romantic getaway, with beautiful gar-dens, tranquil pond, quiet walking trail, and horse-drawn carriage rides (by appointment). Two suites, the Jasmine and Rose rooms, offer private baths with whirlpools and private dining alcoves. Breakfast served in your suite. Two-bedroom farmhouse also available. Restaurant serves southern fare.

Hostess: Kathy T. Stone
Rooms: 2 (PB) + 2-bedroom farmhouse $65-125
Full Breakfast
Credit Cards: A, B, C
Notes: 2, 3, 4, 5, 10, 12

SUMMERVILLE

Linwood Historic Home and Gardens

200 S. Palmetto Street, 29483
(803) 871-2620 (voice and FAX)

Once the home of a 19th-century plantation owner. Gracious hospitality abounds at Linwood, a beautifully restored Victorian home featuring high ceilings, chandeliers, period antiques, and wide porches. Nestled on two acres of lush gardens, Linwood is in the center of the charming village of Summerville, near shops and restaurants. Linwood has a lovely, large inground pool. Famous plantations, golf courses, beaches, and historic Charleston are nearby. Recreation or retreat—we are here to serve you. Recommended by *Southern Living*.

Hosts: Peter and Linda Shelbourne
Rooms: 3 (PB) $75-90
Continental Breakfast and Afternoon English Tea
Credit Cards: none
Notes: 2, 5, 7, 8, 9, 10, 12

NOTES: Credit cards accepted: A Master Card; B Visa; C American Express; D Discover; E Diners Club; F Other; 2 Personal checks accepted; 3 Lunch available; 4 Dinner available; 5 Open all year; 6 Pets

SUMTER

The Bed and Breakfast of Sumter

6 Park Avenue, 29150
(803) 773-2903; (888) SUMTERB;
FAX (803) 775-6943

Charming, 1896 home facing a lush park in the historic district. Large front porch with swing and rocking chairs. Gracious guest rooms with antiques, fireplaces, and all private baths. Formal Victorian parlor and TV sitting area. FAX machine available. Gourmet breakfast includes fruit, entrée, and home-baked breads. Antiques, Swan Lake, and fifteen golf courses close by.

Hosts: Jess and Suzanne Begley
Rooms: 5 (PB) $65-75
Full Gourmet Breakfast
Credit Cards: A, B, D
Notes: 2, 5, 8, 10, 12

welcome; 7 Children welcome; 8 Tennis nearby; 9 Swimming nearby; 10 Golf nearby; 11 Skiing nearby; 12 May be booked through travel agent.

SOUTH DAKOTA

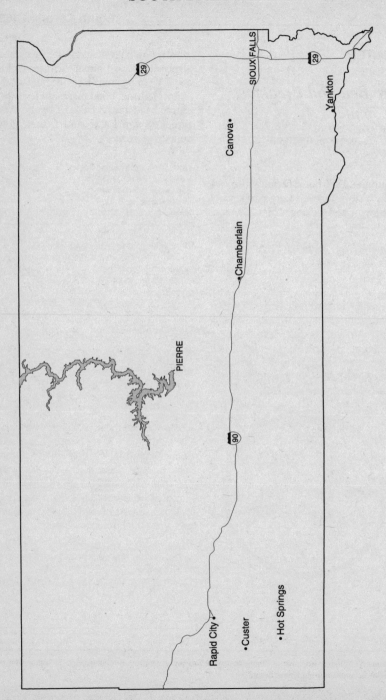

South Dakota

CANOVA

Skoglund Farm

Route 1, Box 45, 57321
(605) 247-3445

Skoglund Farm brings back memories of Grandpa and Grandma's home. It is furnished with antiques and collectibles. A full, home-cooked evening meal and breakfast are served each day. Guests may sightsee in the surrounding area, visit Little House on the Prairie Village, hike, or just

Skoglund Farm

relax. Several country churches are located nearby.

Hosts: Alden and Delores Skoglund
Rooms: 5 (SB) $30/adult; $20/teen; $15/child; children 5 and under free
Full Breakfast
Credit Cards: none
Notes: 2, 3, 4 (included), 5, 6, 7, 8, 9, 10, 12

CHAMBERLAIN

Riverview Ridge

HC 69, Box 82A, 57325
(605) 734-6084
Web site: http://www.bbonline.com/sd/riverviewridge

Contemporary home on a bluff overlooking a Missouri River bend. King and queen beds, full breakfast, and secluded country peace. Three and a half miles from downtown Chamberlain on Highway 50. Enjoy outdoor recreation; visit museums, Indian reservations, and casinos; or relax and make our home your home.

Hosts: Frank and Alta Cable
Rooms: 3 (1PB; 2SB) $55-70
Full Breakfast
Credit Cards: A, B
Notes: 2, 5, 7, 9, 10

NOTES: Credit cards accepted: A Master Card; B Visa; C American Express; D Discover; E Diners Club; F Other; 2 Personal checks accepted; 3 Lunch available; 4 Dinner available; 5 Open all year; 6 Pets welcome; 7 Children welcome; 8 Tennis nearby; 9 Swimming nearby; 10 Golf nearby; 11 Skiing nearby; 12 May be booked through travel agent.

Custer Mansion Bed and Breakfast

CUSTER

Custer Mansion Bed and Breakfast

35 Centennial Drive, 57730
(605) 673-3333 (voice and FAX)

Enjoy the nostalgia of an authentic 1891, Victorian Gothic home listed on the National Register of Historic Places. Transoms, stained glass, and antiques feature Victorian elegance and country charm, with western hospitality. Lovely, individually decorated rooms are named for songs. All-you-can-eat, delicious, home-cooked breakfast. Two honeymoon suites, one with Jacuzzi tub. Central to all Black Hills attractions: Mt. Rushmore, Crazy Horse Memorial, Custer State Park, and many more. Minimum stay of two nights, holidays and peak season; reduced rates, off-season. Recommended by *Bon Appetit*, AAA, and Mobil Travel Guide; member of BBISD.

Hosts: Mill and Carole Seaman
Rooms: 5 (PB) $65-110
Full Breakfast
Credit Cards: none
Notes: 2, 5, 7, 8, 9, 10, 11

HOT SPRINGS

The "B and J" Bed and Breakfast

HCR 52, Box 101-B, 57747
(605) 745-4243

Nestled in the southern Black Hills, this charming 1890 log cabin, decorated in antiques, provides guests with a unique pioneer setting. Enjoy the peaceful mountain scenery while listening to the Fall River that never freezes. Early mornings, deer and wild turkey may be seen. True western hospitality and a good home-cooked breakfast are waiting in Bill and Jeananne's kitchen. Down the entrance road, enjoy horseback riding. One mile south of Hot Springs on U.S. 385/18. In Hot Springs, swim at the historic Evans Plunge, where the water is always eighty-seven degrees. Visit the world's largest find of Columbian Mammoth bones. Golf at one of the Midwest's most challenging and beautiful courses. Minutes to Angostura Lake, Wind Cave National Park, and Custer State Park where buffalo, antelope, elk, and prairie dogs roam.

Hosts: William and Jeananne Wintz
Rooms: 1 (SB) + log cabin (PB) $100-125
Full Breakfast
Credit Cards: none
Notes: 2, 7, 8, 9, 10, 11

RAPID CITY

Abend Haus Cottages and Audrie's B&B

23029 Thunderhead Falls Road, 57702-8524
(605) 342-7788

The ultimate in charm and Old World hospitality. We have been family owned and

---

NOTES: Credit cards accepted: A Master Card; B Visa; C American Express; D Discover; E Diners Club; F Other; 2 Personal checks accepted; 3 Lunch available; 4 Dinner available; 5 Open all year; 6 Pets

operated since 1985 and are the area's first and finest B&B establishment. Our spacious suites and cottages are furnished in comfortable European antiques. All feature a private entrance, private bath, patio, hot tub, and full Black Hill's-style breakfast. Each suite provides a setting that quiets your heart. Our country home, the Cranbury House, has two suites. If the past intrigues you, the Old Powerhouse is for you. (Built of brick in 1910, the facility generated electricity from a water flume into the late '30s.) Das Abend Haus Cottage (the Evening House) is a restful creekside hideaway, tucked into a mountainside; its two suites are designed after a German cottage in the Black Forest. The individual log cottages are also reminiscent of Germany. Soak in your private hot tub and watch Rapid Creek flow along. These accommodations are unsurpassed anywhere.

Hosts: Hank and Audry Kuhnhauser
Rooms: 9 (PB) $95-145
Full Breakfast
Credit Cards: none
Notes: 2, 5, 8, 9, 10, 11

YANKTON

Mulberry Inn
512 Mulberry Street, 57078
(605) 665-7116

The beautiful Mulberry inn offers the ultimate in comfort and charm in a traditional setting. Built in 1873, the inn features parquet floors, six guest rooms furnished with antiques, two parlors with marble fireplaces, and a large porch. Minutes from the Lewis and Clark Lake and within walking distance of the Missouri River, fine restaurants, and downtown. The inn is listed on the National Register of Historic Places.

Hostess: Millie Cameron
Rooms: 6 (2PB; 4SB) $32-52 (seasonal)
Continental Breakfast (Full Breakfast extra charge)
Credit Cards: A, B, C
Notes: 2, 5, 7, 8, 9, 10

TENNESSEE

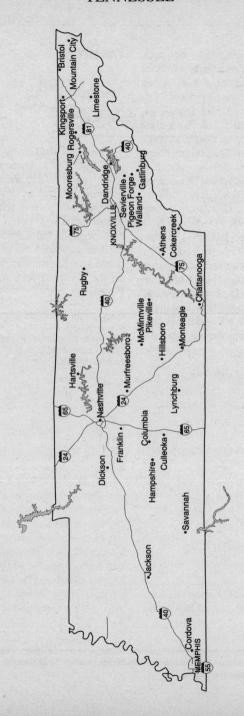

Tennessee

Natchez Trace Bed and Breakfast Reservation Service

PO Box 193, **Hampshire**, 38461
(615) 285-2777; (800) 377-2770

This reservation service is unusual in that all the homes are close to the Natchez Trace, the delightful National Parkway running from Nashville, Tennessee, to Natchez, Mississippi. Kay Jones can help plan your trip along the Trace, with homestays in interesting and historic homes. Locations of homes include Ashland City, Columbia, FairView, Franklin, Hohenwald, and Nashville, **Tennessee**; Florence and Cherokee, **Alabama**; and Church Hill, Corinth, French Camp, Kosciusko, Lorman, Natchez, New Albany, Tupelo, and Vicksburg, **Mississippi**. Rates $60-125.

ATHENS

Majestic Mansion Bed and Breakfast

202 E. Washington Avenue, 37303
(423) 746-9041

Nestled near the foothills of the Smokies, just off I-75 in southeastern Tennessee, this 1909 gracious home adds to historic downtown Athens. Stroll one block to the quaint town square filled with shops, from antiques to women's fashions. Relax in a rocking chair on the wooden porch with cool lemonade or play tennis on the nearby courts. Awake to a power breakfast or a light fitness meal. Ask for either the Ambassador Room with its royal decor and claw-foot tub or the Empress Room with a sunken Jacuzzi and Japanese influence.

Hosts: Richard and Elaine Newman
Rooms: 3 (2PB; 1SB) $65-75
Full Breakfast
Credit Cards: A, B
Notes: 2, 5, 7 (10 and older), 8

Woodlawn

110 Keith Lane, 37303
(423) 745-8211; (800) 745-8213
Web site: http://www.woodlawn.com

Woodlawn, an elegant Greek Revival antibellum home circa 1858, is listed on the National Historic Register. Woodlawn was a Union hospital during the Civil War. It is furnished with gorgeous antique pieces and Oriental rugs that add to its warm feel. Located on five acres in the heart of downtown Athens, a charming historic town filled with antique and specialty shops.

NOTES: Credit cards accepted: A Master Card; B Visa; C American Express; D Discover; E Diners Club; F Other; 2 Personal checks accepted; 3 Lunch available; 4 Dinner available; 5 Open all year; 6 Pets welcome; 7 Children welcome; 8 Tennis nearby; 9 Swimming nearby; 10 Golf nearby; 11 Skiing nearby; 12 May be booked through travel agent.

Woodlawn

Pool on site; golf and tennis nearby; and white-water rafting on the Ocoee River, thirty minutes away.

Hosts: Susan and Barry Willis
Rooms: 4 (PB) $75-110
Full Breakfast
Credit Cards: A, B, D
Notes: 2, 5, 7 (over 6) 8, 9 (on site), 10, 11, 12

BRISTOL

New Hope Bed and Breakfast

822 Georgia Avenue, 37620
(888) 989-3343
Web site: http://www.inngetaways.com/tn/
    newhope.html

New Hope has all the charm of a late Victorian home, yet comfort and convenience were high on the agenda when decorating

New Hope Bed and Breakfast

decisions were being made. Our guests often tell us, "I feel so at home." There are four guest rooms, each with a large, private bath. Our beds are either twin, queen, or king. A full breakfast is served each morning in the dining room or on the wraparound porch, or you may have it brought to your room.

Hosts: Tom and Tonda Fluke
Rooms: 4 (PB) $70-130
Full Breakfast
Credit Cards: A, B
Notes: 2, 5, 10, 11, 12

CHATTANOOGA

Adams Hilborne

801 Vine Street, 37403
(423) 265-5000

Cornerstone to Chattanooga's Fort Wood Historic District; mayor's mansion in 1889. Rare Victorian Romanesque design with original coffered ceilings, hand-carved oak stairway, beveled-glass windows, and ceramic tile embellishments. Old-world charm and hospitality in a tree-shaded setting rich with Civil War history and turn-of-the-century architecture. Small, European-style hotel accommodations in fifteen tastefully restored, exquisitely decorated guest rooms. Private baths, fireplaces, and complimentary breakfast for guests. Fine dining nightly at the Repertoire Restaurant and casual dining at Café Alfresco; wine and liquors available. Ballroom, meeting and reception areas, private dining, and catering available to the public by arrangement. Minutes from Chattanooga museums, fine shops and restaurants, the aquarium, UTC arena, and

---

NOTES: Credit cards accepted: A Master Card; B Visa; C American Express; D Discover; E Diners Club; F Other; 2 Personal checks accepted; 3 Lunch available; 4 Dinner available; 5 Open all year; 6 Pets

other cultural events and attractions. Private off-street parking.

Hosts: Wendy and David Adams
Rooms: 10 (PB) $100-275
Continental Breakfast
Credit Cards: A, B, C
Notes: 2, 3, 4, 5, 7 (by arrangement), 8, 9, 10, 12

Alford House Bed and Breakfast

5515 Alford Hill Drive, 37419
(423) 821-7625

This half-century-old, fifteen-room house is family owned and operated in a peaceful Christian atmosphere. Ten minutes from Tennessee Aquarium, Rock City, and other attractions. In our Gathering Room is a piano, and on wintry nights a cozy fire awaits. Enjoy early morning coffee and breakfast in the dining room or, weather permitting, on the upper deck. Surrounded by tall oaks and bordering the national park. A large collection of antique glass baskets are displayed, and many antiques (some for sale) are found throughout our home. You will be blessed with restful sleep on our beauty-rest bedding. Ask about off-season discounts.

Hosts: Rhoda (Troyer) Alford
Rooms: 4 (PB) $65-135
Full or Continental Breakfast
Credit Cards: none
Notes: 8, 9, 10, 11, 12

COKER CREEK

Mountain Garden Inn

PO Box 171, 37314
(423) 261-2689

Enjoy luxurious, romantic suites and cozy bedrooms, all with private baths and air-conditioning. A stately cypress log inn with wraparound porches and rockers galore. A family-style B&B specializing in reunions—special group rates. Very peaceful setting with a panoramic, three-state view overlooking the Cherokee National Forests of North Carolina, Georgia and Tennessee. Adjacent to historic "Trail of Tears," waterfall hiking, gold panning, and horseback riding.

Hosts: Stephen and Pam Wentworth, Cap and
  Danny Stewart
Rooms: 4 (PB) $40-80
Full Breakfast
Credit Cards: none
Notes: 2, 5, 7

Mountain Garden Inn

COLUMBIA

Locust Hill Bed and Breakfast

1185 Mooresville Pike, 38401
(931) 388-8531; (800) 577-8264;
FAX (931) 540-8719

Historic 1840 antebellum home and two-story smokehouse, both furnished with family antiques, handmade quilts, and embroidered linens. Pamper yourself with morning coffee in your room and evening

---

welcome; 7 Children welcome; 8 Tennis nearby; 9 Swimming nearby; 10 Golf nearby; 11 Skiing nearby; 12 May be booked through travel agent.

refreshments at the fireside. Spacious rooms with private baths and comfortable sitting areas. The gourmet breakfasts feature country ham, feather-light biscuits, and homemade jams. Five fireplaces. Relax in the library, flower gardens, or on the three porches to make this a perfect getaway. Gourmet dining by reservation.

Hosts: Bill and Beverly Beard
Rooms: 4 (PB) $90-125
Full Breakfast
Credit Cards: A, B, C, D
Notes: 2, 4, 5, 8, 10, 12

Sweetwater Inn

Sweetwater Inn

2436 Campbells Station Road, **Culleoka**, 38451
(615) 987-3077; (800) 335-3077;
FAX (615) 987-2525

Experience the southern hospitality of a fully restored, elegant 19th-century home. Rest in one of four guest rooms with private baths. Feast on a southern gourmet breakfast. Located near Columbia, home of President James K. Polk, Saturn car factory, Civil War history and battlefields, and Mule Day Celebration. Near I-65 South. Access to golfing, swimming, hiking, canoeing, and historical homes.

Hostess: Sandy Shotwell
Rooms: 4 (PB) $100-125
Full Breakfast
Credit Cards: A, B, D
Notes: 2, 4, 5, 7, 9, 10, 12

DANDRIDGE

Mill Dale Farm Bed and Breakfast

140 Mill Dale Road, 37725
(423) 397-3470; (800) 767-3471

Nineteenth-century farmhouse located in Tennessee's second-oldest town. Floating staircase leads to three guest rooms, all with private baths. Nearby is fishing, boating, swimming, tennis, golf, the Great Smoky Mountains, Gatlinburg, and Pigeon Forge. Delicious country breakfast.

Hostess: Lucy C. Franklin
Rooms: 3 (PB) $55-72
Full Breakfast
Credit Cards: none
Notes: 2, 5, 7, 8, 9, 10, 11

Sugar Fork Bed and Breakfast

Sugar Fork Bed and Breakfast

743 Garrett Road, 37725
(423) 397-7327; (800) 487-5634

Guests will appreciate the tranquil setting of Sugar Fork, a short distance from the Great Smoky Mountains. Situated on Douglas Lake, the B&B has private access and a floating dock. Enjoy warm-weather water sports and fishing year-round. Fireplace in common room, guest kitchenette, wraparound deck, swings, and park bench by the lake. A hearty breakfast is served family-style in the dining room or, weather permitting, on the deck. No smoking is permitted in the guest rooms.

Hosts: Mary and Sam Price
Rooms: 3 (P&SB) $55-65
Full Breakfast
Credit Cards: A, B
Notes: 2, 5, 7, 8, 9, 10, 11

DICKSON

East Hills Bed and Breakfast Inn

100 East Hill Terrace, 37055
(615) 441-9428

Fully restored traditional home with southern charm, built in the late '40s on four acres with lots of big, tall trees. The home has five bedrooms and a cottage with private baths and cable TV, a large living room, library/den with fireplaces, and an enclosed back porch. Beautifully decorated and furnished throughout with period antiques. Located on Highway 70 near Luther Lake, six miles from Montgomery Bell State Park. Convenient to shopping, hospital, restaurant, and downtown area. Rates include afternoon tea and muffins and a full breakfast in the morning. No smoking or alcohol allowed.

Hosts: John and Anita Luther
Rooms: 5 + cottage (PB) $65-95
Full Breakfast
Credit Cards: A, B, C
Notes: 2, 5, 10

FRANKLIN

Lyric Springs Country Inn

7306 S. Harpeth Road, 37212
(615) 329-3385; (800) 621-7824;
FAX (615) 329-3381
E-mail: patsy@lyricsprings.com
Web site: http://www.lyricsprings.com

Elegant, antique-filled, creekside inn featured in *Better Homes and Gardens*, *Country Inns*, *USA Today*, *Fodor's*, and *Women's Wear Daily*. A haven for romance and retreat. Gourmet food. Picnics. Spa services: massage, manicure, pedicure, facial. Billiards, fishing, hiking, swimming, biking, horseback riding, board games, and puzzles. Music. Waterfalls. Restricted smoking.

Hostess: Patsy Bruce
Rooms: 4 (PB) $145
Full Breakfast
Credit Cards: A, B, C
Notes: 4, 5, 9, 10, 12

Namaste Acres Barn Bed and Breakfast

Namaste Acres Barn Bed and Breakfast

5436 Leipers Creek Road, 37064
(615) 791-0333; FAX (615) 591-0665
E-mail: namastebb@aol.com
Web site: http://www.bbonline.com/tn/namaste/

Quiet valley setting. Poolside deck and hot tub, hiking, horseback trails. Country

welcome; 7 Children welcome; 8 Tennis nearby; 9 Swimming nearby; 10 Golf nearby; 11 Skiing nearby; 12 May be booked through travel agent.

inn offers four theme suites, including the Loft, Bunkhouse, Cabin, and Franklin. In-room coffee, phone, and refrigerator, TV/VCR (movies). Private entrance and bath. Featured in *Southern Living, Horse Illustrated,* and *Western Horseman.* One mile from Natchez Trace Parkway, eleven miles from historic Franklin, and twenty-three miles from Nashville. Established 1933. Reservation requested; weekday discounts. AAA-approved.

Hostess: Lisa Winters
Rooms: 4 (PB) $80
Full and Continental Breakfast
Credit Cards: all major
Notes: 2, 5, 7 (10 and older), 9, 10, 12

GATLINBURG

Butcher House
in the Mountains

1520 Garrett Lane, 37738
(423) 436-9457; FAX (423) 436-9884

Nestled twenty-eight hundred feet above the main entrance to the Smokies, Butcher House in the Mountains offers mountain seclusion as well as convenience. The Swisslike cedar-and-stone chalet enjoys one of the most beautiful views in the state.

Butcher House in the Mountains

Antiques are tastefully placed throughout the house, and a guest kitchen is available for coffee and lavish dessert. European gourmet brunch served. AAA three-diamond-rated; ABBA-rated excellent.

Hosts: Hugh and Gloria Butcher
Rooms: 5 (PB) $79-119
Full European Gourmet Breakfast
Credit Cards: A, B, C
Notes: 2, 5, 8, 9, 10, 11, 12

Cornerstone Inn
Bed and Breakfast

3966 Regal Way, Box 1600, 37738
(423) 430-5064

A delightful country inn with a fifty-foot front porch overlooking a magnificent mountain view. Although very near the arts and crafts community, Dollywood, and the Great Smoky Mountains National Park, the Cornerstone Inn provides privacy and a warm, comfortable atmosphere. Private baths, full breakfast, open all year. Smoking on porches only.

Hosts: Don and Kay Cooper
Rooms: 3 (PB) $85-95
Full Breakfast
Credit Cards: A, B, C, D
Notes: 2, 5, 7, 10, 12

Eight Gables Inn

219 N. Mountain Trail, 37738
(423) 430-3344; (800) 279-5716;
FAX (423) 430-3344, Ext. 51

For the perfect bed and breakfast getaway, Eight Gables is the answer. Reserve your accommodations from among eleven spacious guest rooms that appeal to even the most discriminating taste. At the foot of

---

NOTES: Credit cards accepted: A Master Card; B Visa; C American Express; D Discover; E Diners Club; F Other; 2 Personal checks accepted; 3 Lunch available; 4 Dinner available; 5 Open all year; 6 Pets

Eight Gables Inn

the Great Smoky Mountains National Park, Eight Gables Inn's location is easily accessible to all area attractions. The inn offers bedrooms with private baths and luxurious living space, and has an additional covered porch area. It is AAA-approved, four diamonds. Family owned and operated by Don and Kim Casons.

Hosts: Don and Kim Cason
Rooms: 11 (PB) $99-129
Full Breakfast
Credit Cards: A, B, C, D, E, F
Notes: 2, 3 and 4 (available on request), 5, 7, 8, 10, 11, 12

Olde English Tudor Inn Bed and Breakfast

135 West Hollyridge Road, 37738
(423) 436-7760; (800) 541-3798;
FAX (423) 430-7308
E-mail: tudorinn@smoky-mtns.com
Web site: http://www.smoky-mtns.com/
    gatlinburg/bb

The Olde English Tudor Inn Bed and Breakfast is set on a hillside overlooking the beautiful mountain resort of Gatlinburg. It is ideally located within a few minutes' walk of downtown and a few minutes' drive of the Great Smoky Mountains National Park. The inn has seven spacious guest rooms with their own modern baths and cable TVs (HBO). Each guest is made to feel at home in the large community room, furnished with TV/VCR and free-standing wood-burning stove. Call toll-free for a brochure.

Hosts: Linda and Steve Pickel
Rooms: 7 (PB) $79-105
Full Breakfast
Credit Cards: A, B, C, D
Notes: 2, 5, 7, 9, 10, 11, 12

HARTSVILLE

Miss Alice's B&B

8325 Highway 141 S., 37074
(615) 374-3015; (615) 444-4401

Relax! Enjoy Tennessee's southern hospitality in a restored early 1900s farmhouse. Walk through the woods, read, play horseshoes, sit on the deck, lie in the hammock, have lemonade in the well house, and draw up a bucket of cool sulfur water for a treat. Wake up with a cup of gourmet coffee and afterward enjoy a farmer's breakfast. Area attractions include Stones River battlefield, the Hermitage, Opryland, Cragfont, Vice President Gore's hometown, Cumberland University, and many antique shops.

Hostess: Volene B. Barnes
Rooms: 2 (1PB; 1SB) $65
Full Breakfast
Credit Cards: none
Notes: 2, 5, 9, 10

HILLSBORO

Lord's Landing B&B

375 Lord's Landing Lane, 37342
(931) 467-3830; FAX (931) 467-3032
E-mail: lordslanding@blomand.net
Web site: http://kristallnet.com/lordslanding

Central Tennessee's fifty-acre paradise awaits guests from near and far. You may

welcome; 7 Children welcome; 8 Tennis nearby; 9 Swimming nearby; 10 Golf nearby; 11 Skiing nearby; 12 May be booked through travel agent.

drive in for a relaxing retreat or fly into our 2,400 x 80-foot turf airstrip for a quiet getaway. Located near the base of the Cumberland Plateau, the main house boasts breathtaking views from every window. A leisurely stroll takes guests to the eight-bedroom, seven-bath country cottage, beautifully decorated with antiques and fine furnishings. Fireplaces and Jacuzzi tubs will add to guests' comfort in most rooms.

Hosts: Denny and Pam Neilson
Rooms: 7 (PB) $95-150
Full Breakfast
Credit Cards: A, B, D
Notes: 2, 3, 4, 5, 7, 10

JACKSON

Highland Place Bed and Breakfast

519 N. Highland Avenue, 38301
(901) 427-1472; FAX (901) 422-7994

Highland Place Bed and Breakfast is a stately home of distinct charm, offering comfortable accommodations and southern hospitality. Highland Place is west Tennessee's 1995 Designers Showplace. Each room, hall, staircase, and hidden nook has been designed and decorated by outstanding designers. Experience the pleasure of sharing the surroundings of one of the state's finest homes. Built circa 1911, the inn was totally renovated and reopened in 1995.

Hosts: Glenn and Janice Wall
Rooms: 4 (PB) $75-135
Full Breakfast
Credit Cards: A, B, C
Notes: 2, 3, 4, 5, 10, 12

KINGSPORT

Warrior's Rest

1000 Colonial Heights Road, 37663
(423) 239-8838

Nestled in the rolling foothills of the east Tennessee mountains, Warrior's Rest is the ideal place to withdraw from the battles of everyday life. Spend time with family, friends, or just by yourself. The ninety-year-old farmhouse is within five minutes of golfing, swimming, boating, hiking, and horseback riding at Warrior's Path State Park. The scenic Blue Ridge Parkway and historic Jonesborough are nearby.

Hosts: Charles R. and Suzanne J. Buchleiter
Rooms: 3 (PB) $65-85
Full Breakfast
Credit Cards: none
Notes: 2, 5, 7, 8, 9, 10

LIMESTONE

Snapp Inn Bed and Breakfast

1990 Davy Crockett Park Road, 37681
(423) 257-2482

Gracious circa-1815 Federal-style home furnished with antiques. Come to the country for a relaxing weekend getaway. Enjoy the peaceful mountain view or play a game of pool. Located close to Davy Crockett Birthplace State Park. A fifteen-minute drive to historic Jonesborough or Greenville.

Hosts: Dan and Ruth Dorgan
Rooms: 2 (PB) $65
Full Breakfast
Credit Cards: A, B
Notes: 2, 5, 6, 7 (one only), 8, 9, 10, 12

NOTES: Credit cards accepted: A Master Card; B Visa; C American Express; D Discover; E Diners Club; F Other; 2 Personal checks accepted; 3 Lunch available; 4 Dinner available; 5 Open all year; 6 Pets

Cedar Lane Bed and Breakfast

LYNCHBURG

Cedar Lane Bed and Breakfast

Route 3, Box 155E, 37352
(615) 759-6891 (voice and FAX)

Located on the outskirts of historic Lynchburg (home of Jack Daniel's Distillery). This newly built farmhouse offers comfort and relaxation. You can spend your time antiquing in nearby shops or reading a book in the sunroom. The rooms are beautifully decorated in rose, blue, peach, and green with queen and twin beds. Phones and TVs are available.

Hosts: Elaine and Chuck Quinn
Rooms: 4 (PB) $65-75
Continental Plus Breakfast
Credit Cards: A, B, C
Notes: 2, 4 (by reservation), 5, 7 (over 10), 9, 10

MCMINNVILLE

Historic Falcon Manor

2645 Faulkner Springs Road, 37110
(931) 668-4444; FAX (931) 815-4444
E-mail: FalconManor@FalconManor.com
Web site: http://FalconManor.com

Relive the peaceful romance of the 1890s in one of the South's finest Victorian man-

sions—ten thousand square feet of friendly elegance. Rock on "gingerbread" verandas shaded by giant trees. Indulge in the luxury of museum-quality antiques and enjoy the mansion's fascinating history. Historic Falcon Manor is the ideal base for a Tennessee vacation: halfway between Nashville and Chattanooga, with easy access from I-24 and I-40. Fall Creek Falls Park and Cumberland Caverns are nearby. First-prize bed and breakfast winner, 1997 National Trust restoration award. Historic Falcon Manor is a non-smoking home.

Hosts: George and Charlien McGlothin
Rooms: 6 (4PB; 2SB) $75-105
Full Breakfast
Credit Cards: A, B
Notes: 2, 5, 7 (over 11), 8, 9, 10, 12

MEMPHIS AREA (CORDOVA)

The Bridgewater House Bed and Breakfast

7015 Raleigh LaGrange Road, 38018
(901) 384-0080 (voice and FAX)

The Bridgewater House is a Greek Revival home converted from a schoolhouse that is more than a hundred years old. It is a lovely, elegant dwelling filled with remembrances of travels, antiques, family heirlooms, and Oriental rugs. The Bridgewater House has original hardwood floors cut from trees on the property, enormous rooms, high ceilings, leaded-glass windows, and deep hand-marbelized moldings. There are two spacious bedrooms with private baths. A certified chef and a food and beverage director serve a full gourmet breakfast and pamper guests

welcome; 7 Children welcome; 8 Tennis nearby; 9 Swimming nearby; 10 Golf nearby; 11 Skiing nearby; 12 May be booked through travel agent.

with refreshments upon arriving. The Bridgewater House is located one mile from the largest city park in the United States, which offers sailing, walking and biking trails, horseback riding, fishing, canoeing, and more.

Hosts: Katherine and Steve Mistilis
Rooms: 2 (PB) $90-100
Full Gourmet Breakfast
Credit Cards: A, B, D
Notes: 2, 5

MONTEAGLE

Adams Edgeworth Inn

Monteagle Assembly, 37356
(615) 924-4000; FAX (615) 924-3236

Circa 1896, Adams Edgeworth Inn celebrates one hundred years of fine lodging and still is the region's leader in elegance and quality. Recently refurbished in English Manor decor, the inn is a showcase for fine antiques, important original paintings and sculptures, and a prize-winning rose garden. Stroll through the ninety-six-acre Victorian village that surrounds the inn, or drive six miles to the Gothic campus of Sewanee, University of the South. Cultural activities year-round. Nearby are 150 miles of hiking trails, scenic vistas, and waterfalls, as well as tennis, swimming, golf, and riding. Five-course, fine dining by candlelight every night. "One of the best inns I've ever visited anywhere...." (Sara Pitzer, recommended by "Country Inns" in *Country Inns Magazine*).

Hosts: Wendy and Dave Adams
Rooms: 14 (PB) $75-205
Continental Breakfast
Credit Cards: A, B, C
Notes: 2, 4, 5, 7, 8, 9, 10, 12

MOORESBURG

The Home Place Bed and Breakfast

132 Church Lane, 37811
(423) 921-8424; (800) 521-8242;
FAX (423) 921-8003
E-mail: p.rogers5@genie.com
Web site: http://www.bbonline.com/tn/homeplace

This inn is located in east Tennessee near the Smokies. Adjacent to Cherokee Lake, this home has been in the owner's family since early 1800s. The home is also close to Rogersville, a small town full of history and on the National Historic Registry. The Home Place has four bedrooms; private baths are available, including a Jacuzzi bath, available as a suite. The home was originally a log structure. Full breakfast. First floor accessible to individuals with disabilities. Children okay. No smoking or pets. Lunch and dinner on request, with advance notice.

Hosts: Priscilla Rogers and Jean Shorter
Rooms: 4 (2-3PB; 2SB) $45-100
Full of Continental Breakfast
Credit Cards: A, B, C
Notes: 2, 4, 5, 7, 9, 10, 11 (one and a half hours), 12

MOUNTAIN CITY

Prospect Hill Bed and Breakfast Inn

801 W. Main Street, Highway 67, 37683
(423) 727-0139 (voice and FAX)

As it was a century ago, Maj. Joseph Wagner's 1889 mansion is shaded by tall hemlocks, and the windows look toward the mountains. Sit awhile on the porch

---

swing. Watch the shadows shift and the lightening bugs glow. Prospect Hill is a handmade brick house in Mountain City in far eastern Tennessee. Less than twenty miles from Boone, North Carolina, and only one hundred miles from Asheville. It is central to many nature-oriented activities, including the Appalachian Trail and the Blue Ridge Parkway, Grandfather Mountain, Wautauga Lake and Cherokee National Forest. Robert and Judy chose Craftsman- and William Morris-style furniture in honor of the Rambo family, who bought the hillside mansion in 1910. Guest rooms are large and comfortable, some with stained glass, a porch, or balcony. Most have hardwood floors, queen-size beds, and additional accomodations for a child or adult. There's a tennis court, pool, massive wood-burning fireplace in the summer kitchen, and gardens undergoing development. Box lunches available. No smoking. Opening spring/summer 1998.

Hosts: Robert and Judy Hotchkiss
Rooms: 6 (PB) $99-175
Full Breakfast
Credit Cards: A, B
Notes: 2, 3, 5, 7, 8, 9, 10, 11, 12

MURFREESBORO

Clardy's Guest House

435 E. Main Street, 37130
(615) 893-6030

This large Victorian home was built in 1898 and is located in Murfreesboro's historic district. You will marvel at the ornate woodwork, beautiful fireplaces, and magnificent stained glass overlooking the staircase. The house is filled with antiques, as are local shops and malls. The hosts will

help you with dining, shopping, and touring plans.

Hosts: Robert and Barbara Deaton
Rooms: 3 (2PB; 1SB) $39-49
Continental Plus Breakfast
Credit Cards: none
Notes: 2, 5, 8, 9, 10

NASHVILLE

Bed and Breakfast About Tennessee Reservation Service

PO Box 110227, 37222
(615) 331-5244; (800) 428-2421;
FAX (615) 833-7701
E-mail: fodom71282@aol.com

From the Great Smoky Mountains to the Mississippi, here is a diversity of attractions that includes fabulous scenery, Tennessee's Grand Ole Opry and Opryland, universities, Civil War sites, horse farms, and much more. With Bed and Breakfast About Tennessee, you make your visit a special occasion. Bed and Breakfast provides an intimate alternative to hotels and motels. You will stay in a private home or inn with a host who will share firsthand knowledge of the area with you. This home-style atmosphere includes the offer of a freshly prepared continental breakfast each morning. Send your guest reservation in today so we may place you in accommodations best suited to your needs. Confirmation and directions will be sent to you immediately.

Owner: Fredda Odom
Rooms: 100 (90PB; 10SB) $55-150
Continental Plus Breakfast
Credit Cards: A, B, C, D, E
Notes: 2, 5, 7 (at some), 8 and 9 (at some), 12

welcome; 7 Children welcome; 8 Tennis nearby; 9 Swimming nearby; 10 Golf nearby; 11 Skiing nearby; 12 May be booked through travel agent.

Day Dreams Country Inn

PIGEON FORGE

Day Dreams Country Inn

2720 Colonial Drive, 37863
(423) 428-0370; (800) 377-1469;
FAX (423) 428-2622

Delight in the true country charm of this antique-filled, secluded two-story log home with its six uniquely decorated guest rooms. Enjoy an evening by our cozy fireplace, relax on the front porch to the soothing sound of Mill Creek, or take a stroll around our three wooded acres. Treat your tastebuds to our bountiful country breakfast each morning. Within walking distance of the Parkway. Perfect for family reunions

and retreats. From Parkway, take 321 south, go one block, turn left on Florence Drive, go three blocks, and turn right on Colonial Drive.

Hosts: Bob and Joyce Guerrera
Rooms: 6 (PB) $79-99
Full Breakfast
Credit Cards: A, B, D
Notes: 2, 3, 4, 5, 7, 8, 9, 10, 11, 12

PIKEVILLE

Fall Creek Falls Bed and Breakfast Inn

Route 3, Box 298B, 37367
(423) 881-5494; FAX (423) 881-5040
Web site: http://www.bbonline.com/tn/fallcreek

Elegant mountain inn featured in the August '94 *Tennessee* magazine and August '96 *Country* magazine. Seven guest rooms and one suite, all with private baths and air-conditioning. Some have heart-shaped whirlpools and fireplaces. Victorian or country decor. One mile from nationally acclaimed Fall Creek Falls State Resort Park. Beautiful mountains, waterfalls, golfing, boating, fishing, tennis, hiking, horseback riding, and biking trails.

Fall Creek Falls Bed and Breakfast Inn

NOTES: Credit cards accepted: A Master Card; B Visa; C American Express; D Discover; E Diners Club; F Other; 2 Personal checks accepted; 3 Lunch available; 4 Dinner available; 5 Open all year; 6 Pets

AAA-rated. No smoking. Full breakfast. Romantic, scenic, and quiet.

Hosts: Doug and Rita Pruett
Rooms: 8 (PB) $75-130
Full Breakfast
Credit Cards: A, B, C, D
Notes: 2, 8, 9, 10, 12

ROGERSVILLE (NORTHEASTERN TN)

The Guest House

272 Blevins Road, 37857
(427) 272-0816

View miles of mountain beauty from our front porch or meditate in the woods or at the creek. For great day adventures, we're within two hours of the Great Smokies; Lost Sea; Abingdon, Virginia; or Biltmore in Asheville, North Carolina. Fifty dollars per night includes continental breakfast, or rent by the week/month and do your own cooking in our full kitchen.

Hosts: Mr. and Mrs. Harold McCoy
Rooms: 3 (PB) $50
Continental Breakfast
Credit Cards: A, B
Notes: 3 (make your own), 5, 7, 8, 9, 10 (15 miles), 11 (50 miles), 12

Hale Springs Inn

Town Square, 37857
(423) 272-5171

Tennessee's oldest operational inn, built in 1824 and recently restored to its former glory. AC, central heat. Most rooms have workable fireplaces. Private, modern bathrooms, antique furniture, and poster beds. Dine at fireside in the candlelit dining room. Presidents Andrew Jackson, James Polk and Andrew Johnson stayed

here. Easy one-hour drive to historic sites and mountain resorts.

Hosts: Capt. and Mrs. Carl Netherland-Brown
Rooms: 9 (PB) $45-70
Continental Breakfast
Credit Cards: A, B, C, D
Notes: 3, 4, 5, 7, 8, 9, 10, 12

RUGBY

The Newbury House

PO Box 8, 37733
(423) 628-2441; FAX (423) 628-2266
E-mail: rugbytn@highland.net

Victorian era, beautifully restored. Features include Mansard roof, dormer windows, lovely front porch, shared parlor and sunroom. Newbury House lodged both visitors and settlers to British author Thomas Hughes' Utopian Colony. The National Register village offers historic tours, museum stores, a specialty restaurant, and hiking trails. Victorian cottages are available for families with children.

Host: Historic Rugby
Rooms: 6 (4PB; 2SB) + 2 Victorian cottages
Full Breakfast
Credit Cards: A, B
Notes: 2, 3, 4, 5, 7 (at cottages), 9, 12

SAVANNAH

White Elephant Bed and Breakfast Inn

304 Church Street, 38372
(901) 925-6410
Web site: http://www.bbonline.com/tbbia

Stately 1901 Queen Anne-style Victorian home on one-and-a-half shady acres in the Savannah Historic District. Within walking distance of the Tennessee River,

---

welcome; 7 Children welcome; 8 Tennis nearby; 9 Swimming nearby; 10 Golf nearby; 11 Skiing nearby; 12 May be booked through travel agent.

White Elephant Bed and Breakfast Inn

downtown shopping, restaurants, and churches. Neaby golf and Civil War attractions; ten miles to Shiloh National Military Park. The innkeeper offers battlefield tours. Twelve miles to Pickwick Dam and Lake. Three individually decorated rooms feature antique furnishings, queen beds. Two parlors, antiques, central heat and air, wraparound porches, croquet. No smoking or pets. Traveler's checks accepted.

Hosts: Ken and Sharon Hansgen
Rooms: 3 (PB) $75-85
Full Breakfast
Credit Cards: none
Notes: 2, 5, 8, 10, 12

SEVIERVILLE

Blue Mountain Mist Country Inn

1811 Pullen Road, 37862
(423) 428-2335; (800) 497-2335;
FAX (423) 453-1720

Experience the silent beauty of mountain scenery while rocking on the big wrap-

around porch of this Victorian-style farmhouse. Common rooms filled with antiques lead to twelve individually decorated guest rooms. Enjoy many special touches such as old-fashioned claw-foot tubs, high antique headboards, quilts, and Jacuzzi. Nestled in the woods behind the inn are five country cottages designed for romantic getaways. The Great Smoky Mountains National Park and Gatlinburg are only twenty minutes away.

Hosts: Norman and Sarah Ball
Rooms: 12 + 5 cottages (PB) $95-135
Full Breakfast
Credit Cards: A, B
Notes: 2, 5, 7, 8, 9, 10, 11, 12

Calico Inn

Calico Inn

757 Ranch Way, 37862
(423) 428-3833; (800) 235-1054

The Calico Inn is located in the Smoky Mountains near Gatlinburg and Dollywood. It is an authentic log inn with touches of elegance. Decorated with antiques, collectibles, and country charm. Enjoy the spectacular mountain view, surrounded with twenty-five acres of peace and tranquillity. Minutes from fine dining, live entertainment shows, shopping, hiking, fishing, golfing, horseback riding, and

NOTES: Credit cards accepted: A Master Card; B Visa; C American Express; D Discover; E Diners Club; F Other; 2 Personal checks accepted; 3 Lunch available; 4 Dinner available; 5 Open all year; 6 Pets

all other attractions the area has to offer, yet completely secluded.

Hosts: Lill and Jim Katzbeck
Rooms: 3 (PB) $85-95
Full Breakfast
Credit Cards: A, B
Notes: 2, 5, 7, 8, 9, 10, 11, 12

Persephone's Retreat

2279 Hodges Ferry Road, 37876
(423) 428-7515; FAX (423) 453-7089
E-mail: vnicholson@smokymtnmall.com
Web site: http://www.smokymtnmall.com

A peaceful, rural estate nestled in a grove of huge shade trees. Convenient to Gatlinburg, Pigeon Forge, and Knoxville, but ideal for rest and relaxation from busy tourist activities. An elegant two-story home offers three extremely comfortable bedrooms with private baths and large porches overlooking pastures and a beautiful river valley. Enjoy spacious grounds, yard games, farm animals, miniature horses, and hiking. Children welcome.

Hosts: Bob Gonia and Victoria Nicholson
Rooms: 3 (PB) $75-95
Full Breakfast
Credit Cards: A, B, C, D
Notes: 2, 7, 8, 9, 10, 11, 12

Von-Bryan Inn

2402 Hatcher Mountain Road, 37862
(423) 453-9832; (800) 633-1459;
FAX (423) 428-8634

A mountaintop log inn with an unsurpassed, panoramic view of the Great Smoky Mountains. Greet the sunrise with singing birds and the aroma of breakfast. Swim, hike, rock, rest, read, and relax the day away, then watch the sunset just before the whippoorwills begin their nightly calls. Swimming pool, hot tub, steam shower, whirlpool tubs, library, complimentary dessert, refreshments, and breakfast. Three-bedroom log chalet is great for families.

Hosts: The Vaughn Family (D.J., JoAnn, David, and Patrick)
Rooms: 7 + 3-bedroom chalet (PB) $90-180
Full Breakfast
Credit Cards: A, B, C, D
Notes: 2, 5, 7, 9 (on site), 10, 11, 12

Von-Bryan Inn

WALLAND

Misty Morning Bed and Breakfast

5515 Old Walland Highway, 37886-2539
(423) 681-6373 (voice and FAX)

A three-story log home on eight beautiful acres nestled in the foothills of the Smoky Mountains. The B&B offers a sense of family and southern hospitality with full amenities. A restful getaway convenient to Pigeon Forge, Knoxville, Gatlinburg, Cade's Cove, and Knoxville Airport.

Hosts: Darnell and Herman Davis
Rooms: 2 (PB) $69-89
Full Breakfast
Credit Cards: A, B
Notes: 9 (on site), 10, 11

welcome; 7 Children welcome; 8 Tennis nearby; 9 Swimming nearby; 10 Golf nearby; 11 Skiing nearby; 12 May be booked through travel agent.

TEXAS

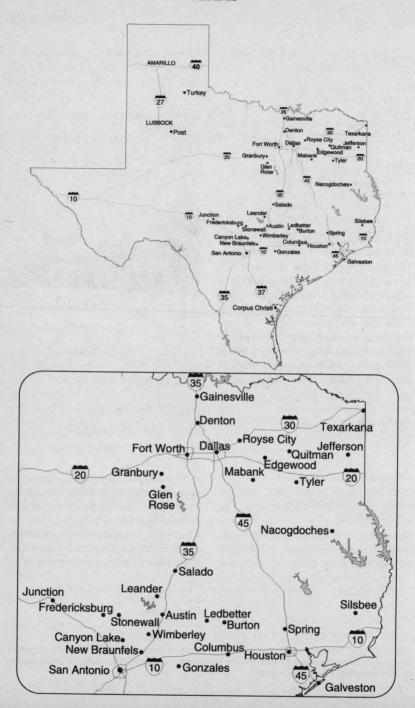

Texas

Reservation Service— Bed and Breakfast Texas Style, Inc.

4224 W. Red Bird Lane, **Dallas** 75237
(972) 298-8586; (800) 899-4538;
FAX (972) 298-7118

Bed and Breakfast Texas Style, Inc., is a reservation service established in 1982. We offer you a wide variety of accommodations in private homes, cottages, and small inns. We carefully inspect and approve lodgings to ensure comfort and convenience. If you prefer more privacy, you may choose a log cabin on a ranch, cottage on a farm, or guest house in the woods. Many of our B&Bs are historical mansions with Victorian decor. Let us know your desire; we will try to find just the right place for your special needs. For more information, call or write us. Approximately 340 rooms; $59-150. Major credit cards welcomed. Ruth Wilson, coordinator.

AUSTIN

Austin-Lake Travis Bed and Breakfast

4446 Eck Lane, 78734
(512) 266-3386; FAX (512) 266-9490
E-mail: jdwyer1511@aol.com
Web site: http://www.laketravisbb.com

Lake Travis Bed and Breakfast, a unique waterfront retreat, is a twenty-minute scenic drive from downtown Austin. The cliffs overlooking this beautiful Texas hill country lake are the setting for your luxurious holiday. Located on a sweeping bend of Lake Travis, all rooms have a spectacular view of the water, where you can experience an inspirational sunrise or a fiery sunset. A romantic, secluded hideaway for adults only, we offer the amenities of a large resort without the hassle. Begin the day unscheduled with a gourmet breakfast tray in bed or on your deck watching the birds and sailboats. A spectacular sunset on your balcony signals the beginning of an

---

enchanting evening and continues with dining at one of the gourmet or waterfront restaurants. Return to a romantic setting of lights dancing on the water, the subtle night sounds and a star-filled sky. You'll know you've found a piece of heaven.

Hosts: Judy and Vic Dwyer
Rooms: 3 (PB) $140-160
Full Breakfast in Bed
Credit Cards: A, B, C
Notes: 2, 5, 8, 9, 10, 12

Austin's Wildflower Inn

1200 W. 22½ Street, 78705
(512) 477-9639; fax (512) 474-4188
E-mail: kjackson@io.com
Web site: http://www.io.com/~kjackson

Austin's Wildflower Inn, built in the early 1930s, is a lovely colonial-style two-story home with a spacious porch. Every room has been restored carefully to create an atmosphere of warmth and comfort. A gourmet breakfast is served each day. We are tucked away in a very quiet neighborhood in the center of Austin. I invite you to come and relax here and enjoy our beautiful grounds and gardens.

Hostess: Kay Jackson
Rooms: 4 (2PB; 2SB) $69-89
Full Breakfast
Credit Cards: A, B, C
Notes: 2, 5, 7, 8, 9, 10

Peaceful Hill
Bed and Breakfast

6401 River Place Boulevard, 78730
(512) 338-1817

Deer watch you come . . . to this country inn on ranch land in beautiful rolling hills. Fifteen minutes to Austin; five minutes to

Lake Travis and the Oasis. Peaceful Hill is a bird-watcher's paradise. Cows, baby calves in field; horses meet you at the gate to be fed carrots. On the porch, enjoy rocking chairs, porch swing, breakfast at a big, round table, soaking in the countryside and the view of the city skyline. Nap in a hammock for two in the treed yard. Warm, friendly, comfortable home—all yours to enjoy. Grand stone fireplace. Sumptuous home-cooked breakfast. Peaceful is its name and peaceful is the game. Deer watch you go. . . .

Hostess: Mrs. Peninnah Thurmond
Rooms: 2 (PB) $60-65
Full Home-Cooked Breakfast
Credit Cards: A, B
Notes: 2, 5, 7, 8, 9, 10, 11, 12

Knittel Homestead

BURTON

Knittel Homestead Inn

PO Box 132, 520 N. Main, 77835
(409) 289-5102 (voice and FAX)

This fully restored Queen Anne Victorian home resembles a Mississippi steamboat, with wrapping porches. Beautifully furnished with antiques and country furniture, the home features three spacious bed-

---

NOTES: Credit cards accepted: A Master Card; B Visa; C American Express; D Discover; E Diners Club; F Other; 2 Personal checks accepted; 3 Lunch available; 4 Dinner available; 5 Open all year; 6 Pets

rooms, each with a private bath. Guests are treated to a delicious, all-you-can-eat country breakfast and complimentary sodas, juices, and snacks. The home is listed in the National Register of Historic Places. Numerous local historical sites are within walking distance.

Hosts: Steve and Cindy Miller
Rooms: 3 (PB) $75-85
Full Breakfast
Credit Cards: none
Notes: 2, 3 and 4 (at our cafe), 5, 8, 10

CANTON AREA

Heavenly Acres Ranch Bed and Breakfast

Route 3, Box 470, **Mabank**, 75147
(903) 887-3016; (800) 283-0341;
FAX (903) 887-6108
E-mail: habb@vzinet.com
Web site: http://www.heavenlyacres.com

Heavenly Acres is a working ranch with three springfed fishing lakes, located twelve miles southwest of Canton. Each private cabin provides unique a decor with kitchen, television/VCR, and porches with rockers that overlook the water. Guests can enjoy the video library, billiards, outdoor game field, mountain bikes, fishing and paddleboats, a barnyard petting zoo, and walking paths. Special group packages and a large meeting/dining hall are available for groups and reunions. No smoking is permitted indoors.

Hosts: Vickie and Marshall Ragle
Rooms: 6 cabins (PB) $95
Continental Breakfast
Credit Cards: A, B, C, D
Notes: 2, 4 (groups only), 5, 6, 7, 8, 9, 10

Texas Star Bed and Breakfast

Route 1, Box 187-1, **Edgewood**, 75117
(903) 896-4277

The east Texas countryside, dotted heavily with large oak and cedar trees, hosts our guest house. Four private bedrooms with private baths, private patios, and two additional rooms with a shared bath in the main house. Each room reflects a different phase of Texas history and/or culture. Enjoy an exhilarating game of volleyball, horseshoes, or croquet, or choose to relax on the shaded porch. Homemade bread and jams are featured in our family-style country breakfast. Within four miles of world-famous Trade Days (flea market) of Canton.

Hosts: David and Marie Stoltzfus
Rooms: 6 (4PB; 2SB) $65-85
Full or Continental Breakfast
Credit Cards: A, B, C, D
Notes: 4, 5, 7, 10, 12

COLUMBUS

Raumonda

1100 Bowie Street, 78934
(409) 732-2190; FAX (409) 732-5881
Web site: http://www.intertex.net/users/ccvb

This grand Victorian home was built in 1887 by Henry Ilse and occupied by his family until 1954. The house was purchased by the Rau family and was completely restored. Raumonda is now open as an elegant bed and breakfast with a gracious host, R. F. "Buddy" Rau, who greets guests with warmth and charm and tells them the history of the house and of

welcome; 7 Children welcome; 8 Tennis nearby; 9 Swimming nearby; 10 Golf nearby; 11 Skiing nearby; 12 May be booked through travel agent.

Columbus, one of the oldest towns in Texas. Raumonda is furnished in lovely antiques and surrounded by an "Old South" garden with swimming pool.

Host: R. F. "Buddy" Rau
Rooms: 3 (2PB; 1SB) $80
Continental Breakfast
Credit Cards: none
Notes: 2, 5, 9 (pool in garden), 10

CORPUS CHRISTI

Sand Dollar Hospitality B&B Reservation Service

3605 Mendenhall Drive, 78415
(512) 853-1222; (800) 528-7782

Properties represented by Sand Dollar Hospitality include residential and ranch guest houses, Padre Island condos, beachfront apartments and carefully selected homes offering rooms with private baths and breakfast. Many of our properties are near the water; most welcome children and several will accept pets with a deposit. Rates: $66-125. Full or continental breakfast is offered. Pat Hirsbrunner, director.

DENTON

The Redbud and Magnolia Inns

815 N. Locust Street, 76201
(940) 565-6414; (888) 565-6414;
FAX (940) 565-6515

The Redbud and Magnolia inns have become home away from home for many business travelers. We welcome you to make our three rooms and four suites your second home. Historic Denton is within walking distance, as are the storytelling and jazz festivals each spring.

Hosts: John and Donna Morris
Rooms: 7 (PB) $56-105
Full Breakfast
Credit Cards: A, B, C, D
Notes: 2, 4, 5, 7, 9, 10, 12

FORT WORTH

The Texas White House

1417 Eighth Avenue, 76104
(817) 923-3597; (800) 279-6491;
FAX (817) 923-0410
E-mail: txwhitehou@aol.com

This award-winning, historically designated, country-style home has been restored to its original grandeur. The home is centrally located near downtown, the medical center, the Forth Worth Zoo, cultural district, Botanical Gardens, and Texas Christian University. Three guest rooms are furnished with luxurious queen-size beds and nice antiques, relaxing sitting areas, and private baths with claw-foot tubs for showers or soaking in bubble baths. Guests are afforded complete privacy; however, if desired, they may enjoy the parlor, living room with fireplace, and large wraparound porch. Breakfast will be a gourmet treat with fresh fruit or baked fruit in compote (seasonal), baked egg casseroles, and homemade breads and muffins, juices, coffee, and tea.

Hosts: Jamie and Grover McMains
Rooms: 3 (PB) $85-105
Full Breakfast
Credit Cards: A, B, C, D
Notes: 2, 5, 10, 12

NOTES: Credit cards accepted: A Master Card; B Visa; C American Express; D Discover; E Diners Club; F Other; 2 Personal checks accepted; 3 Lunch available; 4 Dinner available; 5 Open all year; 6 Pets

FREDERICKSBURG

Gästehaus Schmidt Reservation Service

231 W. Main Street, 78624
(830) 997-5612; FAX (830) 997-8282
E-mail: gasthaus@ktc.com
Web site: http://www.ktc.com/GSchmidt

Put yourself in our place! Plan a stay in one of our traditional B&Bs or guest houses. We offer a pleasing variety of "out of the ordinary" overnight experiences. Whether you want to escape to the country, stay close to town, relive history, or rekindle romance, each home is special and the varieties are endless. You will discover that "our" place is truly "your" place. More than one hundred homes. Open daily. Catalogs available. Donna and Dan Mittel, coordinators.

Kiehne Kreek Farm

1861 Knopp School Road, 78624
(830) 997-5612; FAX (830) 997-8282

Eight miles northeast of Fredericksburg. Restored pioneer home (circa 1850). Four bedrooms: two with queen beds; single and bunk; twin. One and a half baths, living room, dining area, completely equipped kitchen. Hosts' home across the drive and patio. Room to roam and pastures to enjoy the fresh air. Country breakfast foods for you to fix. No pets. Smoking allowed. Children by special arrangement. Central heat/air. TV and fireplace in living room. Phone extension of hosts. Two-night minimum.

Hosts: Nancy and Bill Wareing
Rooms: 4-bedroom home
Country Breakfast (self-prepared)

Magnolia House

101 E. Hackberry Street, 78624
(830) 997-0306; (800) 880-4374;
FAX (830) 997-0766

Circa 1923, restored in 1991. Enjoy southern hospitality in a grand and gracious manner. Outside, lovely magnolias and a bubbling fish pond and waterfall set a soothing mood. Inside, a beautiful living room and a formal dining room provide areas for guests to mingle. Four romantic rooms and two suites have been thoughtfully planned. A southern-style breakfast completes a memorable experience.

Hosts: Joyce and Patrick Kennard
Rooms: 6 (4PB; 2SB) $80-125
Full Breakfast
Credit Cards: A, B, C, D
Notes: 2, 5, 8, 9, 10

Patsy's Guest House and the Cook's Cottage

703 W. Austin, 78624
(830) 997-5612; FAX (830) 997-8282

Enjoy a quiet, romantic stay at the Cook's Cottage, located behind your hostess' home with a private entrance through a screened and furnished porch (ideal for relaxing and enjoying the wonderful antiques). The focal point of the cottage's large, unique one-room suite is a magnificent four-poster cypress lodge pole bed with antique Irish gate headboard. A crystal chandelier is overhead. A few feet away is a large whirlpool for two, handsomely tucked into the corner and surrounded by a creation of Colorado River rocks, slate, and architectural antiques. A gourmet breakfast, delivered to your door by chef Michael Varney, can be enjoyed

---

welcome; 7 Children welcome; 8 Tennis nearby; 9 Swimming nearby; 10 Golf nearby; 11 Skiing nearby; 12 May be booked through travel agent.

in front of a stained-glass window. Patsy's Guest House, a Victorian suite above the private residence, sleeps three.

Hostess: Patsy Swendson
Rooms: 2 (PB) $95-135
Full Breakfast
Credit Cards: A, B, C, D, E
Notes: 2, 4 (additional cost), 5, 12

Schildknecht-Weidenfeller House

Schildknecht-Weidenfeller House

Gastehaus Schmidt Reservation Service: 231 W. Main, 78624
(830) 997-5612; FAX (830) 997-8282

Relive history in this house in the heart of Fredericksburg's historic district. Decorated with antiques and handmade quilts, this guest house accommodates up to ten people. A German-style breakfast is left for you to enjoy at your leisure around the antique farm table in the kitchen. The 1870s German limestone house has been featured on tours of historic homes and in *Country Decorating Ideas*. Member of Historic Accommodations of Texas.

Hosts: Ellis and Carter Schildknecht
Rooms: entire house (8 rooms + 2 baths) $125 and up, according to party size
Expanded Continental (German-Style) Breakfast
Credit Cards: A, B, D
Notes: 2, 5, 7 (12 and older), 8, 9, 10, 12

Way of the Wolf

HC 12, Box 92H, 78624
(830) 997-0711

This B&B retreat, on sixty-one acres in the hill country, offers a swimming pool, space for picnics and hikes, wildlife, and scenic views. The four bedrooms and common living area with fireplace are furnished with antiques. A reconstructed Civil War-era cabin is also available. This destination B&B is peaceful and secluded while only fifteen minutes from shopping, golf, and churches in either Kerrville or Fredericksburg. Assistance in preparing for personal or group retreats is available.

Hosts: Ron and Karen Poidevin
Rooms: 5 (3PB; 2SB) $75-115
Full Breakfast
Credit Cards: none
Notes: 2, 5, 9 (on site), 10, 12

The Yellow House

231 W. Main, 78624
(830) 997-5612 (Gastehaus Reservation Service);
FAX (830) 997-8282

The Yellow House is an original Sunday House built at the turn of the century. It is known as the "little yellow house under the big oak tree." Featured in the June 1994 *Country Living Magazine*, this home has three rooms. The front porch leads you to the bedroom/sitting room with a four-poster queen-size bed situated high off the floor with a fluffy comforter. There is also a fully equipped kitchen and bath with shower.

Hosts: Donna and Dan Mittel
Rooms: 1 (PB) $82
Continental Breakfast
Credit Cards: A, B, C, D

NOTES: Credit cards accepted: A Master Card; B Visa; C American Express; D Discover; E Diners Club; F Other; 2 Personal checks accepted; 3 Lunch available; 4 Dinner available; 5 Open all year; 6 Pets

Yesteryear Gast Haus

Yesteryear Gast Haus

405 E. Morse Street, 78624
(830) 997-5612; FAX (830) 997-8282

Built in 1912, the Gast Haus is in historic Fredericksburg near museums, shops, and restaurants. This large house has been restored throughout and is furnished with beautiful antiques, heirlooms, and decorations from the same time period. Relax on the front porch surrounded by honeycomb rock landscaping, or stretch in the backyard and marvel at the old wisteria that serves as a shaded arbor. Your stay will be nostalgic and tranquil.

Hosts: Janice and George Stehling
Rooms: 2 (1½SB) $95
Coffee Bar Breakfast
Credit Cards: A, B, D
Notes: 2, 5, 8, 9, 10, 12

GAINESVILLE (WHITESBORO)

Alexander Bed and Breakfast Acres Inc.

Route 7, Box 788, 76240
(903) 564-7440 (voice and FAX; call before FAXing);
(800) 887-8794

Charming three-story Queen Anne home and guest cottage nestled peacefully in the woods and meadows of sixty-five acres just south of Whitesboro in the Lake Texoma area. Main house offers parlor and dining room plus third-floor sitting area with TV, and wraparound porch for relaxing; five guest bedrooms with private baths and full breakfast. The two-story cottage has three bedrooms that share one bath; there are full kitchen facilities for preparing your own breakfast, and it is perfect for families with children.

Hosts: Pamela and Jimmy Alexander
Rooms: 5 + cottage (5PB; 3SB) $60-125
Full Breakfast (for main house)
Credit Cards: A, B
Notes: 2, 4, 5, 7 (at cottage), 9, 10, 11 (water), 12

GALVESTON

Madame Dyer's Bed and Breakfast

1720 Postoffice Street, 77550
(409) 765-5692

From the moment you enter this carefully restored, turn-of-the-century home, you will be entranced by period details such as wraparound porches; high, airy ceilings; wooden floors; and lace curtains. Each room is furnished with delightful antiques that bring back memories of days gone by. Enjoy a night or weekend in this 1889 home in a quiet, historical, residential neighborhood. It offers guests a feeling of elegance from the past and the luxury, comfort, and pleasures of today. Featured on Galveston's Historic Homes Tour.

Hosts: Linda and Larry Bonnin
Rooms: 3 (PB) $95-125
Full Breakfast
Credit Cards: A, B
Notes: 2, 4, 5, 9, 10, 12

GLEN ROSE

Bussey's Something Special Bed and Breakfast

202 Hereford Street, PO Box 1425, 76043
(254) 897-4843; (800) 700-4843, 13

Two-story Country Cottage is great for families, with king and full beds, full kitchen, private bath with shower. Cozy Cottage is a romantic getaway with king bed, jet tub, and kitchenette. Both have private porches and yards.

Hosts: Susan and Morris Bussey
Rooms: 2 (PB) $80-100
Continental Breakfast
Credit Cards: A, B
Notes: 2, 5, 7, 8, 9, 10

GRANBURY

Dabney House Bed and Breakfast

106 S. Jones, 76048
(817) 579-1260; (800) 566-1260

Craftsman-style, one-story home built in 1907 by a local banker and furnished with

Dabney House Bed and Breakfast

antiques. It features hardwood floors and original woodwork. Long-term business rates available per request; romance dinner by reservation only. We offer custom, special occasion baskets in the room on arrival, by advance order only. Book the whole house for family occasions, staff retreats, or Bible retreats at discount rates. Hot tub is now available for all registered guests.

Hosts: John and Gwen Hurley
Rooms: 4 (PB) $60-105
Full Breakfast
Credit Cards: A, B, C
Notes: 2, 5, 8, 9, 10, 12

JEFFERSON

McKay House Bed and Breakfast Inn

306 E. Delta Street, 75657
(903) 665-7322; (800) 468-2627;
FAX (903) 665-8551

Jefferson is a town where one can relax, rather than get tired. The McKay House, an 1851 Greek Revival cottage, features a pillared front porch and many fireplaces and offers genuine hospitality in a Christian atmosphere. Heart-of-pine floors, fourteen-foot ceilings, and documented wallpapers complement antique furnishings. Enjoy a full "gentleman's" breakfast each morning. Victorian nightshirts and gowns await pampered guests in each bed chamber.

Hosts: Alma Anne and Joseph Parker
Rooms: 7 (PB) $95-125 (corporate rates available)
Full Sit-Down Breakfast
Credit Cards: A, B
Notes: 2, 5, 10, 12

NOTES: Credit cards accepted: A Master Card; B Visa; C American Express; D Discover; E Diners Club; F Other; 2 Personal checks accepted; 3 Lunch available; 4 Dinner available; 5 Open all year; 6 Pets

Pride House

409 Broadway, 75657
(903) 665-2675; (800) 894-3526;
FAX (903) 665-3901
E-mail: jefftx@mind.net
Web site: http://www.jeffersontexas.com

Breathtaking east Texas landmark. A Victorian mansion in a historic former steamboat port. Myth America lives in this town of 2,200, on the banks of the Cypress, along brick streets, behind picket fences, and in antique houses. Pride House has luscious interiors, luxurious amenities, and legendary breakfasts! We have ten rooms with private baths, big beds, spacious rooms, and just about everything anybody has asked for during the past fourteen years.

Hosts: Carol and Christel
Rooms: 10 (PB) $75-110
Full Breakfast
Credit Cards: A, B
Notes: 2, 5, 7, 10, 12

JUNCTION

Shady Rest at the Junction Bed and Breakfast Inn

101 N. 11th Street, 76849
(915) 446-4067; (888) 982-8292 (voice and FAX)

Junction's one-of-a-kind Victorian-style bed and breakfast offers unique guest accommodations downtown. This beautiful turn-of-the-century home recently has undergone a massive refurbishing inside and out. You can relax on the beautiful wraparound front porch, or leisurely lounge at the umbrella table as you enjoy this picturesque setting nestled between the north and south Llano rivers. You'll be treated to a sumptuous breakfast each morning by candlelight to "Victorian Lovesongs." Shady Rest at the Junction is a nonsmoking home.

Hosts: Bill and Debbie Bayer
Rooms: 1 (PB) $65
Full Breakfast
Credit Cards: none
Notes: 2, 4, 5, 8, 9, 10

LEDBETTER

Ledbetter Bed and Breakfast and Conference Center

PO Box 212, 78946
(409) 249-3066; (800) 240-3066;
FAX (409) 249-3330

Ledbetter B&B, established in 1988, is a collection of multigeneration, family, 1800-1900s homes within walking distance of the remaining 1870s downtown businesses. A full country breakfast buffet can serve up to seventy guests daily. Hayrides, walks, fishing, horse and buggy rides, games, Christmas lights, chuck wagon or romantic dinners, indoor heated swimming pool, VCR, TV. A phone can be made available on advance request. Each unit accommodates approximately four people. Only nonalcoholic beverages are allowed outside private quarters. Only outdoor smoking is allowed.

Hosts: Chris and Jay Jervis
Rooms: 16-22, depending on grouping (most have PB) $70-150
Full Country Buffet Breakfast
Credit Cards: A, B, C
Notes: 2, 3, 4, 5, 7, 8, 9, 10, 11 (water), 12

welcome; 7 Children welcome; 8 Tennis nearby; 9 Swimming nearby; 10 Golf nearby; 11 Skiing nearby; 12 May be booked through travel agent.

NACOGDOCHES

Anderson Point Bed and Breakfast

29 E. Lake Estates, 75964
(409) 569-7445

You won't want to leave this lovely, two-story, French-style home surrounded by three hundred feet of lake frontage. Enjoy sweeping views of the water from every room and a double veranda for dining and dozing. You can stroll around the beautiful grounds or go fishing off the pier. Don't miss the glorious sunsets as you gather in the fireplace sitting room for coffee and conversation. A breakfast pantry will be available every morning. The home and grounds are unique in that no toxic chemicals or fragrances are used. The most severe allergy sufferers will be safe in this pristine environment.

Hostess: Rachel Anderson
Rooms: 2 (SB) $58-68
Continental Plus Breakfast
Credit Cards: B, C
Notes: 2, 5, 6, 7, 9

PineCreek Lodge

Route 3, Box 1238, 75964
(409) 560-6282; (888) 714-1414;
FAX (409) 560-1675

On a beautiful tree-covered hill overlooking a spring-fed creek sits PineCreek Lodge. Built on a 140-acre property with lots of lawns, rose gardens, and a multitude of flowers, deep in the east Texas woods yet only ten miles from historic Nacogdoches. Our rustic lodge features king-size beds in tastefully decorated rooms with phone, TV/VCR, lots of decks, swimming pool, spa, fishing, biking, and much more. We have become the destination for many city dwellers.

Hosts: The Pitts Family
Rooms: 9 + cottage (PB) $55-95
Full Breakfast
Credit Cards: A, B, C, D
Notes: 2, 3, 4, 5, 7, 9, 10

NEW BRAUNFELS

Antik Haus Bed and Breakfast

118 S. Union Street, 78130
(830) 625-6666; (888) ANTIK-71

A romantic Victorian inn filled with food, harmony, magic, and love. Full gourmet breakfast served. Romantic dinner for two available by special request. Fruit and cheese platter/baskets for your room or picnic available. Gazebo, hot spa, landscaped gardens, strombella. Lovely location for weddings, anniversaries, family reunions, and retreats. Fluent German spoken. Bicycle built for two available to guests.

Hosts: Domonique and Jay Rodriquè
Rooms: 4 (SB) $75-125
Full Breakfast
Credit Cards: A, B, C
Notes: 4, 5, 7, 8, 9, 12

Aunt Nora's Countryside Inn

120 Naked Indian Trail, 78132-1865
(830) 905-3989; (800) 687-2887

Our private cottage suites are cozy, with country Victorian decor, including handbuilt furnishings, antiques and old bridal heirlooms—a truly romantic getaway with hill country elegance. The buildings are reminiscent of early Texas, overlooking picturesque hillsides along with a wedding gazebo and arched bridge atop two goldfish ponds with waterfalls. Located just minutes away from New Braunfels, Gruene, the Guadalupe River and Canyon Lake. Private baths, kitchens, decks, patio hot tub.

Hosts: Alton and Iralee Haley
Rooms: 4 cottages (PB) $85-150
Full or Continental Breakfast
Credit Cards: A, B
Notes: 2, 5, 7, 8, 9, 10, 12

Prince Solms Inn

295 E. San Antonio Street, 78130
(830) 625-9169 (voice and FAX); (800) 625-9169

Delightful, registered Texas heritage landmark. Elegantly furnished with European antiques and artwork, the inn has a genteel, refined old-world atmosphere. Picturesque courtyard offers a shady place to relax. Wolfgang's Keller, named in honor of composer Wolfgang Mozart, is a restaurant and bar in the cellar, where excellent continental cuisine is served in romantic surroundings. Places to go: antique shops, historic downtown, Hummel and Sophienburg museums, tubing on the Comal and Guadalupe rivers, Schlitterbahn Waterpark, Wurstfest Grounds and Laura Park, outlet malls, historic Gruene.

Hostess: Deborah Redle
Rooms: 10 (PB) $65-150
Continental Breakfast, weekdays; Full Breakfast, weekends
Credit Cards: A, B, C, D
Notes: 2, 4, 5, 7, 8, 9, 10, 12

The Rose Garden Bed and Breakfast

195 S. Academy, 78130
(830) 606-3916; (800) 569-3296
E-mail: rosegrdn@iamerica.net

Come to our Rose Garden with its designer bedrooms, fluffy towels, scented soaps, and potpourri-filled rooms. Our half-century-old home is only one block from downtown. Enjoy a movie, browse antique shops, or stroll along the Comal Springs—all within walking distance. We offer two guest rooms. The Royal Rose Room has a four-poster rice, queen bed with a crystal chandelier and country French decor. The Country Rose Room has a Victorian-style, iron-and-brass queen bed with pine walls, also done in country French. A full gourmet breakfast is served in the formal dining room.

Hostess: Dawn Mann
Rooms: 2 (PB) $65-95
Full Breakfast
Credit Cards: A, B
Notes: 2, 5, 8, 9, 10

POST

Hotel Garza

302 E. Main Street, 79356
(806) 495-3962
Web site: http://www.innsandouts.com/property/ hotel_garza_bed_and_breakfast.html

This restored 1915 hotel projects the friendliness and history of this "Main Street City" where cereal magnate C.W. Post settled in 1907 to create his "Utopia." Guests can enjoy live theater, colorful shops, museums, and the monthly event of Old Mill Trade Days. The guest rooms boast original furniture. From the comfy library you can look

welcome; 7 Children welcome; 8 Tennis nearby; 9 Swimming nearby; 10 Golf nearby; 11 Skiing nearby; 12 May be booked through travel agent.

Hotel Garza

down on a quaint lobby and the dining area where a hearty breakfast is served. Suites are available.

Hosts: Jim and Janice Plummer
Rooms: 12 (8PB; 4SB) $40-99
Full Breakfast weekends, Continental weekdays
Credit Cards: A, B, C
Notes: 2, 4, 5, 7, 8, 9, 10, 12

QUITMAN

Steinert's Place

Route 2, Box 2738, 75783
(903) 878-2825

Located six miles north of Quitman on a hilltop with a wonderful view of the countryside. Close by is Lake Fork, the bass fishing capital of Texas. It's a thirty-minute drive through the country to Canton for the famous Canton Trade Days. Complete kitchen stocked with coffee, tea, hot chocolate, and juices. Full-size and three single beds with one and a half baths (sleeps five). Living room has fireplace with country decor.

Hosts: Bill and Vivienne Steinert
Rooms: 3 (SB) $60-105
Credit Cards: A, B, C, D
Notes: 2, 5, 7

ROYSE CITY

Country Lane Bed and Breakfast

325 FM2453, 75189
(972) 636-2600; (800) 240-8757;
FAX (972) 636-0036
E-mail: Jaelius@Flash.net

Dallas is a short drive away—yet the casual, country atmosphere beckons you to relax. Your hosts have used their collections of Hollywood classics to decorate the four guest rooms, each of which has a private bath. The Happy Trails Suite and Mae West have queen-size beds and jet tubs, while the Europa Suite and the Rose Room have full-size beds. All have television/VCRs, clock radios, great views.

Hosts: James and Annie Cornelius
Rooms: 4 (PB) $50-95
Full Breakfast
Credit Cards: A, B, C, D
Notes: 2, 4, 5, 7, 10, 11, 12

Country Lane Bed and Breakfast

SALADO

Inn at Salado

PO Box 320, 76571
(254) 947-0027; (800) 724-0027;
FAX (254) 947-3144

Salado's first bed and breakfast is located in the heart of the historic district. Renovated to its original 1872 splendor, the inn

---

NOTES: Credit cards accepted: A Master Card; B Visa; C American Express; D Discover; E Diners Club; F Other; 2 Personal checks accepted; 3 Lunch available; 4 Dinner available; 5 Open all year; 6 Pets

displays both a Texas historical marker and a National Register listing. The inn's ambience is enhanced by its antique furniture, porch swings, and live oak trees, all on two beautifully landscaped acres. A wedding chapel, meeting rooms, and catering complete the amenities offered by the inn.

Hosts: Rob and Suzanne Petro
Rooms: 9 (PB) $70-110
Full Breakfast
Credit Cards: A, B, C, D
Notes: 2, 5, 9, 10

The Rose Mansion

PO Box 613, 76571
(254) 947-8200; (800) 948-1004

Nestled among towering oaks, the traditional Greek Revival-style mansion and complementary cottage and 1850s log cabins offer a return to yesterday, with class. Four acres of beautiful grounds, memorabilia, antiques, shaded seating, swings, and games are complemented by a gourmet breakfast, queen beds, private baths, fireplace, and central heat and air. Elegance in a cozy atmosphere.

Hosts: Neil and Carole Hunter
Rooms: 10 (PB) $90-120
Full Breakfast
Credit Cards: A, B, C, D
Notes: 2, 5, 10

The Rose Mansion

SAN ANTONIO

Beckmann Inn and Carriage House

222 E. Guenther Street, 78204
(210) 229-1449; (800) 945-1449;
FAX (210) 229-1061
Web site: http://saweb.com/beckbb

A wonderful Victorian house (1886) located in the King William historic district, across the street from the start of the Riverwalk. Beautifully landscaped, it will take you on a leisurely stroll to the Alamo, downtown shops, and restaurants. You also can take the trolley, which stops at the corner, and within minutes you're there in style. The beautiful wraparound porch welcomes you to the main house and warm, gracious, Victorian hospitality. The large guest rooms feature antique, ornately carved, Victorian queen-size beds; private baths; and ceiling fans. Gourmet breakfast, with breakfast dessert, is served in the dining room with china, crystal, and silver. Warm and gracious hospitality at its best. AAA-, IIA-, and Mobil-rated, excellent.

Hosts: Betty Jo and Don Schwartz
Rooms: 5 (PB) $90-130
Full Breakfast
Credit Cards: A, B, C, D, E
Notes: 2, 5, 7 (over 12), 10, 12

The Belle of Monte Vista

505 Belknap Place, 78212
(210) 232-4006 (voice and FAX)

J. Riely Gordon designed this 1890 Queen Anne Victorian home, located conveniently in the famous Monte Vista historic district,

welcome; 7 Children welcome; 8 Tennis nearby; 9 Swimming nearby; 10 Golf nearby; 11 Skiing nearby; 12 May be booked through travel agent.

one mile from downtown San Antonio. The house has eight fireplaces, stained-glass windows, hand-carved oak interior, and Victorian furnishings. Near the zoo, churches, Riverwalk, El Mercardo, arts, and universities. Transportation to and from the airport, bus, and train station is available on request. Easy access from all major highways.

Host: Jim Davis
Rooms: 5 (3PB; 2SB) $50-85
Full Breakfast
Credit Cards: A, B, C
Notes: 2, 5, 7, 8, 9, 10, 12

Brackenridge House

230 Madison Street, 78204
(210) 271-3442; (800) 221-1412;
FAX (210) 226-3139

A Greek Revival home (1903) set in the King William historic district with four two-story white Corinthian columns and first- and second-floor verandas. The original pine floor, double-hung windows, and high ceilings are enhanced by antique furnishings, many of them family heirlooms. All guest rooms have private baths and entrances, phones, and minirefrigerators. A bridal suite decorated in all white is available. Breakfast is served in the guest dining room on the second floor. Located only six blocks from downtown, two blocks from the Riverwalk, and one block from the fifty-cent trolley and the San Antonio Mission Trail. Convenient walking to four delightful restaurants.

Hosts: Bennie and Sue Blansett
Rooms: 6 (PB) $89-125
Full and Continental Breakfast
Credit Cards: A, B, C, D, E
Notes: 2, 5, 6 and 7 (in carriage house), 8, 9, 10, 12

Brookhaven Manor

Brookhaven Manor

128 W. Mistletoe, 78212
(210) 733-3939; (800) 851-3666

Recapture the charm and grace of a bygone era in an elegant three-story home built in 1914. Each room is distinctly decorated, from the Murphy Room with a queen-size mahogany Murphy bed to the Country French Honeymoon Suite with private dressing room and marble bath with claw-foot tub. Located in an elite, historic district, five minutes from downtown. Great for walkers and joggers!

Hostess: Nancy Forbes
Rooms: 4 (PB) $75-110
Full Breakfast (Continental for early birds)
Credit Cards: A, B
Notes: 2, 5, 6, 7, 8, 9, 10, 12

The Ogé House Inn on the Riverwalk

209 Washington Street, 78204
(210) 223-2353; (800) 242-2770;
FAX (210) 226-5812
E-mail: ogeinn@swbell.net
Web site: http://www.ogeinn.com

This elegant, historic antebellum mansion is privately located on one and a half landscaped acres along the famous Riverwalk. The inn is decorated in European antiques.

NOTES: Credit cards accepted: A Master Card; B Visa; C American Express; D Discover; E Diners Club; F Other; 2 Personal checks accepted; 3 Lunch available; 4 Dinner available; 5 Open all year; 6 Pets

A gourmet breakfast is served on Wedgewood china with silver and crystal. For business or pleasure, come enjoy quiet comfort and luxury.

Hosts: Sharrie and Patrick Magatagan
Rooms: 9 (PB) $110-205
Full Breakfast
Credit Cards: A, B, C, D, E
Notes: 2, 5, 8, 10

The Riverwalk Inn

329 Old Guilbeau, 78204
(210) 212-8300; (800) 254-4440;
FAX (210) 229-9422

The Riverwalk Inn is comprised of five two-story homes, circa 1840, which have been restored on the downtown San Antonio Riverwalk. Period antiques create an ambience of "country elegance." Rock on our eighty-foot porch. Enjoy Aunt Martha's evening desserts and local storytellers who join us for breakfast. Fireplaces, refrigerators, private baths, phones, balconies, TV, and conference room. A Texas tradition with a Tennessee flavor awaits you. Call for brochure.

Hosts: Johnny Halpenny and Tammy Hill
Rooms: 11 (PB) $110-155
Full Breakfast
Credit Cards: A, B, C, D
Notes: 2, 5, 12

A Victorian Lady Inn

421 Howard Street, 78212
(210) 224-2524; (800) 879-7116;
FAX (210) 224-5123
E-mail: victorianladyinn@msn.com
Web site: http://viclady.com

Rediscover the genteel ambience of a hundred years ago in this 1898 historic mansion. Guest rooms are some of the largest in San Antonio and feature period antiques.

A Victorian Lady Inn

Your pampered retreat includes a private bath, fireplace, veranda, TV, and phone. Fabulous full breakfasts are served daily in the grand dining room. Bicycles and book exchange are on premises. Just blocks away are the Riverwalk, Alamo, and Convention Center. Swimming, golf, horseback riding, and antiquing are all very close by. AAA rating, three diamonds.

Hosts: Kate and Joe Bowski
Rooms: 8 (PB) $69-139
Full Breakfast
Credit Cards: A, B, C, D
Notes: 5, 8, 9, 10, 12

SILSBEE

Sherwood Train Depot Bed and Breakfast

PO Box 2281, 134 Sherwood Trail, 77656
(409) 385-0188

A beautiful wooded setting of a two-story cypress home in the midst of beech and oak trees. Within the home is a unique design of knotty cypress wood. Fireplaced living room that at the ceiling begins a "G" scale "LGB" train system that

welcome; 7 Children welcome; 8 Tennis nearby; 9 Swimming nearby; 10 Golf nearby; 11 Skiing nearby; 12 May be booked through travel agent.

runs on a cypress ceiling-hung rail system; it is 430 feet long and runs throughout the downstairs—even spiraling to the upstairs. You have to see this unusual track layout to believe it. The suite features a king bed, private bath, cable TV/VCR, phone, and two-person hot tub. Guests also can enjoy exercise equipment, walking trails, bird-watching, and much more.

Host: Jerry Allen
Rooms: 1 (PB) $60-75
Continental and Full Breakfast
Credit Cards: none
Notes: 2, 3, 4, 5, 7, 9, 10

SPRING

McLachlan Farm Bed and Breakfast

PO Box 538, 77383
(713) 350-2400; (800) 382-3988

The 1911 McLachlan family homestead was restored and enlarged in 1989 by the great-granddaughter, and her husband, of the original McLachlan family who settled the land in 1862. Set back among thirty-five acres of towering sycamore and pecan trees, neatly mowed grounds, and winding forest trails. It is a quiet oasis that returns guests to a time when life was simpler. Visitors may swing on the porches, walk in the woods, or visit Old Town Spring (one mile south) where there are more than a hundred shops to enjoy.

Hosts: Jim and Joycelyn Clairmonte
Rooms: 3-4 (3PB or 2SB) $75-85
Full Country Breakfast
Credit Cards: A, B, C, D
Notes: 2, 5, 10, 12

STONEWALL

"Heimplatz am Fluss"

Ranch Road 1, PO Box 934, 78621
(830) 997-5612; FAX (830) 997-8282

Located on the Pedernales River, fifteen miles from Fredericksburg in Stonewall, is a charming two-story limestone rock home. Upstairs above the owner's home is *Heimplatz am Fluss* or "Homeplace on the River." Built in the 1880s, this suite offers antiques, including a queen bed, antique love seat and TV. The bath is a tub/shower. Outside the suite is a front porch creating a relaxing atmosphere. A continental breakfast is delivered to your suite. Accommodations for two people only. Guests are invited to enjoy use of the Pedernales River.

Hosts: Hubert and Jeanette Klein
Rooms: 1 (PB) $80
Continental Breakfast
Credit Cards: A, B, C, D
Notes: 2, 5, 8, 9, 10, 12

TEXARKANA

Mansion on Main Bed and Breakfast Inn

802 Main Street, 75501
(903) 792-1835; FAX (903) 793-0878

"Twice as Nice," the motto of Texarkana, USA (Texas and Arkansas), is standard practice at Mansion on Main. The 1895 neoclassical colonial mansion, surrounded by fourteen tall columns, recently was restored by the owners of McKay House, the popular bed and breakfast in nearby Jerrson. Six bed chambers vary from the

---

NOTES: Credit cards accepted: A Master Card; B Visa; C American Express; D Discover; E Diners Club; F Other; 2 Personal checks accepted; 3 Lunch available; 4 Dinner available; 5 Open all year; 6 Pets

Mansion on Main Bed and Breakfast Inn

Governor's Suite to the Butler's Garret. Guests enjoy southern hospitality, period furnishings, fireplaces, and a gentleman's breakfast. Thirty miles away is the town of Hope, birthplace of President Clinton.

Hosts: Lee and Inez Hayden
Rooms: 6 (PB) $60-109
Full Breakfast
Credit Cards: A, B, C
Notes: 2, 5, 10, 12

TURKEY

Hotel Turkey

3rd and Alexander, PO Box 37, 79261
(806) 423-1151; (800) 657-7110
Web site: http://www.llano.net/turkey/hotel

This 1927 hotel is like a step back in time— period furnishings, vintage clothing, and local memorabilia. Enjoy a "peace" of the past, fifteen miles from the beautiful Caprock Canyons State Park. The Bob Wills Museum is located here. We are listed on the state and national Historic Registers. Smoke-free environment.

Hosts: Gary and Suzie Johnson
Rooms: 15 (7PB; 8SB) $69-89
Full Breakfast
Credit Cards: A, B, C
Notes: 2, 5, 7, 8, 10, 12

TYLER

The Seasons Bed and Breakfast Inn

313 E. Charnwood, 75701
(903) 533-0803; FAX (903) 533-8870
E-mail: jbrowntwo@aol.com

Located a few blocks from downtown Tyler, The Seasons Bed and Breakfast Inn was built in 1911 by Sam Littlejohn, affiliated with the prosperous Cherokee County lumber mill. Bricked to its present Southern Colonial style, this wonderful old mansion was remodeled in 1930. The house was approved for the Tyler Register of Historic Landmarks in 1988. The curly pine woodwork that enhances the parlor, music room, dining room, and first-floor bedroom was collected and milled from locally grown timber. Tiger oak floors also are original to the house. The carriage house in the back is a two-bedroom suite. The Seasons is encircled by beds of deep pink azaleas.

Hosts: Jim and Myra Brown
Rooms: 4 (PB) $85-125
Full Breakfast
Credit Cards: A, B, C, D
Notes: 2, 5, 9, 10, 12

WIMBERLY

Southwind Bed and Breakfast

2701 FM 3237, 78676
(512) 847-5277; (800) 508-5277;
FAX (512) 847-5277

Southwind, a prayerful place, sits on twenty-five secluded acres of hills and

---

welcome; 7 Children welcome; 8 Tennis nearby; 9 Swimming nearby; 10 Golf nearby; 11 Skiing nearby; 12 May be booked through travel agent.

trees. Two long porches are provided with rocking chairs so you may enjoy the fresh air, wildlife, and sunsets. Stargazing is especially grand from the hot tub. A guest living room with fireplace and kitchen and dining room privileges complement the three spacious, private guest rooms. A full, tasty breakfast with coffee or tea served on the porch is a wonderful way to start the day at Southwind. There are two secluded cabins, each with king bed, fireplace, whirlpool tub, kitchen, and porch with swing.

Hostess: Carrie Watson
Rooms: 5 (PB) $75-90
Full Breakfast
Credit Cards: A, B, D
Notes: 2, 5, 6 and 7 (in cabins only), 8, 9, 10, 12

NOTES: Credit cards accepted: A Master Card; B Visa; C American Express; D Discover; E Diners Club; F Other; 2 Personal checks accepted; 3 Lunch available; 4 Dinner available; 5 Open all year; 6 Pets

Utah

Mi Casa Su Casa
Bed and Breakfast
Reservation Service

PO Box 950, **Tempe, AZ,** 85280-0950
(602) 990-0682; (800) 456-0682 (reservations);
FAX (602) 990-3390
E-mail: ruthy2425@aol.com

Since 1981, we proudly have listed inspected, clean, comfortable B&B homestays, inns, cottages and ranches in Arizona and the Southwest. We list about two hundred modest-to-luxurious, historic-to-contemporary B&Bs. In **Utah**, we list Alton, Cedar City, Moab, Monroe, Monticello, St. George, Salt Lake City, Springdale, Torrey, and Tropic. Most rooms have private baths and range from $50 to $275, double occupancy. Continental to gourmet breakfasts. A book with descriptions and pictures costs $9.50. Ruth Young, coordinator.

BLANDING

Grayson Country Inn
Bed and Breakfast

118 East 300 South, 84511
(801) 678-2388; (800) 365-0868

Located one block east of Main Street at 300 South. We offer country hospitality

while adding modern conveniences. A private bath and cable TV are available in eight guest rooms. A three-bedroom cottage has three baths, living room, and kitchen for larger groups or a family. We specialize in a home atmosphere!

Hosts: Dennis and Lurlene Gutke
Rooms: 11 (PB) $49-59
Full Breakfast
Credit Cards: A, B, C
Notes: 5, 6 ,7, 12

MOAB

Home Away From Home

122 Hillside Drive, 84532
(801) 259-6276

This bed and breakfast is minutes from Arches National Park, Canyonlands Air Field Airport, and Colorado River rafting, jet-skiing, and kayaking. It is within

---

welcome; 7 Children welcome; 8 Tennis nearby; 9 Swimming nearby; 10 Golf nearby; 11 Skiing nearby;
12 May be booked through travel agent.

UTAH

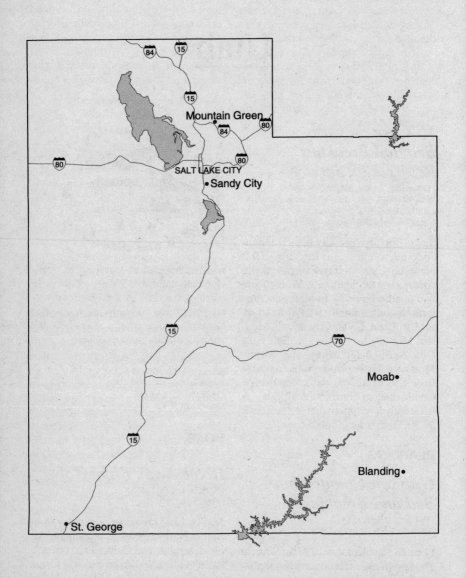

Mountain Green

SALT LAKE CITY
Sandy City

Moab

Blanding

St. George

walking distance of market and shops, mountain biking, and hiking. Horseback riding, water slides, a pool, and golf are a short distance away. Some may enjoy tent camping at the enclosed minipark backyard of the bed and breakfast. Colorado Connection for deer or elk hunting—bow or rifle. Three hours from Telluride. Ski chairlift, winter and summer. TBN dish viewing available in the large living room for guests upon request.

Host: E. M. Smith
Rooms: 4 (1PB; 3SB) $45-75
Continental Breakfast
Credit Cards: none
Notes: 2, 5, 7, 9, 10, 11, 12

Home Away From Home
(Arches National Park)

MOUNTAIN GREEN

Hubbard House Bed and Breakfast Inn

5648 W. Old Highway Road, 84050
(801) 876-2020; (800) 815-2220;
FAX (801) 876-2020

Built in the 1920s, Hubbard House has the warmth and charm of days gone by, with hardwood floors and stained-glass windows. It has awesome views of God's majestic mountains. Three ski resorts are in the area, as are fishing, boating, hiking, and golfing. Piano in dining room. Outdoor whirlpool spa. Additional rooms planned. Can accommodate horses. About a mile east from Exit 92 off I-84.

Hosts: Don and Gloria Hubbard
Rooms: 3 (PB) $60-100
Full Country Breakfast
Credit Cards: A, B, C, D
Notes: 2, 4, 5, 7, 9, 10, 11

ST. GEORGE

Greene Gate Village Historic Bed and Breakfast

76 W. Tabernacle Street, 84770
(801) 628-6999; (800) 350-6999;
FAX (801) 628-6989
E-mail: greene@greenegate.com
Web site: http://www.greenegate.com

Behind the green gates, nine beautifully restored homes provide modern comfort in pioneer elegance. Our guests love the nostalgic charm of the Bentley House with elegant Victorian decor and the quaint Tolley House, where eleven children were born and raised. The Grainery sleeps three in rooms where early settlers loaded supplies for their trek to California. The Orson Pratt Home, built by an early Mormon leader, is on the National Register of Historic Places. Greene Hedge, with one of the village's two bridal suites, was built in another part of town but was moved to Greene Gate Village in 1991. Family reunions or other large groups (up to twenty-two people) may share the comfort and

---

NOTES: Credit cards accepted: A Master Card; B Visa; C American Express; D Discover; E Diners Club; F Other; 2 Personal checks accepted; 3 Lunch available; 4 Dinner available; 5 Open all year; 6 Pets welcome; 7 Children welcome; 8 Tennis nearby; 9 Swimming nearby; 10 Golf nearby; 11 Skiing nearby; 12 May be booked through travel agent.

charm of the Greenehouse, built in 1872. The Greenehouse has a full kitchen, swimming pool, and tennis court. Greene Gate Village also caters to corporate retreats.

Hosts: John, Barbara and Sherri Greene
Rooms: 19 (PB) $55-125
Full Breakfast
Credit Cards: A, B, C, D
Notes: 2, 4, 5, 6, 7, 8, 9, 10, 11, 12

Seven Wives Inn

217 N. 100 W., 84770
(801) 628-3737; (800) 600-3737;
FAX (801) 673-0165
E-mail: seven@infowest.com

The inn consists of two adjacent pioneer adobe homes with massive hand-grained moldings framing windows and doors. Bedrooms are furnished with period antiques and handmade quilts. Some rooms have fireplaces; three have whirlpool tubs. Swimming pool on premises.

Hosts: Jay and Donna Curtis
Rooms: 13 (PB) $50-125
Full Breakfast
Credit Cards: A, B, C, D, E
Notes: 2, 5, 7, 8, 9, 10, 12

SANDY

Mountain Hollow Bed and Breakfast Inn

10209 S. Dimple Dell Road, 84092
(801) 942-3428; (800) 757-3428;
FAX (801) 943-7229
E-mail: KPL@aros.net
Web site: http://www.mountainhollow.com

Mountain Hollow is a secluded eleven-room bed and breakfast located on two wooded acres just fifteen minutes from world-class skiing, Salt Lake City attractions, hiking, mountain biking, and the beautiful Wasatch Mountains. An outdoor hot tub, game room, video library, and breakfast buffet are included for our guests' enjoyment. Come relax and watch the deer and hummingbirds!

Hosts: Kathy and Doug Larson
Rooms: 11 (4PB; 7SB) $75-175
Continental Plus Breakfast
Credit Cards: A, B, C, D
Notes: 2, 5, 7 (over 5), 8, 9, 10, 11, 12

Vermont

American Country Collection of B&Bs

1353 Union Street, **Schenectady, NY**, 12308
(518) 370-4948; (800) 810-4948;
FAX (518) 393-1634

This service provides reservations for eastern **New York**, western **Massachusetts**, and all of **Vermont**. One call does it all. Unwind at any of our more than one hundred immaculate, personally inspected bed and breakfasts and country inns. Many include fireplace, Jacuzzi, and/or Modified American Plan. Budget-minded to luxurious accommodations in urban, suburban, and rural locations. $50-200. Gift certificates available; major credit cards accepted. Carol Matos, owner.

ALBURG

Thomas Mott Homestead Bed and Breakfast

Blue Rock Road on Lake Champlain (Route 2, Box 149-B), 05440-9620
(802) 796-3736 (voice and FAX);
(800) 348-0843
Web site: http://www.go-native.com/inns/ 0162.html

Formerly an importer and distributor of fine wines, your host also enjoys gourmet cooking. His completely restored farmhouse has a guest living room with TV and fireplace overlooking the lake, game room with bumper pool and darts, and quilt decor. Full view of Mt. Mansfield and Jay Peak. One hour to Montreal/Burlington; one and a half hours to Lake Placid and Stowe. Lake activities in winter and summer. Amenities include Ben & Jerry's ice cream, lawn games, and horseshoes. Internet access; boat dock. Gift certificates available.

Host: Patrick J. Schallert
Rooms: 5 (PB) $69-89
Full Breakfast
Credit Cards: A, B, C, D
Notes: 2, 5, 7 (over 6), 8, 9, 10, 11, 12

ARLINGTON

Arlington Inn

Historic Route 7A, 05250
(802) 375-6532; (800) 443-9442
Web site: http://discover-vermont.com/Banner/ arlington.htm

A stately Greek Revival mansion set on lush, landscaped lawns. Elegantly appointed rooms filled with antiques and amenities. All rooms have private baths and AC and include breakfast. Located between Bennington and Manchester.

---

welcome; 7 Children welcome; 8 Tennis nearby; 9 Swimming nearby; 10 Golf nearby; 11 Skiing nearby; 12 May be booked through travel agent.

VERMONT

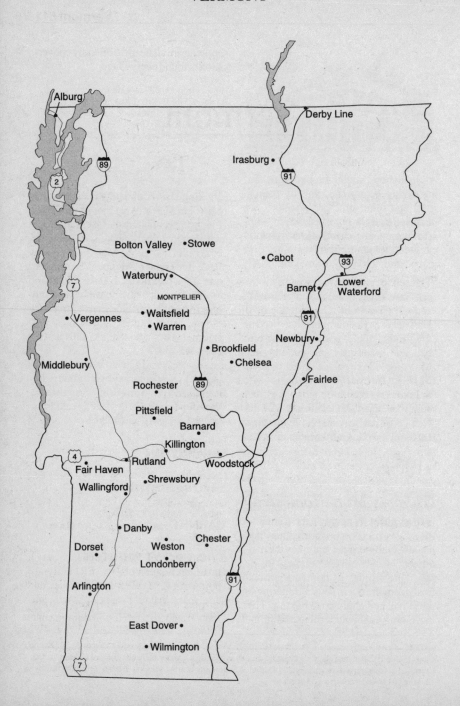

Arlington Inn

Antique shops, boutiques, museums, skiing, hiking, biking, canoeing, fly-fishing, golf, and other outdoor activities are nearby. Tennis on our private court. Outstanding cuisine is served by romantic candlelight in our award-winning, fireplaced dining room. No smoking. AAA three diamonds; Mobil three stars.

Hosts: Deborah and Mark Gagnon
Rooms: 19 (PB) $70-195
Full Breakfast
Credit Cards: A, B, C, D, E
Notes: 2 (deposit only), 4, 5, 7, 8, 9, 10, 11, 12

Hill Farm Inn

RR 2, Box 2015, 05250
(802) 375-2269; (800) 882-2545;
FAX (802) 375-9918

Hill Farm Inn is one of Vermont's original farmsteads granted from King George III in 1775. It has been an inn since 1905 and still retains the character of an old farm vacation inn on fifty beautiful acres between the Taconic and Green Mountains, with a mile of frontage on the Battenkill River. We specialize in warm country hospitality. Outside, relax and enjoy the magnificent views from our porches. Inside, savor the aromas of homemade bread fresh from the oven, soup simmering on the stove, and apple crisp baking. Hiking, biking, canoeing, fishing, skiing, and

shopping are all nearby. Friendly conversation is found everywhere.

Hosts: George and Joanne Hardy
Rooms: 13 (8PB; 5SB) $70-125
Full Hot Country Breakfast
Credit Cards: A, B, C, D
Notes: 2, 4, 5, 6 (limited), 7, 8, 9, 10, 11, 12

Hill Farm Inn

Shenandoah Farm

Route 313, 05250
(802) 375-6372

Experience New England in this lovingly restored 1820 colonial overlooking the Battenkill River. Wonderful "Americana" year-round. Full "farm fresh" breakfast is served daily and is included.

Hosts: Woody and Donna
Rooms: 5 (PB) $65-75
Full Breakfast
Credit Cards: A, B
Notes: 5, 6, 7, 8, 9, 10, 11

BARNET

The Old Homestead

PO Box 150, Route 5, 05821
(802) 633-4016; FAX (802) 633-4924

Vermont's Northeast Kingdom is truly God's Kingdom, and He will shine in your

---

NOTES: Credit cards accepted: A Master Card; B Visa; C American Express; D Discover; E Diners Club; F Other; 2 Personal checks accepted; 3 Lunch available; 4 Dinner available; 5 Open all year; 6 Pets welcome; 7 Children welcome; 8 Tennis nearby; 9 Swimming nearby; 10 Golf nearby; 11 Skiing nearby; 12 May be booked through travel agent.

smile as you enjoy antiques, treasures, collectibles, a cozy fire, a warm sunporch, and lovely gardens. Awake to the sunrise over the White Mountains and Connecticut River and the smell of coffee and fresh-baked breads. Come early and enjoy our afternoon fellowship time.

Hostess: Gail Warnaar
Rooms: 4 (2PB; 2SB) $55-70
Full Breakfast
Credit Cards: A, B, D
Notes: 2, 7, 9, 10, 11, 12

The Old Homestead

BOLTON VALLEY

Black Bear Inn

H.C. 33, Box 717, 05477
(802) 434-2126; (800) 395-6335;
FAX (802) 434-5161

Black Bear Inn, a true Vermont country inn two thousand feet above the valley floor, offers the most magnificent views and sunsets in Vermont. Enjoy more than six thousand pristine acres for hiking, biking, and New England's only "ski in, ski out" country inn for both alpine and cross-country skiing. Located only twenty minutes from Burlington (Vermont's largest city), and twenty minutes from Montpelier (the state capital). Our twenty-four-room inn offers private baths, fireplaces,

Black Bear Inn

Vermont stoves, cable TV, phones, and a romantic fireplace in our lobby. Our hot tubs and heated outdoor pool are perfect after a busy day of skiing. Black Bear Inn is the essence of Vermont hospitality.

Hosts: Ken Richardson and Suzane Wallace
Rooms: 24 (PB) $69-139
Full or Continental Breakfast
Credit Cards: A, B
Notes: 2, 4, 5, 6 (have kennel), 7, 8, 9, 10, 12

BROOKFIELD

Green Trails Inn

By the Floating Bridge, 05036
(802) 276-3412; (800) 243-3412
FAX (802) 276-3412
E-mail: greentrails@quest-net.com

Relax and be pampered. . . . Enjoy comfortable elegance and true Vermont hospitality on our seventeen-acre country estate in the heart of historic Brookfield. Outdoor lover's paradise—biking, hiking, fishing, swimming, canoeing, ice-skating, and cross-country skiing (more than thirty kilometers) from our front door. Scrumptious meals, spacious lounging areas, and comfy beds to fall into at night. Twin-, double- and queen-bedded guest rooms, some with Jacuzzis or fireplace. Fabulous antique clock collection!

Hosts: Sue and Mark Erwin
Rooms: 14 (8PB; 6SB) $79-130
Full Breakfast
Credit Cards: A, B
Notes: 2, 4, 5, 7 (10 and over), 9, 10, 11, 12

CABOT

Creamery Inn Bed and Breakfast

PO Box 187, 05647
(802) 563-2819

This bed and breakfast is not Christian in name only. Its owners have dedicated it to the Lord and put their hearts into providing an atmosphere that witnesses to the Lord's presence. Grace is offered before breakfast. Daily shared morning and evening prayer is available, if desired. The home is used for retreats and teaching seminars. Matthew 11:28: "Come unto Me, all you that labor and are heavy laden, and I will give you rest."

Hosts: Dan and Judy Lloyd
Rooms: 4 (2PB; 2SB) $55-75
Full Breakfast
Credit Cards: none
Notes: 2, 4, 5, 7, 8, 9, 11, 12

Creamery Inn Bed and Breakfast

Shire Inn

CHELSEA

Shire Inn

Main Street, 05038
(800) 441-6908; fax (802) 685-3871
E-mail: shireinn@sover.net
Web site: http://www.innbook.com/shire.html

An 18th-century Adams-style inn set on twenty-three acres in the heart of Vermont. Large guest rooms have high ceilings and tall windows. Canopied beds furnished with hand-ironed, one-hundred-percent cotton sheets. Fireplaces. Casual dining not open to the public. You'll enjoy the best of small Vermont country inn ambience in a wonderfully vintage village. Only a few fellow guests. Your home base for exploring the unspoiled parts of Vermont.

Hosts: Karen and Jay Keller
Rooms: 6 (PB) $90-130
Full Breakfast
Credit Cards: A, B, D
Notes: 2, 4, 5, 9, 10, 11

CHESTER

Greenleaf Inn

PO Box 188, 05143
(802) 875-3171

Beautiful 1860s Victorian just off the village green. Five spacious, quiet guest

welcome; 7 Children welcome; 8 Tennis nearby; 9 Swimming nearby; 10 Golf nearby; 11 Skiing nearby; 12 May be booked through travel agent.

rooms tastefully decorated with antiques, queen-size beds and country quilts. All have private baths. Full Vermont breakfast in our sunny dining room always is included with your stay. Dinner available nightly at our restaurant on the Chester village green. Walk to churches, gift shops, antiques. Swimming, boating, golfing, hiking, biking, and cross-country and downhill skiing are all nearby. Gift certificates are available for that special someone.

Hosts: Jerry and Robin Szawerda
Rooms: 5 (PB) $85-95
Full Breakfast
Credit Cards: A, B, C, D
Notes: 2, 4, 5, 7, 8, 9, 10, 11

Henry Farm Inn

PO Box 646, 05143
(802) 875-2674; (800) 723-8213;
FAX (802) 875-2674

The Henry Farm Inn supplies the beauty of Vermont with old-time simplicity. Nestled on fifty acres of rolling hills and meadows, assuring peace and quiet. Spacious rooms, private baths, country sitting areas, and a sunny dining room all guarantee a feeling of home. Come and visit for a day or more!

Hosts: The Bowmans
Rooms: 7 (PB) $50-90
Full Breakfast
Credit Cards: A, B, C
Notes: 2, 5, 7, 8, 9, 10, 11, 12

Hugging Bear Inn and Shoppe

Main Street, 05143
(802) 875-2412; (800) 325-0519

Teddy bears peek out the windows and are tucked in all the corners of this beautiful Victorian house built in 1850. If you love teddy bears, you'll love the Hugging Bear. There are six guest rooms with private shower baths and a teddy bear in every bed. Full breakfast and afternoon snack are served.

Hosts: Georgette, Diane, and Paul Thomas
Rooms: 6 (PB) $75-95
Full Breakfast
Credit Cards: A, B, C, D
Notes: 2, 5, 6 (limited), 7, 8, 9, 10, 11

CUTTINGSVILLE

Buckmaster Inn

Lincoln Hill Road, RR 1, **Shrewsbury**, 05738
(802) 492-3485

The Buckmaster Inn (1801) was an early stagecoach stop in Shrewsbury. Standing on a knoll overlooking a picturesque barn scene and rolling hills, the inn is situated in the Green Mountains. A center hall, grand staircase, and wide-pine floors grace the home, which is decorated with family antiques and crewel handiwork done by your hostess. Extremely large, airy rooms; wood-burning stove; four fireplaces; and two large porches.

Hosts: Sam and Grace Husselman
Rooms: 3 (2PB; 1SB) $60-70
Full Breakfast
Credit Cards: none (traveler's checks accepted)
Notes: 2, 5, 7, 8, 9, 10, 11

DANBY

Silas Griffith Inn

RR 1, Box 66F, 05739
(802) 293-5567; (800) 545-1509;
FAX (802) 293-5559

Built by Vermont's first millionaire, this Victorian inn was built in 1891 in the heart

Silas Griffith Inn

of the Green Mountains, with a spectacular mountain view. It features seventeen delightful, antique-furnished rooms and a fireplace in the living and dining room. Hiking, skiing, and antiquing nearby. Come and enjoy our elegant meals and New England hospitality.

Hosts: Paul and Lois Dansereau
Rooms: 17 (14PB; 3SB) $72-90
Full Breakfast
Credit Cards: A, B
Notes: 2, 4, 5, 7, 9, 10, 11, 12

DERBY LINE

Derby Village Inn

46 Main Street, PO Box 1085, 05830
(802) 873-3604; FAX (802) 873-3047
E-mail: dvibandb@together.net

Come visit us in the Northeast Kingdom where the rivers run north and the views of the mountains provide peace and tranquillity. Derby Line borders Quebec, Ontario, and is at the midpoint between the equator and the north pole. The Northeast Kingdom is host to many outdoor activities. We invite you to enjoy our warm

hospitality and delicious home cooking at our relaxing and friendly inn.

Hostesses: Catherine McCormick and Sheila Steplar
Rooms: 5 (PB) $65-90
Full Breakfast
Credit Cards: A, B, C, D
Notes: 2, 5, 7, 8, 9, 10, 11, 12

DORSET

Inn at West View Farm

Route 30, 05251
(802) 867-5715; (800) 769-4903;
FAX (802) 867-0468
E-mail: westview@vermontel.com
Web site: http://www.vtweb.com/innatwestviewfarm

The Inn at West View Farm enjoys a tradition of fine hospitality and has welcomed guests since the turn of the century. Our restored farmhouse offers the amenities of a full-service inn in a beautiful pastoral setting and has been chosen by *Glamour Magazine* as one of Vermont's great romantic inns. Our historic buildings have undergone loving restoration and await your arrival. Come experience the tranquillity of a Vermont vacation. In summer,

Inn at West View Farm

welcome; 7 Children welcome; 8 Tennis nearby; 9 Swimming nearby; 10 Golf nearby; 11 Skiing nearby; 12 May be booked through travel agent.

enjoy our wraparound porch and the shade of the majestic maples that dot our lawns. In winter, cozy up to the fireplaces, unwind in the tavern or relax in our cheerful sunroom. AAA- and Mobil-rated.

Hosts: Dorothy and Helmut Stein
Rooms: 10 (PB) $95-145
Full Breakfast
Credit Cards: A, B, C
Notes: 2, 4, 5, 8, 9, 10, 11

EAST DOVER

Cooper Hill Inn

PO Box 146, Cooper Hill Road, 05341
(802) 348-6333; (800) 783-3229

Set high on a hill in southern Vermont's Green Mountains, Cooper Hill Inn commands a view to the east proclaimed by the *Boston Globe* as "one of the most spectacular mountain panoramas in all New England." A small portion of the inn was a farmhouse built in 1797. The inn has ten rooms, all with private baths. The atmosphere is always homey and informal. Country breakfast included in rate. Families welcome.

Hosts: Pat and Marilyn Hunt
Rooms: 10 (PB) $68-110
Full Breakfast
Credit Cards: A, B, D
Notes: 2, 4, 5, 7, 8, 9, 10, 11, 12

FAIR HAVEN

Maplewood Inn

Route 22A S., 05743
(802) 265-8039; (800) 253-7729;
FAX (802) 265-8210
E-mail: maplewd@sover.net
Web site: http://www.sover.net/~maplewd

Rediscover romance in this exquisite, National Historic Register Greek Revival. Elegant rooms and suites boast antiques, fireplaces, AC, cable TVs, radios, optional phone, and turndown service. Gathering room with library, parlor with games and complimentary cordials. Hot beverages and snacks. Pet boarding. Near lakes, skiing, dining, attractions. AAA three diamonds, Mobil three stars, ABBA three crowns. Recommended by more than thirty guidebooks. A four-season inn!

Hosts: Cindy and Doug Baird
Rooms: 5 (PB) $80-135
Continental Plus Breakfast
Credit Cards: A, B, C, D, E, F
Notes: 2, 5, 7 (over 5), 8, 9, 10, 11, 12

FAIRLEE

Silver Maple Lodge and Cottages

RR 1, Box 8, 05045
(802) 333-4326; (800) 666-1946

A historic bed and breakfast country inn is located in a four-season recreational

Cooper Hill Inn

area. Enjoy canoeing, fishing, golf, tennis, and skiing within a few miles of the lodge. Visit nearby flea markets and country auctions. Choose a newly renovated room in our antique farmhouse or a handsome, pine-paneled cottage room. Three cottages with working fireplaces. Many fine restaurants are nearby. Darmouth College is seventeen miles away. Also offered are hot-air balloon packages, inn-to-inn bicycling, canoeing, and walking tours. Brochures available.

Hosts: Sharon and Scott Wright
Rooms: 16 (14PB; 2SB) $54-79
Continental Breakfast
Credit Cards: A, B, C, D
Notes: 2, 5, 6 (in cottages), 7, 8, 9, 10, 11, 12

IRASBURG

Brick House
Bed and Breakfast

Route 14 (just off the Green), PO Box 33, 05845
(802) 754-2108 (voice and FAX)
E-mail: Vermont.Life@connriver.net
Web site: http://www.connriver.net/VermontLife/
    Home

This 1870s brick Victorian home is located in the historic town of Irasburg in the beautiful Northeast Kingdom. One bedroom has twin beds and a private bath. Room

Brick House Bed and Breakfast

with lace-topped canopy bed, queen-size, and full-size antique brass bedroom share a bath. A full breakfast is served country-style and is meant to spoil our guests. In business since 1988. Guest comment: "Everything was wonderful. Every need and more was taken care of."

Hosts: Jo and Roger Sweatt
Rooms: 3 (1PB; 2SB) $45-50
Full Breakfast
Credit Cards: none
Notes: 2, 5, 6, 7, 9, 10, 11

The Peak Chalet

KILLINGTON

The Peak Chalet

PO Box 511, South View Path, 05751
(802) 422-4278

A four-room bed and breakfast located within the beautiful Green Mountains. The exterior is authentically European Alpine. The interior is furnished with a fine country inn flavor and reflects high quality with attention to detail. We offer panoramic mountain views with a cozy stone fireplace to unwind by. All rooms have queen-size beds and private baths. Centrally located within Killington Ski Resort, this is a truly relaxing experience.

Hosts: Diane and Gregory Becker
Rooms: 4 (PB) $50-110
Continental Breakfast
Credit Cards: A, B, C, E
Notes: 2, 5, 7 (over 12), 8, 9, 10, 11, 12

welcome; 7 Children welcome; 8 Tennis nearby; 9 Swimming nearby; 10 Golf nearby; 11 Skiing nearby; 12 May be booked through travel agent.

LONDONBERRY

The Blue Gentian Lodge

RR 1, Box 29, 05148
(802) 824-5908; (800) 456-2405;
FAX (802) 824-3531
E-mail: kenalberti@esi.com
Web site: http://ourworld.compuserve.com/
    homepages/kenalberti

A special place to stay, nestled at the foot of Magic Mountain. All rooms have private baths and cable color TV, and include a full breakfast in the dining room. Seasonal activities on the grounds, a swimming pool, and walking trails. Recreation Room offers ping-pong, bumper pool, board games, and library. There is golf, tennis, fishing, outlet shopping, antiquing, horseback riding, and skiing (downhill and cross-country) nearby.

Hosts: The Alberti Family
Rooms: 13 (PB) $50-80
Full Breakfast
Credit Cards: A, B
Notes: 2, 4, 5, 7, 8, 9, 10, 11

LOWER WATERFORD

Rabbit Hill Inn

Box 55, Route 18, 05848
(802) 748-5168; (800) 76-BUNNY;
FAX (802) 748-8342

Full of whimsical and charming surprises, this Federal-period inn, established in 1795, has been lavished with love and attention. Many guest rooms have fireplaces and canopied beds. Chamber music, candlelight gourmet dining, and turndown service make this an enchanting and romantic hideaway in a tiny, restored village overlooking the mountains. Breakfast and dinner included. Award-winning, nation-

ally acclaimed inn—rated four stars by Mobil and four diamonds by AAA. Our service is inspired by Philippians 2:7. Closed the first two weeks of November and all of April.

Hosts: Brian and Leslie Mulcahy
Rooms: 21 (PB) $189-289
Full Breakfast
Credit Cards: A, B, C
Notes: 2, 3 (picnic), 4, 8, 9 (on site), 10, 11
    (on site), 12

The Middlebury Inn

MIDDLEBURY

The Middlebury Inn

14 Courthouse Square (on the greens), 05753
(802) 388-4961; (800) 842-4666;
FAX (802) 388-4563
E-mail: midinnvt@sover.net
Web site: http://www.middleburyinn.com

Step inside for a memorable experience! Adorned with bright yellow-and-white awnings, representing friendly and cheerful hospitality, the Middlebury Inn has presided on the village greens for 170 years. Elegant rooms, private baths, modern amenities, fine dining, gift shop. In your leisure time, visit the historic, lively, lovely college town of Middlebury: museums, boutiques, art center, and waterfall. Easily accessible to Burlington, Shelburne

---

NOTES: Credit cards accepted: A Master Card; B Visa; C American Express; D Discover; E Diners Club; F Other; 2 Personal checks accepted; 3 Lunch available; 4 Dinner available; 5 Open all year; 6 Pets

Museum, Lake Champlain. Member of AAA and Historic Hotels of America.

Hosts: Frank and Jane Emanuel
Rooms: 80 (PB) $90-260
Continental Breakfast (Full Breakfast at extra cost)
Credit Cards: A, B, C, D, E
Notes: 3, 4, 5, 6 (limited), 7, 8, 9, 10, 11, 12

NEWBURY

Peach Brook Inn Bed and Breakfast

Doe Hill, 05051
(802) 866-3389

Our bed and breakfast is just off Vermont Route 5, which follows the Connecticut River. It is on a country lane with small farms and a variety of farm animals, plus a great farm stand. The house, colonial-style with a carriage house and barn, is on a bluff, giving us a panoramic view of the river, mountains, a village, and farmland. Built in the 1780s, the house gives you a feeling of bygone years with its beams, fireplaces, and antiques. Guests describe the Inn as "beautiful," "peaceful," and "home."

Hosts: Joyce and Ray Emery
Rooms: 3 (1PB; 2SB) $50-70
Full Breakfast
Credit Cards: none
Notes: 2, 5, 7 (over 10), 8, 9, 10, 11 (cross-country)

PITTSFIELD

Swiss Farm Lodge

PO Box 630, 05762
(802) 746-8341; (800) 245-5126

Working Hereford beef farm. Enjoy the casual, family-type atmosphere in our living room with fireplace and TV or in the game room. Home-cooked meals and baking, served family-style. Our own maple syrup, jams, and jellies. Walk-in cooler available for guests' use. Two rooms have queen beds. Cross-country trails on site. B&B available all year. MAP provided November to April only. Mountain bike trails close by. Owned and operated by the same family for fifty years. Lower rates for children in the same room as parents.

Hosts: Mark and Sandy Begin
Rooms: 17 (14PB; 3SB) $50-70
Full Breakfast
Credit Cards: A, B
Notes: 2, 4, 5, 7, 8, 9, 10, 11, 12

Liberty Hill Farm

ROCHESTER

Liberty Hill Farm

RR 1, Box 158, 05767
(802) 767-3926

Come enjoy exploring our award-winning dairy farm in the Green Mountains. Families are welcome to share in the barn chores. Excellent home-cooked meals (full breakfast and dinner included in price) are served family-style in our 1825 farmhouse. Hiking, fishing, swimming, skiing, horseback riding, and golf available. Refresh and restore your spirit and become a member of our "family."

Hosts: Bob and Beth Kennett
Rooms: 7 (SB) $100-120
Full Breakfast and Dinner
Credit Cards: none
Notes: 2, 4, 5, 7, 8, 9, 10, 11, 12

The Inn at Rutland

RUTLAND

The Inn at Rutland

70 N. Main Street (Route 7), 05701
(802) 773-0575; (800) 808-0575;
FAX (802) 775-3506
E-mail: InnatRutland@worldnet.att.net

The inn is an 1890s Victorian mansion that has been restored carefully to its original, elegant charm. The interior is rich with architectural details, such as the leaded-glass window over the formal staircase. All rooms have private baths, remote TVs, and telephones. Breakfast is served in our formal dining room. Relax on the front porch and take in the great views. Close to all Vermont attractions and within walking distance of fine shopping and restau-

rants. Only minutes from three major ski areas. We are a nonsmoking inn.

Hosts: Bob and Tanya Liberman
Rooms: 9 (PB) $69-179
Full Breakfast, weekend; Continental, weekday
Credit Cards: A, B, C, D, E
Notes: 2, 5, 7, 8, 9, 10, 11, 12

STOWE

Brass Lantern Inn

717 Maple Street, 05672
(802) 253-2229; (800) 729-2980;
FAX (802) 253-7425
E-mail: brasslatrn@aol.com
Web site: http://www.stoweinfo.com/saa/
   brasslantern

Award-winning traditional bed and breakfast inn, in the heart of Stowe overlooking Mt. Mansfield, Vermont's most prominent mountain. The inn features period antiques, handmade quilts, local artisan wares, and AC. Most rooms have views; some have fireplaces; some have whirlpools. A hint of romance abounds in each room—an intimate inn for romantics. Special packages include honeymoon/anniversary, romance, skiing, golf, historic, and more. Nonsmoking.

Host: Andy Aldrich
Rooms: 9 (PB) $80-225
Full Breakfast
Credit Cards: A, B, C
Notes: 2, 5, 8, 9, 10, 11, 12

The Siebeness Inn

3681 Mountain Road, 05672
(802) 253-8942; (800) 426-9001;
FAX (802) 253-9232
E-mail: siebenes@together.net
Web site: http://stoweinfo.com/saa/siebeness

A warm welcome awaits you at our charming country inn nestled in the foot-

---

NOTES: Credit cards accepted: A Master Card; B Visa; C American Express; D Discover; E Diners Club; F Other; 2 Personal checks accepted; 3 Lunch available; 4 Dinner available; 5 Open all year; 6 Pets

hills of Mt. Mansfield. Romantic rooms have country antiques, private baths, and air-conditioning; some have fireplaces. New mountain-view suites have Jacuzzis, fireplaces, featherbeds—and views! Hearty New England breakfast. Relax in our outdoor hot tub in winter or our pool with mountain views in summer. Fireplace in lounge. Bike, walk, or cross-country ski from the inn on a recreational path. Honeymoon, golf, and ski packages.

Hosts: Sue and Nils Andersen
Rooms: 12 (PB) $70-200
Full Breakfast
Credit Cards: A, B, C, D
Notes: 2, 5, 7, 8, 9, 10, 11, 12

VERGENNES

Strong House Inn

82 W. Main Street, 05491
(802) 877-3337; FAX (802) 877-2599
Web site: http://www.flinet.com/~bargieleer/
shi_inn.htm

Experience elegant lodging in a grand 1834 Federal home listed on the National Register of Historic Places. The inn, fully air-conditioned, is situated on six acres with walking trails and gardens, and offers snowshoeing and sledding in the winter. Located in the heart of the Champlain Valley, the area offers cycling, golf, skiing, and the Shelburne Museum. All rooms have private baths. Rates include afternoon snacks and beverages and a full country breakfast.

Hosts: Mary Bargiel
Rooms: 8 (PB) $75-165
Full Breakfast
Credit Cards: A, B, C
Notes: 5, 9, 10, 11, 12

Mad River Inn

WAITSFIELD

Mad River Inn

PO Box 75, Tremblay Road, 05673
(802) 496-7900; (800) 832-8278

Romantic 1860s country Victorian inn along Mad River. Elegant but comfortable. Picturesque mountain views, flower-filled porches, gardens, and gazebo. Ten guest rooms, feather beds, private baths, Jacuzzi, and family room with cable TV and billiards. Gourmet breakfast and afternoon tea. Recreation path and swimming along the river. Horseback riding, golf, tennis, Sugarbush and Mad River Glen Ski Resorts, Ben & Jerry's, and Cold Hollow cider mill are nearby. Weddings and groups welcome.

Host: Luc Maranda and Rita Maranda Brown
Rooms: 10 (PB) $69-125
Full Gourmet Breakfast
Credit Cards: A, B, C
Notes: 2, 5, 7, 8, 9, 10, 11, 12

Mountain View Inn

RD 1, Box 69, 05673
(802) 496-2426

The Mountain View Inn is an old farmhouse, circa 1826, that was made into a

welcome; 7 Children welcome; 8 Tennis nearby; 9 Swimming nearby; 10 Golf nearby; 11 Skiing nearby; 12 May be booked through travel agent.

lodge in 1948 to accommodate skiers at nearby Mad River Glen. Today it is a country inn with seven rooms. Meals are served family-style around the antique harvest table where good fellowship prevails. Sip mulled cider around a crackling fire in our living room when the weather turns chilly.

Hosts: Fred and Susan Spencer
Rooms: 7 (PB) $80-140 double
Full Breakfast
Credit Cards: none
Notes: 2, 5, 7, 8, 9, 10, 11, 12

I.B. Munson House B&B Inn

WALLINGFORD

I.B. Munson House Bed and Breakfast Inn

7 S. Main Street, 05773
(802) 446-2860; (888) 519-3771;
FAX (802) 446-3336
Web site: http://www.ibmunsoninn.com

The I.B. Munson House is an 1856 Italianate Victorian totally and lovingly restored in 1992. It features high ceilings, beautiful chandeliers, and five operational, wood-burning fireplaces. Guest rooms and common rooms are finely decorated and furnished with comfortable period antiques and fine art. The grounds and gardens are expertly maintained. Off-street parking is provided for our guests. The inn is located in a quaint, historic village. Boyhood home of Paul Harris, founder of Rotary International.

Hosts: Phil and Karen Pimental
Rooms: 7 (PB) $85-145
Full Gourmet Breakfast
Credit Cards: A, B, C, D
Notes: 2, 5, 7 (12 and older), 8, 9, 10, 11, 12

WARREN

Beaver Pond Farm Inn

Golf Course Road, 05674
(802) 583-2861; FAX (802) 583-2860
E-mail: beaverpond@madriver.com
Web site: http://www.beaverpondfarminn.com

Beaver Pond Farm Inn, a small, gracious country inn near the Sugarbush ski area, is located one hundred yards from the first tee of the Sugarbush Golf Course, transformed into twenty-five kilometers of cross-country ski trails in the winter. *Bed and Breakfast in New England* calls it "the best of the best." Rooms have down comforters and beautiful views. Hearty breakfasts are served, and snacks are enjoyed by the fireplace. Continental dinners are offered three times a week during the winter. Hiking, biking, soaring, and fishing are nearby. Bob will take guests out for fly-fishing instruction. Ski and golf packages are available.

Hosts: Betty and Bob Hansen
Rooms: 6 (4PB; 2SB) $72-104
Full Breakfast
Credit Cards: A, B
Notes: 2, 7 (over 7), 8, 9, 10, 11, 12

NOTES: Credit cards accepted: A Master Card; B Visa; C American Express; D Discover; E Diners Club; F Other; 2 Personal checks accepted; 3 Lunch available; 4 Dinner available; 5 Open all year; 6 Pets

The Powder Hound

Route 100, PO Box 369, 05674
(802) 496-5100; (800) 548-4022;
FAX (802) 496-5163
Web site: http://www.powderhoundinn.com

Enjoy the charm of a country inn with the privacy of your own condo. Two-room suites include kitchenette, cable TV, and deck. Guests may enjoy the outdoor hot tub, pool, and tennis court. Hearty breakfast available at the inn. Dinners are available to groups of twenty or more. The inn features a pub with full bar, pool table, and fun. Close to Sugarbush in the scenic Mad River Valley. Lots to see and do year-round. Pets are always welcome for a small fee. Great for weddings and family reunions!

Hosts: Robin and Cindy Lehman
Rooms: 44 (PB) $68-132
Full Breakfast
Credit Cards: A, B, C, D
Notes: 2, 4 (to groups), 5, 6, 7, 8, 9, 10, 11, 12

WATERBURY (STOWE)

Grünberg Haus Bed and Breakfast and Cabins

RR 2, Box 1595-CB, 05676
(802) 244-7726; (800) 800-7760;
FAX (802) 244-1283
E-mail: grunhaus@aol.com

Grünberg Haus is a handbuilt Austrian inn offering romantic guest rooms (each with balcony, antiques, comforters, and quilts), secluded cabins (each with fireplace and mountain-view deck) and a carriage house suite (with sky window, kitchen, sitting area, and two balconies). The central location is close to Stowe, Burlington, Sugarbush, and Montpelier. All accommodations include a full, musical breakfast. Enjoy our Jacuzzi, sauna, BYOB pub, fireplaces, tennis court, and groomed cross-country ski trails. Help Mark feed the chickens.

Hosts: Chris Sellers and Mark Frohman
Rooms: 15 (10PB; 5SB) $55-140
Full Musical Breakfast
Credit Cards: A, B, D
Notes: 2, 5, 7, 8, 9, 10, 11, 12

Inn at Blush Hill

RR 1, Box 1266, 05676
(802) 244-7529; (800) 736-7522;
FAX (802) 244-7314
E-mail: innatbh@aol.com

Inn at Blush Hill Bed and Breakfast, circa 1790, sits on five acres, high on a hilltop, with unsurpassed views of the mountains. Choose from five individually decorated guest rooms with private baths and featuring colonial antiques, canopy beds, down comforters, and a fireplace or Jacuzzi tub. The large common rooms are spacious and warm, filled with books, antiques, and fireplaces. A full breakfast, featuring many Vermont specialty food products, is served by the garden in summer and fireside in winter. The inn is located "back to back" with Ben & Jerry's ice cream factory, and the skiing at Stowe and Sugarbush is only minutes away. AAA- and Mobil-rated.

Hostess: Pamela Gosselin
Rooms: 5 (PB) $59-130
Full Breakfast
Credit Cards: A, B, C, D
Notes: 2, 5, 7 (over 6), 8, 9, 10, 11, 12

welcome; 7 Children welcome; 8 Tennis nearby; 9 Swimming nearby; 10 Golf nearby; 11 Skiing nearby; 12 May be booked through travel agent.

WESTMINSTER

Blue Haven Christian Bed and Breakfast

6963 U.S. Route 5, 05158
(802) 463-9008; (800) 228-9008;
FAX (802) 463-1454

Explore Vermont's beauty from our 1830 restored schoolhouse. Experience canopy beds, hand-painted touches, and a big country kitchen where hearth-baked Vermont breakfasts are served. Have tea time treats at the antique glass-laden sideboard, or in the ruddy pine common room. Expect a peaceful and pleasant time here. Christian fellowship available. Open to one and all in God's love. Please come!

Hosts: Helene Champagne
Rooms: 6 (4PB; 2SB) $55-85
Full Breakfast, weekends; Continental, weekdays
Credit Cards: A, B, C
Notes: 2, 5, 7, 8, 9, 10, 11, 12

WESTON

The Colonial House

287 Route 100, 05161
(802) 824-6286; (800) 639-5033;
FAX (802) 824-3934
E-mail: cohoinn@sover.net
Web site: http://www.sover.net/~cohoinn

The Colonial House is a unique country inn and motel offering a full breakfast with its rooms. Dinner is available on Friday and Saturday nights year-round and midweek during the summer, fall, and winter holiday periods. Rooms are light and airy. The guest living room has an attached solarium where coffee, tea, and fresh-baked goods are offered each afternoon. Con-venient to all the attractions of southern Vermont.

Hosts: John and Betty Nunnikhoven
Rooms: 15 (9PB; 6SB) $50-88
Full Breakfast
Credit Cards: A, B, D
Notes: 2, 4, 5, 7, 8, 9, 10, 11

WILMINGTON

Shearer Hill Farm

PO Box 1453, 05363
(802) 464-8075; (800) 437-3104
E-mail: ppuseyshf@aol.com
or shfpusey@sover.net

Wake to the aroma of freshly brewed coffee, homemade muffins, and bread at this small working farm on a quiet, pristine country road. Large rooms, delicious Vermont breakfast. In summer, enjoy the Marlboro Music Festival, golf, swimming, fishing, horseback riding, hiking. In winter, enjoy groomed cross-country ski trails on the property and snowmobiling. Near Mt. Snow ski area. Distances: 210 miles to NYC, 120 to Boston, 70 to Albany.

Hosts: Bill and Patti Pusey
Rooms: 6 (PB) $80
Full Vermont Breakfast
Credit Cards: A, B, C, D
Notes: 2, 5, 7, 8, 9, 10, 11, 12

The White House of Wilmington

PO Box 757, Route 9 E., 05363
(802) 464-2135; (800) 541-2135;
FAX (802) 464-5222
E-mail: whitehse@sover.net
Web site: http://www.sover.net/~dvalnews/
    whitehouse.html

The White House of Wilmington—voted "one of the most romantic Inns. . ." (N.Y.

NOTES: Credit cards accepted: A Master Card; B Visa; C American Express; D Discover; E Diners Club; F Other; 2 Personal checks accepted; 3 Lunch available; 4 Dinner available; 5 Open all year; 6 Pets

Times). The 1915 Victorian mansion, converted to an elegant country inn in 1978, sits on the crest of a high, rolling hill amid bubbling fountains and formal gardens. Sixteen elegant guest rooms are available in the main inn, nine with fireplaces and four with two-person whirlpool tubs. Seven rooms are at the adjacent guest house, all with private baths. Award-winning cuisine served by romantic candlelight in front of roaring fireplaces in three dining rooms. Full-service patio lounge. Indoor and outdoor pools, whirlpool and sauna. Cross-country ski touring center on site.

Host: Robert Grinold
Rooms: 23 (PB) $98-195 p.n.d.o.
Full Breakfast
Credit Cards: A, B, C, D, E
Notes: 2, 3, 4, 5, 7, 8, 9, 10, 11, 12

Canterbury House

WOODSTOCK

Canterbury House

43 Pleasant Street, 05091
(802) 457-3077; (800) 390-3077

This 115-year-old Victorian town house is just a stroll from the village green and fine dining. The inn is beautifully decorated with era antiques and is for the dis-

criminating traveler. The inn has won awards from *Yankee* magazine and the American B&B Association, and it is recommended as the best value in town by *Glamour* magazine. Each room is decorated to a different theme. Ten-percent discount for three or more days, except September 15 through October 22. No smoking.

Hosts: Fred and Celeste Holden
Rooms: 8 (PB) $90-155
Full Breakfast
Credit Cards: A, B
Notes: 2, 5, 7 (over 8), 8, 9, 10, 11, 12

Deer Brook Inn

HCR 68, Box 443, Route 4 W., 05091
(802) 672-3713

Handmade quilts, original pine floors, and an immaculately maintained country decor are among the charming features of this 1820 colonial farmhouse. Our five spacious guest rooms, one of which is a two-room suite, have private baths and queen- or king-size beds. Enjoy a crackling fire in the winter or a view of the Ottauquechee River from the porch in the summer. A bountiful breakfast provides the perfect start for your day. Deer Brook Inn is located on five acres, five minutes west of Woodstock Village, fifteen minutes east of Killington ski area. Children are welcome. No pets, but please share our golden retriever. Smoking outside on the porch only. AAA three stars; ABBA excellent rating.

Hosts: Brian and Rosemary McGinty
Rooms: 5 (PB) $70-125
Full Breakfast
Credit Cards: A, B
Notes: 2, 5, 7, 8, 9, 10, 11, 12

welcome; 7 Children welcome; 8 Tennis nearby; 9 Swimming nearby; 10 Golf nearby; 11 Skiing nearby; 12 May be booked through travel agent.

The Maple Leaf Inn

PO Box 273, **Barnard**, 05031
(802) 234-5342; (800) 51-MAPLE
E-mail: mapleafinn@aol.com
Web site: http://www.mapleleafinn.com

The Maple Leaf Inn is an elegant Victorian-style inn resplendent with its gables, dormers, wraparound porch, gazebo, gingerbread trim, and soaring chimneys, nestled within sixteen acres of maple and birch trees. Most of our guest rooms have king-size beds, wood-burning fireplaces, TV/VCRs, telephones, and whirlpool tubs. Stenciling, stitchery, and handmade quilts blend with antique and reproduction furnishings to give each guest room a warm and welcoming individuality. The aroma of our gourmet breakfast will entice you to our dining room for breakfast where your candlelit table awaits. The Maple Leaf Inn has been honored with the AAA four-diamond award.

Hosts: Gary and Janet Robison
Rooms: 7 (PB) $100-175
Gourmet Breakfast
Credit Cards: A, B, C, D, E, F (JCB)
Notes: 2, 5, 8, 9, 10, 11, 12

The Woodstocker Bed and Breakfast

61 River Street (Route 4), 05091
(802) 457-3896; FAX (802) 457-3897

This delightful bed and breakfast sits snugly at the foot of Mt. Tom in one of the country's most picturesque villages. It offers a casual, unpretentious atmosphere where everyone feels welcome. The rooms are exceptionally large and tastefully appointed. The full breakfast buffet and afternoon refreshments are always delicious. In-room kitchens are available—particularly nice for families traveling with small children. The private, five-person whirlpool is a big hit, especially with athletic travelers who spend their days bicycling Vermont country roads or skiing one of many nearby mountains.

Hosts: Tom and Nancy Blackford
Rooms: 9 (PB) $85-145
Full Breakfast
Credit Cards: A, B
Notes: 2, 5, 7, 8, 9, 10, 11, 12

NOTES: Credit cards accepted: A Master Card; B Visa; C American Express; D Discover; E Diners Club; F Other; 2 Personal checks accepted; 3 Lunch available; 4 Dinner available; 5 Open all year; 6 Pets

Virginia

ALSO SEE LISTINGS UNDER DISTRICT OF COLUMBIA.

BASYE

Sky Chalet Country Inn and Restaurant

PO Box 300, Route 263, 280 Sky Chalet Lane, 22810
(540) 856-2147; FAX (540) 856-2436
E-mail: skychalet@skychalet.com
Web site: http://www.skychalet.com

Come to Sky Chalet Country Inn and Restaurant, where spectacular panoramic views, comfortable mountaintop lodging, scrumptious food, gracious service, a charming pub, rustic atmosphere, tranquillity, fireplace, romance, and history all come together. Sky Chalet was built on the mountaintop in 1937 by Germans. Its views, architecture, and hospitality momentarily may make you feel you are in Switzerland—but you are in the beautiful Shenandoah Valley. In addition to rocking chairs, hammocks, and a slow pace, you'll enjoy the area's hiking, snow skiing, grass skiing, golf, miniature golf, horseback riding, tennis, swimming (pool and lake), windsurfing, fishing, canoeing, treasure hunting at the local antique and craft shops, and flea markets. Area attractions include many caverns, vineyards, Skyline Drive, George Washington National Forest, Shenandoah Valley Music Festival, and historic Orkney Springs. Civil War battlefields and museums. We welcome couples, families, and small seminar and special interest groups.

Hosts: Ken and Mona Seay
Rooms: 10 (PB) $34-79
Continental Breakfast
Credit Cards: A, B, D, E
Notes: 2, 4, 5, 6 (with notice), 7, 8, 9, 10, 11, 12

BERRYVILLE

The Battletown Inn

102 W. Main Street, 22611
(540) 955-4100; (800) 282-4106;
FAX (540) 955-0127
E-mail: susie-q@shentel.com
Web site: http://battletowninn.com

Full-service country inn with twelve antique-appointed rooms. All have private baths. Serving lunch and dinner in our main dining rooms, or on the garden patio. Cozy Gray Ghost Tavern upstairs for casual dining. Jazz on Wednesday evenings. We serve new American cuisine combined with old-fashioned southern

---

welcome; 7 Children welcome; 8 Tennis nearby; 9 Swimming nearby; 10 Golf nearby; 11 Skiing nearby; 12 May be booked through travel agent.

VIRGINIA

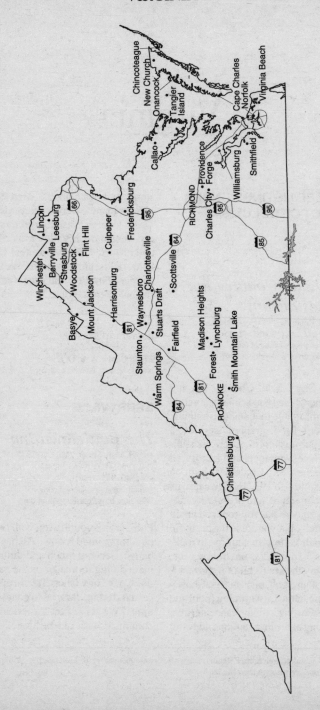

hospitality. The inn is located forty-five minutes from the DC metro area in the Shenandoah Valley.

Hostess: Susi Bailey
Rooms: 12 (PB) $80-105
Continental Breakfast
Credit Cards: A, B, C, D, E
Notes: 2, 3, 4, 5, 7, 8, 9, 10, 11, 12

Blue Ridge B&B Reservation Service

Rocks and Rills Farm, Route 2, Box 3895, 22611
(540) 955-1246 (voice and FAX); (800) 296-1246

Beautiful antique-filled Colonial Williamsburg reproduction nestled in the foothills of the Blue Ridge Mountains, near the Shenandoah River on eleven acres of fragrant Christmas trees. Perfect getaway; ideal for weekend bikers and hikers. Only ninety minutes from Washington, DC. Also a reservation service for numerous host homes.

Hostess: Rita Z. Duncan
Rooms: numerous (most PB) $50-150
Full Breakfast
Credit Cards: A, B
Notes: 2, 3 and 4 (some, with reservations), 5, 6, 7, 8, 9, 10, 11, 12

CALLAO

His Place

PO Box 126, 22435
(804) 529-7014; FAX (804) 529-7187

Come to Virginia's Northern Neck for a relaxing getaway, where the only sounds to be heard are the singing of birds and the humming of lawn mowers. You may stay in the 1974 main house and share Gene's love of music—perhaps even play her baby grand, or choose the private cottage. Furnishings are a mixture of antiques, early-American and traditional pieces. His Place sits on a cove of the Yeocomico River, which runs into the Potomac, leading out into the Chesapeake Bay. Make Callao your base to explore the homes of Lee and Washington, only thirty miles. Play golf at the course two miles away, or use the owner's paddleboat. If you are cruising the Bay or Potomac, you may dock on the property if your boat's draft is not more than three feet—there's a tide. (There are several marinas nearby for larger craft, and pick-up can be arranged.) Callao is 55 miles from Williamsburg, 65 from Richmond, and 115 from Washington, DC.

Host: "Gene" Pehovic
Rooms: 1 (PB) + guest house, $50-70
Full Breakfast
Credit Cards: none
Notes: 2, 3, 4, 5, 10

CAPE CHARLES

Sea Gate Bed and Breakfast

9 Tazewell Avenue, 23310
(757) 331-2206

Located in the quiet and sleepy town of Cape Charles, just steps from the Chesapeake Bay on Virginia's undiscovered Eastern Shore. My home is your home! Day begins with a full breakfast followed by leisure or hiking, birding, bathing, and exploring our historic area. Tea prepares

NOTES: Credit cards accepted: A Master Card; B Visa; C American Express; D Discover; E Diners Club; F Other; 2 Personal checks accepted; 3 Lunch available; 4 Dinner available; 5 Open all year; 6 Pets welcome; 7 Children welcome; 8 Tennis nearby; 9 Swimming nearby; 10 Golf nearby; 11 Skiing nearby; 12 May be booked through travel agent.

Sea Gate Bed and Breakfast

you for the most glorious sunsets on the East Coast. Sea Gate is perfect for resting, relaxing, and recharging away from the crush of modern America.

Host: Chris Bannon
Rooms: 4 (2PB; 2 shared shower) $75-85
Full Breakfast
Credit Cards: none
Notes: 2, 5, 7 (over 7), 8, 9, 10, 12

CHARLES CITY

North Bend Plantation

12200 Weyanoke Road, 23030
(804) 829-5176

North Bend has been in the possession of the Copland family for five generations. George and Ridgely Copland have restored the home and grounds to their original beauty. They began operating a bed and breakfast at North Bend in 1984 and enjoy meeting people from all over the world. A full country breakfast is served with scrumptious homemade waffles, an omelet and biscuits, bacon, sausage, fruit, and juice. Federal-style mantels and stair carvings survive from the oldest portion of the house, as do Greek Revival features from the 1853 remodeling. Enjoy heirlooms and a fine collection of old and rare books. Croquet, horseshoes, and volleyball on site. Awarded excellent ratings by the American Bed & Breakfast Association and *Mobil Travel Guide*. Member of the BBAV.

Hosts: George and Ridgely Copland
Rooms: 5 (4PB; 1SB) $105-135
Full Country Breakfast
Credit Cards: A, B
Notes: 2, 5, 7 (over 6), 8, 9 (on site), 10, 12

Orange Hill Bed and Breakfast

18401 Glebe Lane, 23030
(804) 829-5936; (888) 889-7781;
FAX (804) 829-6453

Located in the middle of fifty acres of working farmland, this newly renovated farmhouse offers the charm and quiet of the country with the luxuries of the '90s. In the heart of historic James River Plantation and only twenty minutes from Colonial Williamsburg, shopping, and golf courses. A full breakfast is served in the dining room, and refreshments are served in the afternoon.

Hosts: Dorothy and Skip Bergoine
Rooms: 3 (1PB; 2SB) $75-95
Full Breakfast
Credit Cards: A, B
Notes: 2, 5, 7 (12 and over), 10, 12

CHARLOTTESVILLE

The Inn at Monticello

Highway 20 S., 1188 Scottsville Road, 22902
(804) 979-3593; FAX (804) 296-1344
Web site: http://www.innatmonticello.com

A charming country manor house built in 1850. The inn sits cradled in the valley at

---

NOTES: Credit cards accepted: A Master Card; B Visa; C American Express; D Discover; E Diners Club; F Other; 2 Personal checks accepted; 3 Lunch available; 4 Dinner available; 5 Open all year; 6 Pets

the foot of Thomas Jefferson's Monticello mountain. It looks out on landscaped grounds toward the mountains. Inside, we offer five beautifully decorated rooms full of antique and period pieces. Each room has its own private bath; some rooms have fireplaces, canopy beds, or a private porch. A full gourmet breakfast is served each morning.

Hosts: Norm and Becky Lindway
Rooms: 5 (PB) $125-145
Full Gourmet Breakfast
Credit Cards: A, B
Notes: 2, 5, 7 (over 12), 8, 9, 10, 11, 12

CHINCOTEAGUE

The Garden and the Sea Inn

PO Box 275, **New Church**, 23415
(757) 824-0672; (800) 824-0672
E-mail: baker@shore.intercom.net
Web site: http://www.bbonline.com/va/gardensea/index.html

Casual elegance and warm hospitality await you at this European-style country inn with its romantic, candlelight, fine dining restaurant. Near Chincoteague wildlife refuge and Assateague Island's beautiful beach. Large, luxurious guest rooms, beautifully designed; spacious private baths, some with whirlpools; Victorian detail and stained glass; Oriental rugs; antiques; bay windows; and patios and gardens. Mobil three-star-rated. We are open April 1–November 26.

Hosts: Tom and Sara Baker
Rooms: 6 (PB) $75-165
Expanded Continental Breakfast
Credit Cards: A, B, C, D
Notes: 2, 3, 4, 6, 7 (limited), 8, 9, 10, 12

The Inn at Poplar Corner

PO Box 905, 4248 Main Street, 23336
(757) 336-6115; (800) 336-6787;
FAX (757) 336-5776
Web site: http://www.intercom.net/local/chincoteague/b-b/popinn.html

The inn was inspired by an old Victorian in Suffolk. Southern hospitality with a family atmosphere will be evident the moment you arrive. Gaze through the parlor at the eclectic mix of antiques, wall coverings, fabrics, collectible treasures, and personal touches. The inn offers a large dining room and wraparound veranda from which breakfast and afternoon tea will be served. The third floor has a sitting room and reading room. Relax or peer out at the magnificent view of Main Street, our famous drawbridge and marshlands, or a sunset over Chincoteague Bay. Guest rooms are comfortably furnished, each with air conditioning, heat, ceiling fan, refrigerator, and large bath with whirlpool tub. Located within walking distance of shops and restaurants; minutes from the Chincoteague National Wildlife Refuge and Assateague's National Seashore.

Hosts: Tom and Jacque Derrickson, David and JoAnne Snead
Rooms: 4 (PB) $99-149
Full Breakfast
Credit Cards: A, B
Notes: 2, 8, 9, 10

The Watson House

4240 Main Street, 23336
(757) 336-1564; (800) 336-6787;
FAX (757) 336-5776
Web site: http://www.intercom.net/local/chincoteague/b-b/watson.html

The Watson House has been tastefully restored with Victorian charm. Nestled in

The Watson House

the heart of Chincoteague, the house is within walking distance of shops and restaurants. Each guest room includes antiques, private bath, and air-conditioning. A full, hearty breakfast and afternoon tea are served in the dining room or on the veranda. Enjoy free use of bicycles to tour the Chincoteague National Wildlife Refuge and Beach. The house is AAA-rated, three diamonds.

Hosts: Tom and Jacque Derrickson, David and Joanne Snead
Rooms: 6 (PB) $65-115
Full Breakfast
Credit Cards: A, B
Notes: 2, 8, 9, 10

CHRISTIANSBURG

Evergreen—The Bell-Capozzi House

201 E. Main Street, 24073
(540) 382-7372; (800) 905-7372;
FAX (540) 382-4376
E-mail: evegrninn@aol.com
Web site: http://www.bnt.com/evergreen

Victorian mansion located in historic area just off I-81 (Exit 114). Private baths, TV/VCRs in rooms, central air, heated pool, poster beds, parlors, library, fireplaces, gallery of local artists, traditional southern breakfasts. Members of PAII and BBAV.

Hosts: Rocco and Barbara Bell-Capozzi
Rooms: 5 (PB) $90-125
Full, Southern-Style Breakfast
Credit Cards: A, B, C, D
Notes: 5, 10

CULPEPER

Fountain Hall B&B

609 S. East Street, 22701
(540) 825-8200; (800) 298-4748;
FAX (540) 825-7716

This grand 1859 Colonial Revival home features tastefully restored and decorated rooms, some with private porch, whirlpool, or sitting room. Common rooms for reading, relaxing, TV, and conversation. Complimentary beverages. Gardens, stately trees, and mature boxwoods. Walk to the quaint historic district; visit antique and gift shops, restaurants, bookstores, and the museum. One mile from Highway 29 between Charlottesville, Washington, Richmond, and the Blue Ridge Mountains. Golf and dinner packages. AAA three diamonds, Mobil three stars.

Hosts: Steve and Kathi Walker
Rooms: 6 (PB) $95-150
Expanded Continental Breakfast
Credit Cards: A, B, C, D, E, F
Notes: 2, 5, 7, 8, 10, 12

FAIRFIELD

Angels Rest Farm

471 Sunnybrook Road, 24435
(540) 377-6449

Angels Rest Farm is located in the beautiful Shenandoah valley just eight miles north

---

NOTES: Credit cards accepted: A Master Card; B Visa; C American Express; D Discover; E Diners Club; F Other; 2 Personal checks accepted; 3 Lunch available; 4 Dinner available; 5 Open all year; 6 Pets

of Lexington. Lexington is home to the VMI and Washington and Lee University as well as a number of historic landmarks and museums. Our home, located on a country road, is nestled in a quiet valley surrounded by pastures with grazing cattle and horses nearby. The pond provides good fishing and a reflected view of the woods as you enjoy the view from either porch. A swimming pool is available in summer, a hot tub year-round.

Hosts: John and Carol Nothwang
Rooms: 2 (PB) $60-70
Continental Breakfast
Credit Cards: none
Notes: 2, 5, 9, 11

FOREST

The Summer Kitchen at West Manor

3594 Elkton Farm Road, 24551
(804) 525-0923

Come enjoy a romantic English country cottage located on a beautiful working dairy farm. This private, restored summer kitchen, circa 1840, sleeps four with fireplace, loft, sunroom, and Jacuzzi. Enjoy a full country breakfast while overlooking six hundred acres of rolling cropland, pastures, cattle, and mountains. Afternoon tea and strolls through the gardens complete each day. Come escape to our country haven. Area points of interest include Thomas Jefferson's Poplar Forest, antique shops, and the Blue Ridge Mountains.

Hosts: Greg and Sharon Lester
Rooms: 1 cottage, sleeps 4 (SB) $115-150
Full Breakfast
Credit Cards: none
Notes: 2, 5, 7, 9, 10

FREDERICKSBURG

Fredericksburg Colonial Inn

1707 Princess Anne Street, 22401
(540) 371-5666; FAX (540) 371-5697

A restored country inn in the historic district has thirty-two antique-appointed lodging rooms, private baths, phones, TV, refrigerator, and Civil War motif. Complimentary continental breakfast included. Suites and family rooms available. Wonderful restaurants within walking distance. Beautiful churches nearby! More than two hundred antique dealers, twenty major tourist attractions, and battlefields. A great getaway! Only one hour from Washington, Richmond, and Charlottesville. Open year-round. AARP welcomed; special group rates on request. Call for more information. Mention ad for discount!

Host: Jim Crisp
Rooms: 32 (PB) $55-75
Continental Breakfast
Credit Cards: A, B, C
Notes: 2, 5, 7, 10

La Vista Plantation

4420 Guinea Station Road, 22408-8850
(540) 898-8444; (800) 529-2823;
FAX (540) 898-9414

An 1838 classical revival country home nestled amid ancient tulip poplars, cedars, and hollies, and surrounded by pastures, woods, and fields. The house retains its original charm, with intricate acorn-and-oak leaf moldings, high ceilings, wide pine floors, and two-story front portico. Guests may choose a two-bedroom apartment (sleeps six) or a huge formal room

welcome; 7 Children welcome; 8 Tennis nearby; 9 Swimming nearby; 10 Golf nearby; 11 Skiing nearby; 12 May be booked through travel agent.

with mahogany, rice-carved, king-size poster bed. Both have AC, fireplaces, TVs, radios, and refrigerators. Brown egg breakfast and stocked pond.

Hosts: Michele and Edward Schiesser
Rooms: 1 apartment (PB) $95
Full Breakfast
Credit Cards: A, B
Notes: 2, 5, 7, 8, 10, 12

La Vista Plantation

HARRISONBURG

Kingsway Bed and Breakfast

3581 Singers Glen Road, 22802
(540) 867-9696

Your hosts make your comfort their priority. The home is in a quiet rural area with a view of the mountains in the beautiful Shenandoah Valley. Hosts' carpentry and homemaking skills, house plants and outdoor flowers, a large lawn, and the in-ground pool help make your stay restful. Just four and a half miles from downtown. Nearby is Skyline Drive, caverns, historic sites, antique shops, and flea markets.

Hosts: Chester and Verna Leaman
Rooms: 3 (1PB; 2SB) $50-55
Full Breakfast
Credit Cards: none
Notes: 2, 5, 7, 9, 10, 12

LEESBURG

The Leesburg Colonial Inn

19 S. King Street, 22075
(703) 777-5000; (800) 392-1332;
FAX (703) 777-7000

You will step back into the 18th century's gracious living but have all the modern amenities (cable, phone, etc.). Conference room available for business meetings. Conveniently located close to Dulles Airport. Approximately thirty miles from Washington, DC, yet located in the center of Leesburg's historic district. Our dining room with fireplace is very inviting; our chef will prepare cuisine for the most discriminating guests, from 18th-century recipes to contemporary cuisine. Once you stay at the inn you will want to return.

Host: Fabian E. Saeidi
Rooms: 10 (PB) $68-150
Full Gourmet Breakfast
Credit Cards: A, B, C, D, E, F
Notes: 2, 3, 4, 5, 6, 7, 8, 9, 10, 11, 12

The Norris House Inn

108 Loudoin Street SW, 22075
(703) 777-1806; (800) 644-1806;
FAX (703) 771-8051
E-mail: inn@norrishouse.com
Web site: http://norrishouse.com

Elegant accommodations in the heart of Leesburg's historic district. Six guest rooms furnished with antiques, and three wood-burning fireplaces. Breakfast served by candlelight. Convenient location with fine restaurants within easy walking distance. An hour's drive from Washington, DC, in Virginia's hunt country, rich in colonial and Civil War history, antiquing,

---

NOTES: Credit cards accepted: A Master Card; B Visa; C American Express; D Discover; E Diners Club; F Other; 2 Personal checks accepted; 3 Lunch available; 4 Dinner available; 5 Open all year; 6 Pets

and quaint villages. Perfect for romantic getaways, small meetings, and weddings. Open daily by reservation. Stone House Tea Room located on the inn's right.

Hosts: Pam and Don McMurray
Rooms: 6 (SB) $85-145
Full Breakfast
Credit Cards: A, B, C, D, E, F
Notes: 2, 5, 8, 9, 10, 12

LINCOLN

Springdale Country Inn

Lincoln, 20160
(540) 338-1832; (800) 388-1832;
FAX (540) 338-1839

Meticulously restored historic landmark, circa 1832. Forty-five miles west of Washington in the foothills of the Blue Ridge Mountains. Bed and breakfast, conference, and wedding site. Sleeps twenty; seats fifty inside, one hundred and fifty outside. Fireplaces, central air, tennis, shopping, antiquing, bike trail within three miles. Civil War battlefield and outlet malls within thirty miles.

Hosts: Nancy and Roger Fones
Rooms: 9 (6PB; 3SB) $95-125
Full Breakfast
Credit Cards: A, B
Notes: 2, 3, 4, 5, 12

LYNCHBURG

Federal Crest Inn B&B

1101 Federal Street, 24504
(804) 845-6155; (800) 818-6155;
FAX (804) 845-1445
Web site: http://www.inmind.com/federalcrest

A warm and relaxing atmosphere awaits every guest at this elegant 1909 Georgian Revival mansion in the Federal Hill Historic District. Magnificent woodwork and architectural details. Amenities include queen canopy beds, whirlpool tub, bedroom fireplaces, AC, luxury linens and robes, arrival refreshments, full country breakfast, gift shop, and much more! Convenient to all area colleges, Appomattox, golf, vineyards, antiquing, and museums.

Hosts: Ann and Phil Ripley
Rooms: 5 (PB) $85-115
Full Breakfast
Credit Cards: A, B, C, D
Notes: 2, 3 and 4 (with notice), 5, 8, 9, 10, 11, 12

MADISON HEIGHTS

Winridge Bed and Breakfast

116 Winridge Drive, 24572
(804) 384-7220; FAX (804) 384-1399
E-mail: pfisterpfamily@juno.com
Web site: http://www.inngetaways.com/va/
winridg.html

Enjoy the warm family atmosphere in our grand country home. Stroll through gardens where birds, butterflies, and flowers abound. Shade trees with swings and hammock. Relax on the large, inviting porches. Scenic mountain views. Hot, hearty breakfasts are served in the dining room. Greenhouse features perennials, unusual annuals, and container gardening. Close to Blue Ridge Parkway, Lynchburg, Appomattox, and Poplar Forest.

Hosts: LoisAnn and Ed Pfister and Family
Rooms: 3 (1PB; 2SB) $69-85
Full Breakfast
Credit Cards: A, B
Notes: 2, 5, 7, 8, 9, 10, 11, 12

welcome; 7 Children welcome; 8 Tennis nearby; 9 Swimming nearby; 10 Golf nearby; 11 Skiing nearby; 12 May be booked through travel agent.

MT. JACKSON

Widow Kip's Country Inn

355 Orchard Drive, 22842-9753
(540) 477-2400; (800) 478-8714
E-mail: widowkips@shentel.net
Web site: http://www.widowkips.com

A stately 1830 colonial on seven rural acres in the Shenandoah Valley overlooking the mountains. Friendly rooms filled with family photographs, bric-a-brac, and antiques. Each bedroom has a working fireplace and canopy, sleigh, or Lincoln bed. Two cozy cottages are also available. Pool on the premises. Nearby battlefields and caverns to explore, canoeing, hiking, or downhill skiing. Bicycles, picnics, and grill available.

Hostess: Betty and Bob Luse
Rooms: 5 + 2 courtyard cottages (PB) $65-85
Full Breakfast
Credit Cards: A, B
Notes: 2, 5, 6 and 7 (in cottages), 8, 9, 10, 11, 12

NORFOLK

Old Dominion Inn

4111 Hampton Boulevard, 23508
(757) 440-5100; (800) 653-9030;
FAX (757) 423-5238
E-mail: calkan@erols.com

Our sixty-room inn opened in 1989 and takes its name from the Commonwealth of Virginia, "The Old Dominion." Located in the heart of Norfolk's west side, just one block south of the Old Dominion University campus and only a short drive up or down Hampton Boulevard from many of the area's busiest facilities. Each Old Dominion Inn room gives you a remote-controlled, color TV with cable service, ceiling fan, and individually controlled heat and air-conditioning. The James W. Sherrill family invites you to share in the warm hospitality of the Old Dominion Inn. As a family-owned business, it is our desire that you feel right at home when you stay with us. We treat our guests like part of "our family." Be our guest for a complimentary, light breakfast each morning of your stay.

Hosts: The Sherrill Family
Rooms: 60 (PB) $65-130
Continental Breakfast
Credit Cards: A, B, C, D, E
Notes: 2, 5, 7, 8, 9, 10, 12

ONANCOCK

Spinning Wheel Bed and Breakfast

31 North Street, 23417
(804) 787-7311

This 1890s folk Victorian home in the historic waterfront town of Onancock, on Virginia's Eastern Shore, has antiques and spinning wheels throughout. All guest rooms have queen beds, private baths, and air-conditioning. Guests can visit Kerr Place (1799 museum), cruise to Tangier Island from Onancock Wharf, and walk to restaurants. Bicycles, tennis, and golf are available. Chincoteague/Assateague Island beach close by. A calm Eastern Shore getaway from DC, Maryland, Virginia, Delaware, and New Jersey on the

---

NOTES: Credit cards accepted: A Master Card; B Visa; C American Express; D Discover; E Diners Club; F Other; 2 Personal checks accepted; 3 Lunch available; 4 Dinner available; 5 Open all year; 6 Pets

Chesapeake Bay, five miles from the Atlantic Ocean.

Hosts: Karen and David Tweedie
Rooms: 4 (PB) $75-95
Full Breakfast
Credit Cards: A, B, D
Notes: 2, 8, 9, 10, 12

and seclusion to travelers. Fine dining can be enjoyed nearby.

Hosts: Howard and Joyce Vogt
Rooms: 6 (4PB; 2SB) $75-105
Full Breakfast
Credit Cards: A, B, C
Notes: 2, 5, 7 (over 12), 10, 12

Jasmine Plantation Bed and Breakfast Inn

PROVIDENCE FORGE

Jasmine Plantation Bed and Breakfast Inn

4500 N. Courthouse Road, 23140
(804) 966-9836; (800) NEW-KENT;
FAX (804) 966-5679

Jasmine Plantation is a restored 1750s farmhouse convenient to Williamsburg, Richmond, and the James River Plantations. Genuine hospitality, historical setting, and rooms decorated in period antiques await the visitor. The home was settled prior to 1683. Guests are invited to walk the forty-seven acres and use their imaginations as to what events have occurred here during the inn's three-hundred-year history. Located 2.4 miles from I-64, Jasmine Plantation offers both convenience

SMITH MOUNTAIN LAKE

The Manor at Taylor's Store Bed and Breakfast Inn

PO Box 533, 8812 Washington Highway, 24184
(540) 721-3951; (800) 722-9984;
FAX (540) 721-5243
E-mail: lande@reu.net
Web site: http://www.symweb.com/taylors

This historic 120-acre estate with an elegant manor house provides romantic accommodations in suites with fireplaces, antiques, canopied beds, and private porches. Guests have use of a hot tub, billiards, exercise room, and guest kitchen. Many other amenities are included. A separate three-bedroom, two-bath cottage is ideal for a family. Enjoy six private, spring-fed ponds for swimming, canoeing,

The Manor at Taylor's Store

fishing, and hiking. Heart-healthy, gourmet breakfast is served in the dining room with panoramic views of the countryside.

Hosts: Lee and Mary Lynn Tucker
Rooms: 10 (8PB; 2SB) $85-185
Full Breakfast
Credit Cards: A, B
Notes: 2, 3, 4, 5, 7, 8, 9, 10, 11, 12

SMITHFIELD

Isle of Wight Inn

1607 S. Church Street, 23430
(757) 357-3176; (800) 357-3245 (reservations only)

Luxurious colonial B&B inn located in a delightful historic, riverport town. Several suites with fireplaces and Jacuzzis. Antique shop featuring tall case clocks and period furniture. More than sixty old homes in town date from 1750. Just thirty minutes and a short ferry ride to Williamsburg and Jamestown; less than an hour to James River plantations, Norfolk, Hampton, and Virginia Beach.

Hosts: Bob Hart and Jackie Madrigal
Rooms: 9 (PB) $59-119
Full Breakfast
Credit Cards: A, B, C, D
Notes: 2, 5, 7, 8, 9, 10, 12

STAUNTON

Ashton Country House

1205 Middlebrook Road, 24401
(540) 885-7819; (800) 296-7819

Ashton is a delightful blend of town and country. This 1860 Greek Revival home is located on twenty-four acres, yet only a mile from the center of Staunton. There

Ashton Country House

are five air-conditioned, comfortable, and attractive bedrooms, each with a private bath. Guests start each day with a hearty country breakfast. Afternoon tea is served in the grand living room or on any porch. Ashton Country House is the perfect place to soothe the spirit, share a weekend with friends, celebrate a special anniversary, or escape to the serenity of the countryside.

Hosts: Dorie and Vince DiStefano
Rooms: 5 (PB) $75-125
Full Breakfast
Credit Cards: A, B
Notes: 2, 7, 8, 9, 10, 11, 12

Thornrose House at Gypsy Hill

531 Thornrose Avenue, 24401
(540) 885-7026; (800) 861-4338;
FAX (540) 885-6458

Outside, this turn-of-the century Georgian residence has a wraparound veranda, Greek colonnades, and lovely gardens. Inside, a fireplace and grand piano create a formal but comfortable atmosphere. Five attractive bedrooms with private baths are on the second floor. Your hosts offer afternoon tea, refreshments, and conversation. Adjacent to a three-hundred-acre park that is great for walking, with

---

NOTES: Credit cards accepted: A Master Card; B Visa; C American Express; D Discover; E Diners Club; F Other; 2 Personal checks accepted; 3 Lunch available; 4 Dinner available; 5 Open all year; 6 Pets

tennis, golf, and ponds. Other nearby attractions include the Blue Ridge National Park, natural chimneys, Skyline Drive, Woodrow Wilson's birthplace, and the Museum of American Frontier Culture.

Hosts: Otis and Suzanne Huston
Rooms: 5 (PB) $60-80
Full Breakfast
Credit Cards: none
Notes: 2, 5, 7 (over 6), 8, 9, 10

STRASBURG

Sonner House Bed and Breakfast

208 W. Queen Street, 22657
(540) 465-4712; (800) 829-4809;
FAX (540) 465-5463

This 1757 weatherboard-over-log home, featured in *Country Home* magazine, has 18th-century hallmarks such as wide plank flooring, original walk-in fireplace in kitchen, and hand stenciling throughout. Primitive antiques adorn the home, which is part of the historic walking tour. Located near Skyline Drive National Park, the Shenandoah River, Wayside Theater, and Belle Grove Plantation (National Trust Property).

Hosts: Sam and Mary Hitchings
Rooms: 3 (PB) $70
Full Breakfast
Credit Cards: A, B
Notes: 2, 7, 8, 9, 10

STUARTS DRAFT

The Elijah Room

Route 2, Box 416K, 24477-9312
(540) 943-7812

The Elijah Room is located on the entire upper floor of a tidy Cape Cod house, via a separate spiral staircase entrance. The neatly furnished bedroom, small den, breakfast nook, and three-quarters bath retain the sweet, country charm of our lovely Shenandoah Valley area. The breakfast/lunch items in the initial visit's welcome basket can be cooked/chilled in the small refrigerator/microwave provided. Accommodations are equipped with air-conditioning, extension phone with separate ring/number, color TV/VCR (no cable), and extra towels.

Hostess: Mrs. L.A. Johnson
Rooms: 1 (PB) $10/person/day
Welcome Basket (only)
Credit Cards: none
Notes: 2, 5, 9, 11

TANGIER ISLAND

Shirley's Bay View Inn

PO Box 183, 23440
(757) 891-2396

Enjoy a pleasant and restful visit to one of the last quiet and remote fishing villages on the Chesapeake Bay. You will stay at one of the oldest homes on Tangier Island, filled with the beauty and charm of days gone by. The beautiful beaches, sunsets, and customs of Tangier Island will make your stay a memorable one, and your hostess will make you feel you are part of the family.

Hostess: Shirley Pruitt
Rooms: 5 (3PB; 2SB) $40-70
Full Breakfast
Credit Cards: none
Notes: 2, 5, 7, 9

welcome; 7 Children welcome; 8 Tennis nearby; 9 Swimming nearby; 10 Golf nearby; 11 Skiing nearby; 12 May be booked through travel agent.

Barclay Cottage Bed and Breakfast

VIRGINIA BEACH

Barclay Cottage Bed and Breakfast

400 16th Street, 23451
(757) 422-1956

Barclay Cottage Bed and Breakfast offers casual sophistication in a warm, historic, innlike atmosphere. Designed in turn-of-the-century style, the Barclay Cottage is two blocks from the beach in the heart of the Virginia Beach recreational area. The inn is completely restored with antique furniture to bring together the feeling of yesterday with the comfort of today. Formerly the home of Lillian S. Barclay, the inn has been a guest home for many years. We have kept the historic ambience of the inn while modernizing it significantly to meet today's needs. We look forward to welcoming you to Barclay Cottage, where the theme is "We go where our dream leads us."

Hosts: Peter and Claire
Rooms: 5 (3PB; 2SB) $70-95
Full Breakfast
Credit Cards: A, B, C
Notes: 8, 9, 10, 12

WARM SPRINGS

Three Hills Inn

PO Box 9, Route 220, 24484
(540) 839-5381; (888) 23-HILLS;
FAX (540) 839-5199

A premier bed and breakfast inn in the heart of Bath County. Enjoy a casually elegant retreat in a beautifully restored historic manor. You'll have spectacular mountain views, acres of woods and trails—serenity at its best! Elegant suites are available, some with kitchens and fireplaces. Three Hills Inn is located four miles from the historic Homestead Resort. Your hosts have missionary backgrounds and speak fluent Spanish. From a romantic getaway to an executive retreat (a meeting/conference facility is available), Three Hills Inn is the perfect choice for the discriminating traveler. Afternoon tea is served on weekends.

Hosts: Doug and Charlene Fike
Rooms: 14 (PB) $59-149
Full Gourmet Breakfast
Credit Cards: A, B, D
Notes: 2, 5, 6, 7, 8, 9, 10, 11, 12

WASHINGTON

Caledonia Farm—1812

47 Dearing Road, **Flint Hill**, 22627
(540) 675-3693; (800) BNB-1812
Web site: http://www.bnb-n-va.com/cale1812.htm

Enjoy ultimate hospitality, comfort, scenery, and recreation adjacent to Virginia's Shenandoah National Park. This romantic getaway to history and nature includes outstanding full breakfasts, fireplaces, air-

---

NOTES: Credit cards accepted: A Master Card; B Visa; C American Express; D Discover; E Diners Club; F Other; 2 Personal checks accepted; 3 Lunch available; 4 Dinner available; 5 Open all year; 6 Pets

conditioning, hayrides, bicycles, lawn games, VCR, and piano. World's finest dining, caves, Skyline Drive, battlefields, stables, antiquing, hiking, and climbing are all nearby. Washington, DC, is sixty-eight miles away; Washington, Virginia, just four miles. A Virginia historic landmark, the farm is listed on the National Register of Historic Places. Unwind in our new spa.

Host: Phil Irwin
Rooms: 4 (2PB; 2SB) $80-140
Full Breakfast
Credit Cards: A, B, D
Notes: 2, 5, 7 (over 12), 8, 9, 10, 11, 12

WAYNESBORO

The Iris Inn

191 Chinquapin Drive, 22980
(540) 943-1991; FAX (540) 942-2093
E-mail: irisinn@cfw.com
Web site: http://www.irisinn.com

The charm and grace of southern living in a totally modern facility, nestled in a wooded tract on the western slope of the Blue Ridge, overlooking the historic Shenandoah Valley—that's what awaits you at the Iris Inn in Waynesboro. It's ideal for a weekend retreat, a refreshing change for the business traveler, and a tranquil spot for the tourist to spend a night or a week. Guest rooms are spacious, comfortably furnished, and delightfully decorated in nature and wildlife motifs. Each room has a private bath and individual temperature control.

Hosts: Wayne and Iris Karl
Rooms: 9 (PB) $80-140
Full Breakfast
Credit Cards: A, B, C
Notes: 2, 5, 7 (over 12), 8, 9, 10, 11

Colonial Gardens Bed and Breakfast

WILLIAMSBURG

Colonial Gardens Bed and Breakfast

1109 Jamestown Road, 23185
(757) 220-8087; (800) 886-9715;
FAX (757) 253-1495
E-mail: colgard@widomaker.com
Web site: http://www.ontheline.com/cgbb

This beautiful home is conveniently located just four minutes from Colonial Williamsburg and five minutes from Jamestown. Situated on a heavily wooded lot in the heart of the city, Colonial Gardens Bed and Breakfast offers the weary traveler a quiet haven of rest and relaxation. The home features English and early-1800s American antiques. Each beautifully decorated bedroom has a private bath. Suites are available. A full plantation breakfast is served. Experience true southern hospitality and Williamsburg elegance at its best.

Hosts: Scottie and Wil Phillips
Rooms: 4 (PB) $95-125
Full Breakfast
Credit Cards: A, B
Notes: 2, 5, 7 (12 and older), 10, 12

welcome; 7 Children welcome; 8 Tennis nearby; 9 Swimming nearby; 10 Golf nearby; 11 Skiing nearby; 12 May be booked through travel agent.

Fox and Grape Bed and Breakfast

701 Monumental Avenue, 23185
(757) 229-6914; (800) 292-3699

Here you'll find genteel accommodations five blocks north of Virginia's restored colonial capital. This lovely two-story colonial with its spacious wraparound porch is a perfect place to enjoy your morning coffee, plan your day's activities in Williamsburg, or relax with your favorite book. Furnishings include antiques, counted cross-stitch, duck decoys, and folk art Noah's arks made by your host. Pat enjoys doing counted cross-stitch. Bob carves walking sticks and makes nursery rhyme collectibles.

Hosts: Pat and Bob Orendorff
Rooms: 4 (PB) $85-95
Full Breakfast
Credit Cards: A, B, D
Notes: 2, 5, 7, 8, 9, 10, 12

Hite's Bed and Breakfast

7041 Monumental Avenue, 23185
(757) 229-4814

Hite's Bed and Breakfast is a charming Cape Cod within a seven-minute walk of Colonial Williamsburg. Large rooms are cleverly furnished with antiques and collectibles. Each room has television, radio, phone, coffeemaker, robes and beautiful bathrooms with old claw-foot tubs. A suite is also available with a nice romantic setting and a large sitting room. In the parlor for our guests' enjoyment is an antique pump organ and hand-crank Victrola. You can relax in the backyard and enjoy the swing, birds, flowers, and goldfish pond as you plan your stay in Williamsburg.

Hostess: Faye Hite
Rooms: 2 (PB) $80-90
Full Breakfast
Credit Cards: none
Notes: 2, 5, 7, 10, 12

Newport House

710 S. Henry Street, 23185-4113
(757) 229-1775; FAX (757) 229-6408

A reproduction of an 1756 home, Newport House has museum-standard period furnishings, including canopy beds. Only a five-minute walk to the historic area. Breakfast with colonial recipes; colonial dancing in the ballroom Tuesday evenings (beginners welcome). The host is a historian/author (including a book on Christ) and former museum director. The hostess is a gardener, beekeeper, 18th-century seamstress, and former nurse. A pet rabbit entertains at breakfast. No smoking.

Hosts: John and Cathy Millar
Rooms: 2 (PB) $120-145
Full Breakfast
Credit Cards: none
Notes: 2, 5, 7, 8, 9, 10, 12

Primrose Cottage

706 Richmond Road, 23185
(757) 229-6421; (800) 522-1901;
FAX (757) 259-0717
Web site: http://www.primrose-cottage.com

A nature lover's delight. In the spring, the front walkway is lined with primroses. In cooler months, the frontyard is abloom with pansies. There are two bedrooms upstairs, each with a large, walk-in closet and private bath. Desks, chairs, and reading lamps add to your comfort. In the morning, the aroma of home cooking rouses even the sleepiest traveler. Within walking distance of the historic area, fine restaurants, and churches. Bikes for guests. Off-street parking. Smoke-free.

Hostess: Inge Curtis
Rooms: 4 (3PB; 1SB) $85-115
Full Breakfast
Credit Cards: A, B
Notes: 2, 5, 8, 9, 10, 12

Williamsburg Manor

600 Richmond Road, 23185
(757) 220-8011; (800) 422-8011;
FAX (757) 220-0245

This 1927 Georgian home was built during the reconstruction of historic Colonial Williamsburg. Recently restored to its original elegance and furnished with exquisite pieces, including antiques and collectibles. Five well-appointed guest rooms, each with private bath, TV, and central AC. A lavish fireside breakfast is prepared by the executive chef. The home is available for weddings, private parties, dinners, and meetings. Ideal location within walking distance of the historic area. Onsite parking. Off-season rates.

Hostess: Laura Reeves
Rooms: 5 (PB) $75-115 (seasonal)
Full Breakfast
Credit Cards: A, B
Notes: 2, 4, 5, 7, 8, 10, 12

Williamsburg Sampler Bed and Breakfast

922 Jamestown Road, 23185
(757) 253-0398; (800) 722-1169;
FAX (757) 253-2669
E-mail: WbgSampler@aol.com

This 18th-century, plantation-style colonial was proclaimed "Inn of the Year" by

Williamsburg Sampler Bed and Breakfast

Virginia's governor. It is a AAA three-diamond and Mobil three-star home within walking distance of the historic area. Richly furnished bedrooms and suites with king- or queen-size beds, private baths, fireplaces, and rooftop garden. A collection of antiques, pewter, and samplers are displayed throughout the house. A "skip lunch" breakfast is served. Internationally recognized as a favorite spot for a romantic honeymoon or anniversary.

Hosts: Helen and Ike Sisane
Rooms: 4 (PB) $95-140
Full Breakfast
Credit Cards: A, B
Notes: 2, 5, 8, 9, 10, 12

WINCHESTER

Brownstone Cottage Bed and Breakfast

161 McCarty Lane, 22602
(540) 662-1962

Enjoy the quiet and peaceful country setting of Brownstone Cottage, a private home in the Shenandoah Valley outside historic Winchester. Hospitality and individual attention highlight your stay. Step across the threshold of this bed and breakfast and feel right at home as you relax in your room or the sitting room, or on the outside deck. Wake to the aroma of fresh-brewed coffee and the beginning of a full country breakfast, featuring Chuck's homemade pancakes or bread.

Hosts: Chuck and Sheila Brown
Rooms: 2 (PB) $75-95
Full Breakfast
Credit Cards: A, B
Notes: 2, 5, 8, 10

Azalea House Bed and Breakfast

WOODSTOCK

Azalea House Bed and Breakfast

551 S. Main Street, 22664
(540) 459-3500

A large Victorian house built in 1892, featuring family antiques and stenciled ceilings. It initially was used as a parsonage, serving a church three blocks away for about seventy years. Located in the historic Shenandoah Valley, it is close to Skyline Drive and the mountains. Many Civil War sites are within a short driving distance. Nearby activities include antiquing, hiking, and horseback riding.

Hosts: Margaret and Price McDonald
Rooms: 4 (PB) $55-75
Full Breakfast
Credit Cards: A, B, C
Notes: 2, 7 (over 6), 9, 10, 11

Inn at Narrow Passage

PO Box 608, U.S. 11 S., 22664
(540) 459-8000; (800) 459-8002;
FAX (540) 459-8001
E-mail: marnpass@shentel.net
Web site: http://www.shentel.net/
　narrowpassageinn

This cozy, historic inn has been welcoming travelers along the Great Wagon Road (now U.S. 11) through the Shenandoah Valley since the 1740s. In the main building, guests can enjoy the large common room with its gleaming pine floors, wing chairs, and massive limestone fireplace. A hearty, fireside breakfast is served in the paneled dining room, with fine restaurants nearby for other meals. The oldest guest rooms feature wood floors, stenciling and the atmosphere of colonial times. Rooms from later additions are decorated in the same style, but open onto porches, with views of the Shenandoah River and the Massanutten Mountains to the east. The inn is fully air-conditioned, and most rooms have private baths and working fireplaces.

Hosts: Ellen and Ed Markel
Rooms: 12 (PB)
Full Breakfast
Credit Cards: A, B
Notes: 2, 5, 7 (well-behaved), 8, 9, 10, 11, 12

Washington

ABERDEEN/COSMOPOLIS

Cooney Mansion

1705 Fifth Street, Box 54, **Cosmopolis**, 98537
(360) 533-0602
Web site: http://www.techline.com/~cooney

The Cooney Mansion is located two minutes from Aberdeen. This 1908 National Historic Register home, situated in wooded seclusion, was built by Neil Cooney, owner of one of the largest sawmills of the time. It captures the adventure of the Northwest. Share the lumber baron's history and many of his original Craftsman-style antiques. Enjoy eighteen holes of golf (in the backyard) or a leisurely walk around Mill Creek Park. Relax in the sauna and Jacuzzi, curl up with one of the many books from the library, or watch TV in the ballroom or living room. Award-winning breakfast.

Hosts: Judi and Jim Lohr
Rooms: 8 (5PB; 3SB) $65-165
Full "Lumber Baron's" Breakfast
Credit Cards: A, B, C, D, E
Notes: 5, 8, 10

Cooney Mansion

ANACORTES

Albatross B&B

5708 Kingsway West, 98221
(360) 293-0677; (800) 622-8864
E-mail: albatros@cnw.com
Web site: http://www.cnw.com/~albatros

Our 1927 Cape Cod-style home offers king and queen beds and private baths in all guest rooms. The quiet living room, patio, and deck areas view waterfront, islands, and mountains. Walk to parks, marinas, fine dining, and inspirational beaches. Close to the San Juan ferryboat terminal for access to the San Juan Islands and Victoria, BC. We are also close to twenty-one churches.

Hosts: Barbie and Ken
Rooms: 4 (PB) $75-90
Full Breakfast
Credit Cards: A, B, C
Notes: 2, 7, 8, 9, 10, 11, 12

welcome; 7 Children welcome; 8 Tennis nearby; 9 Swimming nearby; 10 Golf nearby; 11 Skiing nearby; 12 May be booked through travel agent.

WASHINGTON

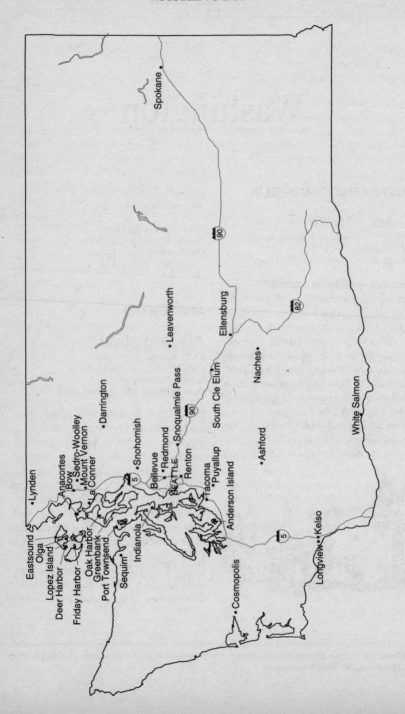

Hasty Pudding House

1312 8th Street, 98221
(360) 293-5773; (800) 368-5588

Celebrate romance in a delightful 1913
heritage home with Victorian decor, fresh
flowers, and cozy window seats. Snuggle
in king and queen top-quality beds; private baths. Breakfast is fabulous! A great
getaway anytime.

Hosts: Mike and Melinda Hasty
Rooms: 4 (2PB; 2SB) $69-89
Full Breakfast
Credit Cards: A, B, C, D
Notes: 2, 5, 8, 9, 10, 12

Sunset Beach Bed and Breakfast

100 Sunset Beach, 98221
(360) 293-5428; (800) 359-3448

On exciting Rosario Straits. Relax and
enjoy the view of seven major islands from
our decks, stroll on the beach, or walk in
the beautiful Washington Park, adjacent
to our private gardens. Also enjoy boating, hiking, and fishing. Three bedrooms
with private baths; one room with a Jacuzzi;
a hot tub is available in a separate building. Private entry and TV. Full breakfast.
Five minutes to San Juan ferries, fine restaurants, and marina. A convenience store
is nearby. Sunsets are outstanding! No
smoking.

Hosts: Joann and Hal Harker
Rooms: 3 (PB) $69-95
Full Breakfast
Credit Cards: A, B
Notes: 2, 5, 7 (over 6), 9, 10, 11, 12

ANDERSON ISLAND

The Inn at Burg's Landing

8808 Villa Beach Road, 98303
(253) 884-9185; (800) 431-5622

Catch the ferry from Steilacoom to stay at
this contemporary log homestead built in
1987. It offers spectacular views of Mt.
Rainier, Puget Sound, and the Cascade
Mountains and is located south of Tacoma
off I-5. Choose from three guest rooms,
including the master bedroom with queen-size "log" bed, skylight above, and private whirlpool bath. The inn has a private
beach. Collect seashells and agates, swim
on two freshwater lakes nearby, and/or
enjoy a game of tennis or golf. Tour the
island by bicycle or on foot and watch for
sailboats and deer. Hot tub. Full breakfast. Families welcome. No smoking.

Hosts: Ken and Annie Burg
Rooms: 4 (2PB; 2SB) $70-110
Full Breakfast
Credit Cards: A, B
Notes: 2, 5, 7, 8, 9, 10, 11

ASHFORD

Mountain Meadows Inn Bed and Breakfast

28912 State Route 706E, PO Box 291, 98304
(360) 569-2788

Experience the authentic Northwest! Built
in 1910 as the home of a mill superintendent, Mountain Meadows Inn is on eleven
quiet acres of tall cedars amongst the grandeur of the northwestern landscape.
Guests enjoy privacy and hospitality on

NOTES: Credit cards accepted: A Master Card; B Visa; C American Express; D Discover; E Diners
Club; F Other; 2 Personal checks accepted; 3 Lunch available; 4 Dinner available; 5 Open all year; 6 Pets
welcome; 7 Children welcome; 8 Tennis nearby; 9 Swimming nearby; 10 Golf nearby; 11 Skiing nearby;
12 May be booked through travel agent.

their romantic getaway weekends. Historic John Muir and Native American displays. Close to Mt. Rainier National Park but away from the crowds.

Hosts: Harry and Michelle Latimer
Rooms: 6 (PB) $75-110
Full Breakfast
Credit Cards: A, B
Notes: 2, 5, 7 (4 and up), 9, 10, 11, 12

BELLEVUE

Petersen
Bed and Breakfast

10228 SE 8th, 98004
(425) 454-9334

We offer two rooms five minutes from Bellevue Square with wonderful shopping, and one-half block from the bus line to Seattle. Rooms have down comforters, and we have a hot tub on the deck. Children are welcome. No smoking.

Hosts: Eunice and Carl Peterson
Rooms: 2 (SB) $60-75
Full Breakfast
Credit Cards: none
Notes: 2, 5, 7

CLE ELUM, SOUTH

The Moore House
Bed and Breakfast
Country Inn

526 Marie Avenue, PO Box 629, 98943
(509) 674-5939; (800) 2-2-TWAIN (OR/WA only)

Former 1909 Milwaukee Railroad Crew Hotel, now offering twelve bright and airy rooms ranging from economical to exquisite and including two genuine cabooses and

a bridal suite with jetted tub. On the National Register, the Inn has a museumlike atmosphere with an extensive collection of railroad memorabilia and artifacts. Nestled in the Cascade Mountain foothills, the house is close to cross-country skiing, hiking, biking, rafting, horseback riding, fishing, and fine dining.

Hosts: Eric and Cindy Sherwood
Rooms: 12 (6PB; 6SB) $49-125
Full Breakfast
Credit Cards: A, B, C, D
Notes: 2, 5, 7, 10, 11, 12

DARRINGTON

Sauk River Farm
Bed and Breakfast

32629 State Route 530 NE, 98241
(360) 436-1794 (voice and FAX)

The wild, scenic Sauk River runs through this farm nestled in a valley of the North Cascades. All-season recreational opportunities await you. Wildlife abounds year-round. The Native American Loft Room is a collector's delight; The Victoria Room offers pastoral privacy. Hallmarks of the farm are its views of rugged mountains, intimate atmosphere, comfortable accommodations, and solitude for those seeking relaxation. Step back in time and sample

---

NOTES: Credit cards accepted: A Master Card; B Visa; C American Express; D Discover; E Diners Club; F Other; 2 Personal checks accepted; 3 Lunch available; 4 Dinner available; 5 Open all year; 6 Pets

Darrington hospitality with its bluegrass music and crafters. Sauk River Farm is a no-smoking bed and breakfast.

Hosts: Leo and Sharon Mehler
Rooms: 2 (SB) $52-65
Full Breakfast
Credit Cards: none
Notes: 2, 5, 11

ELLENSBURG

Murphy's Country Bed and Breakfast

2830 Thorp Highway S., 98926
(509) 925-7986
Web site: http://www.photostar-usa.com/
   kittitasvalley

Two large guest rooms in a lovely 1915 country home with a sweeping view of the valley. Full breakfast. Close to fly-fishing and golfing.

Hostess: Doris Callahan
Rooms: 2 (SB) $70
Full Breakfast
Credit Cards: A, B, C
Notes: 2, 5, 10

FRIDAY HARBOR

States Inn

2039 W. Valley Road, 98250
(360) 378-6240; FAX (360) 378-6241
Web site: http://www.karuna.com/statesinn

Situated in a scenic valley thirteen minutes from town, the inn is located on a sixty-acre horse boarding ranch on the west side of San Juan island. We offer nine rooms, each individually decorated with a flavor of a state's name. Three-diamond rating

States Inn

with AAA. This is a high-quality inn in the middle of the Northwest's most scenic vacation area.

Host: Sandra Jingling
Rooms: 9 (7PB; 2SB) $80-110
Full Breakfast
Credit Cards: A, B
Notes: 2, 5, 12

GREENBANK

Guest House Cottages

3366 S. Highway 525, 98253
(360) 678-3115

Discover privacy, peace, and pampering in each of our seven individually designed cottages in Greenbank, Whidbey Island. Each cottage—four of which are log

Guest House Cottages

welcome; 7 Children welcome; 8 Tennis nearby; 9 Swimming nearby; 10 Golf nearby; 11 Skiing nearby; 12 May be booked through travel agent.

houses—has a private setting on twenty-five acres of island greenery. Every cottage features personal Jacuzzis, fireplaces, kitchens, and TV/VCRs. More than four hundred complimentary movies, an outdoor swimming pool, and a hot tub make for a relaxing retreat for two.

Hosts: Don and MaryJane Creger
Rooms: 6 cottages + 1 suite (PB) $110-285
Full Breakfast
Credit Cards: A, B, C, D
Notes: 2, 5, 9, 10, 12

Longfellow House Bed and Breakfast

KELSO

Longfellow House Bed and Breakfast

203 Williams-Finney Road, 98626-9513
(360) 423-4545; FAX (360) 414-3130

Longfellow House is the ideal private destination for your special occasion or business trip. A secluded cottage for two in a rural setting, one mile east of I-5. The main floor is yours alone. Enjoy our 1913 player piano and collection of works by and about Henry Wadsworth Longfellow. Sleep as long as you like. Wake to the smell of gourmet coffee and the breakfast you've selected being prepared. Fine teas are our specialty. Off-street parking,

phone, modem jack, and business services. Visit Mount St. Helens, Pacific beaches, and Columbia River Gorge.

Hosts: Richard and Sally Longfellow
Rooms: 1 (PB) $89
Full Breakfast
Credit Cards: none
Notes: 2, 5, 8, 9, 10, 11

LACONNER

Benson Farmstead Bed and Breakfast

1009 Avon-Allen Road, **Bow**, 98232
(360) 757-0578; (800) 685-7239, 1930

Located just minutes from the Skagit Valley, tulip fields, the historic town of LaConner, and ferries to the San Juan Islands, the Benson Farmstead is a beautiful, restored farmhouse. The Bensons are a friendly couple who serve homemade desserts in the evening and a wonderful breakfast. They have filled their home with charming antiques, old quilts, and curios from their Scandinavian heritage. The extensive yard features an English Garden and a large playground.

Hosts: Jerry and Sharon Benson
Rooms: 4 (PB) $70-80
Full Breakfast
Credit Cards: A, B
Notes: 2, 5 (weekends only September-March), 7, 8, 9, 10, 11

Rainbow Inn

PO Box 15, 1075 Chilberg Road, 98257
(360) 466-4578; (888) 266-8879;
FAX (360) 466-3844
E-mail: tom@rainbowinnbandb.com
Web site: http://www.rainbowinnbandb.com

For a romantic, peaceful repose in a 1908 Craftsman home where Jesus' love flows,

Rainbow Inn

relax in a hammock or hot tub with a view of the rich Skagit Valley farmlands and Mt. Baker. Fine dining, antiques, quaint shops, kayaking, hot-air balloons, and bird- and whale-watching all are available from LaConner. Miles of flat roads for biking and nearby mountains for hiking and skiing. Grandma's cookies await you after your fun-filled day.

Hosts: The Squires Family (Tom, Patsy, Bruce, and Laureen)
Rooms: 8 (5PB; 3SB) $75-105
Full Breakfast
Credit Cards: A, B, D
Notes: 2, 5, 7, 8, 9, 10, 11

LEAVENWORTH

Bosch Garten B&B

9846 Dye Road, 98826
(509) 548-6900; (800) 535-0069;
FAX (509) 548-6076
Web site: http://www.leavenworth.org

Quiet elegance within walking distance of Leavenworth, a Bavarian-theme village.

Spectacular view of the Cascade Mountains. The facility features warm Christian hospitality, beautiful gardens, king beds, TV, AC, and soundproofing, along with a library, hot tub, fireplace, and multicourse fresh breakfasts. A great area for golf, tennis, rock climbing, hiking, river rafting, downhill and cross-country skiing, sleighing, snowmobiling, etc.

Hosts: Myke and Cal Bosch
Rooms: 3 (PB) $98
Full Breakfast
Credit Cards: A, B, D
Notes: 2, 5, 8, 10, 11, 12

Run of the River

PO Box 285, 98826
(509) 548-7171
Web page: http://www.rofther.com

Imagine the quintessential northwestern log bed and breakfast inn. Spacious rooms feature private baths, hand-hewn log beds, and fluffy down comforters. Or you can celebrate in a suite with your own heart-warming woodstove, jetted Jacuzzi surrounded by river rock, and bird's-eye loft to laze about with a favorite book. From your room's log porch swing, view the Icicle River, surrounding bird refuge, and the Cascade peaks, appropriately named the "Enchantments." To explore the Icicle Valley, get off the beaten path with hiking, biking, and driving guides written just for you by the innkeepers—avid bikers and hikers. Take a spin on complimentary mountain bikes. A hearty breakfast sets the day in motion.

Hosts: Monty and Karen Turner
Rooms: 6 (PB) $95-150
Full Breakfast
Credit Cards: A, B, C, D
Notes: 2, 5, 8, 9, 10, 11, 12

welcome; 7 Children welcome; 8 Tennis nearby; 9 Swimming nearby; 10 Golf nearby; 11 Skiing nearby; 12 May be booked through travel agent.

LONGVIEW

Misty Mountain Llamas Bed and Breakfast

1033 Stella Road, 98632
(360) 577-4772

The hosts welcome you to their little piece of heaven, a five-acre llama ranch. The beautiful new custom home offers you two bedrooms, one with queen and one with twin beds, that share a bath. Large sitting room with wood stove, TV/VCR, games, and a large covered patio, with a view of the Columbia River through the wonderful trees. You may take a quiet walk through the woods or visit the llamas. Enjoy a continental plus breakfast in our great room while watching the llamas graze. Gourmet dinner available with advanced notice. No smoking or pets.

Hosts: Doug and Barbara Joy
Rooms: 2 (SB) $85-90
Continental Plus Breakfast
Credit Cards: none
Notes: 2, 4, 5, 7 (over 12), 9 (Columbia River), 10, 12

LOPEZ ISLAND

Aleck Bay Inn

Route 1, Box 1920, 98261
(360) 468-3535; FAX (360) 468-3533
E-mail: abi@pacificrim.net

Aleck Bay Inn provides the luxurious, quiet, and personal care needed for guests celebrating special events, having a romantic getaway, or just wishing a relaxing time by the fireplace. Coffee always hot and pastry ever present. Repeatedly visited by national and state dignitaries. The inn hosts small weddings, business meetings, retreats, and church outings. Guests can walk our beaches, hike through original forests, relax in a hot tub, enjoy the game room, and watch the wildlife. Near island churches, golf courses, and tennis courts. Kayak instruction and bike rentals available. Special breakfasts are served in our lovely dining room or in the solarium and begin with fresh fruit, followed by a large portion of gourmet selections. Breakfast piano concerts on weekends. Chinese and Spanish spoken.

Hosts: May and David Mendez
Rooms: 4 (PB) $79-159
Full Breakfast
Credit Cards: A, B, C, D, E
Notes: 2, 3, 4, 5, 7, 8, 9, 10, 12

LYNDEN

Century House Bed and Breakfast

401 South B.C. Avenue, 98264
(360) 354-2439; (800) 820-3617;
FAX (360) 354-6910

Located on thirty-five acres at the edge of town, Century House Bed and Breakfast is a 109-year-old Victorian home. You'll find this completely restored bed and breakfast is a quiet retreat with spacious gardens and lawns for your enjoyment. The quaint Dutch village of Lynden is just an easy walk away and boasts the best museums in the area and gift shops galore . . . but sorry, the town is closed on Sundays. You can take day trips to the Cascade Mountains and Mt. Baker, the sea,

---

NOTES: Credit cards accepted: A Master Card; B Visa; C American Express; D Discover; E Diners Club; F Other; 2 Personal checks accepted; 3 Lunch available; 4 Dinner available; 5 Open all year; 6 Pets

Seattle, Vancouver, or Victoria, British Columbia.

Hosts: Jan and Ken Stremler
Rooms: 4 (2PB; 2SB) $65-95
Full Breakfast
Credit Cards: A, B
Notes: 2, 5, 7, 8, 9, 10, 11

Dutch Village Inn

655 Front Street, #7, 98264
(360) 354-4440

For a unique treat, spend a night in a windmill! The Dutch Village Inn opened in 1987 in Lynden's Dutch Village Mall. This extraordinary development, reflecting the tidy Dutch heritage of the area, features a seventy-two-foot windmill, interesting retail shops, an indoor canal that runs through the mall, an Amsterdam-style Sidewalk Cafe along the canal, an indoor miniature golf course, a two-hundred-seat theatre, and six unique hotel rooms, three of which are situated in the windmill. The windmill blades turn and are fully lit until ten o'clock each evening.

Hosts: Chuck and Alice Lee
Rooms: 6 (PB) $69-110
Full Breakfast
Credit Cards: A, B, C, D
Notes: 2, 3, 4, 5, 7, 8, 9, 10, 11, 12

MT. VERNON

Dutch Treat

1777 W. Big Lake Boulevard, 98274
(360) 422-5466

Our modest and very Dutch accommodations are located in a lovely setting on a lake that lends itself to all water sports, including fishing and swimming. A public boat launch is available just down the road.

There is a fire pit on the lake's edge where you can roast marshmallows or sip a glass of wine and gaze at the stars. Across the lake is a golf course and a good restaurant. The area is ideal for biking either through the Skagit Valley bulb fields and farmlands or in the foothills of the Cascade Mountains. In winter, there are the many birds to watch (including eagles, trumpeter swans, and snow geese), or you can ski on Mt. Baker or cross-country ski in the foothills. In summer, a Dutch breakfast is served each morning on the deck.

Hosts: Ria and Peter Stroosma
Rooms: 2 (PB) $55
Expanded Continental Breakfast
Credit Cards: none
Notes: 2, 3 (picnic), 5, 7, 9, 10, 11

NACHES

Apple Country Bed and Breakfast

4561 Old Naches Highway—West Yakima, 98937
(509) 965-1591 (voice and FAX)

Caring hosts welcome you to this remodeled 1911 farmhouse west of Yakima in the Naches-Yakima Valley on a working ranch. Ideal for a traveler seeking a country B&B. Enjoy a luscious breakfast while

Apple Country Bed and Breakfast

welcome; 7 Children welcome; 8 Tennis nearby; 9 Swimming nearby; 10 Golf nearby; 11 Skiing nearby; 12 May be booked through travel agent.

taking in the view of the valley from your large bedroom, decorated with new and antique furniture. A short drive from activities, fine dining, golfing, antiquing, skiing, fishing, hiking, hunting, and wine country tours. "Four-season country."

Hosts: Mark and Shirley Robert
Rooms: 3 (PB) $65-75
Continental Breakfast
Credit Cards: B
Notes: 2, 5, 6, 8, 9, 10, 11

OAK HARBOR

North Island B&B

1589 N. West Beach Road, 98277
(360) 675-7080

North Island Bed and Breakfast is located on 175 feet of private beachfront. Each guest room has a private bath, king bed, individual heating, fireplace, and beautiful furnishings. From your deck or patio you'll enjoy a view of the Olympic Mountains and San Juan Islands. A separate entrance and ample parking are provided. Whidby Island's wonderful attractions are close by.

Hosts: Jim and MaryVern Loomis
Rooms: 2 (PB) $85-95
Continental Breakfast
Credit Cards: A, B, C, D
Notes: 2, 5, 10

ORCAS ISLAND —DEER HARBOR

Palmer's Chart House

PO Box 51, 98243
(360) 376-4231

The first B&B on Orcas Island (since 1975) with a magnificent water view. The thirty-three-foot private yacht *Amante* is available for a minimal fee, with skipper Don. Low-key, private, personal attention makes this B&B unique and attractive. Well-traveled hosts speak Spanish.

Hosts: Don and Majean Palmer
Rooms: 2 (PB) $60-70
Full Breakfast
Credit Cards: none
Notes: 2, 5, 7 (over 12), 8, 10, 11, 12

ORCAS ISLAND—EASTSOUND

Kangaroo House Bed and Breakfast

PO Box 334, 98245
(360) 376-2175; FAX (360) 376-3604
E-mail: kangaroo@Rockisland.com

Kangaroo House Bed and Breakfast, a stately 1907 Craftsman-style home on beautiful Orcas Island, is within walking distance of Eastsound restaurants, shops, and galleries. After breakfast in the sunny dining room, guests can relax by the fieldstone fireplace, curl up with a book or puzzle in the library/game room, relax in the garden hot tub, or explore the island. Rates are approximately 10 percent lower Sunday-Thursday, November-April.

Hosts: Peter and Helen Allen
Rooms: 5 (2PB; 3SB) $75-120
Full Breakfast
Credit Cards: A, B, C, D
Notes: 2, 5, 7, 8, 9, 10, 12

Turtleback Farm Inn

Route 1, Box 650, 98245
(360) 376-4914; (800) 376-4914;
FAX (360) 376-5329

Turtleback Farm Inn is noted for its detail-perfect restoration, elegantly comfort-

---

NOTES: Credit cards accepted: A Master Card; B Visa; C American Express; D Discover; E Diners Club; F Other; 2 Personal checks accepted; 3 Lunch available; 4 Dinner available; 5 Open all year; 6 Pets

able and spotless rooms, glorious setting and award-winning breakfasts. You will be made welcome and pampered by the warm hospitality of Bill and Susan Fletcher and their staff. Orcas Island is a haven for anyone who enjoys spectacular scenery, varied outdoor activities, unique shopping, and superb food. As spring turns to summer, the warm days encourage your enjoyment of nature at its best. Flowers are in full bloom; birds flutter; whales, seals, and porpoises coast lazily through the simmering waters of the Sound. After a day of hiking, fishing, bicycling, kayaking, sailing, windsurfing, or just reading by our pond, return to Turtleback for a relaxing soak in your private bath or a sherry on the deck overlooking the valley below. After a tasty dinner at one of the island's fine restaurants and perhaps a performance at the Orcas Center, guests can snuggle under a custom-made woolen comforter and doze off with visions of the delicious breakfast awaiting you in the morning.

Hosts: Susan and William Fletcher
Rooms: 11 (PB) $80-210
Full Breakfast
Credit Cards: A, B, D
Notes: 2, 5, 7 (8 and over, by prior arrangement), 8, 9, 10, 12

ORCAS ISLAND—OLGA

Buck Bay Farm B&B
Star Route Box 45, 98279
(360) 376-2908

Buck Bay Farm is located on beautiful Orcas in the San Juan Islands of Washington State. Orcas is an idyllic vacation destination with lots of outdoor fun: hiking, bicycling, boating or kayaking, whale-

watching, golf, fishing, and much more. The B&B is a farmhouse recently rebuilt by the owner. A warm welcome and hearty, home-style breakfast await you.

Hosts: Rick and Janet Bronkey
Rooms: 5 (3PB; 2SB) $75-95
Full Breakfast
Credit Cards: A, B, C, D
Notes: 2, 5, 7 (by arrangement), 8, 9, 10

PORT TOWNSEND

Ann Starrett Mansion 1889 Victorian B&B Inn
744 Clay Street, 98368
(360) 385-3205; FAX (360) 385-2976
E-mail: starrett@olympus.net

Just as the Taj Mahal was built as a tribute to love, so was this mansion. The most photographed Victorian in the Northwest was awarded "The Great American Home Award" by the National Trust. A sixty-foot octagonal tower with a free-floating staircase leads to a celestial calendar and frescoed maidens dancing in the clouds depicting Ann. "The Crown Jewel of the Pacific Northwest." Step back in time to serenity and beauty.

Hosts: Bob and Edel Sokol
Rooms: 11 (PB) $75-225
Full Breakfast
Credit Cards: A, B, C, D
Notes: 2, 5, 7, 8, 9, 10, 11, 12

PUYALLUP

Tayberry Victorian Cottage
7406 80th Street E., 98371
(253) 848-4594

Elegant country charm fills the lovely rooms at Tayberry. All include queen bed,

welcome; 7 Children welcome; 8 Tennis nearby; 9 Swimming nearby; 10 Golf nearby; 11 Skiing nearby; 12 May be booked through travel agent.

TV, VCR, and private bath. Choose the canopy bed in the "Suite" or a delightful view from your private balcony in the "Balcony Room," or a lovely European bath with claw-foot tub in the "Blue Room." Bountiful breakfasts and warm hospitality await you in this gracious Victorian.

Hosts: Terry and Vicki Chissos
Rooms: 4 (3PB; 1SB) $65-85
Full Breakfast
Credit Cards: A, B
Notes: 2, 5, 7, 10, 11, 12

REDMOND

Lilac Lea Christian B&B

21008 NE 117th Street, 98053
(425) 861-1898; FAX (425) 883-0285

Custom-built Dutch Colonial on a country dead-end lane, surrounded by large firs and next to eighty acres of wilderness preserve. Quiet, yet just seventeen miles from downtown Seattle. Private cottage with separate entrance, queen bed, TV, and study area. Near hiking and biking trails. Large deck and wooded picnic area available. You're special to us—our only guest!

Hosts: Ruthanne Hayes Haight and Chandler Haight
Rooms: 1 suite (PB) (call for prices)
Self-catered Extended Continental Breakfast
Credit Cards: none
Notes: 2, 5, 8, 9, 10, 11

RENTON

Holly Hedge House

908 Grant Avenue S., 98055
(425) 226-2555 (voice and FAX); (888) 226-2555
E-mail: holihedg@nwlink.com
Web site: http://www.nwlink.com/~holihedg

Country Inn Magazine award-winning, romantic 1901 English country cottage for two. Nestled high atop scenic, historic Renton Hill with a picturesque view of the valley and mountains. Centrally located, less than ten minutes from SeaTac International Airport, fifteen minutes from downtown Seattle and island ferries and five minutes from Lake Washington. The entire cottage reserves for one couple at a time to indulge in the beauty and affordable luxury. Amenities include a private hot tub under a gazebo, outdoor swimming pool, hammock for two, whirlpool bathtub, queen-size heaven bed, fully equipped kitchen, fireplace, vast CD/video/reading library, and glassed-in veranda that overlooks the Green River Valley. Ask about the "Special Occasion Package" and "Spirit of Washington Dinner Train Package." A vacation, honeymoon, corporate travel getaway that will be long remembered and cherished!

Hosts: Lynn and Marian Thrasher
Rooms: 1 cottage (PB) $90-130
Full and Continental Breakfast
Credit Cards: A, B
Notes: 2, 5, 8, 9 (on premises), 10, 11

SEDRO WOOLLEY

South Bay Bed and Breakfast

4095 S. Bay Drive, Lake Whatcom, 98284
(360) 595-2086; fax (360) 595-1043
E-mail: southbay@gte.net

On a hillside overlooking Lake Whatcom is South Bay Bed and Breakfast, a classic lakeside retreat. Wraparound porch, generous hospitality, attention to detail, quiet and restful Lakeview rooms. All rooms have private patios. Breakfast combines the unexpected with good health for deli-

South Bay Bed and Breakfast

cious results. Come, rest, nurture your-self at South Bay.

Hosts: Dan and Sally Moore
Rooms: 5 (PB) $125-150
Full Breakfast
Credit Cards: A, B
Notes: 5, 7 (over 12), 8, 9, 10, 11

SEQUIM

Greywolf Inn

395 Keeler Road, 98382
(360) 683-5889; (800) 914-WOLF (9653);
FAX (360) 683-1487
E-mail: grywolf@olypen.com
Web site: http://www.northolympic.com/greywolf

Nestled in a crescent of towering ever-greens, this northwestern country estate overlooks the Dungeness Valley. An ideal starting point for year-round, light adven-ture on the Olympic peninsula—hiking, fishing, biking, boating, bird-watching, sight-seeing, and golf. Enjoy Greywolf's sunny decks, Japanese-style hot tub, and meandering five-acre woodswalk, or curl up by the fire with a good book. Then retire to one of the cozy, comfortable theme rooms for the night.

Hosts: Peggy and Bill Melang
Rooms: 5 (PB) $65-120
Full Breakfast
Credit Cards: A, B, C, D
Notes: 2, 5, 7 (over 12), 8, 9, 10, 11, 12

SNOHOMISH

Redmond House

317 Glen Avenue, 98290
(360) 568-2042

Enter a world of comfort, luxury, and simple elegance that makes time stand still. Located in the Victorian-era town of Snohomish, Redmond House is within walking distance of the "Antique Capital of the Northwest" with four hundred an-tique dealers, gift shops, and restaurants. The house is graced by beautiful gardens and a wraparound porch. Period antiques. Luxurious bedrooms filled with quilts, lin-ens, and queen featherbeds are available with claw-foot soaking tubs. Near hik-ing, boating, golf, skiing, hot-air balloon-ing, parachuting, wineries, and sports.

Hosts: Ken and Mary Riley
Rooms: 4 (2PB; 2SB) $85-100
Full Breakfast
Credit Cards: A, B
Notes: 2, 5, 7, 8, 9, 10, 11

Redmond House

A Victorian Rose

124 Avenue D, 98290
(360) 568-7673
E-mail: kelnhof@gte.net

A 1904 Victorian located one block from Main Street of Snohomish, the antique

welcome; 7 Children welcome; 8 Tennis nearby; 9 Swimming nearby; 10 Golf nearby; 11 Skiing nearby; 12 May be booked through travel agent.

capital of Washington. Comfortable queen chiropractic beds with Victorian decor. Parlor with fireplace, old books, parlor games, and TV. Formal dining room with full three-course breakfast. Fruit cobblers at night, parachuting, hot-air balloon rides at municipal airport a quarter of a mile away. Gardens and deck overlooking the Kai Pond. We choose to be small and personal. Discounts on your church's visitors and getaways. Appropriate for small wedding reception and outdoor ceremony.

Hosts: Dave and Sheri Kelnhofer
Rooms: 2 (PB) $70-75
Full Breakfast
Credit Cards: B
Notes: 2, 4, 5, 7, 8, 9, 10, 11, 12

SNOQUALMIE PASS

Frantzian Mountain Hideaway

7 Ober Strasse, Alpental, PO Box 174, 98068
(206) 434-6270

Rustic but charming, self-contained, private, fully furnished apartment in hosts' home. Apartment features small kitchenette, living room with fireplace and loft, private bedroom, and bathroom with shower. Great for families or small groups of four to six people. Breakfast provisions provided. Bavarian and Mt. Alpine setting adjacent to four ski areas and the Pacific Crest Trail. Only fifty-five minutes east of Seattle and five minutes to skiing, sledding, hiking, mountain biking, and other outdoor recreational activities.

Hosts: Forrest and Pat Frantz
Rooms: 1 apartment (sleeps 4-6, PB) $55-75
Continental Breakfast (provisions provided)
Credit Cards: none
Notes: 2, 5, 7, 11

SPOKANE

Marianna Stoltz House

E. 427 Indiana Avenue, 99207
(509) 483-4316; (800) 978-6587;
FAX (509) 483-6773

Our 1908 historic home is situated five minutes from downtown. Furnished with antiques, old quilts, and Oriental rugs. We offer a wraparound veranda, sitting room, and parlor, which provide relaxation and privacy. Enjoy king, queen, or single beds with private or shared baths, AC, and TV. A tantalizing, unique, and hearty breakfast is prepared each morning. Located close to shopping, opera house, convention center, Centennial Trail, riverfront park, and bus.

Hosts: Jim and Phyllis Maguire
Rooms: 4 (2PB; 2SB) $75-95
Full Breakfast
Credit Cards: A, B, C, D, E
Notes: 2, 5, 8, 9, 10, 11, 12

Oslo's Bed and Breakfast

1821 E. 39th Avenue, 99203
(509) 838-3175; (888) 838-3175

Oslo's Bed and Breakfast is an attractive South Hill home on a quiet street. It offers comfortable bedrooms with private baths, and living room is available where you may relax and read or visit in a Norwegian atmosphere. The home has central AC. A large terrace overlooking the garden may be enjoyed with a full breakfast served at 9 AM—Scandinavian cuisine, if desired. An earlier breakfast may be arranged, if planned in advance. A small park is located a half block away. It offers tennis courts, exercise stops, and paths for walking. The network of skywalks in downtown Spokane is worth investigating, as well as the Cheney Cowles Museum and the Bing Crosby Library at Gonzaga University.

Host: Aslaug Stevenson
Rooms: 2 (PB) $55-70
Full Breakfast
Credit Cards: none
Notes: 2, 5, 6, 8, 10, 11, 12

TACOMA/SEATTLE

Commencement Bay Bed and Breakfast

3312 N. Union Avenue, 98407
(253) 752-8175; FAX (253) 759-4025
E-mail: greatviews@aol.com
Web site: http://www.bestinns.net/usa/wa/cb.html

An elegant colonial home in scenic North Tacoma with dramatic bay and mountain views. Located in an historic area near quaint shops, numerous fine restaurants, and waterfront parks. Featured in "Northwest Best Places," the inn serves fantastic breakfasts and offers large rooms, private baths, a relaxing fireside area, a secluded garden hot tub, and full services for business guests. Gourmet coffees are served each day.

Hosts: Sharon and Bill Kaufmann
Rooms: 3 (PB) $75-115
Full Breakfast
Credit Cards: A, B, C, D
Notes: 2, 5, 8, 9, 10, 11, 12

WHITE SALMON

Llama Ranch Bed and Breakfast

1980 Highway 141, 98672
(509) 395-2786

Llama Ranch Bed and Breakfast is nestled in a peaceful valley with spectacular views of two mountains. Enjoy free llama walks with hands-on experience. See nature in all its splendor as you hike, horseback ride, white-water raft, windsurf, fish, hunt, cross-country ski, snowmobile, bike, pick huckleberries, or explore caves in the area. Separate bed and breakfast area is complete with kitchen, dining room, living room, and queen beds. Suitable for small group retreats. Children and pets okay.

Hosts: Jerry Stone
Rooms: 6 (1PB; 5SB) $79-89
Full Breakfast
Credit Cards: A, B, D
Notes: 2, 5, 6, 7

welcome; 7 Children welcome; 8 Tennis nearby; 9 Swimming nearby; 10 Golf nearby; 11 Skiing nearby; 12 May be booked through travel agent.

WEST VIRGINIA

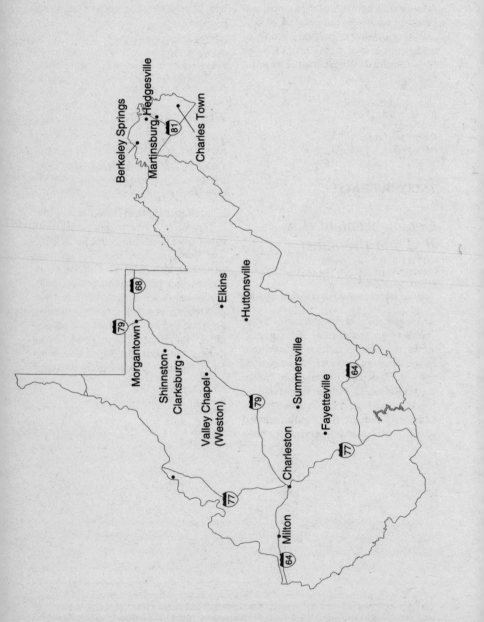

West Virginia

BERKELEY SPRINGS

Maria's Garden and Inn

201 Independence Street, 25411
(304) 258-2021

Peg Perry, devout Roman Catholic, has opened her heart and her door to everyone. A delightful two-and-a-half-story brick colonial home nestled at the foot of the mountain below the Berkeley Castle is within walking distance of the state park, shopping, and antique malls. Peg's motto is "Work as if everything depends on you; Pray as if everything depends on God."

Hostess: Peg Perry
Rooms: 9 (3PB; 6SB) $40-65
Full Breakfast
Credit Cards: A, B, D
Notes: 2, 3, 4, 5, 7, 8, 9, 10, 11, 12

CHARLES TOWN

The Carriage Inn

417 E. Washington Street, 25414-1077
(304) 728-8003; (800) 867-9830;
FAX (304) 728-2976

The Carriage Inn, built in 1863, is a grand colonial home located on a shady acre in the historic district. Generals Grant and Sheridan met here in 1864 to plan Civil War strategy in the Shenandoah Valley. Each of the six bedrooms is large and airy, with private bath and queen-size bed. A hot breakfast is served each morning. Most guest rooms have working fireplaces. Television viewing areas and refrigerated storage are available. This is a nonsmoking inn.

Hosts: Al and Kay Standish
Rooms: 6 (PB) $75-135
Full Breakfast
Credit Cards: A, B

CHARLESTON

Historic Charleston Bed and Breakfast

110 Elizabeth Street, 25311
(304) 345-8156; FAX (304) 342-1572

Historic Charleston Bed and Breakfast is one block west of the state capitol, one mile from downtown and the civic center. An elegant French country home. Hospitality is the main topic of the day. Businesspeople welcome, as well as travelers.

Hosts: Bob and Jean Lambert
Rooms: 3 (PB) $65-75; child's room $15
Full Breakfast
Credit Cards: A, B, C
Notes: 2, 5, 7 (over 10), 8, 9, 10, 11 (1 hour away)

NOTES: Credit cards accepted: A Master Card; B Visa; C American Express; D Discover; E Diners Club; F Other; 2 Personal checks accepted; 3 Lunch available; 4 Dinner available; 5 Open all year; 6 Pets welcome; 7 Children welcome; 8 Tennis nearby; 9 Swimming nearby; 10 Golf nearby; 11 Skiing nearby; 12 May be booked through travel agent.

Main Street Bed and Breakfast

CLARKSBURG

Main Street Bed and Breakfast

151 E. Main Street, 26301
(304) 623-1440 (voice and FAX); (800) 526-9460

Just five blocks from the heart of Clarksburg, our 1872 home is one of the oldest in the county and part of a National Registered historic district. It was built in the Carpenter Gothic style and is decorated in a pleasing, multicolored scheme. The large guest rooms have queen or king beds and comfortable sitting areas.

Hosts: David and Bethlyn Cluphf
Rooms: 3 (PB) $60-70
Full Breakfast
Credit Cards: A, B, C, D, E
Notes: 2, 5, 7, 10, 12

ELKINS

The Warfield House

318 Buffalo Street, 26241
(304) 636-4555; (888) 636-4555;
FAX (304) 636-1457
Web site: http://www.virtualcities.com

Casual atmosphere in elegant turn-of-the-century home nestled among towering oaks, hemlocks, and pines on a quiet corner. Serene setting across from forested City Park in scenic mountain town. Within walking distance of restaurants, shops, and theaters. A sumptuous breakfast of fresh fruit, home-baked breads/pastries and hot entrée will ready you for the day's activities or a nap on the broad front porch. Nearby historic attractions, antiquing, hiking, biking, fishing, and festivals.

Hosts: Connie and Paul Garnett
Rooms: 5 (3PB; 2SB) $75
Full Breakfast
Credit Cards: none
Notes: 2, 5, 8, 9, 10, 11

The Warfield House

FAYETTEVILLE

Wisteria House Bed and Breakfast

147 S. Court Street, 25840
(304) 574-3678

Enjoy southern hospitality in this bed and breakfast located in historic Fayetteville. Just minutes from Bridge Haven Golf Course, within walking distance of the historic Fayette Theatre. Strategically located for rafting, mountain biking, hiking, and

---

NOTES: Credit cards accepted: A Master Card; B Visa; C American Express; D Discover; E Diners Club; F Other; 2 Personal checks accepted; 3 Lunch available; 4 Dinner available; 5 Open all year; 6 Pets

sight-seeing trips. Three air-conditioned bedrooms. Complimentary breakfast. Our southern hospitality is extended in our unique gift shop and our full service barber shop, located on premises.

Hosts: Matt and Denise Scalph
Rooms: 3 (SB) $64
Full Breakfast
Credit Cards: A, B
Notes: 2, 5, 7, 8, 9, 10, 11

HEDGESVILLE

The Farmhouse on Tomahawk Run

1 Tomahawk Run Place, 25427
(304) 754-7350 (voice and FAX)
Web site: http://www.travelwv.com

The Farmhouse is near Martinsburg, ten miles west of I-81. In addition to B&B guests, we host small group retreats for up to sixteen persons. We are trained by the Association of Couples in Marriage Enrichment to lead marriage retreats, which we hold twice each year. Our farmhouse, built during the Civil War, stands beside the springhouse (now on the National Register of Historic Places) and the foundation of the old log cabin. Nestled in a secluded valley beside a meandering stream, it is surrounded by woods, hills and meadows with walking paths. A stone fireplace in the large gathering room contains a roaring log fire on cold evenings. Wraparound porch, rocking chairs and Jacuzzi available. A bountiful three-course breakfast is served by candlelight.

Hosts: Judy and Hugh Erskine
Rooms: 3 (PB) + carriage house, $65-140
Full Breakfast
Credit Cards: A, B, D
Notes: 2, 5, 7, 10

HUTTONSVILLE

Hutton House Bed and Breakfast

Routes 250 and 219, PO Box 88, 26273
(304) 335-6701
Web site: http://www.inns.com/midatl/wv010.htm

Meticulously restored and decorated, this Queen Anne Victorian home on the National Register of Historic Places is located conveniently near Elkins, Cass Railroad, and Snowshoe Ski Resort. It has a wraparound porch and deck for relaxing and enjoying the view, TV, game room, lawn for games, and friendly kitchen. Breakfast and afternoon refreshments are served at your leisure; other meals are available with prior reservation or good luck! Come see us!

Hosts: Dean Ahren and Loretta Murray
Rooms: 6 (PB) $70-80
Full Breakfast
Credit Cards: A, B
Notes: 2, 7, 10, 11, 12

MARTINSBURG

Boydville—The Inn at Martinsburg

601 S. Queen Street, 25401
(304) 263-1448

A stone manor house, set well back from Queen Street. To reach the front door, you turn up a drive through ten acres with over-arching maples on both sides of the road. This is an experience in itself, because it feels as if you are being led away from a busy world into an earlier and more peaceful time. Handsomely appointed and furnished with English and American antiques, the inn dates to 1812. Guests enjoy leisurely walks on the grounds, in the

welcome; 7 Children welcome; 8 Tennis nearby; 9 Swimming nearby; 10 Golf nearby; 11 Skiing nearby; 12 May be booked through travel agent.

brick-walled courtyard, and in the surrounding gardens. Boydville is ideal for a business retreat or romantic getaway. On the National Register of Historic Places.

Host: LaRue Frye
Rooms: 6 (4PB; 2SB) $90-110, 2-night stay
Full Breakfast
Credit Cards: A, B
Notes: 2, 5 (except August), 7 (over 12), 10, 11, 12

MILTON

The Cedar House

92 Trenol Heights, 25541
(304) 743-5516; (800) CALLWVA
E-mail: vickersc@marshall.edu

The home is a spacious, air-conditioned, ranch-style lodging less than one mile from I-64 on five-and-a-half acres overlooking the Milton countryside. Spend the evening in the game room, den, living room, or watching a video in front of a fire in the family room. Work a jigsaw puzzle or play pool, games, guitar, or piano. On warm evenings, enjoy horseshoes, badminton, croquet, or a leisurely walk.

Hostess: Carole A. Vickers
Rooms: 3 (PB) $65-75
Full Breakfast
Credit Cards: A, B, C, D
Notes: 2, 5, 8, 9, 10

MORGANTOWN

Fieldcrest Manor Bed and Breakfast

1440 Stewartstown Road, 26505
(304) 599-2686; (800) 765-0569;
FAX (304) 599-2853

Elegant yet affordable, this eighty-year-old house is surrounded by five beautiful acres.

It offers five bedrooms, all with private baths, TV, and telephone. We are only five minutes from area hospitals, business centers, and West Virginia University campuses/sporting events. Area activities include hiking, bicycling, fishing, hunting, golfing, white water, and Coopers Rock State Park.

Hosts: Susan Linkous and Sarah Lough
Rooms: 5 (PB) $65-80
Full Breakfast
Credit Cards: A, B
Notes: 2, 5, 8, 9, 10, 11

Gillum House Bed and Breakfast

SHINNSTON

Gillum House Bed and Breakfast

35 Walnut Street, 26431-1154
(304) 592-0177; (800) CALLWVA;
FAX (304) 592-1882

The aroma of fresh baking wafts through the house as you enter. Enjoy comfort (robes in closets for guest use), relaxation (all books on the second floor are to be taken home), and good, healthy food (heart-healthy, homemade from scratch).

NOTES: Credit cards accepted: A Master Card; B Visa; C American Express; D Discover; E Diners Club; F Other; 2 Personal checks accepted; 3 Lunch available; 4 Dinner available; 5 Open all year; 6 Pets

Shinnston is a trail head for the West Fork River trail.

Hostess: Kathleen A Panek
Rooms: 3 (SB) $50-55
Continental Plus Breakfast
Credit Cards: A, B

SUMMERSVILLE

Historic Brock House Bed and Breakfast Inn

1400 Webster Road, 26651
(304) 872-4887

Tucked away among towering maples and oaks, Historic Brock House Bed and Breakfast Inn has hosted travelers for more than a hundred years. On lazy summer afternoons, guests can enjoy the rockers and wicker furniture on the wide, wrap-around porch. On cooler days, a cozy fireside is available for quiet moments, a cup of tea, card playing, or visiting with new friends. Guests can choose from a full or light breakfast with various home-baked items. Antique shops, Civil War battlefields, canoeing, water-skiing, horse-back trails, kayaking, rock climbing, and white-water rafting abound in this area.

Hostess: Margie Martin
Rooms: 6 (4PB; 2SB) $70-90
Full Breakfast
Credit Cards: A, B
Notes: 2, 4, 10, 12

Ingeberg Acres Bed and Breakfast

VALLEY CHAPEL (WESTON)

Ingeberg Acres Bed and Breakfast

PO Box 199, 26446
(304) 269-2834 (voice and FAX); (800) CALL WVA
Web site: http://www.tiac.net/users/mann

An unique experience can be yours at this scenic, 450-acre horse and cattle farm. Ingeberg Acres is located in the heart of West Virginia, seven miles from Weston, overlooking its own private valley. Hiking, swimming, hunting, and fishing—or simply relaxing—can be the orders of the day. Observe or participate in numerous farm activities. Craft outlets and antique stores nearby. Come enjoy the gardens, the pool, and the friendly atmosphere. German spoken.

Hosts: Inge and John Mann
Rooms: 3 (SB) $59; cabin $80
Full Breakfast
Credit Cards: none
Notes: 2, 5, 7, 9, 10

WISCONSIN

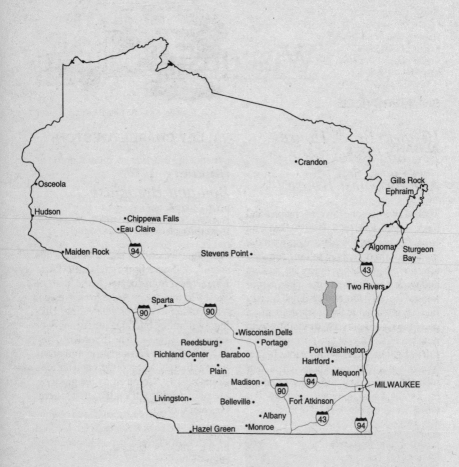

Wisconsin

ALBANY

Albany Guest House

405 S. Mill Street, 53502
(608) 862-3636

A two-acre, parklike setting, with flower gardens galore and a brick walk, is where you'll find the restored 1908 three-story block home. With blooming plants everywhere, you'll find king- and queen-size beds, and a wood-burning fireplace in the master bedroom. Be amazed with the complete, antique, four-piece, solid bird's-eye maple bedroom set, a family heirloom. After a full, wholesome breakfast, recover on the porch swing or rocker, or stroll the

Albany Guest House

grounds before exploring, biking, tubing, or canoeing the river. A great reunion or retreat site.

Hosts: Bob and Sally Braem
Rooms: 6 (4PB; 1SB) $55-75
Full Breakfast
Credit Cards: A, B
Notes: 2, 5, 7 (disciplined), 8, 10, 11

Oak Hill Manor Bed and Breakfast

401 E. Main Street, PO Box 190, 53502
(608) 862-1400; FAX (608) 862-1403
E-mail: glenroth@ix.netcom.com

Step back into time in our 1908 manor home. Enjoy rich oak woodwork, gasoliers, and period furnishings. Spacious, sunny corner rooms have queen-size beds and cozy reading areas. Choose a room with a fireplace, porch, or canopy bed. Relax in our English country garden with gazebo, or lounge in a wicker rocker on our spacious porch. Sumptuous breakfast served by fireside and candlelight. Wake-up coffee. Canoe/fish on the Sugar River or ride/hike the bike trail. Complimentary guest bikes. No smoking. Great

---

NOTES: Credit cards accepted: A Master Card; B Visa; C American Express; D Discover; E Diners Club; F Other; 2 Personal checks accepted; 3 Lunch available; 4 Dinner available; 5 Open all year; 6 Pets welcome; 7 Children welcome; 8 Tennis nearby; 9 Swimming nearby; 10 Golf nearby; 11 Skiing nearby; 12 May be booked through travel agent.

for reunions and business retreats! Gift certificates available.

Hosts: Donna and Glen Rothe
Rooms: 4 (PB) $65-75
Full Breakfast
Credit Cards: A, B
Notes: 2, 5, 7 (12 and older), 8, 9, 10, 11 (cross-country)

Amberwood Inn

ALGOMA

Amberwood Inn

N7136 Highway 42, 54201
(414) 487-3471

Come to Amberwood, a romantic country inn with five large, luxury waterfront suites, located ten minutes from Door County. Enjoy our two-plus wooded acres, three hundred feet of private Lake Michigan Beach, sauna, large outdoor hot tub, and spectacular breakfast. All suites offer private bath, double French doors leading to individual lakefront deck, refrigerator, fine antiques, plush linens, and fireplace. Sleep to the sound of the waves; awaken to a sunrise over the water.

Hosts: Mark and Karen Rittle
Rooms: 5 (PB) $69-99
Full Breakfast
Credit Cards: some
Notes: 2, 5, 7, 9, 10, 11

BARABOO

Pinehaven
Bed and Breakfast

E13083 Highway 33, 53913
(608) 356-3489

Located in a scenic valley with a small, private lake and Baraboo Bluffs in the background. The guest rooms are distinctly different, with wicker furniture and antiques, queen and twin beds. Take a walk in this peaceful country setting. Area activities include Devil's Lake State Park, Circus World Museum, Wisconsin Dells, and ski resorts. Ask about our private guest cottage. No pets, no smoking. Gift certificates available. Closed in March.

Hosts: Lyle and Marge Getschman
Rooms: 4 (PB) $65-125
Full Breakfast
Credit Cards: A, B
Notes: 2, 5, 7 (over 5), 9, 10, 11

Pinehaven Bed and Breakfast

Victorian Rose
Bed and Breakfast

423 Third Avenue, 53913
(608) 356-7828

Nostalgic retreat. A place for all seasons. Spend tranquil moments with memories to

---

NOTES: Credit cards accepted: A Master Card; B Visa; C American Express; D Discover; E Diners Club; F Other; 2 Personal checks accepted; 3 Lunch available; 4 Dinner available; 5 Open all year; 6 Pets

treasure. Nestled in the heart of historical Baraboo. Centrally located to all area attractions. Enjoy the splendor of the Victorian era by resting on the wraparound front porch or relaxing in two formal parlors with beautiful cherub fireplace and TV/VCR. Romantic guest rooms, candlelight breakfast, and Christian hospitality.

Hosts: Bob and Carolyn Stearns
Rooms: 3 (PB) $70-90
Full Breakfast
Credit Cards: D
Notes: 2, 5, 8, 9, 10, 11

BELLEVILLE

Abendruh B&B Swisstyle

7019 Gehin Drive, 53508
(608) 424-3808

Experience B&B Swisstyle. This highly acclaimed Wisconsin B&B offers true Swiss charm and hospitality. The serenity of this retreat is one of many treasures that keeps guests coming back. Spacious guest rooms are adorned with beautiful family heirlooms. The sitting room has a high cathedral ceiling and cozy fireplace. An Abendruh breakfast is a perfect way to start a new day or end a peaceful stay.

Hostess: Mathilde Jaggi
Rooms: 2 (PB) $60-65
Full Breakfast
Credit Cards: none
Notes: 2, 5, 8, 9, 10, 11, 12

Cameo Rose Bed and Breakfast

1090 Severson Road, 53508-9233
(608) 424-6340

Romantic, Victorian country mansion set amid 120 acres of wooded hills and trails.

Enjoy the gazebo porch with wicker swing and furniture, guest living room with fireplace, and tower sunroom. Ultimate quiet and relaxation. Memorable breakfast served on antique china and vintage lace. Five charming, smoke-free guest rooms with king or queen beds, private baths, and central air; one with whirlpool. Ten miles to Madison or New Glarus. Antiques combined with comfort. Welcome!

Hosts: Dawn and Gary Bahr and Jennifer
Rooms: 5 (PB) $89-139
Full Breakfast
Credit Cards: A, B
Notes: 2, 5, 8, 9, 10, 11, 12

McGilvray's Victorian Bed and Breakfast

CHIPPEWA FALLS

McGilvray's Victorian Bed and Breakfast

312 W. Columbia Street, 54729
(715) 720-1600; (888) 324-1893

Built in 1893, this beautifully restored home is furnished with antiques typical of the era. The Georgian Revival/neoclassical home has a portico with two-story columns.

McGilvray's Victorian Bed and Breakfast is located in a quiet west hill neighborhood close to restaurants and unique shops. A delicious breakfast is included, served in the dining room.

Hostess: Melanie Berg
Rooms: 3 (1PB; 2SB) $60-75
Full Breakfast
Credit Cards: none
Notes: 2, 5, 7 (over 12), 8, 9, 10, 11

Courthouse Square Bed and Breakfast

CRANDON

Courthouse Square Bed and Breakfast

210 E. Polk Street, 54520
(715) 478-2549

Guests frequently comment about the peace and tranquillity of the setting. Enjoy birds and squirrels at the many benches placed throughout the flower and herb gardens, or stroll down the hill to the lake through the forget-me-nots and view the wildlife. *The Rhinelander Daily News* wrote: "Traditional hospitality is emphasized at Courthouse Square B&B, and it's evident from the moment you enter this delightful home where tranquillity and peace abounds. You will no doubt smell

something delicious baking in Bess's kitchen as gourmet cooking is one of her specialties."

Hosts: Les and Bess Aho
Rooms: 3 (1PB; 2SB) $52-70
Full Gourmet Candlelit Breakfast
Credit Cards: C
Notes: 2, 5, 7 (ask about 12+), 8, 9, 10, 11

DOOR COUNTY
(SEE—EPHRAIM, GILLS ROCK, AND STURGEON BAY)

EAU CLAIRE

The Atrium Bed and Breakfast

5572 Prill Road, 54701
(715) 833-9045; (888) 773-0094
E-mail: atrium@eau-claire.com
Web site: http://www.eau-claire.com/atrium

The Atrium is named for its most unique feature—the heart of this contemporary home is a 20 x 20-foot garden room where a palm tree and bougainvillea vines stretch toward the glassed ceiling. The home is nestled on fifteen wooded acres on Otter Creek that beckons the explorer. Nearby you'll find bicycling, canoeing, antiquing, and an Amish community. The Atrium offers the best of both worlds: relaxed seclusion, only minutes from numerous restaurants, shopping, and the University of Wisconsin-Eau Claire.

Hosts: Celia and Dick Stoltz
Rooms: 4 (2PB; 2SB) $65-80
Full Breakfast, weekends; Continental, weekdays
Credit Cards: A, B
Notes: 2, 5, 7 (12 and over), 8, 9, 10, 11 (cross-country)

NOTES: Credit cards accepted: A Master Card; B Visa; C American Express; D Discover; E Diners Club; F Other; 2 Personal checks accepted; 3 Lunch available; 4 Dinner available; 5 Open all year; 6 Pets

Otter Creek Inn

2536 Highway 12, 54701
(715) 832-2945

Pamper yourself with breakfast in bed amid the antiques of yesteryear in this spacious, six-thousand-square-foot, three-story inn. Discover amenities of today tucked amidst the country Victorian decor, as every guest room contains a double whirlpool, private bath, phone, AC, and cable TV. Explore the creek or snuggle up inside near the fire to watch the wildlife saunter by. All this country charm is located less than one mile from numerous restaurants and shops.

Hosts: Randy and Shelley Hansen
Rooms: 6 (PB) $79-139
Full Breakfast
Credit Cards: A, B, C, D, E, F
Notes: 2, 5, 8, 9, 10, 11

EPHRAIM

Hillside Hotel of Ephraim

9980 Highway 42, 54211-0017
(414) 854-2417; (800) 423-7023;
FAX (414) 854-4240

Authentic, restored country Victorian inn featuring full, specialty breakfasts and afternoon tea, featherbeds, original antiques, gorgeous harbor view, one-hundred-foot veranda overlooking the harbor, individually decorated guest rooms, claw-foot tubs with showers, and brass fixtures. Afternoon tea served. We have thirteen years' experience and *love* what we do!!

Hosts: David and Karen McNeil
Rooms: 11 (SB); 2 cottages (PB) $80-190
Full Breakfast
Credit Cards: A, B, D
Notes: 2, 5, 7, 8, 9, 10, 11

FORT ATKINSON

The Lamp Post Inn

408 S. Main Street, 53538
(920) 563-6561

We welcome you to the charm of our 122-year-old Victorian home filled with beautiful antiques. Five gramophones for your listening pleasure. For the modern, one of our baths features a large Jacuzzi. We are located seven blocks from the famous Fireside Playhouse. You come a stranger, but leave here a friend. No smoking.

Hosts: Debbie and Mike Rusch
Rooms: 3 (2PB; 1SB) $60-95
Full Breakfast
Credit Cards: none
Notes: 2, 5, 7, 8, 9, 10, 11

GILLS ROCK (DOOR COUNTY)

Harbor House Inn

12666 Highway 42, 54210
(920) 854-5196; FAX (920) 854-9717

A 1904 Victorian bed and breakfast with a new Scandinavian country wing overlooking the quaint fishing harbor, bluffs, and sunsets. The inn has been restored to

Harbor House Inn

---

welcome; 7 Children welcome; 8 Tennis nearby; 9 Swimming nearby; 10 Golf nearby; 11 Skiing nearby; 12 May be booked through travel agent.

its original charm and tastefully done in period furniture. All rooms have Victorian old-world charm, private baths, TVs, air-conditioning, and period furnishings. Two cottages are also available, both with full kitchens and one with a fireplace. Enjoy the inn's fireplace, gazebo, one of the many decks, private beach, Scandinavian sauna cabin, whirlpool, and bike rentals. You can walk to the ferry, shopping, and dining. AAA three-diamond-rated. Open May 1 through October 30.

Hosts: David and Else Weborg
Rooms: 12 + 2 cottages (PB) $55-115
Continental Plus Breakfast
Credit Cards: A, B, C
Notes: 2, 6, 7, 9, 10

Jordan House Bed and Breakfast

HARTFORD

Jordan House Bed and Breakfast

81 S. Main Street, 53027
(414) 673-5643

Warm and comfortable Victorian home furnished with period antiques. Forty miles from Milwaukee. Near majestic Holy Hill Shrine, Horizon Wildlife Refuge, and Pike Lake State Park. Walk to the state's largest antique auto museum, antique malls, and downtown shops. Ask for brochure.

Hosts: Kathy Buchanan and Art Jones
Rooms: 4 (1PB; 3SB) $55-65
Full Breakfast
Credit Cards: A, B
Notes: 2, 5, 7, 8, 9, 10, 11

Jefferson Day House

HUDSON

Jefferson Day House

1109 Third Street, 54016
(715) 386-7111

The quiet, tree-lined street of a romantic river town is home to this luxurious, historic bed and breakfast. The home offers four beautifully designed guest suites, each with private bath, queen bed, double whirlpool and gas fireplace. Wood-burning fireplaces grace the home's formal dining room and main-floor library. Well-planted grounds create a sense of enclosure in the large, private courtyard. Just a short walk away are Hudson's charming downtown streets with one-of-a-kind shops and restaurants. This beautiful house was restored from top to bottom in 1996.

Hosts: Tom and Sue Tyler
Rooms: 4 (PB) $99-179
Full Breakfast
Credit Cards: A, B, D
Notes: 2, 5 (inquire), 6, 7, 8, 9, 10, 11, 12

NOTES: Credit cards accepted: A Master Card; B Visa; C American Express; D Discover; E Diners Club; F Other; 2 Personal checks accepted; 3 Lunch available; 4 Dinner available; 5 Open all year; 6 Pets

LIVINGSTON

Oak Hill Farm

9850 Highway 80, 53554
(608) 943-6006

A comfortable country home with a warm, hospitable atmosphere that is enhanced with fireplaces, porches, and facilities for picnics, bird-watching, and hiking. In the area you will find state parks, museums, and lakes.

Hosts: Elizabeth and Victor Johnson
Suites: 4 (1PB; 3SB) $42
Continental Breakfast
Credit Cards: none
Notes: 2, 6, 7, 8, 9, 10, 11, 12

MADISON

Annie's Bed and Breakfast

2117 Sheridan Drive, 53704
(608) 244-2224 (voice and FAX)

When you want the world to go away, come to Annie's, the quiet inn on Warner Park with the beautiful view. Luxury accommodations at reasonable rates. Close to the lake and park, it is also convenient to downtown and the University of Wisconsin campus. There are unusual amenities in this charming setting, including a romantic gazebo surrounded by butterfly gardens, a shaded terrace, and a pond. Two beautiful two-bedroom suites. Double Jacuzzi. Full air-conditioning. Winter cross-country skiing, too!

Hosts: Anne and Lawrence Stuart
Suites: 2 (PB) $93-129
Full Breakfast
Credit Cards: A, B, C
Notes: 2, 5, 7 (over 12), 8, 9, 10, 11

Mansion Hill Inn

424 N. Pinckney Street, 53705
(608) 255-3999; (800) 798-9070;
FAX (608) 255-2217

The Mansion Hill Inn offers eleven luxurious rooms, each with a sumptuous bath. Whirlpool tubs with stereo headphones, hand-carved marble fireplaces, minibars, and elegant Victorian furnishings help make this restored mansion into Madison's *only* four-diamond inn. A private wine cellar, VCRs, and access to private dining and athletic clubs are available upon request. Guests are treated to turndown service and evening refreshments in our parlor. The Mansion Hill Inn is ideal for honeymoons. It is listed on the National Register of Historic Places.

Hostess: Janna Wojtal
Rooms: 11 (PB) $120-300
Continental, Silver Service Breakfast
Credit Cards: A, B, C
Notes: 2, 5, 9, 12

MAIDEN ROCK

Harrisburg Inn

W3334 Highway 35, PO Box 15, 54750
(715) 448-4500

Our slogan, "a view with a room," does not begin to describe the sweeping vista enjoyed from every room. Miles of Mississippi Valley spread out with boating, fishing, bird-watching, and biking readily available. The Harrisburg Inn nestles on a bluff with the ambience of yesteryear in simple country decor and the beauty of nature pleasing the eye. Hearty food and happy hosts welcome you to Wisconsin's

welcome; 7 Children welcome; 8 Tennis nearby; 9 Swimming nearby; 10 Golf nearby; 11 Skiing nearby; 12 May be booked through travel agent.

Harrisburg Inn

west coast. Explore twelve vintage villages of the Lake Pepin area and "inn-joy."

Hosts: Bern Paddock and Carol Crisp (Paddock)
Rooms: 4 (PB) $68-98
Full Breakfast, Saturday-Monday morning; Continental Plus, Tuesday-Friday morning
Credit Cards: A, B, D
Notes: 2, 7 (weekdays), 9, 10, 11

MEQUON

Port Zedler Motel

10036 N. Port Washington Road, 53092
(414) 241-5850; (414) 241-5858
E-mail: zedler@execpc.com

AAA-approved. Air-conditioned. Convenient to downtown, casino, and excellent restaurants. Twelve minutes north of downtown Milwaukee. Touch-tone, in-room phones. Full private bath/shower. Winter plug-ins. In-room refrigerator and microwave oven on request. Rates include color cable TV (HBO/Showtime). Free parking and ice are available. No charge for children under 12. Senior/AARP/AAA discounts. German is spoken. I-43 northbound, one-half mile northwest of Exit 83 (Highway W. North). I-43 southbound, Exit 82A, one block east and one-and-

one-half miles north on Port Washington Road (Highway W. North).

Hostess: Sheila
Rooms: 16 (PB) $34-95-59.95
Continental Breakfast
Credit Cards: A, B, C, D
Notes: 5, 6, 7, 8, 9, 10, 11, 12

MONROE

Victorian Garden Bed and Breakfast

1720 16th Street, 53566
(608) 328-1720

This 1890 Victorian home has a wraparound porch and a large flower garden. The light and airy interior welcomes you into a pet- and smoke-free home. The sitting room with a baby grand piano, a formal parlor, and an informal parlor with TV are for your enjoyment. A three-course breakfast is served in the formal dining room. The new kitchen is always a favorite spot to enjoy the view of the yard from the bay window.

Hosts: Jane and Pete Kessenich
Rooms: 3 (PB) $70-80
Full Breakfast
Credit Cards: A, B, D
Notes: 2, 5, 8, 9, 11 (cross-country), 12

NOTES: Credit cards accepted: A Master Card; B Visa; C American Express; D Discover; E Diners Club; F Other; 2 Personal checks accepted; 3 Lunch available; 4 Dinner available; 5 Open all year; 6 Pets

OSCEOLA

Pleasant Lake Bed and Breakfast

2238 60th Avenue, 54020-4509
(715) 294-2545; (800) 294-2545

Enjoy a romantic getaway on beautiful Pleasant Lake. While here, you may take a leisurely walk in the woods, watch the birds and other wildlife, enjoy the lake in the paddleboat or canoe, sit around the bonfire, and watch the moon and stars reflecting on the lake. Then relax in one of the whirlpools and enjoy a fireplace. Savor a full country breakfast.

Hosts: Richard and Charlene Berg
Rooms: 7 (PB) $60-125
Full Breakfast
Credit Cards: A, B
Notes: 2, 5, 9, 10, 11

Pleasant Lake Bed and Breakfast

PLAIN

Bettinger House Bed and Breakfast

855 Wachter Avenue, Highway 23, 53577
(608) 546-2951 (voice and FAX)

The Bettinger House is the hostess' grand-parents' 1904 Victorian farmhouse; Grandma was a midwife who delivered three hundred babies in this house. Choose from five spacious bedrooms that blend the old with the new, each named after noteworthy persons of Plain. The home is centrally air-conditioned. Start your day with one of the old-fashioned, full-course breakfasts for which we are famous. The Bettinger House is located near "House on the Rock," Frank Lloyd Wright's original Taliesen, American Players Theater, White Mound Park, and many more attractions.

Hosts: Jim and Marie Neider
Rooms: 5 (2PB; 3SB) $50-65
Full Breakfast
Credit Cards: A, B
Notes: 2, 5, 7 (inquire first), 8, 9, 10, 11, 12

PORT WASHINGTON

The Inn at Old Twelve Hundred

806 W. Grand Avenue, 53074
(414) 268-1200; FAX (414) 284-6885
Web site: http://www.southeastwis.com

The Inn at Old Twelve Hundred is a beautifully restored and decorated Queen Anne. Alls rooms are spacious and have queen or king beds; some offer whirlpools, fireplaces, private sitting rooms, and/or porches. Guest house rooms offer all amenities, including a wet bar, plus privacy. Private baths. TV/VCRs. AC. This is a nonsmoking inn.

Hostesses: Stephanie and Ellie Bresette
Rooms: 6 (PB) $95-175
Continental Breakfast (no breakfast in guest house)
Credit Cards: A, B, C
Notes: 2, 5

welcome; 7 Children welcome; 8 Tennis nearby; 9 Swimming nearby; 10 Golf nearby; 11 Skiing nearby; 12 May be booked through travel agent.

Port Washington Inn

308 W. Washington Street, 53074
(414) 284-5583
Web site: http://www.southeastwis.com

Port Washington is a world apart from the hustle and bustle of everyday life. You can park your car at Port Washington Inn and walk to the lake and downtown. Warm hospitality, thoughtful extras, and peaceful privacy await you. A movie collection, Steinway grand piano, art studio, extensive common areas, and cozy library allow guests a variety of milieus to enjoy. Fine coffees, teas, chocolates, and homemade breads and cookies encourage guests to relax and enjoy.

Hosts: Rita, Dave, and Aaron Nelson
Rooms: 4 (PB) $95-125
Full Breakfast
Credit Cards: A, B, C

PORTAGE

Breese Waye

816 MacFarlane Road, 53901
(608) 742-5281

Breese Waye is an 1880 Victorian home located on Society Hill, which is part of the Portage historic district. Guests enjoy the classic Victorian ambience and warm, gracious hospitality. The Breese Waye is situated within easy access of I-90. It is located near Baraboo and Wisconsin Dells.

Hosts: Dianne and Jack O'Connor
Rooms: 4 (PB) $60-75
Full Breakfast
Credit Cards: none
Notes: 2, 5, 7, 9, 10, 11, 12

REEDSBURG

Parkview Bed and Breakfast

211 N. Park Street, 53959
(608) 524-4333
E-mail: parkview@tcs.itis.com

Our 1895 Queen Anne Victorian home overlooks City Park in the historic district. Many of the original features of the home remain, such as hardware, hardwood floors, intricate woodwork, leaded and etched windows, plus a suitor's window. Wake-up coffee is followed by a full, homemade breakfast. Central air and ceiling fans add to guests' comfort. Located one block from downtown. Close to Wisconsin Dells, Baraboo, and Spring Green. Three blocks from 400 Bike Trail.

Hosts: Tom and Donna Hofmann
Rooms: 4 (2PB; 2SB) $60-80
Full Breakfast
Credit Cards: A, B, C
Notes: 2, 5, 7 (inquire), 8, 10, 11, 12

RICHLAND CENTER

Lambs Inn Bed and Breakfast

23761 Misslich Road, 53581
(608) 585-4301

Relax on our 180-acre farm located in a scenic valley surrounded by spectacular hills. Beautifully renovated farmhouse furnished with country antiques . . . porch for watching deer and other wildlife . . . cozy library for rainy days. Our new cottage has a spiral stair to the loft and a deck on which to relax. Large, homemade break-

NOTES: Credit cards accepted: A Master Card; B Visa; C American Express; D Discover; E Diners Club; F Other; 2 Personal checks accepted; 3 Lunch available; 4 Dinner available; 5 Open all year; 6 Pets

Lamb's Inn Bed and Breakfast

fasts are served at the B&B with home-made breads, egg dishes, and often old-fashioned bread pudding. Twenty-five miles from Spring Green with American Players Theater, House on the Rock, and Taliesen. Close to biking trails and Amish.

Hosts: Dick and Donna Messerschmidt
Rooms: 7 (PB) $75-115
Full Breakfast in B&B; Continental in cottage
Credit Cards: A, B
Notes: 2, 5, 7 (in cottage), 8, 9, 10, 12

SPARTA

The Franklin Victorian Bed and Breakfast

220 E. Franklin Street, 54656
(608) 269-3894; (800) 845-8767

This turn-of-the-century home welcomes you to bygone elegance with small-town quiet and comfort. The four spacious bedrooms provide a perfect setting for ultimate relaxation. A full, home-cooked breakfast is served before starting your day of hiking, biking, skiing, canoeing, antiquing, or exploring this beautiful area.

Hosts: Lloyd and Jane Larson
Rooms: 4 (2PB; 2SB) $75-95
Full Breakfast
Credit Cards: A, B
Notes: 2, 5, 8, 9, 10, 11

Strawberry Lace Inn Bed and Breakfast

603 N. Water Street, 54656
(608) 269-7878
E-mail: strawberry@centurinternet
Web site: http://www.geocities.com/heartland/
    plains/8688/straw.html

Return to an era of romance and elegance. The home is an excellent example of an Italianate Victorian (circa 1875). Rest in your own private retreat with private bath, king or queen bed with mountains of pillows, and distinctive antique decor. Partake in your hosts' four-course breakfast, presented on crystal and linen. Relax by visiting, reading, or playing games on the four-season porch. Known as "the biking capital of America," the area offers bike trails, golf, water sports, antiquing, restaurants, winter sports, and many more attractions year-round.

Hosts: Jack and Elsie Ballinger
Rooms: 5 (PB) $79-125
Full Breakfast
Credit Cards: A, B
Notes: 2

Strawberry Lace Inn Bed and Breakfast

welcome; 7 Children welcome; 8 Tennis nearby; 9 Swimming nearby; 10 Golf nearby; 11 Skiing nearby; 12 May be booked through travel agent.

STEVENS POINT

Dreams of Yesteryear Bed and Breakfast
1100 Brawley Street, 54481
(715) 341-4525; FAX (715) 344-3047

Featured in *Victorian Homes Magazine* and listed on the National Register of Historic Places. Your hosts are from Stevens Point and enjoy talking about the restoration of their turn-of-the-century home, which has been in the same family for three generations. All rooms are furnished in antiques. Guests enjoy the use of parlors, porches, and gardens. Two blocks from the historic downtown, antique and specialty shops, picturesque Green Circle Trails, the university, and more. Dreams of Yesteryear is truly "a Victorian dream come true."

Hosts: Bonnie and Bill Maher
Rooms: 6 (4PB; 2SB) $55-129
Full Breakfast
Credit Cards: A, B, C, D
Notes: 2, 5, 7 (over 12), 8, 9, 10, 11, 12

A Victorian Swan on Water
1716 Water Street, 54481
(715) 345-0595; (800) 454-9886
Web site: http://www.innsite.com:80/inns/
    A000232.html

An 1889 Victorian in the downtown area of a small university town. Antique and modern comforts. Private baths with tubs, showers, and whirlpool. Fireplaces and flower gardens. Walking, biking, and ski trails. Share good food, good conversation, and a great atmosphere in the center of Wisconsin. Special bike tours and gift certificates available.

Hostess: Joan Ouellette
Rooms: 4 (PB) $55-125
Full Breakfast
Credit Cards: A, B, C, D
Notes: 2, 5, 8, 9, 10, 11, 12

STURGEON BAY

Hearthside Bed and Breakfast
2136 Taube Road, 54235
(414) 746-2136

Our 1800s farmhouse has a blend of contemporary and antique furnishings. The old barn still stands nearby. Within easy driving distance are fantastic state parks, beaches for swimming in summer, and areas for skiing in winter. Lighthouses, U.S. Coast Guard Station, lake cruises, airport, ship building, and weekend festivals. The rooms are charming—three with queen beds. Our family room has twin beds with an adjoining room that has a double bed. Guests may use TVs, VCRs, living room, and sunroom.

Hosts: Donald and Lu Klussendorf
Rooms: 4 (PB) $40-60
Full Home-Cooked Breakfast
Credit Cards: none
Notes: 2, 5, 7, 8, 9, 10, 11

The Scofield House Bed and Breakfast
908 Michigan Street, 54235-1849
(920) 743-7727 (voice and FAX); (888) 463-0204
E-mail: scofhse@mail.wiscnet.net
Web site: http://www.scofieldhouse.com

"Door County's most elegant bed and breakfast." This 1902 multicolored, three-

The Scofield House Bed and Breakfast

story Victorian was restored in 1987 by the present hosts. Guests keep coming back for Bill's wonderful gourmet breakfasts and Fran's homemade "sweet treats" served fresh daily. The Scofield House has six guest rooms, of which four are suites, all with private baths, color television/VCRs, and a "free" video library. Double whirlpools, fireplaces, and central AC. Smoke-free environment.

Hosts: Bill and Fran Cecil
Rooms: 6 (PB) $93-196
Full Breakfast
Credit Cards: none
Notes: 2, 5, 8, 9, 10, 11

TWO RIVERS

Red Forest Bed and Breakfast

1421 25th Street, 54241
(920) 793-1794; (888) 250-2272;
FAX (920) 793-3056

We invite you to step back in time to 1907 and enjoy our gracious, three-story shingle-style home. Highlighted with stained-glass windows, heirloom antiques, and cozy fireplace. Four beautifully appointed guest rooms await your arrival. Stroll along our

sugar sand beaches or through downtown antique shops. The Red Forest is located on Wisconsin's east coast, minutes from Manitowoc, Wisconsin's port city, and the Lake Michigan Carferry. Also located midway between Chicago and the Door County Peninsula.

Hosts: Kay and Alan Rodewald
Rooms: 4 (2PB; 2SB) $65-85
Full Breakfast
Credit Cards: A, B, C, D
Notes: 2, 5, 7 (older), 8, 9 (beach), 10, 11, 12

WISCONSIN DELLS

The Buckley House

PO Box 598, 53965
(608) 586-5752; FAX (608) 586-5400

Visit our country Victorian home filled with antiques and charm. A quiet setting secluded in the rolling hills of "God's country." Enjoy breakfast on your balcony or on our wraparound porch. Amenities: whirlpools, sauna, queen-size beds, flower gardens, fishpond, wildlife, bird-watching, star-gazing, bicycling, and hot-air balloon rides. All this—just minutes from Wisconsin Dells, lakes, Amish community, and more. We can help plan your stay.

Hosts: Michael and Kathie Lake
Rooms: 3 (PB) $80-160
Full Breakfast
Credit Cards: A, B

Historic Bennett House

825 Oak Street, 53965
(608) 254-2500

The 1863 home of pioneer photographer H.H. Bennett is warm and inviting in its

---

welcome; 7 Children welcome; 8 Tennis nearby; 9 Swimming nearby; 10 Golf nearby; 11 Skiing nearby; 12 May be booked through travel agent.

casual elegance and welcoming atmosphere. Traveling with another couple? We have the ideal situations for you. Two lovely bedrooms, one with queen canopy bed and English armoire and the other with queen brass bed with wicker accents. Share a carpeted bedroom-size bath with Italian sinks and Bennett's claw-foot tub. You may, of course, reserve just one room. The library has become part of a two-room suite with private bath. View a favorite movie from our hundred-plus collection. Savor a delicious gourmet breakfast, and visit Dells attractions; state parks; Bennett, Rockwell, Circus, and Railroad museums; riverboat tours; skiing; and the C Vane Foundation.

Hosts: Rich and Gail Obermeyer
Rooms: 3 (1PB; 2SB) $70-95
Full Breakfast
Credit Cards: none
Notes: 2, 5, 8, 9, 10, 11

Terrace Hill Bed and Breakfast

922 River Road, 53965
(608) 253-9363

Time stands still at our quiet niche on scenic River Road. Victorian charm, wraparound porch, private parking and a quiet park that wraps around out residences down toward the Wisconsin River promise you a peaceful stay. Our suite is an excellent choice for friends or family traveling together, and our newly remodeled Coral Bells Room sparkles with its canopy bed and in-room whirlpool. Are you first-time B&Bers? We'd love to have you as our guests.

Hosts: Len, Cookie, Lenard and Lynn Novak
Rooms: 5 (PB) $65-110
Full Breakfast
Credit Cards: none
Notes: 2, 5, 7, 8, 9, 10, 11, 12

NOTES: Credit cards accepted: A Master Card; B Visa; C American Express; D Discover; E Diners Club; F Other; 2 Personal checks accepted; 3 Lunch available; 4 Dinner available; 5 Open all year; 6 Pets

Wyoming

BIG HORN

Spahn's Bighorn Mountain Bed and Breakfast

PO Box 579, 82833
(307) 674-8150
E-mail spahnbb@wave.sheridan.wy.us
Web site: http://wave.sheridan.wy.us/~spahnbb

Towering log home and secluded guest cabins on the mountainside in whispering pines. Borders one million acres of public forest with deer and moose. Gracious mountain breakfast served on the deck with binoculars to enjoy the hundred-mile view. The owner is former Yellowstone ranger. Located ten minutes from I-90, near Sheridan.

Hosts: Ron and Bobbie Spahn
Rooms: 5 (PB) $75-125
Full Breakfast
Credit Cards: none
Notes: 4, 5, 7

BUFFALO

Historic Mansion House Inn

313 N. Main Street, 82834
(307) 684-2218

Seven western Victorian guest rooms on historic Main Street. Eleven comfortable motel rooms in annex. Continental breakfast, spa, color cable TV, AC. Located on historic Main Street and Highway 16—scenic route to Yellowstone National Park. Open year-round.

Hosts: Phil and Diane Mehlhaff
Rooms: 18 (PB) $34-55
Continental Breakfast
Credit Cards: A, B, D
Notes: 5, 7, 8, 9, 10, 11, 12

welcome; 7 Children welcome; 8 Tennis nearby; 9 Swimming nearby; 10 Golf nearby; 11 Skiing nearby; 12 May be booked through travel agent.

WYOMING

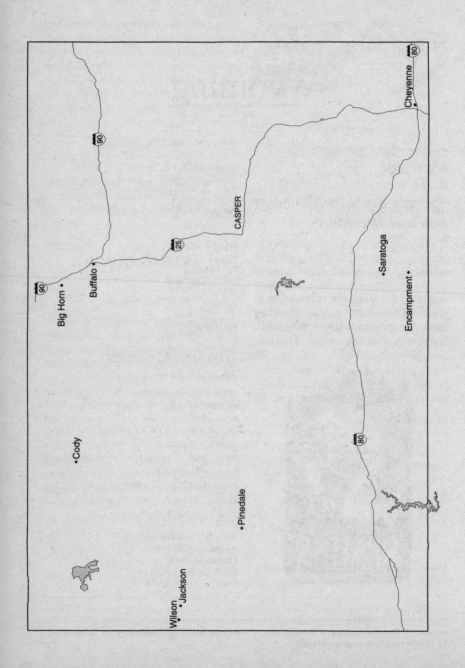

A. Drummond's Ranch

CHEYENNE/LARAMIE

A. Drummond's Ranch

399 Happy Jack Road, **Laramie**, 82007
(307) 634-6042; FAX (307) 634-6042
E-mail: adrummond@juno.com

A quiet, gracious retreat situated on 120 acres near Medicine Bow National Forest and Curt Gowdy State Park. Between Cheyenne and Laramie at an elevation of seventy-five hundred feet. Privacy with personalized service. Hiking, mountain biking, cross-country skiing, llama packing, or simply relaxing. Outdoor hot tubs and glorious night skies. Boarding for horses and pets in transit. Dietary restrictions accommodated, when possible. No smoking, please. Reservations required.

Hostess: Taydie Drummond
Rooms: 4 (2PB; 2SB) $65-155
Full Breakfast
Credit Cards: A, B
Notes: 2, 3, 4, 5, 6, 7, 10, 11, 12

The Storyteller Pueblo Bed and Breakfast

5201 Ogden Road, 82009
(307) 634-7036; FAX (307) 635-9117

Native American art from more than thirty tribes: pottery, beadwork, baskets, and rugs. Contemporary home of country and primitive antiques. Down-home hospitality on a quiet street. Convenient to shopping and major restaurants. Breakfast with all the amenities. Fireplaces and family rooms for your enjoyment. Reservations recommended. Special rates during the last ten days of July.

Hosts: Howard and Peggy Hutchings
Rooms: 3 (1PB; 2SB) $40-55
Full Breakfast
Credit Cards: none
Notes: 2, 5, 7 (by arrangement), 8, 9, 10, 11, 12

CODY

Lockhart Bed and Breakfast Inn

109 W. Yellowstone Avenue, 82414
(307) 587-6074
E-mail: CBaldwin@wyoming.com

Truly your "home away from home" for people who enjoy personal service as well as western hospitality. Enjoy fresh mountain air, blue skies, and beautiful mountain views as you relax on the spacious veranda outside the inn. The historic home of authoress Caroline Lockhart has been beautifully restored with the grace and country charm befitting its tranquil setting in the majestic Rocky Mountains. Just minutes from the Buffalo Bill Historical Center, Old Trail Town, and Cody Nite Rodeo. Twenty-five miles from Shoshone National Forest, fifty miles from the entrance to Yellowstone National Park.

Hostess: Cindy Baldwin
Rooms: 14 (PB) $65-95
Full Breakfast
Credit Cards: A, B, C, D, E
Notes: 2, 3, 5, 7, 8, 9, 10, 11, 12

NOTES: Credit cards accepted: A Master Card; B Visa; C American Express; D Discover; E Diners Club; F Other; 2 Personal checks accepted; 3 Lunch available; 4 Dinner available; 5 Open all year; 6 Pets welcome; 7 Children welcome; 8 Tennis nearby; 9 Swimming nearby; 10 Golf nearby; 11 Skiing nearby; 12 May be booked through travel agent.

Trout Creek Inn

Northfork Route, 82414
(307) 587-6288 (voice and FAX)

Because of our country ranch location, we are a resort as well as a motel. Large, heated pool, private pond/stream fishing, hunting, playground, in the beautiful mountain valley that Teddy Roosevelt—a world traveler as well as American president— said was the world's most scenic. Large rooms, some with kitchens. Watch the deer, elk, and even otters from the rooms.

Hosts: Bert and Norma Sowerwine
Rooms: 21 (PB) $60-80
Full Breakfast
Credit Cards: A, B, C, D
Notes: 2, 3, 4, 5, 6, 7, 8, 10, 11, 12

Rustic Mountain Lodge

ENCAMPMENT

Rustic Mountain Lodge

Star Route, Box 49, 82325
(307) 327-5539 (voice and FAX)

A peaceful mountain view, located on a working ranch with wholesome country atmosphere and lots of Western hospitality. Enjoy daily fishing on a private pond, big-game trophy hunts, cookouts, retreats, pack trips, photo safaries, youth programs, cattle drives, trail rides, hiking, rock hunting, numerous ranch activities, mountain biking and four-wheeling trails, and survival workshops. Individuals, families, and groups welcome! A terrific atmosphere for workshops. Lodge and cabin rentals available. Reservations only. Private fishing cabins available May–September. Write for a complete brochure!

Hosts: Mayvon and Ron Platt
Rooms: 4 (1PB; 3SB) $65
Full Breakfast
Credit Cards: none
Notes: 2, 3, 4, 5, 6, 7, 8, 9, 10, 11

JACKSON HOLE

Nowlin Creek Inn

Box 2766, 660 E. Broadway, 83001
(307) 733-0882; FAX (307) 733-0106
E-mail: nowlin@sisna.com
Web site: http://www.JacksonHoleNet.com/b&bsl

Nowlin Creek Inn is located in Jackson Hole, gateway to Yellowstone and Grand Teton national parks. Located across from the National Elk refuge, Nowlin Creek is convenient for walking or driving to the many area attractions and activities: hiking, biking, fishing, boating, rafting, sightseeing. Nowlin Creek Inn offers many features typical of high-quality bed and breakfasts. We work hard to find those special services like evening beverage, those fine details like thick terry-cloth robes, and that extra measure of graciousness that will make your stay memorable so that you want to return. Stay at Nowlin Creek Inn and enjoy western hospitality at its finest!

Hosts: Mark and Susan Nowlin
Rooms: 5 (PB) $95-210
Full Breakfast
Credit Cards: A, B, C, D
Notes: 2, 5, 7, 8, 9, 10, 11, 12

NOTES: Credit cards accepted: A Master Card; B Visa; C American Express; D Discover; E Diners Club; F Other; 2 Personal checks accepted; 3 Lunch available; 4 Dinner available; 5 Open all year; 6 Pets

PINEDALE

Pole Creek Ranch Bed and Breakfast

PO Box 278, 82941
(307) 367-4433
Web site: http://www.meek.sublette.com/pcranch

Relive the charm of the Old West in our rustic log home with a superb view of the spectacular Wind River Mountains. Stay in one of our rooms or sleep out in the teepee! Enjoy horseback riding; wagon, buggy, or sleigh rides; and evening campfires. Relax in our hot tub under the stars. The peace and beauty of Pole Creek Ranch are unsurpassed.

Hosts: Dexter and Carole Smith
Rooms: 3 (1PB; 2SB) $45-55
Full Breakfast
Credit Cards: none
Notes: 2, 3, 4, 5, 6, 7, 8, 9, 10, 11

SARATOGA

Far Out West Bed and Breakfast

PO Box 1230, 304 N. 2nd Street, 82331
(307) 326-5869; FAX (307) 326-9864

This historic home has six guest rooms that are decorated comfortably with a country flair. All have private baths. Three rooms have king-size beds. We are located two blocks from downtown and one and a half blocks from the N. Platte River, where we have the best fly-fishing in the country. We offer a hot tub, exercise equipment, and large-screen TV in the great room that has a large, round fireplace. Open year-round. No smoking.

Hosts: Bill and B.J. Farr
Rooms: 6 (PB) $95
Full Breakfast
Credit Cards: A, B
Notes: 2, 5, 7, 9, 10, 11

WILSON

Teton View Bed and Breakfast

PO Box 652, 2136 Coyote Loop, 83014
(307) 733-7954

Rooms have mountain views. The lounge/eating area, where homemade pastries, fresh fruit, and coffee are served, connects to a private upper deck with fantastic mountain and ski resort views. Private guest entrance. Convenient to Yellowstone and Grand Teton national parks. Located approximately four miles from the ski area. Closed April and November.

Hosts: John and Joanna Engelhart
Rooms: 3 (1PB; 2SB) $60-90
Full Breakfast
Credit Cards: A, B
Notes: 2, 4, 7, 8, 9, 10, 11, 12

welcome; 7 Children welcome; 8 Tennis nearby; 9 Swimming nearby; 10 Golf nearby; 11 Skiing nearby; 12 May be booked through travel agent.

ALBERTA

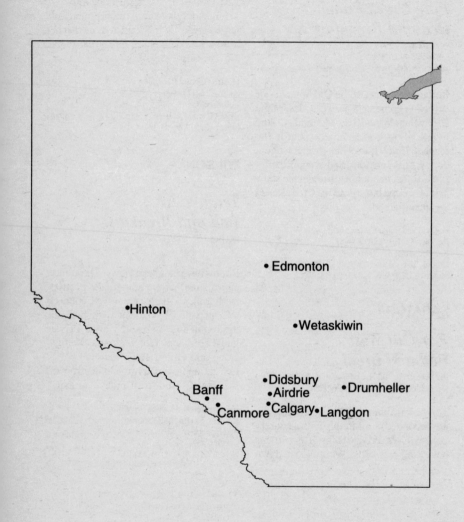

• Edmonton

•Hinton

•Wetaskiwin

•Didsbury
Banff •Airdrie •Drumheller
• •Calgary•Langdon
Canmore

Alberta

AIRDRIE

Big Springs Bed and Breakfast

RR 1, T4B 2A3
(403) 948-5264; FAX (403) 948-5851
E-mail: whittake@cadvision.com
Web site: bigsprings@cadvision.com

Overlooking a picturesque valley on thirty-five very private pastoral acres. Beautifully landscaped and treed. Spacious, five-thousand-square-foot hillside bungalow. Choose from four beautifully decorated rooms with private baths: the Bridal Suite, featuring a hydro-massage tub; the Manor Room; The Victorian Room; or the Arbour Room. Relax in our secluded English Garden sitting room, where furniture groupings are situated so that the garden atmosphere continues to the surrounding green of the outdoors. Elegant gourmet breakfast by certified and experienced hosts. Fireplace, hot tub, evening beverages, and "goodies." You'll find extra personal touches; we pamper our guests. Fifteen minutes to Calgary city limits; twenty-five minutes to airport. Great access to Banff, Lake Louise, Kananaskis Country, Calgary Stampede, and Calgary Zoo. Canada Select three-star rating.

Hosts: Carol and Earle Whittaker
Rooms: 4 (PB) $85-100
Full Gourmet Breakfast
Credit Cards: B
Notes: 5, 7, 9, 10, 11, 12

DeWitt's Bed and Breakfast

RR #1, T4B 2A3
(403) 948- 5356; FAX (403) 277-3113

Enjoy warm hospitality and tantalizing breakfast served in the flower-filled patio or in our dining room, viewing the Rocky Mountains through the trees. Nearby are the world-famous Calgary Stampede, the Western Heritage Center, Calaway Park, Spruce Meadows Equestrian Center, and the many attractions of Kananaskis Country and Banff National Park. Ten-and-three-quarters kilometers west of Airdrie/Highway 2 on the southern junction of highways 567 and 772; twenty minutes to Calgary and the international airport.

Hosts: Irene DeWitt and Wendy Kelly
Rooms: 3 (1PB; 2SB) $75-85 Canadian
Full or Continental Breakfast
Credit Cards: B
Notes: 5, 7, 9, 10, 11

NOTES: Credit cards accepted: A Master Card; B Visa; C American Express; D Discover; E Diners Club; F Other; 2 Personal checks accepted; 3 Lunch available; 4 Dinner available; 5 Open all year; 6 Pets welcome; 7 Children welcome; 8 Tennis nearby; 9 Swimming nearby; 10 Golf nearby; 11 Skiing nearby; 12 May be booked through travel agent.

BANFF

Pension Tannenhof Bed and Breakfast

PO Box 1914, T0L 0C0
(403) 762-4636

Quietly located on the foot of Sulphur Mountain, fifteen minutes walking to downtown on the Eave and Basin (birthplace of Banff and Banff National Park). Featuring a large living room with woodburning fireplace, CCTV, lovely breakfast room, and a homey yet elegant atmosphere. Recreational facilities are within a short walking distance.

Hosts: Ivan and Beryl Taguchi
Rooms: 10 (7PB; 3SB) $70-135 (Canadian)
Full Breakfast
Credit Cards: A, B
Notes: 2, 5, 7, 8, 9, 10, 11

Spray Valley Bed and Breakfast

Box 184, T0L 0C0
(403) 762-2846

"A home away from home" close to the famous Banff Springs Hotel and Golf Course. Hiking trails at your door. Downtown five minutes away. Hostess is knowledgeable of the area will help with your itineraries. Sitting room with fireplace, cable TV, and library. Hostess is a Toastmaster, enjoys good conversation, and speaks German and English. Cash and traveler's checks accepted. Minimum two-night stay.

Hostess: Marvelyne Yarmoloy
Rooms: 3 (1PB; 2SB) $75-110
Continental Breakfast
Credit Cards: none
Notes: 5, 8, 10, 11, 12

CALGARY

Paradise Acres Bed and Breakfast

243105 Paradise Road, Box 20, Site 2, RRH6,
T2M 4L5
(403) 248-4748 (voice and FAX)
E-mail: paradise@cwave.com

Come enjoy our friendly and luxurious setting with country quietness and city access. Paradise Acres features choice of breakfasts, queen-size beds, private baths, plus guest sitting rooms with TV/VCR. Located close to the TransCanada Highway and Calgary airport with a city and mountain view. Airport pickup available.

Hosts: Brian and Char Bates
Rooms: 3 (PB) $55-70
Full and Continental Breakfast
Credit Cards: A, B, C
Notes: 2, 5, 8, 9, 10, 11, 12

Rosedale House Bed and Breakfast

Rosedale House Bed and Breakfast

1633-7A Street NW, T2M 3K2
(403) 284-0010 (voice and FAX)
E-mail: rosedale@cadvision.com
Web site: http://www.cadvision.com/rosedale/
index.html

This large, executive home offers the charm of a turn-of-the-century home with all the

---

NOTES: Credit cards accepted: A Master Card; B Visa; C American Express; D Discover; E Diners Club; F Other; 2 Personal checks accepted; 3 Lunch available; 4 Dinner available; 5 Open all year; 6 Pets

modern conveniences. The guest rooms have en suite bathrooms, excellent queen beds, writing tables, and phone jacks. The lounge offers a TV, VCR, fireplace, pool table, and beverage station with microwave. The full breakfast is served in a formal dining room with linen and china. Excellent central location.

Hosts: Dennis and Beth Palmquist
Rooms: 3 (PB) $80-110 (Canadian)
Full Breakfast
Credit Cards: A, B, C
Notes: 2, 5, 7, 8, 9, 10, 11, 12

CANMORE

Cougar Creek Inn Bed and Breakfast

240 Grizzly Crescent, T1W 1B5
(403) 678-4751; FAX (403) 678-9529

Quiet, rustic, cedar chalet with mountain views in every direction. Grounds border on Cougar Creek and are surrounded by rugged mountain scenery that invites all types of outdoor activity. Hostess has strong love for the mountains and can assist with plans for local hiking, skiing, canoeing, mountain biking, backpacking, etc., as well as scenic drives. The inn has a private entrance with sitting area, fireplace, games, television, sauna, and numerous reading materials for guests' use. Two large guest rooms, one with three double beds, the other with two double beds. Breakfasts are hearty and wholesome, with many home-baked items. Open May to September.

Hostess: Mrs. Patricia Doucette
Rooms: 2 (SB) $60-65 (Canadian)
Full Breakfast
Credit Cards: none
Notes: 2, 3, 7, 8, 9, 10, 11

Grimmon House

DIDSBURY

Grimmon House

PO Box 1268, 1610-15 Avenue, T0M 0W0
(403) 335-8353; FAX (403) 335-3640

"Love in any language, color, or creed fluently spoken here." Relax and enjoy the benefits of a rural experience just forty-five minutes from Calgary. Three rooms charmingly furnished with brass beds, antiques, and quilts. Hearty breakfast overlooking the garden, private entrance, and off-street parking. Wake-up coffee brought to your door. Lemonade and evening outdoor fire, weather permitting.

Hosts: John and Myrna Grimmon
Rooms: 3 (SB) $55-65
Full Breakfast
Credit Cards: none
Notes: 2, 5, 7 (by arrangement), 8, 9, 10, 11, 12

DRUMHELLER

The Victorian House Bed and Breakfast

541 Riverside Drive W., T0J 0Y3
(403) 823-3535

Nonsmoking, pet-free accommodations within walking distance of downtown. We

welcome; 7 Children welcome; 8 Tennis nearby; 9 Swimming nearby; 10 Golf nearby; 11 Skiing nearby; 12 May be booked through travel agent.

have queen, double, and single beds, and private and shared bathrooms. Breakfast served from 6 to 10, with a full menu to choose from. Enjoy a view of the river and Badlands from our veranda and balcony. A quiet location . A guest lounge has TV/VCR with many classical videos.

Hosts: Jack and Florence Barnes
Rooms: 5 (1PB; 4SB) $50-65
Full Breakfast
Credit Cards: A, B
Notes: 5, 7, 8, 9, 10, 11, 12

EDMONTON

Chez Suzanne Bed and Breakfast

18603 - 68 Avenue, T5T 2M8
(403) 483-1845; (888) 483-1849;
FAX (403) 483-1845
E-mail: fils@connect.ab.ca
Web site: http://www.comcept.ab.ca/cantravel/
   suzanne.html

Our residence is in the heart of a west end neighborhood, a stone's throw from West Edmonton Mall and Jasper Highway. Relax and enjoy the privacy of one entire level of our home. Unwind by the fireplace with books, color television/VCR movies, or games. A refrigerator and beverage station are at your convenience for complimentary coffee, tea, hot chocolate, or soup. Three well-appointed bedrooms. Laundry facilities available. Restaurants are a five-minute stroll away. In season, enjoy our deck and gardens. Motor home rentals available in June, July, and August. *Service en français.*

Hosts: Suzanne and Paul Croteau
Rooms: 3 (1PB; 2SB) $60
Full Breakfast
Credit Cards: B
Notes: 2 (in advance), 7 (over 3), 8, 9, 10, 11, 12

LANGDON

Merrywood Bed and Breakfast

124 Newton Street, T0J 1X0
(403) 936-5796

Relaxed accommodation in a quiet hamlet east of Calgary. A rural setting central to the Canadian Rockies, Banff, Lake Louise, Jasper, Waterton Park, Glacier National Park, the Calgary Stampede, West Edmonton Mall, dinosaur areas, dinner theaters, birding and rock-hounding locations, fishing holes, and gardens.

Host: G.M. Chappell
Rooms: 1 (PB) $35-45
Full Breakfast
Credit Cards: some

WETASKIWIN

Karriage House 1908 Bed and Breakfast

5215 - 47th Street, T9A 1E1
(403) 352-5996; (888) 352-5996

Relax in our 1908 home. You have your choice of cozy second-floor bedrooms or a private guest cottage (seasonal). The guest sitting room features a fireplace, a wee library, and antiques. Explore the Curio Shop sunroom. Antique aircraft flights arranged. Breakfasts are generous, wholesome, and delightful—we just love to spoil you!

Hosts: Tom and Sue Chamberlain
Rooms: 3 (SB) + summer cottage (PB) $65-85
Full Breakfast
Credit Cards: B

NOTES: Credit cards accepted: A Master Card; B Visa; C American Express; D Discover; E Diners Club; F Other; 2 Personal checks accepted; 3 Lunch available; 4 Dinner available; 5 Open all year; 6 Pets

British Columbia

ABBOTSFORD

Everett House
Bed and Breakfast

1990 Everett Road, V2S 7S3
(604) 859-2944

We invite you to join us in our Victorian-style home. Easily accessible to the freeway and overlooking the Fraser Valley, our home is the perfect retreat removed from the hustle of the city. It is also that "someplace special" for you while you conduct your business in the Fraser Valley. A stay at our home will provide you with a refreshing break from ordinary life.

Hosts: David and Cindy Sahlstrom
Rooms: 3 (PB) $65-95
Full Breakfast (early departure, Continental)
Credit Cards: A, B
Notes: 5, 7, 8, 9 (public pools), 10, 11, 12

MILL BAY/
VANCOUVER ISLAND

Pine Lodge Farm
Bed and Breakfast

3191 Mutter Road, V0R 2P0
(250) 743-4083; FAX (250) 743-7134

Our beautiful, antique-filled lodge is located twenty-five miles north of Victoria. It is situated on a thirty-acre farm overlooking ocean and islands. Arbutus trees, walking trails, farm animals, and wild deer add to the idyllic setting. Each room has en suite baths and shower. Full farm breakfast. No smoking.

Hosts: Barb and Cliff Clarke
Rooms: 7 (PB) $75-95
Full Breakfast
Credit Cards: A, B
Notes: 2, 12

PEMBERTON

Chris's Corner
Bed and Breakfast

Box 636, 7406 Larch Street, V0N 2L0
(604) 894-6787; FAX (604) 894-2026
E-mail: ceinarson@whistlerweb

Experience the peace and tranquillity of this scenic farming valley, surrounded by spectacular, snow-capped mountains. Enjoy the One-Mile Lake walk, the trail to Nairn Falls, or an evening stroll to the village. Visit the Saturday market. Pemberton also boasts a few excellent restaurants. Three twin/king bedrooms offer shared or private baths; each has its own distinctive flavor. A fireside sitting room is for the enjoyment of our guests,

---

welcome; 7 Children welcome; 8 Tennis nearby; 9 Swimming nearby; 10 Golf nearby; 11 Skiing nearby; 12 May be booked through travel agent.

BRITISH COLUMBIA

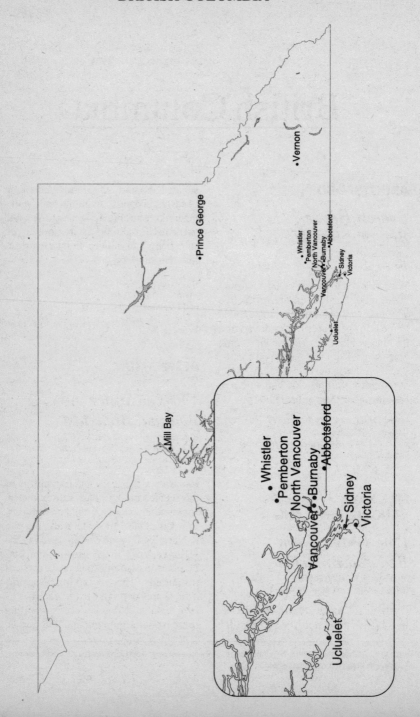

with games, playing cards, books, and TV/ VCR. Relax and view the majestic mountains from the large deck. Swimming spa in summer. Traveler's checks accepted.

Hosts: Christine and Fred Einarson
Rooms: 3 (1PB; 2SB) $50-75; extra person $20
Full or Continental Breakfast
Credit Cards: none
Notes: 3, 5, 7, 8, 9, 10, 11, 12

PRINCE GEORGE

Beaverly Bed and Breakfast

12725 Miles Road, V2N 5C1
(250) 560-5255; FAX (250) 560-5211

Beaverly B&B is located eighteen kilometers west of Prince George on ten acres of beautiful British Columbia wilderness. You will feel very welcome and comfortable in our new home. Many trees surround us, and it is a birder's paradise. We serve a luxurious, full breakfast, and you will enjoy our Dutch touch.

Hosts: Anneke and Adrian VanPeenen
Rooms: 2 (PB) $45-55
Full Breakfast
Credit Cards: none
Notes: 5, 9, 10, 11, 12

UCLUELET

Bed and Breakfast at Burley's

1073 Helen Road, Box 550, V0R 3A0
(250) 726-4444 (voice and FAX)

A waterfront home on a small "drive to" island at the harbor mouth. Watch the ducks and birds play, heron and kingfisher work, and eagles soar. In the harbor, trollers, draggers, and seiners attract the gulls. Loggers work in the distant hills. There is a view from every window. Enjoy the large living room, fireplace, books, and recreation room with pool table.

Hosts: Ron and Micheline Burley
Rooms: 6 (SB) $45-65
Continental Breakfast
Credit Cards: A, B
Notes: 8, 9, 10

VANCOUVER

AB&C Bed and Breakfast Agency

4390 Frances Street, **Burnaby**, V5C 2R3
(604) 298-8815; (800) 488-1941;
FAX (604) 298-5917

A professional reservation agency offering modest to luxurious accommodations. Single, twin, queen, and king beds, private and shared baths. Vancouver, Victoria, and throughout BC. Eighteen years in tourism.

Owner: Norma McCurrach
Homes: 60; $75-160
Full Breakfast
Credit Cards: A, B
Notes: 5, 8, 9, 10, 11, 12

VANCOUVER, NORTH

Sue's Victoria Guest House, Circa 1904

152 E. Third Street, V7L 1E6
(604) 985-1523; (800) 776-1811

Located centrally for many tourist attractions, this lovely, restored, nonsmoking

---

NOTES: Credit cards accepted: A Master Card; B Visa; C American Express; D Discover; E Diners Club; F Other; 2 Personal checks accepted; 3 Lunch available; 4 Dinner available; 5 Open all year; 6 Pets welcome; 7 Children welcome; 8 Tennis nearby; 9 Swimming nearby; 10 Golf nearby; 11 Skiing nearby; 12 May be booked through travel agent.

1904 home is just four blocks from the harbor, seabus terminal, and Quay market. Even closer are restaurants and public transportation. Victorian soaker baths (no showers). Each room is individually keyed and has a fan, TV, video, and phone (for short, local calls). Minimum stay of three nights. Cats in residence; shoes off at door. Longer stays encouraged. Parking behind 152 and 158 E. Third Street.

Hostesses: Gail Fowler, Jen Lane, Sue Chalmers
Rooms: 3 (1PB; 2SB) $65-75 (Canadian)
Self-serve kitchen privileges (4 PM-10AM)
Credit Cards: B (deposit only; cash or traveler's check upon arrival, please)
Notes: 5

Wrays Lakeview Bed and Breakfast

VERNON

Wrays Lakeview Bed and Breakfast

7368 L and A Road, V1B 3S6
(250) 545-9821; FAX (250) 545-9924

Come and relax in the peace and seclusion of our cozy, air-conditioned home in a beautiful country setting. We offer accommodations for up to eight adults. Our guest rooms have private bathrooms. A guest sitting room has a piano and TV, along with a private entrance and parking. Enjoy the view from the deck or balcony.

A full breakfast is served in our formal dining room. Warm hospitality is guaranteed. Adults only. No smoking or pets. Easy access to skiing, golfing, boating, beaches, hiking, dining, and shopping.

Hosts: Irma and Gord Wray
Rooms: 3 (PB) $69
Full Breakfast
Credit Cards: A, B
Notes: 5, 9, 10, 11

VICTORIA

AA-Accommodations West Reservation Service

660 Jones Terrace, V8Z 2L7
(604) 479-1986; FAX (604) 479-9999
E-mail: dwensley@vanisle.net
Web site: http://www.bactravel.com/
    gardencity.html

No reservation fee. Choice locations inspected and approved. Ocean views, farm tranquillity, cozy cottage, city convenience, and historic heritage! Assistance with itineraries that include **Victoria**, **Vancouver Island**, and some adjacent islands. For competent, caring service, call Doreen 9 AM-9 PM Monday through Saturday, 2 PM-9 PM Sunday.

Manager: Doreen Wensley
Credit Cards: A, B, C
Notes: 2, 5, 7, 8, 9, 10, 12

All Seasons Bed and Breakfast Agency Inc.

101-9858 Fifth Street, **Sidney**, V8L 2X7
(250) 655-7173

All the best B&Bs of Victoria, Vancouver Island, and the Gulf Islands. Specializing

---

NOTES: Credit cards accepted: A Master Card; B Visa; C American Express; D Discover; E Diners Club; F Other; 2 Personal checks accepted; 3 Lunch available; 4 Dinner available; 5 Open all year; 6 Pets

in waterfront and garden homes and inns. There's an accommodation style for everyone. When you want to get away from it all, trips are much more enjoyable with a bit of advance planning. You know where you'll be welcome at night, so you can travel for the mere fun of it. Listing approximately forty B&Bs. Visa, MasterCard, and personal checks accepted. Kate Catterill, coordinator.

Craigmyle Bed and Breakfast Inn Ltd.

1031 Craigdarroch Road, V8S 2A5
(250) 595-5411; (888) 595-5411;
FAX (888) 220-5276

Craigmyle is a large old B&B situated only one kilometer from the city center of Victoria in the prestigious Rockland area. Sitting in the shadow of the Craigdarrock Castle, Craigmyle offers a relaxed and quiet atmosphere in the tradition of English-style bed and breakfasts. Craigmyle was built in 1913, designed by the famous Victorian architect Samuel McClure. Craigmyle has been owned and operated since 1975 by Jim and Cathy Pace.

Hosts: Jim and Cathy Pace
Rooms: 17 (PB) $80-95 (Canadian)
Full English Breakfast
Credit Cards: A, B, C
Notes: 5, 7, 8, 9, 10, 12

Top O'Triangle Mountain

3442 Karger Terrace, V9C 3K5
(250) 478-7853; (800) 870-2255;
FAX (250) 478-2245

As I gaze out the window of our solid cedar home atop Triangle Mountain at the splendor of the Olympic Mountains, Juan de Fuca Strait and the City of Victoria, all agleam in the afternoon sun, I stand in awe at God's handiwork. I thank Him for all the wonderful friends we have made during our twelve years of welcoming guests into our home. Good food, warm hospitality, and clean, comfortable accommodations await you.

Hosts: Henry and Pat Hansen
Rooms: 3 (PB) $70-90 (Canadian)
Full, Home-Cooked Breakfast
Credit Cards: A, B
Notes: 5, 7, 8, 9, 10, 12

Villa Blanca Bed and Breakfast

4918 Cordova Bay Road, V8J 2J5
(250) 658-4190; FAX (250) 658-4120
E-mail: VillaBlanca@octonet.com
Web site: http://www.octonet.com/VillaBlanca

A warm and friendly welcome awaits you in our spacious, elegant, Mediterranean-style villa. Well-traveled hosts have lived overseas and are both avid sailors. The atmosphere at Villa Blanca is light and airy and imparts a deep sense of peace. The Villa Blanca displays an impressive collection of hand-made quilts.

Hosts: Vesta Mollins and Dave Wilkie
Rooms: 2 (PB) $75-95
Full Breakfast
Credit Cards: A, B
Notes: 5, 8, 9

Wellington Bed and Breakfast

66 Wellington Avenue, V8V 4H5
(250) 383-5976 (voice and FAX)

You're in for a treat of the finest Victorian hospitality in this 1912, fully restored,

welcome; 7 Children welcome; 8 Tennis nearby; 9 Swimming nearby; 10 Golf nearby; 11 Skiing nearby; 12 May be booked through travel agent.

Edwardian B&B. Inge is an interior designer and each room is specially designed with private bath, queen or king bed, walk-in closet, duvets, and lace; some have fireplaces. A guest living room offers books and relaxation. Only a half block from ocean and bus. A twenty-minute walk will take you downtown through the park. Only minutes from shops, restaurants, and sights. A full, delicious breakfast is served in the dining room.

Hostess: Inge Ranzinger
Rooms: 4 (PB) $65-140 (Canadian) or $50-110 (US)
Full Breakfast
Credit Cards: A
Notes: 2, 5, 7 (over 12), 8, 9, 10, 12

WHISTLER

Golden Dreams B&B

6412 Easy Street, V0N 1B6
(604) 932-2667; (800) 668-7055;
FAX (604) 932-7055
E-mail: golden@whistler.net

Enjoy our world-class, year-round resort just two hours from Vancouver. Be surrounded by nature's beauty and pampered with a wholesome breakfast, homemade jams and fresh breads. Unique theme

Golden Dreams Bed and Breakfast

rooms feature cozy duvets, sherry decanters. Relax in the outdoor hot tub with mountain views! Family room with wood fireplace. Full guest kitchen. Located just one mile from villege express gondolas. Valley trail system and bus route at our doorstep. Bike rentals on site. Many seasonal activities. Now in two locations! Whistler Town Plaza is within walking distance of express ski lifts, fabulous restaurants, and new shops. These new condos feature gas fireplace, entertainment center, full kitchen, spa access, and underground parking.

Hostess: Ann Spence
Rooms: 3 + 2 condos (P&SB) $75-125
Full Breakfast
Credit Cards: A, B
Notes: 2, 5, 7, 8, 9, 10, 11

Nova Scotia

DEBERT

Shady Maple Bed 'n' Breakfast

RR 1, B0M 1G0
(902) 662-3565; (800) 493-5844;
FAX (902) 662-3565

Welcome to our fully operating farm. Exit 12 off Highway 104; travel one and a half miles into Masstown. Or take Exit 14A off Highway 102; six miles to Masstown. Walk through fields and wooded trails, view the milking, pet the animals, have a swim in our outdoor, heated pool, and enjoy the outdoor, year-round spa. In the evening, sit by the fireplace in our country home. Close to the Tidal Bore, Truro, and Ski Wentworth, and only forty-five minutes from Halifax Airport. We offer homemade jams, jellies, and maple syrup. Farm-fresh eggs and an in-house gift shop. Cribs and cots available. Honeymoon package available. Evening snack. Open May 1-October 31.

Hosts: James and Ellen Eisses
Rooms: 3 (1PB; 2SB) $40-75
Full Breakfast
Credit Cards: B
Notes: 5, 6, 7, 9, 10, 11, 12

welcome; 7 Children welcome; 8 Tennis nearby; 9 Swimming nearby; 10 Golf nearby; 11 Skiing nearby; 12 May be booked through travel agent.

ONTARIO

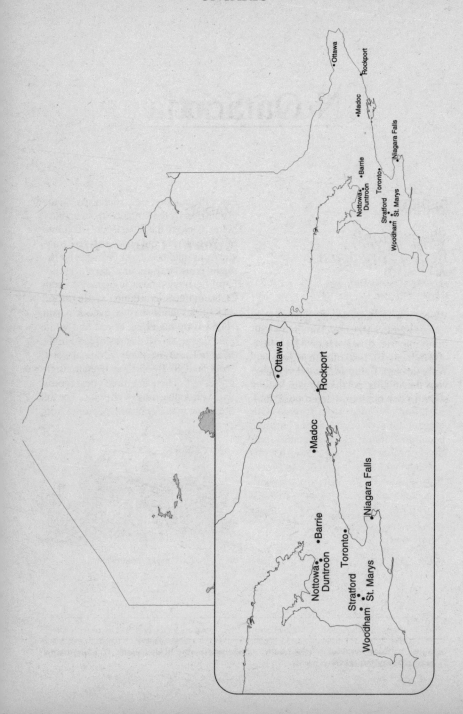

Ontario

BARRIE

Cozy Corner
Bed and Breakfast
2 Morton Crescent, L4N 7T3
(705) 739-0157; (705) 323-3471

A popular location with Georgian Bay—
30,000 islands, Wasaga Beach—on our
doorstep. Close to the Muskoka Lakes,
vacationland to many from the U.S. and
Canada. Site of summer homes of Hollywood celebrities (Kurt Russell, Goldie
Hawn, Rodney Dangerfield, and others).
Only thirty-six miles from Toronto. Our
elegant home offers luxurious and safe
accommodations. Deluxe bedding, hair
dryers, private TV, parking. Suite has private bath with Jacuzzi. Delicious breakfasts and a *joie de vivre* are standard.
Brochure available.

Hosts: Charita and Harry Kirby
Rooms: 3 (1PB; 2SB) $65-110
Full Breakfast
Credit Cards: B
Notes: 2, 4, 5, 8, 9, 10, 11, 12

MADOC

Camelot Country Inn
RR 5, K0K 2K0
(613) 473-0441; FAX (613) 473-0441

Relax in the quiet, country setting of our
1853 brick-and-stone home. It is surrounded by plantings of red-and-white
pine on twenty-five acres of land in the
heart of Hastings County. Original woodwork and oak floors have been lovingly
preserved. There are three guest rooms,
two with doubles, one with twins. The full
breakfast may be chosen by guests from

Camelot Country Inn

NOTES: Credit cards accepted: A Master Card; B Visa; C American Express; D Discover; E Diners
Club; F Other; 2 Personal checks accepted; 3 Lunch available; 4 Dinner available; 5 Open all year; 6 Pets
welcome; 7 Children welcome; 8 Tennis nearby; 9 Swimming nearby; 10 Golf nearby; 11 Skiing nearby;
12 May be booked through travel agent.

the country breakfast or one of two gourmet breakfasts.

Hostess: Marian Foster
Rooms: 3 (SB) $35-45
Full Breakfast
Credit Cards: none
Notes: 2, 4, 5, 7, 8, 9, 10

NIAGARA FALLS

Bed of Roses Bed and Breakfast

4877 River Road, L2E 3G5
(905) 356-0529 (voice and FAX)

Christian hosts welcome you. We have two efficiency units with bedroom, living room with pull-out sofa bed, furnished kitchenette, dining area, bath and private entrance. A full breakfast is served "room service-style." We are located on the famous River Road near Niagara Falls, bridges to the U.S., bike and hiking trails, golf course, and all major attractions. Free pick-up from bus and train station. Family units suitable for up to five people. Come and enjoy your stay in Niagara Falls, Ontario.

Hostess: Norma Lambertson
Units: 2 (PB) $85-140
Full Breakfast
Credit Cards: B
Notes: 5, 7, 10

Gretna Green Bed and Breakfast

5077 River Road, L2E 3G7
(905) 357-2081

A warm welcome awaits you in this Scots-Canadian home overlooking the Niagara River Gorge. All rooms have AC and TVs. Included in the rate is a full breakfast with homemade scones and muffins. We pick up at the train or bus station. Many people have called this a "home away from home."

Hosts: Stan and Marg Gardiner
Rooms: 4 (PB) $45-70
Full Breakfast
Credit Cards: none
Notes: 5, 7, 8, 10

NOTTAWA (NEAR COLLINGWOOD)

Pretty River Valley Country Inn

RR 1, L0M 1P0
(705) 445-7598 (voice and FAX)

Cozy, quiet country inn in the scenic Blue Mountains overlooking Pretty River Valley Wilderness Park. Choose from distinctive pine-furnished studios and suites with fireplaces and in-room whirlpools for two. Spa and air-conditioning. Close to Collingwood, beaches, golfing, fishing, hiking (Bruce Trail), bicycle paths, antique shops, and restaurants. Complimentary tea served upon arrival. Studios and suites available. No smoking.

Hosts: Steve and Diane Szelestowski
Rooms: 8 (PB) $74-120 (Canadian)
Full Breakfast
Credit Cards: A, B
Notes: 5, 7 (well-behaved), 8, 9, 10, 11, 12

OTTAWA

Australis Guest House

35 Marlborough Avenue, K1N 8E6
(613) 235-8461 (voice and FAX)

We are the oldest established and still-operating bed and breakfast in the Ottawa

---

NOTES: Credit cards accepted: A Master Card; B Visa; C American Express; D Discover; E Diners Club; F Other; 2 Personal checks accepted; 3 Lunch available; 4 Dinner available; 5 Open all year; 6 Pets

area. Located on a quiet, tree-lined street one block from the Redeau River with ducks and swans, and Strathcona Park. We are a twenty-minute walk from the Parliament buildings. This period house boasts leaded-glass windows, fireplaces, oak floors, and unique, eight-foot-high stained-glass windows overlooking the hall. Hearty, home-cooked breakfasts with home-baked breads and pastries. Past winner of the Ottawa Hospitality Award, recommended by *Newsweek*, featured in the *Ottawa Sun* newspaper for our Australian bread, and gold award recipient for Star of City for Ottawa Tourism, 1996.

Hosts: Carol and Brian Waters
Rooms: 3 (1PB; 2SB) $62-78 (Canadian)
Full Breakfast
Credit Cards: none
Notes: 5, 7, 8

Auberg McGee's Inn

Auberg McGee's Inn

185 Daly Avenue, K1N 6E8
(613) 237-6089; (800) 2 MCGEES (reservations);
FAX (613) 237-6201

A fourteen-room, smoke-free, historic Victorian inn celebrating fourteen years of award-winning hospitality! Centrally lo-

cated downtown on a quiet avenue, within walking distance of excellent restaurants, museums, Parliament, Rideau Canal, and the University of Ottawa. Rooms have cable TV, phone, and Jacuzzi en suite. Kitchenette facilities for longer stays. Computer-friendly phones with personal voice mail and direct-dial long-distance. Recommended by AAA. Full breakfast served in art deco dining room. All denominations welcome.

Hostesses: Anne Schutte and Mary Unger
Rooms: 14 (12PB; 2SB) $68-150
Full Breakfast
Credit Cards: A, B
Notes: 5, 7, 8, 9, 10, 11

Eagleview Manor Bed and Breakfast

ST. MARYS

Eagleview Manor Bed and Breakfast

178 Widder Street E., Box 3183, N4X 1A8
(519) 284-1811

"St. Marys is a town time forgot." Beautiful Victorian home overlooking a quaint, peaceful town. Minutes from London and Stratford. Sweeping staircase, stained-glass windows, Jacuzzi, quilts, antiques, fireplaces, in-ground pool, and four large

welcome; 7 Children welcome; 8 Tennis nearby; 9 Swimming nearby; 10 Golf nearby; 11 Skiing nearby; 12 May be booked through travel agent.

guest rooms. Nanny's Tea Room available for afternoon or Victorian teas. Reservations necessary. Open year-round. Theme weekends and retreats. Amtrak stops here. Future home of Canadian Baseball Hall of Fame.

Hosts: Bob and Pat Young
Rooms: 4 (SB) $50-70 (Canadian)
Full Menu Breakfast
Credit Cards: none
Notes: 2, 5, 7, 8, 9, 10, 11, 12

TORONTO

Toronto Bed and Breakfast, Inc.

Box 269, 253 College Street, M5T 1R5
(416) 588-8800; (416) 927-0354;
FAX (416) 927-0838
E-mail: beds@torontobandb.com

One call to us and we will arrange your stay at one of our friendly B&B homes. All are centrally located near safe, clean public transportation. You will stay with real Torontonians who love their city and their neighborhoods. This very personal registry has been providing accommodations for eighteen years. Referrals for **Toronto, Ottawa** and **Niagara Falls**! Free brochure on request.

Coordinator: Marcie Getgood
Rooms: 43 (12PB; 21SB) $45-85
Full and Continental Breakfasts
Credit Cards: A, B, C, F

Prince Edward Island

ALBANY

The Captain's Lodge

Seven Mile Bay, RR 2, C0B 1A0
(902) 855-3106; (800) 261-3518

A quiet, secluded bed and breakfast surrounded by flower gardens and fields of clover, grain, and potato blossoms. A short walk to a warm-water beach with red sand, convenient to the Borden ferry. Three guest rooms include private baths, ceiling fans, fresh flowers, slippers, duvets, bathrobes, and a gourmet breakfast. Enjoy the sunporch, TV room, living room, and veranda. No smoking. Resident cat and dog.

Hosts: Jim and Sue Rogers
Rooms: 3 (PB) $70
Full Gourmet Breakfast
Credit Cards: A, B
Notes: 2, 9, 10

MURRAY RIVER

Bayberry Cliff Inn

RR 4, Little Sands, C0A 1W0
(902) 962-3395 (voice and FAX)

Eight kilometers east of Wood Islands Ferry. Private porches. Rooms have antiques, quilts, and rustic decor. Double, single, and queen beds. Two remodeled post-and-beam barns in a scenic farming area "on the edge" of Northumberland Strait cliffs. Swimming, restaurants, seal watching, Rossignal Winery, craft stores nearby. Not suitable for children under 5. Early registrations suggested; deposit required. Open May 15-September 30.

Hosts: Nancy and Don Perkins
Rooms: 4 (PB) $75-125
Full Breakfast
Credit Cards: A, B
Notes: 2 ($50 limit), 7 (over 5), 9, 10, 12

welcome; 7 Children welcome; 8 Tennis nearby; 9 Swimming nearby; 10 Golf nearby; 11 Skiing nearby;
12 May be booked through travel agent.

QUEBEC

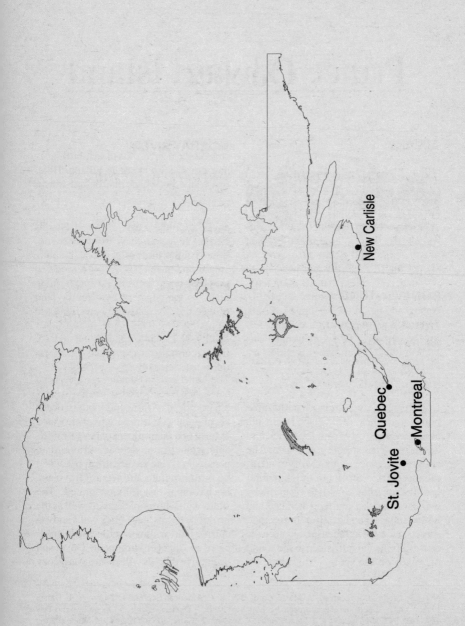

Quebec

Bay View Manor/Manoir Bay View

BONAVENTURE

Bay View Manor/ Manoir Bay View

395 Route 132, Bonaventure East (Mail: PO Box 21, New Carlisle), G0C 1Z0
(418) 752-2725; (418) 752-6718

Comfortable, two-story, wood frame home on the beautiful Gaspe Peninsula across the highway from the beach and beside an eighteen-hole golf course. The building was once a country store and rural post office. Stroll our quiet, natural beach; see nesting seabirds along the rocky cliffs; watch fishermen tend their nets and lobster traps; enjoy beautiful sunrises and sunsets; view the lighthouse beacon on the nearby point; and fall asleep to the sound of waves on the shore. Museums, ar-chaeological caves, fossil site, bird sanctuary, or Bristish Heritage Village. Hike, fish, canoe, horseback ride, or bird-watch.

Hostess: Helen Sawyer
Rooms: 5 + cottage (1PB; 4SB) $35
Full Breakfast
Credit Cards: none
Notes: 5, 7, 8, 9, 10, 11

MONTREAL

Auberge de la Fontaine

1301 Rachel Street E., H2J 2K1
(514) 597-0166; (800) 597-0597;
FAX (514) 597-0496

The Auberge de la Fontaine is a nice stone house, newly renovated, where the twenty-one rooms in a warm and modern decor are of unique style in Montréal. Located in front of a magnificent park. Comfortable, friendly atmosphere and attentive, personal service are greatly appreciated by our corporate and leisure travelers. Each room is tastefully decorated. The suites with whirlpool baths, as well as the luxurious rooms, have brick walls and exclusive fabrics. It will settle you in an elegant and quiet environment. Duvet and decorative pillows will ensure you a cozy

---

NOTES: Credit cards accepted: A Master Card; B Visa; C American Express; D Discover; E Diners Club; F Other; 2 Personal checks accepted; 3 Lunch available; 4 Dinner available; 5 Open all year; 6 Pets welcome; 7 Children welcome; 8 Tennis nearby; 9 Swimming nearby; 10 Golf nearby; 11 Skiing nearby; 12 May be booked through travel agent.

Auberge de la Fontaine

into our comfortable home located on Route 132, Main Highway. Enjoy fresh sea air from our wraparound veranda, walk or swim at the beach. Visit natural and historic sites. Country breakfast; fresh farm, garden, and orchard produce; home baking; and genuine Gaspésian hospitality. Light dinners by reservation. Craft, quilting, and folk music workshops. August Folk Festival. A small cottage is available for $350 per week. English and French spoken.

Hostess: Helen Sawyer
Rooms: 5 (1PB; 4SB) $35
Full Breakfast
Credit Cards: none
Notes: 3, 4, 5, 7, 8, 9, 10, 11

comfort. Breakfast is a given at the Auberg. A delicious variety of breakfast foods are set out each morning, and you have access to the kitchen for snacks. There are no parking fees. We want our guests to feel comfortable and to be entirely satisfied with their stay. Discover the exclusive shops, restaurants, and art galleries of the Plateau Mont-Royal, which is typical of French Montreal.

Hostesses: Céline Boudreau and Jean Lamothe
Rooms: 21 (PB) $99-185 (Canadian)
Continental Buffet Breakfast
Credit Cards: A, B, C, E, F
Notes: 5, 7, 8, 9, 12

NEW CARLISLE WEST

Bay View Farm

337 Main Highway, Route 132, Box 21, G0C 1Z0
(418) 752-2725; (418) 752-6718

On the coastline of Quebec's picturesque Gaspé Peninsula, guests are welcomed

Bay View Farm

QUEBEC

Hotel Manoir Des Remparts

3½-rue des Remparts, G1R 3R4
(418) 692-2056; FAX (418) 692-1125

Located minutes from the train/bus terminal and the famed Chateau Frontenac, with some rooms overlooking the majestic St. Lawrence River, the Manoir des Remparts boasts one of the most coveted locations available in the old city of Quebec. Newly

---

NOTES: Credit cards accepted: A Master Card; B Visa; C American Express; D Discover; E Diners Club; F Other; 2 Personal checks accepted; 3 Lunch available; 4 Dinner available; 5 Open all year; 6 Pets

renovated, it can offer its guests a vast choice of rooms, ranging from a budget room with shared washrooms to an all-inclusive room with private terrace.

Hostess: Sitheary Ngor
Rooms: 36 (22PB; 14SB) $35-75
Continental Breakfast
Credit Cards: A, B, C
Notes: 5, 7, 11, 12

ST-JOVITE

Gîte Les Trois Crables

554 Rue Limoges, C.P. 38, J0T 2H0
(819) 425-6951 (voice and FAX)

We have a charming, two-story stone house in a cottage setting within walking distance of the shops and restaurants of St-Jovite, accessible to nearby Mt. Tremblant Ski and Recreation Area. The interior is pristine-like, having been newly renovated with maple flooring and wood-beamed ceilings. There are two TV rooms with fluffy leather couches and a bright dining area for guests to enjoy.

Hosts: Claudette and Jacques Duclos
Rooms: 5 (1PB; 4SB) $50-60
Full Breakfast
Credit Cards: none
Notes: 2, 7 (over 7), 8, 9, 10, 11

welcome; 7 Children welcome; 8 Tennis nearby; 9 Swimming nearby; 10 Golf nearby; 11 Skiing nearby; 12 May be booked through travel agent.

Dominican Republic

PUERTO PLATA

Casa Gloria

(mail: c/o 5 Abitibi Crescent, Nepean, Ontario, K2G 4J7)
(613) 226-7972 (voice and FAX)

Casa Gloria is a serene hideaway minutes from Puerta Plata. Nestled in the luxuriant shrubbery of Perla Marina. A breathtaking beach and view of the North Atlantic are within five minutes' walking distance. We have a large, impressive guest house with nine spacious guest rooms, seven en suite bathrooms. Indoor lounge areas are available. A Caribbean-style breakfast and dinner with luscious fresh fruits and vegetables are served on the terrazzo overlooking the pool with Jacuzzi. Located minutes from two tourist communities offering a variety of activities (windsurfing, scuba diving, tours, etc.) Traveler's checks accepted.

Hosts: Michael and Joyce Edwards
Rooms: 9 (5PB; 4SB) $80-110
Full and Continental Breakfast
Credit Cards: none
Notes: 3, 4, 5, 7, 8, 9, 10

NOTES: Credit cards accepted: A Master Card; B Visa; C American Express; D Discover; E Diners Club; F Other; 2 Personal checks accepted; 3 Lunch available; 4 Dinner available; 5 Open all year; 6 Pets

Puerto Rico

CABO ROJO

Parador Perichi's

HC 01 Box 16310, 00623
(787) 851-3131; (800) 435-7197;
FAX (787) 851-0560

Parador Perichi's Hotel, Restaurant, and Cocktail Lounge is in Joyuda, site of Puerto Rico's famous resorts of the west. Seventeen years of excellent hospitality and service. Rooms have AC, wall-to-wall carpet, private balconies, color TVs, and telephones. Award-winning restaurant. After sunset, meet friends in the well-stocked, cozy lounge. The banquet room accommodates three hundred persons.

Hosts: Julio C. Perichi
Rooms: 41 (PB) $65-75
Full and Continental Breakfast
Credit Cards: A, B, C, D, E
Notes: 3, 4, 5, 7, 8, 9, 10, 12

SAN JUAN

El Canario Inn

1317 Ashford Avenue—Condado, 00907
(787) 722-3861; (800) 533-2649;
FAX (787) 722-0391
E-mail: canariopr@aol.com
Web site: http://www.canariohotels.com

San Juan's most historic and unique B&B inn. All twenty-five guest rooms are air-conditioned with private baths, cable TVs, and telephones, and come with a complimentary continental breakfast. Our tropical patios and sundeck provide a friendly and informal atmosphere. Centrally located near the beach, casinos, restaurants, boutiques, and public transportation.

Hosts: Jude and Keith Olson
Rooms: 25 (PB) $70-100
Continental Breakfast
Credit Cards: A, B, C, D, E
Notes: 5, 12

Hotel La Playa

Calle Amapola #6, Isla Verde, 00979
(787) 791-1115; FAX (787) 791-4650
E-mail: playita@icepr.com
Web site: http://www.icepr.com/hotellaplaya

Welcome to the Enchanted Island. Since we are a small, family-oriented hotel, we welcome the opportunity to provide a relaxing atmosphere. Our open-air restaurant and cocktail lounge with deck enjoy a cool breeze. Each room has cable TV and AC. Public phones are available in our courtyard. We are located on the beach, and all beaches are public domain.

Hosts: Barbara and David Yourch, Manuel Godinez
Rooms: 15 (PB) $75
Continental Breakfast
Credit Cards: A, B, C
Notes: 3, 4, 5, 7, 9, 10, 12

---

welcome; 7 Children welcome; 8 Tennis nearby; 9 Swimming nearby; 10 Golf nearby; 11 Skiing nearby; 12 May be booked through travel agent.

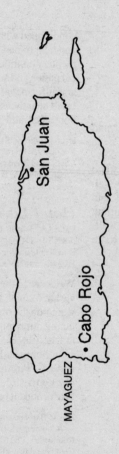

The Christian Bed & Breakfast Directory

P.O. Box 719
Uhrichsville, OH 44683

INN EVALUATION FORM

Please copy and complete this form for each stay and mail to the address above. Since 1990 we have maintained files that include thousands of evaluations from inngoers. We value your comments. These help us to keep abreast of the hundreds of new inns that open each year and to follow the changes in established inns.

Name of inn: _____

City and State: _____

Date of stay: _____

Length of stay: _____

Please use the following rating scales for the next items.
A: Outstanding   B: Good   C: Average   D: Fair   F: Poor

Attitude of innkeepers: _____   Attitude of helpers: _____

Food Service: _____   Handling of Reservations: _____

Cleanliness: _____   Privacy: _____

Beds: _____   Bathrooms: _____

Parking: _____   Worth of price: _____

Comments on the above: _____
_____
_____
_____

What did you especially like? _____
_____
_____
_____

Suggestions for improvements: _____
_____
_____
_____

RECOMMENDATION FORM

As *The Christian Bed & Breakfast Directory* gains approval from the traveling public, more and more bed and breakfast establishments are asking to be included on our mailing list. If you know of another bed and breakfast who may not be on our list, give them a great outreach and advertising opportunity by providing us with the following information:

1) B&B Name _____

Host's Name _____

Address _____

City _____ State _____ Zip Code _____

Telephone _____ FAX _____

2) B&B Name _____

Host's Name _____

Address _____

City _____ State _____ Zip Code _____

Telephone _____ FAX _____

3) B&B Name _____

Host's Name _____

Address _____

City _____ State _____ Zip Code _____

Telephone _____ FAX _____

Please return this form to: The Christian Bed & Breakfast Directory
PO Box 719, Uhrichsville, OH 44683
(740) 922-6045; FAX (740) 922-5948

The nation's **first** and **only** Christian travel magazine!

What do all of these places have in common?

- California's Spanish Missions
- Hezekiah's Tunnel in Jerusalem
- Ireland
- National Cathedral in Washington DC
- Central American Rainforests

They're all upcoming stories in *The Christian Traveler!* Packed with great photos and information, you won't want to miss a single issue! Don't wait—take advantage of the **limited time offer** exclusively for readers of the *Christian Bed & Breakfast Directory!*

The Christian Traveler's Guarantee
You may cancel at any time and receive a full refund for all unmailed issues.

Savings Certificate

Exclusively for readers of

The Christian Bed & Breakfast Directory

Save 50%

Fill out the reverse side of this certificate , clip and mail *TODAY* to:

The Christian Traveler

PO Box 1736
Holland MI 49422

Issue date January 1998

The Christian TRAVELER

Finally...
a travel magazine for Christians!

From America to Asia, from Africa to Europe, experience the richness of Christianity past and present.

- Exciting destinations of Christian significance
  - Add meaning to your travel
    - Plan your own trips

Take advantage of the special **savings certificate** below offered for a limited time **exclusively** to readers of *The Christian Bed & Breakfast Directory*.